READINGS IN
GLOBAL MARKETING MANAGEMENT

READINGS IN
GLOBAL MARKETING MANAGEMENT

Edited by

C. Robert Patty
Harvey L. Vredenburg
Both of Colorado State University

APPLETON-CENTURY-CROFTS
EDUCATIONAL DIVISION
New York MEREDITH CORPORATION

For Helena *and* Cynthia

PREFACE

A number of industries in the United States have reached a competitive standoff; for any one company in these industries the costs of increasing its market share have become prohibitive. Thus, a company may have to choose either stagnation, seeking further growth by marketing products different from the company's traditional line, or exporting overseas the products which have made the company successful in the U.S. market. The latter may not be the riskiest.

In many parts of the world demand is rising at a faster rate than in the United States. Both the need for expansion and the rising world demand have enticed a growing number of firms to investigate global business opportunities. Many firms have found their overseas operations more profitable than their domestic ones, but for others facing increased competition overseas, profit margins are approaching those in the domestic market.

In order to profitably expand overseas, company management must become cognizant of the different environmental conditions—economic, cultural and political—within which global marketing must be implemented.

This book of readings in global marketing management is intended to introduce to the student the concepts and language of global marketing; to introduce some of the problems in investigating and understanding international markets; and to develop certain sensitivities toward behavior overseas.

In order to fit best into the frame of reference developed by most students of marketing, the articles have arbitrarily been grouped as follows: Part I—Analysis for Global Marketing deals with some of the introductory problems involved in the decision to enter foreign markets; the cultural, environmental, and political factors which mold values; and the marketing research methodologies necessary in understanding both emerging and mature economies. Part II—The Strategy of Global Marketing deals with the traditional components of the marketing mix in a global context—product, marketing channels and institutions, and promotion. The articles in Part III—Global Marketing discuss marketing in the more mature industrialized economies, in the developing countries, and behind the Iron Curtain of Europe.

This collection of readings is designed for a variety of uses: (1) as a supplement to a beginning marketing course [the editors are convinced that by studying the role marketing plays in a variety of economies the student can better understand the role of marketing in his own country]; (2) as a text for a senior or graduate seminar in international marketing management; (3) as a supplement to a traditional text-oriented course in international marketing; and (4) as a source from which a marketing executive can introduce himself to or update himself in global marketing concepts and strategies.

We wish to express our appreciation to the many authors for their scholarly contributions and to the various periodical publishers for their permission to include copyrighted articles. We also want to acknowledge the help of our two graduate assistants, Mr. Lawrence King and Mr. Joseph Clithero, and the typing and miscellaneous help of Cynthia and Lani Patty, Helena Vredenburg, and the secretarial staff in the College of Business at Colorado State University.

C. R. P.

H. L. V.

CONTRIBUTING AUTHORS

HENRY ANDERSON
University of Maryland

A. J. ALTON
University of Rhode Island

RAYMOND W. BAKER
Overseas Economic Development Inc. of New York

ROGER W. BENEDICT
The Wall Street Journal

HARPER W. BOYD, JR.
Stanford University

HAROLD BURSON
Marsteller International S. A.

DAVID CARSON
Boston University

WILLIAM COPULSKY
W. R. Grace & Co.

R. J. DICKENSHEETS
International General Electric Company

W. J. DIXON
Wabsasso Cotton Co., Ltd.

S. WATSON DUNN
University of Illinois

ERIK ELINDER
Swedish Sales Institute

LEO G. ERICKSON
Michigan State University

JOHN S. EWING
Stanford University

BEREND H. FEDDERSEN
Institute of East Market Research Inc.

YVES FOURNIS
Paulstra Works

RONALD E. FRANK
Stanford University

JOSEPH R. GUERIN
St. Joseph's College

EDWARD T. HALL
Washington School of Psychiatry

RAPHAEL W. HODGSON
Arthur D. Little, Inc.

RICHARD H. HOLTON
University of California— Berkeley

JEROME KERNAN
University of Texas

EDWIN H. LEWIS
University of Minnesota

JOHN D. MACOMBER
McKinsey & Company Inc.

JOHN G. McDONALD
McKinsey & Company Inc.

WALTER P. MARGULIES
Lippincott and Margulies

WILLIAM F. MASSY
Stanford University

GORDON E. MIRACLE
University of Michigan

CHARLES J. OMANA
Bristol-Myers International

FELIKSAS PALUBINSKAS
*California State College at
Long Beach*

HUGH PARKER
McKinsey & Company Inc.

JERE PATTERSON
Jere Patterson Associates

IVAN PIERCY
Bureau of Commercial Research

RICHARD D. ROBINSON
*Massachusetts Institute of
Technology*

A. COSKUN SAMLI
Sacramento State College

A. A. SHERBINI
*National Institute of Management
Development, Cairo, U. A. R.*

MIHORIL SKOBE
Ozeha Advertising Agency

MONTROSE SOMMERS
University of Texas

CHARLES F. STEWART
Columbia University

ALBERT B. STRIDSBERG
J. Walter Thompson Co.

WILLIAM SUGG, JR.
*Westinghouse Electric Interna-
tional Company*

DONALD A. TAYLOR
Michigan State University

HUGO E. R. UYTERHOEVEN
Harvard University

SUEYUKI WAKASUGI
Mitsui & Co. Ltd.

J. HART WALTERS, JR.
George Washington University

RALPH WESTFALL
Northwestern University

SIMON WILLIAMS
Independent Consultant

YORAM WIND
University of Pennsylvania

MICHAEL Y. YOSHINO
*University of California—
Los Angeles*

MOSTAFA ZOHEIR
*Ain Shams University, Cairo,
U. A. R.*

CONTENTS

RESEARCH

    Raphael W. Hodgson and Hugo E. R. Uyterhoeven

    Before investing overseas, firms must go beyond an anal-
    ysis of technical and economic growth patterns and
    make a financial, economic, and operational analysis of
    competing companies as well.

12. Basic and Economical Approaches to International
    Marketing Research   128
    R. J. Dickensheets

    Often, preliminary and competent international mar-
    keting research can be done from the home office in the
    U.S. if the right resources are known and accessible.

13. On the Use of Marketing Research in the Emerging
    Economies   145
    *Harper W. Boyd, Jr., Ronald E. Frank,
    William F. Massy, and Mostafa Zoheir*

    The authors discuss the obstacles to the use of market-
    ing research in emerging countries.

14. Analyzing Brazilian Consumer Markets   153
    Leo G. Erickson

    A discussion of some of the approaches to marketing
    research in an emerging country.

15. Problems Peculiar to Export Sales Forecasting   176
    Henry Anderson

    Both the nature and the methodological implications of
    problems faced by the export-sales forecasters are dis-
    cussed in this article.

16. Forecasting Sales in Underdeveloped Countries   182
    William Copulsky

    The author discusses the keys to forecasting sales in
    emerging countries.

II. THE STRATEGY OF GLOBAL MARKETING

PRODUCT

CHANNELS AND INSTITUTIONS

The author explores the issues involved in transplanting a modern marketing institution—the supermarket—
into a developing economy.

The functions of wholesaling in an economy of scarcity
are compared with the functions of wholesaling in an
economy of abundance.

PROMOTING

This article isolates seven basic target rings and then
explains their functions in a coordinated international
advertising and marketing plan.

Both the operational and organizational problems of the
global advertiser are analyzed.

The universal needs of people and the stimuli for appealing to those needs are stressed in this article.

The author emphasizes the need for a unified advertising strategy for Europe as compared with the traditional market-by-market approach.

I

ANALYSIS FOR GLOBAL MARKETING

INTRODUCTION

1.

CREATING A STRATEGY FOR INTERNATIONAL GROWTH*

John G. McDonald and
Hugh Parker

GROWING numbers of American companies are spreading their wings abroad. The roster includes not just small- and medium-size manufacturing companies, but some of the largest and most powerful firms in the country. "By 1970, some 50 per cent of our profit will come from overseas operations," predicts the chief of a large diversified company. Du Pont, which once restricted production to this continent, is now producing in Holland, Belgium, and Northern Ireland. The Campbell Soup Company has launched a $30 million assault aimed at capturing a major share of the growing European food market, and I.B.M. World Trade is growing even faster than its ebullient U.S. parent.

The blue-ribbon list goes on and on. Some one thousand American companies have established postwar operations in Europe, most within the past four years. A recent McGraw-Hill survey indicates that the investment plans of American companies call for a $1.7 billion addition to plant and equipment overseas in 1961, 25 per cent more than in 1960. The census of private U.S. investments abroad, recently released by the Department of Commerce, shows that during the year of the census (1957) U.S. firms abroad paid wages and salaries of nearly $7 billion, employed about 3 million people, and spent about $17 billion for materials and services. This international flow of funds and goods is becoming one of the most important economic forces in the world today.

Companies set up manufacturing facilities abroad for a variety of reasons. Some want to enjoy the rapid growth offered by expanding foreign markets. Others seek to reduce their production costs with an eye to world-wide exports—including exports to the United States.

Not long ago, the stay-at-home competitors of these "internationals"

* Reprinted by permission from *International Enterprise: A New Dimension of American Business*, McKinsey & Company, Inc. (1962), pp. 17-24.

3

would have been unconcerned with these moves, but things have changed. Today many stay-at-homes see a threat to their home market position and the possibility of being blocked out of increasingly interesting foreign markets. Some companies are already being harassed in their domestic markets by low-cost goods produced abroad by their U.S. rivals (the 1957 census showed imports of $1 billion from overseas enterprises of U.S. companies). And there is now the prospect of tax and tariff changes that may further cloud their futures.

As a reaction to these threats, actual or potential, many companies are establishing beachheads of their own abroad. Thus for many reasons, some offensive, others defensive, the flood of American companies overseas continues to grow.

Here, based on our own experience and the experience of others, is a report on what these companies find in the way of risks and opportunities, and how they create strategies to minimize these risks.

SPECIAL PROBLEMS IN MOVING ABROAD

Setting up a new production base and marketing organization abroad is far more risky than establishing a new business at home. Manufacture abroad means that large sums of money are invested in plant and equipment for a long period of time in an alien, often changing environment. Management effort and personnel problems take on new dimensions, and profits can sometimes have a long lead time in a new land.

In his home market, the executive moves with ease and confidence; he knows the ground rules. Distribution patterns, trade terms, nuances of consumer tastes and preferences, and competitors' strengths and weaknesses are second nature to him; his judgment in this familiar environment is usually sound, since he operates under a set of fairly stable economic and political conditions. But many of the comfortable assumptions that the executive uses at home may not hold true overseas. In some ways, this is to the good. It permits him to view situations with different eyes and thus grasp opportunities that others do not see. Drawing from domestic experience, he may spot the early signs of a trend for convenience items, packaged foods, or new appliances; or he may see the chance to apply a proven technique in a new situation. But he may also stub his toe. He may assume that foreign consumers react in the American pattern, or he may assume that practices that were successful at home will work equally well abroad. As a result, both the risks and opportunities resulting from executive action abroad are often greater than they would be at home. (See special section below, *Keys to Marketing Success Abroad.*)

Risk comes in many guises and varies from country to country. The political situation, governmental control, or a market unready for a product may be all-important. Several years ago, General Motors, whose European and Australian subsidiaries are currently booming, shut down an expensive assembly plant in India. A prime factor in this painful decision was the unforeseen political climate and the effect of governmental control. In another instance, an American consumer-goods producer moved too soon; after establishing a plant in Belgium, he then found the market was not ready for its product. As a result, he has been conducting an expensive holding operation for the past three years.

Most companies have moved abroad too recently to know how well they will do in the long run, but reports are beginning to filter back. Some companies have been eminently successful, others have run into trouble, and still others have had both successes and failures in different countries. Clearly, long-term success or failure depends on the way a company moves into its overseas adventure. Once a company decides to move and invest abroad, it faces a basic problem: How does it plan its moves to take advantage of obvious opportunities at minimum risk?

KEYS TO MARKETING SUCCESS ABROAD

Leadership in American marketing is no guarantee of leadership in marketing abroad. Some outstandingly successful American firms have been able to duplicate in foreign markets their domestic success with ease and speed. For others success has come slowly and expensively. And for others not at all.

An analysis of the experience of leading American firms in major markets of the world has identified four characteristics of the outstanding marketer. These characteristics describe his fundamental approach to marketing decision-making, which, even in the short run, appears far more important than advantages in price or product.

1. The outstanding marketer exports his approach to marketing decision-making rather than his domestic practices. Foreign competitors are often alert, tough, and aggressive; but many are relatively inexperienced in analytical marketing techniques. This experience—the ability to diagnose the problem, identify the best alternatives, and choose wisely among them—is the American competitor's real advantage. The marketing practices he now employs in the U. S. may be totally inappropriate in the rest of the world; but his technique for developing these practices has application everywhere.

2. The outstanding marketer is keenly aware of the variation from one market to another. He never thinks solely in terms of "the European market," "the Latin American market," or even "the Common Market." He knows that countries, and even sections of countries, differ enormously in almost every factor critical to his market planning:

> *Distribution Channels:* In Italy and France, chain stores are in the ascendant. In Germany, wholesaler groups are growing rapidly. Distribution practices in the north of the United Kingdom are very different from those in the south.
> *Consumer Attitudes:* In Germany, utility may be more important than style; in France, advertising and brand name may play larger roles. Hence product design and promotion have to be tailored to individual markets.
> *Competitive Environment:* In one country, the market for a product may be dominated by a single company; in a neighboring country many firms scramble for their shares.

Market Size, Maturity, and Rate of Growth: An American power tool manufacturer found only replacement opportunities in one market but a completely untapped potential in a country nearby. Within the Common Market, per capita sales of widely used products vary enormously, and rates of growth for the same product differ as much as 100 percent.

3. The outstanding marketer is sensitive to differences in his competitive position. American companies heavily committed to foreign markets are often industry leaders at home. In the U.S., they have become accustomed to the privileges and responsibilities of leadership. They may have a powerful influence on the industry pricing practices. They may be able to avoid discounts and deals. They can limit their distribution to carefully selected outlets. But their domestic position does not travel with them like a passport. The competitive structure of an industry varies widely from one economy to another and so does the industry position of a corporation that competes in several markets around the world. A company that has 30 percent of the American Market may have to fight for 3 percent of a foreign market. And the company that gets 3 percent and more does so with a strategy appropriate for its position in that market.

4. The outstanding marketer combines policy-making at home with tactical decision-making abroad. Only corporate management is in a position to make broad policy decisions and to integrate local plans into a company-wide program. Without this kind of leadership, the most knowledgeable and skilled local marketing people can be only partly effective. But broad policies and plans are implemented best when the tactical decisions are made by local people in each market. There are three reasons for this:

Referral of every problem to the U.S. invites poor decisions and involves unavoidable delay.

Policy-level executives in the U.S. cannot know enough about foreign markets to make every detailed decision.

Information required for operating decisions is often almost impossible to transmit.

A short time ago American corporations found things easier and more profitable abroad than at home; but today margins are shrinking, rates of return are declining, and competition is everywhere more intense. How American companies will fare depends greatly on the way they approach the new problems of international marketing.

STAGES OF FOREIGN INVOLVEMENT

The evolution of a domestic company into a functioning world enterprise normally follows four distinct but overlapping stages.

Stage One: Export-import activity with a minimum of change in management outlook, company organization, or product line.

Stage Two: Foreign licensing and the international movement of technical know-how, still with little impact on domestic operations or management outlook.

Stage Three: Establishment of overseas operations. At this point the company makes substantial international investments in funds and management time, and begins to develop special international skills. But still the domestic operations remain essentially unaffected.

Stage Four: Emergence as a world enterprise with an integrated global approach encompassing both domestic and overseas operations.

These stages will be passed through one at a time, or any one can be bypassed. It is even possible to find a company with its various parts involved in all four at once. But as a rule, the take-off point for moving abroad occurs when a company makes the decision to risk large investments on the prospects of becoming a world enterprise.

It is important that a company re-examine its position at take-off, for it may well have some built-in obstacles to a successful launching of an overseas manufacturing operation. One company, about to enter stage three, fortunately identified such an obstacle in its organizational pattern in time to avoid any delays in achieving its goal. At the take-off point, the company had a group of "international" specialists organized in two departments—exporting and licensing—under one international executive. Ironically, the project team responsible for studying the feasibility of moving abroad found most resistance from the place it expected most support, the export and licensing departments. With the export department already feeling the squeeze from competition built up by the license department, it naturally resisted schemes to squeeze its profits further. Similarly, the licensing department was not cooperating since it foresaw some adverse effects on its profits if single subsidiaries were to replace its numerous licensees in various countries. To surmount this obstacle, changes had to be made in organization and profit responsibility.

Earlier licensing agreements or exclusive distribution rights can also cripple moves overseas. One manufacturer of marine equipment is doing fairly well in Europe, but is encountering tough competition from a German company, which was "educated" with patent exchanges and a licensing agreement several years ago. Many companies that would now like to move abroad are locked out of certain countries by exclusive licensing agreements that seemed wise, low-risk, profitable decisions just a few years ago.

When top management is alert to some of these environmental and strategic problems, it can develop sound organizational plans and safeguards in advance of a move abroad. Step-by-step international experience can become a major asset if it gives a company this foresight. But if top management does not plan its business ahead, existing international activities and agreements can be a major obstacle.

HOW COMPANIES MAKE THEIR MOVES ABROAD

Some companies have been content to move abroad without much planning and have done well; some have been disappointed. Other companies have evolved standard and, in some cases, fairly sophisticated approaches.

The Unplanned Approach

The decision to move into a given country at any time may be based almost entirely on chance. Perhaps the company president has been to the
country and likes it, or he may know businessmen there. Many such
moves are made in response to an invitation.

Some companies have experimented with moving idle production
equipment and setting up shop in another country. Certainly there is a
world-wide market for much secondhand U.S. manufacturing equipment,
but setting up a subsidiary with an obsolete plant can backfire. Local companies are equipping themselves with the latest devices and can sometimes
outproduce and outprice a U.S. subsidiary saddled with old machinery.
This is happening in electronics, where rising European manufacturers
are using the latest automated equipment.

One Midwestern heavy equipment manufacturer, spotting what
looked like a fine opportunity to enter the European market, bought up
a good-sized French company in the same field. The French concern
looked good on paper, but it was actually a high-cost operation on the
verge of losing important markets. The Americans apparently looked at
past performance, not at future trends. They took over just as the new
property started down the roller coaster and have poured in over a million dollars trying to salvage it.

Country-by-Country Analysis

Unplanned approaches have sometimes paid off, but their often fatal
drawback is the absence of an analysis of alternatives. As companies realize this, a number who have already made some moves overseas have
evolved a more systematic approach.

An overseas veteran has a standard approach for analyzing the feasibility of manufacturing in a specified country. Basically, this involves
three steps taken in the order listed:

> The home office conducts desk research on the market, briefly
> reviewing reference material available in the U.S., plus its own past
> international experience and intelligence. This step gives top man-
> agement a quick reading on the investment required and the pos-
> sible financial returns. (It also gives management an estimate of the
> budget, in terms of time, men, and money, required to complete the
> investigation.)
> If the investment looks profitable, a marketing man makes an

on-the-spot investigation. In addition to studying the market, he obtains answers to questionnaires supplied by the manufacturing and financial people. This results in a "first approximation," or feasibility, report.

An on-the-spot confirmation study by a small task force (including a senior member of management) results in the "second and final approximation" report and, later, actual investment, postponement, or rejection of a project.

This type of approach—a study of key information at home followed by on-the-spot investigation of special factors in the target country—is becoming common. It is a useful, and almost textbook-perfect approach. Unfortunately, it can yield critically misleading results. The reason is that no country is so self-sufficient that it is not affected by trends in world trade; therefore, the optimum decision for a single country might be fatal in view of capabilities and economic trends in other countries. If one looks at each country individually, for example, it may seem perfectly sensible to establish manufacturing plants in Italy, Germany, and France. In view of the increasing integration of European economies, a better solution might be to build one large plant.

A NEW APPROACH—GLOBAL PLANNING

A few companies, some American and some European, are building new approaches that minimize the risks of moving abroad. Generally, these approaches begin with one of the fundamentals of good planning—understanding the ultimate goal—and come under the term "global planning."

Global planning assumes that the ultimate objective of any company taking the first move overseas is to expand later without encountering any obstacles created by its first move. It also assumes that the chief executive is willing to extend the scope of his responsibility. Before making any move, he will ask: Where in the world should I invest my company's time, manpower, and funds for the best long-term interests of our stockholders?

Major Advantages

Some of the major advantages of global planning are these:

Setting long-range objectives and developing a long-term strategy before moving abroad enables a company to coordinate all the interim moves so that they do not cancel each other.

Investigating a whole area in depth enables a company to take action in as many countries as desired, so that later integration can be achieved with a minimum of expensive overlapping and duplication.

Developing statutory plans ahead of time gives a company a framework for making country-by-country decisions that will permit later shifts in cash flow without serious consequences (for example, capital gains tax on transfer of appreciated equity ownership).

In effect, the global approach has provided the essential key to long-range planning in the internationalization of American business.

Pitfalls in Global Planning

Like any technique, global planning has its dangers; these stem mainly from some form of misapplication.

One case of superficial application occurred when a billion-dollar corporation, with a few haphazardly placed overseas activities, decided to use the global planning technique to assess the feasibility of its conversion to a world enterprise. Its international division in New York was very powerful politically and, as a peace offering, was allowed to retain all existing remote control powers over foreign subsidiaries. In other words, the company went through the motions of appointing area managers for the various regions of the world, but they were virtually powerless since every decision still had to be referred back to corporate evecutives in New York.

The new area manager for Europe was not given a budget to perform a fact-finding study that would enable him to reappraise and coordinate the company's existing activities, which were spread thinly across Europe. As a result, it was not long before he found that many of the company's subsidiaries were launching new products just because "New York had advised them to do so" and not because they were appropriate for Europe. In effect, therefore, the company had remained domestically oriented while giving lip service to global planning.

Another company ostensibly adopted global planning but continued to allow its domestic divisions to encourage visits from foreign buyers of their products. As a result, the man assigned to set up operations in the European area was constantly being sidetracked in order to chase down special situations for the strong domestic divisions.

Cases of misapplication of global planning also result when a company succumbs to "international fever." This reportedly happened in one Midwestern consumer company. Shortly after a special team had been selected to set up operations in Europe, the team's attractive itinerary caught the eyes of other firm members. Soon letters from hitherto un-known distributors began reaching the company from Asia and South America—each letter suggesting that the company send a man to look over the "fabulous" opportunities in the writer's country. As it turned out, random opportunities did exist in Hong Kong and Brazil. In effect, the global planning technique had been applied partially—that is, in Europe—while plans for the rest of the world resulted from the old un-planned approach. This led to a conflict of interest. One of the European companies that had been selected for acquisition had subsidiaries in the Far East that competed with a property the international division was negotiating for in Hong Kong.

In summary, too often corporate moves overseas are motivated more than a little by the fad to go abroad. Admittedly, real pressures to move overseas are mounting, but the consequences of poor analysis and false moves in this rapidly changing world can be painful. Approaches based on short-term thinking are not sufficient. Any move overseas must be looked upon as an integral part of a clearly defined long-range goal.

There is no magic formula for successful global planning, but com-panies that do it well do possess and make use of one open secret. This is the understanding that only the company president or chief executive officer can successfully implement a series of moves abroad. Only a com-pany president can effectively persuade a board of directors of the value of a move abroad. Only a company president can effectively control and channel the inevitable rivalries and seeming contradictions in policy that simultaneous operation in several countries creates. Only a company presi-dent can successfully create the new marketing and financial controls needed for the new kind of company he will head if he creates a world enterprise.

2.

DEVELOPING INTERNATIONAL BUSINESS*

Richard H. Holton

WHEN we apply the basic principles of marketing strategy to the problem of developing international business, we can well ask why the general approach to marketing strategy should be any different from the approach we use with the development of domestic markets. The end result might well be different; i.e., we might expect to use a different marketing strategy in France than in the United States, but why should there be any significant difference in the way we go about formulating the market strategy? My personal belief is that there should *not* be.

I would like to discuss not the marketing strategy itself but rather the process by which that marketing strategy is shaped when a company enters a particular foreign market. (In doing this, I am quick to admit that this idea is wholly exploratory, and there are no doubt many points at which I am omitting qualifications which should be included in any full blown discussion of the topic.)

Surely most U.S. firms would agree that as a rule the uncertainties surrounding entry into a foreign market are even greater than those encountered in the development of markets here at home. (We should also recognize, however, that diversification into foreign markets is often motivated in part by the desire to reduce uncertainty by reducing the firm's dependence on one market; this is not inconsistent with the view that, for any given new project, the uncertainty faced abroad is greater than at home.)

This greater uncertainty about foreign markets is wholly understandable; it stems from our lack of familiarity with the environment within which the marketing will be carried on. The uncertainty about the level of total demand for the product is greater in the foreign market than at home. We have less insight into who makes the purchasing decision, at least in the case of consumer goods. We know less about the motivation behind that purchasing decision; we are less sure about what features of the product are given what weight by the buyers; we know less about reactions to label and package design.

We know less about the best advertising media or the most effective

* Reprinted from *Sales/Marketing Today*, the Official Journal of Sales and Marketing Executives—International, for January, 1966.

content of advertising. We can be tripped up more easily because we are less sure of reactions to price differences; we know less about how the competition is likely to respond to a new foreign entrant. We are unfamiliar with the details of the performance of different types of marketing channels abroad; the practices and expectations of the middlemen may strike us as peculiar.

In some cases there can even be the possibility of political reaction to a new entrant from the U.S. There is greater uncertainty arising from the various levels of foreign government regulation and the manner in which they are enforced. Uncertainties about one's relations with foreign bankers, shipping agencies and others providing ancillary services can also cloud the picture more than at home. For durable goods there may well be greater problems and uncertainties about post-sale servicing than here at home.

Except for those cases where tariffs or other considerations preclude entering a market without actually producing the good within that market, the U.S. firm *does* have an advantage which helps compensate for this long list of uncertainties. If the firm is well established in this country, any foreign sales it might generate are marginal to its domestic business. Any contribution to overhead and profit from this new foreign business is "frosting on the cake."

The point here is that the company does *not* have to make some massive investment in production facilities in order to enter the market; thus the capital at risk in the development of the foreign market in these cases is usually far less than the capital at risk when a firm tries to establish itself *ab novum* in the U.S.

Against this background of 1) greater uncertainty but 2) usually lower initial cost, the firm expanding into foreign markets is well advised to seek three objectives: minimizing risk; maximizing control; and maintaining flexibility. These three might well be suitable objectives in the development of domestic markets as well, but the greater uncertainty in foreign markets gives these objectives particular relevance when the U.S. firms step overseas. The point here, however, is that it may be helpful to make these three objectives more explicit as the firm shapes its overseas marketing strategy.

These three objectives can easily conflict with one another. For example, a firm might enter markets with minimum risk by using exclusively independent distributors in the individual foreign markets, requiring that the distributors themselves take title to the goods. This avoids tying up any significant amount of capital or administrative time in establishing the exporter's own distribution system abroad.

Although this approach minimizes the risk, it certainly does not maximize control over the marketing process; in fact, it nearly minimizes it. Using independent distributors backed up by missionary salesmen on the exporter's payroll is one means of improving control while still holding the risk at a low level.

One of the more obvious means of reducing the uncertainty surrounding entry into a foreign market is to conduct extensive market research. However, it is apparently fairly common for firms to spend rather modest amounts on market research in foreign markets. The reasons for this seem to be fairly clear, although seldom discussed.

STREAM OF EXPECTED PROFITS

Although it may be difficult to quantify the problem, surely the decision-maker has in mind some stream of expected profits if the market research is not conducted, whereas if the information generated by the market research is in hand, the stream of expected profits would be greater over time. In other words, the marketing research would presumably lead to wiser policies and then to higher profits. At the very least, the variance in the expected profit stream would be reduced by the market research.

The value of the market research can be thought of as the discounted value of the difference between the two streams of profit. The worst expected profit stream can, of course, be negative, i.e., an operating loss. This loss can be very substantial indeed, if a large investment in new production facilities is required to launch the project in question. The greater this risk of loss, presumably the more the decision-maker will be willing to spend on market research designed to be sure that the decision is a correct one.

With this very simplified view of the value of information in mind, what can we say about the likelihood that the U.S. firm will spend much on marketing research before entering a foreign market? Ten years ago the National Industrial Conference Board published a very helpful study, "Researching Foreign Markets," which provides some illustrative material relevant to this question.

HETEROGENEOUS FOREIGN MARKET

The NICB study points out that marketing research abroad faces a different problem, generally speaking, than here at home. The problem is different in a number of respects. *First,* "the" foreign market is a very heterogeneous one. Even within a single developed country abroad, consumer tastes and preferences and marketing conditions sometimes differ more than within the entire U.S. market. As we go from a large homogeneous market to a smaller one, the sample size needed for a given confidence level does *not* shrink proportionally, so the cost of market research, relative to the size of the market, is *greater* for the smaller market.

MINIMUM MARKET KNOWLEDGE

Second, the individual markets abroad each have their own complex of government regulations, packaging requirements, environmental conditions such as climate, nature and reliability of electric current, and so on, which must be ascertained even as a minimum. Since some research funds must be spent to obtain this sort of information for each of several relatively small markets, little is left over for sample surveys and other devices which characterize U.S. research.

Third, the U.S. firm already marketing can rely for market information and advance on its own operating staff abroad. Thus the alternative to a massive market research project prior to entering the market is not a complete absence of market information; a substitute is available. Having the information later and on a smaller scale may not be a perfect substitute, but it can take care of at least the more bothersome problems.

Fourth, market conditions abroad are more likely to be unstable. Political and financial crises can change government policies on imports, repatriation of profits, and the like. Thus, the information one might gain from market research is more likely to become obsolete in the foreign market than in the domestic one. (This point made by NICB is dubious if one sets aside the problems of political instability. The threat of new competition and of new competitive tactics in the U.S. might make for faster obsolesence of marketing knowledge here than abroad.)

Fifth, the NICB study points out that "the foreign operations of a company are almost always subordinate to its domestic operations—in volume of sales, if not in organizational status." Consequently the market research designed to find out what the consumer wants in the way of product design, package size and the like will be done only in the U.S. The company's foreign operations must for the most part content themselves with selling something designed basically for the U.S. market.

We can add to the NICB list the point that the lower investment outlay generally associated with entering a foreign market (compared with entering the domestic market) means that the money being risked in the venture is less, and consequently the value of the information which might be bought in a marketing research project of the domestic variety is less.

If a company knows that in case of a failure abroad it can fold its overseas tent without losing much money, it would be foolish to spend a lot of money to avoid this mistake. Only if the cost of an error is large should the firm spend much marketing research money in an attempt to avoid the error.

UNCOMMON RESEARCH

With these points in mind, we should not be surprised that market research is not used as commonly by U.S. firms entering foreign markets as when they launch new products in the domestic market. The present value of the difference between the two streams of profit is less with a smaller market; it is less if unstable market conditions mean a shorter expected life for the stream of profits; the capital at risk is less (holding to our assumption that production facilities need not be built); and decisions about optimum product design are commonly made on the basis of the domestic market alone.

If there is any validity in this discussion, then certain conclusions about the process for developing a marketing strategy for entering a foreign market would seem to follow. *First,* test marketing in two or three major metropolitan areas as a preliminary to a broadside attempt to enter the entire market would appear to be even more advisable in foreign markets than at home. Given the greater uncertainties in the foreign market, it is easier to make mistakes. If mistakes are made, better that they are made on a small scale.

GIVE ATTENTION TO FEEDBACK

Second, particular attention should be given to the problem of feedback, from middlemen as well as from final users of the product. With greater uncertainty about the reaction of these groups, it is more likely in foreign than in domestic markets that some incipient unhappiness over the product or the firm's policies will come to the surface after the first sales success is recorded. This suggests that the exporter should have his own man on the spot to assure that this feedback is as comprehensive as possible.

Third, the objective of minimizing risk often dictates that first consideration be given the use of independent distributors. Thus, the cost of setting up one's own sales force and physical distribution facilities in the foreign market could be avoided. But, as noted above, this can lead to the U.S. firm having relatively little control over the operating methods used by these distributors. The agreements with the distributors can spell out such matters as minimum inventory levels, pricing policies, market areas and the like, but the U.S. firm may still feel that its product is given too little attention by the distributor, who typically handles a whole line of products. The U.S. firm may also be unhappy with the sales ability of the distributors' sales force. Some U.S. firms have attempted to overcome this problem by having one of their own employees maintain an office with the distributor.

MAINTAIN FLEXIBILITY

Fourth, the objective of maintaining flexibility, although important in domestic marketing as well, would seem to take on special significance abroad because of the greater uncertainties. The marketing strategy should be designed in such a way that it can be altered readily if the initial ideas seem not to work well.

I am reminded here of the case of a firm which first sold through an independent distributor in a particular country, but then after some years' experience decided that they should have a manufacturing operation there. They then discovered that they had signed the distributor to a 20-year contract, and it was costly indeed to buy their way out of this arrangement so that they could operate more as they wished.

MINIMIZE, MAXIMIZE, MAINTAIN

To summarize, the greater uncertainty typically encountered in foreign markets would seem to suggest that in the development of a marketing strategy for international business the U.S. firm should give more attention than they might at home to minimizing risk, maximizing control and maintaining flexibility.

Since these objectives are often in conflict, some balance must be struck. Market research of the sort commonly used in the U.S. is frequently not feasible abroad because the cost of the research is out of line with the value of the information received. Since experimental entry into the market often does not involve the large initial outlays associated with starting a new firm or a new product in the U.S., experimental marketing can be used in essence as a substitute for marketing research. The greater uncertainties in foreign markets, however, suggest that one should enter only a few markets at first, to make one's mistakes on a small scale.

On the basis of this experience, the marketing strategy can be shaped over time. This is in contrast with the more common case in the U.S., where a full-blown marketing strategy typically must be devised from the outset. In the foreign market, feeling one's way more cautiously than at home may be the surest route to solid success over the long pull.

3.

MARKETING ORIENTATION IN INTERNATIONAL BUSINESS*

Michael Y. Yoshino

THE urge to "go international" has captured the imagination of many U.S. business firms. An accelerating commitment to international business in recent years is dramatically illustrated by the following evidence:

Overseas sale of U.S. companies amounted to 28 billion dollars in 1963, a 50 percent increase over 1959.

U.S. manufacturing investment rose to 15 billion dollars in 1963, a fourfold increase over 1950.

1,897 U.S. firms undertook over 4,644 new foreign activities during the four-year period between 1960 and 1964.[1]

Excellent profit opportunities overseas have lured progressive firms from the advanced nations into international business. As a result, competition in the world market is rapidly taking on a multinational character.

This is reflected in a recent study made by McKinsey and Company, Inc. of one hundred corporations which account for over 40 percent of private corporate U.S. investment abroad. The study reports that the overall pretax rate of return of these corporations from overseas operations slipped from 22 percent in 1955 to 14 percent in 1962.[2] The comparable domestic rate in 1962 was 13 percent. The striking difference in profitability once existing between domestic and international markets has all but disappeared.

MARKETING CONSIDERATION NEGLECTED

In spite of these significant developments, a recent study reveals that marketing remains a neglected area in many international investment

* Michael Y. Yoshino, "Marketing Orientation in International Business," *MSU Business Topics* (Bureau of Business and Economic Research, Graduate School of Business Administration, Michigan State University, East Lansing, Michigan), Summer, 1965. Reprinted by permission.

[1] "New Foreign Business Activity of U.S. Firms" (Chicago: Booz, Allen & Hamilton, Inc., 1964), p. 1.

[2] "International Enterprise: A New Dimension of American Business" (New York: McKinsey & Company, Inc., 1962), p. 14.

decisions. Many operating difficulties recurrently observed throughout this study are traceable to this very fact. In the process of the study, the author conducted intensive interviews with executives of 20 leading American firms at corporate headquarters in the United States, as well as American and indigenous executives abroad. This article attempts to identify probable reasons for this neglect, and discuss possible consequences.

A number of firms studied have made a substantial commitment overseas without carefully evaluating relevant characteristics of foreign markets. One such approach is illustrated in the following example: A U.S. manufacturer of electronics products was approached by a foreign firm about setting up a joint venture in a promising Asian market. The president saw a demand for the company's products in that market, and was impressed by its growth potentials. He had his staff make cost comparisons with his operations in this country, allowing for the difference in the scale of operations and wage level. He then concluded that the potential profit appeared to be quite attractive, particularly according to the U.S. standard. Once his interest was aroused, he felt time pressure to beat his competitors in entering the market. He was compelled by the self-generated pressure to establish a beachhead in the market as soon as possible, then devise a strategy to develop it.

Largely ignored in his decision was a host of relevant marketing characteristics such as competitive environment, market maturity, distribution requirements, marketing costs, logistics problems, product policy, promotional facilities, and his prospective partner's attitude toward, and experience in marketing. At the time of this study, the venture, though three years old, was still plagued with problems arising from the inadequate planning surrounding the decision.

Consideration of these and other relevant marketing characteristics should have been an integral part of the entry decision, since these very factors are not only critical in evaluating the attractiveness of a market, but in determining the most suitable entry method, types of production facilities needed, product policy, and the extent of commitments necessary to develop the market.

Evaluation Factors

Evaluation of a foreign market is extremely difficult, challenging the most skilled researcher. In addition, there are two basic factors which prevent marketing-conscious U.S. executives from making objective assessments of a foreign market.

The majority of international investments are traditionally made in economies characterized by severe shortage. For example, some time ago,

an American automobile manufacturer was evaluating entry into a foreign market. The market was experiencing a tremendous shortage of
automobiles of all kinds. Of four hundred thousand motor vehicles operating in the country, 75 percent of the passenger cars and 70 percent
of the trucks were at least ten years old. Nearly one-half were 20 years
old. According to the official government estimate, the country would
need approximately sixty thousand new vehicles every year. Because of
the foreign exchange shortage and lack of a domestic automobile industry, annual replacement was only a fraction of the demand.

Under these conditions, where market size is no longer an unknown
factor, little need was felt for market forecasting or planning. Moreover,
some past international investment decisions have been for a defensive
reason to hold the existing local market, which can be no longer reached
through exporting.

*In spite of much talk about the opportunities of foreign markets,
many U.S. executives are not completely free from prejudice about foreign markets.* Surprisingly, many still regard international business as a
mere appendage to domestic business. International business is segregated
from its domestic counterpart and managed by a group of specialists,
while the top management concentrates on the domestic operations.

Furthermore, in making investments overseas, there is a danger that
top management's attentions are preoccupied with problems such as
selecting a partner, negotiating a contract, seeking government clearances, and constructing a plant. The most important consideration of all
—market characteristics—is pushed aside.

There is often an implicit assumption that since the company is
familiar with marketing problems, its experience is readily transferable
to another market. Some feel that since foreign markets are small or
relatively unsophisticated, they can be penetrated with relative ease. Past
successes in sellers' markets overseas tend to reinforce this illusion.

Top management's overenthusiasm toward certain foreign projects
can also be a problem. While seldom recognized as such, many unwarranted commitments to foreign markets have been made simply because
the president "fell in love" with a country on his inspection trip, or an
influential member of top management acquired a strong emotional commitment to a given area of the world. Excessive zeal can and has inhibited
objective market analysis.

Consequences

The following procedures, with their unsatisfactory results, exemplify
neglect of marketing considerations.

Ill-conceived entry strategy. Basically, there are three routes—export, licensing, and direct investments—to enter a foreign market. Obviously there is no one best route under any conditions. Effectiveness of entry depends largely upon the local investment climate and the capacity and the commitment of a particular firm. Thus an understanding of the advantages and limitations of each method is vitally important. These methods must be viewed as alternatives rather than a sequence of developments to be followed. If any firm confines itself, by default, to any one of the three approaches, it is severely limiting its opportunities in a foreign market. There is, however, a perceptibly inflexible attitude among the firms studied toward devising an appropriate entry strategy to meet the particular requirements of the market under consideration. Frequently an entry method is determined prior to market investigation.

While many factors must be considered in developing an appropriate entry strategy, failure to carefully evaluate the market will most likely result in ill-conceived entry strategy. For example, A large U.S. pharmaceutical firm licensed a new technique to a manufacturer in an Asian market. The licensee promoted the product aggressively and quickly built a substantial volume of business. The U.S. company soon became aware that it was only realizing a fraction of the return, while the licensee was reaping tremendous profit. The situation was particularly regrettable to the American company, since a more direct involvement such as equity participation was entirely possible at the time the collaboration was first proposed. Had the company evaluated the market more carefully, it would have chosen a direct investment route, and could have established itself firmly in this growing market.

When a firm is not aware of the true potential of the market, or lacks a set of carefully thought-out objectives, it tends to neglect proper measures to safeguard its future operations.

In some promising foreign markets, such as Japan, the local investment climate is restrictive as to the scope of activities of any one venture. A single venture, therefore, is unlikely to serve as an effective means for futur expansion. Hence it behooves U.S. firms to define with great care the scope and nature of a particular venture to avoid careless overcommitment of future products and technologies. Under these circumstances, a number of narrowly-defined activities would be necessary for diversified U.S. manufacturers to penetrate deeply into a market. Unless this fact is clearly recognized in the beginning and proper steps taken, future operations in that market would be severely limited.

Ignoring or misjudging the marketing elements critical to the success of the operation. When marketing considerations are neglected in the initial decisions, important marketing decisions are likely to be ignored, or made on a piecemeal basis by nonmarketing executives from the home office, or local executives who lack a proper understanding of marketing.

In the initial phase, the foreign project is usually dominated by production-oriented personnel, because the major problem is frequently viewed as getting the plant into operating condition. These men are understandably preoccupied with production problems and possess little skill or interest in coming to grips with complex marketing issues. Under these circumstances, marketing problems are: ignored, relegated to local partners who have no choice but to follow traditional practices, referred to the corporate headquarters, or based on marketing practices of the U.S. parent organization or its successful foreign subsidiary operating in another market under a different set of circumstances. Any of these alternatives are likely to lead to an unsatisfactory consequence.

One such problem is illustrated in the following example. A well-known U.S. manufacturer of nondurable consumer goods entered the Japanese market in partnership with a local firm. The decision was primarily based upon the general attractiveness of the situation, data furnished by the Japanese firm, and a one-week, on-the-spot investigation by the assistant to the president of the U.S. company. Unfortunately, performance fell far below original expectations. The U.S. company has unsuccessfully tried a crash program to salvage the operation, including replacement of its top management.

Further examination of this case revealed that the investment decision was made on a superficial analysis of the market, with no attention given to relevant marketing characteristics. It was assumed that Japan, being a compact market of 90 million consumers with relatively homogeneous economic and social characteristics and highest per capita income and growth rate in Asia, could easily be penetrated. This illusion was further strengthened by top management's impression of a lack of sophistication in marketing on the part of local competitors. Management also overestimated the built-in prestige of U.S. brands in competition with local or European products. These assumptions led to management's failure to commit the necessary resources to the marketing effort. Particularly damaging was the failure to recognize that the critical element in this industry is to cultivate the entrenched and complex channel of distribution.

Another common area of misjudgment is the selection of equipment for a foreign venture. Not familiar with the true nature of competition in a foreign market, U.S. companies find it extremely tempting to equip a new venture with obsolete machines. This action has backfired in some cases. Some firms that had succumbed to this temptation are finding it impossible to compete with local competitors who are equipped with the most modern production facilities.

Limiting the flexibility of future operations. For example, a U.S. firm which manufactured light industrial machinery began local production in a Southeast Asian market as a result of satisfactory experience with occasional exports. The company was successful in expanding the demand for its products through imaginative promotional programs. Two years later, however, the market was flooded by cheap, local copies of the American product. The American firm has subsequently lost the major share of the market it had created.

What happened here? In shifting to local production, the company management did not bother to evaluate product mix in terms of the market, but decided, by default, that it would manufacture the same product lines it had been exporting. These happened to be the simplest models manufactured for the domestic market. The decision was in part motivated by the U.S. firm's desire to supply the new venture with obsolete equipment sitting idle in one of its American plants. The product decision was made not by the requirements of the market, but the manufacturing capacity of the new venture. It was not until a substantial commitment had been made that the subsidiary learned that their relatively unsophisticated product was within the reach of technology locally available. The only way to overcome the problem was to upgrade the quality of the product. While this was within the technological capability of the firm, it would have required a substantial investment in retooling and the purchase of additional equipment. The local government did not look favorably upon allocating its scarce foreign exchange for this purpose. The company was forced to reduce prices to meet local competitors. At the time of this study, the operation was barely breaking even. This problem could have been avoided had more precise attention been devoted to market characteristics prior to the initial investment decision.

In shifting from export to local production, the assumption is frequently made by the U.S. firm that it should manufacture the *same* product lines exported in the past. This assumption ignores not only local marketing conditions, but also vital differences in the two methods of operation.

Failure to consider local marketing conditions in product decisions severely limits future operating flexibility. The subsidiary is likely to manufacture products, for which strong local competition already exists, which do not reflect the advanced technical skill available at the parent company.

Overlooking opportunities for innovations. It makes little sense for U.S. companies operating overseas to copy local marketing practices, for it is in this area that U.S. firms have a strong competitive advantage over their more tradition-bound, local competitors. However, the manner, as well as the timing, is crucial in introducing marketing innovations. Exclusion of marketing considerations in the initial investment decision overlooks excellent opportunities for introducing new marketing concepts and techniques to foreign operations with a minimum of resistance from the local collaborator.

Most local businessmen interviewed in this study were aware of the advanced marketing concepts and techniques in the United States, and have repeatedly expressed their desire to assimilate them. However, unless this desire is satisfied during the initial period of operation, usually characterized by mutual goodwill, the local collaborators will tend to settle for their traditional practices. Once this happens, they may demonstrate an amazing degree of resistance to any change, as illustrated by the following example. A well-known U.S. consumer goods manufacturer established a joint venture operation in Japan, but neglected to take the initiative in setting marketing policies for the new venture despite the prodding of the Japanese partner. Lacking conscious formulation, the marketing policy drifted and was eventually improvised by the Japanese partner. When the U.S. parent company became dissatisfied with its performance and attempted to introduce changes in the marketing program, it encountered great resistance. During the early stages, the same suggestions by the U.S. firm would have been more than welcome.

Lack of clarification. In setting up a foreign venture, U.S. firms usually make a painstaking effort to retain operating control over production methods, product quality, or financial management. Surprisingly, however, few attempts are made to clarify marketing tasks or responsibilities. This failure has proved to be a major source of conflict in subsequent operations. For example, a large American manufacturer of consumer goods established a joint venture in an Asian market. The American firm was highly pleased with the performance of its local partner in choosing the plant site, setting up the production facilities, and recruiting the personnel. When production began, however, major differences emerged over marketing policies, particularly in the area of promotions and distribution. Both parties were appalled over the magnitude of the differences and wondered why these had not been detected in the initial exploratory stage.

There are two elements, inherent in the very nature of marketing, which complicate an effective working relationship between American and foreign firms. The first lies in the nature of marketing problems and the environment in which they take place. While marketing problems can be real and pressing, they are somewhat intangible and elusive. They are difficult to anticipate, particularly in an unfamiliar operating environment. Moreover, the symptoms of marketing ills are often too subtle to be detected at an early stage. When they are recognized, they are likely to have developed major proportions.

Second, there are some important differences in the basic understanding of and attitude toward marketing between American and foreign executives. Potential local partners, particularly in developing countries, are likely to have indifferent or even hostile attitudes toward marketing. To the majority, manufacturing and marketing, or more accurately, selling, are two distinct activities to be performed by different agencies under different institutional settings. Manufacturers' functions end with the creation of form utility in the narrowest sense of the term. Some even view selling activities with disdain. Even though some "sales" oriented local manufacturers may be highly aggressive and skillful in commercial activities, they view their selling functions not in terms of satisfying consumer wants, but as manipulators of markets. They tend to look for an immediate payoff and are reluctant to make long-term investments to develop a market for their products.

Unless these differences are explicitly recognized in the initial phase of the operations, marketing may prove to be a major source of conflict between the partners.

There is no question that American firms have a wealth of accumulated marketing expertise that can be applied abroad. Alert American firms can gain a competitive advantage over tradition-bound local competitors by carefully blending their domestic marketing know-how with more enduring aspects of the local marketing system.

4.

FOUR MIRAGES OF INTERNATIONAL MARKETING*

Harold Burson

BACK in the days when Arabs were favorite figures in little parables illustrating wisdom, an Arab reportedly answered an American who was bragging about his know-how by drawing a small circle in the sand. "This," he said, "is the humble extent of my own knowledge." Then he drew a much larger circle and said, "And this is the far greater extent of your knowledge." But before the American could warm with a feeling of superiority, the Arab pointed to the limitless desert that lay beyond the largest circle and said, "And there, my friend, is the region of our common ignorance."

As we venture out of the circles of our knowledge of international marketing, we will see on the horizon the beckoning palms of oasis after oasis. Let us take a closer look at these oases, because at least four of them are mirages. They are notions about doing business abroad—or about the nature of business abroad—that have no substance.

SOMETHING NEW

The first mirage is the idea that international trade or marketing is something new. As you read many publications today, you get the feeling that the whole area of international trade is something novel. Of course, it isn't. International trade has been, since earliest times, one of the prime stimulants to advances in civilization. Phoenicians, Carthaginians, and Greeks moved products and ideas along the sea routes of the Mediterranean. Indian, Arabian, and African products moved along the caravan routes of the deserts. The Chinese beat six routes from their country to the eastern and western world. The search for trade routes to the East motivated the great travels and discoveries of the fifteenth century. And the Industrial Revolution brought Western Europe a new impulse for world trade, for markets had to be found for the output of factories.

Nor are we in the United States Johnny-come-latelies in international

* Reprinted by permission from *Management Review* (March, 1963), **American Management Association, Inc.**, pp. 54–56. As condensed in *Management Review*. Published by the American Management Association.

marketing. Before the Civil War, the "Yankee trader" had established himself in places as remote as Shanghai and Hong Kong, and in 1870 our instincts for doing business abroad created an international incident when Perry "opened up" Japan for trading. Names like Singer, W. R. Grace, and Coca Cola have long been known to people in the farthest corners of the earth—and, coming down to modern times, companies like H. J. Heinz, Colgate-Palmolive, and Caterpillar Tractors have derived a major share of their income from overseas.

Neither world trade nor American participation in it is a phenomenon of recent years. What's new is the scale and importance of doing business abroad—which, like the scale and importance of research and technology, have increased tremendously in recent years.

THE MODEST AMERICAN

Let us now turn to the second mirage: the idea that foreign countries won't accept American marketing ideas. It's hard to understand why so many Americans are willing to be scolded for their naivete, brashness, and callowness. We even pay lecturers to come over here and tell us, after they've spent a week in the States, what's wrong with this country.

American businessmen operating abroad are not a bunch of back-slapping boobs who ignore local customs and ignorantly try to impose ideas that have worked back here on the unresponsive natives. The American is different from the European, but this difference is a source of strength in marketing when it is recognized and understood.

AN OVERSIMPLIFICATION

We are told by some people that we must not carry our domestic ideas of marketing over into a foreign area. This is a misleading oversimplification of the truth. The American's organized approach to the subfunctions of marketing—research, sales, product planning, and so on—is just beginning to be understood in Europe. The amusement that the intelligent European feels when he is first exposed to such meticulous methods quickly changes to amazement when he begins to grasp the possibilities. It is true that Americans know little about European markets—but it is also true that Europeans know little more, and often less, about their own markets, when it comes to describing them quantitatively for purposes of planning and prediction.

Europe will scrap traditional marketing habits in favor of American methods. It was said that Europeans would never accept supermarkets—that the women liked to spend hours going from shop to shop. It was said that door-to-door selling would never work. But both have worked, and they will work even more successfully as time goes on. The point is that American business need not pussyfoot when it tries to carry its marketing innovations overseas. Decades ago, many things just weren't done in this country, either—but our progress is measured by the fact that we now do them.

SECRETS OF GROWTH

The third mirage is the belief that the Europeans have discovered a secret of economic growth that we have not. Some Americans have actually persuaded themselves that this is true—and, if it is, wouldn't we be presumptuous to think that we could teach them anything about marketing?

The fact that growth rates in European countries are greater than ours has led to discussions in which there is more heat than light. It is true that the United States trails six other countries with its annual average increase in gross national product of 3.3 per cent; similar figures, also showing the U.S. lagging, are available for productivity increases.

Now, however, we are hearing of problems in Europe that have been familiar here since our own boom began to leak air at the end of 1957. Europeans are beginning to be troubled by a profit squeeze as wage costs, which have been comparatively low, are rising rapidly.

Europeans have no secrets of production or marketing or growth. What they do have is a huge, unsaturated market that offers both them and us great opportunities now and in the years ahead. The secret of European growth is a simple one: Children grow faster than adults.

THE INTERNATIONAL MARKET

The fourth mirage is the idea held by some American businessmen that there is an international market. There is not. There is, instead, a collection of national markets. The approach to establishing an international marketing program is to establish a coordinated series of national marketing programs in countries where there appears to be a potential for a product. Even in a closely knit economic unit like the Common Market, this is still the basis of successful marketing. A company investigating the possibilities of doing business in Europe will find that not one, but five or six marketing studies are required. We cannot use a shotgun approach to overseas market research.

It is important to recognize these four mirages in marketing abroad and to emphasize American strengths. Too much attention has already been paid to real or imagined American weaknesses.

5.

ENTERING A FOREIGN MARKET—
KEY FACTORS FOR SUCCESS*

John D. Macomber

IT is quite evident that successful international marketers are taking a quite different approach now as opposed to the period up through the mid-1950's. Prior to then, most organizations could operate with an "export department" whose major function was to handle the mechanical arrangements necessary for the overseas distribution of domestically produced products. Traditionally, these departments acted as cream skimmers, picking up additional business with no real expenditure of money or effort. They often operated in the almost text-book atmosphere where competition abroad was very limited, or local producers could not make a really competitive product, or the local industry simply did not exist.

Perhaps the most significant single characteristic of the old export department approach was that their operations were governed by the requirements of the domestic market. They certainly were not governed by conditions of the overseas markets. For example, domestic product lines were offered abroad without any significant changes, local selling effort was determined largely on the basis of sales costs, production priority was given to domestic users, investment in the foreign markets tended to be negligible, and the like. Furthermore, in the eyes of top management profits from exports were considered only as a plus return on the company's existing investment for their own domestic market.

The developments since the mid-1950's have caused a basic change in the approach to marketing overseas. Companies seriously interested in developing global markets cannot afford to take the parochial point of view in which emphasis is primarily on one market. The old "export department" approach simply is not adequate for those who want to market globally.

With this in mind, my remarks today are directed at three major areas: (a) the impact of changed global market conditions, (b) the need to take a fact-founded approach in dealing with these changed conditions, and (c) developing meaningful marketing plans that are based on the current facts of marketing life.

* Reprinted by permission from *Indiana Readings in Business,* #38 (1962), The Foundation for Economic and Business Studies, pp. 33–39.

THE IMPACT OF CHANGE

Recent market developments of most overseas countries have been staggering—to put it mildly. For example, the productive capacity in the European countries has increased at an effective rate unlike any other period in history. At the same time suppliers to the new markets have become more abundant, competent and diversified. Seller's markets have turned into buyer's markets. In many cases the aura of exclusivity frequently attached to an imported product has diminished significantly. Simultaneously, trade barriers have been falling to the point where the competition is significantly broader than before. For example, sweaters are being sold in Rome department stores, made of synthetic fiber not only from Italian producers but Japanese, German, Dutch, English and American. (The problems encountered from the recent internationalizing of major markets become more complicated when one considers the different consumer mentalities, languages, distribution systems, financial restrictions and the like which must be taken into account when marketing on a world-wide basis.)

One cannot minimize the effect of these changes upon top marketing management, particularly on the extent of their involvement with nondomestic business. The decision to enter and stay in overseas markets now demands their active interest and support.

Further, the magnitude of the changed market environment has compounded the risks from inadequate analysis and superficial planning. The days have long since disappeared when domestic marketing techniques and procedures can be simply transplanted abroad. Consequently, the major impact of these changes has been to force top marketing management to place far more emphasis upon skillful analysis and planning.

GETTING THE FACTS

It is all important that any company seriously interested in building an overseas position embark on a fact gathering and analysis program before it makes any substantive moves overseas. Only in this way can a company safeguard itself against foreseeable surprises which can completely jeopardize the future developments of its sales abroad. I lay considerable stress upon the importance of getting the facts primarily because there have been several situations where companies relied upon "experience" from local markets instead of developing a fact based marketing program. By way of illustration, here are some of the critical areas that should be explored but which are often overlooked in the press of "getting started."

1. Basic *economic factors* governing market development and growth trends need to be documented. This does not necessarily imply a detailed economic analysis of any country; but it does imply an analysis that is thorough enough to identify the key forces behind a country's economic development. To illustrate, such an analysis should identify the importance of government spending, consumer credit, shifts in population, i.e., those subject to change and which have a real bearing upon the market.

2. *Product opportunities* need to be defined. The basic factors determining the need for the product are frequently vastly different from one market to another. For example, a Chevrolet in Europe has all the connotations of being a luxury automobile—an image that is completely different from the United States. Then too, the success of the scooter in Europe stems largely from the fact that it provided cheap transportation—a need that was adequately met in other ways in the U.S. These illustrations point out a basic fact of marketing life—factors leading to success in one market are often nonexistent in others.

3. Of course, any overseas marketer will be interested in the strengths and weaknesses of his *local competitors*. For example, what is their share of the market, pricing policy, where have their marketing programs been unique, what have been their successes and failures, and the like.

4. A company must have an accurate picture of its *prospective customers*. How do their wishes, needs, habits and beliefs affect the product? What attitude does the consumer have toward imported products in general or toward some radical changes in a long and well-known product? How did they react in the past when confronted with new products, with new promotional techniques? Do they have a favorable or unfavorable impression of the importer's country or his brands?

5. *The legal and financial regulations* governing the marketing of the company's products need to be documented. In addition to trademark restrictions there may be pricing and packaging regulations, labeling requirements, etc. Then, too, sales may be influenced by local taxes unknown in different markets. For example, consider the impact in England of the high purchase tax on the sale of automobiles.

The successful overseas marketer usually does not stint in his analysis of these and other critical areas. Instead it is the marginal operator who compromises in his fact-finding and analysis. The penalty for poor analysis is the inability to develop a truly competitive marketing plan. Stated another way, effective marketing planning depends upon a fact based analysis of the market.

MARKETING PLANNING

Marketing facts become the basis of any good marketing plan and the marketing plan used abroad will be based on entirely different facts than the ones applied in the domestic market. While the total marketing spectrum must be considered in developing a marketing plan, let me focus on three aspects that seem to be most in the limelight today: the product, the distribution channels, and production follow-up.

The product. When a company knows the type of product best suited for overseas markets, it should be in a position to compare the "ideal" product with its own. Quite likely, there will be some variations between the ideal and their own product performance, product specifications, prices, and the like. However, in such cases the company will be fully aware of its product's opportunities and limitations. It can then develop its marketing plan with these strengths and weaknesses in mind, and in a way that will overcome any negative aspects of the product. For example, an American company has had astounding success in selling overseas a higher-priced machine-tool than its counterpart produced in Europe. The reason for this success goes back to a fundamental point in their marketing plan which laid stress upon service superior to competition's.

In other words, a sound marketing plan will avoid such recent product pitfalls as these: (a) the European car manufacturer which did not realize that service was a major factor for their product and tried to sell their cars with little lasting success in the U.S., (b) the American refrigerator producers that marketed the wrong size refrigerator in Europe and thus gave European manufacturers a chance to build a solid share of the market, or (c) the soap company that entered a market with a washing product designed to give best results in boiling water although housewives in that particular market were using lukewarm water for washing. Therefore, the fact-based assessment of a product's strengths and weaknesses is at the heart of a sound marketing strategy.

Distribution channels. Equally important is the choice of distribution channels. Taboos often exist in foreign markets that are unknown in a company's domestic market. Then too, some groups might hold a virtual monopoly on the distribution of certain products. There is the case of the American food company which tried to sell directly to retailers in Germany and avoid the wholesalers altogether—a plan that, for this particular product and in that particular country, was doomed to failure, even though this distribution pattern was a great success in other markets.

In any event, the need to select distribution channels that are consistent with the local market is all important—particularly to the new-comer who is often dependent upon wholesalers for success or failure.

Production follow-up. Any solid marketing plan will have considered its production source—and will have evaluated the repercussions of overseas marketing on supplying the existing markets. All too often, the best laid marketing plans become useless because of inadequate supply. Nothing reduces a marketer's effectiveness more than an inability to deliver the goods that have been promoted and promised.

Therefore, in building a marketing plan, stress today should be placed upon the following:

> *The product must be right.* Product standing in the home market is not reliable. The product may be first class in one market but the taste can be different, the package too large or too small, the color in the wrong shades; the product might fill completely different needs (a necessity in the home market, a luxury in the foreign market), it might have dozens of advantages, but not the important ones for the overseas country (insufficient heating and defrosting systems on cars for northern countries).
>
> *Distribution channels* need to be chosen on the basis of conditions abroad. More than one company has found itself out of step with the market by selecting an inappropriate channel.
>
> *Continuous supplies* must be ensured, which means adequate capacities for overseas markets, sufficient stock in the market and well-organized pipelines.

CONCLUSION

In summary, let me emphasize that all indications point to the continued importance of overseas marketing. The fact that it is more difficult to reap substantial benefits in overseas operations is obvious, yet the opportunities continue to be substantial.

While there are many rules governing success overseas, we have stressed today a few fundamentals that are usually followed by the successful marketer on his home grounds but are often ignored or glossed over when looking overseas. These fundamental rules are (1) the importance of recognizing the impact of changing conditions, (2) the need to get the facts, and (3) the importance of a marketing plan that emphasizes the basics of product design, distribution channels and availability of supply.

6.

TODAY'S MARKETERS NEED
GLOBAL IDENTIFICATION*

Walter P. Margulies

IN the lexicon of modern marketing the terms, "global marketing" and "international marketing," have acquired connotations of togetherness which, though vague and imprecise, often obscure the fact that two different concepts are being talked about.

On the lips of one man, "global marketing" will mean marketing here in the U.S., as well as overseas. To another, even a close associate, economic chit-chat about global marketing registers as "international marketing," but this time the point-of-reference is entirely to those markets outside the U.S. The terms are just not synonymous, even if a semantic happenstance has almost made them so—with an unfortunate amount of confusion the result.

It should be understood that, primarily, I am talking here about global marketing. That is, about products and services developed in and for U.S. consumers—and how they can or are or should be sold in other countries as well.

International markets became a commonplace objective of entrepreneurs soon after bartering began. Global marketing, however, is a relatively new concept. To its disciples, trade has become simply a flow of goods from many sources to many markets.

In principle and practice, this contagious new viewpoint is sweeping across today's business world—bringing organizational changes and new marketing techniques to large companies and small, U.S. and foreign alike. Distinctions such as "foreign trade" and "national market" have been outmoded. For with the growth of new and vigorous competition from all parts of the world, today there is only one market, and that is the global market.

Skeptics may ask does this mean that consumers, willy-nilly have become the same everywhere; that their tastes, desires, and needs are suddenly, singularly alike? Not at all. Consumer differences do exist, as they always have. They are still important, and they still must be taken into account.

* Reprinted with permission from the 4/26/65 issue of ADVERTISING AGE. Copyright 1965 by Advertising Publications Inc.

Here in the U.S., for example, Southerners like to buy insecticide in grocery stores, while New Englanders prefer to purchase theirs in drug and variety stores—and for no clearly evident reason. Karo syrup, however, is produced in two viscosities for the demonstrably valid reason that certain ethnic groups are known to prefer a thicker syrup. And in many countries, frozen foods are strictly taboo, not because of consumer resistance, but because refrigerators and freezers are in such short supply. Even that old standby, the large economy-size package, has little appeal to shoppers who are plagued by storage and freshness problems.

Despite these differences—and there are countless others to contend with—the emergence of the global consumer is closer than ever before. Certainly, this marketing phenomenon is closer than it was ten years ago and, unquestionably, it will be much closer ten years hence.

Perhaps never before in world history have the forces and pressures that stimulate trade among nations been more insistent. The population explosion, a universal striving for a better material existence, increased buying power, and greater economic stability—all these things have helped lay the foundation for what promises to be an unprecedented era of world trade activity and growth.

It is within this affluent framework that the requirements and potential of global marketing must be weighed and developed. There is substantial evidence to indicate that the most successful companies of the next decade will be those in which a full control of global marketing strategy has been established. This does not necessarily imply production facilities in each country. But it will require (1) an international orientation in management thinking that extends beyond licensing arrangements, and (2) a greater degree of consumer orientation than now exists in the marketing operations of many companies.

Quite obviously, the transition from a purely domestic business to a truly global organization cannot be made in one leap. But let us recognize, at least, that it can and should be made with thoughtful long-range planning. The guidelines are available in depth. The techniques have been developed to a high degree. The markets are there. Indeed, international trade on a large scale is still in the development stage. The field is wide open.

Late last month one of the principles of a British agency visited our New York headquarters. Two of the accounts (Unilever and Clairol) handled by his agency are major package goods producers, deeply committed to global marketing. Although his visit was arranged to explore U.S. techniques in relating marketing requirements to package design, our discussions soon showed that he was appalled by the marketing mishaps of many American companies operating overseas.

In particular, he cited the introduction—under another name—of a popular American menthol cigaret in Germany. After spending millions in advertising, promotion, and distribution, the tobacco company involved found that the market was smaller than expected, and that menthol taste differences were greatly varied. Couldn't this have been determined in advance? I was asked. The answer: I'm sure it could, and amazed that it wasn't.

In the detergent field, our visitor noted, Germans also have a very difficult time saying "Dash." It comes out "Das." The copyright laws in Europe, he added, are quite different from those in the U.S. and it is extremely difficult to come up with a good name for a new product. As many American companies are finding, it quite often becomes necessary to go to the computer for a wellspring of candidate names.

Finding the right name, of course, is a universal problem. The famed Sinebrychoff brewery in Helsinki produces "Koff," a beer, and "Siff," a soft drink. Both beverages were being considered for the U.S. market several years ago—until someone explained that both names, though appropriate and appealing in Finland, were loaded with double entendre for giddy American eyes.

All too often the discovery comes after the catastrophe. One U.S. product was recently pulled from Latin American markets, because its name translated as "jackass oil." Another hit the skids because in Swedish the name means "enema."

Already a legend in marketing circles, though possibly apocryphal, is the reaction to a well-known line of baby food products which were unveiled in Africa. Native shoppers, it was said, thought the American company was selling ground-up baby in jars.

Advance knowledge of customs and cultures is essential to successful world trade. To spend years and millions of dollars building consumer acceptance in one country, and then to discover later that the brand name or the product itself is not transplantable—for lingual or cultural reasons—is, at least, foolhardy. It can be costly beyond all economic sense.

Many companies, however, don't even know where, or if, their products are being sold overseas. International distributors are allowed to take over the marketing function, often moving products into countries without notifying the manufacturer. In some cases, local dealers have even switched packaging from one product to another—again, without the manufacturer's knowledge.

Incredible? No, it happens all the time. The frequency of these marketing fiascos makes it evident that an integrated, multilateral system is needed, if global marketing is to be conducted in a climate of consumer confidence and profitable return on investment.

The company that has succeeded on its home ground through understanding and mastery of the techniques essential to a sound marketing program is well-equipped to compete in international trade. "Going international" involves chiefly an extension of function, rather than a change of function.

Perhaps the most glaring need—among package goods producers, in particular—is for a new appraisal of the product manager's function. If the marketing system is to be integrated, if a multilateral approach to global marketing is desirable, even mandatory, then the product manager's responsibility should no longer be confined by national boundaries. In short, with most product lines, he must become a global product manager.

The question will be asked: "How can any one executive be expected to understand, and act upon, all the ramifications of global marketing when it is so difficult now to keep on top of the domestic market?"

In some cases, perhaps many, today's "national" product manager may find the jump to "international" beyond his capabilities. It may be, in fact, that the job will call for a "new breed" with highly specialized talents—just as today's product manager represented a new breed not too many years ago.

Prior to World War II, or even ten years ago, the requirements of world product managership might well have been insurmountable. Not so today. World differences in advertising, selling, promotion, merchandising, and market research methods are sharply reduced, and the gap is narrowing.

Thanks to international television—such as the Eurovision network, linking European cities, and Telstar, linking the world—there will be still fewer communicative barriers to international trade. These developments, coupled with growing global communication through magazines, books, movies, advertising "overspill" and the mounting flow of tourist travel, have clearly shown that the "local" and "national" product manager concepts are inadequate—if not obsolete.

The global product manager, needless to say, will need more help than can be provided by the growth of international communications. He will require the services of experts in foreign customs, credit practices and currency, languages, market research, preferences and prejudices. If not an expert in the social and behavioural sciences himself, and he should be, he will need counsel in the national mores, habits, and cultural influences of many countries.

Fortunately, such skills and services are much more readily available today than they were in years not too far past. Unfortunately, they are not always called into use—or, if called, given a systematic follow through.

It is only natural, I think, that as global marketing continues, those companies which are best understood—that is, those with the best international identity—will be sought out first.

The introduction of a product into a foreign market, whether through export or overseas production, is roughly equivalent to introducing a new product in the U.S. Where, domestically, the goal is to achieve impact through uniformity of expression in all media in all states, internationally the same goal is sought among nations. In changing from one arena to another, moreover, geography is of little importance. From the standpoint of developing a global identity, England is closer to the U.S. than is Mexico.

What's more, the "language barrier" is not as formidable as it might seem at first glance. The customs, mores and preferences that form a hidden "cultural barrier" can be much tougher—even to the point of making a successful product in one country totally unadaptable to another.

As a result, the design elements of a global corporate identity system are of particular importance. For design transcends language—there being but one system of geometry, rooted in scientific fact, that serves all mankind.

It should be remembered that the early traders, lacking knowledge of new cultures, relied exclusively on symbolism for communication. Today, with vastly more sophisticated techniques available, we still find that Esso's white oval with blue border, or Shell's yellow sea shell, serve uniformly around the world to identify the products of large, capable organizations—even when the names are rendered in foreign letters.

There are no pat formulas, however, for developing a global corporate identity system—just as none has been found, or ever will be, for the domestic markets. Each system is unique and must be so, if it is to be effective in presenting the unique identity of one corporation, or family of companies, and one only.

Whether international or domestic, the purpose of a corporate identity system is to put the weight of the entire corporation behind the company's products. An effective system is all the more important internationally, because product diversity is likely to be more extensive overseas. Standards of living, and all the products that such standards affect, fluctuate a great deal more from country to country than region to region in the same country.

KELLOGG, JOHNSON ABROAD

Looking at a global corporate identity system in action, we see Kellogg recording 30% of its sales volume in more than 100 countries in which foreign languages are spoken. Although "Corn Flakes" becomes "Flikk Flakk" in Norway, and the familiar "snap, crackle, pop" becomes "knisper, knasper, knusper" in Germany, one constant selling identity remains —the Kellogg name.

Other companies get a similar result by developing a brand umbrella, such as Betty Crocker, rather than a corporate umbrella. The U.S. Rubber Co.'s recently introduced "UniRoyal" is an outstanding example of global brand identification. Since its introduction, late last summer, the UniRoyal communicative name has begun to be identified with the tires, chemicals, textiles, plastics, and footwear products made and distributed throughout the world by U.S. Rubber and its subsidiaries.

A classic example of global identification, of course is Chrysler Corp.'s "Pentastar." This jewel-like, five pointed figure appears the world over on all Chrysler products and facilities, all advertising and corporate literature, even on shipping cartons, delivery trucks, and water towers. While Simca, Chrysler's French automotive subsidiary, retains its distinctive styling for automobiles, the Pentastar on all vehicles coming from its plant leaves no doubt that this popular car is a corporate-relative of the U.S.-produced Imperial, Plymouth, Dodge, and Chrysler models.

Each of these companies has found that global corporate identity represents an investment in future growth. At the same time, it should not be assumed that their efforts have been confined entirely to the development of distinctive corporate symbols, or brand names with international significance. It is the integration of these elements into a sound long-range system, with appropriate controls for implementation, that gives validity and individuality to the corporate identity concept.

Some years ago, S. C. Johnson & Son found itself in an awkward situation, and was sophisticated enough to recognize what had to be done. Prior to 1957, the company had been known by a variety of names, ranging from simply "Johnson's" to "Johnson's Wax" to "S. C. Johnson" and sometimes "S. C. Johnson & Son." In addition, the company had accumulated a wide assortment of trademarks, including the Carnauba Palm and a representation of the famous Frank Lloyd Wright research tower in Racine—complete with globe to suggest the company's world-wide operations.

With some refinements in recent years, the recommendations made by our firm at that time are still the basis of the corporate identity system that identifies Johnson and its subsidiaries in 70 foreign countries.

The four-point corporate identity policy that began our client-consultant relationship with Johnson in 1957 featured the following:

1. Give as much Johnson's Wax support to your products as you can.

2. Use the trade name "Johnson's" wherever you legally can.

3. Use a consistent signature phrase on all non-wax products to increase association with "Johnson's Wax" even if you can use only the trade name "Johnson's."

4. Adopt a new visual symbol to be carried on all of your packaging and advertising, as well as promotion materials.

The company's role in international markets has since dictated that our original choice for a communicative name, "Johnson's Wax," be shortened to "Johnson." In some countries the possessive "s" makes no sense. In others, "wax" is simply untranslatable. A new corporate signature was designed in 1963 to eliminate this problem.

The new signature also serves as the corporate trademark. The double-diamond symbol, now a familiar mark to consumers, is nested inside the "J" in "Johnson." When the possessive "s" is required, a slant mark replaces the apostrophe. The signature is being applied to all product lines—thus serving the best interests of a unified corporate identity, and allowing each product to benefit from the endorsement of a well-known parent company name.

In their packaging programs, both here and abroad, Johnson enthusiasm for family identity in the design treatment of complementary products is still undiminished. In fact, independent studies, recently conducted by both Lippincott & Margulies researchers and Johnson European managers, have again confirmed that the most important element in packaging for the European market is graphic similarity.

More than most other large corporations, S. C. Johnson & Son has a very lucid picture of itself in its corporate mind. In Europe and elsewhere, it has been as concerned with improving its corporate image as it has with product performance and changing requirements of the marketplace. Call it corporate self-knowledge, or corporate empathy, but it is this attitude that leads to meaningful systems of communications and marketing.

GLOBAL PITFALLS

What sounds like a simple assumption—"international trade starts with having an international product to sell"—is neither simple, nor safe to assume.

For if we translate "product" into the more meaningful term "brand name," it is easy to realize that we have yet to see brand name consciousness existing in world markets to anything like the extent they are found within national markets.

Even some of today's more sophisticated world traders find new problems arising again and again, because their initial marketing strategy failed to include plans for an international product or brand name.

Package design, more than ever before, is of compelling importance in international trade. In the U.S. and several other countries, where advertising and promotion have been developed to a high degree, even a poor package might be forced into a market.

Outside the U.S. market, however, and despite the seeming abundance of foreign competition, few parts of the world can offer the effectiveness of American sales media. In some countries, commercial tv is limited or nonexistent. In many foreign areas, manufacturers face illiteracy rates that greatly reduce the impact of print media.

Thus, for good or ill, package design may be the strongest medium of communication between manufacturer and consumer.

Automotive replacement parts are typical of a product line that offers a stiff challenge in packaging for world trade. The manufacturer often must market these products through primitive distribution systems where reliance on unskilled help is unavoidable—such as in parts of Latin America. Because of the large numbers of basic parts involved, and their many variations in year and model of car, the opportunities for confusion are almost unlimited. Identification by numbers, along with illustration of the parts, is obviously needed—but even more important, our experience has shown, is the uniformity of graphic treatment which identifies the product with its manufacturer.

Take another seemingly small facet of the over-all problem: The selection of a suitable name for global marketing. The proved adaptability of "Schweppes" as a name in world trade, as contrasted to the German hair dressing "Haar Tabac," which might suggest a tobacco product applied to the hair, pretty well typifies the problems that all manufacturers must consider in brand name selection. In their respective countries, both products are well-known brand names with high acceptance, but one name is simply not suitable for some foreign markets.

Ideally, a single world brand name should be used for product identification. This can be done most easily, of course, when a totally new product brand is being developed. Where a successful domestic brand is to be sold internationally, and the existing name is not usable, the closest possible relationship between the new names and packages should be maintained for communications efficiency.

Frequently, phonetic translations can be useful to duplicate at least the spoken name in other languages. For example, in France and Belgium, the name "Klir" can be used for "Klear."

Another approach is to use a lateral, rather than literal, translation with a euphemism that expresses the connotation of the original name. Instant coffee, in this way, can be expressed in French as "café poudre" or "Café prêt à servir" or "café cristallisé"—none of which, of course, is instant coffee.

If the pitfalls of global marketing seem great, the opportunities are even greater. The potential for world commerce in the 60's and beyond is truely staggering. Economic forecasting for Western Europe, Japan, and the U.S. has actually become a risky business, because results often outdistance predictions.

For those with an awareness of the needs and complexities of the world market, the horizon is wide and without visible limits. The development of overseas markets, moreover, not only promises greater opportunities for expansion in good times, but can serve as a buffer against economic dislocation during recessionary periods.

In a very real sense, there are no strictly national markets today. All markets are simply part of one great international market. The companies that accept this one-world market concept—and many have already —are the companies that will be best prepared for the race ahead. International trade is a categorical imperative of our age. It will not, and indeed cannot, be denied.

7.

DEVELOPING AN EXPORT MARKET*

Richard D. Robinson

WHAT to sell? To whom? How much? Over what period of time? Via which channels? To be serviced by whom? To be promoted by whom? To be supplied from where?

These are the questions that come to the mind of an experienced management pondering the export market. And at some point management will also have to consider the restraints that may or may not be permitted to operate via intracompany and intercompany agreements, whether implicit or explicit. Obviously, each of these questions relates to all the others; decisions cannot be made in isolation.

SUBSTANCE OF EXPORT

Unless it has been service-oriented (e.g., research, engineering, architecture, construction, finance, insurance, transport, communications, management consulting, advertising, etc.) in its domestic operations, a management is very likely to look at foreign markets only in terms of merchandise. And, unless the firm has hitherto operated in many different markets and so has introduced a feedback into the design of its products, management will probably see a foreign market only in terms of the goods that the firm has been producing for domestic consumption. The greater the regional variation in its product design for the domestic market (that is, the more market-sensitive), the better prepared is a management likely to be to analyze overseas market opportunities in terms of the most appropriate products, within the capability range of the firm, for a particular market. But, if product is distinguished from service, perhaps no product is really optimum; export need not be limited to merchandise.

Because of their domestic concentration on the manufacture of merchandise and because they have frequently found opportunities for its export, most nonservice organizations do not see themselves in the business of selling services. Yet every manufacturer has a number of valuable

* Richard D. Robinson, "Developing an Export Market" in *Industrial Management Review*, Vol. 7, No. 1 (Fall, 1965) pp. 51–63.

services that he could sell if he chose—skills in management, marketing, production, construction, and research. In addition, many manufacturers have valuable rights that are marketable—process and product patents, copyrights, trademarks, agencies, established brand names, and production secrets. Firms may also find obsolete, but very useful, machinery on hand, or there may be surplus cash for which an investment opportunity is needed. In many foreign markets, the return to be realized from the sale of services, valuable rights, used machinery, and investable funds (for debt or equity in the portfolio sense) may be substantially greater than the profit to be earned on the export of goods or capital (meaning direct investment in foreign-based productive enterprise).

There are two general reasons for this conclusion: political vulnerability and comparative cost advantages.

For a variety of reasons, alien ownership[1] of overseas productive facilities almost always heightens risk. Particularly is this true where the enterprise represents an obvious and relatively large feature on the national economic landscape and the owners are identified with a national state very much more affluent than the host state. The movement of goods into a national state is often more easily subject to immediate control than the movement of services. Sale and purchase agreements are relatively short term, often 30 to 90 days. On the other hand, skills and rights typically move into a national market under the umbrella of relatively long-term contracts, often five to ten years. Very few instances of deliberate breech of such contracts by either individuals or governments have been reported. Rather than risk international harrassment, a state is likely to wait out the term of such a contract and refuse to approve its renewal; in this case the firm may have several years' warning and thus have time to shift its strategy with a minimum of loss. The point is that a contract does not bestow a vested interest unlimited in time, as does the ownership of tangible property. Yet a contract does more or less assure a market for a given period of time, which a simple sale (i.e., export of a product or right) does not.

The second reason for giving careful consideration to the export of skills (which are embodied in people) and valuable rights lies in their possible competitive advantage. Given the widening disparity in material well-being between the richer and poorer nations, the emergence of many new sovereign states (each increasingly sensitive to its own well-being), and the acceptance of rapid economic growth as a national ideology, it is clear that there must be increasing pressure for maximum use of local resources, including labor.

Stated in its simplest form, the theory of comparative advantage

[1] Ownership is equated with management control arising through equity investment. (See also n. 2, p. 47.)

holds that a nation should produce those goods and services that embody relatively more of the cheaper factors of production—that is, those which require resources relatively more abundant within the nation concerned than in potentially competing nations. It is useful to think of six factors, or production inputs:

1. Available natural resources, including arable land.

2. Capital, which is a function of the capacity to produce more goods and services than they consume, past and present.

3. Unskilled labor, labor which requires for productivity very little capital investment except that needed to keep a person alive until he reaches the age of productive labor, which typically is not very long.

4. Skilled labor, labor which requires substantial capital investment in education and training before a return is realized.

5. Entrepreneurship, the psychological set that generates creativity and *risk-seeking* which in turn seems to be a function of heightened expectations, assurance of a socially-acceptable minimum income level, and high-level skill of economic value.

6. Government—public services to assure the maintenance of law and order, development of a currency system, enforcement of commercial law, and public services including health, education, and agricultural extension, all of which tend to generate an integrated national market and a long-lived, educated population.

Risk—and hence cost—is increased for an enterprise in the absence of these production inputs. Cost is also increased to the extent that an enterprise has to provide certain of these services for itself. In addition, the absence of law and order, a currency system, transport and communication services, and effective commercial law renders impossible an integrated national market and, hence, many economies of scale. Furthermore, investment in education and training for high-level skill is uneconomic if public health conditions limit longevity to what might otherwise be considered middle-age.

Capital is embodied to varying degrees in consumer goods, production equipment, development of resources, government services, and the preparation of people for productive roles. Consumer goods embody least capital, and skilled people are most capital-intensive. The other factors lie in between in a generally ascending order. The reason for this ordering of production inputs by capital-intensity lies in the time between investment and return, the so-called "gestation period" of capital investment. Before an individual generates any return on the investment made in him, he must have at least reached a productive age. If high-level skills are involved, the time required may be two to three times greater. In the U.S. today, producing top level professional competence in an individual probably requires a total investment of well over $100,000; in the case of major research involving many highly-skilled persons over many years, this figure is multiplied manyfold.

It may be argued that there are only three true production inputs —resources, people, and capital—that government services, skills, and entrepreneurships are produced by capital. And even the stock of *available* resources may be altered by capital and people. So it is perhaps possible to talk in terms of two factors. However, these factors are capable of very slow change; the stock of people and capital may be changed significantly only in the very long run, and the quantity of *skilled* personnel and the public infrastructure of a nation may be altered only quite slowly. That is, the capital embodied and frozen in skills and government cannot easily be shifted as the result of market pressures operating within the time horizon of most business decisions. The same is true for much resource development. Commitments of capital are made long in advance of actual production. These therefore become independent factors of production within the time with which we are concerned in business decisions.

The United States, having possessed a relatively high capital/unskilled labor ratio for many years, has developed a cost advantage in those goods and services which incorporate large amounts of capital relative to unskilled labor. It has also had relatively high resource/unskilled labor, skilled labor/unskilled labor, government/unskilled labor, and entrepreneurship/unskilled labor ratios. Generally, therefore, it possesses an international advantage in the goods and services that are relatively rich in resources, skilled labor, entrepreneurship, and government services— all of which are a function at least in part of the relative capital wealth of the United States over many decades. This means that in general the greatest markets for U.S. business relate to those goods, rights, and services relatively rich in these factors.

This argument tends to discourage export from the United States of many consumer products; it suggests, rather, that the trend in the direction of exporting products rich in resources, capital, high-level skills, and public services should continue. Most intensive in these factors are the resources, capital, and skills themselves; Government services *per se* do not generally have a direct influence although such services as basic education and preventative health may sometimes be relevant.

For these two reasons, then—political vulnerability and comparative cost—many firms would do well to consider carefully the export of skills, valuable rights (which are produced by high-level skills), and capital in the form of debt or portfolio equity, instead of considering export of merchandise and/or direct investment.[2] It should be pointed out that as nations become more sensitive to the requirements of economic development, to their own economic interests, and to comparative costs, pressure will mount to limit imports from the more developed nations (i.e., those relatively affluent in skills and capital) to those that are rich in skills, risk, and capital. The poorer nations will then be in a position to employ more of their own resources. This pressure, in turn, may heighten the political vulnerability of firms relying upon the export of consumer goods and capital in the form of direct investment. Domestic experience and a history of successful export of merchandise and of direct investment may not be adequate guidelines for the future.

SALES TARGET

It should be recognized that the use of historical export sales statistics to predict future trends of exports is hazardous. Although the figures may possibly be valid in the short run, export sales are subject to discontinuities arising from the collapse of a competitive position (e.g., appearance of local production), imposition of import controls for revenue or consumption control purposes, imposition or release of export controls by the United States, or an official decision to compel local production. In the longer run, imports into the United States of comparable products may be a better guideline to overseas markets. But even imports have a serious flaw; a product may enjoy a substantial demand in a given foreign market but none in the United States due to disparate income and wealth levels, values and institutions, climate, geography, and style of living. In addition, there are many services produced in the United States that have not been pushed into the export stream but which *theoretically* should enjoy substantial overseas markets. Because of their generally capital-intensive nature they do not show as imports into the United States. Therefore, the present flow of international trade in many cases provides only a first, short-run approximation of foreign market opportunities.[3]

---

[2] Direct investment is defined here as investment made for the purpose of acquiring or of maintaining management control, control being defined in terms of the location of final decision-making authority in respect to dividend and investment policies, choice of product, volume of production, discretionary costs, and employment of key personnel.

[3] This is not to deny the importance of these data. The United Nations, U.S. Department of Commerce, Organization for European Economic Cooperation, and various common market and trade bloc organizations publish historical series of trade by commodities, three classification systems being used—the Standard International Trade Classification (SITC) by the United Nations and 85 political entities, the Standard Industrial Classification (SIC) by the U.S. Department of Commerce, and the Brussels Tariff Nomenclature (BTN) by roughly 100 nations and several of the regional trade groups.

Logically, a firm should look periodically at every potential market in order to assure optimum allocation of its resources. Given the limited managerial, production, marketing, and financial resources at the disposal of a firm, a policy of exerting equal energy in developing each national market is obviously not optimum. Stripped to its essence, then, the decision should be a determination of those markets on which the firm should concentrate its efforts, *forgetting for the moment the source from which that market will be supplied.* Does a sufficient demand exist for a product, valuable right, or service within the capability of the firm make that market more attractive than others?[4]

Securing a convincing answer to that question is costly, and herein lies a major obstacle to international business. Detailed studies of virtually every national market, lists of which are published periodically by the U.S. Department of Commerce, are available to the businessman. But management needs a fairly precise notion of the nature of its market before this mass of information is of much value.

Some firms set out the range of goods, rights, and services within their capability and attempt to relate the market of each to certain aggregate national statistical measures. Some of the national measures are per-capita income (bear in mind that comparisons across currency frontiers are very tricky; to secure comparable purchasing powers, dollar figures derived by use of official exchange rates for the poorer countries must be multiplied by a factor of two or three); distribution of personal income (rarely available except for the more developed countries); class structure (may be estimated from educational and occupational breakdowns, and may also be inferred by the differential between rural and urban population); degree of industrialization (may be estimated from sectoral breakdowns of the gross national product data); degree of urbanization (population statistics, rural and urban, are generally available); degree of national integration (may be estimated from the ratio of cargo and passenger transport to the total tonnage of marketable goods and total population); existence of specific industries, services, or agricultural activity (input-output tables are rarely available, although crude approximations may be derived); literacy (local definitions may be misleading); age dis-

4 Eliminated immediately from the list of potential markets for firms controlled by U.S. nationals or legal entities are those closed by U.S. government action through export control, which affects capital equipment, technical information, and skills as well as merchandise. The Export Control Act of 1948 provides for the control of exports to countries other than Canada in order to provide support for U.S. foreign policy, national security interests, and the domestic economy. Most goods can move to non-Communist-bloc countries under a general license which requires no formal application. Validated licenses are required for certain types of strategic goods regardless of destination and in almost all cases for strategic goods destined to bloc countries. In addition, there is a virtually complete embargo on trade with Communist China, North Korea, North Vietnam, and Cuba. Transactions of U.S.-controlled foreign enterprise are similarly restrained.

tribution; and the degree of development of certain natural resources, including water and power.

Unresolved questions include projected trends for each of these factors and the occasional presence of an attractive regional or segmented market. In respect to the first, the inertia of traditional or near-traditional society suggests that changes may appear as discontinuities, not predictable on the basis of a historical series. For example, the Anatolian Turk used a solid-wheeled ox cart for over 3,000 years, but between 1955 and 1965 these carts virtually disappeared from large areas. Rural society may resist urbanization for many years despite great economic pressure; then, almost without warning, the dam bursts. Only skillful social-anthropologists can predict such shifts with any degree of accuracy.

An attractive subnational market may be well hidden by aggregate statistics. Statistics on the poverty of India, considered in the aggregate, do not suggest the existence of a large subnational market for many sophisticated products. The set of cultural variables constituting a market for a given product should not be equated necessarily with a national market.

Even though a given national market may not appear large enough to warrant more than a reading of the statistics, the commitment of company resources may be justified for combined segments of different national markets lying within a convenient geographical or cultural area.[5] In studying such a situation, management should consider its potential competitive position in the market. A rough demand schedule may readily be constructed, but what of the supply side? And where would the firm fit in? Among the relevant variables to be considered are entry barriers[6] (including the displacement of local business and/or present third-country suppliers and their anticipated response; import restrictions, whether in reference to merchandise, services (i.e., visas and official approvals), valuable rights, or finance; the need for special permits or franchises; the degree of cartelization; economies of scale; control of the distribution systems; existence of established brand names; and control by others of relevant patents, trademarks, or copyrights); exit barriers (including barriers to the repatriation of profits and/or capital; legal protection for valuable rights; personal safety of aliens and their property; and restrictions on the export of goods, services, rights, and finance); and competitive barriers[7] (the operating margins of potential competitors; involuntary expense, such as unavoidable costs in manu-

---

[5] Of particular importance in this regard are the many trade blocs, tariff unions, free trade areas, common markets and arrangements in relation to specific industries or commodities. But one should be alert to the fact that "natural" pressures for or against such market integration (e.g., factor complementarily) may well outlive and/or redirect politically-inspired integration.

[6] See [1].

[7] See [2], pp. 60-79.

facture and, in the case of off-shore supply, transport and entry charges; and such discretionary expenses as promotion, development, research, marketing, and profit).

The operating margin may not necessarily reflect either tight or loose competitive conditions. Relevant variables include the scale of production (if large, generous profits may appear even if operating margins are low), the organization of distribution channels (if distribution channels are limited, a high level of discretionary cost may be required), the structure of an industry (if one large company enjoys maximum economies of scale, the operating margin may be wide and competitive conditions severe), and the importance of price in creating demand (if price dominates, a narrow operating margin probably means tight competitive conditions).[8] The point is: "The most important condition of entry is that the company's initial marketing objectives create discretionary margins which are large enough to sustain its growth objectives. Recognizing the importance of maintaining the venture's position relative to industry leaders, management may see that it is not sufficient merely to match their discretionary expenses; it may be necessary to exceed the other firms' expenses substantially. For example, if there is a shortage of distribution channels, the capture of which is critical to achieve success, management may have to spend more than competitors on the product lines, services, or promotion needed to secure these channels."[9] Hodgson and Uyterhoeven admonish against duplicating the programs of industry leaders and urge the new entrant to select his own battle ground. In doing so, they warn that the failure to recognize essential differences in industry or market conditions between the United States and a foreign market may be costly. Such failure "may lead to incorrect assumptions as to a venture's (or a market's) permissible discretionary margin . . ."[10] A careful examination of the involuntary expenses is necessary. Among involuntary expenses differing from those incurred in the United States are likely to be the following:

Labor. In many countries the cost of legally-imposed fringe benefits (social welfare taxes, the "thirteenth month" bonus, payments into a publicly administered pension plan, and termination pay) may add up to a significant percentage of the direct payroll, to which must be added the cost to the firm of accounting for these payments. Also, the true cost of labor includes training costs, which may be aggravated by an unexpectedly high turnover rate. In addition, U.S.-based assumptions as to the number of employees required may not be justified if productivity is substantially different. Labor codes operative in many countries, make termination both difficult and expensive, and labor may therefore be

8 See [2], p. 68.
9 [2], p. 69.
10 [2], p. 70.

more in the nature of a fixed cost. It may sometimes be made more variable by taking advantage of various escape clauses relating to "temporary labor." Such practices may, however, accelerate the turnover rate, thereby adding to training costs. A relevant variable here is how much internal training must be undertaken. In situations where internal training is of vital importance, manning tables should be constructed, rates of disappearance calculated, and projections of needed labor in various skills set up. Unless explicit policy to the contrary has been announced by the firm, graduates of company training schools and courses tend to feel that the firm is obligated to employ them upon "graduation." If the firm does not do so, and if it constitutes an important employer in the local economy, an awkward political situation may be created, further adding to costs.

Materials and power. An inadequate supply may force an enterprise into an integration with which it is not familiar in the United States, thereby adding to cost. Also, because of the economies of scale in power production, power plants serving only a single enterprise may operate at very high cost.

Finance. Local finance may be made necessary by local inflation and foreign exchange controls. However, interest rates and local profit expectations may be high, adding significantly to cost. Differences in taxation, depreciation requirements, working-capital needs, and utilization of debt leverage should, likewise, be considered; all may differ from U.S. practice. For example, distance may mean either high inventories and/or expensive transport.

Management. If American management is deemed necessary for reasons of control and/or inadequacy of local nationals, management may be significantly more costly than in the United States because of special bonuses typically paid to expatriate American managers.

Control. Distance means added cost in terms of communications, travel, misunderstandings, and tardy handling of problems. A generous allowance is required to cover this item. If management is local and does not use English fluently, a significant translation cost may be incurred.

Production. Given a smaller market, either unused capacity and/or more general-purpose machines may be inevitable. In the first case, fixed charges per unit of production are higher; in the latter, more extensive training and supervision are needed. Also, if production depends on imported supplies or components, an uneven allocation of foreign exchange will cause fluctuation in production and, hence, added cost.

Distribution. Control of existing channels by others may make it necessary to open new channels which may be costly due to low volume.

When management has satisfied itself as to the existence of a relatively attractive demand, competitive conditions with which it can live, and apparently feasible costs, the next step is an on-the-spot survey. This is a costly procedure, and management should be relatively certain of its ground before dispatching such a group.

Various methods are available for inplace market surveys. Products may be displayed at local trade fairs, professional meetings, and world trade centers, where response may be measured; potential consumers may be questioned by mail or in interviews; the use of free samples or a concerted sales effort for a given period of time without regard for profit in order to pretest the market; and social anthropologists familiar with the area may be consulted. The choice of methods depends upon several variables: the nature of the market (industrial, professional, or consumer), its size and homogeneity, the geographical concentration of expected consumers, their literacy, the number of markets being surveyed, customer reaction to the questionnaire approach, the availability of dependable surveyers, the resources of the firm, and the availability of competent social anthropologists in the area. There is always the danger of unconsciously making a number of culturally-conditioned assumptions, such as the use of the product being tested and hence the general identity of the potential customers (for example, one firm did not expect its margarine to be eaten like cheese and thereby overlooked that part of the population not using butter on its bread), propensity of people to buy a given type of product, the probability that people will respond to a market survey honestly or at all, the location of the buy-or-not-buy decision-making authority, the relationship between enthusiasm for a free sample and willingness to buy, errors in generalization from a sample (for example, the marketer may fail to recognize significant bias in a sample due to the presence, in undue numbers, of a religious, racial, class, caste, educational, or occupational group).

MARKET PENETRATION

The optimum penetration of the target market is related to the time horizon of management (see below), product quality, design, specialization of product, price, access to channels, and availability of funds for investment in promotion. The really significant questions to be asked are:

1. Are the assumptions made about necessary quality standards really justified in respect to the target market?
2. Is the design of the product such as to generate maximum demand? (Included are such considerations as packaging, marking, color, size, and measure).
3. Is the product necessarily specialized in use or function?
4. Is the product so designed as to rely unnecessarily on the presence of other products or materials in the target market?

5. Can the price be shifted significantly by reason of the above considerations?
6. Would access to channels of distribution become easier and distribution less costly if the firm were to go into partnership with local interests?
7. Is the present promotion budget really optimum if unjustified national bias (bias toward the domestic U.S. market) is eliminated?
8. Are the indicators of potential penetration (income-demand elasticities, for example) used by management reliable in the foreign environment?

It should always be borne in mind that quality is relative to use; it is not an absolute dimension.

TIME HORIZON

Prior to an on-the-spot market survey, management should normally have made explicit the time horizon it will use in determining the return from company resources committed to the exploitation of that market. If the time horizon is very short, only a minimum commitment is justified—possibly no more than a reading of the aggregate statistics and talking with one or two persons familiar with the area. In such case, management will be concerned only with existing conditions in the market, not its dynamics. A short time horizon also normally implies no consideration of supply sources other than those already existing; certainly it implies that there will be no new direct investment in productive facilities either in the United States or abroad from which to supply the target market. Although risk is reduced with a short time horizon, because market conditions of the near future can be predicted with greater accuracy than those of the more distant future, market opportunities inherent in future growth and structural changes in the target market may be hidden from view.

Relevant variables in setting an appropriate time horizon include the firm's available resources, its present geographical spread, the nature of its product, and growth conditions in markets within which the firm is presently operating (particularly in the domestic market). If one or more of these factors does not rule out a time horizon longer than the current fiscal period, then management should not impose such a time restraint on its foreign market strategists. Table 1 suggests some of the relationships that may exist between selection of time horizon and acceptable strategies, but is not meant to be definitive in any sense. The point is that time and effort, and hence money, are wasted if analysts are permitted to consider strategies that management cannot accept. Bear in

TABLE 1—THE TIME HORIZON OF MANAGEMENT AND ITS IMPLICATIONS

Now 1 Year 2 Years	3 Years	4 Years	5 Years	10 Years	20 Years
Sell present product	Consider by-products (i.e., services, rights, finance)		Full consideration of by-products		→
Market research statistical study	Market research – detailed study of selected target markets		On-the-spot market analysis	Continuing market analysis	→
Limited penetration	Moderate penetration		Full penetration		→
Limited promotion (largely spillover)	Some specially-designed promotion		Full promotion		→
No servicing		Provision for some servicing	Full servicing		→
No investment related to foreign sales		U.S. investment related to foreign sales			→
No product modification	Minor product modification		Product redesign	Special products	→
Use present sources	Overseas assembly in leased facilities or contract manufacturing		Overseas manufacturing	Interchange manufacturing possible	→
Direct mail order and/or independent exporters	→ either		Overseas agents or representatives	Foreign sales branch or subsidiary	→
No specialized personnel	Specialized expert personnel		Specialized staff personnel	Internationally oriented staff	Internationally oriented operation
No organizational changes	Slight organizational changes		Major organizational changes	International-oriented organization	Multi-national organization
Tight control from U.S.	Tight control		Looser control	Decentralized control	Near-autonomy for operation
100 per cent U.S. ownership	Contractual relations		100-per-cent-owned foreign subsidiary	Joint ventures	Multi-national ventures

mind that there is a significant difference between what management *can* and *is willing* to accept. This difference should be made explicit after careful study of company resources and its commitment to present markets.

CHOICE OF CHANNELS TO REACH A FOREIGN MARKET

The first decision to be made in choosing channels to a foreign market is whether the firm itself is to undertake the responsibility (i.e., risk) of moving its product to the target market, or whether it will employ an external agency. In making this decision, management should consider the availability of specialized export skills presently within its organization, the desirability of direct relation with its foreign markets (the feedback effect), the likelihood of eventual assembly or manufacture within the target market, the possibility of supplying that market from a third source, and the cost of developing internal exporting expertise. All of these are related to management's time horizon and to the potential importance of the target market in relation to the firm's total sales.

It should be clearly understood that export does require a set of highly-specialized skills having to do with packaging, marking, documentation, selection of carriers, insurance, foreign import and exchange regulations, export finance, and the selection of overseas commission houses, representatives, and/or agencies also the sensitivity to know when direct entry into the market through a foreign sales branch or subsidiary will be most advantageous.

The firm should be prepared to quote c.i.f. the nearest port (not f.o.b. for some point in the United States), give competitive credit terms (not insist on irrevocable letters of credit), provide adequate information about its products in a language and in measures useful to the potential customer, reply promptly and fully to overseas inquiries, provide adequate instructions in a useful language for a product's use, assure overseas customers of supply as regular as to domestic customers. To do these things requires specialists.

In event management opts for an export channel external to the firm, it has the alternatives of using commission agents, foreign buyers (for both government and private principals) resident in the United States, a combination export manager, a cooperative export association (e.g., a Webb-Pomerene Association), an export broker, or an integrated distributor (who buys, stocks, and distributes overseas on his own account). The risk—and, hence, financial liability—is generally least for the firm when it sells outright in the United States to resident foreign buyers and integrated distributors. The risk is moderate in the case of commission agents and combination export managers who operate on a commission basis, somewhat greater for export brokers, who simply negotiate sales contracts but assume little of the risk, and for the combination export manager operating on a flat fee basis. In the case of many communist countries, the firm may not have the option; the only buyer may be an office located in the United States. Lists of all of these services and agencies may be obtained from local Chambers of Commerce, World Trade Centers, Port Authorities and the U.S. Department of Commerce.

Among the many aids to management in planning foreign operations, the least familiar are the combination export managers and Webb-Pomerene associations. The former may provide virtually all of the services of an export department. The relationship rests on an agreement defining territories, products, functions, reimbursable expenses, promotional responsibility, and fees and commissions. A combination export firm generally works for several noncompetitive manufacturers. It conducts business in its own offices, handles all correspondence pertaining to its clients' exports, appoints overseas agents and representatives, and assists in preparing advertising copy and selecting media.

The Webb-Pomerene association is a device by which a group of United States firms may join their export activities without becoming vulnerable to U.S. antitrust prosecution. Such an association, which is a domestic corporation, must engage solely in export trade; foreign manufacturing facilities may not be included. Nor may it engage in any domestic business except that incidental to export. The law authorizes—for export purposes only—joint facilities, price fixing, and the allocation of orders among members; and it is required that members export only through the association. A Webb-Pomerene association may not, however, restrain nonmember exports in any way and may not enter into agreements with foreign companies that are illegal for independent U.S. firms, nor may it have an effect on domestic business contrary to provisions of the antitrust laws.

Management should note that it is contrary to the interest of these external exporting agencies to recommend the development of another source of supply for any particular target market, such as some variety of overseas assembly or manufacturing, even though there be strong arguments in its favor. Hence, even though a management may employ such external agencies, it should undertake periodically an internal or independent check on its foreign markets. Furthermore, a firm using an external agency may find promotion, servicing, and/or product design feedback substantially less than optimum. Management should be forewarned not to finance the *development* of market expertise external to the firm.

The broker in international license, technical assistance, and management contracts is a specialized agency of recent origin. Other relative newcomers are mutual funds concentrating on overseas portfolio investment and specialists in the overseas marketing of used capital equipment.

A firm may in a sense also export its distribution services by buying goods and services of overseas origin—that is, imports—for distribution in the domestic or third markets. Inasmuch as importing, just as exporting, requires a set of highly specialized skills—not the least of which is moving goods through United States customs—the firm anticipating importing is faced with a set of alternatives similar to those in the exporting situation, and similar variables are relevant.

One of the difficulties in comparing the cost to the firm of these various channels is that at least a portion of those activities performed by the firm itself may be charged to general overhead and not be allocated to the export or import function. Therefore, the marginal costs of the various alternatives are not strictly comparable.

The firm that chooses to perform these functions for itself is shouldering the risk of the movement of the goods or services involved to or from the foreign market. It may merely go to the frontier if it is involved only in a mail order or purchase business. Other alternative strategies involve penetration into the foreign market to a greater degree, with the greatest penetration represented by the establishment of foreign sales subsidiaries. In this case the firm comes face-to-face with the internal distribution systems and supply channels of the foreign market. The size of the market, the nature of the product, the importance of the market feedback, and the resources available to the firm (including the necessary associated skills) control the decision. And again, management should be cautioned not to make assumptions conditioned by domestic experience about any one of these factors.

CHOICE OF CHANNELS WITHIN THE TARGET MARKET

A firm may go still further, of course, by pushing on toward the ultimate consumer. Various alternative paths of distribution and the possible functions and characteristics of each level of activity are diagrammed in Table 2. Relevant variables include the ability of one activity (including the manufacturer or foreign sales branch or subsidiary) to perform functions of the next, the degree of control of each activity by competitors, the adequacy of coverage by each activity, the degree to which flow is confined to fixed channels (that is, the extent to which retailers purchase directly from manufacturers in contrast to their purchasing from primary wholesalers), the nature of the customer (mass, industrial, or limited market), the nature of the product (its durability, need for special handling, ease of adulteration, demand for customer service, and unit cost), and the existence of a turnover or transactions tax (which may have a pyramiding effect).

TABLE 2—ANALYSIS OF A DISTRIBUTION SYSTEM

Types of Buyers from Manufacturer or Sales Subsidiary ——→	Primary Wholesaler ——→	Secondary Wholesaler ——→	Retailer ——→	Consumer
Possible Functions of Each Level:				
Storage (various types)				
Inventory				
Credit { Backward / Forward				*
Transport { Backward / Forward				*
Technical service				
Promotion				
Collections				*
Price maintenance				
Accounting				*
Estimate of credit-worthiness of next-level firms				*
Risk-bearing (insurance, product performance guarantees etc.)				
Packaging				*
Characteristics of Each Level:				
Degree of specialization				
Size				
Geographical coverage				*
Performance				*
Tie-in { Backward / Forward				*
Exclusivity				
Ease of entry				

*Does not apply.

CUSTOMER SERVICE

No customer service is required for many consumer goods, although the matter of guarantees of quality and performance may remain. Are such guarantees really necessary and, if not, what is the effect on cost? Where foreign exchange controls operate and time-consuming transport is involved, quality and performance guarantees may be inoperable unless local inventories are maintained. If the complexity, unreliability, and/or use of a product makes servicing necessary, the firm must decide whether to put its own servicing agents into the field or to lease or otherwise contract for these services. Both courses may be unduly costly in the period before a significant market is developed, and so there is pressure for some sort of regional arrangement. This latter is feasible if freedom and cost of movement within the area are reasonable. In some instances a joint arrangement with competitors may be possible, thereby lowering service costs for all concerned. For products exported from the United States, a Webb-Pomerene association may be a useful solution.

PROMOTION VEHICLE

Whether the firm itself undertakes promotion in the target market or contracts for this work with an external advertising or promotional agency depends in large measure upon the availability of the necessary talent, the potential size of the target market, and management's time horizon. If the firm is likely to move into production within the overseas market in the foreseeable future, the rationale for employing an external agency may be somewhat weakened; the necessary talent may reasonably be employed by the firm in preparation for the more complex problems that local production will entail.

Relevant variables in the decision between a U.S. and foreign agency would include the national identification of the given products or services within the target market, the extent of differences between the domestic and target markets, "spill-over effect" and linkages. "Spill-over effect" is the creation of demand in one country by reason of promotion in another. "Linkages" refer to demand created in other than the initial market by reason of either the movement of the product or of the customer, or both; an example is an international hotel system which can be used to channel customers from one hotel to the next; another example is improved cargo handling equipment aboard a ship, which creates demand wherever it is seen in operation. A special type of "spill-over effect" is that created by the "pre-sell," where demand is stimulated in a foreign market by local nationals such as students, participants in professional meetings, and the like who have spent time in the United States or third markets.

There is a further strategy alternative in the selection of an agency: Should it be the agency used by the firm in the United States or a different one? If the latter, should it be foreign—i.e., indigenous to the target market —or identified with a third market? In making this choice, of course, the entire international program of the firm should be considered. Directly relevant are the firm's ownership and control strategies and its likelihood of developing foreign profit centers. Major pitfalls: include centralizing *control* of foreign promotional campaigns in the United States, whether conducted by the firm or an agency; utilizing for overseas promotion a U.S.-based agency which does not have adequate experience or staff to be effective in the target market; failure to have any department, subsidiary, or agency directly responsible for promotion in the target market; and permitting the overseas promotion effort to be overshadowed by and become subsidiary to the domestic effort.

Trade fairs, trade centers, and trade missions are increasingly important in the promotion of certain goods and services in overseas markets. The former tend to be annual affairs in all of the major trading centers of the world. Trade centers often house permanent exhibits and/or market information channels. Trade missions, organized and sponsored by the U.S. Department of Commerce and/or regional world trade centers such as those of New Orleans, Boston, New York, or San Francisco are on an *ad hoc* basis. The varying continuity of each institutional device and the different exposure which each offers determine the relative value to the firm; trade fairs tend to reach a very general audience, trade centers reach commercial buyers, and trade missions are especially effective with specific interested parties.

NATIONAL SOURCE OF PRODUCT

Management should be aware that price alone may not determine optimum strategy in respect to national source of supply. There are several reasons.

Because of balance-of-payments pressure, foreign exchange controls, and high interest rates, the customer may be most concerned about the currency in which payment is to be made; in descending order, his other concerns are likely to be about credit terms, delivery time, durability, and (lastly) price.

Production within the foreign market may be justified even though the resulting product price be higher than for a comparable import; this is because official exchange rates in lesser-developed countries often undervalue (in respect to comparative purchasing power) the local currency in terms of convertible currencies, a circumstance which is equivalent to a subsidy for imports and a tax on exports. That is, the importer is permitted to buy more dollars per local currency unit than is economically justified; the exporter receives fewer local currency units per dollar of value sold. An import-substituting industry should therefore be measured by the recorded value of the imports thereby rendered unnecessary *plus* 20 to 30 percent more for many underdeveloped countries. Up to that inflated unit price, the *local economy* gains even though it could import the same item more cheaply. The point is that, using the official exchange rate, the convertible exchange to be saved is worth more in the calculus of national economic growth than the local resources used. These things are recognized as government economists become more sophisticated, and official pressures favoring the local product can be expected.

In a given target market, certain countries tend to be associated with the more desirable attributes of the product in question—for examples, German optics, Turkish tobacco, English woolen goods, and French wine; in some instances, a foreign-made product is assumed to be "better" than a local manufacture.

In determining the optimum supply source, management should consider trade patterns—often frozen by bilateral commercial agreements, reparations, or foreign assistance—, the extent and sophistication of government trade controls, and comparative costs. For all of the reasons outlined in the previous discussion of relative costs, the optimum supply source cannot be determined by a simple cost comparison built on the U.S. factor mix, the U.S.-designed product, the U.S. definition of a plant (the particular bundle of processes housed on one site), or U.S. scales of economy.

RESTRAINT ON COMPETITION

A firm may limit the sales efforts of its various subsidiaries and associated firms by the device of awarding exclusive territory or by price fixing arrangements. Factors to be considered: legality, product differentiation, enforceability, relative levels of involuntary costs of the various enterprises (including those implicit in collective labor contracts, governmental agreements, and community responsibility), likelihood of intracompany competition forcing revenue below involuntary costs for some enterprises and price-demand elasticities in the various markets. For example, assuming no legal barrier nor product differentiation, a firm might impose an exclusive territorial arrangement if involuntary costs varied substantially among the related enterprises and if price-demand elasticities were negative (that is, if total revenue would fall with a decrease in price) in the markets concerned. Restrictions imposed on foreign entities neither controlled through ownership nor acting as an agency of a U.S. firm are very likely to run afoul of U.S. or foreign antitrust laws; this is particularly true if the associated foreign firm is a manufacturer.

CONCLUSION

In the final analysis, sales strategy must be adjusted and readjusted by reason of the feedback from strategy selections in other areas—supply, management, labor, finance, ownership, legal, and control. That is, no final choices should be made before possible problems in these other areas of decision have been resolved. In a sense, everything could be subsumed under sales strategy, as some marketing "specialists" are wont to do. The international marketeer, sensitive to this reality, maintains close communication with all departments of the firm. Organizational implications are apparent. Any other course which involves isolation of the export or international department may not be in the best interest of the firm.

REFERENCES

1 Bain, Joe S., *Barriers to New Competition,* Cambridge: Harvard University Press, 1956.
2 Hodgson, Raphael W., and Uyterhoeven, Hugo E. R., "Analyzing Foreign Opportunities," Harvard Business Review, March-April, 1962, pp. 60-79.

CULTURE AND ENVIRONMENT

8.

THE SILENT LANGUAGE IN OVERSEAS BUSINESS*

Edward T. Hall

WITH few exceptions, Americans are relative newcomers on the international business scene. Today, as in Mark Twain's time, we are all too often "innocents abroad," in an era when naiveté and blundering in foreign business dealings may have serious political repercussions.

When the American executive travels abroad to do business, he is frequently shocked to discover to what extent the many variables of foreign behavior and custom complicate his efforts. Although the American has recognized, certainly, that even the man next door has many minor traits which make him somewhat peculiar, for some reason he has failed to appreciate how different foreign businessmen and their practices will seem to him.

He should understand that the various peoples around the world have worked out and integrated into their subconscious literally thousands of behavior patterns that they take for granted in each other.[1] Then, when the stranger enters, and behaves differently from the local norm, he often quite unintentionally insults, annoys, or amuses the native with whom he is attempting to do business. For example, in the United States, a corporation executive knows what is meant when a client lets a month go by before replying to a business proposal. On the other hand, he senses an eagerness to do business if he is immediately ushered into the client's office. In both instances, he is reacting to subtle cues in the timing of interaction, cues which he depends on to chart his course of action.

Abroad, however, all this changes. The American executive learns that the Latin Americans are casual about time and that if he waits an hour in the outer office before seeing the Deputy Minister of Finance, it does not necessarily mean he is not getting anywhere. There people are so important that nobody can bear to tear himself away; because of the resultant interruptions and conversational detours, everybody is con-

*Edward T. Hall, "The Silent Language in Overseas Business," HARVARD BUSINESS REVIEW, (May-June, 1960), pp. 87-96. Reprinted by permission.

[1] For details, see my book, *The Silent Language* (New York, Doubleday & Company, Inc., 1959).

stantly getting behind. What the American does not know is the point at which the waiting becomes significant.

In another instance, after traveling 7,000 miles an American walks into the office of a highly recommended Arab businessman on whom he will have to depend completely. What he sees does not breed confidence. The office is reached by walking through a suspicious-looking coffeehouse in an old, dilapidated building situated in a crowded non-European section of town. The elevator, rising from dark, smelly corridors, is rickety and equally foul. When he gets to the office itself, he is shocked to find it small, crowded, and confused. Papers are stacked all over the desk and table tops—even scattered on the floor in irregular piles.

The Arab merchant he has come to see had met him at the airport the night before and sent his driver to the hotel this morning to pick him up. But now, after the American's rush, the Arab is tied up with something else. Even when they finally start talking business, there are constant interruptions. If the American is at all sensitive to his environment, everything around him signals, "What am I getting into?"

Before leaving home he was told that things would be different, but how different? The hotel is modern enough. The shops in the new part of town have many more American and European trade goods than he had anticipated. His first impression was that doing business in the Middle East would not present any new problems. Now he is beginning to have doubts. One minute everything looks familiar and he is on firm ground; the next, familiar landmarks are gone. His greatest problem is that so much assails his senses all at once that he does not know where to start looking for something that will tell him where he stands. He needs a frame of reference—a way of sorting out what is significant and relevant.

That is why it is so important for American businessmen to have a real understanding of the various social, cultural, and economic differences they will face when they attempt to do business in foreign countries. To help give some frame of reference, this article will map out a few areas of human activity that have largely been unstudied.

The topics I will discuss are certainly not presented as the last word on the subject, but they have proved to be highly reliable points at which to begin to gain an understanding of foreign cultures. While additional research will undoubtedly turn up other items just as relevant, at present I think the businessman can do well to begin by appreciating cultural differences in matters concerning the language of time, of space, of material possessions, of friendship patterns, and of agreements.

LANGUAGE OF TIME

Everywhere in the world people use time to communicate with each other. There are different languages of time just as there are different spoken languages. The unspoken languages are informal; yet the rules governing their interpretation are surprisingly *ironbound.*

In the United States, a delay in answering a communication can result from a large volume of business causing the request to be postponed until the backlog is cleared away, from poor organization, or possibly from technical complexity requiring deep analysis. But if the person awaiting the answer or decision rules out these reasons, then the delay means to him that the matter has low priority on the part of the other person—lack of interest. On the other hand, a similar delay in a foreign country may mean something altogether different. Thus in Ethiopia, the time required for a decision is directly proportional to its importance. This is so much the case that low-level bureaucrats there have a way of trying to elevate the prestige of their work by taking a long time to make up their minds. (Americans in that part of the world are innocently prone to downgrade their work in the local people's eyes by trying to speed things up.)

In the Arab East, time does not generally include schedules as Americans know and use them. The time required to get something accomplished depends on the relationship. More important people get fast service from less important people, and conversely. Close relatives take absolute priority; nonrelatives are kept waiting.

In the United States, giving a person a deadline is a way of indicating the degree of urgency or relative importance of the work. But in the Middle East, the American runs into a cultural trap the minute he opens his mouth. "Mr. Aziz will have to make up his mind in a hurry because my board meets next week and I have to have an answer by then," is taken as indicating the American is overly demanding and is exerting undue pressure. "I am going to Damascus tomorrow morning and will have to have my car tonight," is a sure way to get the mechanic to stop work, because to give another person a deadline in this part of the world is to be rude, pushy, and demanding.

An Arab's evasiveness as to when something is going to happen does not mean he does not want to do business; it only means he is avoiding unpleasantness and is side-stepping possible commitments which he takes more seriously than we do. For example, the Arabs themselves at times find it impossible to communicate even to each other that some processes cannot be hurried, and are controlled by built-in schedules. This is obvious enough to the Westerner but not to the Arab. A highly placed public official in Baghdad precipitated a bitter family dispute because his nephew, a biochemist, could not speed up the complete analysis of the uncle's blood. He accused the nephew of putting other less important people before him and of not caring. Nothing could sway the uncle, who could not grasp the fact that there is such a thing as an *inherent* schedule.

With us the more important an event is, the further ahead we schedule it, which is why we find it insulting to be asked to a party at the last minute. In planning future events with Arabs, it pays to hold the lead time to a week or less because other factors may intervene or take precedence.

Again, time spent waiting in an American's outer office is a sure indicator of what one person thinks of another or how important he feels the other's business to be. This is so much the case that most Americans cannot help getting angry after waiting 30 minutes; one may even feel such a delay is an insult, and will walk out. In Latin America, on the other hand, one learns that it does not mean anything to wait in an outer office. An American businessman with years of experience in Mexico once told me, "You know, I have spent two hours cooling my heels in an executive's outer office. It took me a long time to learn to keep my blood pressure down. Even now, I find it hard to convince myself they are still interested when they keep me waiting."

The Japanese handle time in ways which are almost inexplicable to the Western European and particularly the American. A delay of years with them does not mean that they have lost interest. It only means that they are building up to something. They have learned that Americans are vulnerable to long waits. One of them expressed it, "You Americans have one terrible weakness. If we make you wait long enough, you will agree to anything."

Indians of South Asia have an elastic view of time as compared to our own. Delays do not, therefore, have the same meaning to them. Nor does indefiniteness in pinpointing appointments mean that they are evasive. Two Americans meeting will say, "We should get together sometime," thereby setting a low priority on the meeting. The Indian who says, "Come over and see me, see me anytime," means just that.

Americans make a place at the table which may or may not mean a place made in the heart. But when the Indian makes a place in his time, it is yours to fill in every sense of the word if you realize that by so doing you have crossed a boundary and are now friends with him. The point of all this is that time communicates just as surely as do words and that the vocabulary of time is different around the world. The principle to be remembered is that time has different meanings in each country.

LANGUAGE OF SPACE

Like time, the language of space is different wherever one goes. The American businessman, familiar with the pattern of American corporate life, has no difficulty in appraising the relative importance of someone else, simply by noting the size of his office in relation to other offices around him. Our pattern calls for the president or the chairman of the board to have the biggest office. The executive vice president will have the next largest, and so on down the line until you end up in the "bull pen." More important offices are usually located at the corners of buildings and on the upper floors. Executive suites will be on the top floor. The relative rank of vice presidents will be reflected in where they are placed along "Executive Row."

The French, on the other hand, are much more likely to lay out space as a network of connecting points of influence, activity, or interest. The French supervisor will ordinarily be found in the middle of his subordinates where he can control them.

Americans who are crowded will often feel that their status in the organization is suffering. As one would expect in the Arab world, the location of an office and its size constitute a poor index of the importance of the man who occupies it. What we experience as crowded, the Arab will often regard as spacious. The same is true in Spanish cultures. A Latin American official illustrated the Spanish view of this point while showing me around a plant. Opening the door to an 18-by-20-foot office in which seventeen clerks and their desks were placed, he said, "See, we have nice spacious offices. Lots of space for everyone."

The American will look at a Japanese room and remark how bare it is. Similarly, the Japanese look at our rooms and comment, "How bare!" Furniture in the American home tends to be placed along the walls (around the edge). Japanese have their charcoal pit where the family gathers in the *middle* of the room. The top floor of Japanese department stores is not reserved for the chief executive—it is the bargain roof!

In the Middle East and Latin America, the businessman is likely to feel left out in time and overcrowded in space. People get too close to him, lay their hands on him, and generally crowd his physical being. In Scandinavia and Germany, he feels more at home, but at the same time the people are a little cold and distant. It is space itself that conveys this feeling.

In the United States, because of our tendency to zone activities, nearness carries rights of familiarity so that the neighbor can borrow material possessions and invade time. This is not true in England. Propinquity entitles you to nothing. American Air Force personnel stationed there complain because they have to make an appointment for their children to play with the neighbor's child next door.

Conversation distance between two people is learned early in life by copying elders. Its controlling patterns operate almost totally unconsciously. In the United States, in contrast to many foreign countries, men avoid excessive touching. Regular business is conducted at distances such as 5 feet to 8 feet; highly personal business, 18 inches to 3 feet—not 2 or 3 inches.

In the United States, it is perfectly possible for an experienced executive to schedule the steps of negotiation in time and space so that most people feel comfortable about what is happening. Business transactions progress in stages from across the desk to beside the desk, to the coffee table, then on to the conference table, the luncheon table, or the golf course, or even into the home—all according to a complex set of hidden rules which we obey instinctively.

Even in the United States, however, an executive may slip when he moves into new and unfamiliar realms, when dealing with a new group, doing business with a new company, or moving to a new place in the industrial hierarchy. In a new country the danger is magnified. For example, in India it is considered improper to discuss business in the home on social occasions. One never invites a business acquaintance to the home for the purpose of furthering business aims. That would be a violation of sacred hospitality rules.

LANGUAGE OF THINGS

Americans are often contrasted with the rest of the world in terms of material possessions. We are accused of being materialistic, gadget-crazy. And, as a matter of fact, we have developed material things for some very interesting reasons. Lacking a fixed class system and having an extremely mobile population, Americans have become highly sensitive to how others make use of material possessions. We use everything from clothes to houses as a highly evolved and complex means of ascertaining each other's status. Ours is a rapidly shifting system in which both styles and people move up or down. For example, the Cadillac ad men feel that not only is it natural but quite insightful of them to show a picture of a Cadillac and a well-turned out gentleman in his early fifties opening the door. The caption underneath reads, "You already know a great deal about this man."

Following this same pattern, the head of a big union spends an excess of $100,000 furnishing his office so that the president of United States Steel cannot look down on him. Good materials, large space, and the proper surroundings signify that the people who occupy the premises are solid citizens, that they are dependable and successful.

The French, the English, and the Germans have entirely different ways of using their material possessions. What stands for the height of dependability and respectability with the English would be old-fashioned and backward to us. The Japanese take pride in often inexpensive but tasteful arrangements that are used to produce the proper emotional setting.

Middle East businessmen look for something else—family, connections, friendship. They do not use the furnishings of their office as part of their status system; nor do they expect to impress a client by these means or to fool a banker into lending more money than he should. They like good things, too, but feel that they, as persons, should be known and not judged solely by what the public sees.

One of the most common criticisms of American relations abroad, both commercial and governmental, is that we usually think in terms of material things. "Money talks," says the American, who goes on talking the language of money abroad, in the belief that money talks the *same* language all over the world. A common practice in the United States is to try to buy loyalty with high salaries. In foreign countries, this maneuver almost never works, for money and material possessions stand for something different there than they do in America.

LANGUAGE OF FRIENDSHIP

The American finds his friends next door and among those with whom he works. It has been noted that we take people up quickly and drop them just as quickly. Occasionally a friendship formed during schooldays will persist, but this is rare. For us there are few well-defined rules governing the obligations of friendship. It is difficult to say at which point our friendship gives way to business opportunism or pressure from above. In this we differ from many other people in the world. As a general rule in foreign countries friendships are not formed as quickly as in the United States but go much deeper, last longer, and involve real obligations. For example, it is important to stress that in the Middle East and Latin America your "friends" will not let you down. The fact that they personally are feeling the pinch is never an excuse for failing their friends. They are supposed to look out for your interests.

Friends and family around the world represent a sort of social insurance that would be difficult to find in the United States. We do not use our friends to help us out in disaster as much as we do as a means of getting ahead—or, at least, of getting the job done. The United States systems work by means of a series of closely tabulated favors and obligations carefully doled out where they will do the most good. And the least that we expect in exchange for a favor is gratitude.

The opposite is the case in India, where the friend's role is to "sense" a person's need and do something about it. The idea of reciprocity as we know it is unheard of. An American in India will have difficulty if he attempts to follow American friendship patterns. He gains nothing by extending himself in behalf of others, least of all gratitude, because the Indian assumes that what he does for others he does for the good of his own psyche. He will find it impossible to make friends quickly and is unlikely to allow sufficient time for friendships to ripen. He will also note that as he gets to know people better, they may become more critical

of him, a fact that he finds hard to take. What he does not know is that
one sign of friendship in India is speaking one's mind.

LANGUAGE OF AGREEMENTS

While it is important for American businessmen abroad to understand
the symbolic meanings of friendship rules, time, space, and material possessions, it is just as important for executives to know the rules for negotiating agreements in various countries. Even if they cannot be expected
to know the details of each nation's commercial legal practices, just the
awareness of and the expectation of the existence of differences will
eliminate much complication.

Actually, no society can exist on a high commercial level without
a highly developed working base on which agreements can rest. This
base may be one or a combination of three types:

1. Rules that are spelled out technically as law or regulation.
2. Moral practices mutually agreed on and taught to the young as a
   set of principles.
3. Informal customs to which everyone conforms without being able
   to state the exact rules.

Some societies favor one, some another. Ours, particularly in the
business world, lays heavy emphasis on the first variety. Few Americans
will conduct any business nowadays without some written agreement or
contract.

Varying from culture to culture will be the circumstances under
which such rules apply. Americans consider that negotiations have more
or less ceased when the contract is signed. With the Greeks, on the other
hand, the contract is seen as a sort of way station on the route to negotiation that will cease only when the work is completed. The contract is
nothing more than a charter for serious negotiations. In the Arab world,
once a man's word is given in a particular kind of way, it is just as binding, if not more so, than most of our written contracts. The written contract, therefore, violates the Moslem's sensitivities and reflects on his
honor. Unfortunately, the situation is now so hopelessly confused that
neither system can be counted on to prevail consistently.

Informal patterns and unstated agreements often lead to untold difficulty in the cross-cultural situation. Take the case of the before-and-
after patterns where there is a wide discrepancy between the American's
expectations and those of the Arab.

In the United States, when you engage a specialist such as a lawyer or a doctor, require any standard service, or even take a taxi, you make several assumptions: (a) the charge will be fair; (b) it will be in proportion to the services rendered; and (c) it will bear a close relationship to the "going rate."

You wait until after the services are performed before asking what the tab will be. If the charge is too high in the light of the above assumptions, you feel you have been cheated. You can complain, or can say nothing, pay up, and take your business elsewhere the next time.

As one would expect in the Middle East, basic differences emerge which lead to difficulty if not understood. For instance, when taking a cab in Beirut it is well to know the going rate as a point around which to bargain and for settling the charge, which must be fixed before engaging the cab.

If you have not fixed the rate *in advance,* there is a complete change and an entirely different set of rules will apply. According to these rules, the going rate plays no part whatsoever. The whole relationship is altered. The sky is the limit, and the customer has no kick coming. I have seen taxi drivers shouting at the top of their lungs, waving their arms, following a redfaced American with his head pulled down between his shoulders, demanding for a two-pound ride ten Lebanese pounds which the American eventually had to pay.

It is difficult for the American to accommodate his frame of reference to the fact that what constitutes one thing to him, namely, a taxi ride, is to the Arab two very different operations involving two different sets of relationships and two sets of rules. The crucial factor is whether the bargaining is done at the beginning or the end of the ride! As a matter of fact, you cannot bargain at the end. What the driver asks for he is entitled to!

One of the greatest difficulties Americans have abroad stems from the fact that we often think we have a commitment when we do not. The second complication on this same topic is the other side of the coin, i.e., when others think we have agreed to things that we have not. Our own failure to recognize binding obligations, plus our custom of setting organizational goals ahead of everything else, has put us in hot water far too often.

People sometimes do not keep agreements with us because we do not keep agreements with them. As a general rule, the American treats the agreement as something he may eventually have to break. Here are two examples.

Once while I was visiting an American post in Latin America, the Ambassador sent the Spanish version of a trade treaty down to his language officer with instructions to write in some "weasel words." To his dismay, he was told, "There are no weasel words in Spanish."

A personnel officer of a large corporation in Iran made an agreement with local employees that American employees would not receive preferential treatment. When the first American employee arrived, it was learned quickly that in the United States he had been covered by a variety of health plans that were not available to Iranians. And this led to immediate protests from the Iranians which were never satisfied. The personnel officer never really grasped the fact that he had violated an ironbound contract.

Certainly, this is the most important generalization to be drawn by American businessmen from this discussion of agreements: there are many times when we are vulnerable *even when judged by our own standards.* Many instances of actual sharp practices by American companies are well known abroad and are giving American business a bad name. The cure for such questionable behavior is simple. The companies concerned usually have it within their power to discharge offenders and to foster within their organization an atmosphere in which only honesty and fairness can thrive.

But the cure for ignorance of the social and legal rules which underlie business agreements is not so easy. This is because:

- The subject is complex.
- Little research has been conducted to determine the culturally different concepts of what is an agreement.
- The people of each country think that their own code is the only one, and that everything else is dishonest.
- Each code is different from our own; and the farther away one is traveling from Western Europe, the greater the difference is.

But the little that has already been learned about this subject indicates that as a problem it is not insoluble and will yield to research. Since it is probably one of the more relevant and immediately applicable areas of interest to modern business, it would certainly be advisable for companies with large foreign operations to sponsor some serious research in this vital field.

A CASE IN POINT

Thus far, I have been concerned with developing the five check points around which a real understanding of foreign cultures can begin. But the problems that arise from a faulty understanding of the silent language of foreign custom are human problems and perhaps can best be dramatized by an actual case.

A Latin American republic had decided to modernize one of its communication networks to the tune of several million dollars. Because of its reputation for quality and price, the inside track was quickly taken by American company "Y."

The company, having been sounded out informally, considered the size of the order and decided to bypass its regular Latin American representative and send instead its sales manager. The following describes what took place.

The sales manager arrived and checked in at the leading hotel. He immediately had some difficulty pinning down just who it was he had to see about his business. After several days without results, he called at the American Embassy where he found that the commercial attaché had the up-to-the-minute information he needed. The commercial attaché listened to his story. Realizing that the sales manager had already made a number of mistakes, but figuring that the Latins were used to American blundering, the attaché reasoned that all was not lost. He informed the sales manager that the Minister of Communications was the key man and that whoever got the nod from him would get the contract. He also briefed the sales manager on methods of conducting business in Latin America and offered some pointers about dealing with the minister.

The attaché's advice ran somewhat as follows:

1. "You don't do business here the way you do in the States; it is necessary to spend much more time. You have to get to know your man and vice versa.

2. "You must meet with him *several times* before you talk business. I will tell you at what point you can bring up the subject. Take your cues from me. [Our American sales manager at this point made a few observations to himself about "cookie pushers" and wondered how many payrolls had been met by the commercial attaché.]

3. "Take that price list and put it in your pocket. Don't get it out until I tell you to. Down here price is only one of the many things taken into account before closing a deal. In the United States, your past experience will prompt you to act according to a certain set of principles, but many of these principals will *not* work here. Every time you feel the urge to act or to say something, look at me. Suppress the urge and take your cues from me. This is very important.

4. "Down here people like to do business with men who *are* somebody. In order to be somebody, it is well to have written a book, to have lectured at a university, or to have developed your intellect in some way. The man you are going to see is a poet. He has published several volumes of poetry. Like many Latin Americans, he prizes poetry highly. You will find that he will spend a good deal of business time quoting his poetry to you, and he will take great pleasure in this.

5. "You will also note that the people here are very proud of their past and of their Spanish blood, but they are also exceedingly proud of their liberation from Spain and their independence. The fact that they are a democracy, that they are free, and also that they are no longer a colony is very, very important to them. They are warm and friendly and enthusiastic if they like you. If they don't, they are cold and withdrawn.

6. "And another thing, time down here means something different. It works in a different way. You know how it is back in the States when a certain type blurts out whatever is on his mind without waiting to see if the situation is right. He is considered an impatient bore and somewhat egocentric. Well, down here, you have to wait much, much longer, and I really mean *much, much* longer, before you can begin to talk about the reason for your visit.

7. There is another point I want to caution you about. At home, the man who sells takes the initiative. Here, *they* tell you when they are ready to do business. But, most of all, don't discuss price until you are asked and don't rush things."

THE PITCH

The next day the commercial attaché introduced the sales manager to the Minister of Communications. First, there was a long wait in the outer office while people kept coming in and out. The sales manager looked at his watch, fidgeted, and finally asked whether the minister was really expecting him. The reply he received was scarcely reassuring. "Oh yes, he is expecting you but several things have come up that require his attention. Besides, one gets used to waiting down here." The sales manager irritably replied, "But doesn't he know I flew all the way down here from the United States to see him, and I have spent over a week already of my valuable time trying to find him?" "Yes, I know," was the answer, "but things just move much more slowly here."

At the end of about 30 minutes, the minister emerged from the office, greeted the commercial attaché with a *doble abrazo,* throwing his arms around him and patting him on the back as though they were long-lost brothers. Now, turning and smiling, the minister extended his hand to the sales manager, who, by this time, was feeling rather miffed because he had been kept in the outer office so long.

After what seemed to be an all too short chat, the minister rose, suggesting a well-known café where they might meet for dinner the next evening. The sales manager expected, of course, that, considering the nature of their business and the size of the order, he might be taken to the minister's home, not realizing that the Latin home is reserved for family and very close friends.

Until now, nothing at all had been said about the reason for the sales manager's visit, a fact which bothered him somewhat. The whole set-up seemed wrong; neither did he like the idea of wasting another day in town. He told the home office before he left that he would be gone for a week or ten days at most, and made a mental note that he would clean this order up in three days and enjoy a few days in Acapulco or Mexico City. Now the week had already gone and he would be lucky if he made it home in ten days.

Voicing his misgivings to the commercial attaché, he wanted to know if the minister really meant business, and, if he did, why could they not get together and talk about it? The commercial attaché by now was beginning to show the strain of constantly having to reassure the sales manager. Nevertheless, he tried again:

"What you don't realize is that part of the time we were waiting, the minister was rearranging a very tight schedule so that he could spend tomorrow night with you. You see, down here they don't delegate responsibility the way we do in the States. They exercise much tighter control than we do. As a consequence, this man spends up to 15 hours a day at his desk. It may not look like it to you, but I assure you he really means business. He wants to give your company the order; if you play your cards right, you will get it."

The next evening provided more of the same. Much conversation about food and music, about many people the sales manager had never heard of. They went to a night club, where the sales manager brightened up and began to think that perhaps he and the minister might have something in common after all. It bothered him, however, that the principal reason for his visit was not even alluded to tangentially. But every time he started to talk about electronics, the commercial attaché would nudge him and proceed to change the subject.

The next meeting was for morning coffee at a café. By now the sales manager was having difficulty hiding his impatience. To make matters worse, the minister had a mannerism which he did not like. When they talked, he was likely to put his hand on him; he would take hold of his arm and get so close that he almost "spat" in his face. As a consequence, the sales manager was kept busy trying to dodge and back up.

Following coffee, there was a walk in a nearby park. The minister expounded on the shrubs, the birds, and the beauties of nature, and at one spot he stopped to point at a statue and said: "There is a statue of the world's greatest hero, the liberator of mankind!" As this point, the worst happened, for the sales manager asked who the statue was of and, being given the name of a famous Latin American patriot, said, "I never heard of him," and walked on.

THE FAILURE

It is quite clear from this that the sales manager did not get the order, which went to a Swedish concern. The American, moreover, was never able to see the minister again. Why did the minister feel the way he did? His reasoning went somewhat as follows:

"I like the American's equipment and it makes sense to deal with North Americans who are near us and whose price is right. But I could never be friends with this man. He is not my kind of human being and we have nothing in common. He is not *simpatico*. If I can't be friends and he is not *simpatico*, I can't depend on him to treat me right. I tried everything, every conceivable situation, and only once did we seem to understand each other. If we could be friends, he would feel obligated to me and this obligation would give me some control. Without control, how do I know he will deliver what he says he will at the price he quotes?"

Of course, what the minister did not know was that the price was quite firm, and that quality control was a matter of company policy. He did not realize that the sales manager was a member of an organization, and that the man is always subordinate to the organization in the United States. Next year maybe the sales manager would not even be representing the company, but would be replaced. Further, if he wanted someone to depend on, his best bet would be to hire a good American lawyer to represent him and write a binding contract.

In this instance, both sides suffered. The American felt he was being slighted and put off, and did not see how there could possibly be any connection between poetry and doing business or why it should all take so long. He interpreted the delay as a form of polite brush-off. Even if things had gone differently and there had been a contract, it is doubtful that the minister would have trusted the contract as much as he would a man whom he considered his friend. Throughout Latin America, the law is made livable and contracts workable by having friends and relatives operating from the inside. Lacking a friend, someone who would look out for his interests, the minister did not want to take a chance. He stated this simply and directly.

CONCLUSION

The case just described has of necessity been oversimplified. The danger is that the reader will say, "Oh, I see. All you really have to do is be friends." At which point the expert will step in and reply:

"Yes, of course, but what you don't realize is that in Latin America being a friend involves much more than it does in the United States and is an entirely different proposition. A friendship implies obligations. You go about it differently. It involves much more than being nice, visiting, and playing golf. You would not want to enter into friendship lightly."

The point is simply this. It takes years and years to develop a sound foundation for doing business in a given country. Much that is done seems silly or strange to the home office. Indeed, the most common error made by home offices, once they have found representatives who can get results, is failure to take their advice and allow sufficient time for representatives to develop the proper contacts.

The second most common error, if that is what it can be called, is ignorance of the secret and hidden language of foreign cultures. In this article I have tried to show how five key topics—time, space, material possessions, friendship patterns, and business agreements—offer a starting point from which companies can begin to acquire the understanding necessary to do business in foreign countries.

Our present knowledge is meager, and much more research is needed before the businessman of the future can go abroad fully equipped for his work. Not only will he need to be well versed in the economics, law, and politics of the area, but he will have to understand, if not speak, the silent languages of other cultures.

9.

NEGOTIATING INVESTMENT IN EMERGING COUNTRIES*

Simon Williams

TO invest or not to invest in new manufacturing facilities in the under-developed countries of Africa, Asia, and Latin America, or merely to invest in a visit to these places to take a first-hand look, is a decision facing more and more top managers of industrial and financial institutions in the United States—often for the first time.

The pressure to make such a decision is getting greater every day. Despite low average per-capita income, local and regional markets in the less developed areas of the world have a diversity of need and a potential demand that form a powerful lodestone attracting the attention of any management considering overseas expansion. Further, it is becoming necessary for those who have export markets in the developing countries to manufacture at least part of their line locally in order to protect their franchise to sell at all, let alone to protect their competitive position.

Beyond the intriguing nature and size of the market, investment promotion originating in the underdeveloped countries is steadily growing more widespread, more skillful, and more persuasive. It is supported by feasibility studies and based on a wide variety of incentives ranging from tax holidays to tariff protection, anti-dumping legislation, duty relief, and development loans. And, to add further spice and lure to the host-country incentives, the United States extends to the overseas investor guarantees against the risks of currency manipulation, expropriation, war loss, and other dangers, as well as offering low-cost loans for equipment and provisions to share the expense of making feasibility studies.

In all, the challenge of the investment opportunity in the less developed parts of the world rings loud and clear and insistently.

PAINFUL PROCESS

But a too quick response to this challenge, either with a decision to invest or to go see, can be a frustrating, abrading, emotionally disturbing

* Simon Williams, "Negotiating Investment in Emerging Countries," HARVARD BUSINESS REVIEW (January–February 1965), pp. 89–99. Reprinted by permission.

experience. The variables encountered are far more numerous, subtle, and difficult to rationalize than those common to the background of most businessmen from the United States. The art of politics and the concepts of social science can become as important, or even more important, to the success of an investment negotiation as hardheaded technical and financial calculations or a carefully prepared legal and administrative basis for an overseas organization.

Alien customs tend to offend, frighten, and stimulate aggressiveness on all sides. Morality in business and in personal relationships raises sharp and painful conflicts which roil the emotions and raise philosophical issues that long since were thought to have been settled for each of us. Ignorance is easily confused with stupidity; inexperience is soon made synonymous with incompetence; delay soon seems to be opposition.

The inevitable role of the national government in underdeveloped countries may vary at any given moment in a negotiation from that of potential partner, banker, labor relations arbiter, primary customer, judge in passing on applications for tax privileges or tariff protection or profit repatriation to that of a growing child replete with intelligence, ignorance, pride, fantasy, and startling, penetrating frankness. And this demands time-consuming and sensitive attention which can generate many a headache in free-wheeling free enterprisers from the United States.

Indeed, at times it seems there is no path leading to a logical decision that an investment makes sense or that the profit to be made is worth the effort. There is eloquent testimony around the world that potential investors from the United States have arrived at one or another such painful conclusion in large numbers. For example, in 1963, investment in Nigeria in new manufacturing facilities—represented by factories which came into production that year, by plants under construction, and by plans so far along as to be reasonably certain of completion—was reliably estimated at $225 million.[1] Less than 15% of this investment was U.S. money.

Good solid profit has been and is being made by private investors in Nigeria. The country offers one of the most encouraging long-range views of economic growth, political stability, and hospitality for foreigners that can be found in Africa or anywhere else in the underdeveloped world. Yet, while a swelling stream of promoters, bankers, and top-management representatives has poured through Nigeria from the United States since the country became independent of British rule in 1960, most have left without taking action; others have given up after considerable negotiation. Some left angry and frustrated; others, convinced that the promise

[1] An estimate made by Arthur D. Little, Inc., Cambridge, Massachusetts, whose resident staff has been acting as industrial development advisers to the several governments of Nigeria under the sponsorship of the United States Agency for International Development.

of Nigeria is a pipe dream. Some left loaded with superficial observations; others, deeply puzzled and disturbed by their own inability to come to grips with an attractive investment while investments from other countries were proceeding apace.

To a greater or lesser degree, what has happened in Nigeria is happening throughout Africa and Asia; and even in Latin America, where money from the United States may dominate other sources of foreign capital, significant numbers of opportunities for investment are being overlooked or passed over by visitors from the United States whose initial interest and motivation ran high.

Obviously, the successful negotiations and profitable investments throughout the world are mixed with the failures; from both success and failure much has been learned to guide those who would try again or try for the first time to pioneer in production in an underdeveloped country. Dominant among these lessons is one which says: decide before you leave the United States how much you are prepared to give in order to get.

FACT: BRIBERY

Bribery is not the only possible form of giving, as we shall see. But there is no doubt about it as a fact to be reckoned with, no matter whether one decides to use it or not, and no matter what else one does in the way of careful, elaborate negotiating.

In almost every country throughout the underdeveloped world, a businessman can buy protection and grease the skids for a successful negotiation. We Americans call it bribery; some Africans call it "dash," a take-off on the Portuguese verb meaning "to give"; some in Latin America call it "mordida," a lyrical adaptation of the verb "to bite." It goes under a variety of colorful names, but functions in more or less the same way everywhere. Anyone wishing to employ the method can find out how it is done with very little effort.

Probably no aspect of dealing with investment problems in the underdeveloped countries is more disturbing to Americans than the matter of graft. Yet, considering how widely acknowledged the practice is, Americans have done little to prepare themselves in advance to deal firmly with it. One tends to react to it as if surprised. It is talked of behind closed hotel doors. It is sneered at, laughed at, joined uncomfortably, or looked down on. It is fumbled like a hot potato.

How should one prepare to deal with graft? There are no studies published revealing what Americans have actually done. Clearly, some have bribed their way over obstacles while others have fought their way without compromise. There can be no rules in this game to which all will subscribe; one's actions in this respect are intensely personal, and each must decide for himself whether the end justifies the means. Only one thing is certain, and every investor should face this reality: *bribery is a common, universal phenomenon on the economic development scene.*

In fact, it is because of its commonality that a basic philosophical question often arises which plagues those who too easily moralize about right and wrong, but which should be thought through before arriving overseas. In countries where payoff is as much a part of the economic process as payroll, whose ethical standards are right, the visitors' or the natives'? Is management's role that of developer of wealth *and* missionary simultaneously; or is it true that better standards of living are prerequisites to "better" ethics? To win over the opposition, do you join them or fight them?

The temptation to wax eloquent and passionate over the subject of bribery in economic development and what Americans ought to do is great. Each of us feels strongly on the subject. But it is raised here only to emphasize its prominence in the game of investment—in Africa, in Asia, and in Latin America—and to note that it must be considered and a position taken before an investor can move ahead with certainty. Joining with the forces of bribery is no guarantee of success, but it certainly can help. Avoiding graft is no guarantee of failure, either, but success, in this case, depends very heavily on the rules of personal behavior and intellectual effort set forth in the balance of this article.

ALTERNATIVE: INFORMATION

There *is* an alternative way to give; and even if it does not completely eliminate the graft element, it is an essential part of successful negotiation.

A sufficiently profitable investment in manufacturing in any underdeveloped country is rarely possible without some form of protection or subsidy, especially during the early years of production. This truth is universally accepted. Laws setting up systems of protective incentives are in existence everywhere. But few of these laws apply automatically. Most often, benefits (e.g., a tax holiday, a special tariff on competitive imports, duty relief on raw materials, anti-dumping control, currency convertibility, and repatriation privileges) must be requested of and approved by a government agency.

The demand for information during a review of such a request can become the single greatest psychological and intellectual obstacle facing a potential investor from the United States. Months, even years, of effort can go into a negotiation. To appreciate how the demand arises, consider a typical range of requests that reach the desks of ministry officials:

Case 1. A surgical dressings manufacturer with a strong market position agreed to produce a full line locally, provided the foreign government would extend certain benefits. Because the market was small, the granting of a monopoly equal to 80% of current imports was said to be essential. Only at this productive level, the applicant said, could minimum sized process equipment operate reasonably close to capacity. In addition, the applicant requested a tax holiday and tariff protection.

This foreign government's policy was opposed to monopoly; yet there was a growing awareness that to get the first investor in certain industries where market size was marginal relative to the productive capacity of machinery, granting monopolies for a limited time might be desirable. The question raised for the government was: How much supporting data should be demanded of the applicant to justify a claim that a monopoly was indeed the only device feasible? A favorable decision could have opened the floodgates to similar investment requests.

After a year of negotiation, there were still not sufficient data from the applicant to satisfy the government that the existing market could not support a profitable operation, or that the applicant needed a tax holiday and tariff protection. The project was withdrawn. The manufacturer flatly refused to quantify his claim of need.

Case 2. Automobile assembly was proposed by two different investors, one from the United States and one from Western Europe. Each applicant requested the foreign government to establish a wider spread between the import tariff on "completely knocked down" parts and that imposed on fully or partially assembled vehicles. However, the applicant from Europe requested less than half of the change in spread called for by the U.S. producer and, at the same time, expressed a willingness to earn less return on his investment.

Not only is national revenue affected by the level of tariff differential applied, but other questions arise, as well, in considering these alternative proposals: What policy is necessary to attract a third and a fourth investor? Is a uniform policy necessary, or should each applicant be treated within the merits of his case? Should the applicant asking less be granted more in order to get both investments? What information is required to test the validity of the claims made by the U.S. investor?

After two years of negotiation, all parties concerned are still trying to rationalize differences—the investors still explaining, the government still asking for more information.

These examples could be multiplied without end. However, the cases cited are enough to reveal the essential nature of the foreign country's demand for information and why this demand can succeed in trying, then breaking, the patience of the ill-prepared investor from the United

States. Four elements of the demand stand out as being fundamental and contain the key to success or failure—namely:

1. The time given to a negotiation.
2. The attitudes of both investor and civil servant in dealing with ignorance.
3. The attitudes of both investor and civil servant toward sharing responsibility for national economic development.
4. The extent to which the investor can and does document claims covering his need for protection (subsidy).

TIME ALLOTMENT

The critical relationship of time to success is simple: it takes far more time than is usually allotted to get and to give information. The risk of failure to consummate a decision previously made to invest is greater almost in direct proportion to the tightness of a travel schedule. The time referred to is over and above the months that may be devoted to market analyses, technical and financial feasibility studies, and forming an organization and a strategy of operation.

First, there is the time it takes to get a sense of the character of a new country, up to now far outside the ken of most Americans. It takes time to probe the hostile and benign aspects of the climate, the land, and the people, and to decide whether life there is tolerable, no matter what the profit; to listen to the language and learn something of its sweep in expressing feelings and ideas; to feel the surge of social change and its impact on tradition; to walk the byways of history in order to understand and keep pace with current events; to become sensitive to political reality, to the centers of power, and to the interplay between individuals, laws, and institutions.

Then there is the time it takes to make appointments, to meet again and again, to pass from office to office and ministry to ministry, to learn what is wanted and how to provide it. There is the time it takes to make a telephone call, to exchange letters, to get around.

It should not be necessary to labor the point, but it seems to be. One of the persistent gross oversights of the American investor in Africa, Asia, or Latin America is not taking enough time. How vivid is my memory of the president of a U.S. investment syndicate who popped off his plane and dashed into my office, saying: "I heard you were here. I've got two days. How can I make a quick buck?" While this exaggerates, and touches on a matter of attitude to be discussed later, the fact is that too many Americans take two days and treat investment procedure as though they were rushing to the Yukon to pan for gold.

In this regard, it is often argued that the host country, because of its great need and because it must compete, and compete hard, for scarce capital and know-how, should assume the burden of making every minute count when a busy investor comes to town. Maybe. Some countries try harder than others; many have advisers who are busy tutoring invest-ment promotion officers. But the truth is that such planned help is rarely extended. It may be that local officials are really too busy to hold hands with every visitor; when one knows their work-load, this possibility be-comes very real. It may be that pride and arrogance express themselves this way. There are many ways of explaining what may pass for indiffer-ence. The point is that the main burden of patient exploration and ne-gotiation will usually fall on the investor. To carry it can bend the strong-est back. The danger here is that many Americans arrive overseas already strained for easy bending and breaking. Consider:

Case 3. The president of a medium sized U.S. corporation with a good but obsolete (for U.S. market conditions) used-metal-working plant had read newspaper reports of a certain country and become interested in shipping his plant there as his equity in a new industry. In Washington, he talked briefly with people in the State Department and the U.S. Agency for International Development, and was warmly received and encouraged.

Before leaving the U.S. he had become convinced that the country in question needed his plant and his skills, that he would be welcomed with open arms, that U.S. representatives would know all about him and would have paved his way. He arrived. Nobody was at the airport to meet him. His visa was not in order, and he ran head-on into the im-movable bureaucracy that often can immobilize entry into the newly independent countries. It was hot. The airport was dingy. It took hours to break loose.

Then, too, nobody knew of his coming. Nobody had heard of his company. Two days were lost without an appointment, and when ap-pointments were arranged, nobody knew what issues needed discussion. Fury and frustration enveloped this man, and he left, practically yelling, "If they don't want my investment here, to hell with them."

While time is expensive, the need to spend lots of it should be faced before leaving the United States. Unfortunately, there is no way to quan-tify this warning with a prediction of how much time will be needed. A judgment must be reached on the spot within a flexible schedule. How-ever, it may be safely said that a sound judgment cannot be rendered without an honest appraisal of one's attitude toward ignorance—one's own ignorance about the country to be visited, and the ignorance most surely to be encountered there about the business of the investor partic-ularly, and about investment problems generally.

QUESTION OF ATTITUDE

The U.S. investor who arrives overseas is usually an educated, successful man. In the business community back home, he has come to grips with his environment, and over the years he has learned to manage it with skill. He has long since relegated the function of detailed study to his trusted staff. His habit is to synthesize a decision from abstracts of data and recommendations gathered from many sources. He tends to be impatient with any suggestion of "do-it-yourself" when in a foreign country.

With this background and attitude, it is hard for the U.S. investor to be humble and to accept the reality of his profound ignorance and its attendant dangers when dealing with government officials or negotiating a partnership arrangement with local people (or in estimating the cost of sales or operations or a training program) or in handling a thousand and one other details, big and little, which define not only if a project is economically feasible, but if it is humanly tolerable as well.

Observations of literally hundreds of potential investors from the United States in the field reveal that indeed they do find it hard to admit openly their need to learn, and few have taken the time to study. Let us look at two typical situations:

Case 4. A chemical manufacturer began his investment program as a result of meeting his proposed foreign partner while the latter was visiting the United States. A company was envisioned in which the U.S. partner would sell the foreign corporation raw materials. The manufacturing plant would be operated by the foreign partner. Credit arrangements, methods of payment, equity roles, profit distribution, and over-all control were all defined and put into a contract. The American finally visited the foreign country. His partner proved to be as impressive a host as he had been a guest. The company was formed. To get it underway, a large shipment of chemicals was made from the United States.

In six months, the company broke up. The U.S. investor withdrew. Credit terms were not met. Questions arose as to where earnings were going. Power over decisions was in dispute.

It is not possible to suggest what might have been done to ensure success. But the reasons for the failure are clear. The native partner, while a successful businessman, was a known sharp trader in a country where sharp practices are emulated. Default on payment for imports received on credit is common practice. The transfer of cash on hand to one's personal account rather than putting it aside for future payment on the raw materials received could have been predicted by the informed as a normal, even highly thought of, practice. The local partner was powerful politically, and although the contracts made and the laws involved were clear, riding herd on this situation could have been foretold as a wild chase through a dismal swamp.

Case 5. To a certain investor, an unusual opportunity seemed to exist to erect an iron and steel mill. Feasibility analysis confirmed the market and profitability potential. The venture was negotiated, and the mill was built. Within a year it closed. Despite a proper conclusion, made in advance, that jobs were scarce, and hence an ample labor pool would exist, labor's incessant demands for higher wages and other benefits brought on unrest, low output, and poor quality. The building was stripped and the equipment shipped elsewhere.

Management and the technicians who had done the feasibility study in this case had failed to take into consideration the nature of the social and political environment. The area was notorious as a politically turbulent place where private investment had never flourished, even though a strong private sector characterized the country as a whole. Practically all manufacturing in the state was publicly owned and operated and was part of a scheme of social reform on which all local political power was based. Labor had long been encouraged to believe in the threat of exploitation and in the ability of management to pay and pay; furthermore, labor came off very small farms where, in truth, exploitation was common and "owners" detested and distrusted.

In the final analysis, the surge of social reform was more important than jobs—or so it seemed at the time. It had happened thus before; its recurrence might have been anticipated by a sensitive appreciation of the past.

It is worth noting, as the foregoing cases illustrate, that the dangers of ignorance about people and politics may be exaggerated by the fact that the technicians carrying out feasibility studies more often than not also ignore critical behavioristic phenomena. The technician does so for the same reason that U.S. management does. Both start in ignorance and do not achieve sufficient sensitivity to the pragmatic implications of nontechnical, nonstatistical factors in the society. A local technician may also overlook these factors simply because he takes them for granted or will not admit their significance. In this sense, the executive making a final decision cannot depend on staff reports to the extent he may ordinarily do so.

Ignorance & Immaturity

All this reflects but one side of the story. Another side is the ignorance expressed by government officials. Dealing with this is never easy. Language difficulties alone, particularly with reference to technical terms, can render an investment situation austere and full of wrangling. For example:

Case 6. During negotiations relating to the automotive assembly investment described in Case No. 2, a major obstacle which took months to overcome was created by the terms "completely knocked down" and "assembly." The word "completely" was taken literally, and officials were baffled by the use of the term to include fully assembled units such as motors, carburetors, and generators. For a long time they insisted that every part of a car must be wholly fabricated locally for the industry to be legitimate. This insistence was supported by a belief that "assembly" operations were not really industrial but, rather, were a devious scheme to obtain public subsidy under false pretenses and so to multiply profits.

Very often an investor must deal with young men whose immaturity robs the relationship of camaraderie and whose responses tend to be theoretical, heavy with passages taken from university textbooks, and often bombastic. Nor is this immaturity limited only to the young. Men of all ages may be brash and arrogant in dealing with foreign investors; they are part of a new power elite, and they know it and like it. They may also be fearful and evasive as well, for they are part of a political foment which may spew them upward or outward at any time, almost whimsically, and nearly always beyond their control. They may seem overprotective of their country and suspicious, which comes as no surprise when one realizes that these are all children of colonial exploitation whose own memories, and those of their parents, are still vivid and alive.

In all, despite the best of intentions on both sides, the situation is difficult to manage. It is a wonder sometimes why anyone tries. Interviews with scores of successful investors from Europe, the Middle East, and the Far East, as well as from the United States, have been enlightening in this regard.

Need for Respect

It would demean those who have negotiated this tough course to say merely that it was worth it to them to make the resultant profit. While not denying this motivation—most of these people point to profit levels far above those obtainable in their homelands—it should be kept in mind that other attitudes came into play in sustaining the effort. One attitude shared universally is the growth of respect and liking for the people of the host country.

It is hard to mask dislike and distaste. Conversely, it is easy to reflect a feeling of empathy. Either way, relationships become more closed or more open. Here the communication process is exquisitely delicate. Tone and gesture say the same thing everywhere, instantaneously and with precision. They cut through politeness, ceremony, and the superficial joviality of handshakes, cocktails, and curling cigarette smoke. Tone and gesture are heard and watched with infinite care by Asians, Africans, and Latin Americans when dealing with foreigners; early rejection of an investor on intuitive emotional grounds has killed many an investment project.

Experience has shown that Americans are highly susceptible to failure at this point. This fact is interesting in that Americans generally come ready to like their hosts and wanting to be liked. Part of the reason for failure has already been discussed. As a rule, not enough time has been given in advance to the nature of the personal problems liable to be met, or to preparing oneself emotionally and intellectually to deal with such problems. But to say this is not enough; even when the potential American investor has given sufficient time to the learning, adapting task, he will not be effective in dealing with interpersonal relationships unless a fundamental flaw in his thinking and behavior pattern is overcome.

Demand for Self-Discipline

It is in the character of Americans to think of themselves as liking "people," being tolerant of differences, and being a symbol of good will toward all. As a generalization, this image truly reflects our character. Consequently, the businessman arrives in a far-off, strange country prepared to like his hosts, wanting to be liked, but without feeling any need to study or even meet many people on an intimate basis to extend sincere respect and regard. All of this the American will agree to happily, and with justifiable pride.

What he will not agree to so readily, or at all, is that he arrives with some trepidation; he is at heart quite provincial, and easily disturbed when things are not similar to what they are at home—airports, restaurants, service, smells, comfort, language, action, and reaction. It becomes upsetting to be in the minority. In this emotional state, which characterizes him as surely as do his clothes and his idiom, the American is susceptible to errors in behavior which he should admit to, but rarely does until too late. When the going gets rough, when delays and confusion get mixed up with hot weather, poor food, and an upset stomach, verbal response quickly becomes uncontrolled, irritable, complaining, and damaging to attempts to establish a personal basis for negotiation.

No formula is presented here to overcome this weakness in behavior.

None is known to this writer. However, I hope that, by focusing the sharp light of analysis and criticism on the observed behavior of the American investor abroad, the result will be less denial of its existence and more control in dealing with it. Many businessmen who have lived through the experience say that a little laughter, especially at one's own expense, helps enormously.

Sense of Obligation

As surface manifestations of his own ignorance and that of his hosts are penetrated beyond the level of simple bewilderment in dealing with new problems, a second attitude emerges which, in the final analysis, seems to determine whether or not the investor takes on the major share of the burden of making a negotiation work—namely, a sense of obligation to demonstrate the power of superior knowledge.

The typical educated, successful executive from the United States, or Western Europe or Japan, can command superior knowledge in facing an economic development problem. He may not have this knowledge at hand in every instance, but he does have greater access to it, and he has a wider range of experience through which to filter what is learned and extract what is relevant. Failure to solve a problem then becomes a challenge to seek additional facts, to recombine the old and the new, and to present another possible solution.

It can be observed that investors who become aware of, and intrigued by, the power for action vested in them by virtue of superior knowledge also become superb negotiators. It would be unfair to call this a game, but gamemanship is involved, possibly in the same way that it works to stimulate corporate growth when profit per se can hardly be a felt need. Neither can what has been observed be accurately labeled a search for naked power, although the power of accomplishment is a goal and a spur.

In any event, it is fascinating to note that when an investor reaches this state of mind, he will not take *no* for an answer. The challenge to the rational process is too great. This response inevitably leads the investor to a thorough awareness of the state of mind of the government officials with whom he is dealing. And the crowning moment of success can always be recognized when, suddenly, it becomes clear to these officials that their responsibilities are understood and the consequences of their actions appreciated—even shared. Unquestionably, it is a cardinal rule of the game, when negotiating investment in the underdeveloped world, to treat ignorance and inexperience as a challenge to the power of men's minds to teach and to learn and to solve problems. If this rule is followed, it leads to another: *the responsibility for protecting the public interest borne by the foreign government must be shared by investors asking public support.*

SHARED RESPONSIBILITY

The American investor overseas often presents a curious picture. He is the symbol of free enterprise. He is the voice of opposition to government control. Competition is his source of nourishment. So it seems to others, and many Americans believe it to be a true picture. Yet, in a far-off country, the same investor aggressively pursues protection and subsidy. He pleads to eliminate competition. He shrinks from risk. The confusion which results is natural, and U.S. executives have been singularly inarticulate in expressing the real differences between investment in the United States and in an underdeveloped country. Little has been done to spell out the reasons why there is a harmony between the two positions taken in altogether different circumstances.

Thus, when applications are made for a tax holiday or a tariff change or some other benefit under the law, skepticism is commonly expressed. It is charged that the public interest is being exploited to achieve unnecessarily high profit. This accusation tends to infuriate the applicant and exacerbate discussion. The components of ignorance and attitude which influence the course of a negotiation at this point, and the implications for action by the investor to correct errors in interpretation, have already been discussed. What is worth elaborating on briefly, as a guide to the rules of personal behavior governing these situations, is the extent to which successful negotiation involves the investor in sharing responsibility for the public welfare.

Ubiquitous 'Partner'

The role of central government in the economic development of underdeveloped countries is ubiquitous, and it is likely to remain so indefinitely. This need not, and does not, imply a socialistic state; nor does it mean that private investment cannot be made. Rather, the national governments in these countries have had to gather power unto themselves to achieve strength and cohesion. Where there has been an acute shortage of trained people, the trained few have been concentrated in federal agencies. Assistance money has been funneled through the government; combined with its power to tax, this has made the government itself the major source of capital. Planning has been executed and administered as a national function.

These facts and the reasons for their existence are so well known as to need no emphasis or explanation here. What is meaningful to this discussion are the facts themselves, because—no matter what the wish or the political or philosophical persuasion of the U.S. investor—intimate relations with government agencies, their policies, their ministers, and their staffs are an inevitable part of negotiations to invest and of day-to-day operations thereafter. The government is one's partner.

Frequently overlooked is the converse, namely, that *one is a partner of the government*. In point of fact, this is the way governments look on investors, foreign or not, and investment is expected to yield a net gain to the entire economy, not just profit to the company. Admittedly, this result is frequently not achieved, and selfish interests are catered to by one means or another. Nonetheless, the frames of reference are clear and strongly influence how a government official looks on the details of an application for public subsidy and on the persons making the application.

At every turn, the public servant must ask himself whether the cost of protection is balanced by the gain to the national economy from the project. Immediately, as he asks the question, he is generally projected far beyond his competence to supply an answer. The situations raised are various and subtle. To whom does he turn for an honest answer? What is to be the judgment rendered in such situations as *Cases 1* and *2,* or in the following examples:

Case 7. A cement plant is proposed. Application is made to restrict imports in the amount of planned production and to raise tariffs to ensure a satisfactory level of profits during the pioneer years of training a labor force and otherwise developing efficiency in operation and sales. One result would be an increase in the price of cement at a time when construction is booming. Actually, cement is available at the ports at prices well below those set by the proposed local plant, which claims imports are being "dumped" to keep local industry from starting up.

What is in the national interest? Who proves an import is dumped? A local source of cement is thought desirable as a basic industry and for strategic national security reasons. Yet cement making is capital rather than labor intensive, and employment benefits are meager. Higher priced cement would drive all construction costs up. How could a balance sheet be drawn up?

Case 8. Cotton growing has been developed in a country in which cotton fabric imports have traditionally caused a major drain on foreign exchange and have contributed significantly to an imbalance of trade. Spinning and weaving industries have been vigorously promoted. However, the range of goods produced is still limited. A large market for cotton print cloth exists; all prints are imported. In this situation, the project brings to the government its request for full duty relief on gray (raw) print cloth. The investment would be one of the largest ever made. It is known that several other investments in print cloth would be made if the concessions asked for are granted and then made generally available. Total employment would be significant.

But revenue losses would run high. In addition, existing cotton manufacturers vigorously oppose the project on the grounds that it will destroy their incentive to expand in the direction of making print cloth and finishing; that their pioneering efforts should be rewarded by the opportunity to grow; and that as long as duty relief is granted on imported gray goods for printing, they could not compete for this market.

What is the balance to be struck by the foreign government? What assurances can be given to existing industry that, when they can produce print cloth, they will get the market? Who arbitrates a claim that quality and price of local products is right or wrong? Will textile manufacturing be encouraged or discouraged by building in a planned way around a nucleus of existing spinners and weavers, or by allowing a diversity, even if random, of investment to be made?

Case 9. A certain country is a large consumer of refined salt. There are no local sources. During World War II, sources of supply were rendered ineffective, and the shortages which resulted frightened everyone, particularly in the light of troubled world affairs. The country borders the ocean, and there was a determination to become self-sufficient by producing salt from sea water. The determination lasted, but no action had been taken.

A large salt maker proposed a project: enough crude salt to meet national requirements would be imported from low-cost solar evaporated salt pans and refined locally. To satisfy national security requirements, a stockpile would be established sufficient for two years of normal consumption, and much longer than this if rationed. The investor pointed out that nowhere along the nation's coast was there sufficient continuous sunshine and low humidity to effect economic solar evaporation; it was noted that other forms of evaporation had not been competitive anywhere in the world. This proposal stimulated government action, and a feasibility study was bought. The study eventually claimed that evaporating ocean water in boilers could be made profitable, and outlined a very expensive plant for government to build and operate.

What was to be done? Who was to be believed? What is the price a people should be willing to pay for self-sufficiency in a basic commodity like salt? Can national security be quantified as a benefit, and how is partial security to be rated?

Without trusted help, governments can only be arbitrary and secretive in supplying answers to these and other critically important questions. Unfortunately, this is what has happened during the past decade. It has led to a lot of bad investment—bad in the sense of costing the people far more than they have gained. Governments have been led to invest public funds in hordes of factories which have failed or which have drained money endlessly if kept open for political reasons. High-cost, low-quality goods have flooded many a market because of overprotection in the name of industrial development, with resultant loss of purchasing power and a decline in standards of living. What has happened has alerted governments everywhere to the fact that there is no magic in industrial development; it can break an economy as fast as it can make one —even faster, perhaps.

Expert Advisers

It has been partly because of this truth, as it has dawned on both foreign governments and those who would help them, that assistance in evaluating industrial projects has become more widespread. Resident "experts" in underdeveloped countries are now the common thing. They are under the sponsorship of the United Nations; the U.S. Agency for International Development; various foundations; and the technical assistance institutions in England, Western Europe, the Middle East, and the Far East.

However, such expertise has been limited in value. Resident experts, while they may know some industries in depth, cannot be expected to know all industries as well. This has meant that much of such assistance has focused on critical analysis—asking pointed questions, evaluating answers, and shaping law, policy, and administrative practice. Foreign governments and their expert advisers still must depend on the investor to supply certain kinds of specific data, particularly those relevant to cash flow within the company and to and from the company, nationally and internationally.

Growing Involvement

So it is that the investor finds himself deep within a pressure system demanding detailed information the minute he asks for public protection. He becomes a vital part of the process of building a new country, or at least a new economic base. His involvement becomes national and goes far beyond his stockholders, however primary they may remain in reaching a decision; his actions are international in significance as well, as he becomes a visible part of the efforts of the United States to achieve its foreign policy objectives. His industry is not the relatively isolated economic entity it may be in the United States or in Western Europe, but, rather, is an outstanding element of the dynamics shaping social change and political movements. As minutes turn into days, and weeks and months, what is done becomes as much a measure of the man (and what he represents) as of his project.

This is the point. In the years to come, the investor in the developing countries who remains abstracted and aloof will fail to see the means through which to negotiate, and he will be resisted. Neither he nor his industry will be judged automatically desirable. And, conversely, when the local people and their problems become important to the investor, along with his project, he must realize and accept the depth of his commitment in order for it to be effective. On reaching this stage, many Americans face with some sense of shock what they see must be done.

Philosophically, the U.S. investor may be forced to rethink his position on the role of government vis-à-vis the individual in countries ridden with poverty and strife but projected full blast into the hopes and conflicts of 1965. When is a man free and able to demand and support democracy, and when must a government be the trustee of this aspiration and proceed toward achievement with methods sometimes far short of being democratic, as Americans see democracy? How does one work with such a trustee to hasten the achievement? How best does one make a profit for stockholders back home and yet without question have the project contribute to a foreign country's national development? Is the slogan used by some U.S. corporations overseas that they are "here to stay" the right one, or should they be saying, "We will stay long enough to make owners of you and make a profit, too"?

In a practical way, the final deep involvement of the U.S. businessman is most positively challenged when he is asked to reveal all that is necessary to make the best possible estimate of the losses and the gains to the nation which will result when his investment is instituted.

CALCULATED RISK

The essential difficulty in making a constructive contribution to a calculation of national benefits starts with the fact that there is no fully acceptable way to find an exact answer; and, on top of that, seemingly ceaseless exploration of the investor's business is required before the best (most reasonable) answer can be approximated. The balance sheet to be drawn up contains two kinds of elements, both difficult, if not impossible, to quantify precisely:

Elements resulting in a *loss* to national accounts include foreign exchange drain, diversion of resources to low priority use, high prices, low quality, loss of duty revenue, and inflationary impact of payroll if not enough goods are available.

Elements resulting in a *gain* to national accounts include foreign exchange savings, initial capital input to build and equip factory, payroll and its multiplier effect on purchasing power if excess production capacity exists, taxes, purchase of local supplies and services if these have no better alternative use, savings, and training.

The difficulty of tracing the benefits derived from training typifies the tortuous trail that must be followed between losses and gains:

The fact that labor must be trained implies a cost to management and to society for some period of time. There is the actual training cost —the supervisors, the materials, the time. There is also the effect on quality and output which is caused by lack of skill. These must be built into operating costs; in turn, they influence prices upwards and value downwards over an estimated period of time. Yet the cost of training is on a sliding scale, in that labor produces something for sale from the outset and gets more proficient as time goes by.

The fact that labor is being trained, on the other hand, makes the country that much more attractive to the next investor, particularly one in a related industry. This may be charged off as a contribution to development. Labor trained on the job relieves the burden of training in technical schools, and it is legitimate to take a benefit per worker equal to the cost of training in such schools. In fact, income to the economy per worker trained may be thought of in excess of the per pupil cost in a technical school, since learning is accomplished simultaneously with production.

Confusing as all this seems at first, one can reach a figure which summarizes the plus and negative values of a training program, including a correction factor for whether labor has a better use, or whether one is dealing with people who are unemployable prior to training.

Each of the components affecting a balance between gain and loss requires this type of analysis, estimation, projection, and "quantification." It can readily be imagined how much time, patience, judgment, and yielding are required of the group making the calculation. Within the group, the investor becomes the target and the unique resource. Only he can demonstrate how he reached his conclusions as to price, profit, and support requirements; only he can express the risks he feels must be amortized by quick payout. How and when is local ownership to be encouraged? How much use will be made of local services and supplies? Will secondary sources of raw and semifabricated materials be encouraged? If so, how? With loans? With technical assistance? Can training proceed more quickly? Will prices drop as efficiency rises?

Question after question drives deeper and deeper into the quality and extent of the thinking which has gone into a project. The demand reaches into areas of information and policy U.S. business executives do not expect to reveal to anyone outside their own top management.

CONCLUDING NOTE

It must be admitted that this article asks more questions and poses more problems than its answers. But the purpose here has been to emphasize how intensely introspective and personal preplanning investment procedures must be. An article cannot shape a man, but perhaps it can focus attention on the need for honest self-appraisal and careful preparation in dealing with strangers in their homeland—prerequisites generally found lacking in Americans when failures to follow through investment decisions in the underdeveloped countries of the world are analyzed.

The questions raised are questions which have been asked again and again. The situations described are real and illuminate the issues which face investors and foreign governments everywhere and the means through which these issues get resolved. The responses noted are those which have been seen and which reflect how much Americans must learn before the full, rich scope of opportunity for investment in Africa, Asia, and Latin America can be tapped.

10.

MARKETING IN THE INDUSTRIALIZATION
OF UNDERDEVELOPED COUNTRIES*

A. A. Sherbini

INDUSTRIALIZATION is occupying an increasingly prominent position in the development programs of many underdeveloped countries. Its appeal stems from many sources—for example, enhancement of the country's prestige and power, achievement of a higher degree of economic self-sufficiency, and realization of more favorable terms of trade.

However, industrialization has been a painful process in many developing countries. The literature on economic development is indeed flooded with examples of shortcomings that have undermined the efficient functioning of new industrial ventures in these countries. A typical list of pitfalls includes absence of a vigorous growth mentality, difficulties in administration and management, lack of advance planning, poor maintenance, and inadequate financial controls.[1]

Yet, the recent experiences of many underdeveloped countries have shown that marketing problems can be more obstructive than many other deterrents to the process of industrialization. A higher rate of capital formation and relatively large doses of investments in manufacturing have frequently failed to generate the anticipated increase in national income. Poor marketing bears a significant part of the responsibility for this failure.

THE PLANNING PHASE

Industrialization is usually incorporated in a national economic development plan. The benchmark for such a plan is invariably a "macro-economic" program that projects the development of such aggregates as national income and outlay, imports, and exports. This is then refined in a

* A. A. Sherbini, "Marketing in the Industrialization of Underdeveloped Countries," *Journal of Marketing*, Vol. 29, No. 1 (January, 1965), a publication of the American Marketing Association, pp. 28-32. Reprinted by permission.

[1] Albert O. Hirschman, *The Strategy of Economic Development* (New Haven: Yale University Press, 1958), p. 136.

"micro-economic" program that fills in the framework with figures for individual industries, regions, or even some important plants.

What types of goods will have to be produced? This is usually the first question in micro-planning. For the most part, imports provide the shopping list from which new industrial ventures are selected. Thus, few economic planners show due concern about the determination of consumers' generic wants and needs to be served, and the alternative ways of satisfying these generic wants.

Furthermore, the lure of import-substitution often precludes a consideration of other important want-satisfying projects. For instance, certain products have distinct physical characteristics, such as high perishability, which limit their participation in international trade. Also, historically the interests of trade intermediaries and other institutions may have curbed the importation of low-margin, but significant, want-satisfying goods.

Another problem in micro-planning concerns decisions on productive capacity for individual projects. Blind reliance on import statistics has frequently led to grave miscalculations in estimating domestic market requirements.

Likewise, the tendency to overlook marketing considerations has often given rise to the acquisition of improper equipment and other physical facilities. For example: An important section in a bicycle factory was provided for the automatic assembly of bicycle parts. However, it turned out that for several reasons trade channels preferred to receive their shipments unassembled. The assembly section is now operating much below standard capacity.

But the primacy of marketing considerations is not restricted to the micro-planning phase. All too often, marketing is the basic determinant of the destiny of new manufacturing enterprises from the moment they are launched. The remainder of this paper focuses on the role of the marketing in the operating phase.

THE OPERATING PHASE

Generally speaking, the tendency in the early life of new manufacturing concerns is to place primary emphasis on staffing the production, financial, and general administrative departments of the firm. All thinking about sales is generally deferred to the point of actual production. The presence of a ready market and the availability of experienced trade channels minimize executive anxiety. The general assumption is simply that the new firm will inherit the entire assets of the import market; but experience has shown that it also takes over the liabilities.

Product and Production Decisions

In approaching the operating phase, the management of the firm is con
fronted with critical product decisions. A first decision concerns the selection of proper *product attributes* upon which a satisfactory volume of
demand may converge. This may be a difficult task, as imports often tend
to segment the domestic market. The multiplicity of foreign sources of
supply brings to the domestic market an array of products with varying
attributes. Thus, the aggregate demand for a given "product" often consists of many thin and heterogeneous demand schedules that are not addi-
tive.

The demand for even a simple product such as imported sardines
sometimes reflects a high degree of consumer attachment to certain product attributes—for example, shape and type of tin, sauce-packed or oil-
packed, flavor, and price. Foreign exporters who sell in world-wide markets generally find it economically possible and feasible to cater to thin
domestic market segments in underdeveloped countries. But domestic
manufacturing obviously cannot economically serve all thin market segments.

A refrigerator manufacturer may decide to make only electric refrigerators and forego the needs of other market segments for refrigerators pow-
ered by kerosene or butane. The next question concerns the sizes, shapes,
and colors to be manufactured. This is essentially a decision on *assortment* size and varieties. Yet, again, imports condition the market to varieties and assortments not economically feasible for domestic manufacturing.

A third decision pertains to the extent of the *product line*. In general, the advantages of a full product line are not well conceived by the
management of the new firm. The major determinants of line composition are such factors as common raw materials, technical know-how, and
common production facilities. Interrelationships of demand characteristics are usually of minor concern.

This tendency has given rise to many problems. First, a high degree
of unnecessary and misdirected diversification has compounded the distribution problem of many new firms. Many firms begin their operations
by manufacturing many different and unrelated products that sell in distinct markets and utilize diverse trade channels. A second result is that
trade intermediaries in general, and retailers in particular, tend to supplement their incomplete and domestically-based product lines with imported products. Thus, an appliance dealer may carry a refrigerator and
washing machine of a domestic base, together with other household appliances of a foreign base. The higher margins on imported articles have

frequently deprived domestic manufacturers of adequate dealer support.

A fourth area in which marketing problems have led to grave consequences is that of *production planning and control*. One immediate problem concerns the decision on the proper or optimum *product mix*. How
much should be manufactured of the different sizes and shapes of screws,
bolts, and nuts? How much should be produced of the diverse types, accessories, and colors of chinaware or other dinnerware? These typical perplexing questions are encountered by new firms. Secondary sources of
statistics throw little or no light on these knotty points. For many firms,
trial and error, regardless of its extremely high cost, is the only answer to
the product mix riddle.

Production scheduling can also be a formidable problem, particularly for multiple product firms serving the needs of many divergent
end users. For example:

A canvas and netting firm is equipped to manufacture such diverse
products as canvas, heavy cloth, nets, and filters. These products may be
sold to manufacturers of many different articles—footwear, luggage, sails,
tents, furniture, sportsgoods, and fishing nets. Lacking adequate market
information, the manufacturer operates on a job-order basis rather than
engage in mass production in anticipation of demand. The result has
been very high setup costs and very short production runs. Furthermore,
the linkage effect expected from this new industry has been seriously undermined; for instance, cloth filters continued to be imported simply because the importing firm did not know that this item could be manufactured locally.

The lack of crucial feedback concerning inventory fluctuations and
rate of sale at different intermediary levels has often given rise to sporadic
gluts followed by periods of acute shortages. For instance:

A manufacturer of bakery products contracted to sell its entire line
through a sole distributor. One item in the line, a specialty product that
the distributor had not previously sold, was forced on him under a tie-in
arrangement. The news of a serious drop in retail sales during the summer, took a long time in being transmitted to the manufacturer. Because
of dilapidation, large quantities of the specialty product were destroyed,
and many problems ensued at the consumer and retail levels.

Price Decisions

Domestic manufacturers in developing countries often face a dual problem in setting their basic prices. First, imports frequently impose an

upper ceiling on prices, regardless of the adopted policy toward imports. Secondly, prices become rigid once they are set. Price controls and the need for government approval put firm limits on price flexibility.

A mistake in pricing, however trifling, is therefore of grave consequence for the new manufacturer. For instance:

The prices of imported nine-ounce cans of luncheon meat were all "odd" prices. A domestic manufacturer decided to round the price of his product in order to simplify his accounting task. When his sales were not moving as anticipated, a market study was undertaken. It was found that retailers were pushing the competing imports because many customers did not ask for the small change. It took this manufacturer almost six months to obtain permission to change his retail price so as to conform to prices of other competing products.

A major pitfall that has caused many problems for new firms is the tendency to ignore the whole gamut of price differentials and discount structures. Many firms start operations with no specific plans concerning trade margins. Thus, the spread between retail price and factory price is often unplanned and occasionally fails to accommodate the necessary trade margins. To resolve this problem, many manufacturers resort to trade channels that can be accommodated by the given spread; channels that may not be the most desirable for the product in question.

Terms of sale and discount structures also receive little attention. Some firms make no distinction between cash and credit sales in pricing their products, which boosts credit sales and undermines net factory price, since the cost of discounting credit notes is not taken into account. Other firms insist on cash sales and, thereby, do not attain desirable sales goals. The problems of financing, price differentials, and discount structures are often compounded as a result of the need to devise new systems and procedures, which follows the shift from an import-based to a domestic-based source of supply.

Channels of Distribution

Can existing import-oriented channels be effectively used in the distribution of domestic manufactures? How can existing channels be adapted to local manufacturing? These difficult questions confront new firms in many developing countries. Ironically, the new firm has often adapted to the practices and operations of existing channels, in spite of special features that make these channels unsuitable for domestic manufacturing.

The conflicts between import-oriented channels and the needs of domestic manufacturing can be outlined in the following points:

1. Imports not only *segment* the domestic market, they may also *fragment* that market. Large import wholesalers are not prone to create a national market; their businesses tend to cluster in big cities where margins are high and sales are not too costly. Thus, existing channels may not serve the needs of a domestic manufacturer who is contemplating nationwide distribution.

2. Import-oriented channels are generally characterized by a lack of functional specialization. The concept of a channel as a chain of intermediaries directly linked to each other is hardly applicable to this model. Intermediaries may simultaneously assume such different functions as importing, wholesaling, semi-wholesaling, and retailing; their general operating rule is to be present in any capacity when a chance to sell appears. Thus, an intermediary does not sell to a specific link in the channel, but to a *range* of other intermediaries. A domestic manufacturer, on the other hand, would be interested in a *"chain-type"* of channel in which specific tasks can be assigned and responsibilities affixed.

3. Lack of functional specialization is coupled with a high degree of division of labor. Such tasks as financing, storage and warehousing, trucking, shipping and packing, bulking and sorting, grading and packaging, are often performed by separate agencies and intermediaries. Lack of adequate capital and the need sometimes for the simultaneous performance of different tasks account for this. But domestic manufacturing requires a greater integration of these tasks; the manufacturer may assume some of them.

4. An import-oriented channel usually works backward; consumers, retailers, and other intermediaries are always seeking goods. This results from the tendency of importers to throttle the flow of goods and from the sporadic and uneven flow of imports. Inventory hoarding as a means of choking the market can be achieved at relatively low cost and is obviously justified because of its lucrative speculative yields.[2] In contrast, domestic manufacturing ensures a steady stream of merchandise, requiring a smooth flow free from obstructions and stockpiles.

5. The variations in product specifications, resulting from different foreign origins, and in available supplies, lead to certain practices unfavorable for domestic manufacturing. For instance bargaining becomes a standard practice since it makes possible rapid adjustments to any changes in the situation. Profits, in a sense, are not conceived as compensation for the performance of certain tasks; they simply reflect the trader's ability to take advantage of the situation.

6. The credit system utilized in the import-oriented channel may differ considerably from that required by domestic manufacturing. In

2 Harper W. Boyd, Jr., and A. A. Sherbini, "Wholesaling in Egypt," in Robert Bartels (editor), *Comparative Marketing: Wholesaling in Fifteen Countries* (Homewood, Illinois: Richard D. Irwin, Inc., 1963), p. 100.

practice, a commercial bank furnishes the importer with the necessary documentary credit. Upon arrival, the merchandise is stored in the Customs under a Custom bond. The importer need pay the bank only for the specific quantities withdrawn from the Customs. Since these are often sold prior to withdrawal, the importer's business is, in effect, self-financing. But this arrangement is very difficult to duplicate for domestic manufacturing.

Credit also plays a primary role in sustaining and regulating the flow of imports into the domestic market. The marketing channel may be viewed as "a sort of hydraulic system in which the balance of credit pressures at hundreds of larger and smaller couplings determines the speed, direction, and volume of the flow of goods through the system. Most of everyone's time is consumed in pursuing debtors and dunning them, or in trying to wheedle a little more credit from one's creditors.[3] Obviously, this system is not tailored to the needs of modern manufacturing; the latter requires a faster and more direct flow of goods.

7. Because of the above inherent conflicts, some new firms have tried to develop new channels of distribution to serve more adequately the needs of domestic manufacturing. This has often given rise to bitter struggles with existing marketing channels. The existence of strong corporate groups, often based on kinship ties, among larger importers and wholesalers frequently puts the new firm at a disadvantage. Again and again, these middlemen may use diverse means to undermine the position of the new firm—price cutting, coercion, bankrupting other intermediaries who cooperate with the new firm, and spreading devastating rumors about quality and performance of the domestic product.

Promotional Decisions

Of what significance are promotional decisions for the new firm? What is the extent of the monopolistic powers of import-substituting firms? In answering these questions, the following points may be made:

1. A new firm of the import-substituting type is often pictured as a monopolist with no promotional problems. However, imports are frequently needed to supplement domestic manufacturing, and may thereby represent a challenging competitive force.

2. Even when domestic manufacturing is planned to replace imports *in toto,* imports may still continue to flow. Often enough, there seems to be a lack of coordination among government agencies, which results in issuing import licenses for goods that are also produced locally.

3. In many developing countries interindustry competition may be

---

[3] E. E. Hagen, *On the Theory of Social Change* (Homewood, Illinois: The Dorsey Press, Inc., 1962), p. 392.

of great concern to the domestic manufacturer. For instance, the advent of television in Egypt has shown remarkable effects on the sales of other consumer durables. Thus, the stimulation of primary demand may carry greater weight than the emphasis put on selective demand.

4. The new firm often encounters the knotty problem of "domophobia," that is, the mistrust and disbelief in the quality of domestic products. Sometimes, considerable effort is required to establish an acceptable image for domestic manufactures.

5. Dealer cooperation in promoting the domestic product is usually a problem for the new firm. In an import-based system, the costs of distribution are essentially buying costs rather than selling costs; creating an atmosphere of shortages is the classic technique for rapid disposition of merchandise. Domestic manufacturing requires a new philosophy and different behavioral patterns.

In Conclusion

Marketing problems have recently surprised many development planners. The lack of attention given to marketing considerations has resulted in serious flaws in planning and implementing new industrial projects. These concern such things as improper productive equipment, excess or sometimes inadequate plant capacity, and uneconomical plant location.

But marketing problems are not restricted to the planning phase of new manufacturing projects; they remain much at work once the manufacturing process has started. They often turn into obstructive forces leading to the stagnation and decay of ventures that looked hopeful at first.

Marketing is, therefore, a key factor in the success or failure of industrialization programs. Viewed in proper perspective, marketing can play a strategic role in optimizing the utilization of capital resources that are in scarce supply in most developing countries.

RESEARCH

11.

ANALYZING FOREIGN OPPORTUNITIES*

Raphael W. Hodgson and
Hugo E. R. Uyterhoeven

ONE of the most significant business trends of our time is the entry of many U.S. manufacturing companies into foreign markets. How should the managements of these companies size up their opportunities abroad? The approach commonly followed is to analyze present market potentials and assess the prospects of future growth. On the face of it, this approach may seem rational—and certainly it provides *part* of the data top executives need. By itself, however, it is inadequate. As a basis for decision making, it may even lead to more wrong answers than right ones. Here are just a few illustrations to make our point:

The European market for an important line of electronics systems was growing rapidly, and firms participating in this market were enjoying large profits. A U.S. company contemplating entry into this business possessed the skills and resources necessary to gain a competitive market position. At first glance, the company's prospects for doing well looked excellent according to conventional criteria.

Yet closer examination showed that high levels of demand relieved firms of the need to offer a considerable amount of customer service and special systems work normally required in more competitive situations. Given the absence of these sales expenses, profit margins were not as high as one would expect in this industry. Also, product shortages greatly reduced the levels of finished goods and work-in-process inventories, thus requiring less debt and equity capital. Profitability in this business could therefore be expected to decline rapidly as maturing conditions imposed increased sales expenses and capital requirements.

In the late 1950's in Europe, a capacity shortage prevailed in an important plastic. In addition, consumption appeared to be increasing at over 20 percent per year, and prices were very high relative to entry ex-

* Raphael W. Hodgson and Hugo E. R. Uyterhoeven, "Analyzing Foreign Opportunities," HARVARD BUSINESS REVIEW (March–April, 1962), pp. 197-219. Reprinted by permission

penses and plant investments. Most firms felt that the problems of raw material supply and "coproduct" disposal, which are normal to a chemical business, were surmountable in that the huge demand and high price for the plastic relieved management of having to secure either the most economical source of raw materials or the most appropriate distribution for the coproducts. Consequently, the requirements for entry appeared less forbidding than in most other chemical product areas.

It was not surprising, therefore, that the field was entered by almost every candidate capable of doing so, and that capacity mushroomed all over Europe. Worse was to happen. The marginal cost of this product was low, yet capital investment was very high; with a considerable surplus for export already available in the United States, and with low European tariffs, dumping by U.S. producers occurred on a large scale. Today, the compounded effect of dumping by American producers and of large additions to capacity in Europe has collapsed prices to such an extent that a large number of the new business operations will probably become questionable ventures, if they have not already.

Profits were low among many European manufacturers of an important class of electric components, even though the market was a dynamic one. Most firms were under price pressure from two major producers. Investigation revealed that both producers had standardized their production around three basic types of products, thereby achieving higher scales of production resulting in much lower costs. This enabled them to enjoy considerable profits, while keeping prices low. Their low prices even enabled them to extend their market into areas where their products appeared overengineered or extravagant.

Competitors, although still holding the major market share, were making their profits largely on special items which were job-shop runs, while incurring losses on their standard offerings. There was clearly an opportunity for entry by developing a product policy similar to that of the industry leaders and sustaining the necessary production and distribution system. However, this opportunity would not have been suggested by a conventional market analysis.

In 1959 many firms entered the rapidly growing British refrigerator industry on a small scale. At that time, typical high profitability conditions prevailed in the refrigerator business along with a considerable amount of resale price maintenance. Plants of small scale were common, even among the leaders. Since then, however, imports, over-capacity arising from other new entrants, a break in consumer demand, and a break in price maintenance have brought prices down considerably. This trend eluded forecasters using the standard tools.

In short, management's investigation of foreign business opportunities should go beyond judgments of market growth if it is to recognize the opportunities before they become obvious to the world at large and is to spot dangerous situations before investments are unwisely committed. Special reliance will have to be placed on a financial, economic, and operational analysis of competing companies as well as on the technical and economic development of the field itself. We call this broader type of evaluation opportunity analysis.

PURPOSES AND USES

Opportunity analysis provides data and ways of looking at data that help top management with its most important decisions regarding foreign operations. More specifically, opportunity analysis helps executives to recognize:

1. *The limits within which a firm must operate abroad and plan its foreign strategy.* These quantitative limits are essential guideposts in defining the tightness or looseness of competition, which is the principal criterion of whether there is a margin a) for the expense of getting a business started and of sustaining the running expenses and b) for profits.

To recognize and analyze these limits for any given industry is especially important in international operations for two reasons. First, the limits often differ markedly among countries. Failing to appreciate this, companies often look at Europe or another region "as a whole" and thereby draw false analogies. Secondly, these limits change over time. Management often ignores such changes, particularly when planning foreign ventures under currently prevailing high profitability conditions. In many European industries, tighter competitive conditions appear inevitable; in fact, this change has already occurred for some products and has caught several producers off guard. Opportunity analysis assists in determining *when* and *to what extent* the limits are likely to change.

2. *The means of competition in a foreign country.* Only by analyzing how local participants compete is it possible to determine how a foreign entrant can most successfully participate regardless of whether or not he produces locally or exports. Opportunity analysis ensures identification and evaluation of alternatives and avenues which may lead to success. Even within the same industry, competitive methods vary significantly among countries. Therefore, the recognition of their impact on capacity planning, pricing policy, distribution strategy, financial planning, and so on is vital before clear entry and participation requirements for a foreign venture can be formulated.

3. *The critical elements of the industry.* We use the phrase "critical elements" to refer to important factors in operations that vary, not only from industry to industry, but also within the same industry from country to country. For example, variations in depreciation policies, working-capital requirements, utilization of debt, capacity building, operating control, inventory control, product policy, and distribution requirements may be significant.

Opportunity analysis is a valuable tool in appraising the foreign ventures of both established companies and newcomers. It helps the established firm reappraise its operations and judge the merits of expansion or diversification opportunities, and it serves the firm seeking foreign entry for the first time, whether by way of a foreign distributor, licensee, manufacturing partner, suitable acquisition, or an entirely new operation. Opportunity analysis aids not only in judging the value of the products or technology one has to offer (thus possibly increasing one's bargaining power in negotiation with potential foreign associates) but also in judging the competitive standing of potential associates and evaluating the capabilities of foreign competitors. It is, furthermore, of value to security analysts and underwriters in appraising foreign industry conditions as well as the relative strengths of competing participants.

Actually, opportunity analysis would be worth following here in the United States if businessmen were more dependent on formal analysis. At home, however, they can blend investigation, analysis, and judgment with an acute, fine, and, at times, intuitive sense—often the result of many years of experience. Abroad, the American businessman is without this guide; considerable and vigorous analysis, therefore, must take its place.

Coping with Change

Opportunity analysis is most vital in industrialized areas a) if economic and competitive conditions are expected to change markedly and b) if these changes are likely to occur very quickly. Both the amount and the rapidity of economic change magnify the danger of missing opportunities and making unsound investments. This is the situation in European industry today for the following reasons:

Extraordinary growth rates (often as high as 30 percent per year) enable large-scale production in several consumer and industrial sectors, thus reducing manufacturing costs significantly. Firms lagging behind in market share may find themselves priced out of the market.

High growth rates severely tax a firm's financial ability. Yet if it fails to concentrate its resources on keeping up with the growth requirements of its industry, it may sacrifice its future profitability.

Financial burdens will be augmented by the merging of hitherto separate national markets. Until now, industries in each nation have usually been dominated by that nation's own companies, and the narrowness of national markets has frequently limited participation to very few firms. But in the years ahead economic unification will greatly widen the market size while simultaneously exposing predominantly national companies to competition from their foreign neighbors. The impact will be felt both in production and in marketing. For example: The European chemical industry has hitherto constructed its productive capacity in relatively small steps (in contrast to the large capacity additions common in the U.S. chemical industry). A major reason for this difference is that in Europe, with participation in each country limited to a few firms, the risk of forfeiture of opportunity by not engaging in a capacity race has not been too great. This risk, however, will become more acute after the merging of national markets. That it will increase financial burdens, create unused capacity, and aggravate price instability seems all too evident from the U.S. experience.

The task of dislodging national companies from their dominant marketing positions (which is particularly difficult because of structural distribution differences and varying national characteristics) may impose even more severe financial burdens on outsiders. We have already noted that under high growth rates it is a major achievement. This strain will be greatly compounded if a rapid exploration of continental opportunities requires a firm to multiply its position in as many markets as there are nations. In fact, the magnitude of such a task appears to exceed the financial and management resources of a great many European firms.

The need for large-scale plants, the search for low-cost production sites, and the difficulty of breaking into national distribution structures may lead to a considerable number of mergers and acquisitions, thus creating truly continental firms. As a result, companies which continue to limit their activities to their own national market may find themselves at a cost disadvantage. Their local distribution strength will have to be immense to withstand price competition by foreign entrants. However, these high-cost producers may find themselves becoming desirable objects of acquisition by more efficient outside concerns seeking distribution outlets.

Because of differences in product concentration, market sizes, vertical integration, and so on, considerable variations in the costs of materials and parts prevail from country to country. Thus: The French washing-machine industry pays a higher price for its components than does the Italian washing-machine industry, which in turn pays more than the German and British industries do.

British and French refrigerator manufacturers as a whole pay high prices for their compressors, largely because too many of them make their own compressors in small volumes instead of purchasing the very low-cost units made in Denmark and Italy.

The French cathode ray tubes are more expensive than elsewhere because of the lack of price competition among the two big domestic producers, both of whom have important captive television manufacturing outlets.

These differences, which have hitherto been buttressed by national tariffs, are bound to disappear with the progressive reduction of tariff barriers, for purchasers will be able to select the lowest cost suppliers more freely.

The application of technology has been accelerated by international interchange. Thus, a receiving country may go through a technological evolution in five years which took twenty or so years in the country which pioneered in the development. The compression of a long history of U.S. technological change into a short time period in Europe stimulates the already rapid economic growth but also compounds it by creating considerable flux in the product lines of many companies and markets.

Ill-Conceived Ventures

The conditions of change just described allow sizable profits to many corporations today. However, at the same time they invite many new entrants. The additions to capacity may create surpluses of major proportions which, coupled with the coming adjustments required to survive in large unified markets, spell a tightening of competitive conditions. Indeed, the danger signals are already apparent in two of Europe's most dynamic industries—plastics and domestic appliances.

Many a participant will be incapable of withstanding the impact of the new competition. Unfortunately, this does not seem to be appreciated. Current profitable conditions hide crucial weaknesses; they invite complacency in that, because ventures are still so profitable, managements are not disposed to take steps to ensure their future. Conventional methods of analysis do not sufficiently focus on the danger signals or spot the real opportunities.

Errors in judgment are aggravated by the currently fashionable trend to establish operations in Europe. Often a businessman sees a market for his product and is impressed by its growth rate. However, he is pressed for time as he hears competition announcing new ventures; and since he feels he cannot afford to wait, he directs that an arrangement be made right away. Perhaps the contemplated operation is not the best one, but he hopes this can be adjusted afterward; the important thing, it seems to him, is to be in the market on time. He typically assesses the profitability of his contemplated operation by making cost analogies with his existing American operation, allowing for European plant scales and labor rates. The difference between his cost forecast and prevailing price levels usually appears to justify the investment.

Our businessman will, to be sure, ask whether this difference can be maintained in years to come. He expects his future costs to decline with increasing scale of operations. As for future prices, a look at the industry price trend seems to provide him with as good a guess as any. By using this highly respectable approach, he concludes, in most cases, that his costs will decline faster than the industry price trend. The resultant ever-expanding profit margin (how common a phenomenon in company forecasts!) augurs very healthy black figures for the years ahead. Such unrealistic optimism is the cause of many ill-conceived foreign ventures.

At the other extreme, and equally dangerous for sound international business planning, some managements are inclined to exaggerate foreign difficulties and dangers, especially by ascribing inordinately severe price declines to the economic integration process. Opportunity analysis, by *identifying* and *quantifying* the crucial competitive conditions abroad, enables the businessman to put a ceiling on unrealistic optimism and a floor under exaggerated pessimism.

OPERATING MARGINS

A vital tool in opportunity analysis is *operating margin analysis.* The "operating margin" in a business is defined for the purposes of the following discussion as the difference between the sales price and the cost of materials purchased. (For example, in January, 1960, a French manufacturer paid the equivalent of $66 for materials that went into a refrigerator which he sold for the equivalent of $101. His operating margin thus amounted to $35.) It is the margin within which a firm will have to operate, i.e., manufacture, sell, pay for research, conduct all other corporate activities, and make a profit.

In planning foreign ventures, operating margin analysis enables management to reconcile its basic manufacturing, marketing, and growth plan within the price-materials cost limits imposed by foreign competitive environments. It ensures that a venture meet the basic conditions of viability, that the operation of a business be carried out, and that the prevailing prices be met.

We have found it convenient to express the operating margin as a percentage of the cost of materials purchased. Thus, the operating margin for the French refrigerator just mentioned would be (sales price — materials cost) $\div$ materials cost = $35 $\div$ $66 = 53 percent.

Clearly, the operating margin concept is not new. It is often referred to as "value added." It should not be confused with a common accounting usage, according to which operating margin constitutes the difference between sales price and cost of goods sold. This accounting definition has its usefulness in financial statements but is only of limited value for planning management strategy.

Framework of Use

What is novel about our concept is the framework in which we suggest that it be used. Simple in principle, operating margin analysis is complex in its application and interpretation. But in practice we have found the resulting conclusions to be straightforward and revealing.

What makes the approach so useful is that it defines the condition of an industry and not just of an individual firm. The margin limits are almost identical for all competing participants in a given country because each sells his products competitively and buys his materials at approximately the same price. Variations in margin within the same product line do not hinder the approach but invite investigation as to the reasons for the difference. Likewise, different degrees of integration among companies can be reduced to a common denominator by using one of the least-integrated firms as a base and segregating the additional activities of the other participants as separate "businesses."

The operating margin concept is also helpful because it keeps management from placing excessive emphasis on the accounting statements of established firms. Accounting principles leave companies great flexibility, especially in allocating expenses, even in the United States, thus making "true" profit a rather elastic notion. The correct profit figure becomes even more elusive in foreign countries with their different accounting practices, tax laws, disclosure regulations, and so on.

In short, the operating margin as we conceive it is an essential and highly exact element in corporate planning. It is highly exact because its two base points always remain unobscured and untouched by either accounting convention or company practices. Both the selling price and the cost of materials purchased can be determined objectively. In most cases they are common knowledge. If not, they can be readily determined either through trade channels or with the help of an engineer framiliar with the product requirements.

Treatment of Costs

The operating margin becomes particularly useful when its two totally different components, involuntary costs and discretionary expenses, are analyzed.

Involuntary expenses arise from the nature of the firm's business, its scale of manufacturing, the types of processes used, and the degree of product specialization or standardization that has been achieved. They consist mainly of minimum manufacturing costs; they cannot be eliminated unless a firm cuts production. Therefore, they have to be incurred by everyone in the industry. Their level can be recognized by an engineer who is experienced in the product line and manufacturing processes. He also can develop, through careful product appraisal, a schedule of costs for various volumes of production and various manufacturing methods. Thus, relative changes in involuntary costs resulting from volume increases can be predicted with reasonable accuracy.

While involuntary expenses normally constitute the difference between costs of goods sold and cost of materials purchased, there are exceptions. For example: Tooling expenses, though usually included in the cost of goods sold, are really discretionary expenses.

Manufacturing costs which are not absolutely necessary but which may add desirable features to the product line are also discretionary expenses, even though included by accountants in the costs of goods sold.

Discretionary expenses allow a foreign venture to fulfill its marketing and development objectives. Within the framework of competitive conditions, a firm has a certain latitude in determining which and how many discretionary expenses it wants to incur. Corporate strategies among firms vary chiefly because managements put their discretionary money to different uses. One firm may wish to make large profits for distribution to the stockholders or for retention to finance further expansion or diversification. Another firm may direct discretionary expenses toward product development, upgrading of quality, and tooling arising from frequent model changes, or it may incur discretionary expenses to strengthen its marketing position by establishing distribution outlets, creating brand loyalty, improving service to customers, and so forth. Still another firm may surrender discretionary money to reduce its prices.

Discretionary expenses are the lifeblood of a business. They often qualify as true economic investments and should be considered as such even though they are entered into accounting statements as expenses and not as assets. In terms of a company's long-term competitive strength, money invested in building up the distribution position or in creating product differentiation may be no less important than money invested in fixed plant and machinery. During periods of rapid growth, management often emphasizes increases in productive capacity while ignoring discretionary expenses of an investment nature. With the maturity of the industry, however, the emphasis usually shifts from the "capacity to make" to the "ability to sell," thus penalizing companies which in earlier years ignored discretionary expenses for marketing.

Because discretionary expenses of an investment nature in a firm's income statement (in contrast to fixed-asset investment) reduce current profits substantially, a careful analysis of these costs is needed if low profits (or even accounting losses) in growth industries are to be interpreted correctly.

Actually, profits are considered to be part of a firm's discretionary area in our analysis. This is because profit levels are so highly dependent on the types and amounts of other discretionary costs which management needs or wants to incur. In fact, retained profits to be used for further expansion are quite similar to discretionary expenses of an investment nature. On the other hand, rigid profit levels imposed by the need to maintain or increase dividends may reduce other discretionary uses of the money, possibly with perilous consequences.

APPRAISING COMPETITION

Ordinarily, management wants to be sure that a new venture will generate adequate resources for growth and be able to sustain itself for a period of years. The enterprise must, therefore, be able to live within the prices imposed by competition and still generate a sufficiently wide operating margin to achieve growth. For this reason, in determining entry and participation requirements of a foreign venture it is vital to analyze its position relative to the industry leaders. By considering the involuntary costs and discretionary expenses of the leaders, management can predict future price trends. Turning then to the new venture, it can assess its relative capacity to compete and estimate its ability to pay for the necessary discretionary expenses of an investment nature that will be needed to achieve a viable position in the industry.

Analysis of involuntary and discretionary expenses thus enables a firm to plan for possible contingencies by estimating the extent to which industry leaders may be able to lower prices. These reductions will primarily hinge on a) the lowering of their involuntary costs and b), as an industry moves to maturity, the extent to which achievement of product and marketing objectives allows the leaders to lower their discretionary expenses. Even though industry leaders will not in all cases exploit these advantages fully, it is necessary in planning a foreign venture to determine whether it will be able to survive under the most adverse eventuality.

Lower Involuntary Costs

In a dynamic industry, characteristic of so many in Europe today, volume is the prime determinant of the operating margin. Larger scales of production reduce involuntary costs, enabling industry leaders to lower prices. Here is a case in point. In France, the largest firms in the refrigerator industry make 150,000 units a year and operate within a margin of 50 percent, while in Germany the leading manufacturers have achieved a volume of 400,000 units per year and are able to operate more profitably within a margin of only about 35 percent. A manufacturer in Germany making only 150,000 refrigerators a year would clearly be the victim of a price-cost squeeze; indeed, precisely this condition led to the recent withdrawal of a major German electrical manufacturer and of one of the largest U.S. firms.

The extent as well as the timing of price reductions can be fairly accurately predicted by analyzing the leader's involuntary costs and by establishing a schedule of his costs for various increases in volume that can be anticipated with market growth. Price declines will often depend not only on increases in the scale of manufacture of a single product but also on increased production volumes of similar products. In such cases an appraisal should encompass those products as well as the one of main concern.

When these assessments of future price declines, and hence of lower operating margins, are in hand, management is likely to have some interesting questions of strategy to consider. For one thing, a manufacturer contemplating entry into a business in a less mature stage of development must anticipate the conditions under which he could be the victim of a price-cost squeeze. This contingency will occur if prices drop faster than a company's ability to lower costs, which could happen if the industry leaders grow faster than anyone else. Should a price-cost squeeze develop, management may have to incur losses and match the price reductions in order to maintain its relative market share. Otherwise, it may not achieve sales levels which justify increasing its plant scale, to the point where this would ultimately bring the venture's costs in line with the costs of industry leaders.

If no such sacrifice is made, the decline in sales volume will result in even higher involuntary costs. These in turn will reduce the margin available for discretionary expenses and will push management into a vicious circle of still further concessions in the market. The venture will soon have to surrender its growth objectives. Next it will have to abandon its marketing objectives—and from that point on the downward cycle will be repeated, culminating in the loss of the business.

It is therefore essential to establish entry goals, such as market-share objectives, and to decide what production and sales efforts are necessary to achieve them. This will help to ensure that the venture will generate adequate resources at least to sustain its position relative to the industry leaders.

Cuts in Discretionary Expenses

During rapid growth periods, companies are likely to make substantial discretionary expenses of an investment nature, e.g., outlays to establish the product, to strengthen distribution, and to finance expansion. As the growth slackens or as objectives are achieved, however, fewer discretionary expenses of this type will be required, thus freeing the money for price reductions. The magnitude of this drop can also be predicted through operating margin analysis, although it is more difficult to foresee its timing.

High discretionary margins are also vulnerable when competitors lower their profit margins or undertake less expensive marketing methods and resort to price cutting in order to gain a larger market share. Analysis of discretionary expenses will reveal the magnitude of such potential price reductions.

During periods of substantial excess capacity, the temptation may develop to make sales so long as this will cover out-of-pocket costs, resulting in a major price break. Such conditions, however, cannot last indefinitely. As demand catches up with capacity, prices will usually return to a level at which the most efficient industry leaders can still make a reasonable return on their investment.

Conditions of Entry

Often overlooked is the fact that a high rate of growth does not necessarily make for profitable business opportunities. Indeed, dramatic foreign growth rates have often obscured the dangers of low profitability and the difficulty of entry. What is more, even conditions of high profitability may obscure formidable obstacles to foreign entry.

A look at the operating margin provides a first indication. A company experienced in its industry, and thus knowing how much it requires to manufacture, pay for research, sell, and so forth, is able to judge fairly easily whether the operating margin in a foreign industry is either "narrow" or "wide." Such an evaluation is often facilitated—as will be explained later in this article—by using an analytical grid which compares operating margins of the same industry in different countries.

A wide operating margin indicates that a new venture can incur high levels of involuntary and discretionary costs. As would be expected, a margin tends to be wide when, even the industry leaders have a comparatively low scale of output; the industry leaders have high discretionary expenses or cash requirements for marketing, product development, construction of new capacity, or diversification programs; there is insufficient competition; the industry leaders have priced their products to maximize their profits even though this induces smaller competitors to use minor price reductions as a competitive weapon in furthering sales; the leaders are inefficient manufacturers or marketers.

Narrow operating margins, on the other hand, reduce a company's flexibility and are significant hurdles for foreign entry, regardless of whether "tight" or "loose" competitive conditions prevail. A tight industry will be characterized by relatively low profits for the industry leader, while loose competitive conditions permit satisfactory profits to both leaders and followers. It is important to recognize, however, that both loose and tight conditions are possible under a wide as well as under a narrow operating margin.

Combinations of Conditions

1. A *narrow* operating margin in an industry usually results in tight conditions, allowing only few discretionary expenses (including profits) after involuntary costs have been incurred. To illustrate, the German refrigerator industry has margins only 30 to 40 percent above materials costs. Two giant firms are dominating the field. The product lines of both firms consist of stripped-down models. Manufacturers engage in little merchandising, maintain minimal sales forces, offer only limited service, and allow low distribution discounts based on the quantity shipped. The overriding emphasis is on price, effectively forestalling entry by newcomers and threatening the profitability of small followers.

2. Narrow operating margins also permit loose competitive conditions. For instance, the German radio and television industry operated in 1959 within a narrow operating margin, but because of plants of large scale, most participants experienced generous profits. In spite of this high profitability, the narrow margin imposed formidable entry goals for a new venture in terms of production volume and of market-share objectives. Last year, the industry moved to tight competitive conditions as participants used part of their discretionary profit money to cut prices.

3. An industry enjoying a *wide* operating margin may nevertheless experience fierce competition, resulting in *tight* conditions. Given the levels of involuntary costs as well as the discretionary expenses required to compete effectively, profitability may be low. To illustrate again, the French refrigerator industry is, in spite of its higher operating margin, almost as competitive as its German counterpart. The difference in margin is almost entirely absorbed by higher involuntary costs (due to smaller plant scales) and higher discretionary expenses (in view of limited distribution channels). One large firm selling stripped-down products at a low price (much as German firms are doing) is competing with other firms selling better made models at a premium through their own captive distribution channels and engaging heavily in retail promotions.

4. On the other hand, in Europe there are still many industries with *wide* operating margins and loose competitive conditions—what might be called immature industries—in which entry is not only relatively easy to achieve but may also prove highly profitable. However, timing is most important because an immature, loose industry may rapidly move to highly competitive, tight conditions. For example, in 1960 the washing-machine industry in both Britain and Germany experienced wide operating margins under loose competitive conditions. Each market was dominated by one large company which had achieved maximum economies of scale in production. However, in both cases the leading company was not

seriously challenged; and, therefore, it was able to maintain relatively high price levels. Because of low involuntary costs, the leader in each market clearly was able to retaliate quickly and effectively against challengers, thus changing the competitive conditions from loose to tight.

In sum, experience shows that opportunities and difficulties in *entering* a foreign industry are more a function of the magnitude of the operating margin than of the profitability of industry members. A wide operating margin can provide a better opportunity for entry than a narrow operating margin *whether the industry leaders are profitable or not.* For instance, the French refrigerator industry, despite its lack of profitability, probably provided an easier entry opportunity than did the German television industry. On the other hand, a profitable industry with narrow operating margins may be very difficult to enter.

Choosing a Battleground

The most important condition of entry is that the company's initial marketing objectives create discretionary margins which are large enough to sustain its growth objectives. Recognizing the importance of maintaining the venture's position relative to industry leaders, management may see that it is not sufficient merely to match their discretionary expenses; it may be necessary to exceed the other firms' expenses substantially. For example, if there is a shortage of distribution channels, the capture of which is critical to achieve success, management may have to spend more than competitors on the product lines, services, or promotion needed to secure these channels.

However, the wisest strategy may be to undertake efforts that do *not* duplicate the programs of industry leaders. The chances to achieve success are often enhanced if management selects its own battleground instead of imitating what the established firms are doing. If so, the important thing still is to make sure that the new approach is consistent with the discretionary margin it will provide.

One area where a new venture may have considerably more flexibility than industry leaders is pricing. Often, industry leaders wish to maximize their profits by holding the line on prices. This will often be done at a price level that gives considerable discretion even to followers with higher involuntary costs. As a result they can use small price decreases as a competitive weapon to increase their market share and thereby their total profits. In the end, their constant nibbling at the leader's position results in a loss of his market share. For example, in 1960, competitive conditions in the German and the British washing-machine industries were very loose largely because each field was dominated by one firm which was not seriously challenged and because washing machines, unlike refrigerators, justified considerable discretionary expenditures in service, quality manufacture, and demonstration at retail. Instead of matching the leader's heavy discretionary marketing expenses, an entrant might have been able to use price reductions effectively.

Emphasis on price under conditions like these can save many discretionary expenses which, if incurred, would have little impact anyway. To illustrate again, a German subsidiary determined its advertising budget by using the same percentage of sales as its U.S. parent. The subsidiary spent the budget in approximately the same way. Indeed, its whole marketing approach was a mirror of the U.S. parent's program. In the United States, the parent company was one of the leaders in its industry and was, therefore, reluctant to use price concessions. The subsidiary was equally reluctant to use pricing and relied almost exclusively on advertising, even though its market share was only 5 percent compared with 45 percent for the German industry leader. It is hardly surprising that top company executives did not consider the subsidiary's operation entirely successful.

Analysis of the discretionary expense span of industry leaders will also show if a new venture can maintain or improve its relative position by incurring fewer discretionary costs. For example, it is not unusual to see leaders dissipate their resources through unwise diversification, excessive component manufacture, and so forth. These wastes need not be duplicated. Also, a venture may be able to save on discretionary expenses if it is a subsidiary. It may be able to cut down on such items as research and development costs, tooling costs, and design and engineering expenses if the parent corporation has done the needed work in these areas.

CRITICAL CONDITIONS

While fitting the manufacturing, marketing, and growth plan of a business in the limits established by the competitive environment is important, it is not the only task that demands top-management attention. A foreign venture may be unsuccessful if other critical elements are not given equal consideration. We refer to a series of conditions that not only differ markedly among industries, as is well known, but also vary greatly within the same industry from country to country. At the outset of a foreign venture, therefore, it is imperative that management 1) recognize these essential industry conditions and 2) analyze the relevant differences between the United States and the host country. Failure to do so may lead to incorrect assumptions as to a venture's future discretionary margin, resulting in turn in an insecure "plan" or design that is often beyond correction later on by managers in trouble spots. Five industry conditions deserve particular attention.

Impact of Financial Charges

Financial conditions often vary remarkably among countries because of major differences in 1) depreciation policy, 2) working-capital requirements, and 3) utilization of debt leverage.

A recent study provides a case in point. We observed that three companies, one in the United States, one in France, and the other in Germany, were operating under almost identical conditions in the same growth industry. Even though all three were generating approximately the same cash per dollar of gross plant, they were earning 13 percent, 23 percent, and 35 percent, respectively, on their equity investment. The following points are especially noteworthy: In France, and particularly in Germany, rapid depreciation provisions provide growth industries with sizable tax-free funds for reinvestment. In Germany, product shortages enable manufacturers to operate with almost no finished-goods inventories, thus cutting down the working-capital charges. In France, banks lend as much on reputation as on financial analysis, resulting in considerably higher debt-equity ratios than banks would permit in the United States. Consequently, companies in France with a high capital turnover and a good "reputation" benefit from a degree of leverage which is unusual by our standards in the United States.

The utilization of debt leverage hinges partly on the availability of investment opportunities, which in turn depends on the relative maturity of an industry. For example, in the United States during the early 1950's, the cash generated per dollar of gross investment was significantly higher for producers of finished chemicals than for the basic chemical companies. Nevertheless, companies in both ends of the chemical business were earning approximately the same return on their equity, because basic chemical companies were able to offset their disadvantage through greater debt leverage.

Recently, the basic producers have experienced a decrease in profitability. However, this is caused less by a decrease in the cash generated per dollar of gross investment than by the fact that the industry's financial resources available for investment have increased faster than have the available investment opportunities, which in turn has reduced the need for debt and thus cut down the use of leverage.

Burden of Overcapacity

Differences in requirements as to when and how much capacity has to be constructed are vital. To illustrate, compare the household appliance industry with the chemical industry. In the household appliance industry, the ratio of sales to gross plant investment is very high, while profit margins are rather low. The latter element makes low costs imperative, while the high capital turnover requires tight control of capital. The vital implication is that one has to be very careful about building too much in excess of current demand; large plants are vital to mass-production economies, but if constructed too far ahead of the time that demand materializes, the resulting drain on profits can be disastrous.

In spite of these basic truths, several household appliance companies in Europe have succumbed to the temptation of building—far in excess of their market share—huge modern plants which they felt were vital in their type of mass-production industry. United States companies in particular—influenced, perhaps, by the fact that overcapacity is common at home—seem to have lost sight of the heavy burden which surplus capacity imposes if competitors are operating at near capacity and setting their prices on that basis. Their large, not fully utilized, plants in Europe have constituted a severe drain on profits and have become especially burdensome when financed by bank debts.

The profitability conditions of the chemical industry are very different. The emphasis is on process economies and chemical routes with ancillary problems of location, raw materials supply, plant scale, and outlets to the market for several coproducts. New processes, based perhaps on new materials and having different scale economies, may change the competitive position of a particular project markedly, as may new developments in the market. The industry thus experiences a high degree of flux and change.

With most chemicals requiring a large investment in plant for each sales dollar, high profit margins are necessary to justify the investment. Usually, price levels decline with time, while costs mostly depend on scale of operations. Hence, there is a considerable premium on "getting in early" on a new development when profits are large. Early starters, if they succeed in maintaining their initial market position in subsequent periods of maturity for the field, will also be enjoying the cost advantages of large plant scale supported by market leadership. Thus, "thinking early" and "thinking big" are both necessary ingredients in a successful chemical venture.

Specialization and Concentration

Another critical factor to watch is the need for specialization and concentration rather than diversification. Not always are the former important, but in industries where they are crucial, a great deal may hinge on top management's sensitivity to them. As illustrations we can again look at the chemical and household appliance industries. Thinking big in the chemical industry requires a certain concentration of investment funds. Concentration, however, necessitates a high degree of confidence. Lack of sufficient confidence may lead to several small projects to hedge against the failure of any one project. This is undesirable because, while hedging in small ventures to spread risks may ensure survival, it does so only at a subsistence level; it is the bold large-scale operation that makes the money in this industry.

At the same time, specialization and concentration are complicated by what might be called *structural* requirements. Entry usually is not possible without the satisfaction of a wide range of such conditions as having a low-cost and secure source of raw materials and marketing or disposition arrangements for the several coproducts which are simultaneously manufactured in a variety of chemical processes. Also, a successful marketing program may require several complementary products, thus further extending the scope of a chemical operation abroad. It is inability to satisfy these structural requirements completely which inhibits foreign entry by chemical companies in a major way. Thus, even large American chemical firms have experienced major difficulties in entering the European market.

Specialization in the household appliance business is crucial for different reasons. Because of its narrow margin, price and cost control must be very tight, with the result that top management must place a great deal of reliance on the ability of the manager in immediate charge of operations. However, price concessions will always be required to move inventories that inevitably pile up because even the best forecasting cannot fully anticipate all variations in consumer demand. Hence, considerable attention must be given to systems which keep inventories low as well as to the skill of merchandising. The latter, in fact, can be defined in the appliance industry as the ability to move inventories with the minimum concession in price.

Therefore, the type of management necessary is one that combines promotional skill with a fine sense of control. Close familiarity with the appliance business has shown that management will work best when both these qualities can be found in one man. And because so much sensitivity is required in the merchandising job, it is best performed when only one major product is handled. Conseuqently, there are convincing arguments for specialization in the appliance business.

Product Policy

Different income levels in foreign countries often demand different product lines from those offered in the United States.[1] Nevertheless, the major European operations of some U.S. firms are exclusively devoted to manufacturing the U.S. product. Because of size, versatility, quality, or price, American-type products usually occupy a place only at the top of the effective European product line. With most of Europe's current market growth

---

[1] See Raphael Hodgson and Michael Michaelis, "Planning for Profits in World Business," *Harvard Business Review* (November-December 1960), p. 135.

occurring not in these products but in the *basic* models, the result is that the firms mentioned are losing their market shares. This leads to under-capacity operations of plants that are already relatively small, thereby in-creasing costs. Indeed, the U.S.-type products can usually be supplied more economically from American plants than from European sources.

Distribution Requirements

As was mentioned earlier, distribution can be one of the critical obstacles to successful entry into international business. It is therefore vital to ana-lyze the particular distribution requirements for an industry as well as the prevailing conditions in the foreign country. Differences among coun-tries can be most significant, requiring great flexibility and varying poli-cies on the part of international businesses. *Even in the same industry* the distribution setup can favor the entrant in one country, while constitut-ing a major hurdle for him in another country. To illustrate, in the Ger-man consumer-goods industries, wholesalers are by tradition nonexclusive, making it difficult for leading manufacturers to control distribution. The alternative, direct selling, may increase costs more than prices can support. Hence, an opportunity exists for the smaller manufacturer to an extent precluded in countries where there are distribution bottlenecks. However, the situation puts greater emphasis on other marketing elements, such as price and reputation. For instance, it may increase the importance of ad-vertising. This provides an opportunity for the importer who can adver-tise, who can be expected to meet prices, but who usually has difficulty in controlling distribution in a foreign country.

In France, the actual shortage of distribution (a large city such as Lyons has only two really capable appliance wholesalers) puts an extraor-dinary burden on newcomers in the industry. They normally must sell direct, and in France—with its widely dispersed population—this is a very expensive proposition. Also, distributors who are available insist on a full line of white goods (i.e., refrigerators and washing machines), a condition which can tempt manufacturers into a full-line operation that (as we have indicated) is difficult to manage.

In Britain, distribution is similar to what it is in the United States with a relatively large number of exclusive wholesalers. Some manufac-turers have begun to sell direct, a condition which has left their former wholesalers available to importers who wish to use them.

INTERNATIONAL COMPARISONS

By comparing the operating margins of companies in different countries, management can easily recognize the opportunities for entry. The question that executives may face now is: Can the policies and practices which permit a profitable operation at home under a lower operating margin also prove successful abroad? As our earlier discussion of industry conditions has shown, there are inherent dangers in transferring the reasoning that works in an industry from one country to another. Operating margin analysis checks false analogies by providing a useful framework for evaluating them. For example, most electrical components in Europe are sold at a price several times the cost of materials, compared with an operating margin of only 80 percent in the United States. This points to sizable opportunities. But before any action can be taken, it is necessary to ask why operating margins are so much larger in Europe and whether it is appropriate to analogize American involuntary and discretionary costs in determining how a U.S. entrant should behave in this industry in Europe.

Involuntary costs appear excessively high in Europe because of lack of standardization and because a large number of companies have relatively small scales of manufacture. On the basis of American experience, it would appear desirable to standardize the product line around a few basic types, impose it on the industry at a low price, manufacture in great quantities, and "shake the business down." One manufacturer is doing precisely this. At present, this firm cannot meet demand; delivery times are up to 15 months! It has become an outstandingly profitable operation and has not yet been seriously challenged.

In the case of *discretionary* expenses, however, an analogy with U.S. experience does not appear relevant. For instance, discretionary expenses in one U.S. electronic systems industry have become truly defensive; it has become a competitive necessity here to spend between 15 and 20 percent of sales in providing custom-tailored systems engineering to industrial customers. Without this provision, a company's market share would suffer seriously. In Europe, on the other hand, not nearly as much systems work is required. Also, current growth requirements lead to long deliveries, resulting in minimal sales expenses or direct sales of components to large users.

Thus, while U.S. experience in the involuntary cost area appears to be a promising guide, the opposite is true in the case of discretionary expenses.

Threats and Opportunities

International comparisons of operating margins are helpful in still another way. Foreign import threats or export opportunities can be spotted by comparing the domestic operating margin in a given country with importers' operating margins. The operating margin of an importer indicates the degree by which the selling price in the importing country less import duties and freight exceeds the materials cost in the exporting country. It thus expresses for the firm selling abroad the margin within which both the domestic manufacturing and the foreign sales effort must be conducted.

By calculating the operating margin for various exporting nations and using the domestic operating margins, management can construct a grid of opportunity which compares the foreign opportunity with that at home. An example is shown in Table 1. Such a grid also shows the discretionary cash available for any volume of goods to be moved abroad.

TABLE 1—RELATIVE OPERATING MARGINS OF INTRA-EUROPEAN SALES OF 150-LITRE REFRIGERATORS, 1959-1960

(Margins existing in each country are circled.)

Exporting Country / Domestic Sales	Importing Country			
	France	Germany	Italy	Britain
France	(50)	8	(6)	56
Germany	61	(40)	6	68
Italy	81	37	(45)	81
Britain	47	10	(2½)	(75)

NOTE: The operating margin is calculated as follows: 1) from the sales price in the country of destination subtract a) the tariffs, taxes, and freight costs to ship the goods there, and b) the materials cost in the country of origin; 2) divide the figure thus obtained by the materials cost in the country of origin. (Figures in parentheses indicate negative margins.)

Knowing its position relative to that of foreign competitors, a firm can decide whether and how to enter international markets. This analysis will take into account both the industry conditions and the nature of competition in the foreign country (which implies analyzing the discretionary expenses of the established firms). To illustrate the total approach, the opportunity grid in Table 1 shows that in 1959–1960 a German refrigerator manufacturer could expect a 61 and 68 percent operating margin in France and Britain respectively, compared with 40 percent in his own market. However, analysis of industry conditions as well as discretionary expenses in France and Britain during that period showed significant differences. In view of France's acute shortage of distribution, it was necessary to spend a significant portion of one's discretionary money on distribution, especially on direct selling. This aspect, combined with lower plant scales, required higher margins in France than in Germany, while still making for very low profits. In Britain, on the other hand, distribution was less tight and, in spite of high involuntary costs, the industry was enjoying high profits.

As a result, even though German producers could count on almost equal operating margins in both France and Britain, entry into the British market was more profitable and could be more easily achieved. In Britain, price reductions alone proved highly effective; while in France, the situation would also have required a distribution investment (e.g., a full product line or company-sponsored outlets).

Check Points

In evaluating foreign opportunities, three elements are often of crucial importance: *product line, pricing,* and *distribution:*

1. In the preceding example, German refrigerator manufacturers had little difficulty of a *product-line* nature because their product was very similar to British refrigerators. Also, commodities such as chemicals, aluminum, steel, paper, or glass are fairly identical among countries, thus not only saving trouble for the producer but also enabling buyers to switch more easily to foreign sources of supply. However, in many instances product lines will differ in composition from country to country, sometimes requiring expensive adjustments. The cost of these adjustments should be taken into account in drawing up the opportunity grid.

2. Opportunity grids for commodities normally show wide operating margins because a significant portion of a firm's discretionary money is required to meet fixed plant costs. In commodities, as a result, the foreign entrant enjoys wide discretion, giving him greater *pricing* flexibility than that enjoyed by an exporter of differentiated products with their lower operating margins. In short, price cutting is most likely to be effective where there is a wide operating margin, a minimum of product differentiation, and a marked tendency on the part of customers to shop around for low-price suppliers.

3. The *distribution* bottleneck is normally less critical for commodities than it is for differentiated products. Although a domestic commodity manufacturer may have established a firm hold on local distribution, it does not take much foreign competition, even through irregular channels, to put severe strains on the local pricing structure. On the other hand, the earlier examples from the household appliance industry show how distribution may constitute a serious hurdle to the exporter of differentiated products.

In view of these three elements, the level of tariffs that will inhibit trade must be considerably higher for commodities than for differentiated products such as appliances; the former are more sensitive to changes at the top of the "wall" than the latter are. Therefore, the impact of economic integration in Europe with its gradual abolition of tariff levels will most probably be felt more quickly and more strongly by commodity producers. This may force them to become continental in scope more rapidly than manufacturers of appliances and other differentiated products.

CONCLUSION

Opportunity analysis imposes a strong discipline on business planning by ensuring that both the immediate and the ultimate goals of management are consistent with the industry's current and future competitive conditions. Such goals, in turn, can be translated into clear entry and participation requirements for a foreign venture. These requirements have to be consistent with the firm's capabilities and willingness to commit the necessary resources. It is the reconciliation of these interrelated objectives which makes the application of operating margins so useful. For example: Suppose that a venture has a 50 percent operating margin and that management's target is a volume of X dollars. Estimating the involuntary costs at this volume plus the discretionary expenses required to achieve it, executives can determine whether the needed outlays can be covered by the 50 percent margin while leaving an adequate profit. If not, either the venture should be abandoned or the sales objectives must be raised. Perhaps a large marketing investment would produce sales levels of magnitude large enough to lower involuntary costs to the point where an adequate profit could be made within the 50 percent operating margin.

Opportunity analysis enables management to cut through the confusion of current fluctuations and erratic circumstances to the conditions of ultimate success. It will not exaggerate these conditions nor lead to the extraordinary pessimism that, say, a run on prices may otherwise induce. Also, it helps executives to foresee any important differences between the venture under their consideration and the industry leaders'. The very discipline of this exercise may reveal errors in the initial project—for example, by demonstrating that instead of spreading resources over several projects it might be better to concentrate on one, or that the contemplated program is too large for the resources a company is able or willing to commit. Thus, opportunity analysis leads to consistency in planning in terms of:

The immediate goals of a venture
The ultimate goals of a venture
The parent company's capabilities.

12.

BASIC AND ECONOMICAL APPROACHES TO INTERNATIONAL MARKETING RESEARCH*

R. J. Dickensheets

WHAT is the market for electric toothbrushes in France? This is the question so often asked of marketing researchers, and when applied to international markets the question takes on special significance. I don't have the specific answer to my opening question, but with the success of the electric toothbrush domestically, it is a question I can soon expect to be asked. It has been said that only about 35 per cent of all Frenchmen brush their teeth. We shouldn't feel smug, though, because it seems only 40 per cent of all Americans brush their teeth with any regularity.

My objective in this paper is to explore several basic and economical approaches to answering the question—What is the market? I will concentrate on those approaches that are feasible for the researcher working in the United States with a limited opportunity for foreign travel, such approaches being based primarily on the use of secondary data. There is, of course, no substitute for a personal knowledge of international markets, and surely many misunderstandings and perhaps erroneous conclusions are based on the lack of personal experience abroad. Also, at least occasional foreign trips are necessary to make sure the latest and most complete secondary sources are available for use. A surprising amount of good research, however, can be done from a U.S. base, and this talk is intended to explore several approaches in limited detail. Illustrations given will generally be based on experience in the electrical industry although the approaches noted should be generally applicable to many industries.

AN INTERNATIONAL APPROACH—PRODUCT BY COUNTRY

Language and cultural differences, degree of industrial development, and trade restrictions peculiar to individual countries usually invalidate the generalization of research findings to large marketing areas. In addition, the availability of secondary data on production, exports and imports varies by country. It is, therefore, necessary to assemble and evaluate sta-

* R. J. Dickensheets, "Basic and Economical Approaches to International Marketing Research," *Innovation—Key to Marketing Progress*, 1963 Proceedings of the American Marketing Association, pp. 359-377. Reprinted by permission.

tistical data from many national sources. Because of the limited availability of statistics and the many heterogeneous marketing areas, the most meaningful research approach is generally by product by country.

THE FOREIGN MARKETING PATTERN—A MATRIX

Nine reasonably definable "foreign factors" applicable to overseas markets are shown in matrix form in Figure 1. These factors may vary not only by

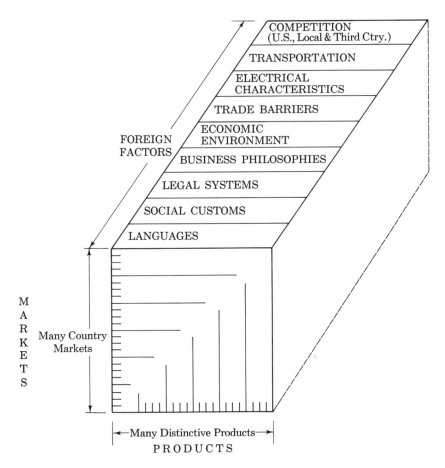

FIGURE 1—THE FOREIGN MARKETING PATTERN

country, but in some cases, electric power supply, for example, by cities within a country. They may also vary by product within any given country, for instance, import duties. Such phrases, therefore, as the "African Market," or the "Latin American Market" are often meaningless from the viewpoint of product marketing. A more specific description by country or local market area within a country is usually necessary to realistically define a "market." When a company manufactures many distinctive products, it can be seen that the complexity of international research is considerably magnified.

ASSEMBLING AN INTERNATIONAL LIBRARY

A basic approach for determining the market for a product is through the use of secondary data, that is, international publications and periodicals. There are specialized libraries available in the larger U.S. cities, and these can often be used to good advantage. For the moment, however, let us assume that it is desirable to have an international library within the international marketing research operation.

At IGE we maintain detailed statistics and supplementary qualitative information for the major producing and exporting countries of the world. In this way, the number of publications to be assembled is kept to a minimum. Since most of the less industrialized developing countries have limited, dated, and often unreliable statistics, this approach allows us to determine local consumption in importing countries from the statistics of the more industrialized exporting nations. This approach has some limitations because of the increasing number of local manufacture or assembly operations being established in many of the developing countries. We have found, however, that information on local manufacture in these developing countries is of such significance that news of this nature is generally picked up by the press and by trade and industry association publications, either U.S. or foreign. Other sources of information on such developments include subsidiary companies, branch offices, local distributors or agents and company personnel traveling to the country or area.

WHAT TYPE OF MATERIAL SHOULD BE MAINTAINED?

Table 1 shows examples of the type of information maintained in our international marketing research library. The completeness and usefulness of these sources, however, varies considerably by country. For some products, officially published information is of limited use either because of the broad categories reported or the dated nature of the information. Further investigation may indicate, however, that very useful and up-to-date data can be obtained by direct contact with the source. Export statistics for the United Kingdom showing country of destination, for example, are published about eighteen months after the close of the year reported. Through direct mail contact with the U.K. Board of Trade, however, cumulative monthly export statistics are available at nominal cost within seven to eight weeks after the close of the month reported. If you have major competitors in the United Kingdom, such statistics can provide an up-to-date indication of what your competitors are doing in third country

TABLE 1—AN INTERNATIONAL LIBRARY
EXAMPLES OF TYPE OF INFORMATION MAINTAINED

I. For Major Producing & Exporting Countries

   A. Official Government Statistics
- Production
- Foreign Trade (Imports & Exports)
- Statistical Abstract

   B. Foreign Industry Associations
- Production, Consumption, In Use, Saturation
- Industry Directory (List of member firms, product scope, etc.)
- Industry Magazines

   C. Foreign Periodicals
- Magazines directed to wholesale and retail trade

II. International Marketing Indicators

   A. United Nations
   B. International Monetary Fund
   C. U. S. Department of Commerce
   D. Regional Organizations, e.g.,
- Organization for Economic Cooperation & Development (OECD)

III. General Background Information

   A. Complementary or Served Industry Publications, e.g.,
- Frozen foods, coffee, steel, shipbuilding

   B. International Press & Newsletters, e.g.,
- "Business International"

   C. Research Organizations, e.g.,
- Ford Foundation

   D. International Banking Publications

IV. U. S. Sources of Industry Information

   A. U. S. Industry Associations' International Publications, e.g.,
- E.I.A. "International News"

V. U. S. Department of Commerce

   A. U. S. Import & Export Statistics
   B. Overseas Business Reports
   C. BDSA Short Market Surveys & Trade Reports
   D. Foreign Service Despatch Loan Service
   E. "International Commerce"

VI. Competition

   A. Annual Reports of Major Competitors. U. S. & Foreign

markets or in the U.S. market. Similar unpublished statistics are also available from West Germany, and in finer detail than are published in the official German foreign trade statistical publication.

Local trade associations, particularly in Europe, are beginning to exchange information between countries. This information is often not available to U.S. manufacturers, however, as many U.S. trade associations have not shown a willingness to reciprocate. These foreign industry associations can be excellent sources, but generally must be approached through local affiliated companies manufacturing in the country concerned. Because of the exchange of data between countries, a good contact with one association in a country may provide information on several additional countries.

A library as extensive as the one described might appear applicable only to companies having a rather wide product scope, but the expense is not great. Such a library should cost under $500 a year to maintain, that is, the cost of the periodicals and publications. The placement of orders, follow-up requirements and the necessity of payment in foreign currency are limitations often mentioned with regard to maintaining such a library. One way of minimizing these limitations is by ordering known requirements with annual orders to an international bookseller. The publications are then ordered as they become available through the year and the ordering company is billed in U.S. dollars. The publisher pays the bookseller his commissions.

BASIC INTERNATIONAL RESEARCH GOAL:
DEFINING TOTAL MARKET

The formula we use to arrive at total market in a given country for a given product is simply: Local Market = Local Production + Imports — Exports.

This formula illustrates the procedure for determining total market statistics. In any one country local market, that is, total consumption, equals local production plus imports into the country less exports from the country. The availability of this type of statistical information varies greatly by country and by product within any one country. In many cases, local markets must be estimated using only one or two parts of the formula, exports and imports, for example. Foreign statistics are generally in the language of the country concerned, are given in terms of foreign currency value, and are often shown in broad categories only. For any one country, production and foreign trade statistical categories are not necessarily comparable.

Figure 2 depicts four markets for a hypothetical electrical appliance. The total market in Venezuela consists entirely of imports from other countries; there is no local production and there are no exports from the country. The Hong Kong market also consists solely of imports from foreign countries. Substantial quantities of these imports, however, are re-exported to other destinations. Belgium offers another variation in that the bulk of the Belgian market consists of local production. West Germany, the fourth market shown, differs from the other three due to the large proportion of local production that is exported. These four examples illustrate the varied make-up of "total market" for a product from one country to another, and suggests the type of approach used in determining total market by country.

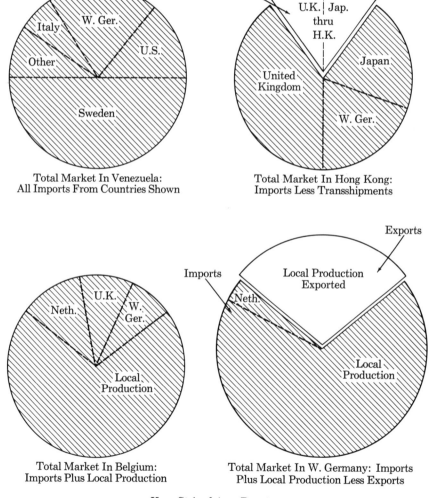

Total Market In Venezuela:
All Imports From Countries Shown

Total Market In Hong Kong:
Imports Less Transshipments

Total Market In Belgium:
Imports Plus Local Production

Total Market In W. Germany: Imports
Plus Local Production Less Exports

Key: Striped Area Denotes
Local Market

FIGURE 2—DEFINING TOTAL MARKET

Data on exports of the same product from several countries may not be exactly comparable. Figure 3 illustrates this situation using Venezuelan imports of vacuum cleaners as an example. As no reliable Venezuelan import statistics for vacuum cleaners were available, the following approach was used.

1. Foreign trade sources of the major exporting countries were investigated.
2. Data published in several foreign languages were translated and interpreted.
3. Data on vacuum cleaners had to be extracted from the broader categories reported. In the Italian and German data, cleaner figures had to be separated from those of floor polishers. For Italy and

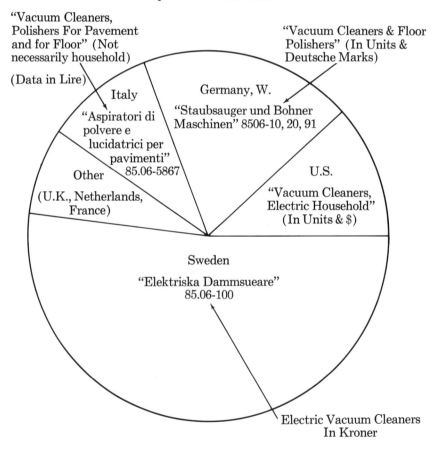

Sources of Data On Vacuum Cleaners
Exported To Venezuela

FIGURE 3—DETERMINING TOTAL EXPORTS TO MARKET

Sweden, data in value terms had to be converted to units. Only the U.S. classification matched the product description desired.

In international marketing research, the analyst is usually faced with the requirement of substantial translation, interpretation and evaluation before one figure for total market can be obtained. Such an approach might be summarized as in Figure 4, the basic elements being as follows:

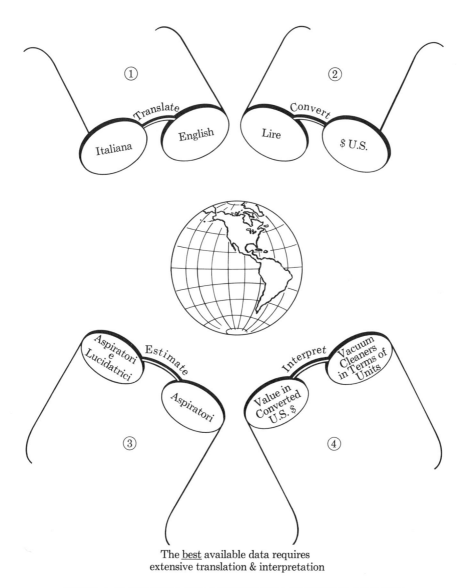

The <u>best</u> available data requires
extensive translation & interpretation

FIGURE 4—TRANSLATION AND INTERPRETATION OF FOREIGN MARKETING
RESEARCH DATA

1. Foreign languages to English
2. Foreign currency to U.S. dollars (presupposes a knowledge and understanding of exchange rates)
3. Broad commodity to specific product; for example, estimating the proportion of vacuum cleaners in the total of vacuum cleaners, floor polishers and parts
4. Values to units; for example, after arriving at the value of vacuum cleaner exports, deriving number of units by estimating an average unit export value

This procedure may not yield exact results for any one exporting country, but the total market figure derived from imports from several countries should be a useful approximation.

Determining the proper classification for a product when using official foreign trade statistics, particularly where the language is unfamiliar, is becoming easier due to the adoption of the "Brussels Nomenclature." This is a numbering system based on tariff classifications that is rapidly becoming international. Most major European countries are using it and many Latin American countries are converting to it as they modernize their foreign trade statistics. Figure 3 shows that while the exact classification will vary among countries, the basic number is approximately the same. The United States and Japan do not use this system as yet, but fortunately the Japanese foreign trade statistics have English translations.

INTERNATIONAL BUSINESS INDICATORS USEFUL IN ESTIMATING RELATIVE MARKET SIZE AND IN FORECASTING MARKET GROWTH

International Business Indicators are perhaps most useful when relatively complete data is available for some countries but not for others in the same region, or where, because of the nature of the product, statistics are very broad or not available. For example, if we are able to compute the market for a product in France, but not in the Netherlands, we may be able to make a reasonable estimate for the Netherlands based on a comparison of several indicators. These might include readily available indicators (for Europe) such as "Gross National Product," "Industrial Production," "Population," "Number of Households," etc.

In making such estimates it is important to use as narrow an indicator as possible for the product area being considered. If we are studying the market for a major household appliance or other durable good, an indicator such as "Private Consumption Expenditures on Durable Goods" might be appropriate. If we are taking an item of industrial machinery, a good indicator might be "Gross Domestic Fixed Capital Formation in Machinery and Equipment."

The indicators just mentioned are available for most industrialized countries although they may be several years old. One source of such indicators is the Statistical Report Series of the Bureau of International Commerce, for example, "Market Indicators for Europe."

Even relatively unsophisticated indicators can be useful in the less industrialized areas. To determine the number of wired homes (potential customers for appliances) in several African countries, we recently used "Newspaper Circulation," "Radio Receivers in Use," "European Population," and "New Residential Construction."

We often hear indicators quoted on a per capita basis, for example, per capita national income, and comparisons made between countries. This type of comparison can be useful when estimating whether the average person or family in a country could afford to purchase such products as appliances or automobiles. Here again, it is important to use as narrow an indicator as possible. It might surprise you to know that in 1959 Per Capita National Income in Venezuela was greater than in France. Per Capita Private Consumption Expenditures in France, however, were considerably greater than for Venezuela; that is, the average Frenchman had considerably more available to spend than the average Venezuelan. National Income is relatively high in Venezuela due to the peculiar nature of the country's oil economy.

In contrast to Venezuela, many countries with limited economic development look worse off than they really are as a substantial portion of business is conducted by barter outside of the money economy. When working with the limited number of indicators available for the developing countries, another considerable limitation is the difficulty of determining appropriate exchange rates to convert to a common currency.

Business indicators are also useful in forecasting, particularly when forecasts of indicators are already available.Organizations such as the National Foreign Trade Council forecast U.S. Commercial Merchandise Exports. The Federal Power Commission forecasts electricity production for many European countries, and the European Economic Community has made forecasts by country of such indicators as "Gross National Product," "Population," and "Per Capita Private Consumption Expenditures." These broad indicators can often indicate plausible rates of growth for exports or consumption of a product, relative rates of growth as between countries, etc.

EUROPE'S FUTURE MAY BE AMERICA'S PAST OR PRESENT

What is presently occurring in many product markets in the United States usually represents the leading trend, and this knowledge often permits us to predict what will happen in the next few years in other relatively affluent countries. Present European growth patterns in the market for many electrical appliances are strikingly similar to what has already happened in the United States. Cultural differences cause exceptions, of course, but more often European markets are increasing at a faster rate than U.S. experience due to the "leapfrog" effect.

There are other useful indicators beside the monetary ones mentioned previously, and a discussion of these ties in closely with our consideration of the present European market as a mirror of America's past. Let us consider, for example, some factors presently affecting the market for refrigerators, and in particular the growing market in Europe for refrigerators with larger storage capacity and freezer compartments. The average European refrigerator is between five and six cubic feet in capacity and does not have a true freezing compartment. Table 2 shows several helpful

TABLE 2—FACTORS AFFECTING THE MARKET FOR REFRIGERATORS WITH LARGER STORAGE CAPACITY

- Food Shopping Habits
- Number of Super and/or Self Service Food Stores
- Automobile Ownership
- Consumption of Frozen Foods
- Per Capita Private Consumption Expenditures
- Employment of Women
- Availability of Domestic Help
- Availability of Consumer Credit
- Cost of Electricity For Residential Use
- Dwelling Construction & Size of New Dwellings
- Refrigerator Saturation in High Income Families

indicators. Information on many of these is available from sources in the United States.

While the refrigerator has taken hold as a necessity rather than a luxury in the European consumption pattern, a development of major importance is the trend in consumer preferences for large capacity refrigerators. If U.S. experience provides a pattern for what will evolve in Europe, it is inevitable that the large capacity refrigerator will steadily gain in popularity in Europe. U.S. experience has shown that the trend in the consumption of large refrigerators achieved its most conspicuous growth during a period when the shopping habits of the American housewife were affected by developments in the marketing of frozen foods and the widespread growth of supermarkets. In a larger context, however, frozen foods, supermarkets and once-a-week shopping were interrelated with such concurrent developments as widespread ownership of automobiles, growing incomes, the working housewife, shortage and high cost of domestic help and the increasing importance of leisure time.

Our research has indicated that Europe is following a pattern remarkably close to that described. While an analysis of available total market product statistics does not conflict with this conclusion, misleading assumptions could be drawn from these total market "numbers" alone.

THE MAIL SURVEY AS A MARKETING TOOL

Selectivity in content and careful preparation of form are both essential to the successful use of the mail questionnaire in international research. Since it is possible to secure only a limited amount of information on one questionnaire, careful planning is necessary to determine and then request only the most important information required.

Considerable attention must be given to the manner in which all questions will be asked. Careful wording is necessary to ensure that the respondent will understand exactly what information is being requested. Illustrative of the confusion that can occur because of wording in these written requests is the point depicted in Figure 5 concerning a washing machine study conducted by a research organization using a brief questionnaire. Information was requested from a German respondent concerning the number of "washers," that is, washing machines, produced in West Germany for a given year. The respondent sent back production data on "washers" but of the flat metal disc variety. As Figure 5 indicates, a considerable length of time is generally required to send out mail questionnaires, and receive responses. The cost of other forms of communication is quite high, making follow-ups to the original mail questionnaire an expensive proposition. These latter points underscore the need for selectivity in the content of the questionnaire.

With questionnaires asking for an open qualitative response, we have found that by sending some information with the questionnaire and then asking for additional information or comments, we have increased the return rate and the completeness of responses. This approach indicates to the respondent that you have tried your best to obtain the required information but that you may not have the complete answer and need his assistance. This would seem particularly helpful in questionnaires to affiliated companies or independent distributors where additional forms from the "home office" are often resented.

Exceptional results can usually be expected where the product area covered is new and of particular interest. We would expect a better return from a questionnaire on color television, for example, than from a questionnaire on tube-type radio receivers. Where there was special interest and where promotional literature was also enclosed, we found that not only was the rate of return greater, but occasionally we received a sample order.

It is preferable to write questionnaires in the language of the respondent but if there are many countries involved, this is not always feasible. If he wants to, the respondent can usually locate someone in his organization who can translate the questionnaire, perhaps verbally. In these cases, however, the answer usually comes back in the foreign lan-

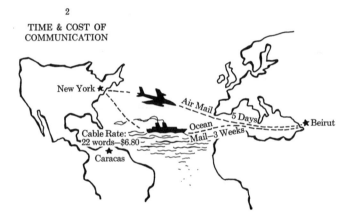

FIGURE 5—FACTORS TO BE CONSIDERED IN THE USE OF THE
MAIL QUESTIONNAIRE

guage. Because of these multiple translations, it is important to use what
might be called "academic" English so that the translations do not change
the meaning of the questions or the responses. This is also important
where English may be the second or third language of the respondent.

It is also desirable, particularly if you are in a large diversified company, to enclose a self-addressed envelope. Otherwise the response may
have difficulty reaching you. Many foreign businessmen seem to have the
habit of addressing returns to a company's headquarters location, even
though proper return addresses are given.

I won't discuss monetary incentives except to say that they have been
used successfully in some selected cases. As customs vary greatly throughout the world, such incentives should be used with caution.

A TOTAL MARKET PROFILE

As an example of our secondary approach to developing total market statistics, Table 3 shows a dummy country market profile for an electrical appliance. Such a summary shows on one page the basics of a country market and provides a quick appraisal of how well we are doing in this market.

TABLE 3—TOTAL MARKET PROFILE

Country A

Summary of the Market for Product X

Market Indicators	1959	1960	1961	1962	Forecast 1970
	- - - - - - - - Thousands of Units - - - - - - - -				
Production	0.000	0.000	0.000	0.000	
(+) Imports	00	00	000	000	
(−) Exports	(000)	(000)	(000)	(000)	
TOTAL LOCAL MARKET	0.000	0.000	0.000	0.000	0.000
New Dwellings	000	000	000	000	
Wired Households	00.000	00.000	00.000	00.000	00.000
Product X Units In Use	0.000	0.000	0.000	00.000	00.000
Saturation (%)	00%	00%	00%	00%	00%
Per Capita Private Consumption Expenditures	$0.000	$0.000	$0.000	$0.000	$0.000

Principal Supplying Nations

Imports From	1959	1960	1961	1962
	- - - - - Thousands of Units - - - -			
France	0	0	0	0
W. Germany	0	00	00	00
Italy	0	0	0	0
United Kingdom	0	0	0	0
United States	0	0	0	0
Others	0	0	0	0
TOTAL IMPORTS	00	00	000	000
Company Sales	0	0	0	0

Major Competitor
Local Manufacturers:

We have quite excellent statistics comparing our export sales against comparable U.S. exports. These are prepared quarterly on a computer and are published in summary reports by sales component, reports showing product by country, and reports showing country by product. These figures tell us how we are doing as compared to our exporting U.S. competitors. But these comparisons can mislead; for example, by showing increasing participation in U.S. exports although our penetration of the total market may, in fact, be falling.

This is one reason why a determination of total market is so important, to show how we are doing as against all competitors. In the hypothetical example shown, if we were manufacturing in the country, sales from local production would have to be added to our export sales in order to measure our true penetration of the market.

The reliability of such a market profile will depend on the product, the country and the general availability of useful statistics. We don't shy away from making estimates, however, because if estimates are based on reasonable assumptions, they generally do not change the meaning of overall conclusions.

DON'T LOSE SIGHT OF THE FOREST

It is easy for researchers to get absorbed in statistical detail, just as we have been discussing statistical sources primarily. I have been suggesting the product by country approach, but from a marketing viewpoint I probably should have been suggesting a business opportunity by country approach. As marketing men, we should understand that we are serving business opportunities and not selling individual products.

In the United States we hear a great deal about the "systems" approach to selling and overseas the same approach is being applied. IGE, for example, is often the prime contractor for a power plant, even though General Electric products may account for only half of the total sales price. By considering ourselves in the business of selling power plants and not just turbines, we are often able to obtain an order against severe price competition. As another example, we are in the business of selling automated steel mills, not just individual pieces of electrical equipment.

We are now finding this project or systems approach more and more necessary in the consumer goods area. In this product area, it is much more difficult to maintain technological leadership over our competitors in the industrialized countries. At the same time, the developing countries are increasingly setting up local manufacture or assembly operations. If we are to maintain U.S. exports of these consumer goods, we must orient ourselves to be marketers of a desired service, rather than salesmen of a specific product. This is not to say that aggressive salesmanship is no longer necessary in exporting—quite the contrary is true—but rather that we are often selling a business or a service and not individual products.

Perhaps a good example of the point I am trying to get across is illustrated by a recent research study of the market for television equipment in the developing countries. We found that in many of the developing countries, particularly in Africa, the Mid-East and Asia, there is strong government control or ownership of communications and TV services. In these cases, the government generally wishes to deal with one supplier. We call this the "project approach," where one company offers a particular country all the essential elements of television service.

A company applying the project approach might, for example, offer the following:

1. TV Transmitters
   —Including technical assistance to train local personnel
2. Station Management and Programing
   —Equipment supplier needs the assistance of an organization experienced in these broadcasting functions.
3. Complete receivers
4. Assistance in setting up local assembly or manufacture of receivers, including:
   —Chassis or kits of parts
   —Sub-assemblies or components
   —Manufacturing machinery and technical manufacturing assistance
5. Financial assistance, equity participation or liberal credit terms

This approach illustrates that we should not consider ourselves in the business of exporting TV receivers, or TV transmitters but rather the business of supplying TV service. By thinking in these terms and by being able to supply the elements mentioned, a company:

a. Can be considered when a country or government agency wishes to deal with one supplier
b. Can capitalize on and continue to export in spite of increasing local assembly programs in former complete product export markets
c. Can offer independent businessmen in developing countries, other than those with government TV ownership, a package particularly appealing if they are not experienced in assembly or manufacturing operations

Further to this last point, a European assembler would probably supply technical specifications and desired quality and styling characteristics when purchasing components. An independent businessman in Nigeria, however, may know only that he wants to be in the TV business, and must depend on the U.S. manufacturer to tell him what he needs. This requires the supplier to be organized and staffed to supply this type of assistance.

It appears inevitable that more and more countries will go to local assembly or manufacture of many less complicated products, particularly luxury consumer goods. The development of economic unions, such as the Central American Common Market, or political and economic unions such as Malayasia, should accelerate this trend. Only by being in the business of supplying a service can a manufacturer expect to maintain exports to these markets. This same analysis might apply equally well to other product areas, for example, refrigerators, other appliances and certain types of less complicated industrial machinery.

DO YOUR HOMEWORK FIRST

In summary, competent international marketing research can be done from the home office in the United States if the right resources are known and accessible. We often tend to overlook that which is readily available. Again, there is no substitute for experiences in the marketplace. Many foreign trips, however, might either be unnecessary or much more productive if the international marketing researcher made use of the information that is available to him from sources in the United States.

The international researcher must not forget that he is first a marketing man and should never lose sight of overall marketing objectives in his search for quantitative or qualitative detail. Rather, he should use his detailed knowledge of foreign markets to point out alternative new approaches to marketing his company's products abroad. The international business environment is constantly changing and only through innovative marketing will a company be able to improve its international market position.

13.

ON THE USE OF MARKETING RESEARCH
IN THE EMERGING ECONOMIES*

Harper W. Boyd, Jr.,
Ronald E. Frank, William F. Massy,
and Mostafa Zoheir

UNDER what conditions, if any, can the United States export marketing know-how to the world's underdeveloped nations? Certainly this is a timely and important question. Peter Drucker [1] has stated that marketing occupies a critical role in the economic development of these nations; yet it is typically the most backward part of the economic system and is treated with neglect if not contempt.

Marketing research should be one of the easiest "areas" in marketing to export, if only because it consists of a collection of techniques which, supposedly, can be applied regardless of the state of economic development as contrasted to certain marketing principles and concepts which have been derived from the American scene. One might assume that the emerging nations would eagerly seek to import marketing research know-how because of their obvious need for information about the market in order to effectively plan and control their economic development.

A unique opportunity to assess the extent to which American market research practices have been exported presented itself during the 1963-64 academic year when 40 teachers of marketing from 18 different underdeveloped countries congregated at the International Center for the Advancement of Management Education (ICAME) at the Graduate School of Business, Stanford University, for a year of study. The countries represented were Argentina, Brazil, Ceylon, Chile, Colombia, Ghana, Indonesia, Israel, Mexico, Nicaragua, Peru, Philippines, Republic of China, South Korea, Thailand, United Arab Republic, Yugoslavia, and Turkey.

The comments to follow are based on informal day-to-day contact with the participants, personal interviews and their responses to a self-administered questionnaire.

Despite some evidence to the contrary, there is little to indicate that

* Reprinted by permission of the *Journal of Marketing Research,* Vol. 1, No. 4 (Nov. 1964) a publication of the American Marketing Association, and the authors, pp. 20-23.

marketing research has to date been used to any great extent in the emerging countries. And while it is true a rather surprising number of these countries have conducted recent censuses or sample surveys of population, housing, agriculture, wholesaling, and retailing, consumer surveys have not been conducted in any quantities. Indeed, in such countries as Ceylon, Ghana, Yugoslavia, Nicaragua, Thailand, and South Korea, one is hard pressed to find even one such study. Outside of Latin America virtually no organizations comparable to the American Marketing Association exist. Those marketing groups which do exist tend to focus on sales rather than the broader concept we call marketing. Only a few of the underdeveloped countries have publications that print articles on marketing research, and these are typically rather specialized, such as the Brazilian sales magazine, *Vandas + Varejo,* the Korean Trade Promotion Corporation's publication, *Trade Journal Monthly,* and the Taiwan *Economic Monthly.*

Still the picture is not all black. A surprising number of business schools in these countries are installing U.S. type marketing research courses in their curriculum. Especially in South America we find the establishment of firms specializing in marketing research. Advertising agencies, particularly those which are branches of U.S. firms, have been important pioneers in the use of marketing research and through demonstration have forced local companies to follow suit.

It is clear, however, that marketing research will not assume great importance in the economic life of these nations for some time to come. This article will attempt to explain the reasons for this lack of acceptance, as well as discuss the difficulties involved in applying U.S. marketing research practices to these countries.

THE LOCAL ENVIRONMENT AND ITS EFFECT
ON THE USE OF MARKETING RESEARCH

Perhaps the major obstacle to the use of marketing research in the emerging countries is the attitude toward marketing of business and government administrators. Most such individuals tend to view marketing largely as a mechanistic process involving at best such functions as transportation, storage, and exchange. In point-of-fact the statement is often made that "we have no marketing problems except, of course, in connection with our export marketing efforts."

The economies of the emerging countries can be characterized as production oriented. In addition, most business organizations—whether located in the private or public sector—are concerned primarily with efficient work systems and procedures, high centralization of authority, multiple layers of supervision, and intense specialization. Such an organization is defended—and logically so—on the basis that demand typically exceeds supply. Thus, there is little concern for the market and how its wants and needs affect the decisions of the organization.

Another deterrent to the use of marketing research is the typical industry organization found in the emerging countries. Because of the limited effective demands for any commodity and the *very* scarce resources available, the government follows the policy of deliberately *not* encouraging competition. Thus, many if not most industries are comprised of one or two firms. This policy, coupled with high tariff barriers, produces a situation where little, if any, competition exists within an industry. Under such conditions little check on the activities of management is made, except that which is generated internally—and this is not likely to be important since, as was noted earlier, most of the firms are production oriented and look "inward" rather than "outward." The fact that all but a very few of these countries have laws which prohibit collusion merely further inhibits competition from taking place.

In addition to limited effective demand, most firms are also constrained by the limited availability of managerial talent, thus further taking the edge off competition. This fact, combined with the higher priority given to production resources, leads to a disproportionate shortage of managerial talent in the field of marketing, let alone in market research.

Most companies in the emerging economies are small by U.S. standards, and many are family owned. The desire for survival is inevitably hinged to a perpetuation of the family's control over the enterprise. This means that many companies do not want to expand or change and that their objective is primarily to maintain the status quo. While this attitude is changing gradually, there is little to indicate that the change will generate greater interest in marketing research, if only because of the small size of the firms. It must also be remembered that many firms tend to be speculators because of their economy's inflation.

Few firms do much in the way of advertising or product development. In the case of the latter, products are largely copies of western products and little or no money is spent on R & D. As a consequence there is little need for marketing research, and there will be no such need until more indigenous products are attempted.

Marketing has always been a relatively low-status occupation in many of the emerging nations. Much of this low status was derived because foreigners were so engaged and, further, because much of what was thought to be marketing was, in reality, speculation. For these reasons, as well as others, the field of marketing has not attracted outstanding men with considerable managerial skills. The fact that few firms have a marketing department per se—or even recognize the marketing function in their organization—has acted as a further restraint on the use of research. Certainly marketing personnel have little opportunity to influence the major decisions of the company. Few men with a marketing background ever succeed to a position of high responsibility within the firm. Rather, such positions are more likely to be reserved for engineers or men with financial experience.

What is true of marketing in this regard is particularly true of marketing research. Few people are qualified to undertake marketing research. Usually these individuals are associated with either government bureaus or schools, not with business firms. Unfortunately the gap between academic and corporate life is considerably greater in most of the emerging countries than in the United States. Firms typically do not look upon the academic community as a source of expert advice. Often otherwise qualified academicians feel that work with a business firm is inappropriate, given their role as educators.

A strong point can be made for the use of marketing research by the governments of these countries, especially in new planning work. Conceptually, at least, knowledge about the market place is necessary if proper allocations of scarce resources are to be made. And given the absence of competition and the inability of the market to influence decisions, marketing research should be able to provide meaningful control and reappraisal data. But one has to take into account the nature of the bureaucratic mind. For the most part, civil servants have little desire to make decisions. Indeed, the reward system in these countries is such that one can only "lose" by so doing. Thus, problems are handed "up" for decisions. In addition, there is a great fear of information that might be used against someone. This insecurity is very real, since within most governmental organizations a number of persons are vying for power at the same time. Hence, marketing research is feared because it might be used as a way of pointing up certain deficiencies. If no information is available, one's persuasiveness can be brought to the fore—perhaps with good results.

The above reasons, however briefly described, point clearly to the fact that marketing is not an important subject to most administrators in the underdeveloped countries. As a consequence, few are concerned with obtaining information that could be provided by marketing research. Since most of these reasons are deep seated and tied to basic economic and attitudinal conditions, they are not likely to change quickly.

TECHNICAL APPLICATION PROBLEMS

Marketing research is considerably more difficult to do in the less-developed countries than in the United States. This is especially true in sampling, data collection methods, and field work. Each of these subjects will be discussed briefly from the point of view of application in the emerging countries.

Sampling

Probability sampling is not used in most of the countries studied. Except for several countries in Latin America (Argentina, Brazil, Chile, Colombia, and Mexico), most reported small or negligible use of probability sampling. Even where it is used, widespread and severe difficulties are encountered, since maps are rarely up to date—if they indeed exist. Such is even true in the case of the larger cities; and, thus, selection of blocks or equivalent land areas is rendered difficult. As might be expected, block statistics are not available, thereby preventing stratification or the opportunity to draw blocks proportionate to population.

Poor transportation often precludes the use of a dispersed sample, as does the fact that field workers are reluctant or refuse to travel alone (especially women). Then, too, some countries have several different languages. Imagine conducting a nationwide survey in India, which has 14 different "official" languages and, in reality, substantially more!

Sampling within blocks presents all kinds of difficulties since dwelling units are not numbered or otherwise identified. It is often difficult to define a dwelling unit. For example, how does one determine how many families are present in a given structure when, because of the prevalence of the extended family, many dwelling units are inhabited by a large number of individuals and several primary family units? It is often difficult to determine who is the "housewife."

The amount of information available upon which to base a sampling plan varies considerably from country to country and city to city. For example, a government agency in the middle east wanted to find out what socioeconomic groups in a given city were more apt to watch broadcasts from the government-owned television station. Only a map of the city was available. The best information about the geographic distribution of population was the research director's own personal judgment. He divided the city into a large number of areas that he felt were about equal in population. Using probability sampling techniques, he selected fifty of these. In each of the fifty, interviewers were instructed to interview a given number of men and women over sixteen years of age. A second round of interviews was planned in advance, so that if the data for any particular socioeconomic group were too sparse for analysis there would be enough time and funds available to conduct additional interviews.

In contrast, the research director of a Chilean firm concerned with an analysis of certain retailing practices in the major cities of his country not only had a map of each city, but also a virtually complete and recent list of retail outlets classified by type, size, and urban district for each major city in the country. He was, therefore, in an excellent position to employ probability sampling techniques. For the most part, however, fortunate circumstances such as these are relatively rare.

The above difficulties make it relatively easy to rationalize the use of convenience sampling, an often relied-upon technique. Even quota sampling, *i.e.*, nonprobability sampling in which interviewing quotas are established for various kinds of respondents, is not typically possible because of the lack of needed secondary data.

Data Collection Methods

Data collection by telephone and mail surveys is almost impossible in the developing countries, and where such is attempted the biases are likely to be substantial. Few persons in such countries have phones: less than 3 percent in Ceylon, while in Israel the cost is so high (the installation charge is $170 and the monthly service fee is $10) that only the very wealthy can afford them. Then, too, there are different attitudes about the use of a phone. Generally speaking, telephone users, particularly women, are highly suspicious of strangers on the phone. Also, because of their respect (even fear) for the instrument, many men and women will not spend much time in talking on it.

Mail surveys are similarly limited. Since many of the emerging countries have low literacy rates, problems often arise as to what languages and dialects to use, even assuming literacy. Postal service is poor—especially in rural areas. In Nicaragua, for example, it is difficult to conduct a mail questionnaire because one can post letters only at a post office. Then, too, some cultures apparently do not believe in writing answers which will be read by a stranger. In some cases the male head of the family will answer the questionnaire *regardless* of the actual addressee.

Response Error and the Field Force

The problem of not-at-homes in most of the cities of the underdeveloped countries is not as great as in the U.S. But this is not true in the villages, where in some countries the younger wife's role is at her husband's side in the fields. Under these conditions, the not-at-home rate may reach as high as fifty percent or more. In contrast, in some of the middle eastern countries, where the wife's traditional role requires her presence in the home a high proportion of the time, the rate is much lower.

In many cities and villages, poor lighting, a high crime rate, and the nomadic nature of the population make evening call-backs difficult to conduct and less effective as a technique for dealing with the not-at-home problem.

Refusals to cooperate also probably are considerably higher than in the States. While the cooperation rate varies by country, the general mistrust of strangers tends to produce considerable difficulty in obtaining satisfactory interviews. Thus, for example, Thai and Indonesian women will not talk to strangers, and an Indian woman will not grant an interview unless an acquaintance accompanies the field worker. In many villages in these and other countries, literally no one will cooperate unless the village elders have sanctioned the study. In many cases the permission of the family head is required and frequently he will grant the interview only if he is permitted to answer the questions. Interviews among the well-to-do are difficult because they are protected by servants.

In an effort to gain cooperation, several countries reported the use of samples or premiums; for example, free product samples (the Philippines, Nicaragua, and Yugoslavia), small gifts (United Arab Republic), and free lottery tickets (Indonesia). Appointments are used in some countries to facilitate interviewing the wealthy, while in others college students are used "to get by the servants."

Many respondents refuse to cooperate (either in whole or in part) or distort their answers because they fear the interviewer may be a tax inspector or some other government official. The director of a household budget study for a middle eastern government expected that less than 50 percent of the households contacted would be willing to cooperate due primarily to mistrust of strangers in general and of the government in particular. Many are suspicious because they believe the interviewer to be a house-to-house salesman. One can understand why those interviewers who either are or look like college students obtain relatively high rates of cooperation.

There is a great reluctance among both men and women to discuss certain subjects with strangers. While the degree to which certain topics are taboo varies between countries, there was unanimity in stating that such subjects as sex, personal hygiene, finance, and household expenditures were difficult to discuss. And further, in a number of countries the subject of consumption habits is thought to be taboo.

Composition of the Field Force

Partly because of their relatively infrequent use, supervisors in these countries are generally poorly trained and controlled.

And it is interesting to note the substantial use of male interviewers in many countries. (While women interviewers are more numerous than male interviewers in Argentina, Israel, and the U.A.R., such is not the case in most of the other countries). Because women are by tradition quite modest, and because their role is not visualized by the male head of the family as that of a worker outside the family unit, it is difficult to recruit workers. Also, although this situation is changing, the number of educated women is quite small in most of these countries. In at least several countries interviewing is typed as door-to-door selling and, therefore, not considered fit work for women. And as was inferred earlier, women are very frequently not permitted to travel, or to work during evening hours.

How does the use of male interviewers bias cooperation and the responses given to certain questions? It seems clear that a male interviewer has more difficulty in gaining the cooperation of female respondents than would be the case if women interviewers were used. Also, males often would not be able to elicit satisfactory responses to questions dealing with female products and the attitudes of other household members on matters having to do with her role within the family unit.

CONCLUDING REMARKS

Marketing research is in an embryonic stage in the vast majority of underdeveloped nations. U.S. techniques would be directly transferable if the appropriateness of their use did not depend on the state of economic development and information and the cultural mores of the population being studied. Despite these problems, our know-how in this area still provides a valuable mine of information. The problem is that the practices and concepts contained in the mine need to be modified (often substantially) before they are suitable for use in a particular underdeveloped nation.

REFERENCE

1. Peter Drucker, "Marketing and Economic Development," *Journal of Marketing,* (January 1958), 252-259.

14.

ANALYZING BRAZILIAN CONSUMER MARKETS*

Leo G. Erickson

THERE is a saying among Brazilians that he who does not have a dog must hunt with a cat. The fact that marketing research is performed at all in Brazil indicates that this saying is more than a simple truism to the Brazilians.

Those sources of information to which the American researcher automatically turns are of limited purpose, and sometimes even nonexistent. For example, trade association information is, so far as the writer has been able to ascertain, simply not available, for the valid reason that trade associations as known in the United States do not exist in Brazil.

Census information is so late in being gathered, tabulated and published that, even if one had confidence in the methods of gathering and presentation, he would still find the information of dubious value. Particularly is this the case in a country such as Brazil where the market situation is so dynamic. When the dynamics of the market are coupled with the questionable reliability of Brazilian census data, a researcher is entitled to some apprehension concerning the results of his own study.

Despite their limitations, census data are in many cases the best available and are useful for certain purposes. Mostly, census reports have value for developing relative measures: relative geographic presence of various factors of importance to marketers and relative changes between census periods.

There are extremely few pieces of research put out by universities. Brazilian scholars may have many laudable attributes (such as their gift for extemporaneousness and rhetoric) but a propensity for doing research is certainly not one of them. There are noteworthy exceptions to this generalization. A rather quasi-academic institution is the Instituto Brasileiro de Economia of the Fundação Getúlio Vargas. This institute employs some excellent economists who *are* research-minded and who turn out some of the best work done in Brazil. In addition, although in the genesis stage, the Escola de Administração de Empresas, São Paulo (also

* Leo G. Erikson, "Analyzing Brazilian Consumer Markets," MSU BUSINESS TOPICS (Bureau of Business and Economic Research, Graduate School of Business Administration, Michigan State University, East Lansing, Michigan), Summer, 1963, pp. 7-26. Reprinted by permission.

a part of the Fundação Getúlio Vargas) is in the process of expanding substantially the activities of its research center. To the extent that such plans materialize, the center should be able to fill in many gaps in knowledge of business practice in Brazil. The Ford Foundation is interested in furthering the research activities of both of these institutions.

There are some good private research companies which perform creditably, all the more so when one considers the handicaps under which they operate. Certain of the advertising agencies, also, maintain research departments which do quite useful work for their clients. Unfortunately the output of these firms is not widely distributed and frequently is limited in scope.

Governmental agencies abound and many publish periodic reports useful to marketing researchers. Reports on sales taxes, geographic distribution of income, numbers and sales of wholesaling institutions are illustrative of the information services supplied by various government bureaus.

For research on most specific marketing problems, the existing sources of information are probably adequate only for background data and for help in formulating hypotheses. Vitally important field research is also handicapped.

SURVEY METHOD

In Brazil, as in the United States, the survey is the predominant marketing research technique. For that reason the emphasis of this article is upon this technique. Even in the United States a good survey is not an easy thing to conduct. There are certain unusual difficulties attending its use in Brazil, whether it be a mail survey, telephone survey, or personal interview type.

Mail Surveys

One of the basic impediments to effective mail surveys is the postal system. Service is not good, either in regard to facilities or in the care that attends handling. Even in the larger, more advanced cities such as São Paulo there are many areas which do not have mail service. It is not uncommon to hear of mail sacks being dumped on vacant lots, or mail being sold for its waste paper value (as perhaps some should be). Consequently, the official estimate that 30 percent of the domestic mail is never delivered comes as no shock. What is surprising is that by implication 70 percent of the mail must be getting through.

Assuming that the questionnaire is delivered to the recipient, the chances of getting a reply are subject not only to the vagaries of the mail system which must return it, but also to the fact that Brazilians are notoriously poor at answering requests by mail. Add to the above the extreme difficulty of compiling a mailing list in Brazil and one can only applaud the efforts of those researchers who are struggling along in spite of inadequate mail surveys.

Telephone Surveys

If mail service is bad, telephone service is simply atrocious. There are very few telephones (the national average is approximately one for every 600 persons). The chances of improvement are not apparent, for there are waiting lists that may run nine to twelve years, or longer, in some areas.

Because of the peculiarities of the system (too complicated to explain here), the name listed opposite a particular number in the telephone directory is not likely to be that of the person occupying the premises where the phone is installed. This situation is no fault of the truly excellent directory service in most Brazilian cities. The directory service does spot the telephone by its correct address. For certain types of area research this may be adequate.

It is unbelievably difficult to complete a call to a business establishment: large manufacturing companies may have only one line; circuits are overloaded. Most of the persons working at business establishments do not have telephones in their homes and so rely upon the business phone for their personal calls.

Personal Interviewing

If the surveyor turns to personal interviewing he finds that he has merely traded one set of difficulties for another. Trained interviewers are virtually impossible to come by. If one is willing to train interviewers, it is not easy to find honest persons with sufficient education or intelligence. These personal characteristics demand a premium and individuals possessing them are not likely to hold themselves available for interviewing work.

An additional difficulty, which is different from the United States situation in its intensity, is that housewives are reluctant to grant interviews, particularly to male interviewers. Regardless of what portion of the population is being interviewed, there is a reluctance to respond because of fear that the interviewer is gathering information for governmental purposes (particularly fiscal).

Transportation is difficult. The interviewer quite likely does not own an automobile. In the larger cities in areas which make up the bulk of the market, bus service is available and usually in quantity. However, it is extremely slow, primarily because of congestion.

The Brazilian reputation for courtesy and kindness has a disadvantage in conducting personal interviews. In the first place there is a tendency not to disappoint anyone by telling him one does not know the answer to a question. Also, consistent with this, a man is likely to tell an interviewer what he thinks the interviewer would like to hear. Characteristics of this sort make one love the Brazilian for his commendable inborn traits, but cause one to become frustrated with the manifestations of these characteristics in certain practical instances.

As a general observation, persons in Brazil are not research-acclimated. Thus far research is not a part of their general environment. As a result, they do not make good researchers or respondents.

U.S. FIRMS IN BRAZIL

One-half of the U.S. firms interviewed for a recent study on marketing in Brazil, undertaken by a Michigan State University faculty member and described in the forthcoming book, *Developing Dynamics: A Study of U.S. Enterprise in Brazil,* stated that they do not engage in any marketing research studies. The rest of the firms, with one exception, are apparently doing work which from any objective standpoint would hardly qualify as marketing research.

Seemingly, there is very little work done by U.S. firms in Brazil in gathering primary data about marketing problems. Considerable reference is made to secondary sources such as publications of the Fundação Getúlio Vargas, governmental agencies, and commercial reports. But even in these instances, one gains the impression that such efforts are likely to be more casual than might be expected. Also, one-third of the U.S. firms stated that they make no reference to secondary sources of marketing data. It is highly unusual among these firms to find the gathering of marketing information functionalized and conducted by a specialized person primarily responsible for this important activity. Instead, the responsibility for gathering marketing information is likely not to be specified or, if specified, it is likely to be an incidental undertaking of someone in the sales department. U.S. firms in Brazil may employ outside agencies on a "one-shot" basis to do a specific piece of research. Here they may turn to one of several management research or service companies. Or they may utilize the research department of their advertising agency. In São Paulo there are three advertising agencies with marketing research departments; two of these are U.S. agencies.

Market Analysis

An initial reaction to this situation may be surprise that American firms in Brazil are not more active proponents of this important activity. However, the situation is perhaps about as one should expect. Prior to locating there the typical U.S. company analyzed the market with considerable care. Isolated instances of research may be undertaken if the firm is considering changing its operation or if it starts to run into trouble. For a production-oriented economy this may be all that is deemed necessary, even within firms in which the top management comes from sales. Particularly is this the case when one considers the aforementioned difficulties in doing objective research in Brazil.

THE CONSUMER MARKET

Describing and analyzing the Brazilian market and its marketing system is a tremendously difficult thing even for a person who has spent all his life in Brazil. It is a country of contrasts and contradictions that refuse to be fitted into generalizations. Further, the nation currently is going through a period of such rapid change (economic, political, and social) that it defies one to keep abreast of new developments which may cause drastic modifications in the marketing structure. Additionally, useful information on Brazilian markets and marketing practices is maddeningly late and of questionable reliability. Or, in far too many cases, the information is non-existent.

For a person who has spent a small proportion of his life in Brazil, regardless of how interested he may be in Brazilian marketing, these difficulties are compounded. Despite such difficulties, a written treatment of Brazilian markets and marketing is needed. Brazil is a country which has captured the imagination and money of many Americans and may well continue to do so in the future if it so chooses. The writer is encouraged in this undertaking because as yet no one more intimately connected with the scene has seen fit to do the job. However, particular attention should be drawn to the fact that much of the material which follows is based upon a paucity of data, often incomplete and often of questionable accuracy.

Insularity

In the U.S. excellent transportation and communication systems have caused the entire widespread population more nearly to become a single economic unit. Brazil as yet has not achieved the degree of excellence in transportation and communications to permit such homogeneity. The consequence is that while in the United States there are, from a marketing standpoint, decidedly more similarities than differences among the several states, the reverse of this situation is true in Brazil. Thus, one is on dangerous grounds in assuming that marketing practices which are appropriate for one Brazilian state are likewise appropriate for another. Despite the fact that similarity predominates in the United States there is still no such thing as a national market. In Brazil, where *differences* predominate, such a statement is doubly pertinent and its implications doubly important. These differences are elaborated in the sections which follow.

Economic Regions

Brazil is composed of 21 states, a federal district (in which Brasilia is located), several small portions of land in dispute between adjacent states, and four territories located in the northwest. For marketing purposes the territories may be excluded from consideration with no real harm. In this writing, the Federal District is also excluded because the recency of its origin prevents comparisons over time. Thus, the concern here is with the 21 states which may be considered by the regional classification used by the Brazilian Embassy in Washington, D.C. in their publication, *Survey of the Brazilian Economy*, 1960.

   The North Central region includes the five states of Amazonas, Para, Maranhao, Mato Gross and Goias, or nearly two-thirds of the area of the states of Brazil. Yet they have only 10 percent of the population and such a low level of income that it is difficult to consider most of this area as being in any sort of a market economy.

   The North East states are Piaui, Ceara, Rio Grande do Norte, Paraiba, Pernambuco, Alagoas, Sergipe, and Bahia. Although there are certain exceptions, such as the cities of Recife and Salvador, this area may be characterized as subsistence and isolated in nature. With the exception of Bahia, these states are individually small in area. As a group they account for roughly 15 percent of Brazil's total area and 30 percent of its population.

   The South includes Espirito Santo, Minas Gerais, Rio de Janeiro, Guanabara, São Paulo, Parana, Santa Catarina, and Rio Grande do Sul. Although differing substantially in individual importance, these eight states form a relatively integrated market. Here is found the highest degree of economic development, the most rapid rate of economic growth, and most of Brazil's industrialization.

   Much of the country's separation into heterogenous areas is due to the existence of a mountain range called the Serra do Mar (Sea Ridge or

Mountain). Although not particularly high, these mountains are so rugged and ubiquitous that they explain in large part why the inland portions of Brazil have never been developed. Additionally, the mountains have caused the rivers to flow backward, away from the sea, thus preventing Brazil from utilizing its natural means of transportation.

There are ethnic, cultural, climatic and historical factors among others, which help determine Brazil's heterogeneity. Reference to certain of these determinants is made throughout this article. However, the most important factor in Brazil's unequal growth is its topography. This alone has been sufficient to cause economic imbalances.

MARKETING'S ROLE

Brazil is still a production-oriented nation, much as the U.S. was until quite recently. Despite the remarkable growth which Brazil has been making in industrial production, the problem of how to produce in sufficient quantities to take care of its expanding population is far from solved. The person with training in engineering is still the most sought after by Brazilian business firms. Logic would indicate that such an emphasis on production would not be likely to be the case for the American firm located in Brazil. The ability to produce efficiently and in quantity can be transplanted. It falls in the category of technology which is probably the American firm's greatest advantage and contribution to the economy. The American firm should be inclined to emphasize the problems connected with serving the complex and strange Brazilian market. And in this connection techniques are not so readily transferable. Although they may leave something to be desired in this respect, the importance attached to marketing problems by U.S. firms operating in Brazil is indicated by the survey mentioned earlier which shows that approximately one-half of the top executives of the American subsidiaries have come from the marketing department.

That the Brazilians have not yet emphasized marketing as a set of business functions is readily observable. When Michigan State University established the first Brazilian school of business administration in São Paulo, the M. S. U. professors soon discovered there was no Brazilian equivalent to the term "marketing." A word had to be coined for it and it is probably true that to this day the typical Brazilian businessman has, at best, only the most hazy notion of what is meant by the term.

Undeveloped Marketing Functions

Brazil's physical distribution system has been sorely neglected. Until just recently the retailing institutions could best be described as primitive, with feiras (open-air markets) and "Mom and Pop" stores predominating. The communication facilities which make possible modern marketing, although developing rapidly, are still inadequate. There is still virtually no trained personnel in advertising, personal selling or marketing research. It is sufficient to state that every function of marketing has remained undeveloped in the process of encouraging production.

A recent study of São Paulo consumer manufacturers[1] shows that two-thirds of the companies interviewed stated that sales policies are determined by production rather than by the sales organization. In fact, only 46 percent even have a sales department. Three-quarters of the salesmen of these firms earned less than $200 per month. More than one-half earned less than $120. Only 50 percent of the firms advertised. All of these comments are consistent with the prevailing philosophy that a company's sales are some function of its production, rather than the contrary view that the market is the determinant of the optimum level of production.

Today increasing numbers of Brazilians are beginning to recognize that marketing must develop concurrent with further developments in production. There is awakening awareness that it is mass marketing which makes possible mass production. Such awareness is evidenced by the introduction of marketing curricula in higher education, short courses on marketing techniques, specialized marketing research departments, and the interest shown in the services of marketing consultants. As in other areas of economic activity, but to a lesser degree, Brazil is making strides in improving marketing methods. It may be safely predicted that marketing will play an increasingly important role in business, but as yet it is far from the stage of development which is consistent with the emphasis placed on increased production.

BRAZILIAN MARKETS

In marketing, as in other areas of social and economic activity, institutions and methodology do not arise simply through chance. Rather, they are a reflection of the particular environment in which they are found. Those institutions which are engaged in marketing, and the methods used to market output, reflect all the environmental factors which are lumped together and called the "market."

There is no such thing as a market in Brazil, the U.S., or any other country. For any single product there usually is a series of markets which may be served with varying degrees of ease and profitability. However, it is common practice to treat markets as though they are divided into two

[1] O Sistema de Vendagem e a Remuneração Dos Vendedores Na Industria de Bens de Consumo Em São Paulo, 1961, P. M. Y., Pesquisas, Mercadologica e Vendas, Ltda.

broad categories: the market for consumer goods and that for industrial goods. Such a broad categorizing has the defect of failing to reveal many important market aspects within each of these two classes. Still, such a division is of basic importance in attempting to generalize concerning methods and agencies. An attendant advantage, of importance to this writing, is that the division into consumer and industrial markets facilitates exposition and makes it possible to describe market elements in relatively less space.

Environmental Changes

Of even greater importance than the advantages mentioned above is the recognition that change and progress in Brazil are occurring so rapidly that it is dangerous to describe current practice with the assumption that such practice will continue. Rather, it is of greater importance to analyze the environmental situation which has given rise to current practice so that one may predict changes in marketing methods which are likely to result from an observable change in the environment. Appropriate comparisons are made with U.S. market factors in order to illustrate certain fundamental differences between the markets of the two countries. Throughout there is a striving for generality at the expense of completeness of description.

The consumer market may be usefully thought of as being comprised of people, with money, willing to spend it. Thus, an analysis of any consumer market may be structured around consideration of population, income and retail sales. Such a structuring is used here. At the outset it should be noted that there are data more nearly current and reliable concerning the first two elements, population and income, than there are concerning the third, retail sales.

POPULATION

Brazil's official population figures are generally termed (somewhat charitably perhaps) as of "questionable reliability." Further, there is usually quite a time lag between the gathering of the figures and their publication (the 1950 census was published in 1956). There are preliminary estimates of the 1960 census of population already available without breakdowns by characteristics. Whether these estimates will be improved to any considerable degree by the final results is doubtful. Therefore, we shall not hesitate to use them here as the best information available.

Brazil is growing rapidly in population. Whereas the United States

increased its population at an average annual rate of 1.7 percent during
the decade 1950-60, Brazil's population increased at a rate of 2.6 percent.
Immigration is an insignificant part of the growth. The explanation is
found in a different direction. Brazilian families average approximately
one and one-half more persons than U.S. families; this despite a higher
infant mortality rate and shorter longevity in Brazil. Brazilians are just
that much more fecund.

If income can increase at a faster rate than population (and thus far
it has) and if efforts are accelerated to insure that this population is productive, the factor of population can have an extremely favorable effect
upon the Brazilian market. A comparison of Brazil and U.S. population
in recent years is shown in Table 1. The manner in which population is

TABLE 1—TREND OF POPULATION, BRAZIL AND UNITED STATES
SELECTED YEARS: 1953-1960

	Midyear Population (000,000)			Annual Rate of Population Increase (Percent)	Area (Square Miles 000)	Population Density Per Square Mile
	1953	1958	1960			
Brazil[1].	55.8	62.7	69.8	2.6	3,287	20
United States[2]. .	160.3	174.8	180.5	1.7	3,615	48

[1]Excludes Territories and Federal District.
[2]Excludes Hawaii and Alaska.

Sources: *United Nations Demographic Yearbook,* 1959, cited in *Cooperation for Progress in Latin America,* Committee for Economic Development, April 1961, p. 12.
Figures for 1960: U. S., *International Financial Statistics,* International Monetary Fund
        Brazil, Instituto Brasileiro Geografica e Estatistica.

distributed geographically is also of considerable importance to a marketing man. Assuming that wherewithal and desire are likewise present, people are markets. As mentioned previously, Brazil's population is anything
but uniformly dispersed. Table 2 shows the population distribution by
states for the census years 1950 and 1960.

It may be observed that every state gained in population numbers
during the decade 1950-1960. There are surprisingly few shifts in relative
importance of the various states in this respect. It is true that some states
lost ground in relative position while others, consequently, gained. Generally speaking, the northern and central states were the losers in position and the southern states the gainers. But the shifts in relative
importance are not striking and, in fact, are less than one might expect,
considering that the south of Brazil has accounted for the greatest portion
of Brazil's economic growth. One might conclude that the relative geo-

TABLE 2—POPULATION OF STATES AND TERRITORIES OF BRAZIL
1950 AND 1960 (PRELIMINARY) (000)

State	No. of Persons 1950	Percent of Total	No. of Persons 1960	Percent of Total	Percent of Change 1950–60
Amazonas	514.1	1.0	721.2	1.0	40.3
Para	1,123.2	2.2	1,550.9	2.2	38.1
Maranhao	1,583.2	3.0	2,492.1	3.5	57.4
Piaui	1,045.7	2.0	1,263.3	1.8	20.1
Ceara	2,605.4	5.2	3,337.8	4.7	23.8
Rio Grande do Norte	967.9	1.9	1,157.2	1.6	19.6
Paraiba	1,713.2	3.3	2,017.9	2.9	17.8
Pernambuco	3,395.2	6.5	4,120.0	5.8	21.3
Alagoas	1,093.1	2.1	1,271.0	1.8	16.3
Sergipe	644.3	1.2	760.3	1.1	18.0
Bahia	4,834.5	9.3	5,990.6	8.5	23.9
Minas Gerais	7,728.8	14.9	9,550.0	13.5	23.6
Espirito Santo	861.5	1.7	1,188.6	1.7	38.0
Rio de Janeiro	2,297.2	4.4	3,402.7	4.8	48.1
Guanabara	2,377.4	4.6	3,307.1	4.7	39.1
São Paulo	9,141.9	17.6	12,930.0	18.3	41.4
Parana	2,129.3	4.1	4,100.0	5.8	92.6
Santa Catarina	1,560.5	3.0	2,146.9	3.0	37.6
Rio Grande Do Sul	4,164.8	8.0	5,448.8	7.7	30.8
Mato Grosso	522.0	1.0	950.0	1.3	82.0
Goias	1,214.9	2.3	1,954.8	2.8	60.9
Federal District (Brasilia)			141.7	0.2	
Territories & Areas in Dispute	367.9	0.7	715.0	1.0	94.3
Total	51,975	100.0	70,517.9	99.7	35.7

graphic distribution of the population was already firmly established prior to the 1950's. If such is the case, there is reason to believe that the so-called "have not" states will not lose drastically in share of population in the near future. Additional weight is attached to such an hypothesis by virtue of the serious development efforts that are to be devoted to Brazil's poorer areas.

Personal Consumption

Casual reflection would lead one to reason that Brazil would have a high rate of consumption, and consequently, a low rate of personal saving. This situation might be expected in an underdeveloped country—the closer the economy is to a so-called basic economy the closer the consumption function should be to 100 percent. As shown in Table 3, Brazil's average propensity to consume, relative both to Gross National Product and Disposable Personal Income, is higher than that for the United States—but not by very much. The reason for this must be found in the inequality of the personal distribution of income referred to earlier. Even with low average per capita incomes, personal savings are relatively high. These savings almost certainly come from the receivers of high incomes. The typical Brazilian is a low income receiver and must have a consumption function of close to 100 percent (or greatr). Not only is this situation attributable to the low income levels associated with under-development, but also to somewhat more subtle reasons of interest to anyone seeking to understand marketing in Brazil.

TABLE 3—PERSONAL CONSUMPTION EXPENDITURES, BRAZIL AND
UNITED STATES RELATIVE TO GROSS NATIONAL PRODUCT AND
DISPOSABLE PERSONAL INCOME 1955-1959

| | Personal Consumption Expenditures as | | | |
| | Percent of G. N. P. | | Percent of D. P. I. | |
Year	Brazil	United States	Brazil	United States
1955	66.0	64.6	93.3	93.6
1956	67.0	64.4	93.6	92.2
1957	67.0	64.4	93.8	92.3
1958	68.6	66.0	99.3	92.3
1959	65.2	65.0	96.3	93.0

Sources: Calculated from figures by Instituto Brasileiro de Economia—Fundação Getulio Vargas and *Statistical Abstract of the U. S.,*1961.

Inflation

Inflation is in itself a major stimulus for consumption on the part of the average Brazilian. Inflation might be expected to accelerate consumption purchases in any economy, but in Brazil the situation is extreme. Interest rates on consumer purchases are, by United States standards, unbelievably high. Yet the Brazilian does not hesitate to use installment credit to the limit allowed by the vendor. His reasoning, quite simply, is that even if interest charges should be as high as 36 percent (which they are), the interest rate will approximately keep pace with the deterioration of his money. Here is the reason why retailers are willing to give substantial discounts from list for cash purchases of durables. The high socalled interest rate is not really an interest rate at all. The retailer (or manufacturer) ties up his money for the period of installment contract with no return in the form of interest.

Additionally, Brazilians are not accustomed to utilize what to North Americans are normal means of personal savings. Historically, the Brazilian has looked to land as the form of saving. However, it is virtually impossible for the average Brazilian to accumulate enough funds to buy real property for other than, at the most, his own personal needs. And land generally is not sold on time. There are corporate stocks available for purchase, certain of which have been demonstrated to be excellent purchases. But an organized stock market is a recent thing in Brazil, and relatively few stocks are offered for trading. Further, many who have the funds to utilize the stock market have not been persuaded of its role in personal savings.

The net result of this emphasis on consumption is that local manufacturers have been able to market virtually any product without fear of critical scrutiny by this market. However, this holiday from normal merchandising responsibility is rapidly drawing to a close and sellers are beginning to recognize that it is unwise to rely solely on an expanding market to move their goods profitably. There is a constantly-increasing number of competitive offerings in most lines today. As competition develops and buyers become more familiar with competitive offerings, the market becomes increasingly sophisticated. Therefore, the seller either must adjust more precisely to demand or face the prospect of splitting the market into progressively smaller shares, all of this at the risk of being driven completely out of the market. Brazilians are still going to buy. The question is rapidly becoming *what* they are going to buy and from whom.

INCOME

The favorable rate of growth in Brazilian income attests to the country's rapid industrialization and development. In constant prices, Brazil enjoyed an 80 percent increase in Gross National Product over the period 1950-1960.[2] During this same period, GNP in the United States was increasing about 38 percent in constant prices.[3]

During the period 1950-1958 it has been estimated that Brazil had an average yearly *real per capita* increase in GNP of 3.7 percent. This compares with the U.S. per capita increase of 2.9 percent for the same period.[4] Since 1958 there is reason to believe that per capita rate of growth in Brazil has declined somewhat. For example, the Brazilian Embassy,

[2] Calculated from estimate published by Instituto Brasilerio de Economia—Fundação Getulio Vargas.

[3] Calculated from figures in *Statistical Abstract of the United States,* 1961.

[4] Figures published in *Cooperation for Progress in Latin America,* Committee for Economic Development, April 1961.

Washington, D.C., supplies a per capita estimate of 2.7 percent increase in GNP for 1959. The situation is far from clear; preliminary estimates from the Fundação Getúlio Vargas do not show such a decline in rate of growth. It should be stressed that comparisons of this sort are of questionable merit because of serious doubts about the reliability of Brazilian estimates, in regard both to the absolute value of production and to the deflators used.

Brazil's classification of industrial origin of product and income is sufficiently different from that employed by the United States to make complete comparisons difficult. However, it is of interest to observe that in 1959 approximately 27 percent of Brazil's domestic income came from agriculture (which still accounts for approximately 60 percent of Brazil's employment). Less than 4 percent of the United States' national income came from agriculture in the same year. In Brazil, in 1959, manufacturing accounted for approximately 25 percent of domestic income, and in the United States about 30 percent. From the standpoint of origin of income Brazil is truly becoming an industrial nation.

Domestic Income

The distribution of domestic income by states is a measure which should be of importance to any person interested in marketing in Brazil. In Table 2 population figures were shown by states. Now, with income figures by states (Table 4) the two most important determinants of markets have been presented. A few comments about Table 4 are in order. First, the term "Domestic Income" (Renda Interna) is a commonly used measure in Brazilian national accounts. It is National Income net of the foreign sector. For purposes at hand it may be considered as synonymous with National Income. Personal income in Brazil is about 93 percent of Domestic Income. Second, the conversion of cruzeiro figures into dollar figures is always a risky business. There are several exchange rates operating in Brazil and there is ever present the question of which to choose. The rate used here has, I believe, the fewest shortcomings. The International Monetary Fund uses this same source for its conversions. Even assuming that the rate selected is satisfactory there is still the danger that one may misinterpret the dollar figures as being a measure of relative welfare between the United States and Brazil. It is not a good measure of such.

National accounts are shown in monetary terms. Many persons in Brazil are simply not in the economy in monetary terms. Although imputations are made for non-monetary income, it is literally impossible to produce accurate imputations. The conversions are made here solely as a convenience to the reader. Most Americans have absolutely no concept of the value of a cruzeiro (with the rate of inflation in Brazil, most

TABLE 4—DISTRIBUTION OF DOMESTIC INCOME BY
BRAZILIAN STATES, 1959

	Domestic Income (000,000) $ Cruzeiros[1]	Percent of Total	Per Capita Domestic Income $ Cruzeiros[2]	Per Capita Domestic Income $U. S.[3]	Bank Order Per Capita Income
Amazonas	12,967.6	0.9	15,061.1	74	10
Para.	17,342.0	1.2	12,334.3	61	12
Maranhao	16,550.4	1.2	8,329.3	41	19
Piaui	7,389.6	0.5	5,640.9	28	21
Ceara.	28,035.9	2.0	8,243.4	40	20
Rio Grande do Sul	12,412.5	0.9	10,378.3	51	17
Paraiba.	19,089.0	1.3	9,398.8	46	18
Pernambuco.	51,556.6	3.6	12,257.9	60	13
Alagoas	12,937.9	0.9	10,425.4	51	16
Sergipe.	8,846.8	0.6	11,733.2	58	14
Bahia.	62,617.2	4.4	10,685.5	52	15
Minas Gerais. . . .	145,809.0	10.2	16,639.2	82	8
Espirito Santo. . . .	15,568.9	1.1	15,919.1	78	9
Rio de Janeiro . . .	65,094.4	4.5	23,214.8	114	5
Guanabara	207,961.6	14.5	66,569.0	327	1
Parana	88,517.0	6.2	25,276.1	124	3
São Paulo	457,887.8	32.0	40,200.9	197	2
Santa Catarina. . .	37,227.5	2.6	18,447.7	91	7
Rio Grande do Sul.	128,793.7	9.0	25,135.4		
Mato Grosso	12,625.0	0.9	19,850.6	93	6
Goias.	22,245.7	1.6	12,866.2	63	11
Total	1,418,445	100.1	22,255.2	109	

[1] Source: Instituto Brasileiro de Economia—Fundação Getulio Vargas.
[2] Source: IBID, Reported in *Comercio Internacional,* Banco do Brasil, July–August, 1961.
[3] Converted at rate of 203.77 (Average end of month rate, Bolsa, Rio de Janeiro).

Brazilians share this confusion). The Bank of Brazil shows in its publications the major imports and exports of Brazil converted into United States dollars. Undoubtedly this is done in large part for the same reason as done here—convenience. However, the conversion is made with more justification because there is a comparison over time and the United States dollar is not considered, for all practical purposes, to depreciate in value.

Apropos of the present writing, the great disparity in the per capita income figures of the various states stands out. On an average, persons in the state with the highest per capita income (Guanabara) receive over ten times the income of persons in the state ranked last in this respect (Piaui). In the United States for the same year per capita income in Delaware, the state with the highest per capita figure, was two and a half times higher than per capita income in Mississippi, the perennial tailender in this regard.[5]

Distribution

There is universal agreement that the distribution of income among persons and families in Brazil, irrespective of geographic location, is extremely uneven. The extent of this inequality is virtually impossible to ascertain from available statistics. There are no data for Brazil comparable to figures for the distribution of income among United States families. Statistics are published showing the amounts of income declared for income tax purposes by number of persons, by income class. Such figures are *worthless for estimating the degree of inequality* in the distribution of income. For one thing, no confidence can be placed in the reliability of the data. Any similarity between amount of income declared and amount received is likely to be coincidental—certainly it is unintentional. But, of even greater importance, the income figures reflect the declared income of only 1 percent of Brazil's population.

On the basis of persons and families not included in the income tax tabulations there is an indication that in 1949, 99 percent of the population was living in family units in which the income earner received less than the cruzeiro equivalent of $450 of gross income. Somewhat surprisingly, this estimate may not be too far from the actual situation. Computations in Table 4 lead one to the conclusion that average per capita income in that year was barely over the equivalent of $100 and family income was slightly in excess of $500.

To whatever extent it exists, the inequality in the distribution of income is not lessened by the Brazilian tax structure. Income tax rates are relatively low and there are many exclusions (e.g., journalists and professors pay no income taxes, a practice which the United States might do well to emulate). In 1960 income taxes accounted for less than 32 percent of the total federal tax revenue. In the same year income taxes were the source of 85 percent of federal revenues in the United States. In Brazil consumption taxes brought in one-third more federal revenue than income taxes.

A strong middle class is a necessity for high level mass marketing. In Brazil such a class is starting to emerge in force. That it is able to do so should provoke some wonder. Not only is there great inequality in the distribution of income but, as mentioned before, the bulk of the population is illiterate and only a small portion of it is in urban industrial employment. Thus the middle class is not large. In addition, its emerging strength is hampered by continuing and severe inflation.

[5] *Statistical Abstract of the United States,* 1960.

Sales Potentials

From the measures of Brazilian population and income presented thus far it is possible to construct an index of sales potential that should have validity for describing the relative geographical opportunity to sell consumer goods in general. Table 5 shows such an index for Brazil by the country's respective states. For ease of exposition, the index is expressed in a manner showing the percent that each state has of the total opportunity to sell consumer goods in Brazil. It is worthwhile to note the great amount of variance among the states in regard to potential. Combining

TABLE 5—TWO FACTOR GENERAL INDEX OF POTENTIAL (BY STATES)

State	(1) Percent of Total Population (1960 Preliminary Estimate[1])	(2) Percent of Total Domestic Income 1959[1]	(3) Sum of Factors (1) (2)	(4) Index of Potential (Percent) (3) (2)
Amazonas	1.0	0.9	1.9	.95
Para	2.2	1.2	3.4	1.70
Maranhao	3.6	1.2	4.8	2.40
Piaui	1.8	0.5	2.3	1.15
Ceara	4.8	2.0	6.8	3.40
Rio Grande do Norte	1.7	0.9	2.6	1.30
Paraiba	2.9	1.3	4.2	2.10
Pernambuco	5.9	0.9	2.7	1.35
Alagoas	1.8	0.9	2.7	1.35
Sergipe	1.1	0.6	1.7	.85
Bahia	8.6	4.4	13.0	6.50
Minas Gerais	13.5	10.2	23.7	11.85
Espirito Santo	1.7	1.1	2.8	1.40
Rio de Janeiro	4.8	4.5	9.3	4.65
Guanabara	4.7	14.5	19.2	9.60
São Paulo	18.5	32.0	50.5	25.25
Parana	5.9	6.2	12.1	6.05
Santa Caterina	3.1	2.6	5.7	2.85
Rio Grande do Sul	7.8	9.0	16.8	8.40
Mato Grosso	1.4	0.9	2.3	1.15
Goias	2.8	1.6	4.4	2.20
Total	100.1	100.1		99.85

[1]Excluding Federal District (Brasilia) and Territories.

Sources: Conselho Nacional de Estatistica, (Instituto Brasileiro Geografica e Estatistica) and Instituto Brasileiro de Economia (Fundação Getulio Vargas).

these states according to the regions described earlier shows the striking dissimilarities that exist.

The North Central states (Amazonas, Para, Maranaho, Mato Grosso and Goias) have 8.4 percent of the potential. When one considers that this group of states has over two-thirds of the area of the country it becomes apparent that this region does not constitute a good market for most products. The three states of Amazonas, Para, and Mato Grosso have 52 percent of the total area of all states and yet have a combined potential of only 3.8 percent.

The North East region of eight states (Piaui, Ceara, Rio Grande do Norte, Paraiba, Pernambuco, Alagoas, Sergipe and Bahia) make a better showing in large part because of the presence in the area of the cities of Salvador and Recife. This region, encompassing approximately 15 percent of the total area, provides 20.4 percent of the total opportunity to sell. The region provides considerable potential which may be exploited by selective marketing techniques.

It is the South of Brazil which provides by far the greatest opportunity for sales. The states in this region (Espirito Santo, Minas Gerais, Rio de Janeiro, Guanabara, São Paulo, Parana, Santa Catarina, and Rio Grande do Sul) provide slightly over 70 percent of the potential market. São Paulo alone has over 26 percent in an area of about 3 percent of Brazil's total. Guanabara (City of Rio), which has only .02 percent of Brazil's total area, has 9.6 percent of the nation's potential. From any logical standpoint these are first-class markets. The other states in this region differ only in degree. This region with less than 20 percent of the total area, and comparatively good transportation covering it, is as close as one might come to defining *the* market in Brazil.

THREE FACTOR INDEX

As a general statement one should expect to be able to improve the above index by adding to population and income retail sales as a measure of willingness to buy. In Brazil this may not be the case. The most recent figures on retail sales (more correctly, sales of retail institutions) are from the census of 1950. It would be unwise to use such out-dated measures in a country where economic growth has been anything but uniformly distributed.

My own estimates of sales of retail institutions for the various states for the year 1959 are based upon information published by *Annuario Estatistico* concerning taxes on sales and consignments collected by each state. The sales and consignments tax is in effect a transaction or turnover tax. Since the goods may be transferred several times before being sold by the retailer to the consumer (as many as 16 times in some cases) the tax figures cannot simply be multiplied by the reciprocal of the tax percent in order to arrive at sales of retailers. The approach used here was to find the relationship which existed in 1950 between taxes on sales and consignments and sales of retail institutions for each state. The ratios derived were then adjusted for changes in the tax percent between 1950 and 1959 and the revised ratio applied to the tax figures for 1959. The resulting estimates of sales are shown in Table 6.

TABLE 6—ESTIMATED SALES OF RETAIL INSTITUTIONS BY STATES, 1959

State	Estimated Sales of Retail Institutions (CR $000,000)	Percent of Total
Amazonas	6,041	1.3
Para	3,803	0.8
Maranhao	3,600	0.8
Piaui	1,769	0.4
Ceara	4,883	1.1
Rio Grande do Sul	2,725	0.6
Paraiba	3,752	0.8
Pernambuco	14,852	3.3
Alagoas	5,698	1.3
Sergipe	1,351	0.3
Bahia	15,415	3.4
Minas Gerais	37,366	8.3
Espirito Santo	4,379	1.0
Rio de Janeiro	30,564	6.8
Guanabara	55,766	12.4
São Paulo	173,840	38.9
Parana	28,488	6.4
Santa Catarina	10,770	2.4
Rio Grande do Sul	40,900	9.1
Mato Grosso	1,041	0.2
Goias	1,177	0.3
Total		99.9

The implicit assumption is that any item sold has been transferred the same number of times in 1959 as in the earlier year. When recognized, such an assumption is troublesome. It is likely that there have been shifts in channels of distribution during that interval. However, these shifts could be offsetting in that, if more goods were sold through retail stores in 1959 than in 1950, this effect could have been counteracted by the wholesaler's decreasing in general importance in the sale of consumer goods. Although there are no data to support such a notion, both of these things may well have happened. As a partial check on the logic of the estimates, a comparison was made of the relationship between personal consumption expenditure and sales of retail stores in 1950 and the same relationship in 1959 using the estimated retail sales figures. In 1950, approximately 27 percent of personal consumption expenditures was made through retail stores. Using the writer's estimates, the relationship would rise to 35 percent in 1959. Such a change would be about what one would expect if there was a shift in importance from open markets, door-to-door selling, etc., to sales made in retail stores. This is all the defense of these estimates that the writer cares to make.

Additional implicit assumptions might be mentioned so that one may judge for himself how much confidence he chooses to place in the figures. One assumption is that there is approximately the same relative

TABLE 7—THREE FACTOR GENERAL INDEX OF POTENTIAL BY STATES (POPULATION, INCOME AND SALES OF RETAILERS)

State	(1) Percent of Total Population (1960 Pre- liminary Estimate)[1]	(2) Percent of Total Domestic Income, 1959[1]	(3) Percent of Sales of Retail Stores 1959	(4) Sum of Factors (1) (2) (3)	(5) Index of Potential (4) ÷ (3)
Amazonas	1.0	0.9	1.3	3.2	1.1
Para	2.2	1.2	0.8	4.2	1.4
Maranhao	3.6	1.2	0.8	5.6	1.9
Piaui	1.8	0.5	0.4	2.7	0.9
Ceara	4.8	2.0	1.1	7.9	2.6
Rio Grande do Norte	1.7	0.9	0.6	3.2	1.1
Paraiba	2.9	1.3	0.8	5.0	1.7
Pernambuco	5.9	3.6	3.3	12.8	4.3
Alagoas	1.8	0.9	1.3	4.0	1.3
Sergipe	1.1	0.6	0.3	2.0	0.7
Bahia	8.6	4.4	3.4	16.4	5.5
Minas Gerais	13.5	10.2	8.3	32.0	10.7
Espirito Santo	1.7	1.1	1.0	3.8	1.3
Rio de Janeiro	4.8	4.5	6.8	16.1	5.4
Guanabara	4.7	14.5	12.4	31.6	10.5
São Paulo	18.5	32.0	38.9	89.4	29.8
Parana	5.9	6.2	6.4	18.5	6.2
Santa Catarina	3.1	2.6	2.4	8.1	2.7
Rio Grande do Sul	7.8	9.0	9.1	25.9	8.6
Mato Grosso	1.4	0.9	0.2	2.5	0.8
Goias	2.8	1.6	0.3	4.7	1.6
Total	100.1	100.1	99.9		100.1

[1]Excluding Federal District (Brasilia) and Territories.

Sources: Conselho Nacional de Geografica e Estatistica and Instituto Brasileiro de Economia (Fundação Getulio Vargas).

error in tax reporting in 1959 that there was in 1950. Another is that errors in reporting are likely to be uniformly distributed among the states so that, percent-wise, similar errors exist. Despite the probable limitations on these estimates it may prove useful to combine them with the population and income figures for a multiple index which measures the three factors of greatest importance in determining potential for consumer goods as a class. This has been done in Table 7.

Table 8 presents a three factor multiple index of population, income

TABLE 8—THREE FACTOR GENERAL INDEX OF POTENTIAL BY STATES (POPULATION, INCOME AND COMMERCIAL ACTIVITY)

	(1) Percent of Total Population (1960 Preliminary Estimate)	(2) Percent of Total Domestic Income, 1959	(3) Percent of Commercial Activity	(4) Sum of Factors (1) (2) (3)	(5) Index of Potential (4) ÷ (3)
Amazonas	1.0	0.9	0.3	2.2	0.7
Para	2.2	1.2	0.5	3.9	1.3
Maranhao	3.6	1.2	0.5	5.3	1.7
Piaui	1.8	0.5	0.4	2.7	0.9
Ceara	4.8	2.0	0.9	7.7	2.6
Rio Grande do Norte	1.7	0.9	0.5	3.1	1.0
Paraiba	2.9	1.3	0.9	5.1	1.7
Pernambuco	5.9	3.6	2.7	12.2	4.1
Alagoas	1.8	0.9	0.8	3.3	1.2
Sergipe	1.1	0.6	0.2	1.9	0.6
Bahia	8.6	4.4	2.5	15.5	5.2
Minas Gerais	13.5	10.2	7.6	31.3	10.4
Espirito Santo	1.7	1.1	1.2	4.0	1.3
Rio de Janeiro	4.8	4.5	5.0	14.3	4.8
Guanabara	4.7	14.5	12.2	31.4	10.5
São Paulo	18.5	32.0	45.7	96.2	32.1
Parana	5.9	6.2	7.1	19.2	6.4
Santa Catarina	3.1	2.6	2.1	7.8	2.6
Rio Grande do Sul . .	7.8	9.0	8.3	25.1	8.4
Mato Grosso	1.4	0.9	0.1	2.4	0.8
Goias	2.8	1.6	0.2	4.6	1.5
Total	100.1	100.1	99.7		99.8

Note: Excludes Federal District (Brasilia) and Territories.

Sources: Computed from various publications of the following: Conselho Nacional de Estatistica (IBGE); Instituto Brasileiro de Economia (Fundação Getulio Vargas); Annuario Estatistica, 1960 (IBGE).

and commercial activity for Brazilian states. Commercial activity is measured by the reported collection of sales and consignment tax by states. These figures have been adjusted to reflect differences in tax rates and are expressed as a percent of all states. The term "commercial activity" is used because this tax reflects sales and consignments at all levels in the channel of distribution. Although the basic data used for construction of this estimate are the same as those used for the estimate of retail sales, the scope is greater for commercial activity because it includes distribution activities of manufacturers and wholesalers as well as retailers.

Estimates of Potential

Certain comments concerning the potential figures shown thus far are appropriate. The fact that the estimates of potential are calculated by states might lead to some misinterpretation. In the first place, most of the market opportunity is centered in or around large central cities. It is unusual to find potential distributed throughout a state with any degree of uniformity. Second, the figures do not reflect the tremendous differences in area among the various states. The largest state (Amazona) is 1,000 times as large in area as the smallest (Guanabara). For one not acquainted with Brazil, a simple ranking of potential by states might be misleading. The question arises as to what extent a particular state is a higher quality market because of concentration of vital market factors and to what extent it ranks higher solely because of sheer size. Conversely, do certain states lose in ranking when consideration is given to their sizes?

   Table 9 shows the potential figures from Table 8 (using commercial activity) with the factor of size introduced. By dividing percent of total potential by percent of total area for each state it is possible to come up with a comparison of states which reflects area differences. For want of something better to call this measure, it is given the name of "quality index of area potential." In general it is found that those states which are lacking in potential rate even more poorly when the factor of area is introduced. There are some notable exceptions, however. Paraiba, Pernambuco, Alagoas, and Sergipe, all low in potential relative to other states, improve relatively as markets when their diminutiveness is brought to attention. The real quality of the São Paulo market is emphasized by its small area relative to potential. The state of Guanabara (actually the city of Rio de Janeiro) shows the astounding amount of opportunity embodied in such a small area.

   A considerable amount of attention has been devoted to sales potentials here. This has been done in part because presentation of sales potentials is perhaps the best way to describe markets in summary fashion.

In addition, a somewhat lengthy presentation is warranted because apparently the concept of sales potentials is one which has not received formal consideration by Brazilians. As in the United States, it has much to recommend its use in Brazil.

TABLE 9—INDEX OF POTENTIAL CONSIDERING AREA

State	(1) Percent of Total Area	(2) Percent of Potential (From Table)	(3) Quality Index of Area Potential (2) (1)
Amazonas	20.00	0.7	3.5
Para	16.04	1.3	8.1
Maranhao	4.26	1.7	39.7
Piaui	3.24	0.9	27.8
Ceara	1.90	2.6	136.8
Rio Grande do Norte	0.68	1.0	147.0
Paraiba	0.72	1.7	236.1
Pernambuco	1.26	4.1	325.4
Alagoas	0.36	1.2	333.3
Sergipe	0.29	0.6	206.9
Bahia	7.24	5.2	71.8
Minas Gerais	7.47	10.4	139.2
Espirito Santo	0.50	1.3	260.0
Rio de Janeiro	0.55	4.8	872.7
Guanabara	0.02	10.5	52,500.0
São Paulo	3.17	32.1	1,012.6
Parana	2.58	6.4	248.0
Santa Catarina	1.21	2.6	214.6
Rio Grande do Sul	3.63	8.4	231.4
Mato Grosso	16.19	0.8	4.9
Goias	7.92	1.5	18.9

15.

PROBLEMS PECULIAR TO EXPORT
SALES FORECASTING*

Henry Anderson

A FIRM'S demand forecast is usually arrived at in two steps. The first of these is concerned with an estimate of industry demand, and the second with the determination of the company's market share. Both phases of the analysis bring the export-sales forecaster face to face with problems unknown in the domestic field.

PROBLEMS IN ESTIMATING INDUSTRY DEMAND

Necessity to Deal with Different Forms of Economic Life

The foreign-sales forecaster must deal with a plurality of national markets in contrast with the domestic analyst's single one. More than that—he may have to employ a plurality of techniques, depending on the diversity of the societies at issue, for political, social, and economic conditions differ from one country to another.

After a fashion, each nation represents a distinct socio-economic organism, which follows its own peculiar causal laws and whose character must be carefully considered in the construction and use of forecasting formulas. Specifically, the following four problems are encountered:

(1) *The quality of given key factors may vary between countries.* That is, conventional market indicators may differ internationally in respect to their predictive efficiency, their measurability, and so forth. This will often preclude the use of an identical forecasting formula for all national markets.

National income, for example, is likely to have considerable estimating power in poor countries; but in rich societies its influence tends to be partially neutralized by a high level of liquid wealth and easy credit arrangements. Hence, a broader formula, which includes these factors,

* Henry Anderson, "Problems Peculiar to Export Sales Forecasting," *Journal of Marketing*, Vol. 24, No. 4 (April, 1960), a publication of the American Marketing Association, pp. 39–42. Reprinted by permission.

may have to be used to estimate market potentials in the more developed nations.

Again, many economically backward societies do not compile satisfactory aggregate-income series.[1] Therefore, analysts may have to resort to the use of suitable substitute series, such as export income.

(2) *Intercountry differences may exist in respect to the time periods marked by normal sales experience.* This raises a methodological problem for forecasters.

Predictive formulas, to be reasonably durable, should be derived from marketing experience free from major disturbances—mirroring the more stable forces at work in the economy. Analysts thus face a dilemma. They may base the estimating expressions for all countries at issue on data drawn from one and the same period. But in the case of some nations that may mean reliance on questionable observations. Alternatively, different periods may be used for different countries as suggested by considerations of normality. But that procedure has the disadvantage of increasing the role played by personal judgment in forecasting.

(3) *The character of the relationship between a given indicator and a given market may lack international uniformity.* The choice of different mathematical functions for the description of sales relations in different nations might thus be justified in certain circumstances.

(4) *The durability of given forecasting formulas may be expected to vary internationally* (even if an identical expression is used for the various countries at issue). It is likely to be low for nations undergoing rapid social and economic change, and high for stagnant socieites. This signifies that the question of indicator selection and weighting must be reopened more frequently in the case of some nations than in the case of others.

Inadequate Data

Many nations as yet lack the means for the periodic determination of aggregate income and other strategic variables reflecting mass behavior. But the export-sales forecaster cannot limit his attention to "statistically developed" countries and thus will generally have to work with inadequate information.

This brings him face to face with a new dilemma. He will be tempted to rely heavily on subjective or mechanical forecasting methods, but these techniques can be shown to be of very doubtful value in the international field. Forecasting on the basis of adequate causal analysis is likely to be more efficient, but in turn also requires more information.

[1] See, for instance, *Statistics of National Income and Expenditure,* Statistical Papers, Series H, No. 5. This United Nations report contains defective income series for Bolivia, Brazil, Colombia, and a host of other countries.

PROBLEMS IN ESTIMATING COMPANY DEMAND

Translating industry demand in a foreign country into an individual American exporter's share is a more complex process than the analogous operation in the domestic field. This is because export sales are importantly affected by several factors that are of little or no consequence in domestic analysis, namely: internal supply possibilities in the foreign countries under consideration or national competition; export supply possibilities in nations other than the United States or international competition; and trade control.

Problem of Heterogeneous Competition

In domestic-sales estimation, foreign competitors of the forecasting firm may be either ignored or lumped together with domestic rivals. In export-sales forecasting, by contrast, a careful distinction must usually be made between national, international, and American competitors of the estimating company. The reason for this is that the three groups of rivals are differently affected by changes in the commercial policies and economic circumstances of the trading countries and may be differently organized.

Their conduct will differ accordingly. A tariff increase in an importing country, for instance, will tend to strengthen the position of national enterprises. Sheltered competition of this kind is peculiar to international trade. Its analysis imposes a task upon the export-sales forecaster which has no exact analogue in the domestic field.

Once national competitors of the forecasting company have been allowed for, the resulting import-demand estimate must be translated into the market share available to American sellers in accordance with a reasonable hypothesis concerning the behavior of rival exporters located outside the United States. The analytical task involved is rendered very difficult by the fact that the strength of a firm's foreign competitors, unlike that of its American rivals, not only depends on factors such as managerial efficiency, special entrepreneurial advantages, and financial resources, but also on international differences in factor costs and in trade policies. This introduces uncertainties into foreign-sales estimation that are absent from the domestic sphere.

The significance that international competition may have for American exporters is demonstrated in Table 1. If it is assumed that, in general, only new cars are imported into Ecuador—a sound hypothesis—the data reflect the number of cars shipped to the Republic in different years.

TABLE 1—PASSENGER AUTOMOBILES IN ECUADOR (CLASSIFIED BY YEAR OF DESIGN)[a]

	1946	1947	1948	1949	1950	1951	1952	1953	1954	1955	1956
Total number of cars in each annual class	242	382	273	400	345	374	367	459	418	650	385
% of American cars	97.1	95.8	90.8	97.2	95.4	96.3	94.8	92.4	79.7	61.8	56.1
% of Fiats	—	—	0.7	—	0.6	0.3	0.5	1.3	1.4	7.4	12.5
% of Volkswagens	—	—	—	—	0.3	—	1.4	0.6	4.5	7.1	9.1

[a]Compiled from unpublished records on file with the Sección de Estadísticas Sociales y del Trabajo, Ministeria de Economia, Quito, Ecuador.

TABLE 2—ECUADOREAN IMPORTS OF WASHING MACHINES (1948 TO 1957)[a]

	1948	1949	1950	1951	1952	1953	1956	1957
Total quantum (in kilograms)	22,823	32,668	6,408	16,169	15,432	17,518	40,126	25,339
% of American machines	97.8	89.4	90.3	86.2	82.2	95.9	85.2	85.1
% of Canadian machines	2.0	1.6	8.8	8.0	2.2	2.4	—	2.1
% of British machines	—	—	—	—	10.4	—	10.7	9.8
% of German machines	—	—	—	—	6.0	1.6	0.9	2.6

[a]Compiled from unpublished records on file with the Sección de Estadísticas Sociales y del Trabajo, Ministeria de Economia, Quito, Ecuador.

The rapid shift away from American models beginning in 1954 is surprising and merits careful analysis. The forecaster must seek to identify the underlying causes (economic recovery of Germany and Italy, etc.) and to measure their effects on American export to opportunities if he wishes to make sophisticated predictions of the kind of competition that U.S. sellers will face in coming years.

Another example of foreign competition in export markets is provided in Table 2. These data also show some displacement of the American export from the foreign market, but the share captured by foreign rivals in this case is less startling than the share taken over in the preceding situation. Again, sound forecasting procedure requires that the analyst go behind the statistical picture and seek to uncover the causes of the observed trend and their typical mode of operation.

Unlike protected local rivals, international competitors are ubiquitous and make their presence felt in all export markets. Empirical evidence for this fact can be found in the information supplied by Tables 3 and 4. It is thus seen that the competitive development observed in Ecuadorean import patterns of recent years is essentially paralleled by Swiss and in fact world sales experience.

An estimate of American participation in a foreign market is not the final goal of export-market analysis. It is an intermediate result which must be converted in one way or another into the forecasting company's market share. This final translation, however, does not present a problem peculiar to international sales estimation. It is a familiar operation in domestic forecasting.

It is possible to merge the analysis of the estimating firm's foreign rivals with that of its American competitors and to determine the company's export-market share in a single step rather than in two. But such

TABLE 3—SWISS IMPORTS OF PASSENGER CARS (IN SPECIFIED YEARS)[a]

	1953	1955	1956	1957
Total number of units	37,093	51,907	50,125	53,409
% of German cars	51.5	54.2	58.8	58.9
% of French cars	11.8	11.6	17.9	17.1
% of Italian cars	11.2	11.4	12.8	9.7
% of British cars	11.1	11.1	5.6	7.5
% of American cars	9.1	8.7	4.8	6.6
% of Canadian cars	3.6	0.1	0.1	0.2

[a]Based on information contained in *Global Automotive Market Survey and World Motor Census,* an annual study prepared by The American Automobile and published by McGraw-Hill International Corporation.

TABLE 4—VEHICLE EXPORTS OF THE "BIG SIX" (1953 TO 1957)[a]

	1953	1954	1955	1956	1957
Total number of units	1,060,122	1,379,413	1,596,175	1,585,332	1,858,716
British % share	39.0	35.7	33.3	29.0	29.6
U. S. % share	27.2	29.1	26.8	23.3	18.0
German % share	16.7	21.6	23.9	30.6	31.4
French % share	9.8	9.6	10.1	11.1	13.5
Italian % share	8.0	3.2	4.7	4.8	6.4
Canadian % share	4.3	0.8	1.2	1.2	1.1

[a] Based on information contained in *Global Automotive Market Survey and World Motor Census,* an annual study prepared by The American Automobile and published by McGraw-Hill International Corporation.

a procedure means slurring over those changes in the relative strength of non-American over American competitors that result from causes peculiar to the international scene.

Treating the two groups of competitors separately makes it possible to take account of the competitive implications of government policy and economic development in foreign countries, as well as of factors familiar in domestic market analysis—sales promotion, distribution management, and the like.

Problem Presented by Trade Control

International sales opportunities are more susceptible to bureaucratic interference than are domestic markets. In fact, that is one of the main reasons why the forecasting firm's export-sales estimates cannot safely be derived in a single analytical step from the relevant industry forecasts— why the company's national, international, and American competitors should as a rule be dealt with separately.

Changes in trade policy may narrow or widen the market that is available to the estimating company in a given foreign country. Foreign-sales forecasting thus cannot be very reliable without some plausible assumptions concerning the regulatory situation likely to prevail during the period at issue.

16.

FORECASTING SALES IN UNDERDEVELOPED COUNTRIES*

William Copulsky

PETER DRUCKER has called attention to the neglect of marketing in underdeveloped countries, in favor of the more "glamorous" fields of manufacturing and construction.[1] The industrial aspects have been highlighted, even though marketing holds the key to success or failure.

Poor planning—or lack of planning—often has resulted from failure to understand or to consider marketing problems. But it is unfortunate that a lack of coordination between marketing and production should hamper development where resources are limited and where every effort should be devoted to obtaining optimum use of capital, manpower, land, and energy.

The proper use of marketing-research techniques can reduce the differences between a country's productive capacity and the demand for its production. Of course, the techniques must be tailored especially to structural changes in markets.

Failure to pay greater attention to marketing problems in underdeveloped countries may be responsible in some part for unnecessary overexpansion, misguided protectionism, and high-cost plants, all of which result in reduced markets. Not all underdeveloped countries have suffered; but closer attention must be given to the relationship of marketing development to industrial development of productive facilities.

FIVE PHASES OF ECONOMIC DEVELOPMENT

In the pre-industrial or commercial phase of economic development characterizing much of Africa, and parts of Latin America and Southeast Asia, there is no elaborate transformation of materials, and almost no use of machines or specialized employees. However, there are transportation, commerce, and an exchange system.

In the next phase—the primary manufacturing phase—resources for

* William Copulsky, "Forecasting Sales in Underdeveloped Countries" *Journal of Marketing*, Vol. 24, No. 1 (July 1959), a publication of the American Marketing Association, pp. 36-40. Reprinted by permission.

[1] Peter F. Drucker, "Marketing & Economic Development," JOURNAL OF MARKETING, Vol. 21 (January, 1958), pp. 252-259.

exports are developed. These involve the processing of metal ores and agricultural products, such as sugar. Examples of other products processed are: rubber in Indonesia and Malaya, sisal in Tanganyika, minerals in northern Rhodesia, and oil refineries in the Persian Gulf.

The third phase of economic development involves production of such non-durable and semi-durable consumer finished goods as paints, drugs, and textiles. Such products usually can be made on a relatively small scale, and require low investment in relation to output. This encourages local manufacture, although initially many materials must be imported. Others are purchased from the developers of the local mineral and agricultural resources just referred to.

In the Belgian Congo, for example, the manufacture of sulfuric acid, powder, and explosives has been initiated to supply materials for the exploitation of mineral resources, as well as the manufacture of such finished goods as soap.

In the fourth phase, as exists today in the Union of South Africa and Latin America, the production of capital goods and consumer-durable goods is initiated—including such products as automobiles, refrigerators, and machinery. These goods create markets for both locally developed agricultural and mineral resources and their derivatives, and the products of the already established consumer goods industries. Automobiles, for example, require textiles, paints, and other products that are sold to consumers as well as to industrial users. In this phase of the economy, manufacturing shifts increasingly from finished non-durable and semi-durable consumer goods to capital goods and consumer-durable goods and their related intermediates.

At first, production in underdeveloped areas is smaller in relation to the total economy than in industrial countries, because more raw materials such as metal ores are exported in relatively unprocessed form, and because secondary manufacturing is often too small to support integration. Tires, for example, can be made locally on a fraction of the scale required to make synthetic rubber.

In the final phase, as the country passes out of the "underdeveloped" status, exports of manufactured products become significant. Exports of manufactured products from underdeveloped countries rarely reach significant volume because: (1) industry is growing rapidly elsewhere; (2) freight rates are rising faster than prices of manufactured products; and (3) underdeveloped countries tend to have higher costs than those prevailing at world levels.

PROBLEMS IN FORECASTING

Underdeveloped countries require new attitudes toward marketing research. In the highly industrialized countries, marketing research can discover or observe specific sales opportunities or marketing channels amidst the complex structure of known needs and requirements. But in underdeveloped countries, where change and progress are much more rapid, marketing research must probe more deeply into underlying economic structures. Here the marketing researcher must combine his commercial know-how with a broad knowledge of basic economic facts and theory.

Marketing research in underdeveloped countries cannot easily discover or observe specific sales possibilities or marketing channels. The marketing requirements of the underdeveloped country are complex and not easily accessible to survey. The task is to discover, and perhaps to define for the first time, the most urgent requirements of the developing economy.

In underdeveloped countries, statistical data are unreliable or completely lacking. Trends are often not observable, nor are there many identifiable historical patterns. Moreover, the fast growth of these economies requires large extrapolations in forecasting, making accurate predictions difficult.

Historical Analogy

When estimating demand, useful comparisons may at times be drawn with countries at similar past development stages and income levels. But this must be done with great care, to take into account a variety of other influencing patterns such as climate and traditional consumption patterns.

In many of the less developed countries, markets may be even smaller than would be thought from the low figures of per capita income. Rarely is the market homogeneous and continuous due to natural barriers, lack of transport, and communication.

Colombia, for example, has four major population centers, poorly connected by ground transportation, and isolated from each other by high mountains. Each of its four major cities has a different climate, population makeup, dialect, and mode of living.

A special condition that should be considered in countries such as Libya and Indonesia is the long coast line which offers easy access to foreign competition.

Disposable Real Income

In rapidly developing countries, historical patterns are easily broken by changes in tastes and variations in relative production costs.

Taking such possible structural changes into account, consumer-goods demand might be projected on the basis of disposable real income. But the productive process utilizes considerable quantities of intermediate goods for which demand is affected only indirectly by changes in real income. Some intermediate goods are very closely linked with final consumer demand such as pulp, cotton, and wool, and to a lesser extent leather, rubber, and wood.

Analysis becomes even more complex, and structural changes in the market more important to anticipate, where multiple uses predominate, as with industrial chemical products. For instance, the demand for caustic soda—a basic chemical building block which is sold to a variety of industries (rayon, paper, textiles, cotton, pharmaceuticals, and construction)—is affected not only by the growth of industrial production, but also by changes in the structure of production.

Input-Output Theory

One applicable forecasting technique, although to be used with caution, is the input-output technique originated by Leontieff.[2] The amount of data required is large and collection costly. Also, most input-output data are static; only one year or at most a few years of old data are available. However, in rapidly developing economies, dynamic input-output data would be essential to show such structural changes, such as movements in relative prices and technological innovations.

The input-output technique was applied to Colombia in a study using otherwise unpublished 1953 Colombian industrial census data in a 16-category input-output table. An International Cooperation Administration manual specifically covers the input-output technique as applied to underdeveloped countries.[3]

FACTORS TO BE CONSIDERED IN FORECASTING

Rate of Industrial Progress

In underdeveloped countries, progress is sporadic, sometimes explosive. Initiation of secondary manufacturing requires the creation of supply

[2] W. Leontieff, *Structure of the American Economy* (New York: Oxford University Press), 1951; Hollis B. Chenery, Paul G. Clark, and Vera Caopinna, *The Structure and Growth of the Italian Economy* (Rome: Mutual Security Agency, U.S. Government), 1953.

[3] Council for Economic and Industry Research, *How to Select Dynamic Industrial Projects* (Washington: Office of Industrial Resources International Cooperation Administration), 1957; *Manual of Industrial Development with Special Application to Latin America* (Washington: Foreign Operations Administration), 1955.

industries, resulting in a burst of activity that tends to quiet down when production becomes regular. A current example is the consumer-durable goods industry of Brazil. Production of household refrigerators went from 85,000 in 1954 to about 200,000 in 1958; washing machines from 36,000 in 1956 to 75,000 in 1958; and motor vehicles from 14,000 assembled in 1956 to 60,000 assembled in 1958.[4]

Obstacles to smooth industrialization are many: social problems, lack of transport facilities, lack of energy, and time needed to build and start up plants. Wars and depressions also affect local industry. World War I provided the first major impetus to industrialization in Brazil when imports were cut off. Industrial output rose 45 per cent from 1931 to 1934, years of depression. During World War II, Brazilian industrial output increased five-fold.[5]

Size of the Economy

Underdeveloped countries may be arbitrarily classified as "large" that have a Gross National Product greater than 3 per cent of the United States GNP, and as "small" with a GNP under 3 per cent.

The GNP level seems to divide into two distinct groups. The "large" countries probably have reached the stage where production of capital goods and consumer-durable goods is beginning to be significant. In the "small" countries, it is doubtful that this will occur in the foreseeable future; and industry in these countries will concentrate on resources development, and finished non-durable and semi-durable consumer goods. In these "small" countries, such operations can probably be economical on a scale commensurate with the size of their markets. But in the "large" countries, markets are large enough to justify both capital and consumer durables as well as supplier industries.

Cost and Price Relationship

In the initial phases of industrialization costs are high as the result of the small scale of operations. High tariffs or other barriers are required to protect these new industries. As markets expand, however, relative costs tend to decrease. Eventually a closer relationship to world prices ob-

[4] National Foreign Trade Council, *Noticias*, Vol. 14, No. 4 (Jan. 28, 1958), p. 6; American Chamber of Commerce for Brazil, *Information Bulletin*, No. 25 (December 16, 1957), p. 5.

[5] George Wythe, Royce A. Wight, and Harold M. Midkiff, *Brazil* (New York: The Twentieth Century Fund), 1949, *Study of Latin American Countries*, Senate Report No. 1082, Interim Report of the Committee on Banking and Currency, 83rd Congress, 2nd Session (Washington: U.S. Govt. Printing Office), March 16, 1954.

tains. Such a condition is developing today in such areas as Latin America and the Union of South Africa.

Undue tariff protection for high-cost local activities retards industrialization. In Egypt a burden is laid on small industries using locally produced chemicals and metals because these protected industries must use high-cost domestic raw materials, fuel, and power.

Costs related to world levels will be high in industries requiring large amounts of capital, where size of plant is comparatively small and where materials costs are high due to high local production costs, the necessity to import, or because of small volumes of production. "Cheap" labor is usually balanced out by lower productivity.

Know-How

Local manufacturing requires technological, managerial, entrepreneurial, and marketing skills and knowledge; and often these skills may have to be imported.

In addition, countries must invest in health, education, and training of workers for effective industrial progress, as well as in physical plant. Without knowhow and competent people, progress cannot be made.

EXAMPLE OF DEVELOPMENT OF CHEMICAL MARKETS

The parallel development of markets and industrial capacity can be illustrated by the chemical industry in underdeveloped countries.

The country passes from the pre-industrial or commercial phase to the manufacturing phase of mineral and agricultural resource development. Industrial inorganic chemicals such as acids and alkalies are then the main requirement, usually converted from local minerals by use of power and fuel. Inorganic chemicals, needed by industries exporting processed mineral and agricultural products, tend to sell in large volume at low prices. Therefore, heavy freight costs encourage early growth of local manufacture of inorganic chemicals.

In the next phase of economic development, the production of non-durable and semi-durable consumer finished goods requires both industrial inorganic and organic carbon compounds. These finished goods may be chemical in nature, such as paints and drugs, or may use chemicals, such as dyes for textiles. In any case these organic chemicals generally are unchanged in chemical structure; they are products of petroleum, natural gas, coal, farm products, and inorganic chemicals.

Finished chemical products for consumers, and chemicals for finished consumer goods—such as pharmaceuticals, dyes, and paints—usually can be made on a small scale, with low investment and high output value. This encourages early growth of local manufacture of such products. However, this manufacturing is usually not large enough to support the production of the low-cost bulk organic chemical intermediates required. On the other hand, the inorganic chemical raw materials required normally are available because local manufacturing of these materials has been developed in connection with the development of resources.

Finally, in the "secondary" manufacturing phase of capital goods and consumer-durable goods—that is, machines, automobiles, refrigerators, etc. —large amounts of low-cost bulk organic chemicals are required. For example, automobiles need plastics made from organic chemicals for molded parts such as tail lights, exterior finish, safety-glass interlayer, and tires. By this time raw-material resources for low-cost bulk organic chemicals have been developed: steel mills with coking by-products, natural gas, and petroleum refineries.

Realistic forecasting then becomes possible, when it is understood what type of demand is created for the chemical industry.

II

THE STRATEGY OF
GLOBAL MARKETING

PRODUCT

17.

WHY PRODUCTS FLOURISH HERE, FIZZLE THERE*

Montrose Sommers and
Jerome Kernan

OF the many forces that bear on buying decisions culture is perhaps the one most often taken for granted. Cultural values typically come in dead last in the parade of exhortations about economic variables, social class, buyers' psyches, and so on. This attitude probably stems from a common misconception regarding the relevance of culture to marketing, the consequence of which is almost always lost sales opportunities.

New products succeed; old products maintain entrenched market positions; promotional campaigns for diet foods, soft drinks, or kitchen appliances stand or fall in direct relation to how well marketers create products and product information which are meaningful and persuasive in the eyes of those who comprise markets. While it can always be said that consumers are individuals with different needs, motivations, or desires, it is also axiomatic that individuals within a culture generally rely on basic hard-core values for all types of decisions—those dealing with consumption as well as others.

This common core of values is reflected in this country in "the American way of life." Part of this way of life results in a characteristic approach to the evaluation of goods and services as well as the product information that supports them. For the marketing manager, a knowledge of this approach and its role in the consumer's evaluation of products and product claims is essential. It helps him to decipher the seemingly random success experience of both new and established products in this country. Further, the ability to compare the characteristics of a number of national markets results in guidelines for adapting domestic marketing strategies to other countries. It is such adaptations that facilitate successful overseas market expansion.

What are the value orientations that underlie characteristic market

* Reprinted by permission from the *Columbia Journal of World Business*, Vol. 11, No. 2 (March-April 1967), Graduate School of Business, Columbia University, pp. 89-97.

behavior? Talcott Parsons[1] and Seymour Martin Lipset[2] isolated six categories to help identify the relevant values. To these authors cultural patterns can be distinguished by the degree to which people: (1) are either egalitarian or elitist; (2) are prone to lay stress on accomplishment or inherited attributes; (3) expect material or nonmaterial rewards; (4) evaluate individuals or products in terms of objective norms or subjective standards; (5) focus on the distinctiveness of the parts (intensiveness) rather than the general characteristics of the whole (extensiveness); and (6) are oriented toward personal rather than group gain.

IF THE PAIR FITS

Where do different cultures find themselves with respect to these paired attributes? Citizens of the U.S. for the most part share the attributes described by the first term of the paired groups discussed above and listed in Table 1 below. In the United States people are encouraged to

TABLE 1—ESTIMATES OF RANKINGS[a] OF COUNTRIES
ACCORDING TO STRENGTH OF THE SIX PATTERN VARIABLES
(RANKED ACCORDING TO FIRST TERM IN EACH PAIR)

Pattern Variable	United States	Australia	Canada	Britain
Equal—Elite	2	1	3	4
Performance—Quality	1	2.5	2.5	4
Material—Nonmaterial	1	3	2	4
Objective—Subjective	1	3	2	4
Intensive—Extensive	1	2.5	2.5	4
Individual—Collective	1	3	2	4

[a] Five of the pattern variable rankings are adopted from Lipset, *op. cit.*, p. 521; the sixth (material-nonmaterial) is from Parsons, *op. cit.*, pp. 101-112.

improve their social position. They can expect: (1) to receive, within limits, recognition for their activities; (2) to be rewarded with material perquisites; (3) to be viewed objectively—what you can do—rather than subjectively—who you are; (4) to be judged in terms of those specific activities pertinent to the situation; and (5) to make evaluations in terms of personal gain. This does not mean that there are no elitist, qualitative, nonmaterial, subjective, extensive or collective values in American so-

[1] Talcott Parsons, *The Social System* (New York: The Free Press of Glencoe, 1964), pp. 101-112.
[2] Seymour Lipset, "The Value Patterns of Democracy: A Case Study in Comparative Values," *American Sociological Review*, Vol. 28, August, 1963, pp. 515-531.

ciety. There very obviously are, but such traits cannot be called dominant in the sense that they are in the British system.

Although in Great Britain values are obviously in flux, the dominant ones are still elitist, qualitative, nonmaterial, subjective, extensive
and collective. The British system does not encourage the individual to
improve his social position; class structure is an acknowledged fact of
life. Recognition is very much bound up with the question of class or
category relationship—the right people or objects do the right things. The
rewards the system offers for appropriate activity, while they include
material perquisites, are to a very important degree positional or status
rewards which confer power or prestige rather than tangible gain. The
evaluation of an individual or an object is made not so much by an impersonal standard applied to specific activities or functions, but rather
by more personal or subjective standards which again vary with group,
category or class. Whereas Americans are more liable to apply an objective standard to a narrow range of activities or functions, the British
apply a more subjective standard across a broader range of activities.
Finally, the British tend to look at persons or objects less in terms of their
uniqueness and distinctiveness (less intensively) than do Americans.

Australia and Canada stand between these two extremes for most of
the paired variables. One exception is the Australian orientation toward
equality. Australians are even more concerned with questions of equality
and general worth than are Americans. It can be maintained that Australians, because of their overriding concern for equality, have value
orientations that are more closely allied with those of Americans and
that the orientations of Canadians generally parallel those of the British.

WHERE THE ACTION IS

In societies where performance, not origin, is key, a high premium is
placed on doing things. The members of such a society seek new activities.
In this sense, then, the reality of a contingency—that is, something that
must be acted upon—is more basic to the United States than to Great
Britain, where there is relatively little stress on action. Americans, for
example, will go to great lengths to consume leisure time. The profusion
of leisure-related products in the U.S. is an example of how this value
orientation influences the marketing system.

When this performance orientation is coupled with a predisposition
to be intensive—i.e., to perceive many separate and distinct needs to be
acted upon as well as a variety of ways in which these needs can be
served—the probability of accepting new contingencies as real is greater
than when an extensive value orientation prevails. Americans see more
separate and distinct activities plus more separate and distinct products

which can be used in their performance than do Canadians, Australians or Britons. Such a disposition supports the market for gadgets, the great array of household and kitchen appliances and accessories, as well as extras for autos, boats, and for almost any other standard item. Intensive evaluation results in specialization within activities and therefore in new products and services. This proliferation of activities is responsible for the long list of American "necessities" that are often viewed by others as frivolous and nonessential.

The pressing desire to solve problems appears most readily in a culture that has strong egalitarian, material and individual value orientations. In the U.S., the opportunity to perform is open to all. It is the superior performance of the individual that results in a superior reward. This kind of an orientation causes *contest mobility*, a situation where individuals compete for and win status and material rewards on the basis of performance. Superior performance in activities is facilitated by specialized products and services—the basic products, accessories and gadgets that are available in the American market.

Contest mobility applies to all and motivates people to search for new solutions. New problems are rapidly perceived, almost as challenges. In a world where performance is important, the more areas that one discovers need to be acted upon, the greater the opportunity to perform successfully. Real contingencies are conceived of as hurdles over which one must jump successfully, and possibly at an increasing rate, in order to achieve both improved status and material position.

The rewards for performance in any society can be increased status, material wealth, or both. Where an equalitarian value orientation is coupled with emphasis on individual performance, rewards tend to be material rather than positional in nature. In the United States, positional rewards are viewed as almost no rewards at all, whereas in Great Britain they are highly respected. Material goods facilitate problem solving and are therefore closely identified with performance. They are perhaps the most important symbols for communicating information about the activities of an individual and they symbolize wealth, position and competence.

In this light, then, we expect Americans (1) to accept or at least try new products and services, (2) to see where small tasks or activities can be successfully performed with specialized products, (3) to feel that everyone is entitled to acquire such products and services and (4) to feel that an individual's social worth will be significantly reflected in the products that he both owns and uses.

The British will not perceive problems and their solutions in the same way as do Americans. Relying more on status and quality, and being more elitist than egalitarian, the Briton lacks the American's contest mobility. His society places less emphasis on performance and therefore he is less disposed to recognize new contingencies as real. Old and established views and methods are more highly valued than the new. When the qualitative approach is joined to an extensive basis of evaluation—i.e., perceiving relatively few separate and distinct problems and solutions—the probability of accepting new contingencies is even further reduced. Thus while Americans view many special-purpose gadgets as necessary for the performance of specific jobs, Britons view the same products as perhaps useful but not particularly necessary because the jobs are not particularly pressing or necessary. At any rate, they are certainly not products which *all* people need, although they may be appropriate for some.

Since in Britain very frequently it is position not performance that results in rewards, the incentive for anything other than basic performance is partly removed and the desire to cope with new problems and to solve them successfully is not strong. Also, because of the emphasis on position, the ownership and use of products is not as infallible an indicator of a person's social role as it is in the United States. Status or position, while it can be recognized by the use of products and services, can also, and probably more easily, be recognized in nonmaterial factors such as family and education.

MATESHIP IN AUSTRALIA

In some ways the Australians are much like Americans and in others like the British, and the same observation can be made about the Canadians. Canadians are more likely to accept the existence of problems and the need for action than Australians because they place greater emphasis on material and objective values, although both countries score the same on performance orientation. And while the contest mobility theme is more limited in Canada than in the United States it is stronger in Canada than in Australia because of the latter's emphasis on egalitarianism. The attitude of the Australians to one another is described by the term "mateship," which is "the uncritical acceptance of recognized obligations to provide companionship and material or ego support as required."[3] The mateship concept implies that an action is acceptable as long as it is not carried to an extreme—the extreme being behavior and appearance that are better than average. This concept is illustrated by the statement[4]: "In England, the average man feels he is inferior; in America he feels superior; in Australia he feels equal." This concern for equality, when

[3] Ronald Taft and Kenneth F. Walker, "Australia," in Arnold M. Rose (ed.), *The Institutions of Advanced Societies* (Minneapolis: The University of Minnesota Press, 1958), pp. 144-145.
[4] Cited in Lipset, *op. cit.,* p. 322.

added to other variables such as nonmaterialism and a subject approach, tends to make Australians less aware of problems and their urgency than Canadians.

MINUTIA MINDERS

In countries where an intensive value orientation is strong, both people and products are scrutinized closely. Americans, for example, are most likely to notice small product differences—slight changes in style, design, coloring, packaging or instructions—and Britons are least likely. A person with a strong intensive orientation would comment: "But this is really different from the others," while a person with a strong extensive orientation would say: "But this is really the same as all the others."

In identifying product features, the relatively strong performance and objective orientation of the American leads him to ask: "What does it do?" or "What is it for?" The objective standards require specific information about performance—speed, precision, ease of operation or implementation, safety in use, etc. In Britain, the extensive value orientation disposes people to be less interested in these details and more concerned with overall classification. Those product features that are readily discernible to an American or Canadian are more likely to be ignored by an Australian or an Englishman, who tend to identify products and ascribe value to them in terms of the maker, the manufacturing process or the accepted use.

PROMOTION MUST ALSO CONFORM

The promotional information which supports products in culturally differentiated markets must also be individualized. The product claims made by promotional information can be thought of as including three components—the meaningful, the plausible and the verifiable. The cultural values of the market will strongly influence the kinds of topics that are meaningful. Similarly, they will control the types of product claims people are predisposed to entertain or consider plausible. Finally, they will influence the basis upon which claims can be rendered verifiable.

In introducing a product in the American market and making meaningful claims on its behalf, it is important to focus on the product in both descriptive and visual terms. The item should be appropriate for all Americans—a legitimate object of aspiration as well as an object that meets basic health and safety standards. At the same time, the product should enhance the individual so that the user will be recognized as influential, important, or as an authority because he appreciates the same functional product attributes as do other important or professional individuals.

Promoting the same product meaningfully in the British market calls for product claims that are based on how the product is related to traditionally performed and accepted tasks, products and materials. A product is not necessarily appropriate for all. The user does not gain more individual recognition but gains recognition as a particular type of person.

An illustration of the differences between American and British buying attitudes can be drawn from an experience of General Mills. The success of the Betty Crocker brand of cake mix in the United States can be attributed to the fact that the mix is designed so that any housewife can produce a "professional" or difficult type of cake that will win her the praise of her family, neighbors and friends. In Great Britain, the Betty Crocker brand (as well as a cheaper line) was introduced in 1959, was heavily promoted ($1,400,000 for both lines over four years), but was withdrawn by 1963. The failure of the program was attributed, in part, to the buying attitudes of the British housewife.

"Market observers here felt the product names might have played a part in their marketing failure. Angel cake and devil's food sounded too exotic for British housewives. And many housewives felt such expert-looking cakes as those on the Betty Crocker packs must be hard to make.

"Perhaps it was traditionalism that finally beat General Mills. The market leader, with 40 percent of the trade in this $10,000,000 field, is Stoddard & Hansforth, which sticks to simple products—its Viota brand of cake mixes features such old favorites as tea cakes, jam surprise, fruit cakes and cherry cakes."[5]

It is apparent from this that British and American housewives differ in their interpretations of what comprises a simple or an exotic product and of what it takes to be an expert or an authority.

BRITISH PRODUCT DESIGN LAGS

In contrasting British and American consumers, Boyd and Piercy comment that "attitudes and habits of many consumers even slow down the trends (toward Americanization) now under way"[6] and point out that a relative lack of desire for change, a willingness to put up with no small amount of inconvenience and conservative tastes still prevail. Such at-

[5] "General Mills Withdraws from British Market," *Advertising Age*, May 20, 1963, p. 4. Excerpted in John Fayerweather, *Inernational Marketing* (Englewood Cliffs, New Jersey: Prentice-Hall, Inc., 1965), p. 99.
[6] Harper Boyd and Ivan Piercy, "Retailing in Great Britain," *Journal of Marketing*, Vol. 27, January, 1963, p. 35.

titudes explain why British consumers think of American products in such terms as: "They're so novel . . . There's something for every occasion . . . What will Americans think of next?"[7] The result is that in clothing, furniture, chinaware, housewares and major and minor household appliances, British manufacturers have been noticeably deficient (relative to Americans) in product design.[8]

The British home is depicted as a private "castle" where nothing changes. "The middle-class (British) housewife is oriented more toward the traditional than the new in home furnishing. She regards the old styles as tried and trusted and, therefore, better than the new—the older the furniture, perhaps the better. Should it become necessary to replace it, she probably does so with the identical style and color."[9]

SAVING SOME FOR THE NEXT CHAP

Observers of the Australian scene are impressed with the similarity between Australians and Americans. One important difference is again the Australian attitude toward achievement. Illustrative of this attitude is a typical Australian comment to an aggressive salesman: "Don't be greedy, mate, you've had yours for this time. Reckon I've got to save some for the next chap. Fair shares for all, you know."[10] Many product claims that succeed in the United States can be used in Australia but themes that focus on the professional aspects of a product or its status enhancement are likely to fail because of the Australian sense of fair play. By the same token, claims of British origin that are based on exclusiveness are likely to run up against this same value orientation.

Claims about British and American products that are introduced into the Canadian market also require some adjustment. Executives of an American-owned Canadian affiliate comment that: "Possibly half of the U.S. prepared advertisements are usable in Canada, but almost never without some change being made in copy or one of the illustrations."[11] Canadians notice physical characteristics and components less and tend to respond to simpler forms and avoid the "gaudy and over-trimmed styling"[12] that are often attributed to American products. Somewhat like

[7] John Ewing, "Marketing in Australia," *Journal of Marketing*, Vol. 26, April, 1962, p. 58.

[8] Harper Boyd and Ivan Piercy, "Marketing to the British Consumer," *Business Horizons*, Vol. 6, Spring, 1963, p. 79.

[9] Harper Boyd and Ivan Piercy, "Retailing in Great Britain," *Journal of Marketing*, Vol. 27, January, 1963, p. 31.

[10] John Ewing, "Marketing in Australia," *Journal of Markeing, op. cit.*, p. 56.

[11] Jack R. Stone, "American-Canadian Co-Operation: Key to Successful Advertising," in Litvak and Mallen (eds.), *Marketing: Canada* (Toronto, Ontario: McGraw-Hill of Canada, Ltd., 1964), p. 262.

[12] B. P. Ohlson, "The Challenge of New Product Development," *Ibid.*, p. 152.

the British, they are predisposed to longer-lasting, more stable products that do not suffer from model-change and obsolescence. More than the Australian, Canadian character is: ". . . balance between the Old World and the New. . . . In matters of tradition, of moral values, of family sociological patterns, Canadians lean toward the point of view of Great Britain. In manner and custom . . . they incline toward the U.S. This sense of balance is shown throughout their way of life. It has often been said that Canadians are conservative in accepting extreme fashions. Yet any successful New York buyer will tell you that Canadian women have an instinctive 'feel' for good style—even though it is not exciting. They are not as eager (as Americans) to try new ideas; it is more difficult to switch them away from the tried and true. They do not respond to hyperboles; they do not like to be conspicuous in any way."[13]

Similar illustrations of the "plausibility" component can be applied to the U.S., British, Canadian, and Australian cultures. While Americans would find most plausible claims that feature opportunities for success, prestige or personal recognition, Canadians and Australians would find these somewhat less plausible, and Britons would see the least amount of relevance in them. Claims dealing with newness, better performance, and materials are most plausible to Americans, less so to Canadians and Australians, and least so for Britons. The claim that a product can be appropriate for all meets the approbation of both Australians and Americans but not so easily that of Canadians and even less that of the British.

VARIETIES OF VERIFICATION

Verifying claims is very much bound up with the use of authority figures and the presentation of information which is considered "proof" in each of these major markets. The authorities and prestige carriers will, of course, differ in each situation. The cultural hero used in an American testimonial is typically an individual who has become an expert in famous endeavors or succeeded in terms of achieving great social mobility. The professional athlete and the show business star have demonstrated both mobility and success or expertise. Similar types of authority or prestige carriers exist in the other countries but their influence is not so widespread. Australians, again because of their militant equalitarianism, would be predisposed toward accepting the American type of testimonial as proof. ". . . Australian advertisements and commercials are characterized by a wide use of Americanism . . . television commercials prepared and used in the United States are often seen on Australian sets, advertising the same products as in the country of origin."[14]

13 Byrne Hope Sanders, "The Canadian Consumer," in Fox and Leighton (eds.), *Marketing in Canada* (Homewood, Illinois, Richard D. Irwin, Inc., 1958), p. 12.
14 John Ewing, "Marketing in Australia," *op. cit.*, p. 58.

FIRST COMES SALABILITY

The concepts of product, market, and promotion provide a basis for understanding the importance of cultural values. The significance of cultural determinants on buying decisions is directly related to the question of market expansion.

It is axiomatic that market expansion depends on salability. Salability in turn ultimately depends on what activities the members of a cultural group (a market) perform or anticipate performing, and what products they consider appropriate for coping with these contingencies. To understand cultural values is, in a very real sense, to know what products *can* be sold in that market. The issue of what products *will* be sold depends upon the ability of marketers to adapt their products and promotional efforts to the contingencies perceived by people in the market. The cultural variable, then, bears on the expansion decision in two distinct, but related ways. First, cultural values determine the position of sanctioned products in a market and thereby answer the question: "Is expansion into a given market advisable?" Second, the dominant value orientations in a market offer strategic clues as to how the product can be marketed.

The United States, British, Canadian and Australian markets are, anthropologically speaking, relatively similar. They share a fairly common linguistic and political heritage. Quite predictably, then, a study of the value orientations of other cultures with less common ground will manifest even greater dissimilarity.

It is well to recognize, however, that virtually any new market will exhibit ethnocentrism—specifically, the opinion that *its* cultural values are superior to all others. This means that overt commercial proselytization is not likely to be successful. For example, Canadians do *not* want to be "Americanized." They want to adopt certain features of American culture, but on their own terms.

In some situations expansion into new cultural markets can be accomplished by using the *same product and the same promotion*. The typical marketing for, say, Coca Cola is one case where an existing product will readily and immediately fit into the market's cultural inventory. This means that the established way of life in the market recognizes the reality of the contingency for which the product is suited. Also, recognition of the differences between the product and substitutes for it are already present in the culture. Finally, promotional product claims—their meaningfulness, plausibility, and verifiability—are universal enough to be acceptable to consumers. In effect, such claims are so innocuous that they benefit from a kind of cross-cultural impunity. What this means is that usually this type of expansion strategy is most appropriate when expanding into a cultural market that is similar to the firm's original market.

Probably more expansion situations involve the use of the *same product but different promotion.* There are two reasons for this strategy. First, the situation simply might be one where the existing product fits into the market's cultural inventory. Real contingencies can be met with it, and the product is recognized as a viable alternative to existing products in the inventory. All the product lacks is cultural sanctioning by people in the market. In this case product claims used in other cultural markets are inadequate, perhaps even disparaging, because they fail to meet one or more of the promotional tests. Promotion must be changed to conform to the particular value orientations of the market to guarantee product acceptance.

This strategy is also appropriate when the existing product fits into the market's cultural inventory, but in a way *different* from other markets, i.e., it is recognized as an acceptable product but it is used differently than in other markets. The same automobile, for example, may be a necessity to an American but is a distinct luxury to a European. Products that are used differently must be promoted differently. Promotional claims made in one market may be totally irrelevant in another market where cultural values define the product another way. The expansion strategy of *same product-different promotion,* whatever reasons prompt its use, tends to be appropriate in situations where the coveted market reflects a culture whose way of life is similar but where implementation of life styles is along different lines.

Another method of expansion must be used in markets that reflect life styles so different from those familiar to the firm that existing products are not included in their cultural inventories. Such markets, if they are to be captured, require different products. These products should be thought of in approximately the same light as their counterparts in other cultural markets. What this means is that in order to expand into Market X, the firm may have to alter its original product—perhaps its color, shape, size, package, etc.—but not the means of promotion. The *different product-same promotion* strategy is used in the multinational marketing of laundry detergents. Typically, the products differ among countries but the nature of promotional claims made in their behalf is similar. Laundering techniques may vary from culture to culture, but the "cleaningest" theme is universally subscribed to.

Finally, the expansion situation may be one where both the life styles and the way they are implemented are "foreign" to the firm's previous experience. The appropriate strategy in such situations is to use a *different product-different promotion* technique. This is the most risky kind of expansion because it involves more than extending the firm's existing production and marketing facilities and it often prompts firms to consider "buying their way into" such markets by acquiring existing firms in the market. This is what occurred when Walgreen acquired the Mexican restaurant-retail chain, Sanborn's.

Merely to admit the relevance of cultural values is not enough for market expansion. When contemplating new markets, management must assess the significance of the cultural attitudes and not just take into account comparative curiosities like polygamy and cannibalism, or merely study such consumer habits as the frequency with which people change their clothes. These approaches may be interesting but are not basic to the expansion decision. What is required is a structural scheme, such as the paired-variable approach discussed in this article.

If products, markets and promotion are thought of in terms of behavioral patterns, both the nature and extent of cultural influence on buying decisions and hence on market expansion are clear. Cultural values determine what activities people perform and what contingencies they perceive. Furthermore, the manner in which members of a culture approach their activities—how they cope with contingencies—determines the acceptance of products by the culture. Cultural values also determine the efficacy of promotional claims made in behalf of products. The extent to which a proposed market reflects different life styles or ways of implementing them should be taken into consideration. Expansion into a new market will be more successful if, based on the patterns discussed, combinations of old and new products and methods of promotion are then introduced.

18

PROBLEMS IN INTERNATIONAL
NEW PRODUCT MARKETING*

William Sugg, Jr.

Ladies and gentlemen, it is a distinct pleasure to be with you today to discuss the international marketing of new products. The subject is, of course, a vast one. Ideal solutions to many such problems have not been found; indeed, it can be said with certainty that there are no *ideal* solutions, no absolutely right answers. In meeting its problems, each company is influenced to a greater or lesser extent by its own historic experience, its current capabilities and commitments. But it must also have the flexibility to strike out in new directions in meeting new problems and opportunities.

The subject of marketing new products raises the question: "What is a new product?", and the answer is not entirely obvious. A product may be well-known in a given market but new to a company which is undergoing an expansion of its line. A product may be well established in other markets but new to the area in which it is being introduced. In that case the product ranks as a new one to potential customers in that market, and the manufacturer faces the problem of educating users and winning acceptance for an idea as well as for a product.

The "new" product may be a small appliance embodying new customer habits, such as an electric hairdryer. It may be an item of power or industrial apparatus appearing on a new application, such as the now familiar gas turbine in a somewhat unfamiliar function of helping power stations meet their peak electrical loads. Or the new product may represent a basic advance in technology, as in the case of the first nuclear power plants, or the first semi-conductors replacing electronic tubes.

While all efforts at expanding product lines and developing new markets have many points in common, each has an even more decisively unique character which arises out of the specific marketing situation.

CULTURAL DIFFERENCES
IMPORTANT IN PRODUCT ACCEPTANCE

The problems which Westinghouse Electric International Company encounters in marketing new as well as old products are strongly rooted in

* Reprinted by permission from *The Marketing Plan in Action* (1964), The New York Chapter of the American Marketing Association, pp. 55-58.

cultural differences from country to country. These take effect along with economic and technical differences, and it is this aspect of international marketing which I propose to highlight today.

In world marketing, we all recognize the existence of highly developed, relatively developed and underdeveloped countries. We also recognize that each country has historical, political and economic development behind it which have conditioned its philosophy, its objective needs and—very important in marketing—its effective wants. This, while Westinghouse would like to sell every new product—in fact, our complete line of products to each country—this is not possible.

The primary problem here and now is: "What *can* we sell?" It is a problem of market readiness; of what is culturally, socially and psychologically feasible in the country. We ask ourselves:
—Are the people ready for a particular consumer product; is their economy ready for a given power or industrial product?
—If not, can they be made ready for it?

TWO KINDS OF ANSWERS

For the answers to these questions we have to rely on two basically different kinds of information. First, we have experts in economic analysis of world markets, who make studies of trends affecting our participation in each market with each type of product. These men make full use of reports, articles and statistics from many sources and, in addition, conduct their own surveys and studies to provide guidance on specific product and market needs.

This is the impersonal side of our study of our markets. It gives us vital clues as to what products we will emphasize, what quantities we can expect to sell, how much money and manpower we will have to expend, and how the picture can be expected to change in the short-term and the long-term future.

This kind of analysis gives us a profile of the mass of people who make up our potential market, but it doesn't provide a good enough picture of the human and individual aspect of our problem, of the realities about what makes people prefer one product, one model to the others. It also does not give us a clear enough picture about what our competition is doing and planning to do to attract the customer, and what are the many economic, legal and other problems and opportunities of each market.

For this close look at each market, Westinghouse relies on "in-country" contacts, particularly on the independent, locally managed and staffed distributor organizations who sell our products in each market. These men have a feel for local conditions and trends; it is they who sell directly to their own nationals, and help us decide when a new type of product can be sold profitably and in quantity in their markets, and what changes in product design are desirable.

By adding up information we receive from these men throughout the world, we can often arrive at a decision to place a different emphasis on our marketing efforts, or go to our manufacturing divisions with new concepts and ideas for product design.

A VARIETY OF DESIGN PROBLEMS

Westinghouse and its distributors are well aware of the many special conditions throughout the world that build up a demand for changes in product design. No company, no matter how large, can design all its products to conform to all the varying electrical and climatic conditions, special customer preferences throughout the world. But the company which does not respond promptly and creatively to changed situations not only through its marketing techniques but through its product design and development of new concepts is going to fall behind in world competition.

One of the traditional problems of electrical products is the wide variation in electrical characteristics. A large and very important part of the world market uses a frequency of 50 cycles. On large power apparatus, the design of each single type of 50-cycle equipment represents a large expenditure of engineering manpower in addition to the original outlay on manpower on the 60-cycle equipment. Yet this effort may be worthwhile to win important contracts.

The problem is so important in the field of consumer products that we have developed a broad line of 50-cycle major appliances for the European and for other markets. We know, too, that we must conform to customer habits and preferences, many of these strongly rooted in local conditions. We have had to develop a self-heating Laundromat for Europe, for example, because Europeans in general use much hotter water for washing their clothes than is used in the United States.

REFRIGERATORS AND SOCIAL CUSTOMS

The size and interior design of a consumer product must fit in with the realities of customer demand. Suppose, for example, that we take a look at the potential for expanding our sales of refrigerators in Great Britain. We will naturally make all the standard economic analyses, including studies of the changing social structure and income of the country, the nature of competition and other factors. They gather a wide variety of data, from the average number of times a family moves to the *per capita* consumption of, say, dairy products.

But we must also know from closer observation how Englishmen use their refrigerators. For example, milk is an item which U.S. families commonly keep in some quantity on their refrigerator shelves; they know it will keep and "it will save a trip to the store." But in most cities of England milk is delivered twice a day so the householder neither needs much storage space nor faces the problem of spoilage. In the English countryside, trips to the store are breaks in a possibly uneventful day, a chance to talk and pick up gossip; or trips may be made by children who don't find it much of a chore.

Such a simple cultural pattern leads back to the average Englishman's difference requirements in shelf arrangement and other features of the refrigerator. On the Continent, of course, the milk container may not be a factor in product design but the liter bottle may have to find a convenient place or the customer may not be interested. The size of refrigerator which the Englishman will buy is affected both by his income and by his commonly more crowded living space as compared with that in the United States. As income has risen in Great Britain and on the Continent, the demand for the larger refrigerators has increased.

Both the economic and technological realities and social preferences must be taken into account in deciding whether and how to gain greater participation in a given market. If the company selects Great Britain as such a target, many alternatives are open, including building or acquiring local facilities, increased supply from the Continent. Naturally direct export from the United States is beset by problems of production cost and other factors. In the case of Westinghouse, we place strong emphasis on licensing arrangements as one means of profitable operation in markets where a high volume of direct exports is ruled out.

If the licensing alternative is chosen, the problem becomes one of finding a British concern with the production, engineering, marketing and financial strength to carry out the complete operation for the national market. The U.S. company must have sufficient leadership in product design and manufacturing techniques before such a licensing arrangement becomes attractive to the British concern. But whether the route to increased participation in a market lies through licensing or any of the other alternatives, a great deal of local advice and adaptation must take place before the product of U.S. know-how is adapted to the individual national market.

All considerations and problems must be discussed and solved, often by compromise, with the English industrial concern. Then, and only then, after all aspects of the program are seen as feasible both culturally and technically, can the actual operation of production, selling and servicing begin.

You will note that I have not touched on financing of such an undertaking, whatever its form, though it is of central importance. Generally speaking, if an operation is sound on all fundamental aspects, the financial means can be found in the financial community.

THREE APPROACHES TO
SALES PROMOTION AND ADVERTISING

Let us assume now that the English industrialist has become a Westinghouse licensee for manufacturing refrigerators. At this point, he will now make and market the refrigerator. But what of the problem of sales promotion and advertising? Our company recognizes the different approaches which may be necessary from country to country, and once again realizes the advantage the licensee has by virtue of being resident in the country.

There are, then, three approaches to the sales promotion and advertising problem. The licensee may elect to take care of the problem himself, he may ask Westinghouse to take care of it, or a combined approach may be used in which we assist in the program, making available all our resources on motivation research, etc., for a financial consideration from the licensee. In this combined approach, the control is in our headquarters, but makes use of the licensee's ideas, etc.

In the case of the refrigerator, the "newness" of the product is not in its basic concept, since it is well established throughout most of the world—but in styling and development of individual features for which U.S. industry has unquestioned leadership. Let me give you an example of a product which is relatively new to many areas of the world but which is rapidly becoming established.

THERMO-KING

Let's take the case of the marketing of the Thermo-King refrigerator unit for trucks. Westinghouse Electric Corporation bought the family-owned Thermo-King Company which already had a small start in Europe. The problem was to expand the market, for even though there was no comparable unit on the European market, the market was still too small. Study showed that the potential market was great, since food spoilage in unrefrigerated transport was great. I have no need to draw out in detail for you all the obvious advantages accruing from the use of the refrigerator unit. They are equally obvious to potential European buyers of the unit.

But the study also showed that there were insufficient facilities for repair and maintenance of the units, with the result that buyers shied away. Nothing could be clearer than the fact that if we were to sell we *must* provide maintenance.

Another study surveyed Europe and found the cross-roads of the refrigerated truck business was Munich. Westinghouse then set up a repair and maintenance facility there, large enough to service all the refrigerated trucks. Further, it set up a fleet of repair trucks to be dispatched to trucks that had broken down and could not get to the Munich facility.

Having done this, all fleet owners of refrigerated trucks were apprised of the facilities, mass media advertising was utilized to spread the information and the sale of the units started to climb. The big profit here is selling the unit, but the problem of service had, in this case, to be solved first.

The case of Thermo-King points up the fact that despite the highly competitive state of the European market, it remains possible to locate new opportunities and to market our products successfully in that area and in other areas.

I have tried to indicate how, in international trade, the universal problems of marketing are overlaid with additional problems arising out of the cultural and social context of each individual market. It is the task of the international market to find the creative combination of product and services for individual markets throughout the world.

19.

LAUNCHING YOUR PRODUCT IN BELGIUM*

Albert B. Stridsberg

THE successful Belgian Economic Mission to the United States demonstrates the tremendous American interest in Belgium as a manufacturing bridgehead into the Common Market. Its advantages over the other five countries for manufacturing operations destine Belgium, in many cases, to be the first *market* attacked by these newly-installed plants. For them, Belgium will be the "test market."

This may be the major reason why Belgium is now talked about in marketing circles as the "test-market of The Six." There are, of course, other reasons. Belgium is among the countries possessing advanced industrialization, and with it, a standard of living outpacing France, the Netherlands, West Germany, and Italy—in fact the highest per capita income in Europe.

Its population density is the second highest in the world, making distribution a seemingly easy matter. Belgium's educational system is one of the most advanced in Europe, providing a public accessible to mass-communications techniques. Thus, it is quite logical that international firms, whether manufacturing in Belgium or not, should look at Belgium as an attractive market.

These companies tend, as a matter of fact, to get involved in a semantic error: because they choose Belgium as their *first* market, they may want to consider it as a *test* of future marketing efforts in other Common Market countries.

The purpose of this article is to counsel prudence. Belgium, with all its features as an excellent market for consumer products, is not necessarily a test market for The Six. The accent in the foregoing sentence should be placed on the word *"necessarily."*

FOUR GROUND RULES

Here are four ground rules: *1. The possibility of applying your Belgian marketing experience in other countries depends on the type of product you are selling.*

* Albert B. Stridsberg, "Launching Your Product in Belgium," *Journal of Marketing,* Vol. 26, No. 1 (January 1962), a publication of the American Marketing Association, pp. 12-18. Reprinted by permission.

This idea sounds trite. Nonetheless, it is easy and so tempting to assume that, *of course,* the Belgian market resembles that of the other countries, with the difference that the Belgians have more money. In point of fact, you have no reason to assume that Belgian consumers should behave like other Europeans in general, or like Frenchmen, or Dutchman, or Germans, in particular. In some cases, they do, and in some cases they do not. Woe betide the firm that assumes they do, without having verified the point in some way.

Some categories of products, such as (for men) cigarettes, passenger cars, movies, or (for women) beauty products, detergents, and household appliances, seem to move easily from country to country using the same marketing strategy in all.

Marketing strategy refers to three elements: (1) the strategy of audience or choice of people to whom you want to sell and the means to contact them; (2) the creative strategy or choice of basic sales message; and (3) the merchandising strategy (or choice of distribution patterns and techniques) to be used in co-ordination with advertising promotion to create sales.

Whence their mysterious universality? Consider two different factors.

First, *high interest.* Some types of products are interesting to all people in all countries, in more or less the same measure. This high interest factor has speeded communications between differing national populations, has "rubbed the edges off," and has created common-denominator ideas. This may not have been true twenty years ago, but today these products are of universal interest (within the confines of Western European/American culture). Cigarettes and automobiles are two examples.

Second, *newness.* A real innovation, or an entirely new category of product with no previous life history, seems to move happily across borders, using the same advertising arguments, the same packaging, and so on. Why? As an entirely new type, it does not evoke upon arrival a halo of psychological associations which may interfere with its acceptance. Confounding all the pundits of motivation research, entirely new products have a good chance of getting purchased the first time for thoroughly rational reasons.

To put these points another way, products universalize best if they appeal to a very basic need, or are so brand new no one has had time to develop prejudices about them.

The relevance of this theoretical analysis is apparent when you face the fact that the Belgian market is very highly segmented, and thus does not automatically resemble the mass markets of other countries. In spite of the high income per capita and other "mass market" symptoms, it is questionable to talk about Belgium as a mass market. Belgium is a number of markets.

Thus, the factors that have forced a flexibility of approach, and a diversification of activity upon Belgium as a manufacturing country suddenly turn against it as a market. The three distinct geographic segments (the Ardenne "massif" plateaus; the ancient estuary basins of "middle Belgium"; and on the northwest the flat tidelands), the two basic languages (and the regional patois within each)—everything seems to conspire to break the so-called "market" into tiny fragments.

The extreme population density that should logically improve communications and create a "mass population" does not function that way. Instead, Belgium is made up of individuals and small groups, a phenomenon that Madame Thérèse Henrot has properly dubbed the "particularisme belge."

If these were casual groupings due to proximity, they would have no special impact on marketing. But all of these groupings, whether social, economic, musical (there are, for example, 848 choirs, 2,090 drum-and-bugle corps, and 1,017 brass bands in Belgium at last count), or trade, or simply for amusement (500 small clubs of this type in Brussels alone), command a fierce variety of loyalty and evoke a sense of the group's history. Despite his acceptance of the political fact of Belgium, the average Belgian *resists* rather than *exists* . . . he uses his "joining" tendencies to express the difference of himself and his group from all other groups . . . and he reacts the same way as a purchaser. As this point, marketing must take into consideration the nature of market segments, and the market becomes many submarkets.

This particularism can have quite dramatic impact on sales patterns. The consumption of food products for example, can be demonstrated to vary widely in the different geographic areas of Belgium, for distinctly different reasons. This affects not only the flavors, but also the quantities consumed, the seasonal curves, and the people consuming. The use of deodorants appears to vary in a similar way.

Thus, for products whose consumption is seriously influenced by such factors as climate, regional industry, socio-economic class, or in-group traditions, you can expect the segmentation of the total market to be of major importance to your product's success or failure. In such cases, advertising and marketing strategies used for the Belgian launching can probably not be transferred to another market, unless the other market has the *same segmentation,* and the *same proportion of population in each segment.*

2. *While Belgium does not represent a "test market" for most products' advertising and marketing strategies, it is an excellent test of European product launching methods.*

Although Belgium is not generally a valid test market for the "content" of the product launching—the basic sales message, the visualizations, the merchandising ideas—it is an excellent test of the "form," that is, the techniques you use. Probably better than any other country in Western

Europe, Belgium will quickly reveal whether or not you have touched all the bases in developing your marketing plan. Despite the country's size, Belgium requires a program more detailed, careful, complex, and balanced than that needed for any of the other five. Failure to remember a single area may lead to complete frustration.

For example, a "pattern-book" launching in France, using American marketing techniques essentially without modification, may have good or even outstanding success. French media are quite effective; with some regional differences, the market displays considerable socio-economic homogeneity; the spine of "tradition" has been broken among the urban masses, making them accessible to new ideas. Thus, a "formula" approach, even though it misses a couple of peculiarities uniquely French, may produce sufficient results that the launching firm is satisfied . . . if slightly disappointed.

Yet the firm might have obtained 25% or—in the long term—100% better results had the "pattern-book" approach been abandoned for a marketing strategy more specifically adapted to France.

Belgium, because of the extreme fragmentation of the market into multiple markets, constitutes a much better test. A "pattern-book" campaign that succeeds will probably succeed anywhere; if it fails, it will fail roundly. But let us take a more important example: a product which in the United States is promoted via the "pressure theory of advertising"—that is, by applying a sufficient amount of advertising pressure directly on the consumer, we can *force* a certain quantity of sales. This theory has been tried many times in Belgium by international firms; it has produced some notable successes, but also some notable failures. Where the failures occurred, the firms involved were forced to admit that, in Europe, additional factors enter into the picture, and you cannot trust in pressure on the consumers alone to bring you success.

Thus, the lesson Belgium holds for European marketing lies in the likelihood of bringing to your attention sectors that require more care and more emphasis, or that may not even exist in American marketing.

What are these factors? To name a few: past product history, wholesaler influence, store lighting, product delivery patterns, politics . . . the list could be much longer.

For example, would an American manufacturer of proprietary pharmaceuticals, accustomed to the U.S. market, immediately realize the importance of the suppository in Belgium? And if he did, how would he deal with competition from a competitive product sold widely in this format?

Would a textile manufacturer realize that, despite what they say about themselves, Belgian textile wholesalers are primarily order-takers, making less than zero effort to promote style, increase retail inventory turn, or teach improved selling techniques?

Would the seller of a luxury beauty product that requires a stylized, delicate package design recognize the danger to package visibility posed by the poor lighting in the majority of Belgium drugstores and pharmacies?

Would any American manufacturer understand, without being told, that wholesale distribution of many products in Belgium is *not* organized on the basis of geographic territories, and that a wholesaler in Bruges may be serving clients in Charleroi or Liège, while a retailer located just down the street in Bruges buys from a different wholesaler located in Charleroi?

There is a reason for every unexpected factor which turns up in Belgium. Not all of them will turn up in France, Italy, Germany, or the Netherlands. But it is probable that the points producing unexpected difficulties or unexpected successes in Belgium are points to be watched out for elsewhere.

3. Product launching in Belgium must follow the rules; no steps can be omitted.

Mistakes cost money and waste time. Therefore, for a cheaper and less painful education on European product launching, it is best to follow with strict precision the classical techniques of product launching—without skipping points which might seem unimportant in the United States.

The standard sequence can be found in any good marketing textbook, and does not need repeating here. Experience shows that, for Belgium, certain areas are absolutely crucial:

> *a. Know, in complete detail, the market segmentation for the specific product you want to launch.*

It is not good enough, or safe enough, to extrapolate from the customer profile encountered in other countries for your product, or in Belgium for other products. Either you know the structure of the market, or you take a calculated risk—safe, for products that are entirely new or of high interest impact, but dangerous for the others. Getting this information may involve you in substantially greater amounts of marketing research than you would normally expect to undertake in the United States.

> *b. Verify the user, purchaser, and retailer acceptance of your product.*

In this area, Belgium—carefully studied—is likely to bring out any problem that might be posed in any other Common Market country. There seems to be a tendency to think that, because the market is small ("only" nine million), this step can be skipped. The results of omitting it have proved costly to many firms.

Also, there may be a tendency to think that a check of consumer *use* is sufficient, forgetting that check of product acceptability at the moment of purchase can make or break the sale, and that if the retailer for some reason does not like the product, it may never be properly displayed and promoted!

Acceptance testing is difficult and expensive, especially with built-in temptation toward dishonesty it entails. The manufacturer, who has spent months and years achieving the product he wants to launch, does not want to hear bad news, or listen to it if told. The advertising agency involved does not want the launching delayed or, even worse, abandoned. Even the research firm, supposedly objective, hesitates to turn in a report that is negative and designed to stop the launching.

Only the consumer, ruthlessly honest because he is disinterested, will turn in a "bad report" without hesitation.

Honesty, while not the most comfortable course, is still the best policy, and honest checking of product acceptability is a vital measure in Belgium. Market fragmentation rarely permits effective post mortems, to find out the "why" of the product's death.

    c. If possible, pretest all the elements of the advertising and marketing plan.

One of the greatest dangers in the "Belgian test market" idea is that it tempts companies to start a national launching of the product without testing the various elements. The temptation is to say: This whole campaign is a test; why test individual elements?

If the cultural differences from the U.S. market, however minor, were not so many, the position might be valid. As it is, any launching depends upon the proper functioning of a chain of detailed steps. Every one of these links must be tested, if possible, and where not tested must be recognized as a risk.

How can you test such elements as ads, sales brochures, and so on? Many of the tests developed in the United States are not only too costly, but also too sophisticated. Relatively simple copy-testing techniques, based on a careful study of how the advertising message is recalled and reworked in the memory of the reader, will generally provide a guide to the effectiveness of the ads proposed. In the event the advertising strategy is liked by the company and agency, but does not seem to satisfy consumers, a minimum number of depth interviews will usually give the information necessary to improve or scuttle the approach. Sales arguments and selling tools can be effectively tested via the "business-games" approach, which is also an indispensable method of training Belgian salesmen to understand and apply American sales ideas. Point-of-sale materials can be checked against retailers' opinions, and also by placement in a test area without advertising support.

These techniques, on the organization level, will permit you to test the individual elements which are to be combined into the launching activity. It is important also to test the balance of the different elements. Generally, two test-market towns (one French-speaking, one Flemish) are used for this purpose. However, it is difficult to find an acceptable pair, due to the fact that the most appropriate areas of Belgium have been hit by economic difficulties affecting only certain industries; thus, once again, the extreme fragmentation of the Belgian market complicates the task.

One school of thought argues that the best test of over-all balance consists of a launching in Brussels, followed by general launching in the four other major retail trading areas. This will undoubtedly produce sales, and supply an index of what the "modern-minded" segment of the Belgian public is likely to do. However, studies of food consumption, cosmetics use, etc., indicate that Brussels' behavior is not necessarily typical of the over-all country, nor does it necessarily predict the attitudes of the general public five years from now.

The answer to testing the over-all balance of a marketing plan probably lies in a careful study of *qualitative* factors involved. Knowing the product, the test market must be chosen in terms of a profile least likely to possess qualitative factors distorting consumer behavior. The linguistic factor may possibly have no influence. If, for example, you plan to market a cosmetic which is known to be best suited for upper-middle class communities, a suburban commune of Brussels may offer a good test, by offering a clear indication of the product's success with a typical group of prime prospects. For a food product of low unit price, to be distributed in as many retail outlets as possible, and suited to all economic and social levels, it is obviously desirable to find a community representative of the population as a whole. Since this is practically impossible, it may be of greater value to use a step-by-step launching, moving one by one through the prime markets until national distribution is obtained, and correcting the marketing balance wherever problems occur. (This technique, usually chosen to hold down costs, is actually a very effective test-market and sales-training method.)

In these examples, the "test-market" concept is revealed for what it really is: a method which cannot be handled simply in terms of statistics, and where it is imperative that the complete profile of the individual test area be thoroughly understood. Test-market sales figures are not enough in Belgium; it is imperative to find out *why* they occur, even if this requires additional consumer survey work before, during, and after the launching of the product.

Even thorough test-market analyses may leave the company faced with a choice: two advertising strategies which seem equally good, and completely different. One must be chosen (unless the company cedes to the perilous temptation of trying to put the best points of both approaches into a single advertising campaign). In this case, the best practice seems to date from the American 20s: comparison of the two advertising approaches via the results from adding a coupon valuable for a certain sum, or a buried offer of a booklet or folder of information value. However simple it may seem, this "mail-order" testing method provides a rough but valid way of taking a practical decision between two apparently equal techniques.

If sales are going well, there is a tendency not to interfere with them, for fear something will be disturbed. If the product launching fails, management usually prefers to let the matter drop. If sales are just so-so, sales managers are preoccupied with driving their sales teams harder and demanding more advertising support. No matter what the case, few people are interested in a painstaking appraisal of results. Yet this is as essential, and as profitable, as any other measure mentioned here.

The first, most obvious element in the appraisal of the now-launched product is an analysis of sales evolution against the evolution of the market. If industry-wide figures are not available through trade organizations, use of a sales auditing operation such as the A. C. Nielsen panels is implied. Where this does not effectively show consumer purchase-and-use trends (for example, because of seasonal usage patterns which do not jibe with consumer purchasing habits), a consumer panel can be set up, or a series of spot-check surveys can be run.

The goal of this appraisal is, of course, to find out what really happened. It is not enough, in present day marketing, to say, "We sold the product," and let it rest at that. In launching your product, did you (1) acquire part of the competitors' share of the existing market; (2) increase the over-all size of the market, and thus take a share in it which, in effect, you created for yourself; or (3) acquire a share in a market that was growing rapidly already, but gain a share proportionately less than your advertising/sales expenditure should have yielded?

This third case is altogether too frequent, and is at the root of a great many subsequent disasters where the products, apparently launched with success, quietly disappeared when competitors reacted with promotional tactics of superior quality.

A second area of appraisal is a qualitative study of the market acquired. No matter how great your success, it is perfectly possible that you are selling to a market you never expected, or that some completely unknown factor is playing a role in sales. If it is a positive factor, you may have a chance to increase the efficiency of your advertising/sales effort; if a limiting factor, you may be able to prevent the bad effects from going too far. Thus, you want to establish a clear profile of who is buying, and why: this inquiry leads directly to a further decision—to speed up the time-table and increase expenditures on the basis of a re-evaluated sales schedule, to maintain the present schedule, or to cut back in terms of inherent limitations in the market. Whether the qualitative study of the market is carried out or not, this decision must be taken. It is obviously better to take it on the basis of accurate information, or as a conscious calculated risk, than to take it on the basis of inertia, fear, or over-optimism.

The final area of appraisal is a study of competitor's reactions. Even if your product did not exist before, by the time you have launched it in Belgium, someone else will be ready to produce a similar one if you show even the most superficial signs of having a success. The impact of this competitive activity cannot be evaluated immediately in terms of sales, whereas spot research can frequently warn you in advance of dangers and/or opportunities which the competition is creating for you. This kind of follow-up is generally carried out by sales managers, much too empirically; the objectivity of an independent research or counseling organization can save much more money than it may cost. Unfortunately, at the present time, there are only a limited number of firms available in Belgium to do this kind of thing, and their schedule loads do not seem to allow for quick service (spot evaluations within fifteen days from order to completion of the report).

4. *Recognize the inherent dangers in Belgian product launchings, and protect yourself against them.*

There is every likelihood that firms will continue to test their products in Belgium; and it is to be hoped that they will take into consideration the factors mentioned here that apply to their case. It will be in their favor to work as methodically as they can in a field which, like all marketing, is essentially a "pseudo-science" whose scientific methods are primarily protective tools for the intuitions of the human brain. But whether they are systematic or not, these firms can save themselves much trouble by avoiding four basic dangers:

a. *The tendency to equate the whole market with its most advanced sectors.*

Most American marketers fail to get sufficiently in contact with the Belgian market to know its retrograde sectors well. The bright lights of the stores in the Borinage or, for that matter, in Brussels' areas of urban blight, such as Les Marolles, would lead you to think that the Belgian economy is uniformly sturdy. Cinema entries, down only 10 percent in face of the arrival of television, and for that matter television itself selling well throughout the country, would indicate a generally modern mentality—free of traditional and provincial attitudes that might limit sales. Yet these examples are treacherous.

The typical American error is, judging from the indexes of economic health usual to American marketing, to deduce an eager, open-minded attitude in Belgium. The comparable Belgian error is to equate the market with its more backward sectors, and to establish marketing and advertising plans in terms of peasants in the Campine and miners in Boussu-lez-Mons. The Belgian market, like most markets in evolution but not arrived at the stage of true mass consumption, is a mixture; and any marketing should be based on evaluating the balance between the product's appeal to the "modern-minded" and its vulnerability to conservatism reinforced by conditions of economic scarcity.

b. *The tendency to discount the opinions of "old hands."*

It may be surprising, in an article advocating systematic marketing techniques with all their checks and balances, to find support for the "old hands" in the field. It is altogether too easy for business-school graduates, whether from the United States or from Europe, to accuse the older marketers of being "gaga." Certainly, many of these men are extremely impatient with the methodical approach advocated in this article: they feel that they "know" their market, in terms of many years of experience, and the strictures of step-by-step work are annoying.

Unscientific as their methods may appear, many of these men do know the market quite well; if they appear disoriented occasionally, it is often a failure to adjust to the new products being marketed, rather than inadequate knowledge of the market itself. The wise course for the systematic marketer, therefore, is to profit as much as possible from the accumulated knowledge of these men, and to avoid the temptation to do the opposite of their counsel, just to make a point about the differences in method.

A most striking example is that of a sequence of firms who have dealt with a well-known Belgian manufacturer over a period of years, insisting that he needs marketing research—while the responsible executive insists consistently that he is carrying all the information he needs in his head. What is interesting is that the firm in question, some ten or fifteen years ago, carried out very thorough marketing and media research, and has consistently updated the research by spot checks and sales evaluation ever since. This information is located in the upper left-hand drawer of the executive's desk; and if he chooses to say that the necessary information is in his head, it is because nothing has so far invalidated the conclusions he reached some fifteen years ago. It is perilous for less experienced men to tell him, "You need marketing research before your next product launching," unless they can demonstrate a major change in the nature, functioning, and structure of his market.

c. The tendency to neglect promotion on secondary levels.

The "pressure theory of advertising" has already been mentioned. This concept assumes a high level of media efficiency, that is, for a given price, to be able to buy a certain amount of pressure on a given consumer group, reaching a high percentage of that group, with an adequate frequency and effective communication of the message.

The firms most closely associated with this theory are, in fact, the ones in Belgium that most consistently back it up with reinforcing promotion to every echelon of the distribution system. Unfortunately, other American firms, frequently with less available money, have tried to cut down on the wholesalers, dealer, and public relations activities, arguing that consumer pressure is the essential part of the plan, and that the other expenses can be eliminated for economy purposes.

Throughout Europe, and particularly in Belgium, the truly mass media have not developed sufficiently to supply the kind of consumer pressure needed to put this theory into effect, at least at a reasonable cost.

The cost-per-thousand figures supplied by many of the media conceal much waste coverage, people who are not ready to buy the product, or many never be ready. In other cases, there exist *no* appropriate media to isolate the target consumers.

At this point, the success of secondary promotion in moving the product along the chain of distribution, and in both convincing the retailer and giving him sales arguments and tools to use, becomes the determining factor in the product launching, as it was often enough in the United States during the 30s, and as it still is, for example, in the sale of such complex products as insurance, pharmaceuticals, or industrial materials.

This is made all the more true by the fact that conservatism, a major problem in the European populations not recovered from some fairly grim economic experiences, is just as prevalent among retailers as among consumers. If the Belgian retailer, independent and thorny character that he is, hesitates to stock the product because he is not convinced, the "advertising pressure" on the consumer may be wasted through poor timing, or lost altogether.

In Belgium, where a market for the type of product already exists, promotion to the chain of distribution, and to "influentials" (doctors, professional groups, industry leaders, etc.) should be studied first, and the advertising effort should be undertaken after satisfactory distribution is assured. Where a market must be created, or where the prime goal is to expand the existing market in a major way, consumer indoctrination through advertising pressure, of course, takes precedence; but it is still extremely dangerous to neglect the "chain of command."

   d. The tendency to "cut corners" in research and counseling.

One of the major problems of U.S. firms involved in launching products in Belgium seems to be that of justifying budget items to state-side comptrollers. No American accountant is likely to object to $10,000 indicated as advertising. Yet when a requisition comes through for $8,000 advertising and $2,000 research or counseling fees, a sudden struggle ensues. As a result, many American firms now entering Europe are attempting to force their advertising agencies to do, at no cost, essential research and marketing analysis. When this cannot be obtained via arguments about "investing in our common future," the companies often enough try to get by on insufficient marketing information.

If your company is entering Belgium for the first time, it will be advisable for you to realize that commissions on advertising will generally not cover the expenses for the kind of research and marketing counsel which you need. In a market where you are already established, much of this work is provided by your own staff, or is drawn from a backlog of knowledge that has been accumulating, possibly without your being aware of it, over a number of years.

Here you need it all, *now,* and you probably start from zero. If you are, in addition, asking for this kind of analysis from your U.S. advertising agency, you have already encountered a resistance to the idea, based on the feeling that commissions do not cover it. (The 1957 Frey Report on the commission system of reimbursing advertising agencies demonstrated with accuracy the inflexibility of the method, and the need to pay for advertising, research, and marketing counsel on the basis of service rendered, rather than the commissions inequitable usually to one side or the other.) Think, then, how much more difficult it is for a Belgian agency to provide the same sort of information, with so much less income (in terms of real revenue from advertising) to finance it.

The alternate method of obtaining this kind of research information without letting the accountant see it is by staffing with knowledgeable people. But this does not always work either, because the people are not available, because there are not enough specialists to go around, or because the state-side management seems to balk even more than Belgian firms at paying top salaries in situations demanding top talent.

In the last analysis, you get what you pay for; and to launch a product effectively in Belgium, you must be prepared to look at the available funds in terms of the amount of work to be done, and the going rate of having it done by the best people.

U.S. management must then be informed, in an effective way, of why —rather than taking advantage of the agency, or attempting to hire away your competition's best people at inadequate salaries coupled with vague promises—you choose to buy research and counseling at market value and obtain top talent for the task to be performed.

CHANNELS AND
INSTITUTIONS

20.

WHOLESALING TRENDS IN WESTERN EUROPE*

Edwin H. Lewis

THE countries of Western Europe are experiencing economic changes without parallel in their modern history. One of the most significant end-products of these changes will be a greatly expanded "middle-income" market which will have major repercussions on European marketing methods and marketing structures.

NEW EUROPEAN MARKET PATTERNS

The emerging market patterns in Western Europe differ from the patterns which have existed in two basic respects:

(1) Historically, these countries have had two quite separate markets: (*a*) a broad market for the basic necessities of life composed of people who constituted the labor resources, and (*b*) a very limited and restricted market for those goods which could be purchased only by the small professional group and by those who controlled the economic and political destinies of their countries.

The upward economic thrust of the past ten years has moved many more people into the bracket where the share of their income which can be used for discretionary spending has steadily increased. The old dichotomy in the market is being replaced, therefore, by a middle class "mass" market which spans the gap between the two extremes.

(2) The markets for any products, and in fact for virtually all products consumed by families with discretionary spending potential, have been urban markets. The necessities of life were sold in the small town

* Reprinted by permission from *Indiana Readings in Business* No. 38 (1962), The Foundation for Economic and Business Studies, pp. 55-64.

and rural markets, but sales of other products in these areas has been negligible.

The economic betterment has had its impact to date primarily in the urban centers, and it is here that the beginnings of a potentially large middle-income market can be seen. Over the longer view, however, the residents in the smaller towns and, eventually, farm families as well will also have more francs, lires, pesetas, etc. to spend for products above those needed to simply live from day to day.

The central point of marketing significance incorporated in these changes is that the concept of a restricted market is becoming obsolete; and, therefore, the marketing system which evolved to serve the needs of a limited market must be substantially revamped to meet the challenge of the rapidly burgeoning middle-income market.

It becomes necessary, therefore, for manufacturers who seek to cultivate this new and broader market and for wholesalers and retailers who attempt to serve it to adopt policies and methods which will make it possible to reach this market efficiently. Among other things, there must be in each country an economically sound wholesale-retail structure through which producers and middlemen can move goods to the consumer.

ROLE OF THE WHOLESALER

Neither the wholesaler nor the retailer—nor the manufacturer for that matter—is the key to the efficient distribution of products, but the role which the wholesaler should play seems to be most commonly misunderstood. There is, for example, the feeling that much of the waste in marketing occurs at the wholesale level, and that the obvious remedy, therefore, is to eliminate the wholesale middleman from the channel.

This idea usually is generated and gains acceptance under conditions in which, in fact, there are wholesalers who are not performing any really significant functions or who are being overpaid for the jobs they do. There is some evidence of this in Europe, even at the present time. In the Spanish economy, for example, which in recent years has been focused on the problem of increasing the output of goods, wholesale establishments have come into being—attracted by easy money—whose principal trading advantage has been that they have had access to scarce goods of some type. Putting buyers into contact with the suppliers, much as a broker would, is about the only function which they perform. Once the supply of goods builds up, however, and manufacturers begin actively looking for markets, these "five percenters," as some businessmen call them, are certain to be displaced.

Another addition to the cost of wholesaling is represented by the two-step wholesaling system under which a large urban wholesaler sells to a smaller wholesaler in the provinces who, in turn, sells to his neighboring retailers. Under conditions in which the small-town and rural market has very limited potential this may have been a justifiable method of distribution, but as the large, aggressive urban wholesalers which are needed to serve the new markets emerge, this double wholesaling also will gradually disappear.

In certain cases manufacturers have used parallel wholesale middlemen in an attempt to broaden distribution. One firm in the building supplies field, for example, has sold through two types of wholesalers: regular service wholesalers, and small volume wholesale-retail middlemen. The company is attempting to build its volume through service wholesalers to the point where the marginal type of distributor can be dropped.

It is one thing to by-pass wholesalers who have outlived whatever usefulness they may have had, as in the examples given above. It is another matter to displace the merchant wholesaler in those commodity fields where his services are necessary in order to minimize the total costs of distribution.

It is a temptation to manufacturer and retailer alike to by-pass the wholesaler in the belief that the wholesaler's functions and his profits as well can be split between them. There are circumstances, of course, wherein direct contact between manufacturer and retailer or user can be the most efficient channel. For industrial goods, bulky items, high-style products, and perishables, the nature of the goods and the sales problems in connection with them may call for more direct distribution. Where a manufacturer has a wide enough line to sell directly, or where sales are made in large volume to retail customers, the wholesaler, likewise, may not be necessary.

But when we consider staple consumer goods in general demand, for example food products, drugs, hardware, tobacco products, etc.—the type of goods which require distribution over wide geographical areas and which we generally call "convenience goods"—the situation is very different. In these lines, experience has shown that the manufacturer who decides to dispense with the wholesaler must exercise considerable caution, because the competitive burden of proof rests with him.

The marketing efficiencies which result from changing the quantities involved at various levels of distribution are so fundamental in the marketing of staple goods that the risks of eliminating the wholesaler must be carefully weighed by all parties concerned. It is clear, therefore, that the full-service merchant wholesaler must be retained in the marketing structure of Western European countries as he has been retained in the United States.

It is equally clear, however, that probing attempts will be made to eliminate the wholesaler in Europe and that to remain in the channel he must perform the functions required of him with efficiency and skill. He must also develop better management techniques and more aggressive sales promotional methods than he has used in the past.

IMPROVEMENTS NEEDED IN WHOLESALE OPERATIONS

One of the major shortcomings of wholesalers, both in Europe and the United States, has been the lack of aggressive sales promotion. Wholesalers, too frequently, have preferred to be order-takers and have considered their function simply to be the supply of items requested by the customer. They have seen no need to recommend one brand over another nor to give active promotional support to any particular manufacturer's products. It has been dissatisfaction on this score which has led some manufacturers to go around the wholesaler.

As one response to the need for stronger selling it may be expected that some European wholesalers will shift to limited-line distribution as have many successful wholesalers in the United States. This reduction of lines permits the wholesaler to sell his remaining lines more effectively. Actually, whether wholesalers limit their lines or not, sales promotion must receive greater attention as these companies struggle for an increasing share of the expanding market. And as wholesalers appreciate the need to work more closely with manufacturers on new products and other special promotions, better-trained wholesale selling organizations will result.

European manufacturers and wholesalers, in commodity fields where selective distribution can be applied, will move ahead faster and avoid some of the problems which have plagued American firms if they will attempt conscientiously to develop close working relationships of the type described. Admittedly, the application of this policy is not easy. It will undoubtedly be difficult to find wholesalers who are educated in this form of operation, at least in some countries. Consequently, the growth of selective distribution arrangements may be slow, but this method of distribution has been proven to the point where its merits are well established and accepted. For many manufacturers, it is the strongest system of distribution which can be devised.

WHOLESALER-RETAILER COOPERATION

Wholesalers cannot, ordinarily, give the type of assistance to retailers which manufacturers can give to wholesalers. However, some 40 or 45 years ago there was started in the United States a type of cooperative arrangement between wholesalers and independent retailers which has come to be known as the voluntary chain. This form of organization is based on a close working relationship between wholesaler and retailer and is generally credited with "saving" the independent grocery retailer in the United States (and the grocery wholesaler as well) from the competitive inroads of centrally owned chains.

The workings of this form of organization are too well-known to need repetition here. Suffice it to say that in the U.S. voluntary chains do nearly 40 per cent of the retail grocery volume, and the voluntary chain idea has spread to drugs, hardware, automotive supplies, and variety lines. In addition, in recent years there have been many franchise operations established in widely diverse commodity and service fields which closely resemble the voluntary chain.

In addition to doing a more effective promotional job, it will also be necessary for wholesalers to give better service to retailers and to industrial customers. The furnishing of technical services to the latter as well as to some types of retail stores, such as drug stores, is another activity of considerable potential importance.

In order for the wholesaler to improve the above services he must have better knowledge of his own markets. Wholesale trading-area data are scarce, and knowledge of market potentials is sketchy at best. Unfortunately for themselves and for the marketing structure as a whole, wholesalers generally are the last among the marketing organizations to adopt sound techniques of market research and analysis.

Since physical handling costs are an important part of the wholesaler's cost structure, careful attention needs to be given to warehousing and order-filling costs. Warehouse layout, the use of materials-handling equipment, and inventory placement and control are all matters to which wholesalers will be forced to give increasing time and effort.

Finally, the office routines—order processing, billing, and credit work—are similarly subject to improvement. In sum, the wholesaler who moves ahead with the expanding European market will find it necessary to re-examine every facet of his operations and to introduce greater efficiency at all levels of his business.

MANUFACTURER-WHOLESALER COOPERATION

In order to bring about this near-revolution in wholesaling, manufacturers will need to work more closely with wholesalers, and wholesalers in turn will need to become more receptive to manufacturers' suggestions and more willing to work with manufacturers in the introduction of new lines. Above all, the wholesaler must be willing to cast his lot with a limited number of reputable manufacturers who agree to work closely with him. In these matters wholesaling has been a tradition-bound industry, and it will take considerable effort on the part of wholesalers to overcome this long-standing inertia.

There are many ways in which a manufacturer can aid wholesalers who are willing to work with him. One of the most important of these is the training of wholesalers' salesmen. Salesmen can be trained individually on the job, or in group training programs sponsored by the manufacturer. In the field of industrial products particularly, the manufacturer can give technical aid and advice, prepare specifications, etc. which will help the wholesaler make a sale. Special seasonal and other promotions, including promotions for new products, can be devised by the manufacturer in close collaboration with the wholesaler.

These aids to the wholesaler can be provided more effectively when the manufacturer follows a policy of selective distribution. Under such a policy, the manufacturer and the distributor can become a closely coordinated team. This team relationship, however, involves responsibilities on both sides. The manufacturer must make it profitable for the distributor to support his line, and he must also be prepared to honor all reasonable requests for aid and assistance. Obviously, the merchandise line must be kept competitive in every respect, and shipments must be made in accordance with the distributor's needs.

For his part, the wholesaler must carry full stocks of the manufacturer's line, give the necessary customer service, and also give full promotional support to the entire line. Furthermore, he must be willing to forgo the sale of competitive lines entirely or to reduce the number of these lines drastically.

In Europe, the first voluntary chain was the "Spar" organization which was started in the Netherlands in 1932. Prior to World War II about the only other voluntary chain activities in Europe were in Germany and Sweden. During the past ten years, however, the voluntary chain idea has spread rapidly throughout Western Europe and particularly in the northern European countries. In southern Europe voluntary chain systems are a more recent development.

A recent study of European voluntary chains made by OEEC indicates that the number of participants is in excess of 1,200 wholesalers and 180,000 retailers.[1] As in the United States, the first growth of voluntary chains has been in the food field. A beginning has been made, however, in hardware and dry goods.

One particularly significant aspect of European voluntary chains is that they have become international in character. Spar International, for

[1] Organisation for Economic Co-operation and Development, *Voluntary Chains in Europe, Structure, Organisation, Results,* Project no. 6/03 E., Paris, 1961.

example, has 165 wholesalers and 24,000 retailers in nine Western European countries.

CONCLUSION

There is a basic need for an expansion of wholesaling activities throughout Western Europe as the level of production rises and standards of living in urban and rural areas gradually improve. Growing competition both within and among individual countries, however, will put pressure on all levels of the marketing system to reduce costs. The wholesaler particularly will find it essential to strengthen his services to both manufacturers and retailers, and to find ways of performing his basic functions more efficiently. A wider adoption of policies of selective distribution by manufacturers would help materially in this respect as would the decision by wholesalers to reduce the number of competing lines which they will carry.

One encouraging development has been the rapid growth of voluntary chain systems in Europe. It may be expected that other innovations in wholesaling will appear, together perhaps with new limited-function or limited-line wholesalers similar to those which have developed in the United States.

Since no way has been found to eliminate the generally accepted wholesaling functions—at least in the distribution of many kinds of goods—the wholesaler will continue to have first claim on the performance of them. It needs to be stressed, however, that this is a claim and not a right. It remains for the wholesaler himself to show that he is the best man for the job.

21.

FRENCH RETAILING AND THE COMMON MARKET*

S. Watson Dunn

WHAT is the role of the retailer in France?

Most analysts overlook the retailer when they assess the chances for success of such well-publicized arrangements as the European Common Market (inner six) and the European Free Trade Association (outer seven). They seem to assume that somehow he will accommodate his operation to the demands of such probable developments as the invasion of strong foreign brands, an increase in consumer advertising by manufacturers, and the relatively free movement of goods from one country to another.

France is of special interest from the retailing standpoint. For one thing, it has reversed its traditional isolationism and has, along with Germany, exercised leadership in speeding up provisions of the Rome (European Common Market) treaty, such as the lowering of internal tariffs. Also France is associated with the earliest developments of modern retailing techniques. For example, Bon Marché in Paris is generally considered one of the world's first department stores. However, the French retailer has been notoriously slow in adopting such recent innovations as self-service supermarkets and national brands. Most Americans tend to consider French retail stores either exasperating anachronisms or quaint reminders of old France.

Two questions need to be answered. First, is the structure of French retailing adaptable to the needs of expanding, dynamic markets? In other words, are there enough of the right types of outlets, too many of the wrong? Second, to what extent are the retailer and his customers adaptable psychologically to the demands of the future? Is he willing and able to make needed changes?

FRAGMENTATION OF RETAIL TRADE

By U.S. standards, the French retailing system is highly fragmented. France has approximately 60 per cent more retail shops per 10,000 popu-

* S. Watson Dunn, "French Retailing and the Common Market," *Journal of Marketing*, Vol. 26, No. 1 (January, 1962), a publication of the American Marketing Association, pp. 19-22. Reprinted by permission.

lation than the United States. Even in wholesaling, the typical organization is a small one.

There are far too many outlets for certain types of merchandise and service. A good example is the café which exists in surprisingly large numbers in almost all sections of every French city. Also one finds in France many small specialized stores which in America would be combined into one. For example, the American supermarket equals the French *épicerie* (groceries), plus *crèmerie* (dairy products, eggs), plus *charcuterie* (specialty meats), plus *boulangerie* (bread), plus *pâtisserie* (pastries), plus *droguerie* (household cleaning supplies), plus *poissonnerie* (fish), plus *boucherie* (fresh meat), etc.

In a middle-class section of Lyons there is one bakery for every 800 inhabitants. As David S. Landes points out, "The small shop is a sort of caricature of the family firm . . . with the objective of high profits on a limited turnover carried to an astonishing degree. There are haberdashers who try to live on the sale of three shirts a day, restaurants which serve six meals at noon."[1]

According to INSEE (French National Council of Commerce), the official French gatherer of statistics, the average French independent food store in 1958 had a gross volume of approximately $23,000. In one random sample of 108 food stores, 27 were found to have an annual volume of less than $10,000.

The INSEE divides the French retailing structure into the following major categories:

Multiple businesses. These include such well-known department stores in Paris and the provinces as Aux Galéries Lafeyette and Au Printemps, and the popular variety stores misleadingly called "one-price stores" (such as Monoprix and Prisunic). There are approximately 1,000 of these, with about 550 accounted for by the popular variety store. They represented approximately 4.5 per cent of the total retail volume in 1958.

Chain stores. There were in 1958 about 37,000 retail shops which were owned by chains having four or more branch stores. Approximately 58 per cent of these were food chain stores. Chain stores accounted for about 6 per cent of retail sales in 1958.

Co-operative societies. Consumer co-operatives are popular and well-established in France. In 1958 there were over 3 million members in approximately 800 co-operative societies. There were 11,000 shops, but 6,500 were run by the 50 largest societies. Part of the remainder were included in the 2,700 co-operatives of shops in private business firms and government services. Co-operative societies, mainly in food, accounted for slightly more than 2 per cent of retail sales in 1958.

[1] David S. Landes, "French Business and the Businessman: A Social and Cultural Analysis," in *Modern France*, Edward Mead Earle, editor (Princeton: Princeton University Press, 1951), p. 342.

Supermarkets. Still a rarity in France are supermarkets. Unlike neighboring Switzerland and Germany, France has only a handful of what most American marketers would accept as supermarkets.

Non-sedentary retailers. There are approximately 95,000 retailers without a fixed place of business (of these, 44,000 handle foodstuffs who account for about 3 per cent of the nation's retail volume).

Sedentary independent retailers. The independent retailer is the perennial backbone of retailing in France. He accounts for approximately 92 per cent of all stores and 84.5 per cent of the total retail sales in France. In the food field the independent retailer is losing a little ground, but the INSEE estimates that the independent food retailers (sedentary and non-sedentary) still handle about 83 per cent of food volume.

What the INSEE calls the "concentrated" form of retail distribution (department stores, chains, co-operatives, and supermarkets) accounts for only 12.5 per cent of the national retail sales. The 95,000 non-sedentary retailers are responsible for about 3 per cent, and the traditional independent shopkeepers handle the remaining 84.5 per cent.

LOW PRODUCTIVITY IN RETAILING

Although the number of retail outlets is decreasing at the rate of more than 6,000 a year, there are too many small outlets, and productivity per worker is low. Table 1 summarizes some productivity statistics.

This table indicates that not only in France but in most of the countries of western Europe the typical store is too small to take advantage of large-scale operation (mass buying, mass advertising, etc.). Productivity per worker, as indicated by employees per million dollars of volume, is much lower than in the United States. Edouard LeClerc, a young Frenchman who is trying to introduce mass retailing and discount selling in France, claims that approximately 21 per cent of the French labor force is engaged in food distribution, as compared with 7 per cent in the United States.[2]

WHAT ABOUT THE FUTURE?

To solve the problem, one must go behind the statistics of French retailing and delve into somewhat imponderable human factors. One must find out what motivates the retailer and his customer.

The retailer presents certain interesting paradoxes. For example, he

2 "Cut-price Grocer Stirs France," *The New York Times,* November 8, 1959, Sec. IV, p. 8.

is more of an individualist than his American counterpart. Most Americans are impressed by the individuality of the average French store. The arrangement of the merchandise, window displays, interior decorations— all tend to reflect the personality, feelings, and prejudices of the owner and even of the family of the owner.

But one finds the French retailer going to all odds to avoid competition as we know it—particularly price competition. He is likely to join a "syndicat" to fix prices and many of the rules of doing business. A few years ago Maurice Gottegno opened two American-style discount houses in Paris; but he encountered strong pressure from groups of his competitors and eventually was forced to go out of business.

Another apparent contradiction stems from the typical Frenchman's great reverence for tradition, but along with this his proven ability to adapt his *modus operandi* to needed changes.

This contradiction has fascinated many historians. In 1915 J. R. Moreton wrote, "The truly remarkable way in which, under the present trial, France has purified herself of her traditional vices and developed virtues which were supposed to be quite alien to her character drives one to the conclusion, not only that the temperamental qualities of nations change more rapidly than we have been accustomed to think, but also that they are often only qualities which have been foisted on nations by noisy minorities."[3]

Forty years later another specialist in French history, Henry Bertram Hill, emphasized France's recuperative power in the face of the French Revolution, the Franco-Prussian War, and the two World Wars and its continuity as a great power.[4] France's adaptability is shown also by her switch from economic isolationism to full participation in the ECM.[5]

Thus, when we note the French retailer's reluctance to make use of modern merchandising techniques, keep in mind that the French retailer may, like his fellow countrymen, eventually change his methods when he is faced by the challenge of international markets.

In the meantime, the retailers are slow to adopt even such standard retailing procedures as advertising and self-service. A department store in Orléans which spends 0.4 per cent of sales for advertising is known as a big advertiser. A large and rapidly-growing food chain in south and central France which spends 0.3 and 0.5 per cent for advertising (all of it in newspapers) is considered by its competitors to be overly aggressive. These percentages would, of course, be considered quite low in the United States for these store types.

[3] J. R. Moreton MacDonald, *A History of France* (London: The Macmillan Company, 1915), p. 6.

[4] Henry Bertram Hill, "The Reliability of France in the European System" in Earle, *Modern France*. Same reference as footnote 1, p. 475.

[5] Edgar S. Furniss, Jr., *France, Troubled Ally* (New York: Frederick Praeger, 1960), Chapter 5 and 7.

Net profit and accumulated surplus are less important to the French retailer than his American counterpart. Instead he is influenced by such considerations as keeping control of his firm within his family, and in maintaining his status within the community. Landes says: "The word *maison* has retained business connotations long since lost by our word 'house.' It is this bond that accounts for astonishing solidarity shown by French families when the integrity or the stability of the firm is imperiled; even today, the social register or family tree is often a better credit reference than the most profitable series of annual statements."[6]

Many French retailers resist expansion because it may weaken family control of the firm. More often than in the United States they let their merchandise stagnate rather than sell it at a "face-losing" reduction. Even when French retailers install self-service, they frequently overlook cutting prices to compensate for this innovation.

WHAT ABOUT THE CONSUMER?

In all fairness, it should be noted that the French retailer has to satisfy a difficult, hard-to-predict customer who is somewhat different from his or her counterpart in other countries. His store is something of a social institution, with many of the attributes of a "club." The proprietor is sometimes as much a social director as a businessman. He must keep his members (his loyal customers) happy, and is often relatively unconcerned about enlarging his circle of customers. Naturally this is more true of the small store than the large one.

An investigation by École Supérieure de Commerce in one of the heavily populated sections of Lyons indicated that many people patronized a certain store because they felt they were thereby members of a privileged group. Buying was a sort of reinforcement of membership rites. The housewives were quite conscious of how they should dress to go to the store (no pin curls, no shorts, no slacks for this venture into the outside world). The daily shopping expedition is an important part of the housewife's routine, bringing her contacts with the outside world. Since she has no P.T.A. meetings, and few social or bridge clubs as a substitute, she is not likely to welcome weekly shopping in bulk, even though it might bring certain savings.

One of the most formidable barriers to marketing progress is the reluctance of the French consumer to accept the standardization implicit in mass production and mass marketing. Even when the French housewife has a refrigerator in which to store her food, even when she has a car to

6 David S. Landes, same reference as footnote 1, pp. 336-337.

transport the entire week's food supply, she will still harbor considerable wariness toward packaged, processed, or canned foods and continue to make daily rounds of her stores. Canned soups have been a failure in France in spite of the fact that soup is a staple item in the French cuisine. It is not feasible to mass-produce fabrics or dresses, because even the most overworked housewives take time to select their own fabrics and sew their own garments, or find a couturière whom they like.

Also, consumption patterns vary substantially from those in the United States. The American is likely to spend the money he or she has left after taking care of food, clothing, shelter, and an automobile . . . for such items as appliances and home furnishings. In France, good wining and dining, along with clothing and shelter, are considered part of basic living costs. What is left is more likely to be spent for services or a vacation than for appliances or other durables.

IMPLICATIONS

The French retailer could well be a real "stumbling block" to successful achievement of European Common Market aims. The retailing system is overly fragmented; and efficiency is handicapped by retailer acceptance of inefficient practices handed down from the isolationist past, a sometimes irrational disregard for maximizing profits, and concerted action on the part of some store managers designed to stem the tide of retailing innovations. The danger is compounded by such consumer characteristics as suspicion of mass-produced items and reluctance to change established shopping habits.

Retailing is being modernized, but the pace is still slow. One encouraging sign is the growth of co-operative chains. These are independently owned and thus not so objectionable to the Poujadists (or other restrictionists) as corporate chains. At the same time they provide the advantages of group buying and merchandising.

A second sign of progress is the success of certain intelligently-run discount houses, supermarkets, and corporate chains. Most of these are managed by people who have studied mass marketing in other countries, yet who know the pitfalls of imposing too quickly foreign retailing methods on the French consumer. Supermarkets have been developing, although progress has been slow and those established so far are more like the Swiss and German types than those in America. However, a genuine American-type supermarket was opened in 1961 on the outskirts of Paris. Several American chains have become quite interested in France, and we may soon see them opening outlets there. Also, it is quite possible that the entry of Great Britain into the Common Market may spur development of more modern retailing methods. As Table 1 indicates, Britain has a higher sales volume per store and a lower number of stores per million dollars of sales than the present ECM countries.

A third encouraging sign is the growth of marketing education. Although university-level courses are but a few years old, some of the graduates are already active in retailing, putting into practice what they have learned. Also, marketing conferences and short courses have helped retailers to find out why some are more successful than others. They are discovering that marketing research and advertising really pay.

TABLE 1—RETAILING PRODUCTIVITY IN WESTERN EUROPE
AND THE UNITED STATES[a]

Country	Stores		Employees	
	Sales volume per store	Number of stores per million $	Sales volume per employee	Employees per million $
France	$15,430	65	$ 8,385	119
Germany	13,970	72	5,415	185
Italy	12,980	77	7,300	137
Low Countries	10,810	93	5,140	195
Belgium	10,980	91	7,080	141
United Kingdom	24,760	40	6,075	164
United States	75,270	13	15,285	65

Source: André Anstett, *Opportunités et Exigences du Marché Commun pour l'Entreprise* (Paris: J. Walter Thompson Company, 1959), p. 17.

22.

LIMITATIONS OF SUPERMARKETS IN SPAIN*

Joseph R. Guerin

IN 1958 Spain was the scene of a marketing experiment: the introduction of a modern marketing institution—the supermarket—into an underdeveloped economy. In this experiment, as in today's medical experiments involving transplanted bodily organs, the crucial question was whether the transplanted marketing institution would grow and prosper in its new environment.

The experiment failed. Over four years later, at the end of 1962, only 44 self-service food stores in Spain met the typical European size criterion for a supermarket—a sales area of at least 400 square meters.[1]

This paper will identify, describe, and evaluate a number of specific factors that limited the growth of Spanish supermarkets. More generally, however, this study offers an analytical framework—a way of arranging those factors—that may be used in studying any country into which a new marketing institution is being introduced, where the question is: to what extent is the new marketing institution likely to displace the existing institutions?

In this framework, retailing services are viewed as a separate product, distinct from the merchandise that the retailer transfers to the consumer. This product consists of a *bundle of services* offered by the new marketing institution, which differs from that offered by the existing institutions. The new marketing institution is, then, a product whose quantity, like the quantity of any other product, is determined by the forces of demand and supply.

The quantity demanded of this product, the new marketing institution, is subject to several limitations: the number of potential customers, their incomes, etc. Each of these sets a different limit on the number of units of the new marketing institution demanded. Likewise, the number of units that could be set up is subject to a variety of limitations—available managerial talent, financial resources, etc.—each of which sets a different limit on the number that could be operated profitably. The actual

* Joseph R. Guerin, *Journal of Marketing*, Vol. 28, No. 4 (October, 1964), a publication of the American Marketing Association, pp. 22-26. Reprinted by permission.
[1] Data supplied by the *Departmento de Autoservicio, Cajas Registradoras National, S. A.*

number of units cannot exceed the number set by the most restrictive demand or supply factor. Growth of the new marketing institution is then contingent upon easing the most restrictive limiting factor.

LIMITED DEMAND FOR SUPERMARKETS

Several major demand factors limit the number of supermarkets:

(1) population density
(2) consumer income
(3) consumer preferences and traditions regarding types of retailing services
(4) the extent to which the existing food stores are able to survive competition from the new supermarkets.

Population Density

A food store which is "super" in terms of physical size or sales volume must have access to a "super" market. One dimension of the potential market of a retail food outlet is the number of people who, considering their geographic location relative to the outlet, could possibly be customers of that outlet.

The limit to the geographic area containing a store's potential customers is set by the transportation facilities at the disposal of the buyers and by their responsiveness to the advantages (price and nonprice) of that store compared with competing stores. In Spain (with 5.7 passenger cars per 1,000 population in 1957[2]) private transportation available to the retail food buyer is next to nil, especially in the rural areas. Rural communities, lacking both high population density and buyer transportation facilities, constitute almost no market at all for supermarkets.

While the incidence of automobile ownership is much higher in the urban areas, the automobile so far has had little impact on the size of the geographic area served by a food retailer. In Spain a supermarket still must be located within walking distance of its customers. A family-owned car is used primarily by the head of the household to get to and from work; it simply is not available for daily food shopping. Because of limited refrigeration facilities and even limited storage space in the typical Spanish kitchen, food shopping is a daily operation.

The requirement that a supermarket be within walking distance of its customers does not limit the potential market for a supermarket too

[2] Dewhurst, Coppock, and Yates, *Europe's Needs and Resources* (New York: Twentieth Century Fund, 1961), p. 296.

severely in urban areas, however, because of the high population density there. Multi-family housing units are typical in urban Spain. The market area could extend beyond walking distance if food shoppers could be induced to use public transportation facilities, where service is both frequent and inexpensive.

Low Consumer Income

A second dimension of the demand for supermarkets is measured by the incomes of those whose physical location makes them potential customers. A supermarket in a heavily populated area will not enjoy adequate sales volume if each buyer's purchases are very small because of limited income; nor will a large volume of such traffic produce adequate profits if purchases are limited to low-margin items. The formula for successful supermarket operation, since the emergence of this institution in the United States in the early 1930s, has been to lower prices dramatically on some items to attract heavy traffic and to keep prices and margins on the rest of the merchandise in line with competition. The formula assumes that once the consumer is inside the supermarket to buy low-margin goods he will also purchase other items carrying normal margins.

In Spain there are many areas, especially in rural regions, where this assumption that consumers will purchase the normal-margin items is not a realistic one because of low incomes. Even in Madrid, where per capita income is about 50% above the national average,[3] 54% of the population in 1960 spent only 17 pesetas (28 cents) per person per day for food.[4] Over 27% of this was spent for items (bread, sugar, oil, eggs) whose margins were kept at very low levels by government controls.[5] For these low-income customers, purchases of high-margin items would be negligible.

Of course, among higher-income families, whose per-capita food expenditure is almost four times that of the poorest class,[6] the premise on which a supermarket operates is justified; and we do find that supermarkets in Spain are located in high-income districts.

The supermarket promises more efficient retailing with lower prices for consumers in the upper layers of the income pyramid; but the supermarket, as we know it, is not viable where incomes are extremely low. As the incomes of the poorest groups in Spain increase, the demand for supermarkets will increase. Until then, the problem of improved marketing institutions for very-low-income consumers remains unsolved.

[3] Banco de Bilboa, *Renta Nacional de España y su Distribución Provincial* (Bilboa, 1963), pp. 17-18.
[4] Comisería General de Abastecimientos y Transportes, Gabinete Técnico de Alimentación, *Propuesto Nacional de Alimentación, Estimaciones de Consumo 1960* (Madrid, 1961).
[5] Same as footnote 4.
[6] Same as footnote 4.

Consumer Preferences

Given an adequate number of persons with sufficient purchasing power, all located sufficiently close to a supermarket, the level of demand for the supermarket's services next depends upon the preferences of consumers between the bundle of advantages offered by the supermarket and the somewhat different bundle offered by the traditional stores.

To enjoy the supermarket's advantages—lower prices, greater selection of goods, quicker service, freedom of choice—one must give up the advantages of dealing with traditional outlets: telephone and delivery service for the well-to-do, credit for the poor, nearness, and whatever pleasure one derives from association with people whose function is to serve. The extent of the demand for supermarkets depends upon how highly people value these competing advantages.

Various economic and cultural reasons have been offered why certain groups of consumers would favor traditional stores over self-service supermarkets. It is alleged that in Spanish society married women, who typically are not gainfully employed outside of the home and who lack other social contacts, find in their daily shopping a welcome opportunity to meet their neighbors.[7] The cold efficiency of the supermarket, peopled with strangers and affording the barest minimum of personal contact, appears a less attractive place than the friendly neighborhood store.

For buyers who depend upon credit extended by the local grocer, the supermarket is ruled out regardless of its other advantages.

Finally, since self-service presumes literacy on the part of buyers, the *illiteracy rate* is a significant index of the extent of the demand for supermarkets. In Spain the illiteracy rate for women ranges from 8.95% for those between ages 20 and 24 to 29.65% for ages 60 to 64.[8]

These economic and cultural factors are related to both income levels and residence: those who depend upon credit have low incomes; illiteracy is more prevalent in rural than in urban areas. In time, with increasing incomes and increasing urbanization, economic and cultural conditions presently influencing preferences away from supermarkets will tend to disappear.

The Response of Traditional Stores

The last demand factor to be considered is the reaction of traditional stores to the new supermarket competition. Demand for supermarkets,

[7] Interview with Spanish sociologists.

[8] Instituto Nacional de Estadística, *Censo de la Población y de las Viviendas 1960, Avance de las Clasificaciones de la Población Obtenido mediante una "Muestra" del 1 por 100* (Madrid, 1962), pp. 4-5.

like the demand for any service, depends in part upon the nature and extent of available substitutes—in this case the small, family-run food store. Disappearance of a large number of such stores under the competitive pressure of the supermarkets would have left the field clear for supermarket expansion; the continued existence of the traditional outlets would have inhibited demand for supermarkets and retarded their growth.

What happened in Spain? In spite of the severe pressure exerted by supermarkets, the traditional stores continued to exist. In the face of lower margins, most small stores kept operating, as the financial press reported, "almost miraculously."[9] Since these stores refused to die, supermarkets were unable to grow.

The undiminished number of small, family-owned stores was probably due to an excess of labor and low wage rates. Spain experienced none of the labor shortage which beset western Europe. In the absence of attractive job opportunities, the owners of small shops continued to operate them even when competitive pressure from supermarkets became severe.

Another factor that kept the small food store in existence was that women, especially married women, are seldom employed outside the home. The shopkeeper's wife, who assisted in running the store, would not have added anything to family income if the store had been closed. Family income might have been lower if the small-store operator closed than if he continued to operate, even with reduced margins.

As a result of this, supermarkets were left with competitors who, despite inefficiency, continued to offer location and services which the supermarket could not duplicate.

This will change:

—a more industrialized Spain will offer more and more attractive job opportunities to both men and women

—the attractiveness of the family food store will diminish

—the transformation from traditional outlets to supermarkets will advance at a quickened pace.

Another noteworthy aspect of the competition facing supermarkets in Spain is the challenge of the *mercados,* or market places. These are usually built by the city government, which leases stalls (ranging in size from about 35 to 350 square feet) to sellers of fruits, vegetables, fish, and meats. In a large *mercado* in Madrid there might be about 200 such stalls.

This marketing institution presents the consumer with a range of items and a variety of qualities that could never be matched by the meat or produce department of a supermarket. Buyers who patronize supermarkets to buy groceries frequently purchase meats and produce at the

9 *El Economista* (Madrid), March 10, 1961, p. 556.

mercados. Thus one-stop food shopping, needed for sales volume, finds little acceptance in Spain.

There are no signs that the *mercados* will soon disappear.

SUPPLY FACTORS WHICH INHIBIT SUPERMARKET GROWTH

Establishment of a supermarket, or any other retailing unit, involves four fundamental operations:

(1) getting merchandise to sell
(2) obtaining a place to sell it
(3) finding personnel to operate it
(4) getting money to finance it.

Difficulties that emerging supermarkets in Spain encounter in each of these operations are the limiting factors on the supply side.

Problems of Packaging and Grading

Self-service retailing requires packaged products. When the manufacturer does not package his product in convenient quantities, the supermarket operator must do it. In Spain this is typically the situation for sugar, beans, noodles, cookies, eggs, and a few other items. Since the scale of this packaging operation is small, unit cost is high. In the sale of items packaged by the retailer, either beforehand or at the time of sale (as with butter, cheese, etc.) the supermarket enjoys almost no advantage over the small grocery store.

Food manufacturers, who presumably could perform packaging operations more efficiently than the retailer, do not do so partly because of limited demand for packaged goods. Traditional service stores do not need prepackaging for their operations and in some cases actually prefer unpackaged merchandise: measurement and packaging in the store at the time of sale allow the retailer to accommodate consumers in very-low-income districts who purchase very small quantities. The self-service stores that need packaged goods comprise only about 1% of all grocery stores.[10]

The packaging situation presents an unfortunate vicious circle: lack of packaged goods forces self-service stores to engage in a costly operation which lowers profits and slows up expansion; and the slow rate of expansion of self-service food stores means no strong demand for food man-

[10] Same as footnote 1.

ufacturers to package their product. Hopefully, the stimulus of demand from self-service stores, when they expand enough, or possibly the stimulus from foreign competition as Spain liberalizes its trade policy, will lead to better packaging by Spanish food manufacturers.

Another difficulty in acquiring merchandise for sale really applies to chain stores rather than supermarkets as such. One reason for lower prices in chain stores is the lower cost of goods due to the chain's volume purchases. But in Spain the large buyer of groceries enjoys little advantage over those who buy in small quantities. This is not due to any legal restriction, such as our Robinson-Patman Act, but rather to the extremely small size of the firms supplying grocery products. A chain of any consequence would not be a large customer of *one* supplier; its purchases could probably absorb the total output of *several* suppliers. Under these circumstances, the large buyer cannot purchase on much better terms than a relatively small buyer.

The large buyer of produce, as well as of groceries, suffers the same disadvantage but for a different reason: absence of a grading system for produce. Produce comes from farm to municipal wholesale market with all grades of quality mixed. In the absence of grading, the volume buyer cannot simply order a large quantity of a commodity of some specified grade but must inspect everything he buys to ascertain its quality. This puts the large buyer on exactly the same footing as the small retailer. Until the wholesale market institutions in Spain improve, this condition will continue to exist.

Finding Suitable Store Locations

Another problem that the expanding supermarket industry in Spain has encountered is finding an appropriate store location. People with above-average income, in whose neighborhoods the supermarkets must be located, usually live near the center of urban areas where free land for building is very scarce. In the outskirts of the urban areas land is available, but in Spanish cities those with low incomes, not a rising middle class, reside in suburbs.

There is commercial space available in the middle-class districts since the ground floor of the typical residential building is designed for stores. Few of these would be large enough for a supermarket, but even these few might not be available to the supermarket operator at a feasible rental. Rents on both housing and store sites are government-controlled. However, whenever a store site is altered in any way (as, for example, conversion to self-service) the owner may request a revision of the legal maximum rent. Since controlled rents are usually far out of line with the

value of the site, the higher rental which the owner of a potential supermarket site could obtain often appears exorbitant to the store operator.
The retailer who converts to self-service and agrees to the much higher
rental must sell his merchandise in competition with other retailers who
occupy locations with rents controlled at low levels.

The location problem is not universal, however. In a few areas housing is being built for above-average-income families, and the necessary
space for a supermarket is provided for on the ground floor of these high-
rise buildings.

Shortage of Trained Personnel

The shortage of trained personnel is still another factor limiting the development of supermarkets in Spain. It is true that when the first supermarkets were introduced in the United States there were no people with
experience in this kind of operation. But in our period of rapid expansion of supermarkets, when the movement was taken over by the chains,
there were many persons connected with the chains who had had experience with large-scale operations.

The chains also had an organizational structure whereby efficient
procedures could be developed centrally and introduced into all of the
individual stores by people who were accustomed to such methods. Spain
today has no corporate-chain organizations of any consequence. It has no
pool of trained management personnel from which a supermarket industry might pick candidates for specialized training.

Lack of Credit

A final factor slowing down the transformation of Spain's food marketing
industry has been the lack of credit to finance this transformation. The
banks in Spain and the various credit agencies of the government traditionally have serviced the credit needs of industry rather than commerce.
The prohibition since 1936 of the creation of new banks has eliminated
the possibility of new banks freed of the old traditions.

Lack of credit might be due in part to the small scale of retailers.
Apparent discrimination against commerce might be mostly discrimination against small borrowers. If so, then the advent of strong corporate
chains in Spain would loosen up sources of credit not presently available
to small independent enterprises. There would also be fewer financing
problems for the expansion of supermarkets if foreign corporations decided to enter this field.

In Conclusion

In spite of these limiting factors of both demand and supply, it is not surprising that supermarkets have made some headway in Spain. A marketing institution that works on a very extensive scale in a developed economy is viable on a limited scale in an underdeveloped economy, because some small segments of the underdeveloped economy have the same characteristics of demand and productive ability common to the developed economy. A small fraction of Spain's population has the income and the tastes and location to constitute an adequate demand for a limited number of supermarkets. A small fraction of its entrepreneurial class possesses the capital and managerial skills required for this kind of operation.

At present the effective limitations are found on the supply side rather than on the demand side. Demand is limited, it is true, to certain parts of the urban areas; but the above-average-income residents of those areas could support a greater number of large self-service food stores if obstacles to their establishment could be overcome.

Successful introduction of supermarkets on a large scale, however, requires conditions which now do not exist in Spain. In the future Spain's general economic development will dissolve the limitations which presently exist.

23.

WHOLESALING IN AN ECONOMY
OF SCARCITY: TURKEY*

A. Coskun Samli

PROBLEMS OF SCARCITY

IN MOST of the underdeveloped and semideveloped countries one of the most significant characteristics is the presence of an excess demand. Individuals in these countries spend most all their incomes on necessities, and greater income would only mean more spending. Since savings are very limited and are completely inadequate for the economic growth aspired to, many industrialization projects of these countries generate inflationary pressures. Projects for electrification of areas, improvement of communications, and advancement of education are all necessary but not immediately productive.

Although money income increases through these undertakings, available consumers' goods do not increase proportionately; and hence there is a lag in real income. This means that demand usually exceeds supply. Such an economy may be called *an economy of scarcity*.

Turkey's per capita income is much lower than in the average Western European country. Also, about 70% of the Turkish population are peasants, making their living in agriculture, and a major portion of the Turkish national income is generated by agriculture. Consider finally that Turkey exports mainly raw materials, and imports finished goods and industrial commodities. All three of these factors are indicative of Turkey's standing (according to Western standards) as a relatively underdeveloped country.[1]

The distinction between an underdeveloped and semideveloped economy is somewhat arbitrary. However the concept of semideveloped is used here to distinguish the Turkish economy from the far Eastern as well as the Western economies.

The fact that demand exceeds supply presents ideal conditions for manufacturers and middlemen. In an economy of scarcity almost any product, so long as there is need for it, is sold with little or no effort.

* A. Coskun Samli, *Journal of Marketing*, Vol. 28, No. 3 (July, 1964), a publication of the American Marketing Association, pp. 55-58. Reprinted by permission.
[1] *Facts on Turkey* (New York: Turkish Information Office, 1959), pp. 38.

There is relatively little need for promotional activities. Advertising, if any, is generally informative rather than persuasive. Since many commodities come from abroad and since the country usually has a foreign exchange shortage, there are many tariffs and quotas to limit imports. This worsens conditions, and in many commodity lines scarcity becomes more acute.

Consequently, the basic problem in Turkey is that of production or availability of goods, rather than marketing.

THE ROLE OF WHOLESALERS

Wholesaling does not present a major problem in an economy of scarcity. Wholesalers in Turkey can sell almost as much as they can handle, provided that they fulfill their functions adequately.

As an economy becomes more prosperous, the position of wholesalers also changes. The economy becomes more competitive, not only within the trade channels but also between channels. Rivalry from other institutions of the distribution complex as well as from other wholesalers also becomes keener. Marketing then becomes the basic problem.

In the United States during the past few decades many manufacturers as well as retailers have tried to do away with the wholesaler by taking over some of his functions.[2] In response to this competition, there have been distinctive changes in overall wholesaling practices; they are being altered to serve changing needs.[3]

Contrary to its counterpart of a century ago, the present American wholesaler renders a number of managerial and research services to customers and vendors, and also is engaged in a number of promotional activities. More specifically, the modern American wholesaler may be involved in any or all of the following functions: (1) location analysis for retailers; (2) store design and modernization; (3) legal assistance; (4) providing opening services; (5) assistance in sales training and merchandising; (6) advertising and promotional services and cooperative promotion; (7) store management counseling; (8) other special services, such as price-marking, shelving, inventory control, and any other special service that may be necessitated in a particular case.[4]

---

[2] See E. H. Lewis, "Comeback of the Wholesaler," *Harvard Business Review*, Vol. 33 (November-December, 1955), pp. 115-125.

[3] Millan R. Karas, "The Historical Development of the Wholesaler During the Past 150 Years," in David W. Robbins, Editor, *Successful Marketing At Home and Abroad* (Chicago: American Marketing Association, 1958), pp. 402-408.

[4] Herman C. Nolen, "The Modern Wholesaler and His Adjustment to a Changing Economy," and Rudolf L. Truenfels, "Some Additional Observations and the Modern Wholesaler," in David R. Robbins, Editor, *Successful Marketing At Home and Abroad* (Chicago: American Marketing Association, 1958), pp. 409-422.

LOCATION OF WHOLESALERS

Turkish wholesalers are clustered in a few large cities, Istanbul by far the most important. The clusters are generally located near vendors rather than the markets. Turkish wholesalers are geographically stationary and almost completely supply-oriented.

The major customers are those retailers who have general stores in the more rural areas. They come to wholesalers during certain seasons to do their buying. Big-city retailers, on the other hand, do not purchase from wholesalers. Usually they are either large enough to have their own production facilities or are near manufacturers and able to deal with them directly. This means that in the big cities the retailers have almost no dealings with middlemen.

Although not usually soliciting new customers or seeking further sales, wholesalers may in "dead seasons" send one or more good-will representatives to their present customers. These representatives not only help maintain good relations but also take orders in advance, and in many cases offer a special discount for these early purchases.

Usually different wholesalers, almost as if by collusion, deal with certain parts of the country only, and with specific types of retailers. This market segmentation almost automatically creates a product differentiation. Since there are many ethnic groups in Turkey with different backgrounds and tastes, the customs and styles vary drastically from one part of the country to another. Hence, if the wholesaler is concentrating on the northern part of the country, he probably will have to carry certain products which will appeal mainly to the people there, but which would not be very attractive to southerners.

FUNCTIONS OF WHOLESALERS

Contrasted with an economy of abundance, the wholesaler has a more significant position in an economy of scarcity. His economic role is by far more important. In contrast to his counterpart in the economy of abundance, he facilitates the distribution of goods and plays the major part in their creation.

In general, he is responsible both for the manufacture and distribution of commodities. This dual role of the wholesaler makes his services indispensable in the Turkish economy. To be able to fulfill this major role the Turkish wholesaler has a number of significant functions which must be considered.

Credit

The Turkish wholesaler extends credit both to small retailers and small manufacturers who could not obtain it otherwise. Although the wholesaler and the manufacturer can sell as much as their capacity permits, large stocks and capital are required. The majority of customers, whether big or small, rich or poor, lack cash, and therefore are either reluctant or unable to pay for their purchases from the wholesaler until after a significant time lapse.

Usually the retailer who buys on credit begins payment between the 90th and 150th day after the transaction. During this time and while he is paying his debt, the retailer is not charged interest. Debts are paid either in installments or in a lump sum. The terms of the transaction and the date and size of the installments vary considerably according to the relationship between the wholesaler and retailer.

Also the retailer's credit rating and the total volume purchased are important factors affecting the credit terms. If the retailer is a personal friend of the wholesaler, has a good reputation, and buys in large volume, he can get more reasonable credit terms than an average retailer.

In the absence of adequate credit sources for small merchants, this credit policy is important for the overall functioning of the economy. Probably without it the Turkish distribution system would collapse.

The wholesaler's credit policy in Turkey creates two distinct situations. First, the wholesaler does not have a high inventory-turnover rate; and second, there are sizeable cash discounts, 3 to 5% or even higher.

The wholesaler still has limited financial resources which force him to wait until part of the total receivables are obtained before another inventory turnover starts. Sources of additional funds for the wholesaler are rather limited. Borrowing from banks, at least for part of the receivables, is common practice; but this is costly and is limited by the bank's generally conservative credit policy. This means that the wholesaler often finds it profitable to allow cash discounts.

Since Turkey is primarily an agrarian country, credits in poor crop years may be extended for periods beyond the original agreement; otherwise the retailer cannot pay his debts. Knowing that he will be paid as soon as possible, the wholesaler prefers to wait rather than to go through complicated and costly bankruptcy procedures. Thus, the burden of poor crop years is usually on the wholesalers' shoulders.

Another facet of the credit situation is consigned selling. In some cases the retailer is given the option of returning any merchandise, provided he pays return transportation costs. Even if the commodities were not purchased on a consignment basis, the retailer fairly commonly takes the liberty of returning them, and the wholesaler almost always accepts these items. The retailer in these cases actually uses the wholesaler's capital without paying interest.

Production

The wholesaler's role in production may take place in three different forms.

First, since Turkey is not highly industrialized, "cottage industries" are still very popular; that is, many people produce goods in their homes during spare time and sell them to wholesalers.

Second, the wholesaler often has an exclusive dealership relation with these people, enabling him to handle their total output. He buys their products and pays them either cash or large installments in a short time; but without a reasonable amount of capital he cannot pay cash to these people while giving large credit to his customers. Sometimes persons in cottage industries work full time and eventually grow into small factories, often by means of constant encouragement and help from the wholesaler. It is, of course, advantageous for the wholesaler to have his vendor growing into an efficient "factory," for his prices may go down and he can produce more.

The third aspect of the Turkish wholesaler's role in production is vertical integration. Many wholesalers have their own production facilities, or have aspirations to integrate vertically. If they have production facilities, these are limited to satisfying their own needs. However, if the productive capacity does exceed his needs, the rest of the output might be "dumped" into the city market. This means competition for the city retailer, but does not create competition for the wholesaler's own customers, as they do not deal with the city markets.

Converting

Besides subsidizing cottage industries or hiring some cottage workers full time, many wholesalers also supply raw materials for these industries. For instance, to obtain a number of woolen sweaters, the wholesaler may buy the raw wool and have it yarned for the cottage industry.

Converting is fairly common among the wholesalers. It often requires large sums of capital; in many cases the wholesaler pays cash to buy and process the yarn, or he gets credit not exceeding 30 to 60 days, which is much shorter than what he gives to retailers.

International Trade

If the type of commodity line carried by the wholesaler requires imported raw material prior to converting or manufacturing, he imports just enough to take care of his own needs. It is mainly the large wholesalers with the necessary capital, of course, who engage in importing.

Sometimes a few small wholesalers may import or export jointly. Semi-finished or finished goods as well as needed raw materials may be imported by the wholesaler. He usually sells the imported commodities wholesale, but some may be sold retail.

In the event of acting as a retailer, the wholesaler pays attention to trade discount principles and does not sell far below usual retail prices. Retailing is engaged in by the wholesaler only to the extent of not competing with his own customers; as pointed out above, he deals with markets separate from his customers.

Exporting also is engaged in to some extent. Although not promoting his products in the foreign markets, the wholesaler will seriously consider an offer received from abroad. Once engaged in exporting, he looks upon it as a "one-shot" proposition; and since he does not expect repeat sales, he may not put forth his best efforts to satisfy the customer.

COMPARISONS WITH OTHER ECONOMIES

Although we have concentrated on Turkish wholesaling, the same observations may apply to other economies of scarcity. There is some evidence indicating that wholesalers in India, Egypt, and Brazil have status similar to that in Turkey.[5] Their role goes farther than being merely a component of the distribution complex. In some cases they may establish and develop the productive as well as the distributive systems.

This may be considered the Clark-Fisher hypothesis in reverse.[6] This hypothesis states that primary, secondary, and tertiary industries in that order will evolve in an underdeveloped country. However, it is possible that tertiary industries, for example, wholesaling, may contribute to the development of primary and secondary industries.

[5] Harper W. Boyd, Jr., Abdel Aziz el Sherbini, and Ahmed Fouad Sherif, "Channels of Distribution for Consumer Goods in Egypt," *Journal of Marketing*, Vol. 25 (October, 1961), pp. 31-32; and Ralph Westfall and Harper W. Boyd, Jr., "Marketing in India," *Journal of Marketing*, Vol. 24 (October, 1960), pp. 11-17, at p. 13.

[6] Richard H. Holton, "Marketing Structure and Economic Development," *The Quarterly Journal of Economics*, Vol. 67 (August, 1953), pp. 344-361; Allan, G. B. Fisher, "Marketing Structure and Economic Development: Comment," *The Quarterly Journal of Economics*, Vol. 68 (February, 1954), pp. 151-154.

Final Comparisons

Wholesaling functions in economies of scarcity and abundance differ
significantly. See Table 1 for a contrast between the functions of Turkish
and American wholesalers.

TABLE 1—CONTRAST IN TURKISH AND AMERICAN WHOLESALING

Function	Turkish Wholesalers	American Wholesalers
Geographically stationary and concentrated	All	Some
Supply oriented	All	Some
Involvement in partial financing of retailers	All	Some
Vertical integration and involvement in production	Most	Some
Involvement in exporting and importing	Most	None
Involvement in consulting and other customer services	None	Most
Involvement in sales promotion	None	All

In contrast to his American counterpart, the Turkish wholesaler does
not engage in promotional activities such as advertising or branding, and
does not perform many other functions such as consulting and servicing.
However, he has other important functions in terms of producing goods
as well as facilitating their distribution. His functions in terms of granting credit, subsidizing production, converting, and importing are basic
to the functioning of the Turkish economy. In short, he assumes the
leadership of distribution channels. In this respect the Turkish wholesaler resembles the American wholesaler of the 1800s or early 1900s when
the American economy was not one of abundance.

PROMOTING

24.

'ON TARGET': SEVEN ASPECTS OF INTERNATIONAL ADVERTISING AND MARKETING PLANNING AND CONTROL*

Jere Patterson

"On Target" is a simple phrase, but as we all know in the marketing field, a very vital one indeed. This is true domestically and no less true internationally. And, it lies at the very heart of effective marketing program evaluation.

Marshalling facts and defining objectives are essential to the development and control of international advertising and marketing programs. Basically, target-oriented planning in marketing and advertising pays off internationally just as it does domestically. When we say "internationally," of course, we speak of the composite of many domestic markets. It is essential to look at each market individually, as well as collectively, just as we do domestically. And, if you are both a domestic and an international company, you ought to plan in such a way that the domestic market is carefully coordinated with the international. Do not compartment your thinking! Market planning is not a U.S. problem, a North American problem, or a European problem. It is a world problem.

THE SEVEN ASPECTS OF INTERNATIONAL ADVERTISING AND MARKETING PLANNING AND CONTROL

A coordinated, well-planned approach to international advertising and marketing planning and evaluation has at least seven basic target rings. Some of these place a certain emphasis on advertising, sales promotion and public relations because if these highly visible and vulnerable items can be thought through and justified, there's a good chance much of the essential marketing thinking has been accomplished. The seven rings are:

* Reprinted by permission from *The Marketing Plan in Action* (1964), The New York Chapter Inc. of the American Marketing Association, pp. 73-76.

- First, marketing objectives—what are they? How do you define them?
- Second, background marketing information available from all sources. Marshall what you know.
- Third, market-by-market considerations that may vary from the general picture.
- Fourth, the world-wide communications budget, embracing advertising, sales promotion and public relations.
- Fifth, analysis and comparison of costs, market-by-market and in various ways.
- Sixth, planning, follow-through and integration.
- Seventh, the measurement of results in order to evaluate and to plan for future modifications and adjustments in the basic plan.

What are some of the important considerations in working out the planning details in each of these areas?

DEFINE MARKETING OBJECTIVES

Let's first look at the marketing targets. Is your business going to go anywhere at home, or abroad without knowing where it's trying to go? What are the objectives and goals? Today this seems so basic, and yet, though we all accept it, how often do our companies and our associates fail to define goals? Short term, long term, one year, five year and ten year. Rarer indeed is the company that really knows where it is going *globally,* or trying to go globally over any protracted period of time.

Here are some of the questions you've got to think through in order to define objectives or targets:

What are your company's international *growth* goals; in terms of size, and position, overall and by divisions, products and areas?

What is the geographic scope and priority of the business abroad?

What are the new and established products to be sold abroad?

What's the comparative future importance of direct exports, compared to sales through overseas subsidiaries?

What are the channels of foreign distribution and their relative importance and stature?

What is the internal organization structure? (If you do not realistically appraise this, you often do not have a knowledge of the framework within which you're truly working.)

What is the present and hoped-for share of world markets, the number and type of foreign customers?

What are the sales abroad by divisions and areas?

What are the profits domestically, internationally, market-by-market and in total?

What are your trade relations, your customer relations? What is your overall image and the degree of awareness of your company abroad?

BACKGROUND MARKETING INFORMATION

Now let's look at the second target ring: background marketing information. Much of it often is right within your reach, very often at headquarters. There's usually much more of it, both within your company and from a number of other sources in this country, than most planners expect to find or know exists. The United Nations, the Department of Commerce, the Stateman's Yearbook and other such sources can give you a great deal of background information on world markets. Assemble the information overall; target it in on each market so you know the relative importance of the market to you.

Now what are some basic facts about your international business that you've got to get:

What are your primary products and brand names?

Which ones are sold abroad and what is the degree of common identity?

What is the location of factories, assembly plants and sales branches? If you, for example, have plants in London, Milan and in Mexico City, from which plant are you supplying Argentina? From all three places plus the U.S.? If so, to what degree and on what product lines? And who's paying for what in terms of local advertising and marketing support of your Argentina operations?

What do your various divisions, subsidiaries or partially-owned companies manufacture? What is your percent of interest in each? If you own a 100% of a business, you've got a different attitude toward it than if you have 10% or 25%.

What is the percent of total international volume and profit of each plant? Do you have licensing arrangements? A licensing arrangement is quite different from a subsidiary arrangement because in a licensing arrangement, the licensee often pays the cost of marketing, advertising and other communications activities. The degree of control and direction you can exercise often varies in direct proportion to the degree in which your money is involved.

What are your major markets; your distributor markets, your export markets versus your manufacturing and your sales branch markets?

What is the international standing of your company; competitive situation, customer awareness, patent, trade mark and legal protection?

What is your basic marketing strategy? What is your basic advertising strategy? How does it relate to your domestic strategy? Is it entirely different? Should it be or is the difference only tactical? There are, of course, profound differences between overseas markets in time, custom, season, knowledge of a company, educational standards, identity of products, etc.; but the differences are often far less in number (and perhaps in importance) than the similarities. Very often basic advertising strategy applicable in the U.S. market is applicable against world markets as a whole, with obvious adaptations to the local scene.

What is the degree of top management interest in your international business? How many foreign customers do you have and where?

All of these you would say are basic questions, but how often or how well do you feel you could answer them right in your home market? I raise the point because if there is shallow lip service to background marketing information at home, you can imagine the dearth of facts and think-through on which many companies base marketing abroad in 80, 90, or more countries.

MARKET-BY-MARKET INFORMATION

We've decided on certain objectives, we've boiled down certain background marketing information. Now for the third target ring: pulling together information on the individual markets.

Make a chart—a chart with basic marketing considerations across the top in a row, next down the left-hand side, list the markets of the world broken down by world areas. Then chart the essential market-by-market facts or considerations. Among these are:

A) Population
B) Number of customers—actual and potential
C) Principal products sold in the market
D) Where the market is supplied from
E) Whether it is sold through a manufacturer, subsidiary, a sales branch, a licensee, or a distributor
F) Extent of sales coverage and distribution
G) Import or other restrictions on sales
H) Degree to which the trade-mark or brand name is protected or unprotected
I) Economic and political conditions
J) Total sales in the market
K) Share of market
L) Extent to which sales are expanding
M) Special competitive considerations
N) Degree of awareness of company and products

O) New products to be pushed
P) Principal marketing objectives for coming year
Q) Comparative cost of advertising
R) Who is paying for the advertising
S) Last year's sales and profits
T) Last year's advertising, sales promotion and public relations expenditure

How do you get all this information? One of the best ways is to get it from the field. Encourage local marketing and top business management to get the information and, in so doing, they will think through these considerations locally. Thinking through the information will help local managers to make the right marketing plans. Without these facts, you cannot properly review, comment, suggest and guide their activities. To do this market-by-market may take a year or even two to five years to establish. But once set up in terms of every market and every division and every product of your company, it can easily and profitably be carried on.

THE WORLD-WIDE COMMUNICATIONS BUDGET

Having thought through marketing objectives, pulled together background marketing information and weighed market-by-market considerations, you are in a position to work out the world-wide communications budget including not only advertising, but sales promotion and public relations. The first step is to set up standard budget categories for the various overseas operations. Care should be taken to distinguish between impact and administrative costs with emphasis on the former.

The prime purpose is to encourage others abroad to prepare effective communications and marketing plans. Pulling together communications budgets for overseas markets is not primarily a matter of financial review. It is a matter of encouraging others to do their homework. In this, good local and international advertising agencies have an important collaborating role to play.

Many companies conduct an overall international media advertising campaign. The degree of coverage of this program and the cost per market can be determined by pro-rating schedule costs country-by-country according to the circulations of the publications used.

When it comes to budgeting advertising, standard categories on the impact side can be set up for 1) newspapers, 2) local general magazines, 3) local trade publications, 4) art and production for space advertising, 5) radio, 6) TV, 7) cinema advertising, 8) outdoors, 9) transportation advertising, 10) other local advertising, 11) advertising research, 12) reserve.

Under the overall heading of administrative expense, standard categories can also be established for a) salaries, b) travel and entertainment, c) occupancy or rental expense, d) supplies, e) shipping costs, f) telephone and telegraph, g) taxes, social benefits, insurance, pensions, h) outside service—local and professional, i) miscellaneous.

Budgets can be worked out country-by-country using these categories and standard definitions of what each category covers. National market figures for each category can then be sub-totaled by regions or marketing areas and grand totaled for all world markets. They can also be cross totaled to arrive at the total impact cost and total administrative cost for advertising in all markets.

A similar procedure can be followed for sales promotion with, of course, different impact categories especially covering such items as direct mail, point of sale, window displays, exhibits, contests, catalogues, films, etc.

The same procedure can be utilized for budgeting public relations. Again the administrative categories can be quite similar with the possible addition of categories for clipping services and memberships and dues. Among the impact categories to be provided for would be obtaining of news, art work and photography, press relations and conferences, special events, company publications, mailing and mimeographing, public relations counsel and other outside services, donations, research, miscellaneous and reserve.

With the establishment of such standard categories covering all phases of communications activity, it is then possible to total up the combined expenses for advertising, sales promotion, and public relations in each market, in each marketing region and around the world as a whole. In this way the stage is set for the analysis and comparison of costs and the measurement of planning and budgeting performance market-by-market in various ways.

MARKET-BY-MARKET ANALYSIS OF COMMUNICATIONS AND OTHER COSTS

The next step is to analyze and compare the total cost of various aspects of the marketing effort; in this case, advertising, sales promotion and public relations, together with all other administrative expenses.

What are the cost differences between markets—past, present and future?

What are our "impact" costs—the costs of reaching individual prospects by various communications channels?

What are the internal administrative costs? Are they disproportionately high? (Often they are.)

What are costs by each key product? Product line?

PLANNING, FOLLOW-THROUGH AND INTEGRATION

Now you get to the most vital thing of all: the elements of coordination and integration. If you put the 12 months of the year across the top of your chart and down the left-hand side you put your world areas and your markets and you mark which of the principal activities or new product launches, or whatever, is due to break where and when, you then have a bench-mark as to the program planning of your various marketing activities—sales, distribution, advertising, sales promotion, public relations, etc. When you do this, you time and integrate the total marketing effort. Also, you are in a much better position to follow through and evaluate the marketing program. You can make all the plans in the world, but if you don't follow through to see that they're executed, the chances are fairly good that they may not be carried out to anywhere near the degree you anticipate.

EVALUATION OF PERFORMANCE—MEASUREMENT OF RESULTS

Lastly, we get down to measuring results. Before you begin any marketing, advertising or communications effort, be it domestic or international, measurements or bench-marks should be established to show where you now stand so that you subsequently can measure where you have gone. You measure at the beginning and you measure again at the end. You do this regularly and periodically because it is the basis for evaluating past efforts and planning future efforts. This is just as true in the industrial product field as in the consumer product field. In the former, advertising and communications activities are naturally less of a factor in the total marketing effort. You fight a harder battle to justify advertising expense than in the consumer field.

You've got to measure and have your facts. For example:

- What is the degree of awareness of your company or its products?
- Are people more or less favorably disposed toward you?
- Have you increased distribution, share of market, number of customers?

These things are all measurable. When the objectives of a marketing program have not been defined, you will find that you can't measure anything because you haven't got anything to measure. If the effort to measure does nothing else, it forces you to think through what your objectives, targets, clearly definable purposes should be for the effort you plan to make.

IN SUMMARY

Internationally, just as well as domestically, industrially, just as well as in the consumer field: define your goals, marshall the background information, outline key points market-by-market, pull together advertising, sales promotion, public relations, budget figures, country-by-country, standard category by standard category. Analyze and compare them, because then you can: check on your timing, check on your follow-through, check on the integration of various elements in the marketing effort, measure results. That's the way to be "on target".

25.

ORGANIZATION FOR INTERNATIONAL ADVERTISING*

Gordon E. Miracle

INTRODUCTION

IN 1964 U.S. commercial exports, plus sales of products manufactured abroad by affiliates of U.S.-based companies, exceeded $56 billion, an amount which is nearly one-tenth of U.S. Gross National Product. These sales are made in part by companies whose headquarters or international division personnel are involved in the planning and preparation of advertising campaigns for use in countries outside of the domestic country. For purposes of this paper, such advertising is defined as international advertising. Thus, international advertising is understood to include advertising in either foreign media or international media when a central authority plays some part in the planning or preparation of the advertising.

The bulk of international advertising by U.S.-based firms is accounted for by large manufacturers, operating in a number of countries. Although the situation is changing and small advertisers are entering foreign markets in increasing numbers, the major lessons to be learned today are from those with experience, primarily the companies that have come to be known as multinational corporations.

The term multinational has been variously defined, but the most popular definition that seems to be emerging contains two essential elements which are important to international advertising organization: (1) the company has a global view with respect to assessment of the relative promise of market opportunities, and (2) the company has a global view with respect to decisions on the allocation of investment funds. In short a multinational company sells or invests in those countries which appear to offer the greatest opportunities for long-run profit or return on investment.

We are interested in multinational companies because they are the leaders in international advertising. Since other firms have much to learn

* Reprinted by permission from *Marketing and Economic Development,* 1965 Proceedings of the American Marketing Association, pp. 163-177.

from the leaders, this paper will be devoted primarily to the *organization for advertising of multinational firms.*

Although the subject of advertising agency organization to serve multinational firms could also fit logically under the general title of this paper, the subject is too extensive to cover in this short paper. Nevertheless, after discussing corporate organization for advertising, a few brief comments will be made about how advertising agencies have adapted to serve multinational clients. Further details on this subject are available in a forthcoming monograph.[1]

THE NATURE OF INTERNATIONAL ADVERTISING

Communication with Foreign Consumers

In planning and preparing international advertising the same basic decisions have to be made as in planning and preparing domestic advertising, namely *what messages* should be run in *which media,* and *how much money* should be spent.

Moreover, scholars and businessmen have come to realize that the basic advertising task is essentially the same, at home or abroad; the fundamental task of advertising is to communicate information and persuasive appeals effectively. Whether domestic or international, the communicator must learn about the intended recipients of messages, define the market as precisely as possible, and study backgrounds and motivational influences in detail before communication is undertaken. It is the advertising environment—language, culture, economic conditions and so on—which changes from country to country, not the approach taken to plan and to prepare effective advertising campaigns. The principles underlying communication by advertising are the same in all nations. It is only the specified methods, techniques and symbols which sometimes must be varied to take account of diverse environmental conditions.

If one agrees with these viewpoints, it follows that knowledge of general principles, approaches and techniques is transferrable to some degree from one market and competitive environment to another.

It has been the realization of these facts about communication and advertising that has led advertisers to the conclusion that some degree of centralized direction, guidance, or perhaps control, can improve advertising within various countries and assist the advertiser in achieving corporate objectives as well as local, branch or subsidiary obectives. This

1 Gordon E. Miracle, *Management of International Advertising: The Role of Advertising Agencies* (Ann Arbor: Bureau of Business Research, Graduate School of Business Administration, The University of Michigan, Michigan International Business Studies No. 5, 1965, in press).

conclusion is one of the factors that have caused some large firms to depart somewhat from the policy of decentralization which has been so popular.

Objectives of International Advertising

Although objectives of international advertising are both numerous and complex, it is helpful sometimes to divide them into two categories, local and corporate. Under some conditions the achievement of both types of objectives can be facilitated by information or guidance from the corporate or central staff.

For example, the communication of specific product information may be primarily a local objective—part of the local marketing mix to serve customers properly. Yet, since management and staff at the top levels ordinarily are responsible for most product research, product development and decisions on basic product lines, they often are able to provide helpful technical information to those who have local advertising responsibilities.

As another example, most companies engage in promotional activities to improve their corporate reputation or image because the image may have an effect on the general acceptance of the company and its products in a market. Since modern transportation and communications media have fostered increased mobility of men and ideas, it is important for companies to have a uniform or at least a compatible image from market to market.

Thus local promotional activities as well as corporate reputation-building activities influence the total company sales and success of operations in multiple markets. A central staff is needed to assure that local and corporate communications objectives, and the methods by which they are achieved, are in harmony with the interests of the company as a whole, in both the short and long run.

Nevertheless, the local management ordinarily is in the best position to judge local market and competitive conditions and to make the final decisions as to *how* the company's communications objectives are to be achieved, that is, the specific messages and media to be employed.

However, local management often needs help even in the planning and preparation of local campaigns. The advancement of knowledge in the field of marketing and communication is rapid. The marketing concept, new developments in communications theory, the application of new techniques in assessing media effectiveness, and the many other new concepts and ideas which are constantly being developed, domestically and in other areas of the world, suggest the need for a clearinghouse or information transferral function for the corporate staff. While all new ideas may not be immediately and totally applicable in all countries, local management needs to be kept informed.

CORPORATE ORGANIZATION FOR INTERNATIONAL ADVERTISING

In order to facilitate analysis and decision making regarding the achievement of communications objectives companies are developing certain organizational patterns and structures. The way a corporation is organized affects the assignment of responsibility and authority, and it affects how functions are performed. Good organization can help to avoid duplication and wasted creative efforts; it can help to avoid the causes of conflict and friction; it can help to create harmonious working relationships to utilize human resources fully.

Generally there are three types of multinational companies that engage in advertising abroad; they may be grouped in terms of their organization structure:

1. Variants of the traditional *international division* structure, all displaying a shift of responsibility for policy and worldwide strategic planning to the corporate level.
2. The *geographic* structure, replacing the international division with line managers at the top-management level who bear full operating responsibility for subsidiaries in assigned geographic areas.
3. The *product* structure, replacing the international division with executives at the top-management level who bear worldwide responsibility for development of individual product groups.[2]

International Division Structure

Some companies with the international division structure are domestically oriented in the sense that the corporate staff has only domestic responsibilities. Under these circumstances the international division staff has the basic responsibility to serve subsidiaries. Other companies are world oriented in the sense that the corporate staff has total corporate and worldwide responsibilities.

The international division structure is best-suited to companies in which foreign subsidiaries have considerable autonomy with respect to

[2] Gilbert H. Clee and Wilbur M. Sachtjen, "Organizing a Worldwide Business" *Harvard Business Review*, Vol. 42, No. 6 (November-December, 1964) pp. 55-67. See also Gordon E. Miracle, *Management of International Advertising: The Role of Advertising Agencies* (Ann Arbor: Bureau of Business Research, Graduate School of Business Administration, The University of Michigan, Michigan International Business Studies, No. 5), Chapter III (in press).

TABLE 1—INTERNATIONAL DIVISION STRUCTURE

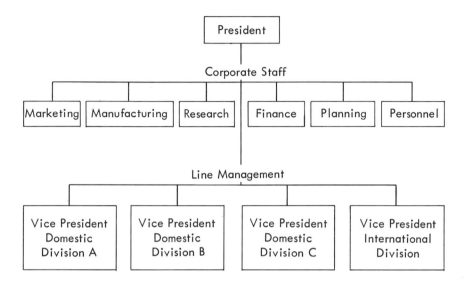

both management control and staff guidance. In such companies relatively little centralized guidance and control are exercised over advertising abroad.

However, there are a few companies with the international division structure which might be described as multinational firms in the sense that the corporate staff and management have established channels of communication and lines of control with the international division staff and management, and in turn with subsidiary staffs and managements, in a manner which permits the development of a global viewpoint on sales and investment decisions. Although such an evolution is difficult to implement, it sometimes is less difficult and disruptive than to abolish the international division and shift to the geographic or product structure.

Generally in companies with an international division, subsidiaries are given a free rein to select the best local advertising agency available without regard to its capabilities in countries outside the subsidiary's markets and without regard to the agency's connections with foreign agencies. Under these conditions a branch of an American agency must compete for the account of each subsidiary on equal terms with foreign agencies. The American agency which has the ability to coordinate local advertising with that of other subsidiaries or the parent company has no "inside track." Even if a foreign branch of an American agency is selected, there is relatively little pressure for such coordination. These conditions do not provide a strong incentive for U.S. advertising agencies to develop the capacity to provide multinational service.

However, companies that are in transition to multinational companies sometimes suggest that subsidiaries utilize the foreign branch of an agency selected by the international division staff, although they may not insist on adherence to the suggestion, especially if the subsidiary has a well-established, successful relationship of long standing with a competent foreign agency, or if the branch of the U.S. agency is unable to provide local service equal to that provided by a local foreign agency.

Geographic Structure

In companies that utilize the geographic corporate structure, the corporate staff has worldwide responsibilities, including some international advertising responsibilities. Although few companies have evolved to the stage illustrated in Table 2, the area concept within the international division is quite common. It appears as if the area structure within the international division is a transition stage which sometimes leads to the full-fledged geographic corporate structure, when the volume of business in each area sufficient to justify divisional status.

The geographic form of organization is particularly appropriate for companies that sell through subsidiaries, distributors or licensees which require substantial local marketing autonomy but still find centralized

TABLE 2—GEOGRAPHIC STRUCTURE

support of value. Under this form of organization, international advertising within each division is coordinated more closely than under the international division structure. The corporate staff has the responsibility to provide whatever guidance and service is required to coordinate between divisions and achieve corporate communications objectives.

The use of the geographic structure has profound implications for advertising agencies. In order to serve the client properly, the agency must be capable of providing services over the relevant geographic areas. This requirement influences agency personnel policies, location and type of branches or offices abroad and internal organization.

Product Structure

In firms that are organized into divisions that have worldwide responsibility for a product group, the corporate staff also has worldwide re-

TABLE 3—PRODUCT STRUCTURE

sponsibilities, including some international advertising functions. Under the product structure the relationships between the corporate staff and divisional staff with regard to strategic planning and operational responsibilities are similar to those under the geographic structure.

The product structure is appropriate for companies that have products that are relatively homogeneous with respect to customer use and marketing requirements, although the products themselves often are of a technical nature and may require individual adaptations. Under these conditions it is appropriate to assign advertising responsibilities on a worldwide basis, especially to provide a mechanism to transfer technical information and marketing techniques, ideas, and materials easily and quickly. Such companies require advertising agencies which are capable of providing service in all markets in which the product division operates or sells.

Corporate and Subsidiary Staff Relationships

The term multinational signifies not only a worldwide perspective with regard to marketing and investment decisions, but it implies an organizational structure to implement that perspective. Table 4 illustrates the corporate staff relationships to subsidiary or divisional staffs which exist in multinational companies.

TABLE 4—CORPORATE AND SUBSIDIARY STAFF RELATIONSHIPS IN THE MULTINATIONAL COMPANY

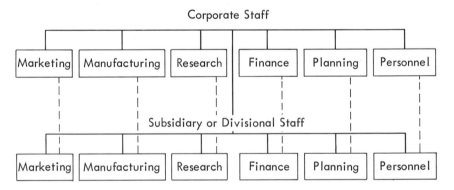

The corporate staff reports to top management, and the subsidiary and divisional staffs are under the line authority of subsidiary or divisional management. The dotted lines indicate the guidance and coordinating function of the corporate staff to counterpart staffs is a characteristic of most multinational firms.

Organization of the International Advertising Department

The position of the International Advertising Manager in the International Division is shown in Table 5.* The organization within geographic or product line divisions tends to be similar.

TABLE 5—INTERNATIONAL DIVISION MARKETING STAFF

```
                    ┌─────────────────────┐
                    │   Vice President    │
                    │ International Division │
                    └─────────────────────┘
                              │
                    ┌─────────────────────┐
                    │   International      │
                    │ Marketing Director  │
                    └─────────────────────┘
                              │
     ┌──────────────┬─────────┴────────┬──────────────────┐
┌──────────────┐ ┌──────────────┐ ┌──────────────┐ ┌──────────────┐
│ International │ │ International │ │ International │ │ International │
│  Marketing    │ │ Advertising  │ │ Product and  │ │ Sales Training│
│   Research    │ │   Manager    │ │   Market     │ │ and Education │
│   Manager     │ │              │ │  Planning    │ │   Manager     │
└──────────────┘ └──────────────┘ │  Managers    │ └──────────────┘
                                   └──────────────┘
```

Since the scope of the International Advertising Manager's functions varies widely, the size and nature of his staff also vary from company to company—from one man, half-time, to staffs of a dozen or more, performing many of the functions of an advertising agency. The form of organization of the international advertising department also varies. The most common structure is illustrated in Table 6.

Organizations of the type shown in Table 6 are characterized by dependence on an advertising agency or agencies to carry the primary creative and advertisement production burden, as well as to handle media placement. The international advertising department staff works with the advertising agency and bears responsibility for approval of agency recommendations in much the same way that a domestic client works with a domestic advertising agency.

---

* This chart is representative of companies that have manufacturing or marketing subsidiaries abroad. For companies that export through the international division, it is common for sales managers, organized by regions or product lines, to report to the International Marketing Director.

Subsidiary advertising personnel work with the local branches or associates of the domestic advertising agency. Ordinarily considerable

TABLE 6—INTERNATIONAL DIVISION ADVERTISING STAFF

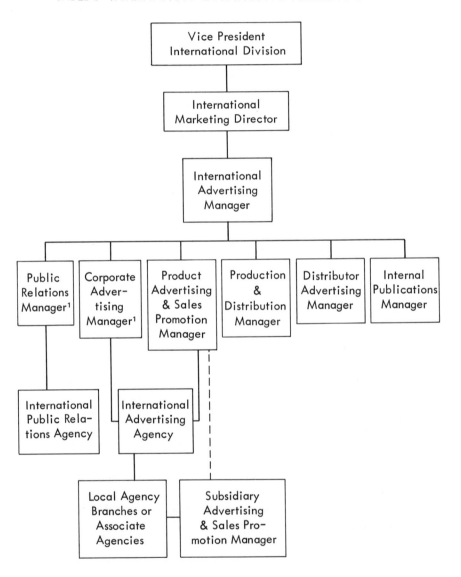

[1] Sometimes the Public Relations Manager or the Corporate Advertising Manager report directly to the International Marketing Director.

coordination is required between the domestic advertising agency and its branches or associates.

Although this form of organization is fairly common, there are examples of companies, usually in specialized product lines such as pharmaceuticals, that maintain their own creative staff and media selection staff; they have relatively little need of the services of an agency. But in other cases the policy of maintaining one's own creative and media selection staff is involuntary; sometimes suitable advertising agency service is not available when required.

In the form of organization illustrated in Figure 6 it is possible to coordinate public relations activities, corporate advertising, product advertising in measured media, sales promotional pieces and brochures, cooperative advertising, and internal publications (house organs) in such a way that subsidiary or divisional advertising managers will be able to formulate an advertising and sales promotional mix which will produce maximum sales at least cost. In multinational companies, in order to improve the planning and preparation of promotional activities, it is common for the international advertising manager or his staff to travel abroad regularly to consult with subsidiaries and to participate in the planning of promotional strategy, development of the budget, and so forth.

THE IMPACT OF CORPORATE AND DEPARTMENTAL ORGANIZATION ON THE CONTROL AND PERFORMANCE OF INTERNATIONAL ADVERTISING FUNCTIONS

The authority and responsibilities of the International Advertising Manager must vary from company to company. One cannot generalize on which particular functions he should perform. However, the range of functions includes participation in:

1. selecting products to promote,
2. planning promotional strategy,
3. preparing advertisements and promotional materials,
4. selecting media, and
5. controlling budgets.

Participation in these activities can range from virtual dictation to modest provision of facts or information when called upon by subsidiaries or divisions to do so. For example, with regard to "preparing advertisements and promotional materials" the specific types of headquarters' aids cover a broad range, including:

1. passing on successful selling appeals from other locations,
2. preparing or passing on art work or photographs,
3. preparing or passing on sample copy or layouts,
4. providing especially prepared print advertisements, or radio, slide or film commercials, and
5. preparing complete prototype campaigns.

There is no general answer to the question whether or not advertising responsibility and authority should be centralized or decentralized. Although we can identify reasons for centralization or decentralization of certain functions, each company must perform its own analysis and make its own decisions. The proper balance for each company is an individual matter, depending on the characteristics of the company, its product lines and the markets it serves.

The degree and type of centralized guidance or control over international advertising can vary from one extreme to another within the three basic corporate structures. However, the tendency is for there to be relatively less centralization under the international division form of organization than under the geographic or product line structures. Thus the geographic and product line structures tend to require more comprehensive control and guidance of international advertising.

Although increasing numbers of companies are tending to become multinational firms, many companies that have sizable foreign operations have not yet moved very far in the transition. Many subsidiaries still are virtually autonomous, operating in much the same fashion as an independent company. Thus, decentralized authority and responsibility with respect to advertising is still widespread, and it likely to continue to be the policy of many companies for some time.

In such companies the International Advertising Manager, with no staff but a secretary or perhaps one or two assistants, will be responsible for a modest amount of advertising in international media, or for keeping subsidiaries posted on general corporate policies such as the limitations on the size of the advertising budget. Under these circumstances subsidiaries plan and prepare their own individual marketing and advertising campaigns, in conjunction with a foreign advertising agency, or with their own creative staffs, as they deem appropriate. There is a minimum of exchange of information and ideas between domestic and foreign, or among foreign subsidiaries, licensees or distributors.

The development of greater corporate or international divisional staff participation at the local level abroad is a slow and delicate undertaking, especially for companies with newly-purchased foreign manufacturing subsidiaries, or partly-owned foreign operations, and particularly in view of the penchant for maintaining subsidiary net profit responsibility. However, the new breed of multinational firms is making progress toward centralized coordination and control of essentially locally-initiated and locally-implemented plans. Such companies attempt to achieve the advantages of coordinating and integrating promotional programs on a worldwide basis. To assist local management in planning local campaigns, the corporate staff and its advertising agency contribute the latest ideas, techniques and approaches to the solution of advertising problems; the corporate staff sets policy to insure effective planning and control procedures. A mechanism is established to convey experience and information from one division of the company to another, which permits full participation in new developments by subsidiaries, licensees, or distributors; they work together and learn and profit from each other.

The trend toward multinational management with local flexibility indicates a growing need for sophisticated advertising personnel in corporate advertising departments. The trend also indicates a growing need for sophisticated multinational service from advertising agencies. While the virtually autonomous subsidiary may be served satisfactorily by a foreign advertising agency, the multinational firm requires an agency capable of providing coordinated service in a number of countries.

TRENDS IN ADVERTISING AGENCY CAPABILITIES TO PROVIDE MULTINATIONAL SERVICE

International billings of U.S.-based advertising agencies are understood to include not only direct placement by agency headquarters in international or foreign media, but also the billings of foreign branches, offices, or associates if such billings originate from, or are influenced or controlled from outside the country in which the advertising is run.

Although a few advertising agencies have served clients abroad for many years, as late as the middle 1950's only six "domestic" agencies and a handful of "export" agencies accounted for over 90 per cent of known international billings of U.S. agencies. By 1964 more than a dozen additional agencies had developed a substantial volume of international billings (over $1 million), and the number of agencies capable of serving clients abroad is continuing to increase rapidly. Nevertheless, the bulk of U.S. advertising agency international billings is concentrated in a small number of large advertising agencies that have the capability of providing service in a number of countries.

In 1953 international billings of U.S. agencies amounted to about $120 million; by 1964 the figure was over $650 million, an annual rate of increase of nearly 20 per cent. Last year (1964) international billings of U.S. advertising agencies accounted for about 10 per cent of total billings of U.S. agencies—a significant share.

U.S. advertising agencies have utilized a number of methods to serve clients abroad:

1. *Fully owned branches,* established from scratch,
2. *Fully owned branches,* bought out an existing agency,
3. *Majority interest,* bought into an existing agency,
4. *Minority interest,* bought into an existing agency,
5. *Joint venture,* an agency formed in partnership with a foreign agency, often depending at least in part on the local partner's staff and facilities to provide service for the clients of the foreign partner.
6. *Associate, affiliate or correspondent relationships* with independent foreign agencies, with the range of cooperation from "personal, careful and close" to "handling the entire relationship by mail."
7. *International agency,* with the range of service from "full service" to mere "media placement."
8. *Direct placement* in foreign media through media representatives which are stationed in the United States.
9. *Direct placement* with foreign media.

Generally most agencies that have clients that require service abroad prefer whenever possible to use branch offices or agencies in which they have at least partial financial interest.

In the past, several large U.S. agencies preferred to start branches abroad from scratch. Today they are in the minority as nearly all agencies that have branches abroad prefer to buy out an existing agency.

Generally, very large agencies prefer wholly-owned branches over partial ownership. Agencies of modest size tend to prefer minority-interest or joint-venture arrangements.

For those agencies which are relatively new on the international scene it is quite common to utilize foreign independent agencies as "associate," "affiliate," or "correspondent" agencies as an interim measure prior to the establishment of branches or joint ventures. Direct placement with foreign media is used only under special circumstances and such billings are relatively small.

CONCLUSIONS

In view of the nature of international advertising problems, and modern advertising technology, there is a need for some degree of centralized direction with regard to basic policies and the approach to the solution of problems. Ther is also a need for competent local management. Modern corporate organizations are evolving which combine multinational coordination with local management flexibility.

Since multinational clients require multinational advertising service, advertising agencies are developing such capabilities. While progress in many ways has been, and must be slow, the pace has been accelerating.

26.

AND NEVER THE TWAIN
SHALL MEET . . . NEVER?*

MANY companies seem to embark on programs of *international* advertising with Rudyard Kipling's famous lines engraved on their minds:
"East is East and West is West and never the twain shall meet."

This preconception is bolstered by evidence of *growing nationalism*
and chauvinism in many parts of the world.

Yet such rigid presumptions of a fragmented world often result in
reducing international advertising's *effectiveness* while *increasing* its
costs.

Unfortunately, the tendency to raise warning signals about the
snares in international advertising is *watering down* many a campaign
and even preventing some from getting off the ground.

It's deplorable, too, that the patter about *pitfalls* in international
advertising is permitted to impair judgment and afflict so many marketers
with *advertising astigmatism.*

UNIVERSAL OR ENDEMIC?

It's dangerous to enter any venture weighed down by taboos, real and
imaginary. This is particularly true if the venture is on *unfamiliar* soil
and in *strange surroundings.*

The "you can'ts" and "you musn'ts" tend to drown out the voices
counseling *courage* and *daring* and pointing to the challenges of opportunity.

The inclinations to look for the *endemic differences* in foreign
countries have been stronger than the impulses to seek the *universal characteristics* of people.

Far too many potentially powerful universal appeals have been need-
lessly discarded in favor of advertising approaches keyed *narrowly* to the
assumed mores and attitudes of each *individual* country.

Obviously, traditional, social, cultural, political and economic differences *do* exist and cannot be ignored for some categories of products.

Possibly a campaign like Pontiac's "wide track" would lack persuasiveness in countries where most roads and streets are narrow.

* Reprinted by permission from *Grey Matter,* Vol. 37, No. 1 (January, 1966), a publication of Grey Advertising.

On the other hand, advertising *unhampered* by mental blocks could change indigenous attitudes. Supposedly, deodorants would have no appeal in cultures where body odors are regarded as less offensive than here. Yet there was a time when we in the United Stats were not so sensitive to body odors until advertising made us *conscious* of B. O.

If advertisers had clung to the idea that tea drinking is so deeply ingrained in Japanese life that it would be *fruitless* to advertise coffee, it would have been a *roadblock* to advertising this beverage in that country.

Yet instant coffee and vigorous *advertising* and *selling* are gradually changing the beverage consumption habits of this nation.

Grey Matter editorial observers noted this change 3 years ago when they wrote (December 1962 issue): "Our Japanese companions invariably ordered coffee rather than tea as we had expected."

Now *coffee houses* are springing up and companies such as General Foods, Nestle, and the Japanese Morinaga Confectionery are battling for this burgeoning market.

Tradition and expediency have too often *inhibited* the universal approach to international advertising for many reasons:

1. Differing policies on *product identities* vs. *corporate image,* and the *presumed* need of a dual approach to segmented national markets, operated *against* universality as an international advertising strategy.
2. Blocking the path to a universal appeal were also the *attitudes* of personnel who staffed the *export departments* of most companies. These people usually started with the assumption that advertising *must* be tailored to local conditions and that headquarter-directed advertising is fundamentally wrong.
3. Complete *local* autonomy, given to branches or representatives and the vested interests which grew up in each country, produced *divisive,* rather than unified approaches to all marketing activities, especially advertising.
4. Preconceived convictions and unwarranted fears have *inhibited* most companies from stating clearly the *copy direction* they desired their advertising to take. Instead, they have left this to local interpretation.
5. The *human* element is a problem. People capable of carrying through a universal advertising theme, with the necessary skill to adopt and adapt locally, are scarce. Local advertising agencies very often are handicapped by their own *chauvinistic attitudes.*
   The spread of American agencies abroad has *partially* overcome this deficiency. However, the new breed of agency talent, capable of carrying an advertising theme *through national boundaries,* is still in short supply and still handicapped by indecision at headquarters.

CHANGES UNDER WAY

But the trend to use universal advertising themes abroad is *accelerating.*

Potent pressures are at work to make such world-wide advertising appeals the dominant strategy of more and more companies.

1. Companies recognize that if they have a great advertising idea at work in one country, it is not only wasteful, but often *suicidal* to junk it in others where change is more for change's sake rather than for important marketing reasons.

   In making such decisions, preconceived notions must be thrown out the window and every method known to *research* must be put to work to find out whether the advertising appeal will work in *every country.*
2. Advertisers are recognizing that political boundaries do not circumscribe *psychological* or emotional *attitudes.*
3. Increasing standardization of products (often made in many countries and assembled in one) adds validity to the universal advertising theme as *sound strategy* in international advertising.
4. Top management is becoming more and more involved in *international* marketing. This acts as a brake on the tendency of middle management to oppose universal advertising and to support "difference" for *difference's sake.*
5. As the marketing concept spreads across the globe, it will lead to more and better *planning,* more *probing,* more *testing.* The mortality rate of sacred cows will rise. As a result, the universal advertising appeal will be regarded with greater objectivity.
6. *Cost control* will play a more dominant role in *evaluating* universal advertising. Unnecessary and expensive duplication of mechanical production costs, country by country, will be avoided where possible. The funds thus saved can be used more productively for additional advertising.

   One company discovered that six divisions in Europe were advertising substantially the *same product* lines in completely *different* ads, often on different pages of the same publication.
7. Most important is the speed with which *new products* are being introduced around the world. Simultaneous launching in many countries is becoming commonplace. Previous lags of years are being shortened to months, as in the case of Kodak's Instamatic.

   The launching *speed* tends to override the *separatist* instinct of local executives and agencies.

UNIVERSALITY GAINING

The list of companies which are moving towards the universal appeal in advertising is more *impressive* with every passing month.

One of the most successful examples is Revlon. (Grey client.)

While Revlon's international organization is *decentralized* in its daily operations, New York headquarters controls *basic* policies such as marketing and advertising.

Revlon is particularly concerned that their international advertising, no matter where it runs, contribute to the *over-all Revlon image*. Latitude is granted field managers in revising individual ads or budgets; but even *these* must be cleared first with headquarters.

AND NOW THEY DO MEET

Can international advertisers ignore the *difference* in peoples? Obviously not. However, isn't it vital to make sure that we aren't letting alleged differences *freeze* our minds and stifle our imagination?

Today Kipling's famous lines could be paraphrased: "East is East and West is West; North is North and South is South; and now they all *do meet*."

SUMMING IT ALL UP

Clear marketing perspective, unhampered by prejudices, indicates that for a large number of products, *basic universal advertising* appeals can be most effective in shifting attitudes and creating or expanding markets abroad.

Hence, it's most important that changing the advertising for each country should be done only after research and investigation have *demonstrated* that this is the most *productive* course.

Changing the advertising country by country, because efficient machinery for international co-ordination does not *exist*, can *dissipate* advertising expenditures and efforts most wastefully.

As space and time shrink, our point of view must *expand*. For as time goes on, more and more of our advertising will reflect what the editors of international magazines have *long understood*. They have successfully demonstrated that the "senses, affections and passions" of human beings are basically the same the world over, and that the people who respond the same way to similar stimuli are legion.

27.

HOW INTERNATIONAL CAN
EUROPEAN ADVERTISING BE?*

Erik Elinder

WHAT would happen if the advertising manager of, say, Coca Cola suggested that his company should run 50 different advertising campaigns on the U.S. market, one for each state? Would you find him on the company payroll next month?

If, on the other hand, he proposes 18 different campaigns and 18 different advertising agencies when marketing a product in Western Europe today, he may be slated for promotion.

And he may have earned it. Up until now there have been a number of obstacles to a uniform approach to European advertising.

While industry all over Europe is undergoing an acceleration of mergers and while at the same time more and more refrigerators, bicycles, safety razors, cigarette lighters, and thousands of other products are being mass produced, too many advertising men in European industry —whether in London, Paris, or Dusseldorf—are wrong about one basic fact.

Unfortunately, they believe that advertising for these goods which are identical in the majority of markets must be formulated differently and "dressed up" in arguments which vary from country to country. Can this be justified?

On the contrary, everything from American hair-spray, Greek tourism, Danish foods, too many other commodities and services can be sold with the same picture material, the same copy, the same advertising approach. This can be done *now*—not just here and there in specialized markets, but throughout Europe in the general market. Moreover, the size and acceptance of this general, overall market is growing daily.

The leveling off in standards of living and habits is accelerating. The technical means for delivering an advertising message on an international basis are steadily improving. There is continued growth in the reading by Europeans of publications from countries other than their own, and the day will come when Eurovision—a *chain* of European television and radio stations—will be a reality.

* Erik Elinder, "How International Can European Advertising BE?" *Journal of Marketing*, Vol. 29, No. 2 (April, 1965), a publication of the American Marketing Association, pp. 7-11. Reprinted by permission.

CAN WE GAIN IN EFFICIENCY?

Everyone knows how European statesmen have worked for years to integrate Europe into two big markets. Powerful groups wish to mold these two into one, but what has been achieved so far is good enough.

International marketers today find an entirely new climate in Europe, and many national companies decide to "go European." This, of course, does not mean that all parts of their marketing mix will overnight be squeezed into an all-European scheme. The sales function, for example, will probably be divided by national or at least language boundaries for a number of years.

But even language boundaries will unquestionably be affected by two main factors: media and mobility. The developments in mass media will influence language to an extent which we have yet to realize. In magazines and newspapers there is a trend toward extended geographical coverage: *Life International, Paris Match,* the *New York Herald Tribune,* and the *New York Times* international editions are examples of this. Some time ago *Punch* had a cartoon of an Englishman looking up from his paper and saying to his fellow clubmember: "By Jove, *Le Monde* has bought the *Times!*"

However, the advertising medium which is really going to break language barriers on a large scale will be television. Already people in southern Sweden watch television programs from Denmark and vice versa. In southern Denmark people watch German TV, Austrians watch German TV, and a large number of Frenchmen too. Germans watch TV programs from Holland and Belgium. Italians watch Swiss TV. And so on.

Recently the Swiss government decided to allow domestic commercial television, because Swiss producers had begun to lose business in their own market to foreign producers advertising on German and Italian commercial television. Several European governments are already "worried" because the children especially seem to absorb foreign language and culture by watching television programs from neighboring countries.

But above all else, when through technical development TV programs can be relayed over a satellite without earth-bound intermediary stations, the influence on children and adults of one-language (English) TV programs and advertising will be enormous.

This is definitely *the* change to be foreseen in Europe. In comparison with this barrier-breaking influence, other factors are no more than "peep holes" in the walls.

Nevertheless, mobility—tourism and migration—must be taken into account in today's European marketing. Five million Germans went to Italy as tourists in 1960. One million Italians are today working in Germany.

All this means that advertising must be synchronized to fit the all-European media, and must take advantage of border-crossing tourists, readers, and viewers. Advertisers will gain by "going all-European" now.

An interesting example of how a strictly national approach produces a loss of efficiency is seen when several national brand names are used for the same product. Even Unilever with its sophisticated marketing organization can attest to this by sad experience. One of its major detergents is sold under the name of Radion in Germany; but for special reasons a similar Unilever detergent in Austria—according to a Unilever executive—bears a different brand name. The great majority of Austrian housewives read German magazines, and a substantial number are also exposed to detergent advertising over German commercial TV. But this considerable geographical "extra-spread" of German advertising is of no value if Austrian housewives cannot find the name Radion among the detergent boxes in their shops, although the product *is* there but under another name.

Standardized brand names offer the most obvious examples of the advantages of all-European uniformity. However, if we believe in a certain "repetition effect" when advertising certain consistent copy themes in the United States, this ought to apply also when marketing in Europe. The impact of an advertising theme for detergents, cigarettes, or foods must be greater if, for example, a Swiss consumer meets practically the same advertising theme when reading *Life International* magazine, watching Swiss TV commercials in the French language, watching TV commercials from Western Germany, going to England on business, or when visiting Italy or Spain or Greece as a tourist.

The Swiss "perceptional sphere" is by no means only the *Neue Zürcher Zeitung* and the nearest TV and radio station, but something much wider, something almost all-European. There are such substantial arguments in favor of a common "copy platform" that advertisers ought to give serious thought to the possibility of standardizing copy themes used in Europe.

This goes for picture material as well. A picture, of course, is the most international conveyor of a message we have; and if we believe in a recognition effect of pictures and symbols in U.S. campaigns, why not accept it on the European continent, too?

THE EUROPEAN CONSUMER

When Europeans think of the United States of America, the great differences that still exist between East and West, North and South, rich and poor, are likely to be overlooked. We see the American people as "one big happy family," with gleaming teeth gathering around a corn-flake breakfast, drinking Coca-Cola in the afternoon sunshine, raiding a well-stocked refrigerator, cruising along parkways in sleek automobiles, and gathering to see spectacular TV shows, with a leading brand of Scotch in their glasses.

This picture may not be correct, but what we should not forget is that the lack of trade barriers within the United States is a force which tends to "even out" differences between different regions. In this process and in shaping the pattern of life, coast-to-coast advertising has played a vital part. And this leads to the following point: *To the consumer industries considering how best to formulate their messages to European consumers, it is more important to take into account trends in European consumption habits than the "national traits" and "traditional characteristics."*

Twenty years ago there were those who seriously claimed that the Swedish savings bank promotion program in northern Sweden should be different from that in southern Sweden because of differences in traditions. Today such a claim would be laughed off in the same way that future readers of this article may wonder how advertising could ever be limited by national boundaries.

Is it not true that we in Europe already have a gigantic all-European indoor market, where everybody has the same needs and desires for practical labor-saving kitchens; restful, comfortable living space; beautiful bathrooms, etc.? And do we not have a Euro-American outdoor market, which is largely identical in climatic conditions? What differences are there between the beach resorts of Italy, Spain, Florida, and California? Are the airplanes so different, or the automobiles we use for commuting and leisure trips? Can anyone honestly claim that all these internationally accepted goods and services must forever be marketed in one way in the U.S.A. and in a number of different ways in Europe?

The European consumer—does he really exist? *Yes! Right now there are millions and millions of Europeans living under largely similar conditions, although they read and speak different languages.* They have about the same incomes after taxes. They may live in private houses or in modern apartments, with bathroom, TV, radio, and refrigerator. By and large they tend to have the same drinks, and their food becomes more and more all-European every year. They see the same films and plays. They read the same magazines or syndicated articles. Their vacations are spent on the same European roads or at the same European summer resorts. Wherever they work, their factories have much the same kinds of machinery; and office equipment is so standardized that you can almost find your way through a modern office in the dark, no matter in what country.

Industry and trade in Europe are at the forefront of internationalism in their consumption. Most of their technical inventories and raw materials are bought without the least regard to national barriers.

Go into the nearest record shop, the nearest self-service store, household appliance store, beauty shop. Make a list of the products made locally by local companies. Make a similar list of all the products that have foreign names, manufactured under license or imported. It may surprise you how all-European, how international, European consumption is as of today. Soon it may be only advertising which stubbornly "refuses" to adjust itself to the new situation. Europe right now is a melting pot of goods without the label "made in . . ." National origin is usually of little or no importance. The *possession* and *availability* of certain goods is changing people's lives into a more uniform pattern—just as tools, materials and techniques have had a great influence on living habits and spiritual outlook in all historical cultures.

In Europe people read about largely the same products. But the picture material is not the same, nor the copy, nor the persuasive appeals —even in the thousands of cases where there is no necessity whatever for them to differ.

It would be unjust to blame advertising managers for not having used an all-European approach in the past, but today *differences* in living habits are rapidly diminishing. The time is ripe for advertising practitioners to take this into account.

LEGAL AND ADMINISTRATIVE OBSTACLES

When the plans for integrated tariff unions were drawn up in Europe, the politicians were quite aware of the fact that some governments might tend to misuse various legal and administrative rules to protect domestic industries from foreign competition. There have been some tendencies in that direction, but on a much smaller scale than originally feared.

Advertising has not been particularly protected by any such means. However, the rules governing the remuneration to an advertising agency using material from an agency in another country have hampered this particular form of unification.

As production costs for advertising are of relatively minor importance to the advertiser—compared with the negative effects of non-uniform copy, layout, pictures, etc., produced by national agencies—this is not too serious a matter, although negative attitudes may have been created among advertising agencies toward the broader concept of an all-European approach.

STRUCTURAL OBSTACLES

Have differences in distribution structure among various countries prevented the use of unified European advertising themes?

In some cases this has unquestionably been so, as the total marketing strategy is generally dependent on the type of outlet used. On the other hand, when it comes to fast-moving consumer items such as typical food and drug articles, we are rapidly moving toward an all-European distribution system. In 1961 the number of inhabitants per self-service store was some 1,300 in Sweden, 1,900 in Western Germany, 2,200 in Norway, 2,700 in Switzerland, 2,900 in Denmark, 4,000 in Holland, 4,800 in Austria, and 5,900 in England—all very favorable figures compared with those only five years earlier.

Retail development in Western Germany can best be characterized as an "explosion"—from 1,400 self-service stores in 1956 to 30,700 in 1961. In Sweden the self-service share of total retail sales is now 40%, and in England 16%, as compared with 85% in the U.S.A. Only France has lagged behind.

Foresight is, of course, a profit-producing factor in marketing. Those Swedish manufacturers who foresaw the great switch to self-service and non-food items in the domestic food trade after World War II were able to increase their market shares and to strengthen their positions, at the expense of competitors who kept on fighting for shares in the shrinking or "stagnant" retail branches. It would be a good idea for U.S. corporations to have their European headquarters not necessarily in a large country, but in one of those which are ahead of others in living standards, distribution, structure, etc.

Another structural factor making European advertising heterogeneous is the way in which the European advertising business is organized. Some of the national agencies have established or taken over agencies in other countries and built up bigger or smaller "chains." The drawback is that these so-called international agency chains have remained local. Their ambition seems to be to create *national* campaigns for *international* products. Swedes, Danes, and Norwegians, who speak practically the same language, meet *entirely different advertising campaigns* even for a product like razor blades that is used in exactly the same way by consumers enjoying the same standard of living!

Large American, British, German, French, and Scandinavian advertising agencies have built up a number of voluntary chains. It is surprising that they almost always present themselves as international chains of national agencies.

In the United States there are hundreds of executives of advertising agencies who consider the whole of the United States as their sales territory, and who plan and think on the basis of coast-to-coast advertising. But there is no single European agency today that has systematically built up its business for bigger markets, not to speak of all-European advertising.

People who try to promote a European "common market" dwell almost exclusively on its advantages to producers. Yet in the long run the advantage will be far greater in the distribution sector. In many cases industry is responsible for only 20 to 30% of the final consumer price. The most important benefit of a European common market would be to lower the costs of marketing, which in numerous cases account for 60 to 80% of product prices.

CURRENT OBLIGATIONS

I have never yet heard an American marketing man speak of insurmountable difficulties in applying brand advertising and centralized marketing strategy directed at the highly disparate mass of human feelings and emotions called the American consumer. But I am every day "up against" real resistance to the thought of an all-European approach in advertising.

Some of the objections relate to subordinate matters, such as differences in legislation as to the advertising of liquor, pharmaceutical products, etc. Others point to the differences in language, climate, sales channels, and physical distribution, and draw far-reaching conclusions based on insufficient knowledge.

The business leaders of Europe ought to follow the American example, and step by step build up their advertising on a greater-market basis. Too many businessmen emphasize only the differences and constantly overlook the similarities in the European market picture!

The swelling flood of practically identical products used in the same way all over Europe to cover identical needs demands a unified strategy in advertising. So does the great increase in migration across national and language border lines. So does the great expansion of tourism. So does the development in retail and wholesale structure in the various countries. So does the political determination to "even out" differences in legislation.

Consider the fact that all over the world the slogan used in advertising Lux soap is "9 out of 10 film stars use Lux"—the self-same slogan (in different languages), the same beautiful girls, the same name, and the same success.

The point is that advertising *must become* international. Advertisers, advertising agencies, and media need to play as active a part as possible in speeding up this process of development.

The coordination possibilities are much greater than ever have been imagined. The responsibility of advertising men is to support the serious attempts to internationalize the European market.

28.

MANUFACTURERS BOOST FOREIGN SALES BY EASING RESTRICTIONS ON CREDIT*

Roger W. Benedict

U.S. exporters, long timid about selling on credit to foreign buyers, are increasingly being forced to reverse course.

The pressure is coming, not surprisingly, from astute marketers in other Free World countries who are intent on expanding volume outside their borders and are finding credit is an almost irresistible sales lure.

"Credit is becoming as important to making an export sale as the price of the product," asserts Matthew Provenzano, credit manager of Jefferson Chemical Co. in Houston. He reports his company is extending more export credit and granting longer terms to meet competition. Altogether, he estimates Jefferson's export accounts receivable in the past three years have risen 21% faster than the growth in total foreign sales.

At the beginning of this year, American companies (other than financial institutions) held $2.7 billion of short-term paper from foreigners, more than four times the $593 million they held five years before. Only slightly smaller gains were recorded in export credit by banks. The credit increase far outstrips the growth in export shipments themselves, which climbed a much smaller 55% during the same five-year period.

ROLE IN PAYMENTS DEFICIT

The rising use of credit has helped spur a rapid growth in exports, a strong plus in the nation's efforts to reduce a persistent balance-of-payments deficit. With this in mind, the Federal Reserve Board granted such credit top priority when early this year it called for voluntary restrictions on foreign lending by U.S. banks. The restrictions are aimed at holding foreign loans to no more than 5% above the total on last Dec. 31.

Nonetheless, these restrictions—plus the crippling effects of the now-ended dock and ship strikes—may well slow the growth in export credit this year, but exporters say any slowdown is certain to be temporary. They argue the use of credit is so essential to overseas selling that it's bound to grow.

* Reprinted wih permission of *The Wall Street Journal*.

To get around the restrictions, in fact, many companies are beginning to fall back on their own working capital to finance foreign sales rather than turning to banks for such financing. "We carry our own paper on export sales and I think this is true of most big companies these days," says Louis Candee, credit consultant for Witco Chemical Co. in New York City. "We don't expect the Government's voluntary restrictions to slow the export credit trend. We're certainly not going to lose export business because of inability to extend longer terms. We'll find ways to do it and others should be able to do the same."

BILLING ON "OPEN ACCOUNT"

What's more, U.S. exporters are increasingly selling and billing foreign customers directly on "open account," the same as they do with nearly all domestic buyers. On such selling, the goods or services are simply charged to the customer's account for payment at some future date. Its use in overseas transactions is in marked contrast to the traditional practice of requiring confirmed and irrevocable letters of credit, under which the customer's foreign bank and the exporter's U.S. bank assume the risks and guarantee payment. These letters of credit are more secure ways of doing business but they are costly, time-consuming and irksome to many foreign customers.

"Until a year ago, we were only selling open account overseas to our own distributors," reports Kenneth H. Knox, credit manager for Tektronix, Inc., Beaverton, Ore., manufacturer of electronic test instruments. "Now we're selling nearly half our export volume that way, and it's working out well. It has definitely gained us new customers, particularly in Latin America where the cost of money is often the difference between a customer buying or not buying."

Extension of longer credit terms and assumption of more direct credit, of course, requires a sharp increase in the amount of credit checking U.S. firms must do overseas and many are finding the field has its own special hazards. "In West Germany, companies keep one set of books for the government, another for their banker, and still a third for themselves," reports one New York banker. Adds the president of a small leather goods company: "When we checked up on a potential customer in Nigeria who was ordering $3,000 worth of leather on credit, we found his assets totaled just $25." The credit manager of a Houston manufacturing company says ruefully, "One of our Latin American customers paid our bill to his bank on time, but the bank went bankrupt."

Despite such problems, bad debt losses in foreign countries remain remarkably low. J. Stewart Gillies, director of the Foreign Credit Interchange Bureau, New York, which collects overdue debts for 1,500 U.S.

exporters, says, "Our volume of uncollected bills never runs over $1.5 million, and for most U.S. companies foreign credit losses are infinitesimal."

On top of worrying about the customer's credit status, exporters must also ponder the political and economic stability of the country in which a customer is located.

"Nine times out of 10, foreign customers are willing to comply with terms of an export transaction, but getting your money out of some countries can be a problem," says Leo E. Kucera, general credit manager for Consolidated Foods Corp., Chicago. "Restrictive currency regulations, changes in exchange rates and internal political troubles can raise havoc."

But U.S. exporters are getting some important protection against such adverse developments from an insurance program set up three years ago. Provided jointly by the Government's Export-Import Bank and by the Foreign Credit Insurance Association, a voluntary group of more than 70 stock and mutual insurance companies, the program covers exporters on up to 85% of their loss from any commercial risk and up to 95% on losses from political cause such as expropriation.

About 3,100 companies currently are insuring export loans with the FCIA, double the 1,549 at the start of last year, and insurance in force has climbed to more than $1.5 billion from $660 million during that time, says Henry Sheehy, the association's president. He predicts 10,000 companies will be participating by 1970.

This Government backing is helping U.S. exporters better compete against West German and British firms that have had such coverage for many years, but Mr. Sheehy says U.S. companies still aren't making enough use of export credit. "U.S. companies had it so good so long in foreign markets, they are just beginning to realize the need for credit terms in foreign trade," he asserts.

Certainly most companies who have relaxed credit restrictions on foreign selling seem enthusiastic about the results. George E. Gaba, credit manager of J. P. Stevens & Co., New York textile maker, says that since it began making open account sales to foreigners in 1963 it has had no credit losses on the transactions. "We now sell on open account in Scandinavia, Germany, France and Israel and we're lengthening terms in other countries," he says. "For instance, we're giving up to 120 days in Italy now, compared with payment on delivery a few years ago."

But the remarkably low ratio of losses in foreign selling doesn't mean U.S. companies haven't experienced some credit headaches, particularly in sales to Latin America. Notes an Atlanta banker: "You just have to expect a normally higher rate of delinquency on paper outstanding in Latin America, because companies down there are continually short of working capital, and are also slow to collect their own receivables. So they just take a free ride on the exporter's capital as long as possible."

Insisting on prompt payment isn't always the solution. Filing of a formal protest for slow payment is considered in many countries to be the equivalent of an involuntary bankruptcy proceeding, and almost certainly would cost the exporter a customer. Some exporters try to speed payments by charging interest for late payment, but this has hazards, too.

"Charging interest on overdue export drafts is just an invitation to foreign buyers to delay payment still longer," says Sylvester F. Majestic, vice president of Chemical Bank New York Trust Co. "After all, 6% is darn cheap interest in most foreign countries. We don't like drafts going beyond due dates and insist on prompt payment."

Perhaps the greatest roadblock to extension of more export credit in many countries is the fact that foreign governments often insist on letter-of-credit transactions to better control currency and trade.

"We could treble our sales of commercial aircraft overseas except for restrictions foreign countries place on use of credit due to their dollar shortage problems," reports Frank A. Boettger, senior president of Cessna Aircraft Co., Wichita. "The less-developed countries that could most use airplanes, due to lack of roads and railways, usually bar use of credit, and that greatly reduces the number of potential buyers."

29.

SALES PROMOTION IN EUROPE . . .
IT'S TOUGH!*

"THERE'S no one way to promote a product with premiums throughout Europe."

This fretful exclamation comes from a marketer who was naive enough to view the Continent as "one market"—and has now found out it just isn't.

True, the Common Market philosophy and all it entails promises a uniformity of marketing legislation which will make life simpler for companies with an international outlook. But these promises may take a long time to materialize.

Until that utopia arrives, marketers intent on selling to our Free World cousins will have to contend with a potpourri of sales promotion statutes that indicate little regard for the American way of selling.

To illustrate just how varied and tough these European laws really are, Sales Management has culled some data on legislation governing the use of premiums in several countries from a study conducted by Intam Ltd., London-based international advertising and marketing consulting organization.[1]

AUSTRIA

Premium offers to consumers of non-luxury products come within the Discount Law. This law prohibits any cash reductions which would give preferential treatment to different groups of customers. Since most premium offers would be judged as doing this, they are normally not allowed. Exceptions to this rule are: quantity discount offers, trade offers, and special offers to employees of the advertiser. Loyalty rebates are also permitted. The manufacturer who gives a loyalty rebate normally puts a coupon in the product package. A number of these may be traded for a gift or cash prize.

* Reprinted with permission of *Sales Management, The Marketing Magazine.*
[1] The complete 46-page report is available from Intam Ltd., 399-401 Strand, London, W.C. 2. Price: £3 ($8.40).

BELGIUM

Self-liquidators are allowed on condition that neither the value of the item offered, nor the difference between the claimed value of the item and the sum required, is too great. In other words, the purchase price must bear a reasonable resemblance to the actual value of the product. Unfortunately, there is no fixed percentage, and cases are judged individually.

For example, it is unlikely that there would be any objection to a pair of stockings retailing at 40 francs being offered at 25 francs plus two box tops. However, if the stockings were worth 60 francs and were offered at 10 francs plus box tops, proceedings might be taken against the company concerned.

DENMARK

Regulations on special promotions in Denmark are less restrictive than in the other Scandinavian countries. The main legislation in the Law of Competition which, for the most part, restricts the use of giveaways.

Free gifts which are obtainable only on purchase of a particular product are forbidden unless they are of minimal value. There is no precise definition of the term "minimal," but it is related both to the value of the gift and to its value in proportion to the value of the main product.

Any kind of advertising mentioning free gifts is forbidden. Another limitation on promotion in this country is the tax system. For example, consumer prizes exceeding D. Kr. 200 ($28.95) are taxed at 15%, which is usually paid by the contest sponsor.

FINLAND

Finnish law allows considerable scope for special promotions. The main regulations are designed to ensure that contests do not unfairly coerce consumers to buy products.

Premium offers are allowed, but the word "free" can't be used in announcements promoting the offer.

FRANCE

The decree of August 5, 1961, prohibiting premiums, came into force on February 6, 1962, and most forms of premium offers are no longer possible. It is illegal to sell a product at less than cost price, or to offer the consumer a gift or premium which is conditioned by the purchase of another product. This means that the advertiser cannot demand proof of purchase. Such a demand is regarded as an obligation to buy, and is an offense.

Nor can a manufacturer or retailer offer products which are of a different kind from those in which he deals (e.g., a detergent manufacturer cannot offer clothing or kitchen utensils).

Giveaways are permitted, provided the gift is of a low intrinsic value and, in any case, less than 5% of the purchase price of the product in question. It must be stamped indelibly with the manufacturer's name and must obviously have been given for publicity purposes. Giveaways must always be given to the consumer at the time of purchase. In no case can they be given later on.

WEST GERMANY

In Germany, the laws on special promotions—as on many other facets of advertising—are extremely strict. They are so voluminous and complicated that any advertiser contemplating a promotional campaign should consult a lawyer.

Most kinds of promotion are allowed, with reservations. For instance, premium offers and contests may be used, but not conditionally upon purchase of a particular product. Cash prizes are not allowed at all. Free sampling is permitted, but samples should always be smaller than the standard pack.

GREAT BRITAIN

The Betting and Lotteries Act of 1934 contains the only legal restrictions really applicable to promotions. Otherwise the law in Great Britain is relatively liberal.

There is no limit on value of prizes, and a company may insist on proof of purchase of its product.

Contests are somewhat restricted. They must be decided by skill; otherwise sponsors run a serious risk of prosecution under the 1934 law. Ad agencies can lose out, too. The courts have held that if a contest should in fact be a lottery, and therefore unlawful, the agency cannot enforce payment for the media arrangements made on the client's behalf.

ITALY

Italian law divides special promotions into two main groups. These are "Concorsi a Premio" (prize contests) and "Operazione a Premio" (gift offers). Briefly, it can be said that for certain types of product groups, contests and gift offers are normally prohibited. A list of the products is published annually by the Ministry of Finance. At the present time it includes butter, coffee and coffee substitutes, rice, pasta, processed meats, many other processed foods, most dairy products and all vegetables.

NETHERLANDS

In Holland promotional activities are covered by regulations incorporated in the "Wet Beperking Cadeaustelsel" Law. The law is mainly concerned with restricting giveaways to products which are directly connected with the parent product (such as cups with coffee).

Also, there are special laws and regulations limiting the promotion of cigars, cigarettes, pharmaceuticals, alcohol and cosmetics. Apart from these products, however, it is generally true that items associated with the parent product can be used as giveaways or offered at a lower price. Cash may be given away at any time.

NORWAY

Premiums are more restricted here than in any of the other Scandinavian countries. The main legislation is contained in The Competition Act. Advertisers may not, as a general rule, demand proof of purchase for premium offers or contests, since this is considered putting the consumer under an obligation to buy. It's also illegal to bring pressure on retailers to promote one particular product.

The only way in which Norwegian regulations are more lenient than those in other countries is that contests do not necessarily have to be based on skill.

SPAIN

Premium promotions of the type used in the more sophisticated European markets have been used in Spain only in the last two and a half years. Consequently, the government has not yet formulated specific regulations to deal with each type. Instead, permission must be obtained from the Direccion General de Tributos Especiales for individual cases. To date, permission has always been granted.

But there is a levy on giveaways (the same rate as the advertising tax, i.e., approximately 1% of value). However, the application of this tax is arbitrary.

SWEDEN

Regulations on special promotions are strict, and limit the activities of the advertiser, although not quite as extensively as in Norway. The main legislation is contained in the Lottery and Games Act of 1939, which covers a wider field of activity than its name implies.

Under this act, no one may arrange a lottery without a government license, and no lotteries are permitted for advertising or promotional purposes. The definition of the term "lottery" covers all contests which are based on an element of chance.

The only exceptions to this are newspapers and magazines, which are allowed to conduct contests provided that the top prize does not exceed S. Kr. 200 ($38.50). Contests must require an "intellectual achievement" from contestants, and must be judged by an "Award Jury."

Any prizes or premiums which are of "substantial value" cannot be conditioned by purchases of a product, and should be offered to all comers.

SWITZERLAND

The main difference between Swiss and other European legislation is that no time is allowed. In other words, once a premium offer (or money-off pack) has been launched, the consumer must be able to continue to get it whenever she requests it.

Also, promotions of this type may not be advertised. For instance, the words "special offer" are prohibited. However, within these limits, a certain amount of promotional activity is permitted.

III

GLOBAL MARKETING

IN INDUSTRIALIZED COUNTRIES

30.

THE MARKETS OF EUROPE
OR THE EUROPEAN MARKET?*

Yves Fournis

EVER since Europe became conscious of the need to perfect its institutions, industrialists have been confronted with the problem of evaluating the prospects of foreign markets.

Undoubtedly, the problem is not new; products have probably crossed political and natural frontiers for centuries. But the threats of competition from abroad have now assumed other forms: the cancellation of quotas, the lowering and disappearance of duties, the free movement of goods, men, and capital, the equalization of burdens, and the prohibition against agreements. These measures have, however, aroused industrialists to search for permanent foreign markets.

The evaluation of the prospects of foreign markets has too long been limited to a search for favorable rates of exchange, import duties, and raising of quotas. Today, industrialists must find lasting markets using all the care and scientific precision that they have shown during the last few decades in the study of their domestic markets.

However, they encounter two main difficulties. The first stems from the fact that the broad context of the domestic market can be felt, appraised, and measured independently of all scientific knowledge. When an industrialist maintains long-standing relations with his customers and sees political parties with well-known viewpoints succeed each other, he is generally not surprised at changes in national economic conditions. Such is not the case in a foreign country, where everything can take one by surprise. Population changes, standards of living, and buying habits can be completely different and are in general misunderstood by outsiders.

The problems of evaluating the prospects of foreign markets necessitate an understanding of previous developments, the level of present

* Yves Fournis, "The Markets of Europe or The European Market," *Business Horizons*, Vol. 5, No. 4, Winter 1962, pp. 77-83.

developments, and buying motivation. This understanding precedes all action and must eventually incorporate an understanding of the mechanisms of interaction, which will not fail to arise as the exchanges develop.

Finally, in the long run, these interactions can lead to a complete modification in the appearance of domestic markets, a modification that offers an opportunity for lasting business ventures, not just temporary solutions.

The methods used to evaluate long- and short-term market prospects are the same ones used for the study of domestic markets: statistical analysis and studies of markets and motivations. Therefore, the second difficulty is that the application of these methods necessitates gathering and studying foreign data or carrying out research in foreign countries, both of which are further complicated by the language barrier. Because the application of these methods must be preceded by concise studies of various countries, and because repeating these studies in individual countries multiplies costs, they are used only in those countries that seem worthwhile.

On the other hand, the methods to be used for a long-term study of the European market are less familiar. Research will have to be developed in order to find valid instruments and, at the same time, certain data will have to be collected for the whole of Europe.

We will consider these differences in methods for (1) the short-term evaluation of the prospects of the markets of Europe, and (2) the long-term evaluation of the prospects of the European market.

SHORT-TERM EVALUATION

Perspectives of Development

Too often we visualize the Europe of tomorrow as a bloc, pit it against an American or Russian bloc, and evaluate its strength in millions of inhabitants, tons of coal, or kilowatt hours of power available. This view may provide a basis for judging the relationships between forces, but it invites false ideas about future markets.

Population shifts differ in each country of the European Economic Community (see Table 1). While the 1960 population of Italy was higher than that of France by almost 10 per cent, the population growth of France by 1970 will be greater (3.50 million) than that of Italy (3.15 million).

If the market study emphasizes total population, the most interesting countries will be, in this order, Germany, Italy, and France, which represent 88 per cent of the E.E.C. population. If the market is being studied according to population growth, the most interesting countries are the same, but their order changes: Germany, France, and Italy, which repre-

TABLE 1—E.E.C. POPULATION GROWTH (IN THOUSANDS)

Countries	Total Population			Percent Change 1960-70
	1960	1965	1970	
Germany	53,040	55,660	57,980	9
France	45,355	47,070	48,855	8
Italy	49,260	50,890	52,410	6
Netherlands	11,417	11,936	12,528	9
Belgium	9,114	9,405	9,697	6
Luxembourg	315	325	335	6
Total	168,501	175,286	181,805	9

Source: Statistical information of the E.E.C.—July–September, 1961.

sent 87 per cent of the total growth. If the emphasis is on the active population, the ranking will again be different: Germany, Italy, and France. In importance of growth of population the order is Italy, France, and Germany (see Table 2).

TABLE 2—E. E. C. ACTIVE POPULATION (IN THOUSANDS)

Countries	Total Active Population			Percent Change 1960-70
	1960	1965	1970	
Germany	25,545	26,037	26,637	4
France	19,803	20,356	21,072	6
Italy	20,670	21,530	22,120	7
Netherlands	4,149	4,524	4,834	6
Belgium	3,690	3,763	3,889	5
Luxembourg	140	145	150	7
Total	73,997	76,355	78,702	6

Source: Statistical information of the E.E.C.—July–September, 1961.

This elementary examination shows that the global view of a domestic market is not sufficient and that only a searching analysis can permit one to discern the relative interests. More notable differences appear if one extends the analysis still further. For example, Table 3 shows peak differences of the young active population in the various E.E.C. countries. For those products whose market is bound to the development of the young active population, France will offer the largest avenues of trade with Italy, the Netherlands, and Belgium following far behind, and Germany forming a regressive market.

TABLE 3—CHANGES OF YOUNG ACTIVE
POPULATION SINCE 1961

Countries	Units	Year
Germany	− 601,000	1964
France	828,000	1968
Italy	248,000	1966
Netherlands	199,000	1966
Belgium	196,100	1966

To evaluate the prospects of the foreign markets solely upon presentation of global figures leads to erroneous conclusions. First, a systematic study of detailed estimates is necessary lest considerable differences appear in the development of the various countries.

Stages of Development

European countries are, of course, at different stages of development in per capita income and levels of investment. But the differences, essential in themselves, also have greater significance than merely as indications that a market is open to a given product. In effect, the present level conditions the future level, since the development curves of the per capita sales of a product have the appearance of a growth that depends essentially on the peaks of the curve.

For example, the annual per capita consumption of rice in 1959-60

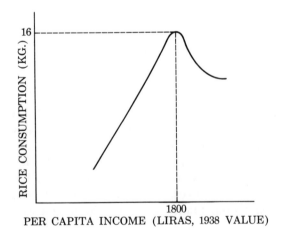

FIGURE 1—RICE CONSUMPTION AND INCOME

was Germany, 1.9 kg.; France, 1.9 kg.; Netherlands, 2.5 kg.; and Italy, 6.3 kg. On the basis of these figures only, one can infer either that the German and French markets offer the greatest development potentials, or that French and Germans are not too fond of rice, and that it would be better to direct efforts to the Dutch and Italian markets.

Figure 1, which relates rice consumption in Italy to per capita income of the individual (compared to the total per capita consumption), shows that rice consumption increases as income drops, and decreases when income exceeds, 1,800 liras. The rice market will expand or contract in Italy according to the predicted per capita income.

For a product such as butter, consumption increases as the peak of the income curve approaches, but there comes a saturation point where the consumer consumes no more. In hard goods, saturation occurs when a certain percentage of homes is equipped. Saturation curves appear well defined (logistical curves), and the differences between the curves of various countries are the result of a time lag between countries.

Future development depends on more than time lag, however. The maximal saturation point varies according to population structure, relative size of socio-professional group, or other factors (percentage of bachelors and servants, amount of electric power, and so on), and the curve varies according to the country (increase in incomes or the price index of the product in relation to the general price index).

Finally, ways of life, tastes, and motivations cause the relative saturation curves of a product to differ among countries.

Motivations

An economic context, a common way of life, a shared culture, a certain atavism, and a more or less acute sense of what is national all characterize a nation and form its special tastes. If the Italians are great consumers of rice, it is because rice has been produced in their country for a long time; if the French drink wine, it is because they have it in abundance. But when the free movement of goods makes Italian rice and French wine accessible to Germans, will they consume more? Will the custom of eating a large breakfast extend beyond Great Britain, or will the leisurely French noon meal find adherents? Will French housewives continue to boil their washing each week in huge washing machines, or will they change to a daily washing in a smaller machine with hot rather than boiling water? Why did Italian-style shoes sweep Europe and even the United States?

These questions are quite risky to answer, and they show the danger to which a product exposes itself when it seeks to penetrate a foreign market. If the product is not currently in use there, will it succeed in getting in? Is there an opposing motivation? What is its nature? Can one hope to overcome it?

A product's origin can be a contraindication. Motivation studies have shown, in effect, that each country imagines that others are favorable to the sale of certain products and unfavorable to the sale of others. Buying perfumes, champagne, and dresses in France is consistent with the image of this country as buying steel and chemicals would not be. To what extent can one hope to overcome this resistance to buying? Must we present our products as being particularly French, German, or Italian, or must we disguise them by changing their characteristics, uses, packaging, and appearance? Must we adopt an international image, as certain well-known brands are doing, or a European image, as an automobile manufacturer has done?

Only studies of motivation and consumer behavior, only sociological studies, can provide solutions to these problems. Perhaps every study of a foreign market should be preceded by a study of motivation to predict the reactions of a foreign country.

Interactions

Each suppression of barriers creates currents that slowly give way to a new state of equilibrium. But it is generally difficult to foresee what this state of equilibrium will be. Hydraulic engineers are well acquainted with this problem. In order to solve it, they are forced to test models of ports, dams, and estuaries. But because we cannot create a model of the Europe of tomorrow, we must trace the development of certain changes in order to imagine what the final condition will be.

A few problems can be resolved. Thus we have established, for the Europe of the Six, a table of interindustrial exchanges (Leontieff's Table), which permits us to evaluate the influence of the modification of certain factors: for example, by how much will it be necessary to increase steel production if we wish to increase automobile production by 10 per cent? But this table can only give answers for very wide areas of activity. Now the interactions exist in numerous areas: what will happen to the breweries in Germany if the Germans begin to consume wine? Inversely, if German auto production finds wider outlets in Europe, and increases its manpower to meet the expansion, will this shift in manpower hurt other German industries that, when their production lags, will open outlets to their foreign competitors? Will the disappearance of reciprocal agreements, which favor the introduction of the products of one country into another, change business trends?

The authors of Europe have acted wisely in providing for delays that will permit the new balance to materialize slowly, but those who want permanent export markets cannot be content with a short-term outlook. They must consider their position in the Europe of the day after tomorrow, that is to say in "the" Europe.

THE LONG-TERM EVALUATION

Will the Europe of tomorrow produce a standard type, like the American who drinks Coca-Cola, chews gum, and smokes king-size, filter-tip cigarettes, or will the French remain faithful to Gauloise and the Dutch to their aromatic tobacco? Will Europe, like Switzerland, retain different languages, national traditions, and cultures?

It is likely that, even in fifty years, little progress will have been made in the direction of uniformity, since one does not readily give up customs, traditions, language, and literature. To create the "European" will undoubtedly take many generations, not including the time needed to overcome the inevitable opposition to the creation of this type.

But one fact is certain: if Europe is realized, the abolition of frontiers, quotas, duties, and various other barriers will make it easier for an industrialist in Northern France to get supplies in Belgium rather than in Lorraine and Alsace; and every European consumer will be able, if he desires, to drink French champagne chilled in a German refrigerator and served in Italian glassware.

First Phase

In a first phase we will probably concentrate on the sectors that have lower power rates, an abundance of raw materials, and fertile soil, so as to increase productivity and be better able to take our place in the European market or in the export markets.

Large zones corresponding to just such requirements clearly appear in Europe: Rhineland, Northern and Eastern France, Benelux, Paris region, Switzerland, Lyon region, and Milan region. Moreover, these zones have as an axis two natural routes of communication, the Rhine and the Rhone, which will form the heart of the Europe of tomorrow as much from the point of view of industrial activity as from those of transactions, transportation, population density, and so on. By a well-known effect of attraction (Reuilly's Law), the zone will attract to itself adjacent zones still sparsely populated and thinly industrialized, which will become the suburbs of this main zone: Burgundy, Alsace, and Bavaria.

This first phase will eventually make difficult the exploitation of ventures that resist concentration, for they will be in hard competition with larger and better situated producers.

Two courses of action are possible at this point:

1. To participate in this concentration through mergers and agreements apportioning the zones of influence, always remembering (1) that such agreements cannot aim at artificially prolonging the life of badly located companies, and (2) that such operations must be considered with a view toward realizing the economic optimum.

2. To build up a market that does not compete with the markets of the large manufacturers, either by aiming at small or medium production or limiting operations to a geographic regional market.

This latter aspect is particularly important, for the suppression of frontiers must incite each manufacturer to reconsider natural and economic regions and zones of concentration, rather than political frontiers. Already in the United States certain manufacturers of high-consumption products have remodeled their sales organizations around television stations, which they use as their support for publicity. This contributes to the creation of a concentration of buyers, which assures better returns.

The first phase, which we are going through now, is thus a phase of concentration and organization during which we are seeking a certain optimum while avoiding a waste of energy and manpower through high transportation costs, low-yield exploitation, and dispersed and costly distribution.

This phase came about through the European Coal and Steel Community, which plans new investments by lowering future prime costs; but, on the other hand, this phase also led to a discontinuance of business operations that were badly located in Belgium or France.

Second Phase

It is likely that a united Europe will not be able to subsist if profound disequilibriums continue between regions. Europe will thus have to concern itself with its underdeveloped zones in order to assure their progress while taking into consideration their unique calling: climate, population, existence of raw materials, and potential of land under cultivation.

Moreover, certain countries can facilitate the development of this phase through the extension of atomic and solar energy facilities and of those facilities related to the harnessing of tides, all of which will permit the creation of power production centers far from the zones of traditional production (coal and waterfall regions).

In other respects, it will be necessary to reckon with the exhaustion of natural resources and to consider the new production methods for synthetics which may cause displacement of certain industries. The development of man-made fibers from agricultural products (rilsan) is an example of this. When certain resources stocked by the nation are finally exhausted, the only possibilities left for manufacturing will be through those techniques used by plants or animals, techniques involving natural elements: oxygen and hydrogen from water, oxygen and nitrogen from air, and carbon from plants. In the future, agriculture will ensure the production of raw materials, and new concentrations will have to be considered in the best agricultural regions.

To this one must add that, in order to prevent her prosperity from causing envy, notably in the African world which she is raising to independence, Europe will have to favor the development of African and Middle Eastern countries. Europe should expect to furnish them with a minimum of food, clothing, light industry, and power so that these peoples can carry out their own industrial development in peace.

Thus Europe cannot look upon itself as a closed market limited to ensuring its own needs under the best conditions. It will be necessary to produce for others, which should prompt development of operations along the Mediterranean and in those countries adjacent to the Near East.

As probable as they may be, these projections are not certain enough for a business concern to gear its policies to them. However, their consideration depends almost wholly on the business concerns and the governments. If we want Europe to create itself and to continue to exist, it is necessary to think for the future and to include these thoughts in some evaluation plans in order to verify their coherence and acceptability. The large European enterprises in particular owe it to themselves to favor such plans if they wish to control their destiny and not submit to it.

31.

THREE EUROPES, ONE BOOM*

U.S. businessmen are more and more tuning their marketing antennas to the new sound of Europe's booming economy. Though the sound itself is sometimes chaotic, the message is clear: The European consumer, as his American counterpart did long ago, is becoming a mass consumer.

Prosperity, and the shared effect of the Marshall Plan and the Common Market, have broken many of the rigid molds of Old World culture. In the process, they have made traditionally frugal Europeans almost as anxious to spend as to save.

Perhaps the most remarkable change of all, on a continent that treasures its heritage, is the attitude toward change itself.

"Need has become caprice," says Robert LeDuc of the A.F.P. Bates & Co. advertising agency in Paris. "Fashion, which used to reach only a narrow segment of the population, now is reaching more people with more strength." Fun, a German adds, is no longer immoral. Debt is O. K. You don't have to keep old things for years, much less generations.

Even thrifty Hollanders are getting used to the idea of living with the "wastemaker" philosophy. "It used to be that a Dutch housewife couldn't imagine throwing things away," says Joop Swart, managing editor of a half dozen magazines published by Amsterdam's Illustrated Press. "Now there's a new sense of freedom. She doesn't have to mend socks any more."

New hands. For such an attitude to become as widespread as it has, obviously peace and prosperity were required. But required even more was a new generation.

"The young are running away with the world," notes Lois Pavlis of J. Walter Thompson Co. in Frankfurt—and manufacturers are running after them. As a market category, age has become virtually as important as class, income, or nationality. And it affects even the preserves of elegance: Richard Ginori, Italy's top china maker, has had to venture beyond its famed traditional patterns to bring out modern ones for young. Britain's Doulton & Co. has done the same.

Above all, youth has generated an optimism unknown in prewar days. "Before the war, horizons were stagnant," says Emile Touati of

* Reprinted from the September 10, 1966 issue of *Business Week* by special permission. Copyrighted © 1966 by McGraw-Hill, Inc.

Agence Havas, in Paris. "The feeling that 'I'll be living better in five years' is a postwar phenomenon."

With that optimism has come a fervent buying spirit that extends far beyond London's Carnaby Street. What has been called "the revolution of rising expectations" has affected virtually all of Western Europe—and to a degree unthinkable in prewar days.

I. The Several Europes

A year ago, Mark Abrams of the London Press Exchange told the American Marketing Assn. that there are not one, but three Europes. He defined them this way:

New Europe is such big cities as Stockholm, Paris, London, and Hamburg—and their environs, and such highly industrialized, high population areas as Switzerland and northwest Italy. Per capita income in New Europe is about $2,000 a year.

Emerging Europe lies in the "semi-urbanized hinterlands"—in southern France, northern Italy, southwest Germany. Its per capita income is just over $1,000 a year.

Old Europe is the difficult farming land of Portugal, Spain, southern Italy, and northwest Scotland. The top per capita figure in these areas is $600.

Spending habits, of course, differ from group to group and from country to country. But in underscoring the similarities, Abrams points out that all three Europes exist everywhere. And the New Europes, with their ever swelling bag of possessions, tend to look more and more alike.

Two of the major contributors to that trend are transportation and television.

II. Travel, TV, and Trade

Europe is admittedly travel-happy. Gerhard Schroeter of Infratest, a large market research concern in Munich, reports that some 40% of Germans travel each year, a third of them abroad. Perhaps 60% of Britishers leave home on vacations, estimates Social Surveys (Gallup Poll), Ltd. of London—though only a small number leave the country. Nyman & Schultz, a large Stockholm travel outfit, this year expects to take the startling total of 300,000 Swedes—of a population of 7.6-million—on charter flights to the Mediterranean and to the sunny Canary Islands.

If holidaymaking inspires much European travel, hardship is also a contributor. In 1962, 145,000 Italians went to Switzerland, 105,000 to Germany, and 45,000 to France to seek better jobs. Such emigrés typically stay a year or so. When they return, often it is with a car or television set that makes them the envy of their village.

The tube. Television has been a second major homogenizer of European culture. The British estimate that 80% to 90% of their households have television. Some other approximate figures are: Sweden, 70%; Netherlands and Germany, over 60%; Italy, 45%; France, 30%. For better or worse, television has opened doors to ideas and manners working class Europeans never previously had access to, and it will open them wider as prosperity puts more antennas on rooftops. Already they can be seen sprouting incongruously from pitched Bavarian roofs, among multi-chimneyed Scottish cottages, and next to Dutch windmills.

Food and drink have also become increasingly cosmopolitan. Pizzerias thrive in Germany, a Stockholm supermarket sells lasagna, and even the British institution of fish and chips has passed on to the Continent. Whisky sales in France are now substantial—and the French drank none at all as recently as 1950. Whisky is also increasing in popularity with the Germans, many of whom acquired their taste from U.S. soldiers stationed there. Some 15% drink it today; 10 years ago, only 5% did.

Even a limpness of national spirit can contribute to a sense of Europeanism. As a nation, Italy is just about 100 years old, and northern Italians tend to feel more at home in Switzerland than they do with their Mediterranean compatriots. Bavaria, a sovereign state until after World War I, still considers itself a bit apart from the rest of Germany. Besides, with "a bad experience with nationalism in its recent past," as one German describes it, Germany tends to bend over backward to assure itself and others that it is part of the European community.

Yet even a German, trying to view himself as a European, knows he is still German. A marketer who today banks on the notion that Europe is in fact a common market does so at his peril.

The old order is changing, certainly. Mass communication is helping to diminish national differences and to promote the "need" for the same goods everywhere: better housing, cars, appliances, luxuries such as fashions, holidays, and fun. But the old ways die hard, for they are rooted in language and history.

An English businessman protests that marketers are trying to force a homogeneity on a Europe that is not homogeneous. An Italian adman warns there's no such thing as a European consumer—yet. The concept of a united Europe is superimposed on a patchwork map of highly individualized groups—and the differences are alive and kicking.

BRITISH ISLES

"There is nothing comparable on the Continent to the youth rebellion here," says the same Mark Abrams who defined today's "three" Europes.

A fashion coordinator adds: "This isn't a fashion change. This is revolution. It began when Lady Pamela What's-her-name said she liked to eat fish and chips in her bedroom because it was so lovely and dirty."

While the British are a little tired of hearing about "swinging London"—after all, London isn't all of Britain—they do admit something extraordinary has happened. Along with the loss of its traditional elegance to the garish aesthetics of rock 'n' roll, Mod, and Pop Art, London has been afflicted by a spirit of youthful rebellion for its own sake. More than anywhere else in the increasingly permissive West, the discotheque-happy young have made themselves heard in Britain.

The current economic crisis may slow the swinging tempo and slow a lot else besides, but in any case Britain has prospered more than it likes to admit. Britons protest that their postwar progress has been less notable than that of other countries, but the fact is that consumer expenditures rose from $34-billion in 1954 to $59-billion in 1964. Last year, car population rose nearly 700,000—to 9-million. Licensed radio and television sets come to over 13-million, nearly 3-million ahead of 1960. Gallup in London reports over 40% of households have refrigerators and over 50% have washing machines.

Attitudes have changed more than living habits. "We had a very rigid class structure," says James Pilditch of Allied Industrial Designers, Ltd. "This has been smashed. So you have to get help where you can find it—on how to think, how to behave. The help doesn't come from Cambridge any more but from some smart guy in Liverpool."

At sea. For the great universities are at sea, too. Their function had been to train an upperclass to run an empire. No more. To fill the void at the top, a brand new elite—of the young and talented—has rushed in.

In fashion, the young dominate to the virtual exclusion of everyone else—or so notes Julius Schofield, editor of a new publication called Trends, Fabrics, and Fashion. "The whole social climate is for them," he says, pointing out that the miniskirted young want to dress for fun rather than for an occasion.

That attitude "affects the fabrics you put into a dress, how well the clothes are made. It helps push extreme fashion. You can afford to be extreme in a costume you're going to chuck in a week."

In distribution, the young are abetting what some call a revolution: an explosion of boutiques sporting such names as Habitat, Casa Pupo, and A Carrot on Wheels, and selling everything from imported knick-knacks to contemporary furniture. "Why?" asks a bewildered onlooker—and answers his own question: In buying, too, the young have opted for "fun."

Throwaway lines. It's not so much fun for traditional retailers. "Harrods built on service and broad assortments and high standards," asserts D. G. Anthony, merchandising director. And, as T. R. McKie, general manager of Selfridges Ltd., puts it, "The young want clothes to throw away."

A buyer explains: "A few years ago I wouldn't carry a particular designer's line. It wasn't up to our standards. Then the young people came in and said, 'What kind of dump is this that it doesn't have his clothes?' So we carry them."

There is still an important market that wants all the service a Harrods offers: a fine food shop, where meats are cut to order; a unique rental library; a bank; a "secondhand" furniture department where pieces from fine old houses are refinished in a special way and sold.

So the market is split. Older people want service. The young like self-service. The older ones pay cash; the young like credit. As the demise of fair trade pinches profit margins, retailers are pondering how to keep both worlds happy.

Even with much higher wages, many are unhappy with the postwar world. "After the war they promised us Eden," one woman recalls. "All it was was more taxes and more austerity. It's the best country in the world for the lazy and the poor."

While many who remember the old days find the loss of world leadership bitter, there is another view. "A great weight was lifted when the empire was dissolved," says Shaun Dowling of J. Walter Thompson in London. The Gallup Poll finds people almost evenly divided as to whether they would prefer their former imperial status.

Working women. In the new, unimperial England, the changes are many. Women make up nearly half the work force, ancient slums are giving way to modern apartments, and launderettes have become the social equivalent of the sewing bee.

Progress isn't always popular. The English "mum" doesn't really take to big, American-type supermarkets. According to a Swedish study, self-service stores do less of the food business in Britain than they do in Sweden, West Germany, or the Netherlands.

Whatever her reactions to supermarkets, the English housewife is a pushover for health, says John Clemens, managing director of McCann-Erickson in London. She'll buy vitamins for the children, and gallons of disinfectant. To increase her motivation in other areas, package design is being "romanticized," and the Design Council is helping to improve a taste in furnishings and architecture that most marketers admit is deplorable.

Social tastes are something else. Once, says Nicholas Faith of the Economist, you could identify a man's class by the wine he drank—the dryer, the higher. It's not so pat any more. "Classless" steak houses are a more recent sign that the walls are falling.

But the old order dies hard. Abrams tells of a young man who wanted to date a girl in his office. She was attractive and intelligent—but still he didn't dare. "Find out if she's of the working class," he begged, "because I can't tell."

WEST GERMANY

Germans have become such devout consumers it scares some of them. "There's no Puritan ethic here," asserts Axel Bremer of Divo-Institut in Frankfurt. "The German is a wasteful, restless consumer who lives for Sundays and holidays."

But the "economic miracle" that boosted consumer income roughly a third between 1960 and 1964 carries in its own name an expression of doubt. Can a miracle be for keeps?

There's an almost superstitious anxiety below the surface—a feeling uncovered in a survey earlier this year by EMNID Institut in Bielefeld, when 60% of Germans said, "We have it too good." J. Walter Thompson researchers call it a latent fatalism—an expectation that war may come again after all.

Some of it is undoubtedly worry about security and rising prices. "We feel that we have for rent the things that we have," says Gerhard Schroeter of Infratest in Munich.

Lasting hopes. And some of it goes deeper. For Munich women, dreams and fears are bound up in a word—peace. A German, who with her husband operates a Rosenthal china studio, says: "Women come to buy china for their daughter's wedding, and they say, 'I hope it lasts.'" They remember china of their own that didn't last, 20 years ago.

Divo's Eugen Lupri thinks Germany is a nation of taboos. One taboo is the subject of a divided Germany. Germans don't talk about it, they just live with it. Again, Germans are torn between pride in their nation's recovery—"We have assimilated 9-million emigrés from East Germany," one says—and a feeling that "our un-coped-with past" is still to be coped with. Reports of a revival of Nazism in the Nuremberg area bring troubled explanations.

Yet neither fears nor constraints halt spending. Some 9.8-million cars ride the highways. According to Marplan, in Frankfurt, 66% of the 20-million households have TV sets; 70%, refrigerators; and 47%, washers.

For many Germans, the dream is a little house or apartment of their own. Since "social" housing, put up with government aid after the war, is inexpensive, only 15% of consumer expenditures goes for rent and fuel—and there's more to spare for other goods. But there's a catch. Social housing is limited in space, and people want more room.

Clothes horses. Nondurables are booming. Working women spend "very, very much" on clothing, reports Bessie Becker, a Munich designer. The young, her special customers, appear to be putting all their money on their backs. And for young and old, style is in greater demand than ever.

As in Britain, women have stepped in to plug the manpower gap—they represent about a third of all employed. Some work to avoid boredom: The car, for all its contributions to the new Germany, has not yet liberated the housewife. Men drive to work, leaving their womenfolk stranded at home for the day. But most women work for "unneeded income," to raise their living standard.

Saving plans. The government has worked out a variety of plans to encourage saving. You put so much in the bank, add so much every year, and get an annual bonus, and another if you have a child. Once you have saved enough for a downpayment on a house you can get a loan on good terms.

One study indicates that 42% of money saved goes for emergencies; nearly 39% is earmarked for a special purchase. Marplan reckons that 11% of all households are repaying debts—mostly for cars.

With economic shifts come social changes. The authoritarian papa is disappearing—if slowly—from family life. Children speak before spoken to, and have a say in such matters as whether or not to go on a picnic. Their fathers had no such voices when they were small.

Since the wife doubles as wage earner, her husband doubles as hausfrau. The German husband pitches in with household chores as few Italian or French husbands do. And if he goes out for a social evening, his wife goes along.

In theory, shorter hours and longer vacations should produce more leisure. But ask a career woman where her spare time goes and she laughs. She rushes from her job to the store, which closes at 6:30, then home to dinner, and cleans up afterward. Nor do men have all the leisure one might think. Do-it-yourself chores—painting, gardening, polishing the car—absorb much of a man's Saturday. But come Sunday, the family piles into the shining car and takes off for boating, camping, or perhaps a soccer game.

Look, ma. German youngsters are going their own way—if a bit less flamboyantly than the London youth. "They earn so much," as one observer puts it. They can buy their own cars or motorcycles, they have their own restaurants and their own chess cellars. Sexual freedom is increasingly taken for granted. Lois Pavlis, of J. Walter Thompson, paraphrases one result of it this way: "Look, ma, I'm pregnant. We're getting married."

The doubts that haunt their elders don't touch the young. All-out optimism keynotes their mood—too much so, some say. "Always dancing—dancing and amusement," one business woman comments. "Never in house. Nothing in head. Too much money. It is not good for the character to have too much money."

Germans of all ages share a traditional respect for law and order, a respect perhaps implicit in their authoritarian history. It also shows up in today's economic structure—in work contracts that run three and sometimes five years.

This attitude of order first also tells in the market place: Impulse buying is almost a dirty phrase to Germans. The well-constructed household budget calls for planned expenditures.

Quality first. A spokesman for Braun, which has become a design pace-setter for quality appliances and home electronics, insists that quality still makes the sale to a German consumer. Braun itself rejects the notion of style obsolescence, but concedes that people now think in terms of perhaps a five-year life for appliances. The proprietor of the Wohnberatung, a quasi-public institution in Frankfurt that helps people plan their homes, says people now tend to refurbish their houses after the children have grown. Marplan finds that kitchen furniture, which is booming, is out of date after five or ten years.

Turnover. In cars, Germans are catching the new-model fever. Though one marketer insists it is the functional excellence of the Mercedes that wins the motorist, the "commercially biased" are beginning to turn in their cars every year.

The supermarket is thriving—though the housewife still prefers her little service store. This will change as more second cars free the housewife for marketing farther from home and as new houses with bigger kitchens permit bigger refrigerators.

There can be no mistake: Germany has joined Europe. One reason Germans fret less about the Wall than they do, a man says, is, "We are on the right side of it." On a pleasant Sunday, Berlin's parks have a cosmopolitan air—with not only German families, but also Italian workmen, Filipino businessmen, and Negroes in sports clothes enjoying the air.

Yet the park bank plays the good old sentimental schmaltz, and the pleasure boats chugging up the river with their holiday crowds bear such nostalgic names as Lohengrin and Vaterland.

FRANCE

"We have de Gaulle. Nobody else has him."

Thus does Nicholas Leboeuf of J. Walter Thompson, Paris, explain the French.

Never a notably meek nation—it's the Paris cabbie, after all, who takes on a fare if and when he feels like it—the French lost some of their traditional élan in the bleak war years and in the years of splintered government that followed. Now, says Marplan's Pierre Baccon, "de Gaulle has given us back our pride—whether we like him or not."

And pride is not just a political matter. France's economic progress has been remarkable: Per capita income grew from $985 in 1960 to $1,100 in 1964, and household income during the same period climbed 25%.

As it does with most Europeans, housing comes high on the French "most wanted" list. While most city dwellers are well enough off, many of them want a second home in the country, and about 1.3-million have them. Country dwellers want modern improvements, particularly running water. In 1962, only 31% of French households had a bath or shower.

French frugality. If the French are buying more cars and appliances and traveling more than in years past, France is "not yet a genuine consumer country." Or so thinks Emile Touati of Agence Havas. He adds: "The need to economize, to save, is still very strong." By his count, two-thirds of the French just make ends meet. About 11% are in debt; some 23%, however, do manage to save.

There is general agreement that the great consuming wave is still to come. Besides a native aversion to being too free with money, there is another sort of conservatism that inhibits spending. The French cherish their tradition of fine cuisine—and spend nearly 40% of disposable income on food and drink. Even the tiny country bistro considers it a point of honor to serve a fine meal—and that means traditional dishes, especially in the provinces. In Brittany, for instance, it's unthinkable not to have cream with your vegetables.

Choice convenience. All of this makes for a rather cool reception for convenience foods. The French prefer to take their convenience in the form of the best cuts of meat—the quick-cooking steaks and hams.

In any case, the French have always admired the man of moderation, or "l'homme de mesur," points out A.F.P. Bates' Robert LeDuc. Presumably, the French also admire the woman of moderation because miniskirts show up less frequently than in London. A French designer theorizes that French girls want to look elegant whereas English girls want to look cute.

Yet, in other areas, conservatism is wanting. "The magic word is 'new,'" says Cecilia Walter, consumer specialist for J. Walter Thompson. Such new products as high fidelity sets and tape recorders are big sellers. With almost 9-million cars for some 48-million people, France has one of the highest car ratios in Europe.

In Paris, as in London, the yen for novelty is changing fashion trends. People used to buy coats to last several seasons, says Mlle. Milliers La Croix, a buyer for the big store, Galeries Lafayette. "Now, instead of something useful, they want the latest."

Many marketers feel that if there is a Gallic urge to keep up with the Joneses it's minimal. A proper Frenchman, after all, doesn't care what anyone thinks. So it's quality, rather than style or status, that sells cars. Besides, performance has to count when gasoline and taxes come so high.

One France. Once all France was divided into two parts: Paris and the provinces. That gap is closing. Maria Moutet, who under the name Maria Carine produces ready-to-wear adaptations of couture models, says wealthy provincial women want what the wealthy Parisienne wants.

Because about a third of the women work, and servants are scarce, housewives are often harried. Elle magazine preaches: Organize your time. To cut down those time-consuming, twice-a-day shopping trips, perhaps you should buy a freezer or a bigger refrigerator. Then you can get the sofa you want.

Stocks low. A study by Agence Havas asks how people would spend a hypothetical increase in income. About 20% put it to better daily living; 18% would spend it on the household; 30% would invest in land or an apartment. Only 8% would keep it for a rainy day; only 4.5% would invest it. The French tend to view stocks with suspicion, preferring to put their money in postal accounts, where they can get their hands on it readily, or in some other accessible spot—like the family washing machine.

As good individualists should, the French have different notions of what's worthwhile. Women old enough to remember the war put peace at the top. Youngsters, suffering perhaps from too much money and freedom, are weary of such abstractions as liberté and fraternité. They yearn for a good, solid cause, like Algeria.

The French homme wants peace, too, with perhaps a little friendly controversy. Above all, he wants to be let alone, to rule lord in his castle. It is the dream of a moderately unreconstructed individualist. It reflects the essence of Leboeuf's summing up: "There's a little piece of de Gaulle in each of us."

ITALY

The Italians are individuals with one particularly strong group loyalty —to the family. The average family of the industrial North spends $3,000 a year—substantially more than in the rural South, where outlays, even with larger families, average $1,800.

Socially, the sections seem worlds apart. "The northern woman is emancipated," says Giovanni Bianco, of Milan's Management Methods, Inc. The southern housewife rates "with the dog asleep under the porch."

Tradition strong. Still, the extent of that northern emancipation is

314 of 530 GLOBAL MARKETING MANAGEMENT

open to question: North or South, tradition lays a heavy hand on the people. The woman is strongly protected—first by her parents, then by her husband.

An Italian is apt to feel it reflects on his honor if his wife works. So perhaps no more than 25% of women take jobs, usually only until they are married.

Even in the "emancipated" North, women's work is not taken for granted. A Milan businessman tells of a young married assistant, rich, educated, who worked simply because she liked to. When he wanted her to go to Rome on business for several days, she had to say no. Her husband wouldn't permit it.

With the old ways so strong, the wonder is that Italy responds to new ideas at all.

Cold fish. Joseph Maranelli, assistant to the president of Motta, a big food packager and distributor, finds Italians eager for new experiences. Frozen foods are gaining, with some 60% of Motta's frozen sales fish.

Like most Europeans, Italians dream first of all of a "bella casa." But they leap at other durables, too. More than half of all households have refrigerators; almost half have TV.

Italians insist that quality and style make sales. Yet one observer finds their judgment weak. "The hardest thing to sell in Italy is a 57¢ toothbrush," he says. "The easiest thing to sell would be a gold-plated one."

Discount sells. Some manufacturers complain the discount is what sells. The first thing people say, is "How much off?" General Electric Co. has begun a determined campaign to advertise the features and values of its lines.

Though Italy is still smarting from the economic crisis of a few years ago, big retailers—who account for only some 5% of total sales—are steadily upgrading their products. La Rinascente-UPIM, a department and variety store, offers couture fashions and antiques today that 10 years ago would have been out of the question.

Standa, a chain of popular-priced general merchandise stores, reports a boom in such leisure items as tennis racquets, sportswear, underwater gear, and skis. Nowadays, a tailor assures you, you must be as elegant on the ski slope as at the dinner party.

Supermarkets growing. The supermarket, now 10 years old in Italy, has a good image, even an elegant one says a Rinascente spokesman. There are perhaps 500 scattered in cities and towns. Though prices run 14% below those of conventional stores, Motta's Maranelli says quality, not price, has converted women to supermarkets. It's not uncommon to see a well-dressed customer, list in hand, with a chauffeur pushing the cart behind her.

Yet because there are not the autos in which to take large grocery loads home, nor large enough refrigerators in which to store them, most customers do a lot of short-order buying.

"You'd be amazed," says Andrea Ringler, marketing director of Mc-Cann-Erickson in Milan, "if you looked in those carts: maybe a little piece of cheese, a bottle of Coke, and a piece of soap—that's all."

Government efforts to encourage industry to move south have had only moderate success. The southerners lack technical skills, and like all Italians, they are "the devil to organize," one businessman says. "The Italian is very, very individualistic," he adds. "He is not at all team-prone."

Italy has managed to double consumption between 1950 and 1965. Recent figures from Pier Paolo Luzzato-Fegiz, of the Central Institute of Statistics at Rome, show that food—which still gets the lion's share (from 42% to 46%)—did not quite double in that period. Transportation outlays, including cars, tripled.

Progressive. Once people make progress, however, they generally want more. Italians take no special pride in their so visible past. "They are more interested in the future," Luzzato-Fegiz says—and a bit grim about the discrepancy between the 1% who are millionaires and the vast bulk who are poor.

But if the gulf between haves and have-nots breeds discontent, it also breeds a rich and eager market, says Bianco of Management Methods.

The Italian has an enduring quality. "He isn't concerned with the large problems," an observer says. "He is too busy going about the business of meeting his daily problems. And one way or another, he does this very well."

. . . AND A LOOK AT OTHER COUNTRIES

In the less populous countries, too, people are spending. Even Spain and Greece, where per capita income averages less than $500, markets are fast expanding. And Sweden, with a population of 7.8-million, remains Europe's foremost example of an affluent society.

In its current spending binge, Sweden may be reacting to a long history of isolation and poverty. As recently as a few decades ago, marketing consultant C. K. Squires of Stockholm recounts, Swedes sealed themselves up during their long winters, fortified with barrels of pickled tidbits—the ancient forerunner of the smorgasbord—and with 30 pairs of sheets to last them from autumn's last big washday to spring's first.

In the postwar years, however, with a rising demand for steel, lumber, and other resources, Sweden's economy caught fire. Today, some 46%

of Swedish households have a car; 75%, television; and perhaps 25%, a boat—the latest status symbol.

Self-service affluence. Some 8,700 self-service food stores account for two-thirds of food sales, the highest such ratio in Europe. And for those who like their affluence straight, a self-service department store, Stockholm's cooperative OBS, started selling Piper aircraft this summer.

Swedes fret at the tax bill, which last year took from 40% to 59% from most earners to pay for, among other things, such welfare-state staples as old-age pensions and health benefits. But Stockholm's Enskilda Bank contends that counting hidden taxes, France's taxes are higher as a percent of gross national product, and West Germany's nearly as high.

Uncertain. Currently, marketers describe Belgium's 9-million people as hesitant. Higher prices and new taxes curtailed department store sales this spring.

With half again as many people aged 20 as it had five years ago, Belgium marketers look for increased sales in new products. A country that likes the supermarket, Belgium has one food outlet for every 60 families. But the little shops are folding—four and five a day.

Though Holland is fully part of the New Europe, it retains some of the old provincialism. "When my wife and I came home from a trip recently," says an executive of De Bijenkorf, an Amsterdam department store, "we thought our country looked friendlier, neater, just a little more taken care of." The Dutch housewife would seem to live up to her reputation—a high 75% of households contain washing machines.

The Dutch are also conscientious about their religion. One adman advises clients that there's no use advertising rich foods in Protestant magazines there because their readers frown on rich diets.

The Austrians don't—and with their fondness for fine food, have come big refrigerator sales.

Spain's 30-million people, tasting prosperity for the first time, are bullish—and not just over el toro. Consumer spending is expected to rise 65% over 1963. For Spain's young women, the traditional mantilla and cape are dying; Madrid's fancy Serrano Street boutiques are chalking up impressive sales in London and Paris fashions.

Wine and Coca-Cola. While older farm people still wash their day's thirst away with wine, Coca-Cola sales have risen so fast that Spanish wine producers have had to launch a rather defensive national campaign. Its slogan: "Drink 10% more wine."

One of the more remarkable European consumer developments is the transformation of the Greek housewife. Not too long ago, she was strictly a homebody—sewing her own clothes, and washing them in a cauldron over a wood fire—and she didn't even shop. Her husband took care of that on his way home from work.

Big change. Today, she shops at the supermarket, goes to a hairdresser once a week, washes clothes in a machine, and nags at her husband for a refrigerator, vacuum cleaner, an electric cooker.

Since these products must be imported, the country suffers from a trade gap. To counter it, the government resorts to various protective devices—and sometimes retail prices are increased as much as 200%. The government has slapped so many taxes on cars that to put a new one on the road costs a Greek from twice to four times the factory price. Then he has road taxes ranging from $10 a month on a small European car to $35 for a U.S. make. And still car sales have been rising at a steady 20% for the past six years.

It's the housewife, though, that most marketers are concentrating on. It is she who persuades her husband to switch from Turkish coffee for breakfast to instant coffee.

32.

MARKETING TO THE BRITISH CONSUMER*

Harper W. Boyd, Jr. and
Ivan Piercy

TODAY, Britain is a major importer of American capital and goods as well as American marketing practices. More than 750 American companies have a direct investment in some form of British manufacturing activity. In 1958-59, the United States invested $329 million (bringing its total investment to more than $2 billion) and exported $864 million in goods to Britain. In 1958, the United States received more than $300 million in profits, after taxes, from its investments there.[1]

A substantial part of the investment is in the form of fully owned, large firms such as those manufacturing automobiles, rubber tires, agricultural machinery, and printing equipment. But such food producers as General Mills, Campbell Soup, and H. J. Heinz Company hold important shares of the British food market. To these and other American companies, the marketing component of the British economy holds considerable interest and challenge. After substantial setbacks in their initial marketing operations in Britain, several prominent American companies have realized that the marketing techniques that had worked so well at home would not succeed overseas.

Because Britain has trailed America in perceiving the importance of the marketing concept and in being consumer oriented, important British industries, for example, motorcars and trucks, textiles, and office machinery, have lost large parts of the world market. However, American marketing concepts and practices are having a substantial impact, and change is evident. The growth of the Common Market and the possibility that Great Britain will ultimately join it have intensified the desire for change.

The primary objective of this article is to describe and evaluate some of the major characteristics of the British marketing system for consumer goods. Wherever possible, reliable secondary sources are used to substantiate statements, especially where statistics are presented. But to a consid-

* Harper W. Boyd, Jr. and Ivan Piercy, "Marketing to the British Consumer," *Business Horizons*, Vol. 6, No. 1, Spring, 1966, pp. 77-86.

[1] U.S. Department of Commerce, *U.S. Business Investments in Foreign Countries* (Washington: U.S. Gov't Printing Office, 1960), pp. 89, 92, 98, and 126.

erable extent the authors have had to rely on their own observations as well as discussions with British marketing and advertising executives.

BACKGROUND

The Economy

Great Britain, with a 1961 population of 52.6 million, covers an area slightly smaller than that of the state of Oregon. In 1959, Britain's gross national product was $77.7 billion, about one-sixth that of the United States and twice that of Canada.[2] Although GNP has increased substantially over the past ten years, increased prices are responsible for much of the gain. Britain's rate of increase in productivity has been much slower than that of West Germany, Japan, France, and Sweden.[3]

Industries in the engineering and allied trades category (such as shipbuilding, agricultural machinery, machine tools, heavy electrical plants, radios, electronic equipment, appliances, and vehicles) contributed 43.3 per cent of the value of net output of all manufacturing industries in 1957. Textiles, leather, and clothing comprised 13.4 per cent; metal manufacture, 9.3 per cent; chemicals and allied trades, 8.8 per cent; and all others, 16.1 per cent.[4]

In 1958, Britain imported goods and raw materials worth more than $10.5 billion. Food, beverages, and tobacco accounted for more than 40 per cent of total imports, and, of this amount, meats, fruits, and vegetables made up more than half. The more important manufactured products exported were machinery, road vehicles, aircraft, chemicals, electrical apparatus, and appliances.[5]

From 1957 to 1959, the government promoted a sharp rise in consumer spending, exports, and industrial production by easing restrictions on long-term borrowing, removing controls on installment buying, stepping up public investments in roads, and lowering income and sales taxes. But because of a substantial deficit in Britain's current account during the first six months of 1961, the government was forced to reinstitute certain controls to slow consumer spending.

[2] Central Statistics Office, *United Kingdom Annual Abstract of Statistics, No. 96* (London: 1959), pp. 1, 6, and 13 also, see *The Economist* (July 29, 1961), p. 437; *Preliminary Report of United Kingdom Census of Population, 1961;* and *The New European Market* (New York: The Chase Manhattan Bank, no date), p. 48. The GNP cited has been adjusted to reflect the purchasing power of the British currency.

[3] United Nations, *Statistical Yearbook, 1961,* pp. 73, 76, and 79.

[4] *United Kingdom Annual Abstract of Statistics, No. 96,* pp. 128-29.

[5] *United Kingdom Annual Abstract of Statistics, No. 96,* p. 213. The value of the British pound in U.S. dollars has remained relatively constant at about $2.80, which is the conversion rate used in this article. See British Information Services, *Britain, In Brief* (London: 1960), p. 32.

Consumer Habits

The population of Great Britain has remained relatively static, increasing an average of less than 0.5 per cent a year. In 1960, approximately 45 per cent of all income earners received $1,400 or less annually after taxes, and nearly 75 per cent less than $2,100.[6] Only about 1 per cent earned $5,600 or more annually after taxes. Food accounts for more than 29 per cent of all personal expenditures (up from 26.7 per cent in 1948), and food, alcohol, and tobacco for about 45 per cent.[7]

For the average housewife, shopping has always been a social event to some degree. Many housewives spend an hour or more shopping for six to ten items and may visit as many as six shops in the process. The excursion is frequently capped by joining friends for coffee or tea. Service in Britain has always had a status appeal. Combine these factors and one can understand why many housewives, especially those belonging to the upper lower class, resent to some degree the trend toward self-service.

Most shopping is local, partly because only one family in three has a car and partly because only one in four has a refrigerator (and the amount of storage space in British kitchens is generally small). Consequently, most housewives do their shopping locally and frequently, thus minimizing two of the more important advantages of self-service—economy of time and purchase of large, economy sizes.

The home is very important to the typical British family because of their love of privacy and their general dislike of communal life. There is little in-home entertaining and people do not "drop in." Nor are children given free run of the house. Given such attitudes, it is not difficult to understand the desire to have a home where "nothing changes." Then, too, the middle-class housewife is more oriented toward the traditional than the new. She tends to regard the old styles as better than the new because they have been tried and accepted.

Product

With the exception of the food industry, British manufacturers have been noticeably deficient in their product designs. This has been particularly true of clothing, furniture, chinaware, housewares, and major and minor

---

[6] *One-Hundred-and-Fourth Report of Commissioners of Inland Revenue* (London: 1961).

[7] Central Statistics Office, *National Income and Expenditure, 1959* (London, in *Whitaker for 1960*), p. 601; and *Monthly Digest of Statistics* (London: 1962).

household appliances. In this connection, it is interesting to note a comment by an agency of the British government regarding the availability of U.S. goods in British stores at Christmastime: "If you ask English women what they like about American goods, the answer is likely to be 'They're so novel'; then when pressed, 'so convenient and well designed,' 'There's something for every occasion,' 'Everything is such fun, and finally, 'What will Americans think of next?' "[8]

In recent years, and to an ever-increasing extent, consumer goods manufacturers have engaged in more research and development work. While firms with American connections tend to rely to a considerable extent upon work done in the United States, many such companies do a surprising amount of product research work of their own, and more firms are testing their new products at the consumer level before releasing them. This also applies to those firms that receive a product already marketed successfully in the United States. The appliance manufacturers do a good deal of continuous testing of their products against those of their major competitors.

For various reasons, British consumers have always been more concerned about the quality of the goods they buy than American consumers. In 1957, the British Standards Institution's consumer advisory council started the distribution of *Shopper's Guide,* and the Consumer's Association began the publication of *Which?* The circulation of these magazines in early 1962 were 44,000 and 300,000 respectively. The readership of *Which?* is estimated to be more than 3 million adults a month. The BBC recently launched Friday radio and TV shows that report on the results of comparative tests of named goods.[9]

The growth in private branding has produced some quality control problems. Only a few distributors do an effective job in policing quality or in setting meaningful specifications for the manufacturer to follow. Among the excellent private labels are St. Michael (Marks and Spencer), Boots (a drug or chemists' shop chain), and Harrods (a large department store noted for the quality of its offerings).

In general, the packaging of most consumer goods is adequate, if not imaginative. Packaging of many consumer food products, especially those produced by American companies, is similar to the American manner. Package sizes tend to be smaller than those sold in America because of the lack of storage and refrigeration space in the home. Most products sold by the greengrocer are not packaged, but supermarkets sell prepackaged fruits and vegetables, for example, potatoes that are washed, cut, and peeled.

[8] " 'Made in U.S.' Goods for Christmas Make Britons' Shopping Brighter," *British Information Services* (Dec. 17, 1959).
[9] *The Observer* (Feb. 11, 1962).

CHANNELS OF DISTRIBUTION

Britain tends to use the same two major distribution channels that the United States does: manufacturer to retailer to consumer, and manufacturer to wholesaler to retailer to consumer. A pre-World War II study estimated that these two channels were of equal importance—about 40 per cent each.[10] But the changing retail structure, with the increase in multiples (chains) and average-size stores, has caused more manufacturers to sell direct. In fact, several large sellers are undertaking considerable revisions of their sales force in view of the growing concentration at the retail level. Such firms have noted that a higher caliber, more versatile person is required to negotiate with chain buyers. In particular, the salesman who deals with chain headquarters has to know more about advertising and in-store promotions.

The sale of consumer durables, especially appliances, is accomplished primarily through exclusive outlets. In such situations, the manufacturer typically sells direct. More and more, the salesmen for these companies find themselves doing an educational job with their accounts, especially in the areas of administration and promotion.

Wholesaling

Over the past several decades, wholesale merchants of consumer goods have been relatively more important in Great Britain than in the United States because of the prevalence of small-scale retailing. But for reasons already noted, many of these wholesalers are fighting for their lives. Some have been instrumental in forming voluntary chains of independent retailers. In these arrangements, the wholesaler offers more favorable terms, monthly billing, promotional aids and programs, and management advice. In return, the retailer agrees to buy all or most of his goods from that wholesaler. About one-third of all independent grocers belong to some kind of a voluntary group organization and account for nearly 50 per cent of the sales of independent grocers. While group members have undoubtedly increased their sales, they have done so largely at the expense of other independents rather than chains.

The tendency to sell direct to the retailer has caused wholesalers to provide better service without increasing their margins. Thus, many have improved their deliveries, have developed a more aggressive sales force, and have begun to carry larger stocks. While some mechanization has

[10] Central Office of Information, *Britain, An Official Handbook* (London: 1960), p. 471.

taken place in materials handling, order filling, stock control, and billing procedures, the average British wholesaler badly lags behind his U.S. counterpart in these respects.

Some wholesalers have developed self-service departments in an attempt to trim selling expenses. Rather than send out salesmen, the wholesaler encourages the retailer to come in and "serve himself." The idea appeals particularly to small retailers, since it provides flexibility in purchasing and helps them to avoid the problems of excessive inventories.

As would be expected, packaged food and household products are the most important items distributed through wholesalers, followed by textiles and agricultural produce. London's wholesale market is by far the largest in the distribution of produce. Covent Garden, for example, handles about $200 million worth of fruits, vegetables, and flowers each year.

Frozen food manufacturers deliver direct to the retailer, and thus frozen food distributors are not yet of any great importance. This direct selling has occurred because Bird's Eye has a virtual monopoly in the field, and also because of the small size of the country.

RETAILING

The British retail structure remained relatively static until 1950. Since that year, and especially since 1958, the situation has changed dramatically. It seems certain that British retailing practices have been and are following those already established in the United States. In 1961, total retail sales in Britain were estimated at $24.5 billion (up some 70 per cent from 1950 and 15 per cent from 1957) excluding sales of petrol, oil, coal, building materials, grain, agricultural supplies, and motor vehicles.[11] Retail establishments are classified as (1) independent traders; (2) multiple traders; (3) retail cooperative societies; or (4) department stores.

The independent trader classification covers independent retail businesses and branches of small chains (that is, comprising less than ten shops) and includes variety and dry goods stores, specialty shops, independent general stores, door-to-door and other types of direct retailing, and general mail-order houses. This group contains more than 80 per cent of all retail establishments and in 1961 handled nearly 57 per cent of total retail sales (down from 60 per cent in 1950).[12] A deterrent to the growth in size of the independent retail outlet has been the almost confiscatory nature of the surtax on income in excess of £5,000 ($14,000)— until very recently the surtax was applied on income in excess of £2,000-

11 U. K. *Census of Distribution and Other Services, 1957* (London: Board of Trade, 1959), p. 7, and estimates from indexes released by the Board of Trade (London: 1962).
12 U. K. *Census of Distribution and Other Services, 1957.*

2,500 ($5,600-7,000). Most small retailers feel that it would be foolish to expand when they can keep but a small part of any increase in profits.

The multiples classification includes those organizations (other than cooperative societies and department stores) with ten or more branches. In 1957, some 982 enterprises owned 10.2 per cent of all retail units and accounted for about 24 per cent of total retail sales. From 1957 to 1961, the sales of multiples increased 29 per cent (to 27.6 per cent of total retail sales), while independents increased 11 per cent, cooperatives 7 per cent, and department stores 22 per cent. Sales for all retailers increased 15 per cent.[13] As would be expected, the multiples have been extremely active in the grocery field; for example, Finefare (Associated British Foods) has 200 supermarkets and plans to invest $75 million in new stores over the next several years. In the drug field, both Timothy White and Boots have been active. Marks and Spencer, a large ready-to-wear clothing chain selling private label merchandise, has made impressive gains.

Retail cooperative societies are nonprofit organizations that sell not only to members (who control the operation and receive a dividend based on purchase volume) but to the general public as well. Traditionally— and emotionally—this group has been an important force in British retailing. Its part of total retail sales, however, has dropped from 11.2 per cent in 1950 to 10.8 per cent in 1961, for various reasons including: failure to reconcile their social goals with the drive for efficiency and innovation required to match their competitors (co-op managers are rarely fired); political affiliations (their left-wing politics limits their class appeal); a deferred system of rebates that is less attractive to the housewife than price reductions (the "divi" has been falling over the past several years—it now stands at about 5 per cent); lack of capital for expansion; and persistence in promoting their own labels despite growing popularity of manufacturers' brands. Although probably the first to use self-service in food retailing, cooperatives have not responded as well as multiples to the recent trend toward supermarkets.[14]

From 1950 to 1961, department stores dropped in importance from 6.1 per cent of total retail sales to 5.3 per cent because of increased sales of grocers and provision outlets and household goods stores. Further, few branch stores have been opened because of the lack of new shopping centers. Despite the growing interest in food departments, which generate traffic, few have actually been set up.

One major change has to do with the growth of self-service stores in the food field. About 10,000 such stores (there were less than 1,000 in 1950) account for about 28 per cent of total grocery sales. On the average, these stores are substantially smaller than their American counterparts. At the end of 1961, approximately 750 supermarkets (about 200 opened that year) claimed 6 to 7 per cent of total grocery sales. More than 50 per

---

[13] *U. K. Census of Distribution and Other Services, 1957.*
[14] *The Financial Times* (March 8, 1961), p. 10.

cent are operated by multiples, 35 per cent by cooperative societies, and the rest by independent retailers and department stores. The number of supermarkets and their average size will not develop along the same lines as large American supermarkets for four reasons: (1) the lack of consumer mobility; (2) the absence of new shopping centers, reflecting a relatively static population; (3) the high cost of space; and (4) frequent shopping because of the lack of refrigeration and storage space in British homes.

Scrambled merchandising has increased substantially in recent years. The supermarket has effected a form of vertical integration by selling items that formerly were the exclusive prerogative of butchers, fishmongers, poulterers, greengrocers, fruiterers, and bread and flour confectioners. All of these have experienced a decline in numbers. Selfservice stores —and especially supermarkets—are introducing more and more nonfood items. A main reason for this drive to expand the range of goods offered is the higher gross margin associated with nonfood items. Chemist shops have also expanded their lines of goods and now commonly sell housewares, small furniture, garden hand tools, fertilizer and seeds, and lamps.

Many smaller shops are old and dingy, to say the least, and a high percentage of the self-service stores are merely older stores altered slightly. The newly built supermarkets do not, of course, fall into this category. Only a few individuals specialize in store modernization and the result has been poor store layouts and bad space allocations. British stores do not invest as heavily in equipment as do American stores.

PROMOTION

Advertising

Advertising and promotion expenditures in Britain in 1958 approximated $1 billion, of which 28 per cent was spent in national and provincial newspapers, 19 per cent in magazines and trade publications, 14 per cent in television, 10 per cent in catalogs and leaflets, 1 per cent in window and interior displays, 7 per cent in outdoor displays, 4 per cent in exhibitions, and 6 per cent in free samples and gift schemes. The remainder went for production costs, films and slides, administration, and miscellaneous (including radio).[15] Television has made impressive gains since 1958, largely at the expense of press advertising. Nineteen companies, each spending more than £1 million ($2.8 million) on press and TV advertising in 1958, spent a total of more than £56 million ($156 million). Unilever, the Beecham group, and Thomas Hedley were the three largest advertisers, totaling almost £24 million ($69 million) in 1960.[16]

[15] From an article by Mark Abrams in *The Financial Times* (June 1, 1959).
[16] *The Financial Times* (Aug. 18, 1961).

Of the approximately 700 advertising agencies in Great Britain, at least 300 are small agencies and not officially recognized. Britain has a substantial number of large, outstanding, integrated advertising agencies, including J. Walter Thompson, London Press Exchange, Foote, Cone & Belding, S. H. Benson, Erwin Wasey, Ruthrauff & Ryan, Ltd., Massius & Ferguson, and Young and Rubicam. Each of these agencies billed more than $15 million in 1961. Advertising agency personnel have been extremely important in stimulating the management groups of their clients to place greater emphasis on marketing and to adopt many American marketing techniques and practices.

The number of agency employees per $1 million billing is higher in Great Britain than in the United States. The reason is not a greater range of activities or services offered by British agencies, but greater efficiency and effort by American clerical and executive employees.

Britons read more newspapers per capita than any other people in the world although it must be remembered that their newspapers are typically quite "thin"—especially when compared to those of the United States. Circulations of the three largest newspapers (all weeklies) are *News of the World,* 6.7 million; *The People,* 5.4 million; and *Sunday Pictorial,* 5.3 million.

More than 1,700 trade and technical magazines and about 2,000 general magazines are distributed in Great Britain. The leading weeklies are *Radio Times,* 6.1 million; *T.V. Times,* 3.8 million; and *Woman,* 2.9 million. The leading monthlies are *Reader's Digest,* 1.1 million, and *Everywoman,* 0.3 million. In recent years, magazines have had difficulty maintaining their circulations, partly because of the growing popularity of television.

Although the British Broadcasting Corporation inaugurated the world's first public television service as early as 1936, the first commercial station (referred to as Independent Television) did not begin transmitting until September, 1955. Television Audience Measurement, Ltd. estimates that 86 per cent of all homes now have television. Radio is relatively unimportant as an advertising medium since the only available commercial station is not in Britain but in Luxembourg. This station reaches an estimated one-third of all British homes.

British print ads and TV commercials are more subtle than those in the United States. This difference of hard sell versus soft sell comes about in part because American commercials must compete against many more commercials for audience attention. Also, the average Britisher is far more conservative in his tastes than the American. Many organizations, and even M.P.'s, will do battle in the press against manufacturers who stray in their advertising claims. The average Britisher applauds such action, since he still views advertising—especially TV commercials—with considerable suspicion. In print advertising, especially in magazines, the best American advertisements are far better than the best of the British, partly because of superior color fidelity.

While more and better in-store display material is being produced, much more needs to be done to meet the special requirements of the self-service outlets. Showcards and cartons designed for counter use are, of course, not suitable for self-service stores, which are more interested in the freestanding display unit. The British manufacturer faces a dilemma here, since the clerk service retailer is still of great importance, despite the rapid growth of self-service stores. Furthermore, many manufacturers have learned the hard way that the big retailer is more interested in displays that suggest additional sales than in those aimed at switching sales from one brand to another.

Manufacturers are making use of fifteen-second tape-recorded commercials, known as storecasts, played at short intervals between music broadcasts. Two contractors presently offer this service, mainly in the London area.

Personal Selling

As the British economy moved from rationing to competition, manufacturers found it increasingly difficult to get their products stocked and sold, and hence began to pay more attention to their sales force operations. Between the prewar years and the early 1950's when rationing began to disappear, there had been little need to develop an aggressive sales force. Since then, more and more companies have placed greater emphasis on the selection, training, and control of their salesmen. Even so, only a handful—excluding American companies—have done an effective job (by our standards) of building a sales force.

British companies are now making every effort to attract better men to their selling activities. They have been willing to increase the starting pay and provide marginal benefits in the form of a car and expenses. Most companies are doing a reasonably good job of recruitment, and some use the services of consultants to help make the final selection. The consultants prepare advertisements, filter out unqualified applicants, interview the more promising men, and make final recommendations. Their fees range from 10 to 15 per cent of the salesman's first-year salary.

The extent and caliber of sales training vary considerably between companies. A number of larger ones operate their own training schools complete with a full-time specialized staff. Most companies have a sales manual. Associations such as the Institute for Marketing and Sales Management have been active in promoting better sales training and have published a considerable amount of helpful literature on the subject.

Most salesmen are paid a salary plus commission; some are paid a salary only, and few companies remunerate their salesmen by commission only. The years of rationing and the inevitable concern with allocation versus selling greatly affected the compensation system. Growing interest in providing better incentives for the sales force has prompted the establishment of realistic quotas so that individual salesmen can be paid a commission on the amount over the quota.

In 1960 it was estimated that the field cost of a typical salesman was:[17]

Basic salary	£ 700	($1,960)
Commission bonus	£ 300	($ 840)
Pension	£ 70	($ 196)
Car	£ 300	($ 840)
Expenses	£ 300	($ 840)
Supervisory overhead	£ 250	($ 700)
Total	£1,920	($5,376)

Recently, several independent companies have been organized that specialize in supplying salesmen on a contract basis. These men are high-pressure selling specialists, usually with considerable experience. Commander Sales Force and Sales Force, Ltd. are two of the better known firms.

As British consumer goods manufacturers increase their emphasis on preselling their brands through advertising and promotion, and as retailers grow in size and in their use of self-service, the sales force operation of many such companies can be expected to become less important.

PRICING

The 1956 Restrictive Practices Act permitted manufacturers to fix retail prices upon application to a Restrictive Practices Court. To date, few of these court actions have been successful. While resale price maintenance is still important in the sale of appliances, pharmaceuticals, tobacco, periodicals, cars, and cosmetics, it is all but dead in the grocery field where low-cost retailers have demonstrated the effect of low prices on volume. Also, the multiples now have sufficient volume to promote their own brands, a possibility that has not gone unnoticed by most manufacturers.

At the retail level, the consumer is exposed to considerable price competition, especially in the grocery field. The supermarkets follow to a considerable extent the same pricing practices as those employed in the

[17] E. B. Graves, "Cost of a Salesman," Published Papers 99, *The Incorporated Sales Managers' Association* (London: 1960).

United States: low markups are taken on such volume items as tea, sugar, bread, and coffee and high margins on frozen foods, drug and personal care items, and packaged bakery goods. Only a few retailers use any sort of stamp plan. The handful of so-called discount houses operate very differently from those in the United States in that they sell very few manufacturer brands and concentrate essentially on unbranded soft lines.

During 1961, and for the first time, many electrical appliances could be purchased at substantial discounts off list price. Some appliance manufacturers, such as Hotpoint, were planning to reduce prices and retail margins for the spring of 1962, while others, such as English Electric, were planning large advertising campaigns to stimulate sales. Because of the heavier purchase taxes recently installed, consumption has increased of the less expensive brands of cigarettes, beer, and lower octane gasolines.

The growing importance of the supermarket has caused some decline in the use of credit. Durables can be bought on time, but typically only from certain merchants who specialize in such activities and who charge a high rate of interest. Banks require security before providing personal loans or overdraft privileges.

All the arrangements for hire purchase are made through the retailer with a hire purchase specialist, who charges interest rates similar to banks. The total hire purchase debt has about doubled since 1958. In 1961, it was over $2.5 billion, of which about half could be attributed to cars.

Marketing in Great Britain is characterized by institutions and practices that, in many ways, are similar to those in the United States. But the British are only just beginning their marketing revolution, as evidenced by supermarkets, which account for only an estimated 5 to 6 per cent of total food sales; discount houses, still virtually nonexistent; product design and styling, which lag behind most Western countries; resale price maintenance, still important in the sale of many commodities; and new products, more often than not "borrowed" from other countries.

The marketing concept, relatively well known in America (although subject to many interpretations), has only recently gained any recognition in Britain. Relatively little attention is paid to marketing by most British firms, although notable exceptions are found in Unilever, Hedleys, Beechams, Nabisco, S. C. Johnson, and Heinz. In very few companies does one find a marketing vice-president who is responsible for coordinating such activities as advertising, personal selling, merchandising, and marketing research.

But Britain is undergoing a transition, and the importance of marketing is increasingly being recognized. The growing importance of the Common Market, coupled with the possible entry of Britain, will undoubtedly accelerate the interest of most British businessmen in marketing. Certainly, men with marketing skills are scarce, and the result has been a rapid rise in the salaries of senior marketing personnel and the growing use of brand managers.

Any attempt to explain what has happened to British marketing over the past ten years or so must keep in mind such factors as: (1) the years of rationing and the time required to rebuild the nation's industrial plant; (2) the letdown following a long war that led to a socialistic economy where complacency was, and to some extent still is, prevalent; (3) the high income taxes and the heavy purchase taxes; (4) the lack of any significant population increase; (5) the lack of venture capital; (6) the high cost of space and the lack of cheap land, which have slowed new retail formation; (7) the general prevalence of resale price maintenance until the late 1950's; and (8) the investments made by American interests in the British economy. The latter were extremely important, because American subsidiaries inevitably used American marketing methods that were, for the most part, successful.

And one must not forget that the attitudes and buying habits of British consumers tend to slow the trends now underway. Such factors as conservative tastes, willingness to put up with inconvenience, lack of mobility, lack of desire for change, and the status of service have all played an important, if negative, role.

What can one predict for British marketing? Certainly as it grows in importance many changes will occur, including the development of more consumer-oriented products, more efficient sales forces, increased advertising expenditures, some reduction in prices, and a retail and wholesale structure that more nearly resembles that of the United States. There appears to be a definite lead-lag relationship between marketing practices in the United States and those in Great Britain. Nowhere is this more true than in retailing, although the future retailing structure will differ substantially from that of the United States. Stores will be smaller and less capital will be invested; the highly specialized small service retailer will remain a vital part of the scene.

33.

MARKETING IN FINLAND*

A. J. Alton

ALTHOUGH the Scandinavian country of Finland shares 700 miles of common frontier with the Soviet Union, marketing in Finland may best be characterized as definitely "Western." Although there are instances of marketing which are antiquated by modern American standards, one can find striking examples of "up-to-the-minute" marketing performance and institutions which compare favorably with the best in the United States.

Modern retail and wholesale establishments are found in many cities. The rapid influx of self-service food stores, the approximately 50 advertising agencies, the sprinkling of ultra-modern, smart specialty shops, and the appearance of planned shopping centers are evidence of a rapidly-expanding, modern marketing economy.

THE FINNISH MARKETER

A portion of the business community may be described as astute practitioners who are well-qualified to "take charge" of the marketing operation of a domestic firm in the United States. Businessmen are becoming increasingly consumer-oriented and look to the United States for marketing innovation. Visits to leading American advertising agencies, research organizations, and marketing-oriented firms keep these practitioners abreast of the latest developments in the United States.

Membership in the American Marketing Association by marketing academicians and practitioners in Finland typifies the expanding international flavor of the Association. The full array of American marketing periodicals is as commonplace in some Finnish firms as in the United States. In contrast to the marketing-minded businessmen, however, there are many who do not as yet appreciate the importance of marketing.

One advantage which observant marketers in Finland possess is that of capitalizing upon "hindsight." Finland's economic and social development is sufficiently advanced to permit the successful transplanting of American marketing ideas. Although marketing techniques and institu-

* A. J. Alton, "Marketing in Finland," *Journal of Marketing*, Vol. 27, No. 3 (July, 1963), a publication of the American Marketing Association, pp. 47-51. Reprinted by permission.

tions cannot be transferred from the United States to Finland per se, careful study permits the adaptation of certain marketing methods under appropriate conditions. Pitfalls and errors of American marketers may also be avoided.

THE MARKET

Finland, the size of Montana, has a population of 4½ million. Approximately two-thirds of the people inhabit rural areas; and Helsinki, the capital, accounts for 10% of the population. The northern third of Finland is sparsely populated, the central portion is somewhat more populated, and most of the people live in southern Finland.

The proportion of two-thirds rural to one-third urban population in Finland is similar to that in the United States at the turn of the century. Projections indicate that one-half of Finland's people will live in urban areas about 1980, a condition reached in the United States about 1920.

Gross national product is $1,182 per person, approximately at the midpoint among Western European nations.[1] The comparative figure for the United States is $2,885.[2] The consumer market is expanding both in numbers and buying power. On a percentage basis, population increase for the decade of the sixties is expected to approximate that of the United States. Economic indicators such as real income, cost of living, prices, and industrial production are continuing favorably. Three successive boom years have helped to maintain a state of full employment, and the rate of economic growth has ranged from 5 to 7% per annum.

Finland's ties with the West are exemplified both by her marketing innovations and by her foreign marketing activities—80% of both her import and export trade is with the West.

Statistical data concerning the market and other sectors of the economy are well developed. A major advance in marketing statistics was the institution of a census of retail and wholesale trade in 1953. It compares favorably in detail and variety of information with the censuses of retail and wholesale trade in the United States.

RETAIL TRADE

Finland's first and most recent census of retailing reports 33,352 retail establishments with sales of $1.2 billion for 1953.[3] Sales for 1961 were $2.1 billion.

1 *Economic Review* (Helsinki: Kansallis-Osake-Pankki, Issue 1, 1962), p. 40.
2 *Survey of Current Business* (June, 1962), pp. S-1 and S-2.
3 1953 General Economic Census, Volume II: Trade (Helsinki, 1958), p. 30.

Based on census reports, there was one retail establishment with average sales of $36,700 for every 124 people. In comparison, similar figures for the United States in 1954 were $98,724 of sales per establishment for every 94 people. For the same years, per capita sales of retailers were approximately $300 in Finland and $1,047 in the United States.

These figures reflect, in part, the dominant rural population of Finland and the numerous small stores necessary to meet the needs of rural communities. General stores, characteristic of rural areas, account for more than one-third of the 33,352 retail establishments and 36% of retail store sales. General stores are approximately 1% in number and sales volume in the United States.

Most of the kinds of retail establishments in the United States are found in Finland; but several which are not characteristic of Finland are the variety store, discount house, mail-order house, and drug store. The latter, as Americans know it, does not exist in Finland. A Finnish consumer must visit four stores in order to purchase the array of merchandise that the typical American drug store carries. These are the apothecary, dispensing prescriptions and over-the-counter drugs, the "chemical" shop which stocks toilet goods, the "paper" shop which stocks stationery supplies, and the "kiosk" which carries candy and soft drinks.

Multi-stop shopping still prevails to a great extent in the food store field as well. A Finnish homemaker often visits three types of food stores to fill her market basket—a dairy-bakery store, a meat-and-poultry outlet, and a store that stocks dry groceries. The number of food stores carrying all food items is growing rapidly, and also the number of self-service food stores. Of the approximately 6,500 retail establishments classified as food stores, 623 are self-service.

Shopping Centers

Undoubtedly the most striking advancement in Finnish retailing is the development of planned shopping centers, found in Helsinki. Population mushroomed by more than 250% in the suburbs during the 1950s, while it declined in the old city proper. The first of seven major shopping centers was opened in December of 1959; and a well-balanced variety of retail stores and service establishments comprise this initial center. During the same month two smaller centers were dedicated.

Well before construction began on the first center, planning had been under way to insure that the downtown shopping area of Helsinki would continue to thrive. This simultaneous attack upon shopping-center planning and preservation of the downtown section represents a coordinated effort in marketing strategy by the city government and cooperating business interests.

Retail Chains

The retail-chain store movement has been significant in Finland for a number of decades. Whereas the major category of chain in the United States is the "corporate" ownership type, the most important central ownership type in Finland is the consumer cooperative. The latter is a realistic counterpart of the corporate chain of the United States.

Political and economic conflict between independents and chains has existed in Finland as in America. The consumer cooperative chains account for one-third of all retail sales, with the strongest showings in the general store category (51%) and food stores (44%). There are few chains of central ownership other than the consumer cooperative chains; and these are confined usually to one of the larger cities, especially the capital. A corporate food chain in Helsinki of about 34 outlets is the largest of these.

An effective rival of the consumer cooperative chains is a nationwide group of independent retailers of a number of merchandise lines known by the trade name Kesko. This unified effort might be classified as a type of voluntary chain, with ownership and control of warehouses and sales branches vested with the independent retailers.

The success of this venture can be attributed to the fact that the problem of competing effectively with the cooperative chains was met in other than just the buying function. Emphasis upon marketing research and attention to all the functional marketing areas is exemplary.

WHOLESALE TRADE

Wholesaling is highly developed and plays an important part in the marketing structure of Finland. In the principal lines of trade, retailers obtain their supplies almost exclusively from wholesalers. There is little direct selling by manufacturers; and when orders are solicited by manufacturers' salesmen, wholesalers usually perform the billing function.

The first census of wholesaling lists 4,030 wholesale establishments with sales of $1.505 billion.[4] Sales for 1961 were $3.015 billion. Merchant wholesalers comprise the major category, totaling 3,045 establishments and accounting for more than 95% of total sales. Agents and brokers number 985, with sales of approximately 1% of the total.

The diversity of Finland's wholesale trade structure is illustrated by census enumeration of 15 major classifications and 34 subclassifications by kind of business. The most important category, as measured by sales

[4] Same reference as footnote 3, at p. 28.

volume, is the general merchandise wholesaler. Although relatively few in number, this group accounts for 23% of sales of all merchant wholesalers. The vast majority of these establishments are among the very largest of all wholesale establishments—largely because of two consumer cooperative complexes and a retailer-owned wholesale enterprise. All but 2 of the 50 general merchandise wholesale establishments are operated by one of these three organizations. Not only do these establishments serve the needs of general stores, but also single-line stores in a number of merchandise categories.

Following the general merchandise wholesalers in importance are food, dry goods and hardware-builders' supplies wholesalers with 17, 9 and 8% respectively of total sales of merchant wholesalers.

Competition at the Wholesale Level

The competitive struggle between independent retailers and consumer cooperative retail chains in Finland is apparent at the wholesale level. Kesko, reputed to be the largest wholesale enterprise in Europe in terms of sales volume, is the creation of independent retailers. Over 11,000 retail stores, fully one-third of all the retail establishments in Finland, are regular customers of Kesko. Sales for 1961 were $313 million. This retailer-owned wholesale enterprise "blankets" most of the country with a network of sales offices and warehouses. It was created in 1941 when four regional wholesale buying organizations of retailers were merged. These four had been established during the 11-year span from 1906 to 1917.

The successful development of consumer cooperative retail chains during the latter half of the nineteenth century and the establishment of wholesale institutions to serve these cooperatives threatened the existence of independent retailers. The forerunners of the several regional wholesale buying organizations of the independent retailers were a number of loosely-knit retail buying groups which were established to combat the growing number of consumer cooperatives.

The two consumer cooperative wholesale enterprises and Kesko carried on programs to advance the management practices of retailers they served. In contrast, independent wholesalers were lax in this regard. Although the Finnish Wholesalers' Association was founded in 1920, it was not until 1949 that a systematized program of instructional and advisory work was formulated which individual wholesalers provided for their retail customers. Previous to that time the Association efforts were confined largely to a public relations program. Financial support for the program comes from member wholesalers of the Association. Despite the earlier shortcomings of independent wholesalers, they are as a group the dominant body at the wholesale level of trade.

Eight categories of wholesalers comprise the direct-firm membership of the Association. In addition, there are eleven separate associations of wholesalers by product line that also comprise the membership of the national Association. Most firms operate on a full-service basis, including transportation. Credit is granted usually for a 30-day period. The members of the Finnish Wholesalers' Association have found it necessary to pool their purchasing power in order to compete successfully with other segments of wholesale trade.

A comparison of the three major components in Finland's wholesale trade shows that independent wholesalers belonging to the Finnish Wholesalers' Association continue to lead in sales. Their share of the combined sales volume of the three segments is 45%, followed by the cooperatives with 36%, and Kesko with 19%.

ADVERTISING

Advertising Agencies

In appearance, operational methods, and organization there are great similarities between American and Finnish advertising agencies. The oldest agency was founded in 1923; and today there are approximately 50 agencies, ranging in size from one-man operations to the largest with 150 employees and billings of $3.3 million. A policy of agency "recognition" is practiced by Finland.

The employee-billing ratio for agencies in Finland with billings from $1 million to $3½ million is 40 employees per $1 million of billings. This is a considerably higher ratio than in the United States, although comparable to a number of other Western European nations.

Total advertising expenditures were estimated at $30 million in 1960, amounting to 0.8% of national income or $7 per capita.[5] The $30 million excludes retail window display and forms of interior store devices, which are included in certain summaries of advertising volume in Scandinavia. In contrast, advertising expenditures in the United States were 2.9% of national income in 1960 or $66 per capita. European nations' advertising expenditures per capita ranged from Switzerland's high of $28 to a low of $3 for Italy.

Reaching all of the public by means of advertising is somewhat complicated because Finland is a bilingual nation, with both Finnish and Swedish as official languages. However, the fact that 92% claim Finnish as their mother tongue alleviates the difficulty to a great extent.

[5] *Advertising Age* (April 16, 1962), p. 51.

Media

Newspapers are the dominant advertising medium, as in many other European countries. There are more than 60 daily newspapers, as well as numerous newspapers published from one to four times per week. National advertising coverage is offered by one national daily. The ratio of circulation of daily newspapers to population is one of the highest in the world. Illiteracy is practically unknown. Typically, the largest agencies' billings for newspapers range from 50 to 65% of total billings. There is a Finnish "Audit Bureau of Circulations" which certifies and analyzes circulation figures.

Magazines rank next in importance to newspapers as an advertising medium. Approximately 20% of billings of larger agencies are derived from this medium.

Finland also allows advertising on television; and there are two "networks," one government-owned. The larger agencies report that approximately 8% of their billings are from television.

Other advertising media are outdoor, direct mail, transit, business papers, point-of-sale, and films. The latter—frequently in color and expertly produced—are presented in movie houses and precede any features.

OTHER MARKETING ACTIVITIES

Manufacturers' brands and brands of middlemen vie for consumer loyalty. Branding in all product lines is carried on extensively. Domestic products compete with those from the United States and other foreign lands. The battle of brands in the cigarette and soap industries is "Americana" reproduced in the far north. Many domestic products have American names for brand names as well as slogans.

Packaging is of considerable concern to Finnish marketers. With self-service becoming increasingly important and with the television medium available, effective color and labeling are carefully considered.

Frozen foods are the most recent innovation in the packaged-food lines, but the small size of home refrigerators limits the market as does the high price. Habit also plays a part in determining the growth of frozen-food marketing. The general lack of storage space in apartment living fosters the continuance of the traditional daily food shopping, and encourages the Finnish homemakers to purchase the less expensive canned or fresh foods.

Advertising has progressed to a more advanced state than personal selling. This may be partially explained by the reticent nature of the average Finn, who is not likely to feel at home in the role of a reasonably aggressive salesman. The broad role of sales management is also characterized by its relative "backwardness" compared to advertising. On the average, far more of the Finnish business community has grasped the role of advertising and its strategy and techniques than the many facets of modern sales management.

To date, installment selling has been of little significance in the Finnish marketing picture. It is on the rise, however, and the contention is that it will be only a matter of time when it will be of some importance. Saving and not being in debt, except for home financing, is still a Finnish virtue. However, hard goods are being purchased more and more frequently on the installment plan, and some soft goods are sold in this fashion.

Finland has not as yet experienced the type of pricing revolution that the United States has at the retail level. Throughout Finland's entire economy the emphasis is on stability of prices, be they retailers', wholesalers', or manufacturers' prices. Cartels have been important and are cited as a force which fosters price stability. Although resale price maintenance legislation does not exist, there is great reluctance on the part of retailers in all lines of business to compete with emphasis on price.

Uniformity in pricing characterizes retailing throughout. It is claimed that margins are so low in some lines of retailing that pricing as a competitive weapon would be disastrous to all. Nevertheless, proposed legislation to prohibit "fair trading" and post-war statutes which have tended to dissipate restriction of competition may typify a trend away from price rigidity. Clearance, and other types of sales, are a minor element in the attempt to move merchandise.

MARKETING IN THE FUTURE

Finland presents an interesting study in comparative marketing. Socioeconomic conditions in Finland are sufficiently similar to those in the United States so that America's marketing past is to a great extent Finland's present, and America's present is seen evolving as Finland's future. However, the evolutionary process in marketing is much more rapid in Finland than it was in the United States.

Greater progress needs to be made in marketing research. Although there are scattered examples of excellent research in many of the functional areas of marketing, overall developments have not been noteworthy. Much can be done in areas such as sales forecasting, market potential, product development, and activities concerned with management of the sales force.

Finland is fortunate to have four independent collegiate schools of business, two of which have celebrated a half-century of training young people for business careers. The emphasis upon the several functional areas of business has followed the same evolutionary proces which characterized collegiate chools of business in the United States. Economics dominated the curriculum during the early years, followed by accounting and finance; and marketing as an academic discipline is the last "arrival" in Finland, as it was in the United States. Today, however, marketing is recognized by Finnish colleges of business as an important part of Finland's business scene. Individual firms and industry groups also show an increasing awareness of the importance of marketing, with emphasis given to it as a subject in advanced management institutes and seminars.

34.

MARKETING IN SPAIN*

Edwin H. Lewis

MODERN Spain is a multi-faceted country of some 30 million people whose strong regional ties and loyalties make them primarily Castilian, Catalan, Basque, Sevillian, Valencian, or Galician—to name some of the regional groups—and only secondarily, and sometimes grudgingly, Spanish. Even though united under a strong central government, Spain is still essentially an aggregation of regional cultures.

Marketers should recognize the regional characteristics of the country; and sales and distribution organizations must be set up in such a way that each region receives the special attention it requires. While the Spanish language is understood by all inhabitants and is the language of the advertising media, personal contacts are more effective if made in the local Spanish idiom or the regional tongue—Catalan in the area around Barcelona, Basque in the North.

REGIONAL TRADE CENTERS

The regional trading patterns of Spain have not been carefully studied, but several important trade centers exist. The two primary market centers, roughly equal in population, are Madrid and Barcelona. Although essentially a political center, Madrid is the commercial hub of the central and western parts of the country. Barcelona, considered to be the leading industrial and commercial city of Spain, is also an important Mediterranean port. It is the gateway to the "Costa Brava" and is the distribution point for the northeastern provinces—the region known as Cataluña.

The central Mediterranean coastal area, the Levante, is served from Valencia, a port, the center of the citrus industry, and the third ranking commercial city in Spain. The southern provinces, which make up Andalucia, hinge on the fourth largest commercial city, Seville. Bilbao, located on the northern coast in an area of heavy industry, and La Coruña (in Galicia) are the leading commercial centers in the northern part of the country.

* Edwin H. Lewis, "Marketing in Spain," *Journal of Marketing*, Vol. 28, No. 4 (October, 1964), a publication of the American Marketing Association, pp. 17-21. Reprinted by permission.

STANDARD OF LIVING

Although the Spanish market reflects wide extremes of income, the average per capita income is only $360 per year, the lowest—except for Portugal—in Western Europe, and one-fourth or less of that in the leading Western European countries. In the fall of 1963 the Franco government established a new minimum wage of 60 pesetas ($1.00) per day. Even at these levels, substantial improvement in the Spanish economy has occurred during the past decade. Since 1953, when defense and economic-aid agreements were signed with the United States, Spain has received more than $1 billion in military and economic aid.

Signs of growing prosperity appeared first in the larger cities. Tangible evidence is the vast number of new apartments and the rapid increase in the number of automobiles. During the period 1955-61 the output of automobiles increased three and one-half times. Still, in 1960, there were only 10 automobiles per 1,000 population in Spain, compared with 98 in Great Britain and 335 in the United States.

The small towns and rural areas have not shared in the new affluence; life there is hard, and comforts are few. Agricultural workers are frequently under-employed, especially on the small, fragmented farms of the North; and the vast wheat and grazing areas of the central *meseta* are over-populated. Consequently, per capita income in agricultural areas is about two-thirds of the national average.

CHANNELS OF DISTRIBUTION

Manufacturers whose products are distributed throughout the Spanish market sell through agents (*agentes comerciales*), their own salesmen, or both. The term "distributor," in Spain, frequently is applied to an agency operation, and some agents work under a so-called "distributor agreement." Agent compensation is typically straight commission, but key agents are sometimes paid a salary plus commission.

In the postwar years many agents were used primarily because of their contacts. Some have close ties with the major industrial-banking groups, which have had a powerful influence on the Spanish economy. Under conditions involving a shortage of capital, business activities of many types have been influenced by financial relationships. Also, prior to 1959, merchandise shortages were such that access to a supplier was of major importance. Agents often provided this access. Now that governmental controls have been considerably relaxed in both the financial and commodity spheres, some manufacturers are dropping those agents who have performed few services other than serving as a contact.

Even where they presumably perform a selling function, agents have been criticized by manufacturers as being mere order-takers. Top-grade agents with promotional ability have been difficult to find in Spain. Some manufacturers encourage their agents to carry stocks, and may, in fact, require it in areas where field stocks are desirable. As this change in function occurs, agents may evolve into regular distributors.

Manufacturers have very limited control over their agents. Although agents are usually assigned to specific areas, the almost total lack of satisfactory market-potential data makes it difficult to establish performance controls. Also, like their counterparts in the United States, Spanish agents usually represent several lines, and this increases the control problem. In areas large enough to permit the use of subagents, the agent holding the franchise is responsible for the activities of his subagents, and in the industrial field for the installations they undertake.

Some manufacturers sell through their own sales organizations in major markets, as in Barcelona and Madrid, where they may maintain sales offices and warehouses. Agents are then used to cover the remainder of the market.

Major industrial lines, such as chemicals and industrial apparatus, may be sold by company salesmen directly to users. Sales engineers can be hired and trained for this purpose, but their training presents problems. Seldom are educated Spaniards sales-oriented. If they are going into business instead of a profession, they tend to prefer general office work. Industrial salesmen are located in such primary trade and industrial centers as Barcelona, Bilbao, La Coruña, Madrid, Seville, Valencia, and Zaragosa.

Governmental controls determine the market structure of some products. In the drug industry, for example, the government decrees the channel to be used and the allowable margins. Furthermore, all parts of the industry are licensed. The channel specified is manufacturer-wholesaler-retailer, and the margins permitted are 15%, 12%, and 30% respectively. Manufacturers must submit cost data for new products to the government and must get approval for the product and for the price schedule.

The bulk of the steel output of the private companies is sold through a long-established industry sales organization. Central Siderurgica, S.A. This organization receives orders from industrial customers and wholesalers and allocates them to its members. Orders in excess of 500 metric tons may be placed by industrial users directly with the sales organization. Smaller quantities must be purchased from wholesalers, who in turn buy through the sales organization. Wholesalers are registered; there were some 500 in 1961. Some are classified as subwholesalers and, as such, cannot deal directly either with the mills or with Central Siderurgica. Instead, they must buy from wholesalers in a higher class.

Prices of several products are fixed by the government. These include coal, cement, iron pyrites, some paper, lubricating oils, lead, super phosphates, industrial alcohol, sugar, antibiotics, and some iron and steel products. Fixed processing margins have been established for wheat and sugar. The entire Spanish wheat crop is purchased by a government organization, Servicio Nacional del Trigo. Livestock slaughtering is controlled by the individual municipalities under a system of fees and taxes that vary by area.

MERCHANT WHOLESALERS

Although industrial products are sometimes sold directly to users, it is not always efficient, even for large manufacturers, to do so. A manufacturer of chemical products, for example, might sell through a specialized wholesaler who has been able to develop technically trained salesmen. However, when no provision for such middlemen exists in the trade-discount schedule, they are forced to operate on the quantity discounts earned.

Smaller types of industrial products are sold typically through wholesalers. Thus, a manufacturer of electric motors and switchgear sells through 40 wholesalers, some of whom have their own branches. These distributors are not permitted to carry competing lines.

Consumers' goods that require broad distribution (for example, drugs, small household items, and paint) are also sold through wholesalers. Products whose outlets are more limited, such as shoes and phonograph records, are sold directly to retailers. A record manufacturer indicated that he had attempted to sell through wholesalers, but found that they would not give enough attention to the line; therefore, it became necessary to sell directly to retailers.

Merchant wholesalers in Spain are of two basic types: *mayoristas,* large national or regional wholesalers selling to retailers and/or small wholesalers in the provinces; and *meñoristas,* small wholesalers serving a local market. The latter may also make some sales at retail. The governmental licensing provisions specify higher fees for *mayoristas* than *meñoristas.*

Especially when they engage in some retail business, *meñoristas* are gradually being removed from the customer lists of the larger manufacturers because they cannot perform the necessary wholesale services. From the manufacturer's point of view, the most satisfactory wholesalers are large, merchandising-minded firms that carry allied but not directly competing lines; that will take the responsibility for a market and do an effective job of promotion; and that can assume the installation and servicing functions. Since it is difficult to find wholesalers who meet these specifications, manufacturers frequently find it necessary to aid them in every way possible, even to the point of securing turnover orders from retailers.

The salesmen for one manufacturer of consumers' goods, for example, call on retailers regularly, perhaps as often as once a month. Orders received are turned over to wholesalers designated by retailers. This manufacturer also trains new jobber personnel and holds annual sales-training clinics for wholesalers. In this instance, wholesalers handle only the small, routine orders. Key accounts involving large orders, special formulations, and special services are sold direct by the manufacturer.

A drug manufacturer uses 80 detail men to cover the country, and to secure turnover orders from retailers. As in other commodity lines, the drug wholesaler is essentially an order-taker. His main function, in effect, is to operate a warehouse. Much of his selling is done by telephone; and daily, or twice-daily, calls are made to regular customers. One reason for this is that retailers carry low stocks of prescription items and expect immediate delivery or pick-up service.

Approximately 277,000 retail establishments and 28,000 wholesale establishments are operating currently in Spain. Detailed statistics for wholesale and retail trade are not available. In 1961, wholesale and retail trade accounted for 13% of the gross domestic product, ranking third after manufacturing (23%) and agriculture (18.5%).

RETAIL TRADE

The typical Spanish retail establishment is small-scale. Many of those in small towns and neighborhood areas of cities are one-man shops, carrying a limited stock of merchandise and doing no promotion. Still, the entrepreneur serves the needs of his trade. Although he carries no inventories in depth, he can at times produce a surprising range of items—some of these may be a little shopworn, but nobody seems to mind, so long as the product functions.

Stores in Spain frequently specialize more than in the United States. This is most noticeable in food, where the shopper must make daily rounds, stopping at separate stores to purchase dry groceries (and perhaps produce), meat, seafood, poultry and eggs, milk, bakery products, and fresh fruits and vegetables. In the cities and larger towns, the public market is an important institution. Here fruits and vegetables, meats, and a wide range of seafood may be beautifully displayed in stalls.

The *supermercado* is making its appearance in Spain, although more slowly than in other parts of Western Europe. These markets need improvement in cleanliness, display, promotion, and merchandise assortment.

Drugs and toilet goods may be sold in *droguerías* (which may also handle household supplies), *farmacias* (which do a prescription business and also sell packaged drug products), and *perfumerías* (which specialize in soaps, toilet goods, and cosmetics).

Hardware items of the type used in the home are purchased in *ferreterías* (ironware shops). Lines are narrow, and typically exclude the housewares and sporting goods lines that American hardware stores have added.

Petroleum products are distributed by a partially government-owned monopoly, Companía Arrendataria del Monopolio de Petroleos, S.A., generally known as CAMPSA. Prices of petroleum products are standardized throughout the country. Gasoline is bought at curbside pumps, although there are some drive-in type stations. Most of these establishments sell gasoline only, in two grades.

The tobacco industry is another monopoly. Tobacco products, especially cigarettes, are sold in several types of stores. In the cities, specialized tobacco-products stores may be found. Cigarettes may be purchased in neighborhood stationery stores, or in cafés. The street vendor is a unique element in cigarette distribution, and many of his sales are individual cigarettes.

Automobile tires are sold by automobile and automobile-accessory dealers and a few specialized tire dealers, found only in the largest cities. Spanish gasoline-filling stations have not sold tires in the past, but some tire manufacturers are attempting to establish dealerships among these stations.

Most tire dealers prefer to carry several brands. Some manufacturers have attempted to set up limited distribution arrangements, expecting that the dealer will give primary if not exclusive attention to his line. In Northern Spain, manufacturers have had some success in building dealer loyalty, but elsewhere multi-line arrangements are the rule. Where exclusive contracts covering a large market are used, the dealer may set up subdealerships.

Women's outerwear in Spain is generally custom-made; and every Spanish woman in the middle and upper classes patronizes a *modista* (dressmaker). Men's outerwear also is frequently custom-made. Consequently, many yard-goods stores are in existence. Although most shoes are ready made, it is not uncommon to have both shoes and gloves (especially women's gloves) custom-made.

Retail shoe stores, customarily of the family type, buy the products of several manufacturers. Purchases are made twice a year from manufacturers' agents. Manufacturers operate independently with respect to style, and industrywide styling of the type used in the United States is not followed. One interesting feature of the industry is that the retailer often is permitted to ask for design changes. Brands are unimportant. Retailers sell on the basis of price and style. The range of retail prices is wide. Little attempt is made, on the part of either retailer or manufacturer, to increase the demand for shoes.

Large-scale retailers, especially of the chain and mail-order types, are virtually unknown in Spain. A few large general-merchandise or department stores, such as SEPU, operate with open counters and displays. Merchandise promotions are aggressive and based on price appeal. Innovations such as air-curtain entrances also are used.

The opportunities in large-scale retailing undoubtedly led Sears, Roebuck and Company to choose Spain for its first European venture. The company plans stores in Madrid and Barcelona. A wholly owned subsidiary, Sears Roebuck de España, will handle buying and retail activities.

Spanish retail operations typically are geared to low-key promotion. Price appeal is seldom used; even special promotions based on price are uncommon. Merchandise tends to stay on the shelf until it is sold, with no price reduction on shopworn items.

Since plenty of low-cost clerical help is available, there is no pressure toward self-service. On the contrary, labor is used for purposes that would seem extravagant to Americans. Some specialty stores—for apparel, for example—set up elaborate and attractive after-store-hours displays, installed and removed every day.

Most stores use a centralized cashier system, requiring that the clerk supply sales slips which the customer must present to the cashier. Most sales are on a cash basis; little use is made of bank checks and open accounts. Collections, when involved, are usually handled by a *cobrador* (collector), who calls at the home to secure payment. *Cobradors* are used regularly by all types of business establishments.

ADVERTISING

Accurate data on the aggregate volume of advertising in Spain are not available; but advertising activity is expanding rapidly, and technical competence is improving.

Publication media (newspapers, consumer magazines, and trade papers) account for about half of the media expenditures. The greatest demand for space is in the "top" metropolitan papers, especially those in Madrid and Barcelona; and because of limited printing facilities it has been difficult sometimes to schedule space. Space sales in the leading Barcelona paper, *La Vanguardia,* for example, have been running several months ahead.

Agency commissions vary inversely with the quality of the newspaper. They average about 10% for the leading dailies, but may be considerably higher for the smaller papers. Standardized circulation data, comparable to the American reports of the Audit Bureau of Circulations, are not available. At times agencies make their own checks of newsstand sales and home deliveries.

Expenditures for radio advertising are mounting; they quadrupled in the 1958-60 period alone. One reason is that 80% of Spanish women are reported to be radio listeners. Most of the approximately 200 radio stations are privately owned, low-power, local stations; these are combined into several private networks. A government-owned network, Radio Nacional de España, also accepts advertising. The larger stations are on the air from 8 a.m. to 1 a.m. Advertising rates remain the same, regardless of the time of day.

Commercial television, introduced in 1958, is government-owned but carries paid advertising. Although there is considerable interest in television, the cost of a set is too high for most Spanish families. Sets may be found in many of the innumerable cafés. Bullfights and soccer are major attractions, and the cafés fill up on afternoons when an important *corrida* or *futbol* game is being shown.

Television has become a much-sought advertising medium; and it is difficult to buy time in the prime evening hours. This time has been controlled by a few agencies. This problem arises from the fact that during the development period only one channel was used. Most programs have originated in Madrid or Barcelona, and then have been sent out over transmitters located in other cities. As a result of new transmission facilities in Barcelona, Asturias, Mallorca, and the Canary Islands, 93% of the population is now within the receiving range of a TV station.

Many of the large number of so-called advertising agencies in Spain (trade estimates range up to 400) hold the exclusive rights to sell space in a particular medium and, therefore, are more properly classified as media representatives. The number of agencies equipped to give full-agency service of satisfactory quality is very small. Some American clients have felt that until very recent years there have been none in this category. This situation undoubtedly accounts for the recent acquisition of two Spanish agencies by American agencies. The largest agencies, located in Madrid or Barcelona, frequently maintain branches in other cities.

The absence of market data, combined with a lack of research competence and interest on the part of Spanish agencies, has resulted in little advertising research of any kind; nor are agencies involved in packaging research. The product and the package are taken as given, and the agency then proceeds to work up a campaign.

THE OUTLOOK

The next 10 years will be a period of rapid change for the Spanish economy. Major shifts in resources will occur, especially in use of land; and the income of the industrial and service sectors will show a great increase.

A booming tourist trade is already being experienced. The Economic Development Plan (1964-67) calls for an annual increase of 6% in the gross
national product (at constant prices), and establishes specific goals in
virtually all sectors of the economy.

To meet the demand created by increased output and rising incomes,
the Spanish marketing structure will need strengthening in several respects. Further decontrol of prices, further reduction of marketing restrictions, and an acceleration of the movement toward freer competition
are needed. In some channels, agents and small wholesalers not making
an adequate contribution to distribution will be eliminated. Large aggressive wholesalers are greatly needed, who can work closely with manufacturers and give them proper support. In fact, a need for a stronger sales
orientation is evident at all levels—manufacturing, wholesale, and retail.

The present retail structure cannot cope with the growing volume of
goods. Retail operations need to be generally upgraded. Probably this will
have to be done by a new generation of retailers who are willing to operate on a larger scale than in the past.

Advertising facilities and services will need to be broadened, and the
competence of agencies must be enhanced.

Above all, better-trained marketers are needed. A few schools are
now operating at the collegiate level, but the state universities do not
recognize marketing as a subject area.

All of these matters pose a challenge. The Spaniards are now demonstrating a will to speed up the changes that will bring improvements in
their standard of living.

35.

MARKETING IN ITALY TODAY*

David Carson

ITALY has been described as a Janus-headed being peering toward the future with one face, while riveting its second set of eyes firmly on the past.

The nation's marketing structure and operations have long been prime examples of this "schizoid" characteristic. There are increasing signs, however, that Italy is becoming more interested in catching up with the economic leaders of the Western world than in extolling the grandeurs of the Roman Empire and the Renaissance. Marketing is advancing rapidly.

THE MARKET

Italy is roughly the size of New England and New York State combined. Approximately 52 million people live on the mainland, the major islands of Sicily and Sardinia, and the small isles. Its population density of 440 people per square mile is almost nine times that of the United States. The population is highly concentrated in the industrial triangle formed by Milan, Turin, and Genoa in the Northwest, and around Rome, Naples, and other major cities.

Italy is regarded by some as one of the oldest nations in the world; on the contrary, it is relatively new. From the fall of the Roman Empire until the establishment of the Italian Kingdom in 1861 Italy was a collection of separate states ruled by princelings, by the papacy, and by various foreign powers. Fascists controlled the monarchy from 1922 to 1945; but since 1946 Italy has been a republic.

Following the devastation of much of its productive facilities during World War II, Italy embarked on an era of industrial expansion in the 1950s with considerable aid from the United States. From 1952 through 1962 its average annual increase in industrial production was 9.2%, a record high among Western European nations.

* David Carson, "Marketing in Italy Today," *Journal of Marketing*, Vol. 30, No. 1 (January, 1966) a publication of the American Marketing Association, pp. 10-16. Reprinted by permission.

Some indication of what this meant for the Italian consumer is the increment in automobile ownership from 11 per 1,000 persons in 1952 to 49 in 1962. Measured on the same population basis, radio ownership increased from 90 to 170, and telephones from 30 to 85. These rates of increase were far above the Western European average.

Accompanying this rapid industrialization was a decline in unemployment from well over 2 million people in 1951 to approximately 500,-000 by the end of 1963; a shift in the proportion of the total labor force engaged in agriculture, from 53% in 1951 to 40% in 1963; and the emigration of almost 3 million people from the rural South, largely to Italy's North.

Despite governmental and private efforts to equalize economic opportunities, *per capita* net income in the North remains almost twice as high as in the South—with regional results for 1962 ranging from a high of $944 in Lombardy (the Milan area) down to $272 in Basilicata, located in the "instep of the boot."

PRODUCTION

Extraordinary contrasts exist among manufacturing enterprises in terms of size, ownership, technology, and marketing methods. Approximately half of Italy's industrial production is controlled by the federal government, largely through the IRI and ENI groups.

IRI (*Istituto per la Ricostruzione Industriale,* or Institute for Industrial Reconstruction) is largely a holding company, administering much of the nation's production of pig iron, steel, cement, ship-building, and machinery, as well as such services as telephones, maritime shipping, road-construction, banking, the radio and television networks, and the national airline.

ENI (*Ente Nazionale Idrocarburi,* or National Petroleum Group) engages in all facets of petroleum production and distribution, both at home and abroad.

IRI subsidiaries tend to be operated like private business firms in their financial as well as in their marketing operations. Customers are sought out and serviced by well-trained sales staffs backed up by technical specialists. Relations with private business are generally good.

ENI, on the other hand, was described by Enrico Mattei, its late chief, as a state within a state; and the organization has retained not only a strong individualistic stamp but also its antagonism toward private business. Its policy of vertical integration, ranging from petroleum prospecting to gasoline service stations and motels, has tended to insulate ENI against contacts with private business firms and with other governmental units.

Fiat, with over 125,000 workers, is the nation's largest private employer, producing 90% of the domestic automobiles and considerable amounts of steel, machinery, household appliances, etc. Other industrial firms employing more than 50,000 people each are Montecatini (chemicals, minerals), Pirelli (rubber products, cables), Olivetti (office equipment), and Snia Viscosa (textiles).

Yet when la Rinascente, Italy's largest retail group, was in need of major suppliers of women's and children's apparel to meet the postwar demand for ready-to-wear, it was forced to set up its own manufacturing affiliate, APEM, in tandem with Snia Viscosa. On the other hand, the Marzotto group of textile manufacturers, interested in expanding men's ready-to-wear, integrated "forward" not only to men's apparel plants but also to a 17-unit retail chain. These large-scale consumer goods firms have integrated their operations from raw materials through retailing because of weaknesses in scale of production and in channels of distribution.

In spite of the industrial giants, producers of consumer goods are typically small, family-centered, artisan-type firms. Operations are generally oriented toward production, and to a lesser extent finance. Little direct selling is done by small manufacturers; and distribution is generally handled by commission agents who take the initiative to seek out these small producers. Large retailers also generally take the initiative in such producer-retailer contacts. Among manufacturers where oligopolistic conditions prevail—such as automobiles, talcum powder, or textile bleaching—marketing efforts are equally weak.

Yet conditions are changing, and manufacturers are beginning to upgrade marketing organizationally to the same echelon as production and finance. Much of the impetus for this move comes from the hundreds of foreign companies now operating in Italy. American firms alone opened over 300 enterprises in Italy between 1958 and early 1964.

Indoctrination in modern marketing concepts has also been encouraged by several schools for business executives, backed principally by the larger private and public industrial enterprises; by foreign and domestic management consulting firms and advertising agencies; by increasingly close relationships among major Italian business executives and their counterparts abroad; and by mass tourism converging on Italy from all sectors of the globe. Even so, the use of the English word "marketing" in Italian may be indicative of the foreignness of the marketing concept.

The prominent role played by design has been a particular feature of Italy's productive growth during the past two decades. Designer-architects such as Nervi, Nizzoli, and Ponti are of first-rank international note. Pinin Farina and Nuccio Bertone are, if anything, better known among automotive circles in Detroit than among the general populace of their homeland. A list of names of outstanding designers would include Aponte,

Biki, Brioni, Capucci, Fabiani, Ferragamo, Fontana, Galitzine, Garnett, and Pucci. The significance of the *Compasso d'Oro* (Golden Compass) award in fostering design excellence has been recognized in special exhibitions sponsored by the Museum of Modern Art in New York and by many other organizations throughout the world.

DISTRIBUTION

In Italy most distributive firms, including wholesalers, retailers, itinerant merchants (largely retailers), and public businesses (that is, restaurants, bars, hotels, etc.) must be licensed by municipal boards before they can operate—a practice introduced by the guild system of the Middle Ages.

Since an applicant must prove a "need" for a proposed outlet, and since local merchants are well represented on these boards, obtaining a license usually calls for considerable political acumen, if not chicanery. There are approximately 70 types of retail licenses, though the categories vary considerably from area to area.

In certain localities license classifications are so "refined" that a merchant must obtain one license for aluminum housewares and another for plastic items. Although department stores and supermarkets have been specifically exempted from the "need" proviso, red tape often delays the issuance of a license. Even though all licensed businesses are not in operation nor are all firms in operation licensed, official statistics of the distributive trades are generally based on licenses.

Latest available comparative data for the distributive trades show that in 1960 Italy had 1,045,900 establishments employing 2,326,500 individuals.[1]

By comparison, Great Britain had 573,988 establishments with 2,568,886 employees; and the United States had 2,161,462 establishments with 13,318,091 employees. There was an average of 2.22 employees per establishment in Italy, compared with 4.48 for Great Britain and 6.16 for the United States.

Inhabitants per establishment were 47.3 in Italy, 87.4 in Great Britain, and 80.9 in the United States, while national inhabitants per employee in distribution averaged 21.3 for Italy, 19.5 for Great Britain, and 13.1 for the United States.

Thus, Italy's distributive enterprises tended to be much smaller than those of Great Britain and of the United States, although relatively fewer of Italy's inhabitants (1 to 21.3) were engaged in these trades than in Great Britain (1 to 19.5) or the United States (1 to 13.1).

[1] *Commissione per la elaborazione di uno schema organico di sviluppo nazionale, dell'occupazione e del reddito—Gruppo Commercio, Primo Rapporto* (Rome: March, 1962).

The number of distributive units in Italy increased at an annual rate of 1.66% from 1951 through 1955, but slowed down to 1.26% from 1956 through 1960. During this 10-year period the number of employees engaged in distribution increased at an annual rate of 2.6%, indicating an average gain in the number of employees per establishment.

Many reasons have been offered for the comparatively large number of enterprises in the distributive trades:

1. The surplus of manpower in the past has forced the establishment of marginal enterprises. Until the recent years of almost-full employment, there was tacit acceptance of this "make-work" function of distribution by many members of the political and economic elite.
2. Difficulties in transportation and communications have encouraged the growth of localized activities.
3. Small amounts of capital are generally required for entry.
4. Middlemen are also partial producers and finishers of numerous products, such as ready-to-wear. Their customers often prefer individualized merchandise and services to less personal ones.
5. The consumer has become accustomed to short-term credit, the delivery of small orders, and similar services offered by small retailers and wholesalers.
6. Political and legal pressures discourage large-scale distribution. Among these are the aforementioned license requirements; the *dazio,* an "import" tax levied on almost everything brought into a city; and the turnover tax, averaging about 3%, applied against all transactions *except* at the retail level.

The government—particularly at the federal level—is involved in distribution to a much greater extent than in many other Western nations. Quasi-public provincial agricultural cooperatives (*Consorzi Agrari*) coordinate the planning, purchasing, and selling of much farm produce.

Other quasi-governmental units distribute bananas and pasteurized milk, and at times control the sale of sugar. Rigid state monopolies regulate sales of tobacco, matches, lighters, cigarette paper, salt, and quinine, all of which are sold in tobacco shops.

The government may become even more deeply involved in distribution by aiding existing wholesalers and retailers to modernize their operations, and possibly by establishing supermarket chains. Although these activities would be directed at the federal level, actual operations would be carried out by the municipalities.[2]

[2] Report of June 27, 1964, meeting of *La Commissione Nazionale per la Programmazione Economica* (c.n.p.e.), a governmental commission of economists representing government, business, and certain professions. Special supplement published by MONDO ECONOMICO, July 4, 1964, on *Bozza del Programma Quinquennale Quinquennale 1965-1969.*

WHOLESALING

The most recent census for which complete data are available (1951) indicated that approximately four-fifths of the wholesale enterprises were individually owned, most of the rest were jointly owned, and the number of publicly owned enterprises was negligible. About 88% of the wholesale establishments employed fewer than six persons, compared with 59% in the United States. Over 0.11% of the Italian wholesale enterprises employed over 100 persons each, compared with more than 1.0% of the total number of American wholesale firms.[3]

Italian wholesaling is thus essentially a family business, with low volume and small net profits. The heavy concentration of wholesaling in the North resulted in a ratio of only 8.1 retail establishments for each wholesale business in 1958, as compared with 14.3 in Central Italy and 21.6 in the South.

Wholesalers in all trades generally extend credit to their customers; but except for textiles, few do so to suppliers. Although most wholesalers carry merchandise inventories, they seldom provide their customers with special services such as technical assistance. Because of this reluctance to service customers more fully, increasing numbers of manufacturers are bypassing wholesaling and selling directly to retailers and to industrial accounts.

Since the end of World War II many large manufacturers of consumer goods have increased direct sales to retailers, particularly in foods and in toiletries. Therefore, the proportion of goods passing through wholesalers has declined. In a few fields—notably pharmaceuticals—wholesalers have maintained their position despite the establishment of networks of detail men by manufacturers.

RETAILING

Fragmentation of the market is particularly prevalent in retailing, where at the end of 1961 there were 1,216,616 outlets, of which 908,344 were stores and 308,272 itinerant merchants.[4] An average of only 1.8 persons was employed in each retail enterprise in Italy, one of the lowest figures in Western Europe.[5] One explanation is the high proportion of itin-

[3] Article by Pietro Gennaro on "Wholesaling in Italy," in Robert Bartels, editor, *Comparative Marketing: Wholesaling in Fifteen Countries* (Homewood, Illinois: Richard D. Irwin, Inc., 1963), pp. 37-46.

[4] *Ministero dell'Industria e del Commercio, Caratteri Strutturali del Sistema Distribuitivo in Italia nel 1961* (Rome: Ugo Pinto, 1962), p. 72.

[5] James B. Jefferys and Derek Knee, *Retailing in Europe* (London: The Macmillan Company, 1962), p. 30.

erants, one-fourth of all retail enterprises—a record high for Europe—
where vendors in street markets, door-to-door salesmen, and "sellers-on-
the-fly" are considerably more prevalent than in the United States.

Italy has lagged far behind the United States and the more highly
industrialized European nations in developing modern forms of retailing. The first department store, la Rinascente, was opened in Milan in
1917. Its customers, in the habit of haggling, could not understand why
a salesperson had to abide by the fixed prices clearly marked on the
merchandise.

Prejudice against mass-produced goods also had to be overcome. In
1928 la Rinascente launched UPIM, now a chain of over 100 junior department stores. The second-largest retail group, Standa, has approximately the same number of stores as UPIM. However, ten of these are
supermarkets and the remainder are junior department stores, the majority containing sizable supermarket "departments" in the French manner (as examples, Prisunic and Monoprix). The junior department stores
are one-stop shopping centers designed primarily for pedestrians, and
are dispersed among residential districts of the large cities.

After several false starts the first *real* supermarket was opened in
Milan in 1958 by combined American and Italian interests. The latest
count indicated just over 300 supermarkets, of which 129 were departments of junior department stores. The majority of the separate supermarkets were small, with selling space slightly more than 2,000 square
feet per store.

Compared with the 4,000 supermarkets in West Germany or the
2,600 in France,[6] Italy may seem backward. But the social and economic
infrastructure of supermarkets is well advanced, ranging from the growth
of a sizable middle-income group, to the disappearance of the household
"slavey," to the increased annual production of refrigerators (from 100,-
000 units in 1954 to 1,700,000 in 1963). Certain sectors of the food industry, particularly meat and produce, cannot supply supermarket groups
effectively. American supermarket chains are aiding their Italian counterparts either through occasional advice or by outright managerial and
financial commitments.

At the end of 1962 there were only 74 voluntary chains servicing
7,200 associated retailers, and 126 cooperative buying groups with 8,211
retail members.[7]

Of the 15,411 store members in these two categories, fully 73.8%
were located in the North, 22.6% in the Central regions, and a mere 3.6%
in the South. The number of retail stores in these groups is growing
rapidly, having increased 17% from 1961 to 1962. Consumer coopera-

[6] *Camera di Commercio Internazionale, Il Supermarcato—Nel Sistema Distribuitivo
Italiano* (Milan: Giuffré, 1962), p. 9.
[7] Same reference as footnote 4, at p. 130.

tives, weak by general European standards, do exist, largely as offshoots of centrist and left-wing political parties.

The degree to which retail distribution in Italy differs from that of Western Europe as a whole is indicated in Table 1. The relatively weak positions of consumer cooperatives, specialty store chains, variety store chains (principally junior department stores), and department stores are readily apparent.

TABLE 1—ESTIMATED SHARES OF TOTAL RETAIL SALES BY TYPE OF RETAIL ORGANIZATION: ITALY AND WESTERN EUROPE[a] 1960

Type of Retailer	Italy	Western Europe[b]
Consumer cooperative	2.7%	6.2%
Specialty store chain	0.1	8.2
Variety store chain	1.6	2.6
Department store	0.4	3.6
Independent specialty store and others	95.2	79.4
Total	100.0%	100.0%

[a] Source: James Jefferys and Derek Knee, *Retailing in Europe* (London: The Macmillan Company, 1962), p. 65.
[b] Includes Austria, Belgium, Denmark, Finland, France, Germany, Iceland, Ireland, Italy, Netherlands, Norway, Sweden, Switzerland, and United Kingdom.

From time to time studies have been made, comparing operating results of Italian retailers with those of other countries, particularly the United States; but they have invariably bogged down in a morass of inconclusive judgments. Principal handicaps to achieving adequate comparability have been international differences in accounting procedures; variations in tax structures, and in accounting classifications of taxes; the Italian penchant for secreting operating results; and the haphazard accounting methods found among smaller firms, where owners' household expenses are often intermingled with business records.

Based upon net sales, tentative conclusions of comparisons between general merchandise retailers in Italy with those in the United States indicate that gross margins in Italy range from 7% to 10% lower; wages and salaries, from 5% to 7% lower; social security expenses, about double those of American companies; and markdowns, roughly half.

Italian retailers often prefer warehousing seasonal merchandise to taking sizable markdowns. Stock rotations are lower, as Italian suppliers do not keep merchandise inventories on hand to the same extent as American manufacturers. Conditions in the Italian supply markets are changing, though, encouraging higher rates of stock turnover.

FACILITATING FUNCTIONS

Fifteen years ago advertising in Italy was concentrated largely on movie flash signs and radio spots. Since then advertising agencies have grown at a rapid pace, often with financial and personal assistance from American, British, and other foreign agencies. Media uses have broadened considerably, and copy and art work have become more sophisticated.

Despite the increase in advertisements in magazines and newspapers, advertisers are handicapped by the limited circulation of such media as well as by the reluctance of publishers to furnish circulation figures. Total advertising expenditures were only $3 per capita of population in 1960, compared with $13 for all of Western Europe; and yet Italy's costs for printed media were apparently the most expensive.[8]

In 1959 movie-theater advertising in Italy set a European record with its estimated 8% of total advertising expenditures. With 205 cinemas per million people—again a European high—such an expenditure was hardly surprising. Television is cutting into movie spots, however, with the number of receivers increasing from 88,000 in 1954 to almost 5 million by the end of 1964. Since the government-owned TV networks severely limit the total TV advertising time and individual advertiser's time, this medium has not expanded as rapidly as the ownership of receivers. Another deterrent has been the networks' close censorship of "taste" levels of advertising.

A wide variety of sales-promotion media are used, ranging from contests and awards to premiums, samples, and trading stamps, many of which the Ministry of Trade must approve, particularly premiums.

The development of manufacturers' brands has been phenomenal, particularly in foods, appliances, and clothing. To some extent this has been due to the establishment of Italian affiliates by American and other foreign enterprises. Still a rarity in 1950, in 1963 at least 80 different brands of refrigerators alone were produced in Italy. Private brands have been "pushed hard" by the two major junior department store chains.

Marketing research, almost unknown in Italy in 1950, has been spurred largely by management consulting firms, many with international contacts of high professional status. Very few manufacturers or distributors have their own marketing researchers. As in advertising, able practitioners are in such short supply that most firms are forced to use outside agencies. Italians, long conditioned to prying by governmental tax

---

[8] Costs of printed media based on advertising per 1,000 copies circulation in most of the important daily newspapers and in women's magazines. Ilmar Roostal, "Standardization of Advertising for Western Europe," *Journal of Marketing*, Vol. 27 (October, 1963), pp. 15-20 at pp. 17-18.

agents, frequently transfer this suspicious attitude to marketing research interviewers, thus creating problems for interviewers, especially in regard to obtaining income data. However, techniques are being evolved to cope with this situation.

Small-scale consumer credit extended by shopkeepers is centuries old. Formal charge accounts are relatively rare, though; and those retailers who have them often bestow them only on specially favored clients.

Increased sales opportunities for automobiles and household appliances have stimulated the growth of large-scale consumer credit schemes, particularly time-payment. In the big cities these credit plans are commonly sponsored by commercial banks, frequently in cooperation with retailers.

HANDICAPS TO FURTHER DEVELOPMENT

Despite the significant advances of marketing in Italy, severe handicaps face its further development. These obstacles may be classified as (1) taxation, (2) political stability and fiscal policies, (3) licensing, (4) regional disparities, and (5) other factors.

1. Taxation

One of the most onerous taxes is the *dazio,* the municipal "import" tax harking back to the Middle Ages when a large part of Italy consisted of independent or semi-autonomous city-states.

Rates vary considerably among municipalities, as do the basis and rate of charge; but typically the *dazio* is 7% of wholesale value of merchandise items and of certain services (for example, electricity). Collection costs are high, as indicated by a recent study made in Palermo that showed that 40% of the funds taken in were expended on the collection process.

Evasions are said to be common, particularly among smaller merchants vending such small, high-value items as perfumes. Larger (and often more efficient) retailers who cannot afford to indulge in "smuggling" are placed at a disadvantage pricewise. Parliament has been considering changing the *dazio,* but by early 1965 no solution was in sight.

Direct taxes in Italy account for only 19% of total government income, as compared with 78% in the United States. Major responsibility for collecting the indirect taxes is imposed on the various echelons of marketing, particularly for the *dazio,* the sales turnover taxes, and state-controlled commodities and services.

Even direct company-income taxes often work against efficient distributors, since the tax for an individual firm is set largely by bargaining between the firm and the revenue agents. Small wholesalers and retailers commonly do not keep adequate accounting records. Larger firms must necessarily maintain more accurate records, and are therefore more vulnerable to proper payments. This means that greater efficiency of operations may be turned into a tax disadvantage.

2. Political Stability and Fiscal Policies

The fragmentation of political parties must bear some responsibility for the governmental instability existent since 1946.

The largest party, the centrist Christian Democrats, has been unable to muster a majority in the lower house. In recent years, therefore, it has turned increasingly to the left for support, and found it in the socialist parties. Since the four federations of labor are linked with the political parties, socio-economic governmental measures usually have strong political overtones. Increasingly powerful opposition from the Italian Communist Party—the largest Communist group in Europe outside the Soviet Union—is directed against government and business.

Much of the national legislation passed in recent years has been labor-oriented, excessively so, in the opinion of many. Private investors, disillusioned by the government's expropriation of private electrical utilities and threats to enter other segments of hitherto private industry, react characteristically by holding back on investments. Investment in real terms rose by 19% in 1960 and by 11% in 1961, but fell to 7% and 8% in 1962 and 1963.

Increased possibilities of near-confiscatory business taxes and of government-supported retail chains have added to investors' feelings of insecurity. Following the 1950s, when wages rose somewhat less than productivity, labor-management contracts supported by the government called for annual gains of 20% or even 30% in certain industries during the early 1960s. Personnel costs for one large distributor jumped 62% from mid-1962 to mid-1964!

In 1963, under pressure of money wages, sales of consumer goods increased by 16%, and investment goods by 14%. Automobile sales alone were up 45% in value. Flight of the lira to Switzerland and other havens was a common reaction of investors.

In addition to social-security charges of over 50% of basic wages—by far the highest rate in the European Economic Community—the celebration of as many as 17 public holidays per year has been particularly burdensome to wholesalers and retailers because of the disruption of operations. Mandatory store closings of from two to four hours at midday is another consideration. So is the stance of government-backed labor unions against inovations encouraging operational efficiencies.

One retailer, noting the advantages of part-time personnel in the United States, was informed by his unions that he would have to pay part-timers a wage rate 50% higher than full-time employees. Additional conditions included a guaranty of a minimum or a half-day of work each day. And this was in an area which has experienced a severe labor shortage for at least ten years!

3. Licensing

Italy's restrictions on the distributive trades are the most severe in the European Economic Community, due largely to the system of licensing. Initially designed to restrain undue competition among small-scale merchants, applications of this law have not achieved its original purpose; instead, it has prevented the entry of more efficient distributors.

Even though department stores, junior department stores, and supermarkets are now exempt from the licensing statutes, municipal agencies continue to obstruct new entries. Despite the growth of large-scale wholesalers and retailers, particularly the latter, the distributive trades remain essentially strongholds of small-scale entrepreneurs of dubious efficiency.

Although large numbers of major foreign manufacturers have entered Italy since the end of World War II, retail firms from other nations have remained aloof, despite considerable "border-hopping" by retailers into other Western European countries. The licensing system, taxes, and the high cost of real estate have generally discouraged them.

In recent years a "trickle" of foreign entries has appeared: Spar, the European supra-national voluntary chain of food stores; several American supermarket chains; Prénatal, a French group specializing in clothing for babies and pregnant mothers. These newcomers have been few in number, however, and their commitments small.

If the European Economic Community continues to develop according to plan, licensing and other restrictions may need to be abrogated. This would encourage more competitive practices in marketing, particularly in the distributive trades. Until then, small-scale distribution will probably be perpetuated as an "alternative to the dole."

4. Regional Disparities

Although billions of liras have been poured into the economic development of the South, this area remains a socio-economic "drag" upon the nation. Marketing progress has invariably stemmed from the North, and remains strongly entrenched there. However, newer systems and methods of distribution are seeping into the South, keeping pace with the spread of general economic growth. Before World War II major cities were clearly classified into fashion categories: Milan at the top, then Rome, Naples at the low end, and Cagliari (Sardinia) very low.

Apparently Sicily was "unmentionable"; at least, it was not even included in a rating made by a top-fashion merchandiser. Historically, the South usually has been one to two years behind the North in style for women's wear. Today, though, due to mass communications, identical fashions are displayed almost simultaneously throughout the country, the differences being accounted for by climatic variations.

5. Other Factors

Inefficiencies abound in all modes of transportation, especially in freight clearances at ports of entry and at customs. Educational standards are low for a "modern" nation. It has been estimated that 850,000 children aged 8 to 14 do not attend school at all; and adult illiteracy is 8%.

Marketing—particularly retailing—is often the catch-all for socially marginal individuals once absorbed by agriculture. The idol of the educational system is Castiglione. The Renaissance humanist, rather than the citizen of an industrialized, democratic land. Business finds it difficult to interest able young people in careers, and to inculcate them with a modern approach toward commerce. Marketing is particularly abhorrent to college graduates, since it is commonly equated with tiny retail shops and street marketplaces. Although the subject of Marketing is taught in several universities under various names, not a single institution has a professorial chair in this subject.

Manufacturers, even large ones, are so often engrossed in production and finance that they lose sight of marketing; and hundreds of thousands of small retailers look upon their enterprises more as extensions of family life than as business firms. Suggestions for improving marketing efficiency are often unwelcome.

One question for the immediate years ahead is—what is the future of marketing in Italy?

36.

JUST A LITTLE BIT NORTH . . .
JUST A LITTLE BIT DIFFERENT*

W. J. Dixon

UNLESS he is extraordinarily close to his company's Canadian operations, the average American marketing executive probably tends to forget many of those subtle differences between the U.S. and Canada that
have a not-so-subtle effect on selling to his neighbors to the North.

In fact, should he suddenly be called upon to evaluate a marketing
plan for Canada, to help train a man for a Canadian sales post, or even
take charge of marketing there himself, his first efforts to reopen his own
mental file on Canada would probably bring forth a rush of similarities,
along with a few of the most obvious differences, between the two great
North American countries.

Actually, this would be quite natural. But, unless this recalled knowledge is quickly joined by some of the more down-to-earth comparisons of
marketing problems, the results could be dangerous indeed.

Since the turn of the century, American capital and ideas have pre-
dominated on Canada's industrial growth, both at the labor and management levels. The cultures are similar, business values are parallel and
the free enterprise system predominates in both countries. Canadians and
Americans compete for status in their work, use the same symbols as
standards of success and believe in the concepts of hard work and outward conformity.

In fact, about 90% of all Canadian purchasing power is within about
a hundred miles of the U.S. border.

Perhaps the most readily recognizable difference between the two
countries lies in the fact that Canada has not yet achieved the assimila-
tion of ethnic groups enjoyed in the United States. Language as well as
cultural differences exist in a segment of the market which represents
about a quarter of the total purchasing power of the country. (A full
31.4% of the Canadian people are French-speaking, and most of these are
in Quebec, Canada's second most populous province, which is 87.5%
French-speaking. These and all demographic figures to follow are taken
from the June 10, 1962 Sales Management Survey of Buying Power.)

Another fairly obvious difference between the two nations is in the

* Reprinted by permission from *Sales Management, The Marketing Magazine,*
September 21, 1962, pp. 111-116.

effect of government on business, particularly in the handling of tariff and customs duties. There is a wide difference between the two major political parties in Canada in their approach to trade policies, and this difference can seriously limit the accuracy of long-range industry forecasts and confuse marketing plans.

But the most meaningful differences, and often the most easily forgotten, are the result of Canada's geographic and demographic composition.

Obviously, Canada is a large country; its land area is somewhat larger than the 50-state U.S. But remember that its population of 18,488,300 is only about a tenth that of the U.S., or about the same as the population of Illinois and Michigan combined. Canada's total effective buying income is slightly larger than the effective buying income of Illinois.

Of course Canada's population, like that of the U.S., does tend to center in metropolitan areas. The country's 34 standard metro areas contain 58.4% of the total population (the U.S. has about two thirds of its people in 300 metro areas), and fully a quarter of all Canadians live in the three largest of these—Montreal, Toronto, and Vancouver. (Top three areas in the U.S. account for only about 13% of the total.)

While this concentration into metro areas is a plus factor for marketers, and although all the metro areas are located in the southern third of the country, there are still some very substantial distances between thse population centers.

REGIONAL AND ECONOMIC DIVISIONS

One result of this is the existence of fairly clearly defined geopolitical regions which tend to be economic entities as well. The West, for example, is largely an agriculturally based economy. The Maritimes depend on the fishing and coal mining industries to sustain their economy. British Columbia depends on the export of forest products.

Because of the limited population and the reliance on the country's rich resources, the Canadian economy is less diversified than that of the U.S., and the standard of living tends to reflect the somewhat higher proportion of non-skilled jobs.

Also, this dependence on resources, coupled with the fact that Canada exports about a fifth of its gross national product (as opposed to about 3% exported by the U.S.), subjects the country to severe short-run cyclical and seasonal variations in income and employment.

Don't forget that any discussion of marketing in Canada must take into account the many ramifications of distance, of weather, of income, of cultural isolation and whatnot. If marketing is done through a Canadian manufacturing subsidiary, the differences between Canada and the U.S.

are most outstanding. If products are merely exported north of the border, some of these demographic and geographic differences will be vastly more important than others.

Take the very product and its package as an example. The marketer will, of course, assess and determine how far product development can go toward establishing the components of quality, style and package that will be acceptable to all the regional tastes of consumers, making sure that no one region is given undue preference over another. But where chemical or physical change can take place in a product or package that is subjected to Canada's extremes in temperature, then product or package stability must take precedence over preferred quality or appearance.

And, while a package obviously must be attractive to the Canadian consumer, extra consideration must be given to the design to ensure its ability to withstand the long hauls and considerable handling it will get on its way to the country's scattered markets.

On the other hand, the ramifications involved may be limited to just a very small percentage of marketers in special situations. For example, the Canadian marketer of resort wear (or other summer goods) will have his line ready for the market in April and he has only this one chance to make good in any year. Unlike the American marketer, he has no Florida to turn to to clear his line if he happens to miscalculate in planning his summer sales. While this is, of course, an oversimplification, it does demonstrate the tremendous differences brought to bear on marketing in certain situations.

THE SUBTLE VARIATIONS

There are a great number of other subtle, but extremely important, variations between the American and Canadian marketing scenes. Some have a broad application, others a more narrow effect; in toto, they range the entire marketing spectrum. Here are some that shouldn't be forgotten:

• Because of the regional composition of the country, special care must be taken when considering elimination of the less profitable items in a product line. Does the product to be eliminated offer in some regions special inducements that are responsible for the distributor's continuing interest in the whole line? Does that particular product offer the entire line protection from strictly regional competitors in certain areas? Is it the wanted product that makes the line "complete" in certain areas of the country? With such a regional economic diversity, the answers to these questions are often affirmative.

• Where consumer motivation research is being done, it is dangerous to apply the results of one area study to the total market. Because of the importance of obtaining as wide as possible an acceptance of products and because of the relative narrowness of the total market, the marketing department must do intensive regional studies at considerable extra cost, or risk losing the all-important volume of one of the regions.

• Like the U.S., Canada has substantial variations of income from region to region. What may be a specialty item in one section will be a shopping good in another; what may be a luxury item in one may be almost completely out of range in another. This holds particular significance for marketers of higher-price products.

In Canada, 15.9% of families have incomes of $7,000 or more, while in the U.S. the figure stands at 27.3%. Only one of the 11 provinces claims an average annual household income greater than $6,000, though there are 32 states that do.

NO ALTERNATIVE MARKETS

What this means can best be shown by an example: A market of hi-fi stereo equipment has been selling his product profitably only in sizable metro areas where over 15% of households have an effective buying income of $7,000 or more. In Canada this means he must go all the way west—to Alberta and British Columbia—to find his expansion. And, if he should happen to overestimate the potential in these markets, he is stuck with his excess; he has no alternatives, no place else to go into. Unlike his counterpart in the U.S., this marketer has no wide market, no hope that his overestimation will be balanced by a low forecast elsewhere.

• The marked cultural and income differences among regions in Canada means that there will also be marked differences in the effectiveness of product promotions. To spend the money and effort for promotion without first assessing the various markets in relation to types of promotional approaches to be used can mean poor results in relation to the expenditure.

In addition, seasonal and economic factors can change rapidly from region to region, so special consideration must be given to the timing of promotional campaigns or new product introductions.

• Handling the sales and service organization takes on a new dimension because of Canada's great physical size and limited market. When goods are marketed on a national basis, a firm will usually have a number of district offices from which salesmen work and take direction. Regardless of the organization, the sales manager in Canada will have special problems created by the great distances and smaller markets. Where the American manager may have to travel several hundred miles to be in contact with several salesmen, the manager in Canada may have to go twice as far to see one. Because of the distances, time and costs involved, the salesman not only lacks the personal contact with his manager, but management loses the opportunity to understand in depth the special regional problems faced by each man as well as to become familiar with his abilities.

VARIATIONS IN COMPENSATION

Various regions will also call for distinctive types of salesmen. When a man is doing a sound job, there can be a tendency to maintain the status quo rather than to rotate men to broaden their experience and prepare them for promotion. Wide variations in market potential also mean that the basis of compensation has to be set on a regional basis.

This problem is doubled for those industrial and consumer hard goods marketers that must maintain far-flung service organizations as well as sales forces.

Marketing is concerned with subtleties, slight peculiarities in the cultural, social, economic and geographic composition of its markets. It is precisely these oft-hidden subtleties that make the difference between Canada and the U.S. They might hardly be noticed in many business or personal situations. But in marketing they are magnified, and their importance must not be forgotten.

37.

IN FRENCH CANADA, VIVE LA DIFFERENCE*

"IT is we who make Canada different," says Quebec's Minister of Industry Gerard Levesque—a French Canadian. "Without us there would be nothing distinctively Canadian. We want to continue to be an asset to Canada, but in the context of mutual understanding."

The demand that the French Canadian "difference" be recognized has found its most explosive expression in the ferment of political nationalism. But the French Canadian has another way of voting for his national pride.

He does it millions of times each day at the cash register. The businessman who wants to deal in the French Canadian market must understand this force.

I. MOTHER TONGUE

Quebec's Province population in April of this year was 5,453,000. Of this, an estimated 2-million live in what is generally considered to be the Montreal metropolitan area (pictures), a complex including Montreal proper and about 20 additional communities. The total French population is just under 29% of the nation's. It is a ripe, homogeneous, and relatively easy-to-reach part of the Canadian market, which, except for southern Ontario, is diffuse, dispersed, and difficult to sell to profitably.

In this marketing area, according to the last census, 37% of the residents speak only French, 23% speak only English, and 38% speak both French and English. In actuality, more than 38% are bilingual when they are forced to be. But for 63% French is the mother tongue—the one that responds to the marketers' blandishments and that is the outward structure of a whole complex of thoughts and habits and attitudes.

"My grandfather always told us, 'We're too poor to buy cheap goods,'" says a French-Irish executive of the Montreal branch of a national department store chain. He explains: "French Canadians buy the same type of goods as other Canadians, but they tend to buy proportionately more of the better quality lines. That's because their motivations are different. Remember, they have relatively lower incomes and bigger

* Reprinted from the November 12, 1962 issue of *Business Week* by special permission. Copyrighted © 1962 by McGraw-Hill, Inc.

families than in Ontario, at least, so they are more conscious of their pennies. What they buy must last."

Getting and Spending

In 1961, the last year for which figures are available, average personal income in Quebec was $1,332, only 86.6% of the Canadian average and barely 70% of Ontario Province's $1,829. It is the closest to the national figure Quebec has come in two decades. Disposable personal income in 1961 was $6.45-billion, an all-time high. Only once before since the beginning of World War II did disposable income get closer to the all-Canadian amount.

But just as relatively-rich Ontario brings a heavy weight to bear on Canadian statistics as a whole, so the culture, traditions, and living patterns of the French Canadian cast their own light on Quebec's statistics.

Under the pressure of rapidly advancing industrialization and urbanization, Quebec Province's personal incomes are rising. The French Cana-

TABLE 1—HOW SPENDING SOARS IN QUEBEC PROVINCE

	Millions	
	1952	1962
Groceries	$588	$1,064
Autos	409	645
Department stores	176	285
All clothing	176	264
Furniture and appliances	107	195
Hardware, lumber, building materials	110	169
Restaurants	116	152
Drug stores	53	98

Data: Dominion Bureau of Statistics.

dian has money to spend, and he is willing to spend it (chart above). In 1952, the total estimated retail trade in all outlets in Quebec was $2.6-billion; in 1962 the total was $3.7-billion.

How It Went

Behind these figures are some significant facts about the 1952-62 decade:

• While total retail expeditures in the country were going up a shade under 50%, Quebec's rose some 65%.

• In clothing and hardware and building supply outlets, nationwide spending rose 25%. In Quebec the increase was 50%.

• Canadians as a whole spent about 33% more on automobiles. Quebecois boosted it to about 66%.

• In purchases at furniture and appliance stores, the total for the country went up some 30%. But in Quebec the total zoomed 85%.

French Canadian traditionalism affects all buying decisions, and Quebecoise are less prone to shop in chain stores than their countrymen. Last year about 21% of all Canadian store purchases was in chain stores. In Quebec it was 18% of the total. Yet traditionalism works two ways. Marketers in Quebec agree that once you capture a French Canadian customer, he is more loyal than the English Canadian.

"In Toronto, customers seem to drive miles to chase a special," says Jack Lavine, sales vice-president of Montreal-based Steinberg's Ltd., supermarket chain. "In Montreal, the customer shops hard, but she trusts her store to give her consistent value."

II. A MATTER OF TASTE

The French Canadian may want goods that last, but he doesn't buy drabness.

"They go for the bright, loud, and tawdry," says an executive in one discount store. But another immediately replies: "Absolutely not. In fact, please don't tell that guy how wrong he is. They do tend toward brighter colors, but the French Canadian woman has more style and chic than the rest of us. It is true, though, that she isn't quite so concerned with seasonal style variations. She can't afford to be."

Beyond the hard hunt for value, other differences show up between the French and English Canadians. The big deal for the younger set in Quebec City in midwinter is to drive through the streets in a convertible with the top down and a pretty girl not visibly frozen at your side. But because of income, Quebecers on the whole buy smaller cars than others in Canada. Still, they coddle their possessions. According to Bernard Hymovitch, a Montreal market researcher, Quebecers buy a bigger percentage of premium gasoline than is sold in Ontario.

And when it comes to entertainment, eating out, or liquor, French Canadians are right in there with the best. They don't drink cocktails before dinner to relax, they are likely to drink convivially at any time. And they pay the price. The leading rum seller in Quebec is Bacardi, Hymovitch reports. The leading gin in Gordon's, and the leading whisky is Seagram VO. All are higher priced items than lead the trade in the rest of Canada or in the U.S.

III. IT PAYS TO ADVERTISE—RIGHT

In reaching the French Canadian market more than an awareness of regional differences is needed. What is involved, also, is a grasp of a basic tool—language.

"When you put the French marketing mix together," says Lavine, "it changes your entire communication pattern. Your words must be different than they would be in English because the needs you are trying to meet are different. The emphasis is different, just as the culture is different."

Like many non-French-owned Quebec companies—and many others that operate in Quebec but have their headquarters elsewhere—Steinberg's once simply translated its ads or labels from English to French and let it go at that. They do it no longer. The results were not only bad French, with meanings twisted and idioms tortured, but often were grotesque.

Good and Bad

In a recent issue, Canadian Marketing magazine cites a number of examples of both good and bad use of the language:

A series of newspaper ads promoting Toronto's Royal York Hotel was planned to run in both languages, using the same art. One ad, picturing a paintbrush, was headed, "How to paint the town without this." The idiom had no connotation in Quebec. The French don't paint the town, they "make the bomb." The ad was scrapped.

Another, showing a baseball glove, worked nicely in both languages. Baseball is a much loved sport in Quebec. The English ad read, "Why be out in left field on a business trip? The French ad, literally translated, read, "Why be out in the field far from your goal?" Equally important, the art in the ad was usable with both English and French copy because it had the same meaning for both peoples. This is an important consideration in Canada where the small market makes production charges a relatively large part of total advertising cost.

Two of Seven

British Petroleum Co., Ltd., of Canada, which consistently takes advantage of both French and English creative teams, found that in one planned campaign only two of seven proposed English ads were adaptable to French.

One never considered for French use employed the words "horse sense" with a picture of a new BP pump and a horse in the background. In French, "horse sense" would imply stupidity rather than wisdom. But another—which was run in French—showed the pumps with a pile of hay and a pitchfork and used the words, "Ménagez votre foin," or, "Have your hay." In Quebec slang, "foin" is money, thus "Save your dough" was an easily recognized, properly rustic double entendre.

Since the French Canadian simply won't accept promotion that isn't of his milieu, every important retail chain in Quebec uses separate creative staffs for the two languages. Many go further and insist that their suppliers do the same. Lavine says Steinberg's might tolerate an all-English label on a product it has to import from the U.S. on a temporary basis, but a Canadian product, to get on the shelf, must have a "good" bilingual label. And all the promotional backing by the manufacturer must be soundly bilingual.

French Canadian advertising and promotion men are keenly aware of the bilingual situation.

"For old, established products that always have treated the French housewife fairly and honestly, this new awareness hasn't made much difference," says one ad man. "But a new product can have a terrible time if it doesn't come on the market as French."

Instant Identification

The French Canadian's pride in family heritage is tied to his love of home and family. Chase & Sanborn coffee was one of the first to take advantage of this to turn a feature that could have been scorned into an asset.

Coffee drinking, according to Hymovitch, is a much more ceremonial function in French homes than in English, and the preparation of "real" coffee is one of the French housewife's touchstones in the role she conceives for herself. Instant coffee—casual, inelegant, relatively inexpensive —did not fit into the French pattern.

But C&S began running French commercials on television in which the convenience of preparation was not mentioned or pictured at all. What was shown was a loving, presumably married couple relaxing (upright) on a sofa with a handsome coffee service on a table before them. While the wife served ceremoniously, a soft-voiced announcer murmured the message. It described the coffee's "caressing flavor."

At the same time, the TV commercial on Montreal's English stations was an animated jingle that touted all the usual instant coffee advantages.

The two commercials combined to nearly double C&S's share of the instant coffee market in three months, according to Hymovitch.

Penalties

Failing to adapt can lead to some painful experiences. One large, Toronto-based hardgoods distributor of a wide variety of household items—a subsidiary of a Chicago company—is recording rising sales throughout the rest of Canada but a sharp drop in Quebec. It uses no sales promotion of literature with the French point of view.

Perhaps the easiest way to bite off a bigger chunk of the French market—assuming the manufacturer has followed the other rules of the road—is to make a premium or a price offer. "The French housewife isn't suspicious of a manufacturer's motive," says one sales researcher. "A price offer or a premium should be, and usually is, more effective in French Canada."

One soap brand still is distributed with towels in the box in Quebec four years after the promotion ended in the rest of Canada. Coupon returns nearly always are greater in Quebec than elsewhere. But Lavine, who continually stresses the French housewife's loyalty, thinks in this case the response is purely economic. He says the highest coupon return area in Montreal is one economically depressed English suburb.

Still, a good promotion will pull from all levels of French life. A drug company promotion to French doctors, a top income group, included a reply card offering to send information and a sample. It pulled an astonishing 90% in only 48 hours. The come-on: a small bottle of brandy.

The Bandwagon

The industrial advertiser must be aware of the "French fact," too. Of 430 business and professional publications, 41 are French. More are aimed at the professions than at the trades, most are small, few are first-rate, but they all are better than they were three or four years ago. They are better because they are getting more advertising, and the advertising comes to them in part because in Quebec, you have to go French.

Where there is a product that can be adapted to the French treatment, the results are almost always good. One advertising man recalls one of the few industrial campaigns his agency took beyond basic translation for the French market. It was a series of roofing ads to run in French building and architectural magazines. The ads were illustrated with pictures of roofing jobs on parish churches. It did the trick.

38.

MARKETING IN AUSTRALIA*

John S. Ewing

THE Australian Market resembles that of the United States in many respects. Languages, legal and political structure, standard of living, way of
life, and particularly willingness to consume are comparable or rapidly
becoming so. Research, advertising agencies, media, channels of distribution, and other elements of the marketing function are familiar and easy
for Americans to use.

It seems safe to generalize: If it works in marketing in the United
States, it will work in Australia. But there are some problems, as we shall
see.

MARKET CHARACTERISTICS

Area and Population

Australia is much the same size as the United States. But it contains only
a fraction of the population: 10,227,000 people in the only country to
occupy a whole continent.[1] Small wonder that one executive rejected
operations in Australia with the remark, "We have a much greater market
potential within sight of the Empire State Building."[2]

Yet to consider Australia solely or primarily from the standpoint of
the area population relationship is misleading. Some important differences from American demography exist. Largely because of climate and
the location of natural resources the country's three million square miles
are unevenly inhabited. Most of its people live in a narrow fringe of land
along the east and southeast coasts; and within that fringe they are concentrated in the large capital cities.

* John S. Ewing, "Marketing in Australia," *Journal of Marketing*, Vol. 26, No. 2
(April 1962), a publication of the American Marketing Association, pp. 54-58. Reprinted by permission.

1 This and subsequent population figures are estimates from the Australian Bureau
of Statistics, March 1, 1960.

2 James Robinson, Vice President of Textron, Inc., quoted in John Fayerweather,
Management of International Operations (New York: McGraw-Hill Book Co., Inc.,
1960).

Thus, the states of New South Wales and Victoria alone contain about 66 per cent of the population, and their capitals of Sydney and Melbourne themselves have almost 38 per cent. The addition of Queensland to the north increases the eastern market area to 80 per cent, and its capital of Brisbane raises the urban share to 43 per cent.

Transportation

Shipping from the eastern capitals to the relatively few other large population centers involves mainly coastal steamers, much used but slow, or long rail hauls through sparsely settled areas. A variety of gauges adds to rail costs. From Brisbane in the east to Perth in the west, a journey comparable to but somewhat shorter than that from New York to Los Angeles, requires six changes of trains which run over three gauges. Some progress has been made toward standardization, but the rail network is far from this goal.

Transcontinental road transportation is almost nonexistent, for obvious reasons. But Australians rank fourth in the world in vehicles per head of population, and major centers are linked by hard-surfaced relatively good roads. There is considerable movement of goods between these centers, and often over incredibly bad roads, between smaller cities and remote settlements.

Air transport is highly developed. The air service networks are extensive and in some districts provide the only long distance transportation. Passenger and freight rates are relatively low.

Consequently, air shipment enables the marketer to widen distribution into areas which road or rail haulage would make uneconomical if not impossible. In relation to population, the volume of freight traffic handled by Australian airlines is heavier than in other countries. Passenger traffic on the same basis is exceeded only by the United States.

TRADE CONSIDERATIONS

General Channels of Distribution

As in America, for years the wholesale merchant provided the traditional link between manufacturer and retailer, but the growth of the Australian economy has developed changes in the pattern. Combinations of retailers buying in bulk, and large department stores buying directly from manufacturers or in many cases having their own factories, account for a considerable volume of goods.

Many manufacturers have established their own organizations for direct sales to retailers through salesmen, from vehicles carrying stocks, or through agents or branches equipped to offer after-sales service. Smaller manufacturers frequently sell directly to retailers in the metropolitan area around their factories and use agents for coverage elsewhere.

Mail-order purchases by country people are relatively more important in Australian retailing than in more closely settled countries. Such selling is carried on chiefly by the mail-order offices of department and specialist stores; but large, purely mail-order houses along the lines of the early Sears, Roebuck or Montgomery Ward did not develop.

Margins on all levels of distribution are generally claimed to be lower than in the United States. However, there is considerable variance, and in some trades margins are equal to or higher than in this country.

The Wholesaler

Faced with usurpation of his functions by both retailers and manufacturers, the Australian wholesaler has fought back, in some instances by extension of his own operations into manufacturing and retailing. In small city and country distribution, wholesalers have for years been vertically integrated, but such integration is of recent development in the large cities.

In neighboring New Zealand the voluntary chain, wholesaler inspired and modeled after those in the U.S. food industry, is important. Australian wholesalers have been slow to attempt this form of competition but it has been making an appearance. One wholesaler of soft goods in the north of Queensland adopted a modification of the voluntary chain in 1960. He selected certain outlets on which to concentrate, provided uniform accounting procedures, advice on store layout, and the advantages of large-scale buying through grouped orders.

Distribution in Small Cities and Country

In many parts of Australia, notably the north coast which trades with New Guinea and the Pacific Islands, and which cannot be easily served from a large center, vertical integration is found. This derives from the need for self-sufficiency among trading companies set up originally to exchange goods for copra and other regional products, and now much wider in scope.

Such concerns may make some of their goods or may contract for their manufacturer. They act as distributors for some manufacturers and as wholesalers for still other manufacturers and distributors. And they may sell through their own retail stores; for example, one operated a large chain of variety stores emphasizing textile goods in Queensland for some years. Not all functions are carried on in the same trading area.

There are problems in the use of these companies by manufacturers. Their dominant position in some areas enables them to strike hard bargains with suppliers. Some carry own-label lines competitive with those of principals. Independent merchants or the controlled outlets of other trading companies may be reluctant to deal with them as distributors or wholesalers. However, in view of the costs involved in other forms of distribution in the markets served, anyone wishing to sell there has little alternative to their use.

One interesting characteristic of retailers in small cities and towns has significance for sales promotion and training in Australia. These retailers welcome salesmen cordially as visitors from an outside world they seldom see but like to hear about. To encourage calls, it is sometimes alleged, they divide orders with a sense of fair play if not business logic.

Too much persistence in selling may lead to such remarks as: "Don't be greedy, mate, you've had yours for this time. Reckon I've got to save some for the next chap. Fair shares for all, you know." If this does not discourage the presentation, the result may be no order at all as a warning not to overdo it next time.

Urban Retailing

No such sentiment characterizes urban retailing. Large department stores are very much features of Australia's cities and are well up to American standards. They are in aggressive competition. Price is one of the weapons used, to the degree that retail price fixing permits it, and so are sales promotions, stores services, and private brands.

Supermarkets and self-service stores in Sydney and Melbourne have been slow to develop, although Perth, in Western Australia, had some before World War II and Brisbane also adopted them earlier. One of the reasons for the delay in the two largest cities may have been the heavy emphasis on food retailing by department and variety stores. Another is the curious tendency of some Australian marketers in one city to ignore what is happening elsewhere in the country.

Suburban shopping centers on the American pattern and scale were also late in reaching the Australian scene. One of the first opened in Melbourne in 1960 under the stimulus of the city's largest department store. There had been some small-center developments earlier, usually of the neighborhood type and generally without special parking provision.

Toward the end of 1960 discount houses made their appearance. For years these had been thought of by many marketers as impossible, thanks, they felt, to Australia's low retail margins. Nevertheless, a discount house opened in Perth in late 1960, and in December one called Shoppers Fair occupied a disused motion picture theater in a Sydney suburb. Roundly attacked by the Retail Traders Association, the 4,000 square-foot store featured nationally- advertised products, and appeared at the end of the first few months of operation to be a success.

While the same predictions which were once common in the United States are heard in Australia, about the inevitable failure of discount houses "when the public has come back to its senses"—these did not inhibit their development.

The Shoppers Fair company planned others in the Sydney area, operators in Melbourne intended to follow suit, and overproduction in some consumer-goods industries seemed to insure supplies. While some manufacturers were known to have withheld their goods from the discounters, others were openly selling them despite threats from retail associations, and customers apparently were happy.

One somewhat singular aspect of Australian retailing lends support to the thesis that American marketing methods will work effectively in Australia. At times the transplanted American might be forgiven for wondering if he had really left home. Woolsworth and Penney stores stand close by on the main street in Brisbane. In Sydney shoppers may patronize Macy's, where "It's smart to be thrifty." There are many opportunities in other parts of Australia for housewives to buy groceries at Big Bear, Food Fair, Safeway, and Stop and Shop.

Yet none of these retailers has any connection or ever has had with firms of the same name in the United States. However, much Americans might wonder about the choice of names or speculate on the number of Sydneysiders to whom Macy's is familiar, or of Brisbaneites who have heard of the American Penney's, Australian retailers are convinced that such names are effective.

Retailing Restrictions

Retail price maintenance by agreement among manufacturers and with retailers, widely used although not legally enforceable, has held an "umbrella" over the small merchant. Despite this, he is threatened now by continued expansion of both chains and department stores, by the introduction of merchandising methods clearly attractive to customers, and by the discount houses. He is fighting back by conversion into superettes, by limited use of voluntary chain organization, and by offering services such as credit and free delivery.

The small merchant competes also by appealing to the Australian sense of fair plan and bigness. In this he receives some support from the retail labor union, fearful of the impact of such new methods as self-service and resistant to changes in working hours. In Sydney, the country's largest market, the Shop Assistants Union has for many years prevented night or Sunday opening of stores except under specific restriction of type and area—drug stores, for instance, or food stores in resort areas—despite a membership of less than half the clerks employed.

In some areas limited night opening exists, but everywhere most stores close from noon on Saturday until Monday morning. This is particularly irksome to men who may want to shop with their wives, especially for big-ticket items, and who do not want to give up Saturday morning for the purpose.

It is likely that some liberalization will follow, but it is doubtful that the extent of American retail hours will be reached. However, automatic vending may become quite popular.

Two interesting examples of vending-machine success in Australian conditions may be mentioned. One is the coin-operated pump, permitting gasoline sales after service-station hours, which are rigidly controlled and usually shorter than in the United States. Popular in Victoria, the pump has been fought in New South Wales by the Shop Assistants Union and by some retailers as unfair competition to the vendors who might not be able to install them, and to their employees. The argument has found little favor with the motoring public, often plagued by the problem of finding an open station after 6:00 or 7:00 at night.

The other unusual use of vending machines is their installation in some private homes to sell cigarettes. Companies, reporting a surprising number of these, believe their popularity is in homes with several heavy smokers. Apparently fearful of running out when shops are closed, these smokers prefer putting coins in the machine for another package to adoption of the American habit of carton-purchase.

ADVERTISING

Media

The Australian marketer has, in metropolitan areas at least, as wide a choice of media as has his American counterpart. Outdoor media are probably the least used nationally, whereas newspapers are the most widely used.

National magazines are relatively few, but at least one woman's magazine, a weekly, has a circulation of more than 3 million copies a month. Newspapers lack the typographical excellence of the best American papers, but are generally good in quality. A feature is a wide use of classified advertising, running to half the paper, on Wednesdays and Saturdays in several cities.

Two radio systems—one, governmental without advertising—exist. No network radio for the whole country operates, but there are state networks; and national coverage can be bought, if not entirely at the same time. The pattern is very similar to that in this country, and American trends are watched closely.

Television, again with both governmental and commercial stations, began in 1956. By the end of 1960 stations were operating in all the state capitals, and hearings were under way to decide on licensees in smaller cities. In Sydney and Melbourne there are three stations—two commercial, and one governmental. In other state capitals there is one of each; and plans in smaller cities call for one commercial station.

The commercial station has features reminiscent of the United States, Canada, and England. No networks exist, but there are plans for facilities to enable simultaneous transmission. Strict restrictions on ownership make anything like the American networks impossible. The advertiser has more choice of program association for his advertising messages than in England, but his freedom is more restricted than in Canada and the United States. Unlike those in Canada, governmental stations carry no advertising.

Advertising Agencies

For many years only one American advertising agency, J. Walter Thompson Co., was active in Australia, and in a sense it was more Australian than American. Agencies generally limited activities to advertisement preparation and placement, on a commission basis similar to that of the United States and Canada. A popular saying in agency circles was to the effect that if the *Saturday Evening Post* were denied admittance to the country, all copywriters would be out of work. Research was almost nonexistent, and agencies provided little service or competitive information to clients.

Several things have combined to change this. One is television, with new demands on creative staffs and on agencies to justify its use. Another is the high standard of service from agencies expected by American firms which entered Australia after the war. Finally, in 1959 the purchase of an Australian agency by an American firm (McCann-Erickson, Inc.) noted for its aggressiveness and emphasis on marketing research led to a flood of rumors of impending invasion by other American agencies, to defensive mergers by Australian companies, and to a general strengthening of local agency operations.

Research in particular has received attention. Not only have most agencies of any size installed research departments, but numerous specialized research organizations have begun operations. Some are branches of

American or British firms, drawing on their principals for help, and others are Australian-owned. Post-war interest in statistical reporting by government departments has helped marketing-research development, although the level and extent of such reporting is not always up to American standards.

Advertising Messenger

Like retailing, and like other aspects of advertising, Australian advertisements and commercials are characterized by a wide use of Americanisms. Despite the over-all improvement in technical standards in recent years, agencies and advertising departments still borrow freely from the United States, and also England.

Thus, the use of a man in a black eye-patch to advertise men's shirts and the claim that a certain cigarette "tastes good as a cigarette should" are American-born, whereas "Eata Egga Day" and "Have a Good Rum for your Money" are English imports. Campaigns may be duplicated in entirety or individual advertisements only used.

This is particularly evident in television. Much program content, on both governmental and commercial stations, is American. Listeners are attuned consequently to American accents and feel no great resistance to these in commercials. As a result, television commercials prepared and used in the United States are often seen on Australian sets, advertising the same products as in the country of origin.

While the impression should not be left that American-prepared advertising dominates the Australian scene, it is a very important factor. Lack of consumer antagonism has enabled Australian companies with American connections to keep advertising cost down and quality high.

CONCLUSIONS

1. Similarity of the Australian to the U.S. scene in so many ways makes entry simple and operation relatively easy. To recapitulate, what works here will work there, as the successes of many American firms testify.

2. The very receptivity of the Australian market to American ideas has some hazards. Thus, in 1960 the cigarette-smoking public in Australia, conditioned to smoking an Australian cigarette because it tasted good as a cigarette should, was bemused to be offered an American cigarette (made in Australia) which tasted good *like* a cigarette should.

An American firm relying heavily on trade marks, distinctive sales promotion, or a particular advertising campaign and also with even a slight plan to enter Australia in the distant future should thus keep the importance of protection in mind. Laws vary from state to state, but the general result is that registration of a trade mark confers protection for a period of time, without manufacture and sale, five years in most instances. There are cases of American companies that have discovered prior registration which could effectively debar them from use of their own trade marks for that period.

3. Instead of seeking national distribution, the marketer considering entry should ignore total population and geography statistics. Selection of areas is indicated, and the concentration of population on the east coast makes this easy. In addition, the Australian population is increasing rapidly and 15,000,000 are forecasted for 1980.[3] A company might logically confine its activities to Melbourne, Sydney, and their surrounding areas, with further expansion indicated only in terms of incremental revenues versus incremental costs.

Although the size of the Australian market is not large by American standards, it is well worth consideration because of the attitudes of the consuming public, the successful records of American firms, and the long-range growth projections for the country and its economy.

[3] Projection by Economics Dept., W. D. Scott & Co., Pty. Ltd., management consultants, Sydney, N.S.W., Australia.

39.

THE MIGHTY JAPANESE TRADING COMPANIES*

Sueyuki Wakasugi

THE central role played by Japan's great trading companies in the phenomenal renaissance of that nation's domestic postwar economy suggests
this guiding implication: a specialized international trading network may
be today's answer to the problems of tomorrow's world economic community. Considering their size, their hundreds of years of cumulative
experience, and their rapidly progressing internationalization, Japan's
top trading organizations may very well become the future trading arms
of the world's aggregate domestic industry.

Because they are the lifeblood of commerce—providing effective, balanced interchange of goods and services—Japan's trading companies have
prospered through vigorous and thorough application to their purposes,
and continue to prosper on the very economic advances they foster. In the
face of the enormous production and consumption potential of awakening economies all over the world and the urgency for economic development in newly independent nations, Japan's giant trading companies
may prove to be the only available key to that unprecedented equalization of national economic differences upon which a truly stable international community of nations depends.

Three factors help the observer to grasp the potential importance of
Japanese trading companies to international executives in a growing
world economy:

1. Their part in Japan's domestic commerce and import-export
2. Their role in third-country (triangular) trade beyond Japan and
Southeast Asia
3. Their present and projected steady growth relative to physical
assets, world-wide facilities, services, market coverage, and diversification
in all of these.

HOW THEY GREW

About 300 years ago, when Japan's oldest trading company, Mitsui, was
first organized, the country's means of transport and communication were

* Sueyuki Wakasugi, "The Mighty Japanese Trading Companies" *Business Horizons,*
Vol. 7, No. 4, Winter 1964, pp. 5-19.

primitive. Manufacturers and their markets were geographically isolated. The visionary who established the first trading company recognized that goods made in one area should be transported to other areas where they were needed. But he soon realized that to assure the continuance of this service, the means of supply to manufacturers had to be maintained. To assure that finished goods moved out into the right markets, trading companies then began to locate new markets with the appropriate demands.

The steady growth of Japan's trading companies from this basic pattern was a long and complex process. As their intermarket activities developed, they came into close working contact with other elements of Japan's domestic business—banking, finance, transport, contracting, wholesaling, distributing, insurance, and real estate—until today they have an integral, entrenched position in the entire spectrum of the nation's internal commerce. As their coverage of Japan's domestic business increased, their range of activities extended to import and export, foreign sources of industrial raw materials, and trading with foreign markets. In this way, for over three centuries, trading companies have grown into today's vast international organizations. These trading organizations have an invaluable background of long experience (a bank that is part of one trading firm's family group of commercial and industrial companies in Japan antedates even the Bank of England) in all the functions of trade interchange that are now emerging as the best practical means of bringing the worldwide economic community closer to reality.

Position in Japan

A modern Japan without its major trading companies would be inconceivable. There are 6,465 of these unique organizations in Japan today, all intimately tied up with Japan's economic destiny. To consider the nation and the companies separately would be impossible even for academic argument. Japan's geography and limited natural resources gave birth to its trading companies, and its trading companies now support and sustain Japan.

What they have accomplished in Japan holds the key to what the international executive can accomplish with their help through worldwide marketing. About 300 of the trading companies are engaged in some foreign as well as domestic trade, handling about 80 per cent of the country's imports and exports. Altogether they employ 130,000 people, including thousands of specialists in every phase of commerce and transport, and operate a total of 1,434 branch offices outside Japan. This is quite impressive for organizations that are neither manufacturers nor retailers, and indicates the thoroughness of their services.

The great bulk of Japan's foreign trade is channeled through a few major trading firms, each capitalized at more than $28 million, with 75 per cent of it going through the twenty largest. The top two, Mitsui & Co., Ltd., and Mitsubishi Shoji Kaisha, Ltd., based in Tokyo, each do current annual over-all business of more than $3 billion on a c.i.f. basis, while the next two, Marubeni-Iida Co., Ltd., and C. Itoh & Co., each does business in the vicinity of $2 billion. Rounding out the top five is Sumitomo Shoji Kaisha, at about $1.8 billion. These figures demonstrate the close alliance between the country's trading companies and its export-import lifelines. Japan's total foreign trade in 1963 amounted to $12.15 billion—a sum almost equal to the combined annual business of the top five traders alone.

Japan and the World Market

Since Japan became a full member of the Organization for Economic Cooperation and Development (OECD) in early 1964 and accepted equal status with member nations under Article 8 of the International Monetary Fund—laying her economy open to the full brunt of free competition in the world market—it has had to deal as an equal partner with countries both larger and smaller than itself. Were it not for its huge trading companies, it is doubtful that Japan could have managed this as successfully as it has. Their worldwide network of facilities and market contacts has allowed Japan to maintain a workable balance between manufactured exports and imports, between imports of industrial raw materials and domestic consumer demand, and between Japanese goods and competing goods on the world market.

Even though some firms active in the Japanese market prefer to maintain their own direct or joint organizations, an increasing number of foreign companies are turning to trading companies for a better and less costly selling job. Even large manufacturers handling their own overseas sales might find marketing costs running as high as 5 per cent and more. While each contract calls for its own particular distribution methods, similar marketing services provided by trading companies generally cost less.

WHAT THEY DO

To those involved in international commerce, trading companies are probably known primarily as importers and exporters. But although this is an important part of their activities, it is no longer the most important. Their accomplishments foster growth above all else, and because they thrive on the very growth they foster, Japan's trading companies have moved into areas of international business not traditionally connected with exporting and importing but necessary to their continuance—areas such as marketing, sales representation, financing, door-to-door transport as a link in the international chain of distribution, participation in overseas joint ventures, market research and consultation, engineering and technical consultation, insurance, claims adjustment, plant construction, general contracting, overseas efficiency investigations, real estate, freight forwarding, transshipment, atomic energy for industry, and a host of others. In fact, about the only commercial services they do not perform are the actual production and retailing of the goods and commodities they handle. They are not manufacturers but service specialists, charting the course of commercial goods between origin and consumer destination.

Henry Kearns, former U.S. Assistant Secretary of Commerce for International Affairs, once characterized Japanese trading companies as organizations that will "find it . . . finance it . . . formulate it . . . construct it . . . mine it . . . refine it . . . place it . . . machine it . . . ship it . . . insure it . . . and compound it—and do it faster."

The functions of the large Japanese trading company today fall generally into four categories: import and export, financing, joint ventures, and technological exchange.

Import and Export

The companies are most experienced and quite expert in this area; a seller wanting to export to Japan from any country in the world can probably find no better agency for his needs. A trading company will examine the seller's product, determine the best market for it, analyze potential demand and competitive conditions in the selected markets, and advise the seller accordingly. When the contract is made—usually in about forty-eight hours by international Telex cable—the trading company will undertake as much of the physical transaction as the seller wishes to contract for. That is, the company will supervise the overseas shipment in all stages from packing, warehousing, dockside storage, and loading, to distribution to proper wholesale outlets in the selected market in Japan.

If a potential buyer needs a product, the Japanese trading company performs the same services in reverse. It finds the best seller of the best product for the buyer's needs—either in America or anywhere in the world—and supervises the transaction from contract negotiation to delivery of the goods to the buyer's doorstep. This includes all those services necessary to the physical movement of the goods, such as customs clearance, obtaining proper permits, covering import-export duties, and marine insurance—even salvage arrangements and claims adjustments when necessary.

Raw Materials, Commodities, Consumer Goods. The big Japanese trading company is primarily an importer of raw materials and commodities, but with a growing emphasis on importing consumer goods and production equipment. The large companies act not only as agents but also as merchandisers, buying foreign goods for resale in the Japanese market, sometimes under their own trademarks.

Major categories of commodities, foodstuffs, equipment, and merchandise imported by the big traders are: iron ore, steel, scrap, and other steel-making materials; iron and steel products; nonferrous ores, concentrates and metals; coal, petroleum, and refined oil products; chemicals and raw materials for chemical production; nitrates, phosphates, and other fertilizer materials; logs, lumber, and building materials; paper and pulp; grains, soybeans, feeds, oils, fats, hides, sugar, livestock, and provisions; natural and chemical fibers and textiles; rubber, resins, and nonmetallic minerals; machinery, motor vehicles, aircraft, and scientific apparatus; and sundries, a category which includes hundreds of raw materials, appliances, medicines, cosmetics, and consumer goods of every description.

It is difficult to conceive of any product not imported by Japanese traders, except a diminishing number of products specifically excluded by protectionist barriers. In any business—iron and steel, buttons or toys, fish or plastics—the traders probably have a specialist who knows the market trends, manufacturing techniques, cost and distribution, and other important factors that can make a difference in a corporation's profit.

Doing Business. Trading organizations as vast as Japan's two giants handle Japanese overseas trade in a number of ways.

One of the foreign purchaser's contacts with Japanese products is the large importer. Trading companies do a sizeable business with importers, mainly in consumer goods, because major importers have a diversified stock list with great aggregate volume. In certain categories, businessmen need quantities too small to import economically. In this case, the importer is the ideal middleman, because his policies permit low operating costs. A trading company can ship single-order sundries profitably, the importer can import a diverse product list profitably, and the buyer can obtain from the importer the products needed in profitable quantities. Everyone saves on costs because of volume. This essence of trading companies' service is generally applied to mass shipments of essential goods and commodities.

If a buyer for a steel mill wants large quantities of Japanese steel, for example, and wants to deal directly with the producer, he will be referred to a large trading company. In Japan's economy a steel producer is concerned almost entirely with producing steel, not with selling it overseas. He depends on trading companies' foreign market contacts and selling organization.

Trading from Stock. Although trading companies are primarily service specialists not normally operating from stock position, they often commit themselves to purchasing large percentages of Japanese industries' output, taking advantage of fluctuations in international freight rates. Such products enjoy steady and continuous demand, and they are considered a safe risk. Widespread facilities and a steady flow of customers allow shipment of goods taken on a temporary long basis with the greatest efficiency and economy consistent with demand, and under the most advantageous shipping situations. By keeping operating expenses to a minimum, savings are passed on to customers through lower service charges.

Marketing in Japan. Japan's economic dependence on its trading companies is so complete that in many cases these organizations are not only the best commercial avenues in and out of the country but the *only* ones. Foreign businessmen who attempt to approach major Japanese manufacturers directly today are often advised by the manufacturer himself to call Mitsui, Mitsubishi, or Marubeni, or whichever trading company he happens to be most closely associated with. Japanese manufacturers have not generally developed overseas representation because trading companies do the job for them—in most cases better and more economically than they could themselves.

Financing. Japanese trading companies very often create new business ventures by extending credit for long-term production or sales programs on the most favorable terms—in many cases more favorable than equivalent financing from another lending institution. This is made possible by their international position, their great financial resources, their extremely stable financial position through diversified investment, and their solid position with the world's major lending institutions, enabling them to obtain funds at inexpensive terms. A manufacturer or major seller who wants to take advantage quickly of a favorable market opening but has no ready funds benefits from this financing source.

FUTURE PROSPECTS

Problems

Transacting overseas business through a Japanese company is not without its occasional problems. Those engaged in international trade are geared to large-scale operations, mostly in gross commodities and bulk shipments. However, most trading companies maintain a sundries department that handles business not in the traditional categories, and a moderate-sized order is an unconventional type of product many take somewhat more time to finalize. A trading company will make every effort to find practical and profitable business opportunities in any proposal presented to it, and, if unable to accept an order, will refer a prospective customer either to another trading company or to another type of agency.

Another type of problem involves joint ventures in certain industries, or large importations of certain products into Japan. Import-export trade transactions on a major scale must have the approval of the Japanese Ministry of International Trade and Industry (MITI), and in cases of foreign capital investment a client must have approval of the Ministry of Finance. These government agencies are responsible for maintaining a balance in domestic commerce protecting insofar as possible the balance of international payments, and providing for an evenly distributed growth of Japan's domestic industry.

Trading companies work in close harmony with government agencies and government policy, and, consequently, an overseas manufacturer wishing to export to Japan large quantities of a product already enjoying a strong position in the local market might not be guaranteed approval. This applies as well to joint venture establishments. Foreign capital wishing to invest in a plant, utility, or other enterprise in a category which is either nascent or well-established domestically, may encounter similar hesitancy (if not official opposition) on the part of the government in granting approval. On the other hand, joint ventures in industries contributing to a well-rounded, diversified internal commerce—domestic industries either weak or lacking, but needed—are likely to receive the fullest government cooperation. Such policy is predicated on the desire to neither discourage the development of home industries nor to saturate a given market so as to create an unhealthy competitive situation.

A third problem that sometimes arises is a cultural one—the differences between Japanese business methods and practices and those of the country in which overseas business is transacted. The Japanese, historically accustomed to a calm and easy pace attended by much social amenity, sometimes frustrate foreign businessmen accustomed to faster-paced schedules.

But the practice of employing seasoned local businessmen in foreign countries offers a ready solution. An experienced, respected, and sometimes well-known local business figure is relied upon for advice and direct contact with the local business community.

IN DEVELOPING COUNTRIES

40.

MARKETING IN INDIA*

Ralph Westfall and
Harper W. Boyd, Jr.

MARKETING is probably the least developed aspect of the Indian economy. It is considered a wasteful activity. Middlemen and salesmen of all types are regarded as schemers trying to profit at the expense of the public.

Retailers' margins in India are extremely low, probably about 10 per cent, and wholesalers' margins are less than half as much. Both figures are well below those in the United States; even so, marketing in India must be considered inefficient. Losses from poor physical distribution methods are undoubtedly large, as are losses resulting from the failure of the marketing system to integrate consumer wants with production resources. The greatest waste, however, probably comes from the failure of marketing to furnish the force necessary to start the economy on a period of growth.

THE MARKET

India is only about one-third the size of the United States, but has more than twice as many consumers—almost 400 million. Virtually all of these consumers have a very limited income. Gross national product is only about $72 per person, one of the lowest in the world, as compared with $2,343 for the United States.[1] Personal consumption is, of course, even lower—about $54 per person per year—as compared with $1,664 for this country. About $32 of Indian consumption represents cash purchases; the rest is consumption of home-produced items.[2]

---

* Ralph Westfall and Harper W. Boyd, Jr., "Marketing in India," *Journal of Marketing*, Vol. 25, No. 2 (October 1960), a publication of the American Marketing Association, pp. 11-17. Reprinted by permission.

[1] *Facts and Figures* (San Francisco: International Industrial Conference, 1957), pp. 5 and 8.

[2] *Second Five-Year Plan: The Framework* (New Delhi: Ministry of Information and Broadcasting, 1955), p. 12.

The majority of Indians are still living in an economy that is only partially monetized. In the villages, where some 85 per cent of the population lives, there are still village potters and carpenters who produce for all members of the community in return for a certain share of the harvest. This share has been fixed by tradition and is not subject to bargaining.

Indian shopping habits differ markedly from those in the United States. In the cities the housewife makes a daily shopping trip to buy fruits and vegetables. There are no refrigerators except in a few wealthy homes. A certain amount of grain may be stored in earthen jars in the household.

Shopping for items other than food is unusual and so becomes a significant undertaking. A day may be devoted to shopping for a sari or other items of clothing. Neither the vendor nor the shopper feels right if the sale is made without some bargaining. The vendor usually quotes an initial price well above that at which he is willing to sell; the buyer offers less than he expects to pay. Both can then "give" a little. In only a few of the finest shops in the largest cities is there a one-price policy.

CHARACTERISTICS OF MARKETING IN INDIA

Importance of Marketing

Some idea of the low relative importance of marketing in the Indian economy can be gained from the employment figures in Table 1.

TABLE 1—ESTIMATED EMPLOYMENT BY TYPE OF EMPLOYMENT
IN INDIA, 1955–56, AND IN UNITED STATES, 1958[a] (MILLIONS)

Type of Employment	India		United States	
	No.	%	No.	%
Agriculture & allied pursuits	109.5	72.0	5.0	8.8
Mining & factory establishments	4.0	2.6	16.8	29.6
Household enterprises & construction	12.0	7.9	2.9	5.1
Communication, railway, banks, insurance	1.6	1.1	4.1	7.2
Wholesale & retail trade & transport other than railways	10.0	6.6	11.6	20.5
Professions, services, & government administration	14.9	9.8	16.3	28.8
Total	152.0	100.0	56.7	100.0

[a] *Second Five-Year Plan: The Framework* (New Delhi: Ministry of Information and Broadcasting, 1955), pp. 42 and 98. *Survey of Current Business* (April, 1958), p. S-11. Classes shown are for Indian data. U.S. data are for approximately similar classes.

As would be expected, employment varies greatly between India and the United States. The total number employed is almost three times as large in India as in the United States, but over two-thirds of the employed Indians work in agriculture. The United States actually has more people employed in wholesaling and retailing than has India, even though the typical Indian merchant handles a far smaller volume than his counterpart in this country. The data undoubtedly understate the marketing activity in both countries since many farmers and factory employees spend at least part of their time in marketing activities.

Channels of Distribution

Channels of distribution are similar in type to those in the United States. The most common channel for manufactured products is the orthodox manufacturer-wholesaler-retailer-consumer. In cases where production is concentrated geographically but dispersed among many small firms, there are often two wholesalers, one which concentrates production from a number of producers into larger quantities near the point of production (local wholesaler), and one which disperses products to retailers (consumer wholesaler) near the point of consumption. Commission agents who operate essentially as manufacturers' agents are also common. They usually represent manufacturers in distant markets and sell to wholesalers.

Channels for agricultural products are also similar to those in the United States. Local buyers assemble large quantities for shipment to wholesalers in consuming areas, who in turn sell to retailers. Thus, the middlemen in India are similar to those in this country in the general processes they accomplish; but their methods of operation are far different, as are the marketing activities of manufacturers.

Marketing by Manufacturers

Manufacturing in India is primarily a hand process carried on in homes or in small establishments. There are occasional exceptions, for example, the great Tata steel plant. The household utensil and the shoe-polish industries are fairly typical of the small establishments. Of eleven utensil manufacturers selected at random from among sources used by wholesalers in Punjab State, the largest had an annual volume of approximately $50,000. All but three had annual sales of less than $15,000. All of these manufacturers sold to wholesalers, and four also sold some direct to retailers. Only two had sold to as many as fifty customers during the entire previous year. Only one had any salesmen—that one had three. All sold on credit, but only two had a published price list. Two manufacturers sold branded products and did some advertising, but the annual advertising expenditure of the two totaled only about $700.

In the northern region of India there were fifty shoe-polish manufacturers in 1956.[3] Total production was 1,250,000 pounds, of which about 400,000 pounds were made by one producer. The other forty-nine firms produced an average of about 17,000 pounds each which resulted in sales of about $7,000 annually.

Wholesalers Important

Wholesalers are standard in most channels of distribution in India. Many of the wholesalers combine their wholesaling functions with retailing or with manufacturing. A number of large companies accomplish the physical distribution function of the wholesaler without relinquishing title, through the use of "stockists." There are retailers or wholesalers who perform a function similar to the public merchandise warehouse. Hindustan Lever (the Indian Lever Brothers firm) often uses stockists. For example, Lever arranges for the merchant to stock Lever soap and vanespati (hydrogenated oil). Title to the merchandise remains with Lever. The dealer will sell the stock for cash, at a price set by Lever, to any customer who presents himself. He deducts his charge for the service and forwards the balance to Lever.

Among thirty household utensil wholesalers in Punjab State, the median annual sales volume was approximately $4,000 in 1957. Fourteen of the wholesalers had no employees, and only one had more than three. Wholesale margins are low as compared with those in the United States. The utensil wholesalers have margins on various items that vary from 1.5 to 4 per cent. Wholesalers' margins on soap are 3 to 4 per cent. One bicycle wholesaler buys cases of six bicycles at $140 per case and sells them at $23.25 each for a total of $139.50. The only profit is made by selling the crate to a furniture company for $1.40. This wholesaler is a relatively large merchant. His expenses indicate why he can operate on such a small margin:

Rent	$ 6 per month
Wages (4 employees at $12)	48 per month
Electricity	1 per month
Entertainment of customers	12 per month
Total Expenses	$67 per month

[3] *Boot Polish*, Small-Scale Industry Analysis and Planning Report No. 9 (New Delhi: Ministry of Commerce and Consumer Industries, 1956), p. 6.

The initiative for exchange at the wholesale level comes primarily from the buyer. On their last purchase, twenty-seven out of thirty utensil wholesalers bought from manufacturers and three from other wholesalers. Fourteen of the thirty visited the manufacturer to make their purchase, and four others sent their orders by mail. In eleven cases, vendor salesmen called on the wholesaler to make the sale, and in one case a selling agent called on the wholesaler. During the preceding year, twenty-six of the thirty utensil wholesalers were visited by salesmen from more than one source, but four were not. Three wholesalers had bought from only one source during the entire preceding year, but the median number of sources was four.

Selling effort is very limited among Indian wholesalers. The traveling salesman scarcely exists; in the utensil survey none of the thirty wholesalers had a traveling salesman. One wholesaler received calendars from a manufacturer and sent them to retailers as a promotional device. None of the others had any promotional materials. Twenty-eight of the thirty utensil wholesalers gave a 30-day credit, and twenty-six admitted to bargaining on prices with their retailer customers.

Retailers

Retailing in India differs in many respects from that in Western countries. Self-service is not feasible because of the pilferage problem. In many of the better stores in large cities, the goods are kept locked behind glass or mesh doors which have to be unlocked every time a sale is made. In stores in which sales people other than the owner wait on customers, two different employees are used to prevent stealing. On employee writes the sales check and another accepts the money. There are no department stores in the standard sense, but there are a few examples in the largest cities of what might be called department stores in small U.S. towns. There is not a single supermarket in all of India.

Outside of the principal shopping centers in cities of over 1,000,000 population, the typical retailing center is a bazaar where many shops are clustered together. Each shop is typically about ten feet square, so that the proprietor can sit in the middle of the floor and reach his entire stock.

In the small villages, where most of the population lives, there are no retail shops. Individuals buy very little. Hawkers travel to villages, selling frequently purchased items such as utensils and cloth which they carry on their backs and heads. They often make exchanges by barter or partially by barter, accepting old utensils, clothes, and shoes in full or partial payment. For special occasions such as a wedding, when the parents may give the bride and groom some household utensils, villagers will go to neighboring towns to buy.

There has been no census of retailers in India. In Madras State, how-ever, all retailers with annual sales of more than 7,500 rupees, approximately $1,500, are required to register under the sales tax law. Madras State had a population of 56,000,000 in 1951. In 1955-56, 103,000 dealers registered; of these, 58,000 had annual volumes between approximately $1,500 and $2,000. The remaining 45,000 dealers with volumes over $2,-000 were distributed by size and type of business as shown in Table 2.

TABLE 2—MADRAS STATE RETAILERS CLASSIFIED BY TYPE OF BUSINESS AND SALES VOLUME[a]

	Approximate Sales Volume				
	$2,000 to $5,000	$5,000 to $10,000	$10,000 to $20,000	Over $20,000	Total
Hotels and restaurants	3,149	621	322	151	4,243
Cloth	3,467	1,099	549	653	5,768
Grocery	7,816	1,997	867	970	11,650
All others	16,138	5,872	1,736		23,746
Total	$30,570	$9,589	$5,248		$45,407

[a]National Council of Applied Economic Research, New Delhi.

The number of retailers with volumes of less than $1,500 is not known, but many Indians believe there are more with sales below $1,500 than above. If this is correct, it means there are more than 206,000 retailers, perhaps about 250,000, in Madras State. On a similar per capita basis, there would be about 2,000,000 retailers in all of India—a slightly larger number than in the United States.

Small Retail Margins

Indian retail margins are unusually small as compared with the 30 per cent and larger margins common in this country. Accurate margins cannot be measured directly because most retailers have no accounting records. Data gathered from fifty-eight utensil retailers in 1957 showed that dealers specializing in earthenware utensils had gross margins of approximately 20 per cent; but the highest margin of any dealer on metal utensils (aluminum, cast iron, brass, moradabadi, bell metal, and stainless steel) was 8 per cent, and some were as low as 2 per cent.[4] These were margins on individual sales; each dealer's margin varied from transaction

[4] Survey conducted by the National Council of Applied Economic Research, New Delhi, in which one of the authors participated.

to transaction, as both wholesale and retail prices were subject to bargaining.

Retailers' Sources

Purchasing is not easy for the retailer in India. Most merchants must visit the source, either wholesaler or manufacturer, or order by mail to purchase new stock. Wholesalers have no traveling salesmen. Of sixty-eight utensil retailers questioned, forty-two had visited the source to make their last purchase and twenty others had ordered by mail.

Retailers often travel considerable distances to make their purchases. Among the utensil dealers studied, purchases were made every two to three months by most; the median distance to the source was between 100 and 125 miles, considerably farther than the typical wholesaler traveled to make his purchases. In the small town of Lonavla, about 70 miles from Bombay, most retailers go to Bombay to buy. One hardware retailer goes to the city twice a month, a 6-hour round trip, to buy from a manufacturer. Another has a monthly train ticket to Bombay, and has his son go almost every day to make small purchases from a wholesaler. No salesman has ever called on either retailer.

WEAKNESSES IN INDIAN MARKETING SYSTEM

Demand Creation

There is little demand creation effort in India. Although there are branches of some of the top U.S. advertising agencies in India, such as J. Walter Thompson Co., there is little advertising.

There are good reasons, however, for this. National advertising is impossible. There are some fifty-one dialects spoken by one or more million people each. No one language is spoken by more than about 50 million of the almost 400 million population. Only about 15 per cent of the population is literate in any language.

There are no communication means by which the advertiser can reach any large proportion of the people. Newspapers are confined to the major cities, where less than 20 per cent of the population lives, and a majority of them are in English. Radio reaches only a small segment because there is no electricity in most of the villages, and few people can afford radios. In addition, Indian radio is controlled by the state and does not use commercials. Radio Ceylon does permit commercial messages and is beamed over much of India, but its audience is limited. There is no television.

A more fundamental problem in using modern demand creation methods lies in the character and culture of the people. On the one hand, Indians have shown themselves to be natural merchants; in many countries to which they have emigrated they have become major factors in the country's internal trade—Burma, South Africa, and Fiji, for example. On the other hand, Indians have a philosophic outlook on life which tends to make them less interested in materialistic things—at least as compared with the typical U.S. citizen. Their thinking in this respect is similar to that in Europe in the Middle Ages.[5] As a result, the businessman seeking a profit is considered unworthy, and this is particularly true for a merchant who takes an aggressive approach to selling something which he did not make but which will bring a profit to himself. Thus, the initiative for exchange typically comes from the buyer's side. At the same time Indians are great bargainers and, once negotiations are started, will strive to make a sale and secure a price advantage.

The Indian village of the past was not a market economy. Each person performed his job, largely determined by his caste, and shared in the village's produce on the basis of a complete system of shares. There was no market valuation of either the services of the artisans or the produce of the farmers.[6] In such an economy there was no place for selling. The attitudes developed over centuries of this type of economic thinking cannot be changed quickly. Since approximately 85 per cent of all Indians still live in villages and many are still living partially in a communal system, this lack of understanding of a market economy is a major factor.

Under the circumstances, American demand creation methods cannot be directly and immediately transplanted to India. The success of a few promotional efforts adapted to the local situation, those used by Hindustan Lever, for example, indicates definitely that demand can be created.

Transportation

Transportation difficulties are a barrier to effective marketing. The transportation system of India is a mixture of the ancient and modern. A bicycle made in Madras may travel by railroad to Delhi; move to Ambala by truck; go to Ambala Cantonment by bullock cart; and go from the shop there to some consumer by hand cart or on the top of someone's head.

The railroad industry is one of India's sources of pride. It is rela-

5 Marquis W. Childs and Douglass Cater, *Ethics in a Business Society* (New York: Harper and Brothers, 1954), p. 12.

6 Walter C. Neale, "Reciprocity and Redistribution in the Indian Village," in Karl Polyanyi and others, *Trade and Markets in the Early Empires* (Glencoe, Illinois: The Free Press, 1957), pp. 218-234.

tively modern; however, it operates on three different track gauges, so that extra handling of goods is sometimes necessary. The trucking industry is somewhat less well developed, but can still be considered modern. It has the same problem of differing load limits among the various states as in the United States.[7] The competition between the railroads and trucks is intense, as it is in this country; however, in India the railroads are owned and operated by the Government, while the bulk of the trucking industry is owned privately.

Government ownership plus pride in the railway system has led to artificial limitations on the development of trucking.[8] Length of haul has been particularly limited. It is not possible for a truck registered in one state to go beyond an immediately adjoining state. If the shipment is to go further, it must be transferred to a truck registered in the second state which can go to the third, and so on.

More restrictive than this, however, is the effect of octroi, a tax on all goods shipped into a city. This limits trade to some extent, but the greater limitation arises on goods passing through a city. A truck going one hundred miles may pass through perhaps six towns and octroi duties. At each of these towns the trucker must wait in line for his turn to be checked and must then pay the octroi. The octroi will be refunded at the other end of the town if the goods go through, but the refund system is so complicated and time consuming that a middleman has sprung up to handle this for a slight additional fee.[9] Some local governments hold the octroi collections on goods going through a town. The Indian Supreme Court has held this tax on goods in transit to be illegal, but as late as August, 1958, Delhi widened its city limits to take in a bypass road and held the octroi duties collected.[10]

Limited Storage Facilities

In the non-monetary subsistence economy in which the vast majority of Indians have lived for centuries, there has been little need for commercial storage facilities for food products, particularly grains. Each family has stored its own grain in urns. With the growth of a monetary economy, more grain is moving in trade, and more storage facilities are needed. The first grain elevator in India was completed in 1957. Storage facilities at all wholesale levels are inadequate. In the city grain markets,

[7] "Quick Redress of Road Transport Problem Needed," *Motor Transport,* Vol. 14 (July, 1958), p. 25.

[8] S. K. Patil, "Road Transport Has Come of Age," *Motor Transport,* Vol. 14 (July, 1958), p. 19.

[9] "Rising Taxes," *Motor Transport,* Vol. 14 (March, 1958), p. 11.

[10] "Terminal Tax on Goods in Transit by Road," *Motor Transport,* Vol. 14 (August, 1958), p. 17.

sidewalks get completely blocked by sacks of grain piled there for lack of any other place. Such poor storage facilities, of course, lead to spoilage and to seasonal shortages and surpluses.

Wide and erratic price fluctuations have plagued the lac industry for years. (Lac is the raw material from which shellac is made; it is secreted by insects that infest a specie of tree native to India.) A survey among the members of the lac industry in 1957 disclosed that the vast majority believed prices could be stabilized to some degree with more adequate storage facilities.[11]

Some of the storage problem stems from the basic shortage of capital, but there are differences in outlook that make it difficult to install modern methods. When the first Indian grain elevator was officially opened in 1957, an American was pointing out the advantages to an Indian official. Among other things he mentioned that the elevator would protect the grain so that rats would not eat it. To this the Indian replied: "We look at that differently. We think the rats also have to eat."

Adulteration and Standardization

Indians buy household utensils by the pound instead of by the unit. If they did not, they suspect the manufacturer would pound the metal thinner than the buyer believed it to be. Sugar is sold only in extremely coarse crystals—partly because it is more difficult to adulterate in that form. Almost all consumers buy grain and grind it themselves. Flour can easily be adulterated with chalk dust. Even grain must be sorted, virtually kernel by kernel, or sand and other foreign matter will be slipped in to add to the weight. There is a flourishing market for empty containers for cosmetics, toilet goods, and medicines. Unless the labels are destroyed when the contents are used, the jars, bottles, and cans will be refilled with substandard products and sold as the original. In 1957 health authorities in Delhi estimated that 25 per cent of all the food bought in that city was adulterated.[12] Sawdust, husks, colored earth, and ground seeds were found in various foodstuffs, accounting for 10 to 50 per cent of the total weight of the products.

Since there are few brands, most products have no reputation to uphold. A manufacturer who tries to establish and maintain a standardized quality for his product faces a difficult task.

"Because of severe competition, small factories where more or less scientific methods are adopted, find themselves in a perplexing situation. They cannot market their goods in competition with manufacturers work-

[11] *Export Markets for Indian Lac* (New Delhi: National Council of Applied Economic Research, 1957), p. 39.
[12] *The Times of India,* August 28, 1957.

ing on crude lines because (1) their cost of production is higher on account of using better raw materials and working on modern lines with machinery which necessitates large investments, and (2) the consumers are unwilling to pay them a higher price, believing that the quality of all Indian brands is equally bad. On the other hand, in competition with large scientific manufacturers they are handicapped because people are not prepared to purchase their brands, believing that invariably the foreign brands are superior."[13]

CONCLUSIONS

A steel mill or a fertilizer plant may be transplanted from Pittsburgh to Jamshedpur, India, and the machines will run the same way and chemicals will react as expected.

The same is not true of marketing. Social customs, individual attitudes, education, business institutions, methods of communication, and governmental influences and control differ markedly between India and the United States. Modern-day marketing methods in this country cannot be directly transplanted successfully to the Indian economy. Change must be more gradual, and American methods probably will never fit exactly.

There are a number of aspects of marketing, however, in which improved methods would aid Indian economic development. One of the main deterrents to effective advertising is being overcome. Education is expanding the percentage of literates rapidly. As more people learn to read, there will be more newspapers and magazines which can be used as advertising media.

The physical handling of goods also offers opportunities for great improvement. Administrative barriers hamper an already limited transportation system and storage facilities are far short of needs. Standardization of quality is almost unknown; but, as demand creation techniques develop, thus permitting brand names to establish franchises, standardization will undoubtedly become more common.

13 *Boot Polish,* same reference as footnote 3, p. 13.

41.

MARKETING IN BRAZIL*

Donald A. Taylor

A visitor to one of the large industrial or commercial centers of Brazil would find it difficult to detect differences in marketing practices over those found in the USA. In fact, the similarity on outward appearance is striking. It is only after considerable time that the practitioner begins to realize he must re-examine every idea he ever had about marketing. Sometimes the facts are such that he will arrive at a course of action similar to that taken at home, sometimes a similar course of action but for different reasons, and sometimes an altogether different action is called for. Since the economic and cultural facts differ from those found at home it should not be surprising that marketing action in Brazil is different from marketing in the USA. The key to successful marketing in Brazil is a broad knowledge of the economic and cultural environment and the ability to analyze facts in a manner which will contribute to corporate success. The purpose of these remarks is to demonstrate the way in which differences in economic and cultural environment affect marketing practice and the role of education in Brazil in promoting the analytical ability to utilize facts in a meaningful marketing manner.

CONTRASTS AND CONTRADICTIONS

It has been said that Brazil is a land of contrasts, and this is equally true in the field of business behavior. A few examples of marketing behavior in the fields of pricing, advertising and distribution will serve to demonstrate the differences; however, all explanation is purely conjectural.

Pricing

A story is told of a banker who had purchased a large quantity of piggy banks as a promotional device in a savings campaign the bank was con-

* Donald A. Taylor, "Marketing in Brazil," *Marketing and Economic Development,* 1965 Proceedings of the American Marketing Association, pp. 110-115. Reprinted by permission.

ducting. Later the campaign was expanded and he tripled the order to the piggy bank maker, who in turn immediately increased the price. After much explanation by the banker about the reduction in production cost because of the quantity, the increased use of the already amortized moulds, the producer responded that this was all very true "but the demand was up." In discussing a pricing case on a ready-made man's shirt (an innovation at the time in Brazil), a large proportion of the students argued that the price should go up because the idea of ready-made shirts was accepted and the demand had increased. There was absolutely no consideration of the supply cost factors involved.

Stepping up a level in the plane of distribution, an interesting contradiction occurs at the wholesale and retail level. Since 1957, Brazil has lived with rampant inflation, which reached as high as approximately 86 per cent in 1964. Prices increase monthly on almost a reflex basis. However, practically all retailers offer old stock at a lower price. In fact, a frequent comment is, "you are lucky, that is old stock, the new ones are 50% more." There seems to be a notion that it would not be "just" to charge the same price for an item that cost less as for one that cost more. In the sense that the only way a retailer can stay in business with such a pricing policy is to draw down on net worth or borrow to replenish inventories, the concept of a "going concern" is practically nil.

How can these two types of behavior be explained? Manufacturers set the price and wholesalers and retailers take a set mark-up regardless of the cost price. However, there may be another explanation which serves this seemingly contradictory behavior. Industrialization in Brazil is relatively new. Up to a few years ago practically all manufactured goods were imported. Variations in manufacturing supply costs were of little concern. Goods came in at a landed price and pricing from there on was simply assessment of demand. This same historical background may account for the "one deal" mentality of pricing at the retail and wholesale level. Each ship-load was a deal and when that was gone the merchant simply waited for another good deal.

These tendencies are still very strong in Brazil today. However, there is some indication that they are disappearing. Some of the larger foreign firms have cautiously departed from these practices, and the Brazilian managements are emulating rapidly. The term cautiously was used purposely since even large foreign firms are afraid to unleash the wrath of nationalistic elements in the country.

Closely related to the above are price-volume-profit concepts. In general, most Brazilian businessmen espouse a low volume, high mark-up attitude. The absence of a mass market mentality probably can be explained by the distribution of income. It is true that in Brazil, there is a very rich and a very poor class as well as a rapidly developing middle class. In the case of automobiles, one educated Brazilian observed that the market for autos was saturated as all those who could afford a car already owned one. Therefore, rather than try to expand the market it was a sounder policy to produce less and make more money on each item sold. The mentality expressed above may explain the structure of business enterprise in Brazil and the existence of mark-ups in the neighborhood of 100 to 150 per cent. Although there are a few large enterprises in Brazil the majority are small or medium size concerns. Comfortable profits may be maintained at relatively small volume when the size of the mark-up is considered. It may seem that the high mark-up is an inflation phenomenon, and of course, this has had an influence, but historically mark-ups have always been high.

Advertising

Advertising practice in Brazil is very similar to that found in the U.S. In fact, most advertising in Brazil was introduced by branch offices of the large North American firms. Upon closer scrutiny there are differences. Many products that are not considered to be highly advertisable receive a large part of the total marketing budget in Brazil. To spend large sums on advertising men's ties and textile piece goods seems contrary to U.S. practice. Until it is recognized that the bulk of this advertising is primary demand advertising, simply announcing the fact that these goods are now produced and available in Brazil, there seems to be no explanation for this kind of expenditure. Not so many years ago all goods were advertisable as a means of announcing their availability.

Similar media are available in Brazil but there is a difference in the use of outdoor billboard advertising. The same advertisement will be repeated 50 or 60 times along a wall in the center of the city. At first, this seems to be a waste of advertising materials. All one needs to do is witness a single political campaign in Brazil and a possible explanation is found for this kind of practice. The literacy rate is not high and much advertising simply tries to create brand recognition through a high level of repetition. Although the result is somewhat unsightly, it does work.

Distribution

There are two dominant characteristics of the distribution system. First, it is a localized or regional system. To speak of national distribution in Brazil even today is somewhat of an anomaly. The transportation system makes this most difficult. Consequently, most companies sell in a relatively small area. The distribution of population is such that a large percentage of the total market can be reached by serving the large cities along the seaboard. However, the improvement in transportation is changing this characteristic rapidly. Because distribution is somewhat local there is a prevalence of direct sale—manufacturer to retailer to consumer. In part this is a result of the availability of efficient distributors, but more so because of the concentration of customers with the attendant ease of solicitation.

Second, there is a high degree of specialization at the retail level. Particularly is this true of the large cities where the bulk of retail trade takes place. This is partially a result of the legal framework within which business is allowed to operate. Brazil is a civil law country, and there is extensive fiscalization of all business activities. Every type of retail outlet is recognized in law and therefore, legalized. These statements of legal recognition define the outlet and broadly categorize the goods handled. Lack of legal recognition for a type of outlet can be a serious matter. For example, the supermarket is not legally recognized in the state of S. P. Although it had its origin in Brazil in this state, supermarket operators could theoretically be put out of business overnight. This is particularly true if their greatest competitor, the large cooperatives controlling the outdoor fairs, wished to exercise their political power. There is much more scrambling of merchandise today at the retail level, but the old traditions still are evident in the high degree of retail specialization found.

These few examples hopefully demonstrate some of the differences which do exist. They should not constitute a problem for marketers in Brazil as they simply must be taken into consideration in designing marketing strategy.

42.

MARKETING IN NIGERIA*

Raymond W. Baker

AFRICA has rushed into the realm of world awareness with amazing speed during the last decade. Once the dark continent, it is today catching the fancy of industrialists and commercialists from every corner of the globe.

TROPICAL AFRICA

For the 195 million people living in tropical Africa, per capita GNP averages less than $100. With the achievement of self-rule for the majority of these Africans has come a corresponding increase in national hopes and expectations. Ambitious development plans are being adopted and supported by substantial blocks of foreign aid largely for the improvement of transportation, communication, power, and education facilities. In virtually all the newly independent tropical African nations, the people are conscious that a better standard of living for themselves is possible and with rare exception are ready to participate fully and energetically in the process of their own advancement.

Along with the ambitions, problems, and developments common to Africa today have come changes in patterns of buying and selling. Consumer products of many kinds are being introduced for the first time. Individual African retailers are beginning to feel their way into new product lines and larger trading units. National governments are discouraging more diverse foreign activity in the retail sector and are striving to obtain a larger basis for African participation in the importing and wholesaling sectors. The establishment of industries is being encouraged, most commonly to produce for the local markets. Product preferences and techniques of advertising and promotion are changing, as competition increases and as literacy spreads.

Nowhere is the economic potential of tropical Africa more evidenced than in the number of foreign firms taking an interest in the commercial

* Raymond W. Baker. "Marketing in Nigeria," *Journal of Marketing* Vol. 29, No. 3 (July, 1965), a publication of the American Marketing Association, pp. 40-48. Reprinted by permission.

possibilities of the area, and nowhere is their interest more concentrated and committed than in the large and progressive Federal Republic of Nigeria.

NIGERIA

Situated on the West Coast, Nigeria is rapidly gaining stature as a major political and commercial leader in tropical Africa. More than 300 foreign firms have registered to do business since independence was gained in 1960. British, French, Swiss, Dutch, German, Italian, Scandinavian, American, Canadian, Brazilian, Greek, Lebanese, Indian, Chinese, and Japanese businessmen are competing to build successful enterprises and to demonstrate their ability and willingness to participate with Nigerians in the economic life of the country.

Economic Data

With an officially reported population of 55 million people, Nigeria is the home of one out of every four tropical Africans. The value of foreign transactions, above $1 billion, is larger than that for any other tropical African country, and the gross national product, in excess of $3 billion, is nearly triple that of the second-ranked nation. The infrastructure in Nigeria is reasonably well established. Postal, telephone, and telegraph services are widespread, if overworked.

Buying Patterns

Marketing systems in Nigeria are of two broad types—the large foreign-owned wholesaling and retailing networks and the small individual African traders. Both systems operate, however, primarily for the simple needs of the average Nigerian consumer.

Rural Nigerians, constituting somewhat over 60% of the population, are important as suppliers of primary products but are less important as buyers than the people who live in or near cities and towns. These urban Nigerians, active participants in the commerce of the country, have an average cash income of about $100 per year. Approximately 85% of this must be spent on food, clothing, and shelter (Table 1).

Considerations of both need and status are important to the Nigerian. The latter is thought to arise partly as a result of 1) a long history of respect and admiration for the position and affluence of traditional tribal authorities, and 2) a long history of essential sameness in the economic

TABLE 1—CONSUMERS' EXPENDITURES BY CATEGORIES
(Thousands of Dollars)[a]

	1950[b]		1954[b]		1957[b]		1960[b]	
	Value	% of total expenditure	Value	% of total expenditure	Value	% of total expenditure	Value	% of total expenditure
Drink	23.5	1.4	33.9	1.6	43.7	1.9	48.4	2.0
Tobacco	41.2	2.4	49.3	2.3	50.4	2.2	46.5	1.9
Fuel and light	20.4	1.2	27.2	1.3	33.0	1.4	39.2	1.6
Clothing	137.2	8.0	198.8	9.2	216.2	9.5	206.4	8.5
Other nondurable goods	24.0	1.3	57.4	2.6	84.0	3.7	—	—
Durable goods	28.6	1.7	50.7	2.3	52.9	2.3	88.5	3.6
Travel	22.1	1.3	39.2	1.8	58.5	2.6	71.4	2.9
Education	21.9	1.3	28.3	1.3	55.4	2.4	—	—
Miscellaneous service (including housing)	68.9	4.0	74.8	3.4	86.2	3.8	239.1	9.8
Sub-total (non-food items)	386.1	22.6	559.4	25.8	680.4	29.8	739.5	30.3
Food	1,316.3	77.2	1,600.5	73.7	1,590.4	69.7	1,682.5	69.1
Consumers' expenditure in Nigeria	1,702.4	99.8	2,159.9	99.6	2,271.6	99.5	2,422.0	99.4
Less: Expenditure by non-residents	−0.3	0.0	−1.7	−0.1	−2.5	−0.1	−3.4	−0.1
Plus: Expenditure by Nigerians abroad	4.2	0.2	10.6	0.5	14.3	0.6	17.4	0.7
Total consumers' expenditure[c]	1,706.3	100.0	2,168.9	100.0	2,283.4	100.0	2,436.0	100.0

[a] Source: The Northern Nigeria Ministry of Trade and Industry, *The Industrial Potentialities of Northern Nigeria* (Kaduna , Nigeria, 1964), p. 35.

[b] Based on constant 1957 prices. (It should be noted that complete, accurate, and current statistical information is not always available. The data presented in this and subsequent tables are as up to date as possible.)

[c] Errors in addition due to rounding.

conditions of the majority of the people. Thus, while the Nigerian may limit his food consumption to that which is merely filling, he will almost certainly own at least one expensive "national dress" for special occasions. And while he may live in a simple mud hut, he may at the same time own and be proud of a fine imported radio.

The Nigerian is a frequent buyer of small units, such as a tin of fish, two ounces of soap, or three cigarettes. In making his selections he exhibits two fundamental characteristics—a lack of education but an intense curiosity. He may study a range of sandals for 20 minutes, then make his choice in a seemingly offhand manner. Except in situations where brand image is entrenched and decisive, the Nigerian's process of selection is almost totally incrutable to the inexperienced foreigner.

IMPORTING AND WHOLESALING

Channels of distribution in Nigeria are well organized, though sometimes protracted and cumbersome. Products enter the trading channels either from local production or by import. Subsequently, it is not unusual for an article to change hands five or even ten times before reaching the ultimate consumer.

Local Primary Production

Agricultural products constitute by far the largest part of indigenously produced items. Those for local consumption are usually bought by a Nigerian trader in the producing area, resold to an urban wholesaler, who will then sell again to smaller wholesalers and retailers. Commodities for export, including palm products, groundnuts, cocoa, timber, cotton, and rubber, are bought by large trading companies of English, Swiss, French, Levantine, or Indian ownership, or by government marketing boards. Minerals, especially tin, columbite, and oil, may be exported by the extracting concern or again by a large trading company.

Foreign Importers, Wholesalers, and Agents

Several large foreign-owned trading firms have been active in Nigeria, and indeed in other parts of Africa, for over 50 years. Their integrated import, wholesale, and retail organizations are largely a result of their having to supply complete marketing services, and today their bulk buying powers and widespread distributive networks are impressive.

Both the integrated trading firms and some 100 or so foreign agents or manufacturers' representatives oversee the importation of products of

TABLE 2—IMPORTS BY MAJOR COMMODITY GROUPS, 1957-1963
(Thousands of Dollars)[a]

Commodity group	Imports						
	1957[b]	1958[b]	1959[b]	1960[b]	1961	1962	1963
Food and live animals	51,318	50,862	58,369	66,951	63,622	65,780	61,326
Beverages and tobacco	15,529	15,708	16,178	17,226	17,108	13,353	8,151
Crude materials, inedible, except fuels	5,264	5,636	5,746	6,009	6,871	6,745	8,708
Mineral fuels, lubricants and related materials	22,988	25,040	29,002	31,724	37,464	39,407	43,450
Animal and vegetable oils and fats	126	185	221	182	176	235	244
Chemicals	22,518	23,220	28,314	34,250	35,272	34,530	40,482
Manufactured goods classified chiefly by material	175,885	184,548	184,383	227,175	245,059	204,582	207,676
Machinery and transport equipment	87,718	110,278	119,554	144,592	141,075	135,145	141,635
Miscellaneous manufactured articles	37,458	43,448	49,955	66,956	66,506	60,628	59,772
Commodities and transactions not classified according to kind	8,106	7,137	7,815	9,430	9,579	8,019	9,495
Total[c]	426,910	466,063	499,534	604,495	622,728	568,425	580,936

[a] Source: *Nigeria Trade Summary*, Federal Office of Statistics, Lagos, Nigeria, (December issues, 1957-1963).

[b] Figures for 1957 through 1960 include former British Trust Territory of Southern Cameroons.

[c] Errors in addition due to rounding.

TABLE 3—IMPORTS OF SELECTED CONSUMERS' GROUPS,
1955, 1960, 1962, AND PROJECTED 1967
(Thousands of Dollars)[a]

Commodity	1955[b]	1960[b]	1962	1967
Meat, fresh, chilled or frozen	237.7	1,028.1	680.3	1,876.0
Jams, jellies, marmalades, etc.	406.7	1,582.0	1,510.5	2,520.0
Sugar, beet and cane, refined	6,807.5	10,601.1	9,038.3	13,160.0
Beer, ale and stout	7,641.6	10,914.6	7,911.8	14,000.0
Salt	4,297.9	5,221.4	5,634.5	7,840.0
Prepared paints, enamels, etc.	1,821.6	3,361.1	2,708.0	8,120.0
Miscellaneous medicinal and pharmaceutical products[c]	4,307.3	8,569.7	9,501.4	16,800.0
Bottles, flasks, etc.	293.3	1,225.1	1,496.9	3,360.0
Handtools and implements, including agricultural	1,409.3	1,952.9	1,783.3	3,920.0
Metal hardware	1,347.6	2,483.0	2,156.8	3,360.0
Nails, nuts, bolts, screws, etc.	1,334.7	2,200.9	1,392.6	3,080.0
Metal stoves, furnaces etc.	206.9	481.2	666.0	1,120.0
Typewriters and other office machinery	612.7	1,475.5	1,802.2	2,240.0
Aid conditioning and refrigerating equipment[d]	540.5	2,569.2	1,961.2	4,480.0
Radio receiving sets, domestic	742.3	4,042.0	2,474.5	6,580.0
Dry cell batteries	957.8	2,634.1	2,923.2	4,620.0
Hurricane lamps, oil burning	702.8	626.8	627.0	1,260.0
Travel goods, handbags, etc.	942.2	2,349.8	1,966.0	3,920.0

[a] Source: U.S. Department of Commerce, *Market for U. S. Products in Nigeria,* Washington, D.C., 1964, p. 6 (compiled from unpublished computations of Nigerian Federal Ministry of Commerce and Industry, Economics and Statistics Division, Arthur D. Little, Inc., technical advisers).
[b] Figures for 1955 and 1960 include former British Trust Territory of Southern Cameroons.
[c] Excluding vitamins and vitamin preparations; bacteriological products, sera and vaccines; penicillin, streptomycin, etc.; opium, alkaloids, etc.; ointments and liniments; and bandages, wadding, etc.
[d] Excluding nonelectric refrigerators.

foreign manufacturers (Tables 2 and 3). Most agents operate on an "indent" and commission basis—handling orders, documents, import licenses, and so on, but arranging for direct shipment to trading firms and other buyers.

Two factors have adversely affected foreign representatives in recent years. First, competition has become intensified and profit margins squeezed as more and more manufacturers are seeking markets for their products in Nigeria. Secondly, many import lines have been dislocated with the very rapid expansion of products manufactured internally

TABLE 4—GROSS PRODUCT OF MANUFACTURING SECTOR
AND OF PRINCIPAL INDUSTRIES (Thousands of Dollars)[a]

	1950[b]	1954[b]	1957[b]	1960[b]	% increase 1950–60
Total manufacturing production	8,762	18,127	30,589	43.820	398
Baking	53	185	588	885	1,550
Oil milling	1,018	999	6,053	7,308	618
Margarine manufacturing	7	34	51	51	630
Brewing and bottling	773	2,075	4,714	7,840	911
Tobacco manufacturing	3,908	6,234	5,882	6,132	57
Textile manufacturing	13	140	1,056	1,716	1,350
Rubber processing	55	386	1,665	3,858	7,080
Tanning	17	47	110	113	586
Sawmilling	1,396	3,652	4,288	5,040	261
Cement manufacturing	0	0	1,043	3,248	—

[a] Source: The Federal Ministry of Economic Development, *National Development Plan 1962-1968* (Lagos, Nigeria, 1962), p. 9.
[b] Based on constant 1957 prices.

(Table 4). Since 1960 industrial production has more than doubled, major increases occurring in textiles, rubber products, cement, concrete, beverages, vehicle assembly, plastics, oil, tobacco products, flour, paint, and aluminum.

Nigerian Wholesalers

While a number of entirely Nigerian firms are active as importers, a much larger number function as wholesalers. These Nigerian wholesalers—and there are as many women as men—typically buy from an expatriate wholesaler or agent and resell to a myriad of smaller wholesalers and retailers.

In his first dealings with a foreign firm, the Nigerian wholesaler will probably be required to pay cash for his merchandise. As a satisfactory trading relationship develops credit can be extended, sometimes eventually in amounts of over $100,000! Then, too, the wholesaler may expect to receive a monthly commission on the volume of his purchases, perhaps 1% or 2% or more. It is not at all uncommon for an especially aggressive Nigerian wholesaler, working on extremely thin margins, to sell at slightly less than his cost, making his profit at the end of the month on the commissions he receives from his suppliers. And even without commissions, some Nigerians will still sell quickly at less than their costs, then do what is called "gold coasting"—trade with the cash generated for 30 days in order to earn a profit before having to pay back the credit extended.

It is the policy of the Nigerian government to encourage Nigerians to participate increasingly in the importing and wholesaling activities of the commercial trade. New foreign firms wishing to establish in this sector are discouraged. In time the greater part of the distributive functions of the country will be in the hands of the local people.

RETAILING

Retailing in Nigeria is conducted on two distinct levels—the large foreign-owned stores and branches and the local Nigerian collective markets. Between these, the middle ground of independent small stores and specialty shops is very limited, the reason being that this type of undertaking has not been particularly attractive to the majority of more prosperous Nigerians who have preferred to expand backward into wholesaling.

Expatriate Networks

Almost all of the foreign trading firms operate large retail outlets in major cities as an integral part of their businesses. In Lagos, the capital of Nigeria, there are some eight department stores and five individual supermarkets. These stores, now managed largely by Nigerians, are well stocked with a wide selection of products to appeal to Nigerians as well as to the diverse nationalities of expatriate residents.

Several of the foreign firms have networks of smaller general stores throughout the country. However, since independence there has been a move to "Nigerianize" these outlets as well, either by appointing Nigerian managers or in some cases by actually relinquishing ownership of the branch to a Nigerian manager, then functioning as his adviser and supplier.

Nigerian Collective Markets

By far the greater volume of goods sold at retail are, however, not sold through such department stores and branch outlets. Rather, collective market areas, somewhat like bustling farmers' markets in the United States, are the retail shopping centers for the average Nigerians. These collective markets constitute indisputably the heart of the economy, and an understanding of them is essential to an understanding of the mainstream of commercial activity in Nigeria.

Collective markets represent an effective adaptation of the needs and facilities of the people to the environmental setting of the land. The controlling factors are several, as they are to varying degrees in other tropical developing countries: 1) a hot, humid, and deteriorating climate, 2) a profusion of edible products, 3) a high population density, and 4) a low per capita purchasing power. Food, accounting for about 70% of the average Nigerian's purchases, is the basic need which the collective markets must serve.

The result is a rotating market, forming at traditional time intervals of four, five, or seven days, setting up in temporary facilities, drawing from a ten to twenty-five mile radius, then moving sequentially to other markets in the area. In this way fresh food and other products are brought frequently to the buyers, small unit purchases can be accommodated, and investment by sellers in permanent facilities for preservation or display of goods is not necessary.

A good-sized market, such as Jankara in Lagos or the famous Onitsha market in Nigeria's Eastern Region, may attract 5,000 sellers and as many as 25,000 to 100,000 customers in a single day. The general impression given by a market is one of activity—the movement and noise of thousands of people, the maze of colorful product displays, the fusion of many odors. Some markets specialize, for example in textiles or meats, but most sell a very broad range of consumer products, including vegetables, fruits, meat, fish, fowl, staples, tinned foods, medicines, cosmetics, soaps, earthen and metal pots and pans, plastics, glassware, textiles, clothes, shoes, adornments, basketware, hardware, and candies. Sellers of similar products learned long ago to group together, and therefore markets tend to be divided into organized sections.

Some metropolitan markets have covered areas for the food sellers and stalls for others, but many sellers must simply find a small open area. Business begins by 8 a.m. Prices vary somewhat at first but then find a common level, as customers move from seller to seller seeking the best buys. Volumes of trade are hugely expanded for a week or so around the change of months, because wage earners are commonly paid on a monthly basis, sometime between the 24th and 28th.

Market Traders

The great majority of market traders are women. Traditionally, trading for women has been a logical differentiation from the more laborious farming and fishing activities of men. Also, gathering in the collective markets provides a social outlet for women, to such an extent that trading is not usually regarded as a particular type of occupation.

Most market traders specialize in a narrow line of products, for example peppers, jewelry, enamelware, or cloth, but some will sell broader, related lines such as soaps, medicines, and cosmetics together. A trader's quantity of goods available is limited to what she can carry on her head for the distance she must walk to market, possibly with the assistance of her children. Thus her stock is seldom large. Competition is extremely keen.

Displays are meticulously arranged so that each item is visible. As much as two hours may be spent stacking up goods several feet high to attract the eye of the shopper. Bargaining is the general rule, sometimes animated and vociferous, sometimes quite subtle. A price once offered can be changed if accepted too quickly, thereby reinitiating the bargaining process. Daily sales volumes may range from $1 to $20 or higher for traders in some lines such as textiles.

A trader does not expand by setting up branch operations. Usually the people working with her are too few, limited to members of her own family. Rather she will develop a portion of her trade as wholesale, gradually making the backward transition complete.

Within or around the edges of most market areas can be found such tradesmen as tailors, carpenters, blacksmiths, tinsmiths, goldsmiths, grain millers, and repairmen for bicycles, shoes, and watches. Bars, food shops, and refreshment kiosks also are common. And never absent are the "hawkers," usually young girls started early in life by their mothers selling prepared food, nuts, or biscuits from baskets carried on their heads.

In many larger cities the "mammy traders" have organized themselves into local market associations, numbering hundreds of women each. These associations can be extremely powerful in lobbying for improved physical facilities, tax reliefs, or other matters such as better schools for their children. The market traders do, after all, largely control the cash of the economy. Their place is paramount in the commerce of Nigeria and therefore most important in the development of the country.

ADVERTISING AND PROMOTION

To comprehend marketing in Nigeria requires not only an understanding of wholesale and retail channels of distribution but also an understanding of the rather unusual requirements of advertising and promotion. Successful marketing programs, whether for new product introductions or for maintenance of established brand images, are developed consistent with a few very basic considerations.

Essential Considerations

Most important are the degrees of literacy and the levels of education of the people. About 80% of the adult population of Nigeria have had little or no formal education and cannot read or write. Under these conditions local marketing programs are generally most effective when they are direct, forceful, and continuous. For example, the ubiquitous slogan, "Guinness gives you power," next to the bulging biceps of an African arm has made Guinness stout the biggest seller in Nigeria. And again,

"Buy Raleigh, the all steel bicycle," on radio, billboard, and poster has kept this manufacturer's product tops for years.

With only a very small part of his income discretionary, the Nigerian is a careful shopper. He is not inflexible in his preferences; on the contrary, the Nigerian is ready to try the new if it is presented to him properly. But he does want value for his money, and while he is cautious in his selections his concepts of value may be difficult to determine.

Finally there is a broad range of cultural and personality factors that must be recognized as peculiarly African, indeed even distinct to each geographically concentrated tribal group. A deep-seated impression of recent colonial rule is one that permeates widely. Status consideration is another, though appropriate symbols can vary. Personalities are important but dissimilar; the Yoruba of the Western Region is a very outgoing and friendly individual, while the Hausa of the Northern Region is rather quiet and reserved. Religious preferences are primarily Christian and Moslem, and each demands a certain awareness of its respective precepts. Colors may be important; for the Yoruba blue is widely favored. Even the direction of hands and eyes is sometimes significant.

In essence, what is important to realize is that marketing in Nigeria must be considered with an appreciation for the tribal and cultural background as well as the education and income of the local people.

Media and Technique

Radio is considered a particularly effective advertising medium, since it does not depend on the literacy of the people. Motion picture advertising is very popular, and some commercials are absolute marvels of creative and adaptive advertising genius. Newspapers and magazines enjoy extremely high readerships per copy (Table 5).

Paper, cardboard, and metal posters and signs, nearest the point of sale, are perhaps the most widely used advertising materials. Billboards are also popular and effective, since the movement of people in and out of metropolitan areas and trading centers each day is tremendous.

Personal selling takes on major importance, because Nigerians enjoy and appreciate the efforts of aggressive salesmen in hotly competitive situations. Sampling is a widely practiced technique but handled indiscriminately can cause unbargained-for problems of crowd control from the enthusiastic Nigerians. Multilingual sales promoters, operating from vans with loudspeakers, are very active around market areas, most commonly in connection with drug, soap, food, or drink products.

Organized public contests, drawings, and bonuses are sometimes employed. Seven-Up has been particularly effective with this type of promotion, such as offering prizes to the highest bidders competing with Seven-Up bottle tops.

TABLE 5—VARIETIES AND COVERAGES OF ADVERTISING MEDIA[a]

Media	Disseminating	Receiving (Estimated)
Radio	5 broadcasting stations	1.5 million sets in use
Television	4 broadcasting stations	14,000 sets in use
Motion picture	90 theatres	5 million persons annually
Local English language newspapers	4 major dailies	Circulations from 47,300 to 114,600
	4 major weeklies	Circulations from 28,000 to 147,300
Local English language magazines	4 major monthlies	Circulations from 25,000 to 108,000

[a]Source: U. S. Department of Commerce, *Market for U. S. Products in Nigeria,* (Washington, D. C., 1964), pp. 48-51.

Consumer-motivation analysis, as an aid in planning marketing programs, has not yet been developed to a point where its value can be assured. Until questionnaire, sample, and interview procedures are improved, it may be preferable for new entrants to seek sales guidelines by test marketing, despite the higher cost involved.

FUTURE

Marketing patterns in Nigeria are changing, and these changes are taking place at an accelerating rate. While some of the present recognizable trends will require a good many years to gain significant momentum, it is nevertheless possible to ascertain now what forces are at work.

1. Perhaps most important are the increasing degrees of Nigerian participation in all phases of commercial activity of the country. Collective markets have always been completely Africanized. But wholesaling and importing, years ago almost totally foreign controlled, are now being entered by more and more Nigerians. Similarly, large retail stores are being managed increasingly by Nigerians. With a keen trading instinct and an eye for the mass display, the Nigerian is becoming skilled in this area as well.

2. A trend toward enlargement of trading units is also noticeable. The government is encouraging this, as can be detected in the design of new collective markets with orderly arrangements of larger stalls. Also,

more Nigerians are beginning to establish retail specialty shops in down-town areas removed from the traditional collective markets. Parallel de-velopments in both these systems will continue, with the new pattern eventually becoming the more dominant. The intensity of competition as it now exists among petty traders may have some economic advantages, but the greater impact of larger, stronger buying and selling units, whole-sale and retail, is expected to have more.

3. Along with the enlargement of trading units is coming a shorten-ing of channels of distribution. The growing wealth of the people ap-pears to be engendering more sizable and possibly less frequent consumer purchases. The proliferation of locally made products, often distributed through manufacturer-owned or -appointed outlets, is also contributing to a shortening of channels. The day is passing when a product can change hands almost a dozen times before being sold to the ultimate user. The formation of larger units at the level of the collective markets and small shops will mean more direct buying from primary wholesalers. Unlike now, the demarcation between wholesaling and retailing will be-come distinct. The mechanisms of credit, already important, will prob-ably be broadened in use and effectiveness.

4. Gradual changes can be expected to take place in techniques of advertising and promotion. The intensity of competition between alter-nate consumer products is already bringing on changes, and, in the long run, improvement of the education and literacy of the people will bring further changes. Status appeals and exaggerated advertising may in vary-ing degrees be supplanted by straightforward product differentiations and emphases on utilitarian values. Product advertising expenditures may require a larger percentage for development of brand image. And intro-ductions of new items may become possible through media campaigns instead of more costly personal promotions.

5. Quite obviously, some products will lose volume and others will gain. Broadly speaking, the relative losers will in time be the home-pre-pared and craft-fabricated items, and the gainers will be processed and manufactured items. Also losing will be many that have false values, such as all-purpose medicinals and wool garments, giving way to products of a more practical nature for a more discriminating consumer. Products made in Nigeria will continue to increase in volume, with the encourage-ment of government industrialization programs and also with the ex-pressed preferences of the people.

6. Finally, industrial and consumer markets as a whole can be ex-pected to grow and expand. Disruptive political crises are not likely. While competing for the prize of Pan-African leadership, Nigeria is de-termined to keep her own house in order. Political stability should be one of the key attributes contributing to Nigeria's continued economic development.

43.

MARKETING IN SUB-SAHARA AFRICA*

Charles J. Omana

THE South African Negro market (usually referred to as African or Bantu) is the *largest* purchaser of most of the consumer type products which our leading American overseas companies handle. It is also the most sophisticated and the most advanced economically. For this reason many companies commence with the South African Bantu, expanding their African coverage after having gained experience in this market. It is an excellent starting point in a discussion of marketing to the indigenous African. Specific knowledge of the South African Bantu's marketing environment is also important to those marketers interested in the rest of Sub-Sahara Africa. It amounts to approximately 18 per cent of the urban African market. It accounts for an even higher percentage in terms of actual purchasing power.

BACKGROUND

In Africa the whites are called Europeans, the mulattos are called colored, the East Indians are called Asians, and the Negroes are called Africans. There are nearly 4 million Europeans, $1\frac{3}{4}$ million colored, and $\frac{3}{4}$ million Asians living in Sub-Sahara Africa, most of these groups being concentrated in Southern and East Africa. The African segment of the market accounts for 97 per cent of Sub-Sahara Africa's population.

Sub-Sahara Africa covers a land area of approximately 8,300,000 square miles. This is $2\frac{1}{2}$ times the size of the United States. Of its 217,-000,000 people, only 21,000,000 live an *urban* existence (in cities and towns of more than 10,000).

Focusing on the South African portion of the continent, we find a country nearly twice the size of Texas with an area of 472,359 square miles.

* Charles J. Omana, "Marketing in Sub-Sahara Africa," *Marketing and Economic Development,* 1965 Proceedings of the American Marketing Association, pp. 128-139. Reprinted by permission.

South Africa has 16,000,000 people with a diverse racial composition:

Europeans make up 19% of the population
Coloreds (Mulattos)—9%
Asians (Mostly Indians)—3%
Africans—69%

Economy—General

South Africa has a most buoyant economy. Its net national income has more than trebled in the 15-year period, 1948-1963. The European South African with a per capita income of $1,200 a year enjoys one of the highest standards of living in the world.

The urban South African Bantu's per capita income is comparable to several south European countries and exceeds the per capita incomes of the other African countries.

As we know, per capita income figures can be deceptive, for these figures do not take into consideration such items as cost of living indexes, disposable income, etc. While the Europeans have the highest living standards and the Africans the lowest, the Asians and the colored fall somewhere in between.

The African's Role

Though the African accounts for 69 per cent of the South African population, his income represents only 27 per cent of that country's total net national annual income.

It is interesting to note that in 1936 the African's income accounted for 19 per cent of South Africa's national annual income. This means that his income is increasing at a faster rate than the European's.

What about the future? All indications are that the African's earnings and living standards will continue to grow at an *even faster* rate. It is estimated that by 1972 the African's earnings will be nearly three times what they are today.

We can therefore reasonably expect:

a. That the present day's wage earner's salary will increase materially. (The rate of increase today is about 7 per cent a year.)

b. More rural and tribalized Africans will enter the money economy, hence new customers for our goods.

Now let's look at the living and marketing environment of South Africa. Much of what is said here can be applied to the other markets of Sub-Sahara Africa, particularly in the urban areas. The differences would be largely quantitative rather than qualitative.

MARKETING IN SOUTH AFRICA

The largest city in South Africa (in fact, in all of Africa south of the Sahara) is Johannesburg. It has a population of 1,100,000. One South African cigarette advertiser refers to Johannesburg as the biggest growing city in the world. It was founded in the late 19th century. South Africa has four other modern cities and towns with populations exceeding 100,000.

Supermarkets

South Africa's dynamic progress is mirrored in its supermarkets and self-service stores. The country already has 2,000 supermarkets with a predicted growth rate of 400-500 a year.

A glance at the interior of South Africa's supermarkets shows that in-store merchandise in this country is every bit as progressive as it is in the U.S. They don't have to envy us in this regard. There is no color bar in the South African shops, though apartheid applies to the ownership.

European Way of Life

European South Africans live in houses and apartments comparable to what we have in California, Texas, and Florida. (One out of every three persons in this group has a car. Swimming pools abound in the upper and upper middle class homes. I dare say there isn't a group of people anywhere in the world who have a higher standard of living than the European South African.

African Way of Life

What about the 11 million Africans?

  a. Tribal. Four million Africans live a tribal existence in separate homelands far removed from the city environment I have just described. These homelands account for 13 per cent of South Africa's land area. They are occupied by eight distinct ethnic groups or tribes. The

Government's plan is to eventually make these African homelands self governing. One of them already is—the Transkei located on South Africa's east coast (between the cities of Durban and East London).

　　b. Urban and non-urban classification. Of the remaining 7 million Bantu, half live in or near the cities and are classed as urban, while the other half live and work in white man's farms.

　　c. Importance of urban Africans. From a consumer goods marketing point of view, we are mainly concerned with the 3½ million urban Africans. This 30 per cent of the Bantu population controls 60 per cent of the total Bantu buying power. They are westernized to an extent that few other Africans anywhere have become. They are in degree of education, way of life, and general spirit more like American Negroes than they are like their tribal forefathers.

　　Their number is increasing:

> In 1950 28% of nonwhites lived in towns
> In 1960 37% of nonwhites lived in towns
> In 1970 45% of nonwhites predicted to live in towns

　　i. Bantu Earning Power

> 10% skilled $120-225 a month
> 25% semi-skilled $60-$120 a month
> 65% domestics and laborers less than $60 a month

　　It is estimated that subsistence level for an average family (six persons) is $75. If we consider that the average household has two wage earners, very few households would be living at the below-subsistence level. This factor, however, has been questioned, and there is also documentation to the contrary.

　　It is interesting to note that 74 per cent of what is earned above the subsistence level is spent on consumer goods.

　　In fact, you might be curious just how the Bantu spends his money. According to a regional survey which was done by the University of Africa at the end of 1961, the following spending patterns emerged:

Food	40%
Clothing	8%
Housing	10%
Fuel & Light	6%
Personal & Hygiene	5%
Transportation	5%
Medical	1%
Taxes	.7%

About ¼ of income is spent on discretionary items, the more important being:

Alcoholic beverages	4%
Cigarettes	3%
Installments	4.5%

Housing constitutes a mere 10 per cent of his income. That is because the greater part of the housing is subsidized.

ii. Living environment

Seventy per cent of the urban Bantu live in townships or locations which are situated near large cities and towns. The other 30 percent of urban Bantu are domiciled within the city areas in quarters provided by their employees. These are mainly the domestic servants. This figure is going to change as a new law is being enacted which will stipulate that no more than one domestic servant can live in with a European family.

iii. Typical African shops

As mentioned before, the shops in the towns and cities are not segregated. The African is free to do his shopping in the cities and towns or in the township where he lives.

iv. African supermarket development

The development of supermarkets in the African townships is in its infancy. In fact, there is only one supermarket in the Johannesburg township. It is interesting to observe the number of children outside this supermarket, the reason being that most of the shopping in the township is done by children, one very good reason why supermarkets haven't taken hold in the African townships.

v. Mining concessionaires stores

Mining occupies more Africans than any other industry outside of agriculture. Over ½ million are employed in the mines. They enjoy high purchasing power and buy mostly in the mine concessionaire stores.

vi. Pertinent comparisons with other Sub-Sahara Markets

In other parts of Africa, particularly in the West Coast where European influence is not as pronounced, most consumer goods are bought in the open market place, the main figure being the Mammy Trader, who is a combination wholesaler and retailer. Some of these Mammy Traders are quite successful and affluent. There is one in West Africa who has a credit line exceeding 1 million pounds. It is also interesting to note that 90 per cent of the Africans in business in this part of the world are women. The wholesalers in West Africa are generally Syrians and Lebanese, while in East Africa the wholesalers and retailers are usually Indians.

Summary—Living and Sales Environment-South African Market

Up to this point I have endeavored to give you some economic background, as well as a glimpse of the South African living environment and its relation to the market place for packaged consumer goods. You will note that I have emphasized the African segment of the market. From the point of view of relative importance, the emphasis should have been given to the European segment.

However, it doesn't take as much explaining to make you familiar with the European market as it does not differ markedly from our own middle and upper class market in the U.S. The African market, as you have already gathered, is considerably different from any market that exists in the U.S. and a great deal more complex. We are dealing with an alien culture and environment.

ADVERTISING TO THE AFRICAN MARKET

Preface

For this reason it behooves us to take a close look at the African consumer. Let's see what makes him tick, and let's consider what we must do in order to win him over to our products.

Even though the African market is far from being homogeneous, there are denominators common not only to the South African's African market but to the whole of the African market south of the Sahara. My remarks will endeavor to concentrate on these common denominators.

The African Consumer

Let's start with a thumbnail sketch of our prime target: The African consumer. I would describe the average African consumer as very *unsophisticated* and more often than not *illiterate*.

However, he is very quality conscious—to the point of being suspicious! And more important, he is *willing and very able to learn*. This means that he is susceptible, in fact, *very receptive* to advertising.

In other words, give the African a *quality product, priced within* his means, advertise it in a manner which will reach him, and you will *develop* a customer with *an unprecedented degree of brand loyalty*—as Nestles has been able to do with its condensed milk.

However, don't be surprised if the African puts familiar products to a different use than you and I would. In advertising and marketing to the African, one might as well forget standard practices and start from scratch. *If there was ever a case for adaptability and flexibility, this is it!*

The Advertising Approach

How do we reach this market? What *appeals* shall we use? What *pitfalls* must we avoid?

a. The Basic Premise (Be simple and direct)

First of all, I would like to stress that the approach must be *simple* and *direct*. While this is a *desirable* principle to follow in the U.S., it is an *essential* one for Africa, for what can be considered simple in America can be interpreted as complicated in Africa.

b. Illustration and Art Work

i. Simplicity

Let's first consider the illustration of the advertisement.

I would say that one of the first *rules* would be to avoid ABSTRACTIONS. In other words, do what I just said: KEEP IT SIMPLE.

ii. Avoid the use of perspective

What would you say this picture represents? (Slide projection.)

It appears to me to be a caricature of two lions a short distance apart. That is the way *we* see it, for we are familiar with the principle of perspective. We are able to perceive a third dimension—depth—on a two-dimensional flat surface.

The African, on the other hand, has not yet mastered the principle of perspective. He sees the illustration in only two dimensions. He sees a large and a small lion. However, we shouldn't be too critical. We didn't master perspective until the fifteenth century with the advent of the Italian Renaissance.

iii. Avoid a "Before and After" approach

Besides abstractions and perspective we should avoid the *"before and after"* illustration, for the African in his singularly logical way reasons that no one can be in two places at the same time; therefore, these two people who *look a little different* must be somebody and "his brother." The entire intent of the advertisement would therefore be lost.

c. Copy

i. Avoid alliteration

What about copy? Again we should strive for simplicity. For example, we should avoid the use of alliteration. You know, stuff like that dog food commercial that says, "It's might, it's meaty, it's mighty mighty meaty!" It falls flat to African ears.

ii. Avoid inferences

We should also *avoid commercials which proceed at too fast a pace* and which *jump* from one situation to another. The average African cannot follow them, as he does not possess the same mental shorthand we do. That is why many American and European commercials have not succeeded with the African.

iii. Be mindful of standards of values

We should avoid approaches which would be *foreign* to their standard of values. For instance, the "keeping up with the Joneses" approach would be difficult for the African to comprehend.

iv. Be aware of cultural patterns

We should be aware of their *cultural patterns.* Take as an example the status of women. African men regard their women as chattels; therefore, *it would not be wise to appeal solely to women in advertisements,* for it is the man who approves of the purchase. This situation, however, is changing.

d. Positive Aspects

I have given you some examples where the African's background and habits make our selling and advertising job more difficult. There are also instances where it can help.

i. Established Habits

One case in point is in the sale and promotion of toothpaste and toothbrushes. Africans have appreciated white teeth for generations, and their use of *rubbing sticks* probably goes back further than the Europeans' toothbrushing habits.

ii. Use of totems and symbols

Use of animals is something which advertisers rely heavily upon in Africa, for they *symbolize important intangibles and values associated with everyday African life.* Among the more popular and generally recognizable symbols with the Bantu tribes of Southern and Central Africa are the lion, the leopard, and the elephant, for they represent *strength and vitality,* a subject which I will cover in a moment.

An example of a product which successfully makes use of the lion symbol is the Rhodesian beer—Lion Lager. This press campaign, which incidentally makes excellent use of a second color, ran for three years. During that period the market share for this beer increased from 5 per cent to 48 per cent.

From what I have said so far, you would think that all this stress on simplicity and directness would take away much of the need for creativity and cleverness. Does it really? Perhaps in Africa the really clever thing to do is *not* to appear to be clever!

Let's now examine some of the main considerations which should be taken into account when planning a creative strategy in Africa.

Formulating the Creative Strategy

A. The African's Main Preoccupation

The lion, like the leopard and other similar animals, is a symbol of strength, and therefore, you see its frequent use in African advertising. *Why?*

The African is overly preoccupied with *health, strength, and vitality,* which is commonly conveyed by the word "power." This emphasis on "power" can be compared to the widespread *use of sex in our U.S. advertising.* In order to appreciate this ad, one must realize that the African does not regard sex in the same way as the Western. Pin-ups and similar symbols have no meaning for him. Furthermore, his interpretation of sex does not include the undertones of piety and self-sacrifice that are an ingrained part of our culture's mores. The African does not link sex with responsibility. Plainly speaking, sex to the African is the satisfying of an appetite and nothing more; therefore, the African advertiser would be wise to limit his use of the sex theme to the health, strength, and vitality approach.

B. Special Approach to the African?

i. Success of Glenryk's Canned Fish

Let's take as a case in point Glenryk's Canned Fish, for their advertising campaign is now a classic. Prior to the campaign the sale of canned fish to the Africans in South Africa was virtually nil, and the chances for getting the African away from his traditional corn meal diet seemed very slim. Today you will find Glenryk's canned fish widely sold in the African stores of South Africa. You can't help noticing it—Glenryk's canned fish stands out like a neon light on the African grocers' shelves.

ii. Rationale

How far should we go in developing a special African approach? This is one of those subjects to which there are many answers and opinions. First, we must keep in mind that the African is extremely conscious and aware of his having been exploited and fooled by unscrupulous advertisers. *Therefore, one of his reactions is to reject products which he feels have been specifically created for him.*

iii. The "white" image is essential

It is therefore important that the advertiser convey the idea that the product being advertised is popular with the European population as well. This is fairly easy to do in parts of Africa with a large

European population, for there are usually available media which reach both races, South Africa being a prime example. However, for a product to attain this essential "white man's image" in areas where the European population is negligible, such as in West Africa, will require the creation of a special atmosphere. The use of an American, European, or even a *worldwide* backdrop showing *whites using the product,* is one way of handling the problem.

Another excellent way to convey a "white man's product" image is to show the product being used by Africans in ultra-sophisticated Western-world backdrops. The use of an African personality who has been accepted and acclaimed by the white world can also be employed to good advantage.

iv. White image for "blacks only" products

How about products that are obviously for Africans only—for example, a skin whitener or a hair straightener? Can and should they too be given a "white man's image"? My feeling is that they should.

Many successful advertisers achieve this by running ads in newspapers and magazines that cater to Europeans but also have a substantially large African readership. These ads feature European models using the essentially African products. Later on in the campaign, ads are placed in African media, and African models are utilized.

v. Alternatives

How would you tackle the problem? A lot of course would depend on your product and the particular African market involved.

a. Elimination of models

For instance, you might be one of those who would skirt the use of models altogether, as was recently done by one of the four successful beer companies.

b. Similar ads

Or you might wish to run identical or similar ads, one showing African models and the other showing Europeans, making sure that the Africans would see both ads. This strategy, through outdoor media, left no doubt in one's mind that Castle Beer is for Europeans as well as Africans. The same tactic was used by a competitor, Lion Export Beer, except the medium used was press.

c. Use of white models

Perhaps you might want to emulate South Africa's most successful cigarette manufacturer, Anton Rupert. His cigarettes virtually control the market. He uses only European models.

C. Package Design and Size

i. Minimize charges

The redesigning and changing of a successful product's package is at times highly desirable in this country. However, it should be studiously avoided in Africa. Quite often the African has been sold inferior goods in a package very similar in appearance to an established quality product. For this reason the African looks at even the most *minute* deviation in package or design with suspicion.

If a manufacturer feels that he has to change his package, he should first *test it*, or he may risk losing a sizeable share of market.

ii. Size

I mentioned earlier that the African is an excellent judge of quality. Therefore, it makes good marketing sense to avoid selling him inferior merchandise. However, his purchasing power is low. What is the solution to this dilemma? Market *low-cost, small-size units*. This is precisely what we have done with our dentifrices and deodorants in Africa.

D. Influences and Expectations

While the African can generally be described as *unsophisticated,* he certainly cannot be considered uncomplicated. He is subject to many influences and preoccupations, which must be taken into account when formulating brand and copy strategies.

i. Money and power

A major preoccupation is money. However, he does not want money for its own sake but rather because he believes it to be a source of power. Power is something he craves, for he has been subjugated for too long a time. In looking at his European bosses and the way they live, he has come to the conclusion that they obtained power because they have earned and saved money. I am sure that this is one of the reasons why the banks are such heavy advertisers. They are very wisely taking advantage of a tailor-made opportunity.

ii. Education

The African's craving for power is also behind a virtually insatiable thirst for education. He does not look to education as an end in inself but rather as a means of earning more money, which, in turn, will mean more power. If you would pick up an issue of any of Africa's leading magazines, you would be likely to find several advertisements for correspondence schools.

iii. Future and success (American example)

Another strong influence in the African's life is his respect for things American, for America symbolizes a way and manner of life toward which he is striving. Advertisers, both local and foreign, take advantage of this fact. It is not uncommon to hear American accents and see American spelling to advertise products.

F. Languages

The multiplicity of languages in Africa adds to the mounting list of variables facing the African advertiser. As I mentioned earlier, there are nearly 100 languages and dialects in Sub-Sahara Africa. Obviously, it would not be practical to advertise in all of them. However, in order to reach the markets which we are after, we have to consider advertising in the main languages, such as Hausa in West Africa; Swahili in East Africa; Susoto, Zulu, and Xhosa in South Africa; not to mention Hindi and Guarati, spoken by the East Indians who form an important and affluent segment of the populations of East and South Africa.

G. Unconventional Media

For the most part, my remarks dealing with a special approach to the African have been in the area of what we consider mass media—press, radio, T. V., cinema, and outdoor advertising. *However, in Africa concentration in these media is usually not enough.* There are other media which are more important because it is considerably harder to reach the African consumer by conventional means, high illiteracy rates and geographical inaccessibility being prime factors. Hence, in Africa we rely heavily on sound trucks, roving movie vans, sampling, promotional teams, and contests.

i. Sound trucks and roving movie vans

The sound truck is by far the number-one medium in Sub-Sahara Africa with the exception of South Africa, where they are not permitted. These vehicles are expensive but most effective in getting the advertising story across, particularly when a new product is involved. Some sound trucks are outfitted with film projectors and offer regular movies and live entertainment in addition to advertising. This operation is not too different from the roving medicine man shows that were popular in this country during the latter part of the last century.

ii. Sampling

These vehicles also offer a springboard to other important forms of advertising and promotion; for instance, sampling, which is the most effective method of introducing and increasing the usage of many products.

iii. Promotion teams

Then there are sales promotion teams, which consist of trained propagandists stationed in special booths outside retail outlets. They demonstrate and extol the benefits of the product they are selling or describe and promote a special offer.

iv. Contests

And finally there are contests. This form of promotion is particularly successful with Africans with entries running as high as 25 per cent of the total readership employed. In order to be successful, contest rules should be simple, and a large number of prizes (of a useful nature) should be offered rather than a few extremely valuable ones. Simplicity is rule #1 as far as contests to the African are concerned.

44.

THE ROLE OF MARKETING IN ISRAEL*

Yoram Wind

IN many of the underdeveloped economies, marketing is sorely neglected. Indeed, "it is generally the most backward of all areas of economic life."[1]

The emerging nations can gain great advantages, however, from seeking, above all, to please and satisfy the consumer. In some countries marketing is receiving considerable and increasing attention; this is especially true of the State of Israel.

In 1964, U.S. exports to Israel amounted to about $200 million, one-fourth of Israel's total imports. Clearly, however, the relative smallness of the Israeli market makes it of only limited interest to American exporters. Israel moved from an "underdeveloped" stage of around $400 per capita Net National Product at factor cost in the early 1950s to a "middling-European" level of $934 per capita NNP in 1964—a year with a GNP per capita in Israel of about $1,130. Israel's transition from the underdeveloped to the present modern marketing-oriented economy took only about one decade.

In the early 1950s Israel's marketing system was more selling-oriented than marketing-oriented. The retail outlets could have sold almost anything, even though the channels of distribution were inefficient and the products of low quality. Almost no promotional activities existed, nor marketing research, and no official regulations governed either restraints of trade or deceptive marketing practices.

Yet ten years later Israel could be described as a quasi-modern, marketing-oriented economy, and with a quasi-capitalistic value system.

THE NATION

The 8,000 square miles of Israel, approximately the area of New Jersey, contain over $2\frac{1}{2}$ million people, 75% of them under 30 years of age.[2]

* Yoram Wind, "The Role of Marketing in Israel," *Journal of Marketing*, Vol. 31, No. 2 (April 1967), a publication of the American Marketing Association, pp. 53-57. Reprinted by permission.

[1] Peter F. Drucker, "Marketing and Economic Development," *Journal of Marketing*, Vol. 22 (January, 1958), pp. 252-259, at p. 252.

[2] *Facts About Israel,* Israel Ministry for Foreign Affairs, 1964-65, at p. 41.

About 85% of the Jews and 37% of the 11% non-Jewish population reside in the 65 urban settlements. This urban-rural ratio is similar to that of the western countries—69.9% of the total United States population in 1960 was classified as urban,[3] and represents quite a different pattern from the "typical" underdeveloped country.

Both the small size of the nation and the urban concentration facilitate marketing activities. Transportation by rail, and more particularly by road, is efficient (even though far below road-standards in the United States).

Newness is everywhere. Many towns are planned from their inception as part of the "New Development." Typically, they have central shopping centers surrounded by residential and industrial areas. Differing sharply from their U.S. counterparts, these centers contain small specialty stores which provide standard goods rather than luxuries. In comparison with U.S. shopping centers, they do not feature a central department store, and they are much smaller.

More than one-third of the people live in the three principal cities: Tel Aviv, Jerusalem, and Haifa. The trend has been away from mixed residential and commercial areas toward a centralization of commercial activities in the "downtown" districts, and an outward dispersion of purely residential districts. With improved private and public transportation and rising levels of living, high-income suburbs are being developed, even in the smaller towns.

THE ECONOMY

Israel now supplies most of its own needs for foodstuffs. Local foods are generally of high quality, plentiful, and cheap.

The greater part of the demand for furniture and furnishings is met by local production. Refrigerators and other household appliances are also locally produced. To encourage local production, taxes and duties are high.

Clothing, textiles, and footwear are highly-developed industries, and account for more than one-sixth of industrial output.

Imports have been necessary to feed, house, and employ the large number of immigrants (about 1¼ million from 1948 to date), and to provide raw materials and essential equipment for industry and agriculture. In 1949 the returns from exports amounted to only 15% of the cost of imports and services. By 1963, however, the percentage had risen to 52%. Changes in types of imports are indicated in Table 1.

Despite few natural resources, the average rate of growth of the Gross

[3] *Statistical Abstract of the United States* (Washington, D.C.: United States Department of Commerce, Bureau of the Census, 1965), at p.15.

TABLE 1—ANALYSIS OF ISRAEL IMPORTS BY DESTINATION[a]

Form of imports	1952		1965	
	in U.S. $ (millions)	In %	in U.S. $ (millions)	In %
Total imports	576.4	100.0	819.7	100.0
Consumer goods	324.0	56.2	83.9	9.4
Raw materials for production	185.0	32.1	554.6	66.3
Investment	67.4	11.7	181.2	24.3

[a]Sources: For 1952: *Statistical Abstract of Israel* (Central Bureau of Statistics, 1964). For 1965: *Review of Economic Conditions in Israel* (Bank Leumi Le-Israel B.M., No. 54, July, 1966).

National Product has been approximately 10% annually since 1950. About 25% of the rate can be ascribed to higher inputs of labor, 35% to more capital, and the remaining 40% to increase in over-all efficiency.[4] This growth has been achieved by a mixture of governmental and private enterprise, heavily supported by foreign aid. In 1964, for example, imports were 38% of the GNP.

Approximately 20% of all industrial undertakings are government-owned, 15% represent cooperative ventures, and 65% are privately-owned. Over 80% of the agricultural sector, on the other hand, is owned cooperatively or collectively.

But there has been inflation, and a number of official devaluations of the Israeli pound. The last one was in February, 1962, when the pound was devalued from IL 1.80 (= US$ 1.00) to IL 3.00 (= US$ 1.00). Price-levels rose by 9.5% in 1962, but by only 6.6% in 1963 and by only 5.0% in 1964.

THE CONSUMER

The total real disposable income of Israeli consumers has increased steadily, despite the continued rise in the cost of living. Per capita disposable income rose from IL 1.645 in 1960 to IL 2.820 in 1964.[5]

Income levels are widely dispersed over the various segments of population, mostly due to education and occupation differences. Improvements in the living standards are indicated in Table 2.

The heterogeneity of the population makes a single profile of the typical Israeli consumer difficult. But it can be said that in 1964 89% of

[4] A. Hovne, *The Economy of Israel*, "Israel Today Series," No. 23 (Jerusalem: October, 1965), p. 12.

[5] Figures based on data from *Bank of Israel Annual Report, 1964*, Hebrew edition (Jerusalem: May, 1965), p. 25.

TABLE 2—THE COMPOSITION OF CONSUMER
EXPENDITURES[a] (At Current Prices as
Percentages of Total Expenditures)

	1956–57	1963–64
Food	47.3%	35.7%
Housing	9.1	8.3
Clothing and footwear	13.9	11.4
Furniture and household appliances	5.6	10.8
Health, education, and entertainment	12.0	16.2
Cigarettes, transportation, and personal services	9.4	15.6
Donations and subscriptions to organizations, etc.	2.7	2.0
Total	100.0	100.0

[a] Source: *Bank of Israel Annual Report, 1964* (Hebrew Edition), at p. 58.

Israeli homes had radios; 85%, stoves or hot plates; and 69%, electric refrigerators. Also, 27% of the homes had washing machines, 24% two radios, 14% electric-mixers, and 10% vacuum cleaners. But only 7% of the families owned private automobiles.[6]

The majority of lower-income homes have very few durables other than a radio, stove or hot plate, and a refrigerator.

CHANNELS OF DISTRIBUTION

The majority of local producers and importers utilize wholesalers, independent agents, and/or their own sales force to distribute their goods through retailers. A few prefer to sell directly to consumers, either through their own retail outlets or through a sales department within the plant.

The Wholesaling Function

In 1961 only about 13% of the total volume of trade was sold through the 1,500 wholesalers.[7] Of these, 1,100 operated stores or warehouses, while

[6] *Bank of Israel Annual Report, 1964,* Hebrew edition (Jerusalem: May, 1965), p. 63.
[7] Akiva Ilan, "Wholesaling in Israel," in Robert Bartels, Editor, *Comparative Marketing: Wholesaling in Fifteen Countries* (Homewood, Illinois: Richard D. Irwin, Inc., 1963), pp. 106-122.

400 were truck-jobbers. Of the 1,100 about 650 were in the grocery business, 100 in small housewares and kitchenwares, and the remainder in paper, textiles, and toys.

As with the general pattern of industry, so with wholesaling—a few large organizations account for approximately 45% of the total volume handled by wholesalers. Some of these companies are also importers and have integrated vertically until they either own or control their own manufacturing plants and retail establishments. Most of the large wholesalers are general merchants, whereas the small organizations specialize within one or two allied product groups and operate regionally rather than nationally. The truck-jobbers in the produce-market serve the small retailers, but other jobbers trade in any product which appears to be profitable. They sell for cash and deal largely in the cheaper, unbranded lines of merchandise.

The larger manufacturers bypass the wholesaler in order to achieve greater control and market penetration. As may be seen in the United States, however, they often use wholesalers to reach the smaller, more remote stores that their other channels cannot serve economically.

Independent agents, who are the primary channels in some industries such as the garment industry, provide some wholesaling functions. They furnish the marketing functions of selling, collection, and market "feedback," but not the warehousing and credit functions.

The Retailing Function

Vending machines and mail-order houses do not exist in Israel; and door-to-door selling accounts for only an insignificant share of sales. The largest proportions of goods of all types are retailed through specialized stores—clothing stores, appliance stores, furniture stores, butcher shops, automobile dealers, hardware stores, and so on.

Nonfood Outlets. Most sales are through the estimated 20,000 to 25,-000 privately-owned specialty stores. Filling stations are smaller and fewer than in the United States, with competition among the four gasoline companies essentially nonprice in nature. Department stores are found only in the three major cities; they are more similar to Woolworth's than Macy's, but have fewer departments and a more limited offering of goods than either. The only exception is a new store in Tel-Aviv that resembles U.S. department stores in size and line of merchandizing. Department stores and specialty stores extend credit to customers, usually for 30 to 90 days.

In Israel, two department-store chains are of real importance. One operates approximately 15 stores and is part of the collective sector of the economy, while the other, similar to a U.S. Army PX, is owned and controlled by the Ministry of Defense.

In the smaller towns, small general stores stock a limited range of a large number of products. These stores are similar to those in smaller rural communities elsewhere.

Discount stores, as known in the United States, do not exist in Israel. Peddlers and small street stalls are still common, but mainly for low-quality low-unit-cost items.

Food Retailing. In 1957, the first supermarket in Israel was established by a company headed by C. R. Bronfmans, President of the House of Seagram. Today this company (Supersol, Ltd.) operates ten supermarkets, with meat and produce departments as well as dry groceries, but few nonfood items.

In the late 1950s, the cooperative movement resulted in a number of self-service grocery stores being established, replacing some of the traditional cooperative stores ("Tzarchanioth") of the larger cities. Israeli supermarkets do not offer credit, but they do provide free home-delivery. For improvement of their facilities and appearance, the Ministry of Commerce and Industry has made loans available to the small stores—there are approximately 6,000 of them in Israel.

Many food products are sold through small food stores specializing in one or two lines. Meat is sold through small, privately-owned butcher shops, and virtually all fruits and vegetables through special stores which buy produce directly from the wholesale market or from jobber-truckers. "Delicates," similar to American delicatessens, are found in the main cities.

The consumers' cooperative movement controls a large segment of the food-retailing business and is the largest single retail organization in Israel. The food markets in the cities and towns mainly are selling produce, but also have some other food items. In general, they cater to those with low and middle incomes, and their prices are lower than the neighborhood grocery stores. Home-delivery is virtually restricted to milk, although in some areas neighboring farmers sell their produce, mainly eggs, on a door-to-door basis.

Resale price-maintenance exists basically by private surveillance in some industries. It is important in the sale of appliances, cigarettes, newspapers, and magazines. Attempts to maintain resale prices for food products failed.

Private-label merchandise is found in the top-quality stores and supermarkets, but is not nearly so prevalent as in the United States. Trading stamps were introduced in 1964 in both food and nonfood retailing; but because of retailer resistance not very successfully. Self-service in nonfood retailing has not been successful either, largely because of the dependence of consumers on the sales staff for guidance and advice. Few stores of any kind are air-conditioned, showroom and window displays are few, and parking facilities are very seldom provided; but improvements are being made.

ADVERTISING AND PROMOTION

Total advertising expenditures in Israel in 1964 were about IL 45 million (= US$ 15 million).[8] Annual per capita advertising expenses in Israel are just over $5, as compared with $65 per capita for the United States, $35 for Canada, and $25 for Great Britain.

Israel has no television, and of the two radio stations owned by the government, only one carries commercials. The great influx of migrants from virtually every nation of the world has led to a proliferation of newspapers and magazines. Yet only 15 of the 25 daily newspapers in Israel are in Hebrew, the most commonly used language. Because of the language-ethnic segmentation of the market, a company advertising convenience-type products to the total market must use several different newspapers, magazines, and periodicals.

Israel has no drive-in theaters, but there are approximately 270 standard theaters with a capacity of around 160,000 seats. On the average, each person aged 15 and above attends the cinema 24 times a year.[9] Movie-goers are exposed to extensive advertising in the form of slides and short commercial films.

Of the 116 advertising agencies in Israel, all Israeli-owned, about 20 offer and are capable of providing the full range of advertising services normally expected of U.S. agencies, including advertising research and public relations.[10]

MARKETING RESEARCH

The amount of marketing research of a commercial nature is limited, because management still concentrates primarily on production.

Even those who stress marketing do not generally recognize the importance of marketing research, and rely heavily on judgment only and indirect informal feedback from consumers and other channels of information. There is a scarcity of skilled marketing research personnel. However, marketing research is facilitated by numerous reports issued by government agencies, particularly the Central Bureau of Statistics.

8 *Advertising Investments Around the World* (New York: International Advertising Association, 1965), p. 11.

9 *Statistical Abstract of Israel.* (Jerusalem: Israel Central Bureau of Statistics, 1964, No. 15) p. 565.

10 Same reference as footnote 8.

GOVERNMENT REGULATION

One of the major reasons for the rapid development of the Israeli economy has been the government's attitude toward private enterprise.

In marketing, government control is slight. The comprehensive controls of the early days were progressively reduced from 1952 on. The
Cartel Law enables groups of business firms to request approval of marketing arrangements—such as allocation of market territories, conditions
of sale and discount policies, and upper- and lower-price limits.

Credit is a business necessity but is discouraged by the government,
which wants to channel consumers' uncommitted funds toward savings.
Thus, the use of consumer credit is relatively small; and credit cards are
unknown, except for limited operations by a few international credit organizations. The major source of credit is the store itself.

The government exercises considerable influence over the marketplace by its tariff structure, taxation, and policy of encouraging industries
essential to the economy by means of grants, loans, and subsidies. The
Ministry of Commerce and Industry does grant government assistance.
Investment in marketing organizations is recognized as an approved investment; and 5-year development budget loans from up to 50% of the
total investment are granted.

IMPLICATIONS

Israel does not have a typical "underdeveloped" economy, and yet Israel
cannot be considered a "typical" modern economy. This is mainly because
of two factors. (1) Entrepreneurship is relatively lacking, with major segments of the private and corporate sector relying strongly on government
aid. (2) Dependence on foreign assistance continues to be considerable, as
reflected in a large import surplus.

The Israeli experience emphasizes the interdependence of the economic development of a country and the penetration of the marketing
orientation to its socio-economic system.

45.

THE CHANGING MIDDLE EAST MARKET*

Charles F. Stewart

FOR MOST of its history the Middle East has been a commercial cross-roads of the world. It is only since World War II, however, that the region, without abandoning its function of way station, has begun to assume the role of market. The reason is not hard to find. In 1956 the Middle East supplied 23.6 per cent of the free world's 5½ billion barrels of crude oil. Production and transit royalties to governments in the area exceeded one billion dollars, and additional millions were poured into local economies through purchases and wage payments by oil companies.[1]

As for future prospects, it was reported that the Middle East had 74.4 per cent of the free world's proved reserves. The Sheikhdom of Kuwait, less than half the size of Connecticut, alone contained 24 per cent of the total, while the whole United States could claim but 14.7 per cent.[2] Taken by themselves, the figures suggest a market well worth the attention of many firms in foreign trade. The attraction becomes even greater when one considers that, except for oil, there is a relative paucity of local natural resources suitable for manufacturing.

Other factors, however, must be considered in making an appraisal of market potential, and it is the thesis of this article that the more strategic ones generally serve to keep the potential in the Middle East small. Among these factors are (1) market environment; (2) character of demand; (3) product promotion, advertising, and services; (4) nature of competition; and (5) pricing and credit. While there may be differences in detail among the countries covered (Lebanon, Syria, Jordan, Iraq, Saudi Arabia, and Kuwait), there are also striking similarities.

MARKET ENVIRONMENT

When the question of market environment is posed, the foreign trader, in making his assessment, undoubtedly thinks of a host of political, so-

* Charles F. Stewart, "The Changing Middle East Market," *Journal of Marketing*, Vol. 25, No. 3 (January, 1961), a publication of the American Marketing Association, pp. 47-51. Reprinted by permission.

1 *Survey of World Oil* (London: The Financial Times, 1958), pp. 9, 43.

2 Same reference as footnote 1, p. 9.

cial, and economic factors. Since space limitations preclude adequate treatment of all these factors, discussion must be confined—and somewhat arbitrarily—to a very few. Included are the political climate, trade barriers, the trade pattern, and inland transport facilities.

The Political Climate

The Middle East is characterized by frequent political upheavals. (The Suez affair, the Lebanese crisis, and the Iraqi revolution all took place within twenty-one months.) It should be pointed out, however, that political trends move much more slowly than the recurring crises suggest. The foreign trader, consequently, should not lump trends with events, but make his appraisal on the basis of their separate contributions to market environment.

TRADE BARRIERS

The picture concerning trade barriers is mixed. Lebanon has no exchange controls, and its tariff structure is largely a revenue type. In addition, the principal port of Beirut has a thriving free zone which provides excellent storage and processing facilities for goods destined to the local market as well as for those in transit to the hinterland. Kuwait's trade policy is also liberal (the tariff schedule is a flat 4 per cent *ad valorem*), but elsewhere the situation is different.

Syria has developed a protective tariff structure as encouragement to certain local industries, and does not hesitate to impose import licensing and exchange controls whenever deficit wheat and cotton crops threaten the currency. Iraq provides some protection to industry, but less than Syria; exchange problems do not arise in the former since earnings from oil royalties overwhelm the effects of a bad agricultural year. If left alone, Jordan would not be able to sustain even present low levels of living. A chronic problem of payments is alleviated partly by extensive controls but mostly by American aid. In Saudi Arabia, tariffs go as high as 35 per cent; and extravagant public expenditure has recently led to the imposition of exchange controls.

Trade Pattern

The pattern of trade in the Middle East can best be described as nodules of effective demand surrounded by expensively-crossed physical space, much of it desert. All, thirteen in number, are cities, and each is a commercial center and/or capital.

Transportation Facilities

Inland transport is costly, because generally poor. The rail system—with the exception of a relatively short line in Saudi Arabia—is characterized by two gauges (necessitating costly trans-shipment), round-aboutness, antiquated rolling stock, slowness, and large merchandise losses through damage and pilferage.

Highway facilities are not much better—with a few local exceptions. Intraregional truck traffic relies mostly on desert tracks or maintenance roads running alongside oil pipelines. Under these conditions, equipment life is short, and freight charges are correspondingly high. An alternative to rail and truck transport is air shipment, but of course this method remains very expensive.

Trade barriers, the particular trade pattern, and costly transport all serve to narrow markets and, in the case of trade barriers, to direct demand into certain channels. The degree of effectiveness of these factors in a specific case, however, depends not only on the product, but also on the skills of the seller in meeting their challenge. For the skillful seller with the "right" product, trade opportunities remain. To show them requires a closer examination of demand.

CHARACTER OF DEMAND

Despite the oil revenues, a large part of the estimated 20 million people in the area are not yet in the market at all. Distribution of income is extremely skewed, on both a geographical and a personal basis. Oil deposits, for the most part, are located in countries with relatively sparse populations; at the same time, much of the income from oil accrues directly to the ruling class in the capital cities, a class which makes no distinction between personal and public finance. In cases where "conspicuous consumption" and public outlays do not totally absorb income, the balance is found largely in personal bank deposits and portfolio investments abroad. Another concentration of income is found among merchants in the commercial cities who supply the rulers' wants. This helps to account for the pattern of trade described earlier.

Under the circumstances, income filters down very slowly and sets a like pace on the emergence of a non-ruling group with discretionary income. Nevertheless, there is at least one piece of evidence that such a group is appearing. A 1954 survey of Beirut revealed that roughly 30 per cent of the estimated 35,000 families had incomes over $1,500 per year, the amount considered necessary for a minimum of health and decency; 4

per cent of these had incomes over $8,000.[3] Unfortunately, no comparable data are available for other Middle Eastern cities.

To the upper end of income scales throughout the area must be added the foreigners. For example, there are an estimated 2,500 Americans alone in Beirut. In the Persian Gulf, the Arabian-American Oil Company and its associated contractors have approximately 6,500 foreign employees, of whom 2,900 are highly-paid Americans with 3,400 dependents.[4] The Americans are not only a market in themselves; they are also ambassadors of American products through the "demonstration effect."

Product composition, of course, emanates primarily from the pattern of income distribution and tastes. In the Middle East, it is the well-to-do "locals" who make the market for consumer durables—autos and home appliances—and the governments and oil companies which account for the purchases of capital goods. The foreigners, having carried over consumption patterns developed at home, are largely responsible for the sales of imported consumption goods. Purchases by Middle Easterners are increasing, however, especially in Kuwait.

Some idea of the magnitude and composition of purchases from the United States can be gained from representative import figures. Dollar imports of Kuwait in 1956 totaled almost $31 million, of which a little more than $20 million consisted of machinery and vehicles.[5] The value of food products exceeded $3 million. In the same year, Lebanon's imports of U.S. machinery and vehicles reached almost $11 million, out of a total of $35 million.[6] Dollar imports of Syria amounted to $22 million in 1956, with more than half in the category of machinery and vehicles.[7] The importance of oil companies can be shown by referring to the case of Saudi Arabia. Imports totaled $185 million in 1955, and the Arabian-American Oil Company accounted for just short of $63 million, or about one-third.[8]

PRODUCT PROMOTION, ADVERTISING AND SERVICES

Product promotion is confined largely to lotteries in which consumer durables are awarded as prizes. Advertising, barred from government-controlled radio stations, is conducted through the press and movie

[3] Charles W. Churchill, *The City of Beirut, A Socio-Economic Survey* (Beirut: Economic Research Institute, American University of Beirut, 1954), p. 23.

[4] David H. Finnie, *Desert Enterprise: The Middle East Oil Industry in its Local Environment* (Cambridge: Harvard University Press, 1958), pp. 110, 211.

[5] *The Middle East* (London: Europa Publications, 1958), p. 52.

[6] U.S. Department of Commerce, Bureau of Foreign Commerce, *Marketing Potentials in Lebanon* (World Trade Information Service, Part I, No. 58-17), p. 1.

[7] Syrian Republic, *Statistical Abstract of Syria* (Damascus: Ministry of National Economy, 1957) pp. 14, 91.

[8] Same reference as footnote 4, pp. 149-150.

houses. The effectiveness of these latter media is doubtful, and thus they fail to sustain the impact of promotion. The newspaper field is characterized by a host of small dailies, few with circulations more than a couple of thousand. Movie advertising generally takes the form of slides shown at the beginning of the program.

In making promotion and advertising budgets, local businessmen belong to the "all-you-can-afford" school, the appropriation being based on volume of past sales. They are frank to admit that results are unknown.

Undoubtedly more effective than local outlays is advertising in those American periodicals which have a broad circulation in the Middle East. English is read and spoken by a substantial number in the upper classes and by some in the lower ones as well. Although the figures for Beirut undoubtedly represent the extreme case, it is estimated that 22 per cent of the heads of households there are proficient in English.[9]

Large unskilled labor pools mean that services are cheap. Delivery service in food lines is universal, and customers inside the store are also showered with attention. The retailer who opened Lebanon's first "supermarket," for example, supplied not only carts à l'américaine for the shoppers, but also young boys to push them.

Service goods are another story. Dealers in appliances are inclined to assume no responsibility after sale; very few maintain any repair facilities at all. Most auto dealers have repair shops, but these are generally deficient in spare parts. Low sales volume partly accounts for the lack, but so does the practice of rebuilding which, with inexpensive and in the case of automobiles, often skilled labor, is usually cheaper than replacement. Apparently no cost allowance is made for the time that the vehicle is immobilized.

NATURE OF COMPETITION

The nature of competition differs markedly at the three relevant levels in the channel of distribution—the foreign exporter, the importer-wholesaler, and the retailer.

The Foreign Exporter

Americans, relative newcomers in the Middle East market, encounter strong competition from the long-established British and French, but even more from Western Germany and Japan, both well-equipped with up-to-date plant and equipment and with aggressive trade policies. The

---

9 Same reference as footnote 3, p. 9.

most recent arrivals have been from the Soviet Union and certain satellites, particularly Czechoslovakia and Hungary. The eastern countries trade almost exclusively through bilateral agreements with Lebanon, Syria, and Iraq; the fact that, in almost every case, both parties have had difficulty fulfilling the terms suggests that the agreements are more political than economic.

The Importer-Wholesaler

The exclusive agency contract predominates among importers of branded products. Because markets are geographically concentrated, the importer is also likely to do his own wholesaling. Because markets are narrow, he often carries an array whose components have in common only the facts that they are branded and that they usually originate in the same country. Thus, one Lebanese importer is exclusive agent for famous American brands of automobiles, electrical appliances, cosmetics, paints, and drugs. Another in Kuwait has all these and frozen foods too.

The Retailer

Retail distribution is characterized by large numbers of little shops with small capital investments, much imitation, low turnover, high margins, and high mortality. Most food stores possess all these characteristics; many appliance stores do also. Understocking is a feature; an annoying refrain for the newcomer is that the retailer will have the desired item in an hour, a day, or next week. Store layouts are haphazard; there is no stock control; and only the most elementary accounting records are kept. Under these circumstances it is little wonder that a 12-hour day, 7-day week is often necessary for the owner to remain solvent.

Relatively minor exceptions to the above pattern have appeared in food, department, and novelty stores, where one chain in each line has been established. The food chain is British owned, while the department stores are dominated by French interests. The novelty chain, consisting of five units, all located in Lebanon, is owned locally. All have adopted the corporate form, unlike the typical retail operation which is family owned and operated. None has been successfully duplicated thus far.

PRICING AND CREDIT

In pricing and credit, the Middle East picture is a hybrid of western and traditional practices; this is especially so in the case of pricing.

Pricing

If Middle East governments have produced little thus far by way of higher living levels for the masses, they have taken some steps to make their poverty less odious. Among these is price control of certain items in common use. Often included are kerosene, flour, sugar, salt, rice, and meat. Government purchases of capital goods are on a bid basis, and the same generally holds true for the oil companies.

Where merchants have price freedom, practices vary from American-style fixed prices (the three chains follow this system), to oriental-style haggling. Both types may occur in stores within the same block and for the same goods. Discounts are never advertised, and there is no open price competition. One Lebanese retailer in photographic supplies, impressed by the successful price cutting of Paris's "Mister Twenty Per Cent,"[10] toyed with the idea of becoming his Middle Eastern counterpart, but lost his nerve at the last minute. In the jargon, he felt that, in moving big-ticket items such as cameras, demand was price inelastic.

Credit

Competition in credit extension is found in dealings between foreign firms and importers. The Europeans, many of whom have government support, extend credit anywhere from three months to a year on consumer goods, and up to three years or more on industrial equipment. The Americans are far behind in this respect, since it is the practice of most to ask for cash against documents, if not with order.

At the retail level, credit extension by food stores is almost universal, and is certainly an important reason for high gross margins. Consumer durable financing, on the other hand, is not well developed. Liquidity-conscious bankers, without the support of strong central banks, are reluctant to finance anything other than imports on short term. Merchants are consequently limited to their own financial capacity and to the small amount of paper they are able to discount with commercial banks. There is no direct consumer financing by banks, and there are no commercial credit companies.

CONCLUSIONS

The Middle East market is much narrower than the figures for oil revenues would suggest. Barring a broader distribution of this income

[10] Gilbert Burck, "The Transformation of European Business," *Fortune,* Vol. 56 (November, 1957), p. 151.

through radical political change, hopes for a larger market must come from development programs. Land reform and rural improvement projects are under way in Syria and Iraq, which should eventually have favorable income effects in those countries. Highway construction and port improvements (Syria, Iraq, Jordan, Saudi Arabia, and Kuwait) can also be expected to make their contribution through reducing delivered costs.

The fact that the market is increasing only slowly probably accounts for the persistence of distributive methods developed for another age and for the continued concentration of many disparate lines in the hands of a single agent, with the consequent lack of attention that each requires. The absence of strong central banks is responsible, at least in part, for the dearth of consumer credit.

All of this adds up to a small market; but a small market is not necessarily a negligible one. For the marketing man whose product falls into the category of consumer durables or capital goods, the Middle East market may well be worth investigating, with caution.

BEHIND THE IRON CURTAIN

46.

MARKETS BEHIND THE IRON CURTAIN*

Berend H. Feddersen

PRIORITY LIST

IN the Communist planned-economy systems, some products are considered more important than others. Government planning committees decide which products have priority over others, that is, which products should be produced and offered to their people. There is a demand for many products; the Russian, Polish, Hungarian, and other Eastbloc trade presses write regularly about serious shortages. If such shortages were reported in the Western trade press, the news would be seen immediately as providing business opportunities.

Some representative examples of shortages described in Eastern trade journals and technical magazines follow:

In the November, 1965, edition of *Kautschuk i Resina* (Natural and Synthetic Rubber), Machorcht and others report on "Some Results of the Activities of the Rubber Industry in 1964." This sentence appeared in the middle of the article: "Because of the lack of caoutchouc, soot, and technical fibers the production of many rubber-made technical articles is heavily blocked."

A few weeks later, there was another hint concerning the same problem. In the edition of the Russian trade journal *Planned Economy* of February, 1966, page 5 and following, W. Bibichew in "Problems of the Chemical Industry" pointed out difficulties with nearly the same words: "Due to the lack of caoutchouc, soot, and technical fibers the production of rubber-made articles is blocked."

Another example: "In the *Economic Revue,* No. 8/1966, page 17 and following, W. Dykin discusses a specific cotton blend in Russia and its problems: "For 1966 there is a demand for 5,200 kilos of bright orange

* Berend H. Feddersen, "Markets Behind the Iron Curtain," Journal of Marketing, Vol. 31, No. 3 (July 1967), a publication of the American Marketing Association, pp. 1-5. Reprinted by permission.

dye. But the Moscow chemical plant Derbenewo is able to supply only 1,200 kilos. Although 20,000 kilos of Bordeaux-colored dye are needed, the supply amounts to only 5,000 kilos." This description of shortages continues.

Do the above paragraphs mean that markets are available for these products? Not at all. No matter how great the demand and how serious the need is for a certain product, the product will not be imported if the planning commission has decided that other products are of greater importance to the economy. Imports must be carefully selected, as the Eastern countries are quite short of Western currency.

So the first advice to any businessman interested in doing business with the Eastbloc is to find out the position of his product or product category on the priority list. Lack of this information has been extremely costly to hundreds of Western companies that showed their products at various Eastbloc fairs and that were bitterly disappointed because they did not "make their sales" in spite of the interest shown in their products.

A number of Western companies do a great deal of business with Communist countries. These companies include well-known firms such as Krupp, Montecatini, and Imperial Chemical Industries as well as new and unknown companies whose business with these countries accounts for 50% and more of their total exports.

The amount of goods exported by the Western countries to the Eastbloc is, of course, rather small compared to total exports. In 1965, only 3.5% of German exports went to Eastbloc countries, but 3.5% meant 2.7 billion Deutsche Marks ($680,400,000). This is a sizable amount considering that only a limited number of companies participated. How did they do it? Is there a closely-guarded secret way to sell to the Eastbloc countries? The answer is no. But trading with the Communist countries required experience, understanding, and careful study of the market situation. Some companies have the advantage of a long historical background of trading with the East. Before World War II, 15.3% of Germany's export business was with the now Communist countries. However, there are some progressive companies in Germany, as well as in Great Britain, France, and Italy, that did not sell to the Communist countries before the War and who now export part of their products to the Communist world. These firms collected their information and studied market opportunities the same way that any other company could have.

EASIER ACCESS TO FACTS

For many years it was almost impossible to obtain exact market information from the Communist world. Now there *are* sources open to everybody. If most Western companies have not done any marketing research in these countries, the chief reason has undoubtedly been that they believed they could not collect economic or technical information from the Communist countries that was useful and reliable for planning. There are, of course, no available facts about strategic goods. But, in all other fields, a Western company today can get practically all information needed to plan economic contacts with the different Communist nations. It is necessary to be prepared with all vital facts in advance because the Eastbloc officials usually know exactly what is happening in Western business circles.

One example of how much conditions have changed is seen in this anecdote: Until recently, production and consumption of diamonds was one of the best-hidden secrets of the Soviet economy. The Soviet Union (in capitalistic manner) sold its surplus of diamonds to the Western World through the De Beer's Syndicate in London. When their contract expired, and it seemed as though the Soviet Union would sell the surplus of diamonds directly to the West, nobody knew whether the prices on the diamond market would be affected. How great was Soviet production? How big was their surplus? Was this perhaps the beginning of an export offensive? The answers to these questions were found "hidden" in various articles in the technical journals of the Soviet Union.

Although many companies in the Western world believe it is nearly impossible to get reliable information about Eastbloc economies, their problems, and their needs, the contrary is true. A market researcher can collect the same sort of information from these economies as he collects before launching a business offensive in any Western market. This will come as a surprise to many businessmen, but the researcher can get more and better information from published official sources in the Communist countries than he can get in most other countries in the world.

ANALYZING THE MARKET

The procedure for analyzing markets behind the Iron Curtain must be different from the procedure used in the Western countries. Six successive questions must be answered in every market study of the Communist countries.

National Product Goals

What plans have been set up by the planning commission for a given product for the next five years or so? What is the goal? How many units or tons have to be produced in what period?

Production Plans

In what way is the demand for this product going to be satisfied? That is, what are the production plans?

National Industry Capability

Is the industry of the country able to supply the planned amount of the product without outside help?

Competition from Other Communist Countries

Can another Communist country supply the needed product? (If there is a difference between amount of production planned and ability to produce, a Western company cannot necessarily step in and furnish the balance. The potential supply for a given product in all other COMECON countries must be considered. Before importing a product from a non-communist country, a Communist country first tries to fill the gap from other Communist countries.)

Position on Priority List

If there really is a difference between planned production and actual production, and if no other COMECON country can supply the product, the researcher next must find out the position of a given product or product category on the list of priorities established by the planning commission. There is no chance for a Western company to get an export contract, if the product occupies a rather low position which, for instance, is true for all consumer goods. But if the product ranks high on the priority list, it must be imported from non-communist countries.

Specifications

Finally, what are the exact quantities needed, what quality or qualifications are preferred, and what conditions are most acceptable?

POSSIBLE COMPETITORS

One of the problems stemming from the planned-economy system is that one factory or industry that completes its plan suddenly may have a surplus because the factory or industry needing this product did not meet its quota. The result will be that one of the Eastbloc countries will try to sell surpluses to non-communist countries, hoping to get the necessary currency to import goods. This has happened and has caused serious trouble for Western companies. The Eastbloc countries should be regarded not only as future clients but also as possible competitors, and Western firms should analyze the Eastbloc markets from this viewpoint. The oil industry, for example, has made such a study.

SOURCES OF INFORMATION

This article excludes all official regulations, embargo lists, or other business limitations imposed by Western governments for political reasons.

There are three major sources of useful information. First statistical yearbooks and statistical journals are published regularly by the Eastbloc governments. Second, there are hundreds of trade journals and highly-specialized technical papers. The third source consists of the excellent monographs and technical books published in ever-growing numbers for different industries.

Can anyone obtain all these sources of information? The answer is a definite *yes*. A Western company, without difficulty, can subscribe to statistical journals or technical papers dealing with production lines from any Communist country (with perhaps the exception of the Chinese world). An order for a monograph or technical book will usually be filled more quickly than an order for, say, a Spanish book. It should arrive in three or four weeks from date of the order.

One should first study the statistical yearbooks and statistical journals to find out how much is being produced and how production has developed in recent years. Unfortunately, except for the Polish and Hungarian data, these figures are so inadequately recorded that this source of information does not provide detailed analyses. Nevertheless, these data do provide quick and easy-to-get first general reviews.

The trade press and the technical journals are numerous. The articles are of high caliber and can well be compared with those of the West.

Reliability of Sources

It is often said that the information published in the trade press of COMECON countries is full of propaganda, that it is written to show the superiority of the Communist system. There are, of course, many publications that are entirely Communist propaganda, written for the non-communist world or for the simple Soviet citizen. But there is no propaganda at all in the technical and scientific journals, in the trade press, and in the monographs or technical books. These are written by experts for experts. The language of technicians, plant managers, and scientists is not the language of politicians.

There is a surprisingly large number of different technical journals in every area. Each journal deals with only one part of an industry, and there is little overlapping of readership. The problems of the chemical industry are the subject of some 50 different journals. There are eight different journals for the petrochemical industry alone. Added to these are the special journals published by universities.

One of the eight petrochemical journals covers only the problems of plastic production. The problems of plastic manufacturing are dealt with in another publication. One deals with the problems of fiber production; the problems of fiber manufacturing are the subject of still another publication. These articles are written on an extraordinarily high technical or scientific level. As they are written by Eastbloc experts for other Eastbloc experts, they are completely outspoken in their discussion of techniques, problems, and production capacities.

In the Polish trade journal *Review of the Candy and Sugar Industry,* February, 1966, Henrik Podsiadly discusses the "technical progress of the baking industry." In this article, the ten plants that produce machinery for the baking industry are mentioned as well as their capacities, type of machinery produced, production plan up to 1970, and problems of production. He says, "Although the production of this type of machinery could be improved greatly, the demand could not be fully satisfied. Imports will be necessary in 1966." According to the author, machinery for the baking industry for 15 million sloty ($3,750,000) would be imported in 1966, one-third from Western countries.

In the Soviet trade paper *Economic Questions,* November, 1965, page 49 and following, one of the outstanding experts of the Soviet economy, Professor N. Federenko, writes about "Ways and Possibilities of Applying More Chemistry in the Soviet Economy." He says, "At present half of the world production of washing powder is detergents. In the USSR only 3% of the demand for detergents can be satisfied. Up to now our chemical industry can supply 30% of the demand our farmers have for herbicides."

It is generally true that more valuable material can be found in these articles than in articles published in similar journals of the Western trade press. The explanation for this is that the authors, usually leading managers or scientists in the Eastbloc plants, need not be afraid that their competitors can use this information. It is an absolute necessity that production problems be discussed at the earliest possible time, especially if the problems might lead to failure to fulfill a fixed goal. In a free economy with heavy competition among different producers, a plant can easily switch from one supplier to another if the first one is not able to supply him with enough. This is not so in a planned economy.

For one seven-year plan, an expert of the Soviet Union assumed that the production of raw phosphorus would be large enough to guarantee a sufficient amount of phosphate fertilizer and that the Soviet industry would be able to supply the necessary sulphuric acid. In the course of the seven-year period, however, it became clear that the Soviet industry was not able to build plants for sulphuric acid according to the original plan. So the Soviet Union suddenly had a tremendous surplus of raw phosphorus while they were extremely short of surphuric acid and of phosphate fertilizer. That this would happen was clear to everyone who followed the constantly-growing discussions of the problems in the technical press, starting at a very early stage.

More Than One Source

Usually all necessary information cannot be found in one source. In general, many articles in many trade journals must be studied. Since the trade press in Communist countries is so highly specialized, by knowing where a given product comes from, what it is used for, and what machinery is needed, the number of journals needed for study can usually be limited to eight or ten for each country.

It is best to cover these journals written during the past five or even ten years to learn how conditions have changed. A researcher may end up with 200 or more sources. This happened in the oil industry, in an advertising agency that analyzed problems of distribution, and in an electrical company that wanted to find its possible markets. In the sources quoted by authors of these articles, the most valuable sources of all can be found, namely excellent monographs. They are so full of economic and technical data that market situations can be analyzed much more thoroughly by studying them than by desk research on Western markets.

This published information is more precise and reliable than any information gathered from so-called "confidential sources."

MARKET SITUATIONS

When a market researcher has collected and analyzed the data he needs, he will be confronted by one of four different market situations:

Excess Production Capacity

The capacity for production of a given product is bigger than the demand in the analyzed country or in the other countries of COMECON. There is at least the possibility that the Eastbloc countries will start an export campaign. Then it may be worthwhile to think about importing the product and trading it in non-communist countries.

Production in Line with Requirements

Capacity and production of a given product or product line satisfy the needs of the Eastbloc countries. Then it is useless to offer that product. This is true even if the product can be sold more cheaply or is of better quality than the various Eastbloc countries can offer each other.

Needed Product Low on Priority List

There is a demand for a given product because production did not come up to the original plan. The product, however, is believed to have a low position on the priority list fixed by the planning commission. The difference between the goal and the production capacity may be very large but because of a shortage of hard currency, the Eastbloc country will not import the product from non-communist countries.

Needed Product High on Priority List

The analysis has shown that the demand for a given product is much bigger than the production, and the product is of great importance to the entire economy, that is, it has a high position on the priority list. *Then, and only then,* is it worthwhile for a Western company to make contacts with the Eastbloc country, to appear at the different Eastbloc fairs, even to advertise the product in the trade journals.

Officials of the Communist countries are pleased that companies from Western countries exhibit their products at Eastbloc fairs, and they try to persuade their companies to visit them. Every interested company should know, however, that a careful analysis has led to the conclusion that more than 50% of all products offered to the Communist experts at fairs had no chance to be sold in those countries. Millions of dollars have been wasted over the years, and exhibitors disappointed; these companies usually did not know why.

ACCELERATING THE PROCESS

Some Western companies have found a way to accelerate the process of selling to Eastbloc countries. Systematically a company identifies the plants, combines, or factories that have a demand for their product. Then the product is offered *at the same time* to the plants, the centralized trading companies, and the ministry responsible for that area—informing each of them that the offer has been made to the others. Certain Western companies have been able to sign contracts a few weeks after their offers were submitted.

CONCLUSION

The Eastbloc countries are interested not only in goods, but also in know-how. One difficulty in trading was eased when the USSR joined the Paris Patent Convention in March, 1965.

Trade winds are blowing between East and West with more force than at any other time since the end of World War II. Western firms will find trading with countries behind the Iron Curtain different from trading with other nations. But it can be profitable—as the experiences of many European companies have proved.

47.

WHAT CRACKS IN IRON CURTAIN
MEAN TO AMERICAN MARKETERS*

PART I

WHAT do the widening *cracks in the iron curtain* promise to American marketers?

Are they a cue for a "great leap forward?" Or is this a time for waiting until the *improving* marketing climate has become more constant and marketing opportunities for manufacturers of the Western world clearer?

A survey we made among American and European marketers in collaboration with our International Partners indicates a *wide range* of answers to these questions.

Western marketers do agree that all the countries of Eastern Europe (including Mother Russia) *want* to trade with the West.

Some American and many European manufacturers to whom we talked are either *already* marketing in East bloc countries or are *gearing* for entry into this market to get a jump on competition.

Many have a "wait and see" attitude. "Let others get their feet wet," they say. "We'll plunge in when the *time is right*."

Still others say (and their number is substantial): "There are enough undeveloped marketing opportunities in this country and other developing parts of this world without our *risking* the uncertainties behind the iron curtain."

As usual, there is something to be said for each of these positions. Obviously, *no blanket policy* can realistically be set for marketers generally. Also obviously, we shall make no attempt to set one.

However, there is one approach that should be common to all marketers looking to Eastern Europe: segmentation.

East-West Trade Already Growing

Poland, Czechoslovakia, East Germany, Hungary, Rumania, Bulgaria, Yugoslavia and the Soviet Union can no longer be considered surrounded

* Reprinted by permission from *Grey Matter*, Vol. 38, Nos. 1 and 2 (January and February, 1967), a publication of Grey Advertising Inc.

by a *single* impenetrable Iron Curtain. Instead, each has high individual areas for successful marketing and, in turn, offers *distinctly different* opportunities for trade.

Each must be considered by *itself* because there is ample evidence of the tide of nationalism which is buoying up at varying tempos the aspirations of the people of these countries to higher levels of living.

Although there is considerable uncertainty among American businessmen about the immediate prospect of profitable marketing in Eastern Europe, there is a *general thaw* in their attitudes.

News out of Eastern Europe reveals to them that vital changes are under way . . . changes which point to growing opportunities which may merit a calculated risk.

Headlines in newspapers and the business press document these changes.

"American Motors Plans Sale of Cars to Reds"
"American Concern Buys Soviet Hydrofoil Ships"
"Trade with Reds Relaxed by U.S."
"First Direct New York–Moscow Flights to Begin in Spring by Pan American and Aeroflot (Soviet Airlines)"
"Poland Produces Fiats"
"France to Import 1,500 Moskvitch Cars from U.S.S.R. in 1967"
"Soviet Opens First Store Outside Communist Bloc in Brussels"
"EFTA Hopes for Yugoslav Trade Links with the West"
"Eastern Europe Moves Toward Market Economics"
"Bulgaria Touts Tourist Attractions"

These headlines tell the story of *increased trade, travel and tourism.* They also suggest why—for many alert U.S. manufacturers—the long-term prospects are well worth intense study.

Let us take a closer look at some of these social, political and economic changes in the Communist countries which may hold the *promise* of a new climate for East-West trade.

The much discussed "economic reform" sweeping through the U.S.S.R. and Europe's other Communist states does *not* mean socialism is the *end* and the *onset* of capitalism. It means, rather, a new stress on *economic flexibility,* local initiative and pragmatism to meet rising consumer demand for the better things of life.

The likely result—already apparent in several countries—is a greater flow of *consumer goods* and, in turn, an ever more *discriminating consumer* with broader and more varied wants to be satisfied.

In the Soviet Union the acceleration of response to popular demand for consumer durables is dramatically illustrated in the following production figures:

	1953	1960	1965
Refrigerators	49,000	529,000	1,675,000
Washing machines	3,000	895,000	3,400,000
Television sets	84,000	1,726,000	3,700,000
Radios	1,640,000	4,165,000	5,200,000
Clocks and watches	12,838,000	26,038,000	30,600,000

And if current Kremlin targets are met, such growth could be even more impressive by 1970. Russia *plans* to produce 800,000 cars by 1970, quadruple 1965 production and a far cry from a 1953 total of 77,000.

Perhaps the ideological shift which underlies the changing economy of Russia is nowhere better symbolized than in the *contrasting leadership:*

From Khrushchev with his well-known *aversion* to private car ownership and the type of society such consumption represents, to Kosygin, who rose to the managerial level in the textile industry and came to power partly because of his *stress on the role of the consumer goods* industry in raising the Russian standard of living.

Incidentally, one reason for the current tremendous emphasis on autos, according to reliable sources, is Russia's recognition of the significance of the auto industry in *powering the U.S. economy* and Russia's desire to harness the dynamic thrust of the automobile to their own development.

Consumer not Commissar

The first significant trend in the economies developing behind the iron curtain is that the *consumer,* rather than the *commissar,* is increasingly determining the course of industry's output, prices and styles.

Once despised terms and techniques, now being freely used reflect this.

A key Czech economic planner stresses the necessity for *"free price competition,"* as that country's strangled economy seeks to shed the shackles of state planning for a system of *local factory "profit"* accountability and bonus incentives.

A Hungarian writes that his country's economy has "already reached the phase of 'mass consumption,'" and describes how "by the use of *modern methods of market research,* new avenues were opened to determine consumer demand."

From Yugoslavia's already aggressively *market-oriented* system of planning to the still doctrinaire *statism* of Rumania, each of the curtain countries is moving at different speeds toward "demand" rather than "command" economy.

Significant for Western marketers is another aspect of the pressure of consumer aspirations behind the iron curtain:

Eastern European consumers are *hungry* for *basic consumer necessities,* now being slowly supplied by the ponderous revolutions of their economic systems: from mini-skirts in Moscow to patterned stockings in Prague . . . from Beatle records in Budapest to lipstick in Leipzig . . . the iron curtain consumer, particularly the youth, craves the status and excitement of Western fashions and fads.

As new channels of communication, travel and tourism open up, this demand is certain to *grow,* not diminish.

Want Western Ways

The second significant trend is the tremendous effort now being made by the Eastern bloc to improve and increase *trade relations* with the West.

Behind it: the recognition that Western skills, technological and machine resources and hard currency are essential to the swift and efficient expansion of a consumer goods production base.

To that end, the Soviet Union and the satellite governments are sparing no effort to *promote tourism and trade,* including a growing use of advertising.

Five Eastern European nations ran *advertising sections* in the International Edition of the New York Times this year. Russia and Czechoslovakia bought sections in the U.S. edition.

All stress *tourist attractions*—since earnings from tourism represent an important source of the exchange needed to trade with the West. Most also contain advertisements for *products,* from Polish hams, textiles and trucks to Czech motorbikes and shoe fashions. They promote trading organizations such as Czechoslovakia's new "Merkuria," selling "light consumer metal goods," or "Vreshposyltorg," a Soviet firm just established to retail Soviet *merchandise in ninety countries,* including the U.S.

The ads indicate that the would-be traders are *not unaware of the power of brands and brand names.* One Czech ad for Skoda-export and Techno-export states proudly that they "represent Czechoslovak heavy industry export products of manufacturers of *world-famous trademarks,"* 15 of which are reproduced graphically.

So eager are the Eastern bloc countries for hard currency that they have turned to *unorthodox means* to build reserves:

> Yugoslavia's state tourist office promotes six casinos devoted to that *malaise of capitalism,* gambling—but hard currency only buys the chips.
>
> Czechoslovakia's Tuzex Emporium offers savings on items from Skoda cars to Scotch for tourists or nationals with *gift dollars* from the West.
>
> The same goes for Moscow's "dollar stores"—with receipts from *cut price* caviar and chocolate bars accounting for tens of millions of exchange yearly.

European Break-Through

But trade is a two-way street. And currently, the nations of Western Europe have far *outpaced U.S.* in tapping East bloc markets.

Some of the reasons for this are *political,* as well as economic; e.g., de Gaulle's interest in *political rapprochement* with Russia while disengaging himself with the Western Alliance.

Others are *economic,* such as the willingness of Europeans to extend the longer term credits so badly needed by the exchange-shy Soviet bloc.

Geography plays a role, too. The proximity of the East bloc makes it an attractive export market for West European manufacturers seeking to reduce per unit costs as production capacity begins to surpass consumption potential at home.

It is worthy of note that some American marketers are also taking advantage of *geographical proximity* by using their facilities in West Germany and Austria as entry points to the Eastern markets.

However, such American companies are still a *distinct minority.* The simple fact is that the Europeans are entering the holes in the iron curtain in an aggressive manner and on a broad scale.

France's improved relations, dramatized by a constant exchange of iron curtain and French dignitaries and top-level trade missions, has produced *concrete results.* These range from persuading Russia to accept the French color television system rather than the U.S. or German systems, to plans for Renault to begin producing cars in Russia as early as 1968.

From Machinery to Cosmetics

Meanwhile, Germany, England and Italy are finding *lucrative markets* for a variety of products from machinery to cosmetics. Some smaller German firms do over fifty percent of their business exporting to the East. Italy's Fiat landed the biggest contract of any Western firm to build autos in the U.S.S.R., another in Poland. Olivetti of Italy is helping Russia's automation program in banks and offices.

European businessmen are not afraid to *cooperate* with each other in industrial projects in order to ease balance of payment problems and gain a foothold in iron curtain markets. Thus, on the heavy industry level, you'll see a Swiss manufacturer working with a Hungarian firm to provide a power station in Yugoslavia.

In the New York Times supplement, Hungarian Miklos Marton describes the advantages of this industrial cooperation:

> "The essential feature of industrial cooperation is that it is based on mutual benefit. It helps Hungarian companies to speed up technical development, and improves the quality of both the manufacturing process and the product itself, but it is, of course, also advantageous to the Western partners. As a result of it, trade in both directions increases. The Western firms participating lay a foundation for their exports, and increase their own competitiveness in the market."

European firms are also willing *to adapt to local demands* and requirements. An Italian apparel maker ships cut fabrics behind the iron curtain for completion there.

It all adds up to the very real danger that American marketers will find themselves facing *firmly entrenched* European competitors if they wait too long to approach marketing to the Soviet bloc.

The figures tell the story:

> In 1965 Western European Trade with the East reached *nearly $7 billion*—compared with a U.S. total of some $277 million.

Changing Climate in U.S.

Small wonder then, as President Johnson calls for better and broader U.S. trade ties with the East, that American businessmen are taking *another look* at the opportunities.

They are heartened by the *thaw* in a heretofore chilly official U.S. government position, which had held many back. This has taken the form of such *concrete steps* as: raising the level of diplomatic exchange with Bulgaria and Hungary; lifting export controls from some 400 nonstrategic items; extending Export-Import Bank credit guarantees to Poland, Hungary, Czechoslovakia and Bulgaria.

It could mean *market possibilities* for companies in fields ranging from margarine and mayonnaise to radio and TV equipment and textile machinery to medical equipment and machine tools.

One indication of new interest:

Recent tours arranged by Time magazine, in which executives of companies like Alcoa, Ford, Goodyear, Bendix, Eli Lilly, Borg-Warner, Seagram's, Armco and the New York Stock Exchange spent ten days in Prague, Warsaw, Bucharest, Budapest, and Belgrade.

Billed as a general education tour, the visits included frank discussions about the economics of the countries visited with local planners, managers and government officials.

Is There a Black Lining Behind the Silver Clouds?

Unquestionably, the attitude of a large body of American businessmen towards doing business behind the iron curtain is *warming up*.

President Johnson's easing restrictions on trade with Russia and the East zone is accelerating such business dealings.

The rapidity with which West European competitors have moved and are moving into East European markets spurs U.S. business to examine the cracks in the iron curtains more *realistically*.

Businessmen to whom trading with Communists might be abhorrent are beginning to wonder whether they shouldn't cast their prejudices aside and not give up these markets by *default*.

If peering through the iron curtain reveals merely what we have described above, few would *hesitate* to plunge through the gaps and go after business.

But the alert businessman looks beyond the obvious.

Roadblocks on Both Sides

Impediments to marketing in East Europe are not so easy to brush aside.

In the United States, there are laws on the books hindering such commerce. These are powerfully backed by *influential organizations* sincerely afraid of Communist expansion.

Last year Firestone Tire & Rubber Company broke off talks with Rumania for building a synthetic rubber plant because, according to reliable reports, of *pressure by anti-Communist groups*.

Laws such as the East-West Trade Act, designed to give the President authority to grant most favored nations treatment to imports from Communist countries, were shelved by the last Congress. The new legislature is hardly likely to *rush its passage.* Only Poland and Yugoslavia have favored nations treatment now.

However, the President has been able to take steps on his own, as we have noted.

Deterrents to Quick Thaws

Difficulties encountered by American manufacturers in establishing trade relations with the East under the Eisenhower and Kennedy Administrations are a *lingering deterrent* to immediate thaws in the American attitude toward increasing trade with Eastern Europe.

Continuous virulent propaganda against the United States has had the effect of *steeling a large number of American businessmen* against any dealings with countries even tinged with Communist ideology. They set their own ideology against the Communists. They regard as siren's songs the current Communist calls to "come and trade."

Another large body of American businessmen cling to their skepticism about expanding trade with the Communist East because they can see no *economic nor political advantages.* They point to the fact that American exports to these countries in the first half of 1966 amounted to only a shade over $100-million.

Some Western European nations are finding that trade with the Eastern group is *not* as two-way a street as they had anticipated. It was reliably reported that during Soviet Premier Alexei N. Kosygin's visit to Paris in December, the French Government expressed disappointment at the level of Soviet *imports* from France. French leaders blamed their businessmen in part for their failure to explore Soviet market opportunities.

However, Michel Debré, Economics and Finance Minister of France, believes that one of the fundamental problems is that Soviet economic planners are primarily interested in making the Soviet Union *self-sufficient* in every product category.

A complaint often heard among American businessmen is that since Communist countries do not produce very much which Americans desire, they are *short of dollars* and often propose barter arrangements which are distasteful to U.S. marketers.

Nor do many businessmen believe that the credit records of Communist countries warrant the risk of dealing with them.

Another block to expansion of American marketing behind the iron curtain is the *fear* in this country that, despite the struggle between fundamentalist China and the mellowed Soviet Union, Communism is still a *threat* and Communist countries must still be kept at arm's length.

An essay in Time magazine concludes:

"Communism today is unquestionably a failing creed. Yet it is precisely in decline and decay that ideologies, like empires, can prove most dangerous."

Then there are the *warnings* by responsible government figures, such as Walt Rostow of the State Department, that by rushing into trade with Eastern Europe because of "a false sense that the cold war is coming to an end, out of boredom or domestic preoccupations, or a desire to get on with purely national objectives, we will open up new opportunities for the Communists to advance."

True, the move from a "command" system to a "demand" system cannot be effected so easily. Yet it is under way even though attacks are mounting on these changes as "leaning too much toward capitalism."

In the February issue of Grey Matter we shall examine more closely the pitfalls and booby traps likely to be encountered in *penetrating perforations* in what was once a solid iron curtain around Eastern Europe.

PART II

In the January issue of Grey Matter we examined some aspects of marketing in Eastern Europe by American manufacturers.

We pointed out that the countries behind the iron curtain *want* to trade with the West; that some American and European marketers are *already* doing business with the Eastern bloc; that others are poised and ready; but that a large number have closed their eyes and their minds to *any* dealings with Communist countries.

We tried to make it clear that a *realistic* look at that part of Europe reveals that the term "iron curtain" is an anachronism.

There is *no one* curtain.

There are *separate* curtains for each of the so-called Soviet satellites. Even these drapes are shot full of holes.

East–West Trade on the Rise

The fact is that trade between East and West is *increasing* and the long-term prospects for trading with the Communist bloc are *well worth intensive study.*

We emphasized particularly that a significant economic trend, developing in what are called the "countries behind the iron curtain," is that the *consumer,* rather than the commissar, is increasingly determining the course of production of goods, techniques of marketing and patterns of distribution.

Especially important to the American marketer is the fact that the nations of Western Europe have *far outstripped* the United States in tapping the markets opening up in East Europe.

Yet there are roadblocks to overcome in *both East and West.*

We noted some of them in the January issue.

On the following pages we shall take a *closer look* at these impediments to expanding trade between American marketers and Eastern Europe.

We shall also add up some of the pros and cons as *thought prodders* and *action stimulants* to those of our readers who may be inclined to let marketing opportunities go by default.

If Thaw Becomes Freeze Again

Although the U.S. and the U.S.S.R. are moving toward cooperative agreements on freer trade, air travel, and possible nuclear non-proliferation, there is little evidence of change in *military plans* on either side.

Nor is there any letup in the denunciation of the United States about Vietnam by Communist countries.

Also, more recently, for the *first time since the Korean War* ended, the Soviet Union and nine other nations in its bloc asked the United Nations for "withdrawal of all United States and other foreign forces occupying South Korea under the flag of the United Nations and dissolution of the United Nations Commission for the Unification and Rehabilitation of Korea."

The Russian anti-missile system threatens to set off a *new arms race.* Should this occur, the thaw can well turn into a freeze. What would happen then with Russo-American business dealings?

It would be foolhardy for marketers to think that in this 50th year of Soviet power the U.S.S.R. has *completely* settled down to a system in which the need for economic reform will dominate political considerations.

Eastern Europe has lived under a system where the Communist Party (or its leaders acting for it) *controls* both its political and economic policies.

A question which needs an answer in the foreseeable future is whether this *duality* of function can remain *compatible.*

There is considerable uncertainty about the future even among some clients of our West European partner agencies, who are already marketing *their own brands* in Communist countries.

Examples: a client marketing a consumer product in East Germany under his own brand believes that a substantial increase in volume is not probable because his local competitors are *"state aided."*

Another client selling his own brand of packaged goods in Yugoslavia says the *future* of his business is "dependent on political developments."

Marketing Brands to the Communist Bloc

Although, as we have noted, the Eastern European countries recognize the values of *brands,* the American marketer who is thinking of distributing his international or American brands there will find obstacles.

• • • The *consumers* in these countries may harbor a fondness for American brands, but there is no evidence that their governments share this attitude.

• • • Since the channels of distribution are directly or indirectly government owned, the Western marketers may find it difficult to inject *his* brand if the bureau or agency he deals with insists on a national (rather than producer's) brand.

• • • It is important for marketers of consumer brands to be sure to investigate the status of trade-mark protection in each country, regardless of whether that nation is a signatory to the so-called Madrid arrangement or not.

Nevertheless, opportunities for some manufacturers' brands in certain products *are* opening in some of these countries. This applies especially to goods previously *low* on that country's *priority* list of consumer products destined to be funneled into the distributive stream.

It's conceivable that in cigarettes, cigars, cameras and films, cosmetics, packaged cereals and other prepared foods, the manufacturers' labels which have already established themselves *internationally* under a *company's* trade-mark will have superior opportunities for market entry.

> The comments of one manufacturer surveyed, whose sales are still limited to tourist shops, reflect a bullish attitude. Speaking of the future, he claims to be "very encouraged" about a "relatively untapped market" and to be determined to "pursue possibilities of increasing activity directly . . . as conditions get better."

Consumer Goods vs. Industrial Products

But the bald fact remains that marketers' labels in most *consumer* product categories will face *formidable* but not necessarily insurmountable *hurdles,* while *industrial* products will have smoother sailing because of their position on the priority lists.

One indication: A client of a partner agency selling industrial and home appliances in practically *all* the satellite countries under his own trade-mark considers the future potential good and "expects expanding business."

An informal survey of U.S. companies already doing business in countries of the East bloc also shows that those most optimistic about prospects are companies in *heavy or light industrial* categories or *consumer durables.*

Most stress "future potential" and look for business to "increase steadily," especially in Yugoslavia, Poland, Czechoslovakia, to a lesser degree Rumania and Bulgaria—but with little or no volume and not much hope for selling to either East Germany or Albania.

So the first major practical pitfall faced by the would-be trader to the Communist East is the question of the *position* of his product on the *list of priorities* set up by each government planning commission.

This will vary from country to country and year to year, depending on a number of factors. These include:

• • • the *long-range* (generally five year) plan for supplying the product (is it to be manufacured or assembled nationally or imported?)

• • • the *current situation* (have local plants met their targets or can the product be obtained in another country within the East bloc?)

• • • if not, is exchange available for import from the West?

Information and Communications gaps

Beside the problem of priorities, U.S. marketers of consumer products are likely to face other unexpected difficulties, growing out of the *primitive state* of Communist *distribution systems* and the almost total lack of elements considered essential to marketing in the West.

First there is the *time-consuming* necessity for dealing through bureaucratic state-owned trading organizations.

All the U.S. and European companies surveyed which are doing business with the East bloc, handled their operations through *government trading bureaus* in all countries except Yugoslavia, where a certain amount of private distribution is licensed by the government. Except for a few Czech plants, factories are not allowed to import or export directly.

To speed up the ponderous decision-making process of these trading organizations—which can mean a time lag of months between an offer and the final order—Western marketers have devised *ingenious methods* of spurring action. They attack on a number of fronts, such as identifying the plants or retail organizations which can use the product and submitting it simultaneously to them, to the central trading organization and to the ministry in the area.

But tactics like these require *detailed information* about specific factories and combines. Such market information, though becoming increasingly available, is still hard to come by and compile.

Advertising and Research

Market research, just beginning in countries such as Poland, Hungary and Yugoslavia—where it is run as an independent, profit-making service by the government—is still in *embryonic stages* by Western standards.

The rapidly expanding interest in market and media research on the part of the Soviet Union and the Eastern European Countries, according to Dr. Leo Bogart, President of the World Association for Public Opinion Research, "represents a new development of great potential interest. It is the first application of the survey method to the systmatic study of public opinion in these countries. Once the survey mechanism is set in motion within a country it cannot be confined to the minutiae of consumer preference."

To the marketer of consumer goods, this can mean an improving political and socio-economic climate in which to do business.

With relaxation of security restrictions, there is now an *abundance of market and technical data* being published by bloc governments and trade and professional journals. However, compilation from many sources is difficult and language barriers remain obstacles for most U.S. companies.

Then there is the problem of *advertising*.

Undeniably, understanding of the power of advertising is *on the rise* and its function in a demand economy is getting increasing *recognition*.

The Journal of Advertising Research reports the translation of an article from a Soviet trade journal entitled, "What Advertising Does," which relates how a store in Novosibirsk increased sales 30 times by an "inexpensive coordinated advertising campaign using TV, local radio, newspapers and point of sale." Concludes the article:

> "We should spare no effort in the organization of *good advertising*. Neither should we economize on advertising, because expenditures for it are repaid a hundredfold."

However, for the Western marketer, facilities in terms of agencies and media are still woefully *inadequate*.

At this point the would-be marketer must turn to yet another state monopoly—the country's *centralized advertising agency* (AGPOL in

Poland, RAPID in Czechoslovakia, PRESTO in Hungary, INTER-
WERBUNG in East Germany) or small regional agencies.

These agencies, originally merely space brokers, are growing in the
advertising *services* they atempt to provide. PRESTO, for example, which
was founded 15 years ago, had only 27 employees three years ago. Today
its staff numbers 160. AGPOL is attempting to solve the lack of trained
advertising personnel by sending employees to the West for training: six
are currently working in various European agencies.

In fact, Eastern European countries which are marketing or want to
market products and services in the West are calling *increasingly* on *Western agencies* because of the lack of advertising know-how at home. Would-
be marketers to Communist countries must recognize the delicate problem of trying to function in collaboration with the *state-owned* advertising "agencies" now springing up in the Eastern bloc.

Media a Problem

Finally, the U.S. marketer faces the problem of finding the right medium
for his product. For certain products there are a number of choices; Hungary has 60 trade journals, Poland 10 national newspapers and 40 local
ones.

In their desire to advertise to Russian buyers, some American companies are asking the United States Information Agency to open up to
advertising the pages of "America Illustrated," the magazine printed in
the Russian language and distributed inside the Soviet Union.

Broadcast advertising, on which U.S. packaged goods advertisers are
accustomed to rely heavily, is practically non-existent by Western standards. Poland's one national TV channel takes about *40 minutes* of advertising per day; Hungary has the same amount per *week*. Poland's four
national and 20 local radio channels can carry 30 commercials *a day*.

Trade fairs, often touted as a prime way to promote products behind
the iron curtain, also present problems. According to Berend H. Feddersen, a German specializing in East European market research, "A careful
analysis has led to the conclusion that 50 per cent or more of all products
offered to the Communists at different fairs did not have the slightest
chance to be sold."

Adding It All Up

1. Cracks in the iron curtains of Eastern Europe are *opening* progressively wider, so that in truth the words "iron curtain" are more a
   political *symbol* than an economic *reality*.

2. *Urbanization,* the development of a *middle class,* and the pressure of the consumer for a higher standard of living are gradually *forcing* shifts in the economics of these countries from "command production" decisions to "consumer demand" decisions. Not equally in all countries, but to some degree in every country.
3. The nations of the East bloc are still more interested in building tourism, getting long-term credit, acquiring Western skills and techniques in *consumer goods production* than they are in *importing* such goods.
4. There are many obstacles on both sides of the curtain obstructing a free flow of consumer goods. But some of these obstacles are gradually being surmounted.
5. Despite growing permissiveness on the part of Russia and more independence among the satellite nations, we must not forget, as one authority put it, "It was Mr. Destalinization Khrushchev" who sent the tanks to Hungary. It would be unrealistic to assume that the sword of Damocles has been sheathed.

In fact, some experienced observers insist that, in Hungary, behind the official *facade* there are increasing evidences (rarely seen by guided tourists) of an incipient popular *explosion.*

Still "Command Economies"

6. Except for Yugoslavia, the other satellite countries are still *"command production"* economies, though they are changing slowly.

For example, in a 16-page special color roto section advertisement run by Hungary in the New York Times (International Edition) there is an article headed: "Background and Purpose of the Economic Reform." The writer is quick to correct any impression that the country's economy is adopting profit as a goal. Says he:

> "The Western press occasionally misinterprets the Hungarian economic reform. A frequently recurring statement is that the socialist economy is changing its course and from now on profit will be its guiding principle. This is, of course, wrong. The reform does not divide the system of planning and economic management from socialism; on the contrary, it is designed to realize the possibilities inherent in socialist planned economy by more modern methods and with greater efficiency."

7. Obviously, marketers of American products in Communist countries will have to recognize the difficulties of fitting their *marketing conceptions* into undeveloped production-distribution systems.

The deficiencies of distribution in Eastern Europe are most evident in *consumer goods*. Students of these economies are generally in agreement that distribution will be one of the most difficult problems for the majority of consumer goods products.

8. *Continuing problems* are still posed in dealings between Western companies and countries of the socialist bloc.

This is illustrated in the construction of a $6 million luxury hotel in Hungary, financed by Tower International, Inc., controlled by Cyrus S. Eaton, Jr. The hotel, to be called The Budapest Intercontinental and planned as one of several in East bloc countries, was begun some months ago. However, the loan for construction had to be made by a Swiss subsidiary rather than by the American parent company, because "of U.S. laws that prevent a U.S. national from extending credit to a Communist country or certain countries that are in default on debts to the U.S."

As we noted, Americans contemplating operations in Eastern Europe may be forced to deal through Swiss or other European subsidiaries.

New Impediments Will Spring up in U.S.

9. For the American marketer, new impediments to free trading will continue to spring up *right here* in the United States. Many will be born of domestic politics.

For it is difficult to separate the *political* and *business* aspects of international trade. A case in point:

> In the closing days of 1966, the sale of surplus foods to Yugoslavia was reluctantly suspended by the Administration because of new Congressional restrictions on the Food for Peace program.

Unquestionably, this decision is a *setback* for the expansion of our economic relations with the most independent of the East-European bloc countries. It is indicative of the Administration's problems with Congress rather than a desire to *decrease the help to Yugoslavia,* which that country needs to finance a more liberal, decentralized economy.

10. Nevertheless, a European businessman who trades with Eastern Europe told us:

> "The future potential of trading with the countries behind the iron curtain is great. In planning for marketing there, it should be noted that for the most part they work on a quinquinquennial basis.
>
> "First they produce their own technical goods. Gradually, as their needs increase beyond their capacity to produce, they import.
>
> "After that they contemplate copying and then producing the goods themselves. Thus, manufacturers from other countries who

deal with them and wish to retain these markets must be always ahead of them with new products or with improvements in existing products."

Conclusion

Despite difficulties and obstacles, the possibilities of marketing in the Communist countries are worthy of serious consideration. There can be rich potentials for mutual profit.

Courageous, imaginative planning by American government and business is necessary to prevent U.S. manufacturers losing this market by *default*.

The rest of the world is already exploiting it and the number of American companies set to go is increasing.

For many American marketers, right now the word is "GO"—but the *strategy* should be to

LOOK BUT NOT LEAP
PLAN BUT NOT PLUNGE

48.

THE GROWING IMPORTANCE OF MARKETING IN SOVIET RUSSIA*

Feliksas Palubinskas

MARKETING AND IDEOLOGY

MARX had great contempt for marketing; he considered it unproductive and unnecessary. From the very beginning of the Soviet state it was held that the development of a Communist society and the expansion and development of trade are contradictions. Since Soviet Russia was established on Communist principles and still professes to be gravitating toward a Communist state, marketing and its functions should, accordingly, have been swept away or at least well on the way out, especially since it was declared in 1960 that by 1980 Soviet Russia is to become a fully Communist society.[1]

The purpose of this study is to examine the status of marketing and its functions in the Soviet centrally planned economy. Although there had been early attempts to eliminate not only marketing but the whole orthodox economic system, these attempts were discontinued because of the resulting chaos. None of the six basic marketing functions: merchandising, preparation of goods for marketing, handling of merchandise, financing risk and incentive, and dispersion of goods, nor their main subactivities were successfully eliminated. Attempts at alterations resulted only in a changed performance or a shift in the point of performance rather than in an elimination. Since marketing functions as such are universal and not organizationally determined, nothing else could have been expected. As an alternative to the desired complete elimination, Soviet marketing was greatly simplified and developed into a crude system of distribution for the allocation of scarce consumer goods. Although much effort had

* Reprinted by permission from the *Western Economic Journal*, Vol. III (1964–66), pp. 274-287.

To a considerable extent this paper is based on a doctoral dissertation written by the author under Professors H. W. Huegy, D. P. Flanders, and C. H. Sandage, at the University of Illinois. The antecedent of this paper, "Marketing—The New Soviet Solution to the Problem of Distribution," was presented at the Thirty-Ninth Annual Conference of the Western Economic Association.

[1] B. Miroshnichenko, "Some Problems of National Economic Planning at the Present Stage." *Voprosy Ekonomiki*, 1960. Reprinted in *Problems of Economics*, November 1961, p. 10 (hereinafter referred to as *P of E*).

been devoted to consumer goods allocation before 1950, this was always done within the framework of the existing organizational system. In the 1950's consumer goods became more plentiful. They were of poor quality, but there were more of them, and for a while, this was sufficient to the consumer-goods-starved Soviet buyer. After a few years, however, goods of poor quality began to remain on the shelves for extended periods of time. The existing distribution system was unable to cope with the new conditions. In 1961 S. Partigul, a Soviet economist, declared that experience had disproved the notion that the development of a Communist society and the expansion and development of trade are contradictions and that it is clear that trade is a necessary factor in the creation of greater material well-being for a Socialist society.[2] Thus, marketing is coming into its own in Soviet Russia, and it is being regarded as the new solution to their old problems of distribution.

Let us glance at each of the marketing functions and note the problems encountered and the solutions advanced.

MERCHANDISING

Marketing Research

It comes as somewhat of a surprise that the Soviet society, which is based on extensive economic planning, possesses virtually no mechanism for demand study. During the period of severe scarcity of consumer goods, the Soviet planners did not have to rely on consumer studies: only the barest necessities were produced and, furthermore, in a sellers' market the seller is the king—it is thus not surprising that this period showed a complete disregard for any type of a consumer study. With the increase of consumer goods in the 1950's, however, the problem of proper assortment arose. Soon it was realized that in a somewhat more affluent society the lack of knowledge of demand causes risks of either overstocking or facing shortage of some consumer goods in demand. To escape this situation of uncertainty it was proposed that a demand study be initiated.[3] The recognition of the necessity for market research had been born within the Soviety economy.

Presently the general demand study is primarily the responsibility of the Soviet planning bodies. They accomplish it through statistical studies of consumer money incomes and the structure of expenditures to arrive at the purchasing power of the whole population—by territories and on

[2] S. Partigul, "Statistical Study of Population Demand," *Vestnik Statistiki,* 1961; *P of E,* December 1961, p. 29.
[3] P. Maslov, "Consumer Demand Must Be Studied Better," *Ekonomicheskaya Gazeta,* No. 3, 1961; *P of E,* April 1962, pp. 38-42.

the social group basis.[4] To supplement the data of the government accounts, regular and special surveys are conducted by the Central Statistical Administration of the Union of Soviet Socialist Republics Council
of Ministers.[5]

The "100 Family Budgets" study[6] is an example of a survey of working family budgets conducted from 1951 to 1961 in Moscow, Ivanovo,
and Gorky. The results are presented as "typical of the budgets of the
working people of the USSR." The representatives of the sample is questionable, but this attempt at market research is still worth noting. A centralized study of goods by categories is also in progress. Inventories for
some 150 to 160 items have been taken on January 1 since about 1956.[7]

In 1963 the State Trade Committee set up a demand and marketing
department to deal with market research problems. Unfortunately its staff
consists of only ten employees serving hundreds of thousands of stores
handling tens of thousands of types of goods. Data are obtained through
nonstaff correspondents in 40 cities. The correspondents observe the state
of trade in their localities and send in reports to the demand and marketing department. From these reports, a survey of the market situation is
drawn up.[8] At the republic level a selective survey of commodity assortment versus demand is carried on through quarterly reports of sales and
inventories by stores dealing in manufactured goods and food stores with
complex assortment.[9]

That the study of consumer demand is still not only backward but
also rather rare at the Soviet retail level is indicated by numerous articles in the Soviet press.[10] As a result of the inadequate study of demand,
the above-norm inventories of unsold goods are on the rise and the
amount of losses resulting from price cuts is increasing every year.[11]
Nevertheless, market research at the retail level is definitely increasing,
although slowly. Actually, the Moscow Finance Institute had been
conducting one-time demand investigations since 1940. During such an

[4] Partigul, op. cit., p. 29.

[5] I. Matiukha, "Studying Family Budgets of Collective Farmers," Ekonomika
Selskogo Khoziaistva, No. 11, 1960; P of E, May 1961, pp. 45, 46.

[6] Report: "100 Family Budgets," Ekonomicheskaya Gazeta, January 4, 1964. Reprinted in The Current Digest of the Soviet Press, February 5, 1964, p. 10 (hereinafter
referred to as CDSP).

[7] Partigul, op. cit., p. 32.

[8] A. Druzenko, "Concerning the Study of Trade Factors," Izvestia, March 26, 1964;
CDSP, April 22, 1964, p. 30.

[9] Partigul, op. cit., p. 34.

[10] N. Arshinchikov and M. Kholmatov, "They Will Answer for This," Kommunist
Tadzhikistana, April 12, 1961; CDSP, May 24, 1961, pp. 34-36; Prof. P. Petrov, "Commodity Dictionary," Ekonomicheskaya Gazeta, No. 13, October 30, 1961; CDSP, December 13, 1961, pp. 46-48; and Rachel Golden, "Recent Trends in Soviet Personal Income and Consumption," Dimensions of Soviet Economic Power (Washington: U.S.
Government Printing Office, 1962), p. 362.

[11] V. Veselovsky, "Light Industry Will Work in a New Way," Nedelya, October
25-31, 1964, pp. 4, 5; CDSP, November 11, 1964, pp. 7, 8.

investigation several dozen students of the Institute visit some department store. They are posted at all entrances, the cashiers' offices, next to each sales person, and at the checking points. Their investigation consists of counting customers who enter the store, counting those who pay, and registering the satisfied and unsatisfied demand.[12] Maslov and Partigul also cite several examples of market research conducted by individual enterprises themselves.[13]

Although the existing demand study is crude, consisting mainly of a simple statistical count and concerned primarily with either past or present performance of a good on the market, it is nevertheless significant that its use is beginning to be considered essential; and, in fact, late in 1964, it was proposed to set up an all-Soviet Union research institute to study the demand for consumer goods.[14] More significant is the fact that there is a growing realization that a more effective market research can be carried out at the initiative of individual trade organizations rather than the unwieldy statistical agencies of the State Planning Commission.[15] For example, the Bolshevichka Production Association decided to make a better study of the demand for its products. For this purpose a showroom for the sale of semifinished goods was opened at the factory. An almost ready-to-wear suit could be purchased there, and a master tailor would then sew the final stitches according to the purchaser's specifications. On the basis of the sales results in this showroom, the Association drew conclusions as to what its customers like or what they do not like.[16]

Assortment

Soviet distribution of consumer goods was formerly accomplished through the allocation of goods among individual trade enterprises on the basis of a central plan and through the system of funds allocation. Since the flow of goods has increased considerably it is felt that for the majority of goods the method of distributing them through allocation is outmoded and it thus is becoming a hindrance to the effective operation of the trade system.[17] In lieu of the former allocation from the top of the organization, attempts are now being made to provide the individual en-

12 Maslov, *op. cit.*, p. 39.

13 *Ibid.*, pp. 39, 40 and Partigul, *op. cit.*, p. 33.

14 "Direct Ties," *Ekonomicheskaya Gazeta*, October 28, 1964, p. 4; *CDSP*, November 11, 1964, pp. 8-10.

15 Maslov, *op. cit.*, p. 42.

16 M. Kunznetsova, Chief Economist and Assistant General Director of Bolshevichka Production Association, "Demand, Quality, and the Plan," *Pravda*, October 4, 1964, p. 4; *CDSP*, November 4, 1964, pp. 12, 13.

17 M. Denisov, Chairman of the Board of the Russian Republic Union of Consumers' Cooperatives, "Not for 'the Gross' but for Man," *Izvestia*, January 11, 1964; *CDSP*, February 5, 1964, p. 32.

terprises with more say-so as to the assortment of goods they wish to handle. The planners still decide on the total figures of the operation categories, but the individual enterprises place individual orders with the various producers. Producers, however, are often unresponsive to the needs of trade.[18] This is a result not only of the still-existing shortage of some goods but also due to the fact that there is no incentive for producing enterprises to cooperate with the trade system.

The lack of cooperation between production and trade results, among other things, in poor assortment of goods. Although the quality and variety of goods have recently increased considerably, queues were still a frequent occurrence in city stores even in 1962.[19] In spite of the fact that some stores are jammed with goods, customers leave unsatisfied because these goods are of the wrong assortment,[20] in terms of quality and variety.[21] For example, nine plants make 800,000 pieces of an identical fruit dish.[22] Or, again, men's raincoats are so uniform in color, style, and finish that their wearers appear to be in uniform.[23]

With the growing supply of consumer goods, the buyers are becoming more selective.[24] Some commodities are completely rejected or remain long in stock because of poor workmanship, little selection, or low quality of materials.[25] At the same time a very serious problem is encountered in obtaining replacement parts,[26] as well as supplies.[27] Such disorder in assortment is irritating to the consumers and is becoming costly to the economy.

The poor assortment of consumer goods is blamed on faulty planning,[28] lack of incentive to the producers for making goods the consumers

[18] The 130-man raid brigade, consisting of *Izvestia* worker-correspondents, and including several city deputies and officials of public trade departments, "Negligence behind the Counters," *Izvestia,* February 7, 1962; *CDSP,* March 7, 1962, p. 27.

[19] *Ibid.,* p. 26.

[20] N. Koshelev, "Trade, Don't Distribute," *Izvestia,* August 8, 1959; *CDSP,* September 9, 1959, p. 23.

[21] The 130-man raid brigade, *op. cit.,* p. 27.

[22] I. Serebrennikov, "In Debt to the Buyers," *Pravda,* January 30, 1961; *CDSP,* March 1, 1961, p. 36.

[23] N. Zhukov, "Cultivating Taste," *Novy Mir,* No. 10, October 1964, pp. 159-76; *CDSP,* December 29, 1954, p. 3.

[24] G. Sakhnovsky, Ukraine Republic Minister of Trade, "Production, Trade, and Demand," *Pravda,* September 30, 1963; *CDSP,* October 23, 1963, p. 27.

[25] Imogene Erro, "Trends in the Production of Consumer Goods," *Dimensions of Soviet Economic Power* (Washington: U.S. Government Printing Office, 1962), p. 371.

[26] Serebrennikov, *op. cit.,* p. 36.

[27] *Ibid.*

[28] N. Kopyevsky, Correspondent, "The Pharmacy's Measure," *Trud,* October 7, 1962; *CDSP,* October 31, 1962, p. 19; Zhukov, *op. cit.,* p. 10; Partigul, *op. cit.,* pp. 31, 32; S. Partigul, "Demand and Supply under Socialism," *Voprosy Ekonomiki,* No. 10, 1959; *P of E,* February 1960, p. 13; and M. Lifits, "Certain Questions of Commodity Circulation in the USSR at the Present Stage," *Voprosy Ekonomiki,* No. 11, 1959; *P of E,* March 1960, p. 36.

need and want,[29] as well as the cumbersome machinery used for approving a new product for production. The story of white sandals illustrates this latter point especially well. A model of white sandals is manufactured at the Progress Shoe Firm in Lvov. Before the factory could start producing the sandals, an approval had to be obtained from the Artistic Council of the Lvov Economic Council, the Republic Artistic Council in Kiev, the Artistic Council of the All-Union Institute for the Assortment of Light Industry Articles and Clothing Standards in Moscow, and the price bureau of the USSR State Planning Committee. All this took six months. And then production of these sandals was delayed another six months because it took two months to set up production and four more months to obtain materials.[30]

As the Soviet citizens move upward on the scale of living—with some of their income beginning to fall into the "discretionary" buying-power category with which "optional" goods may be bought—the Soviet distribution system has to deal with the all-to-familiar "fickle" consumer of a well-to-do economy. The trade people are beginning more intensely, and perhaps rather desperately, to search for ways of solving the problem of consumer goods assortment. And the formerly mentioned greater freedom on the part of individual retail outlets for deciding on the assortment they will carry is one example of a "new" solution. Furthermore, after considering the fact that in a capitalist society the market controls the assortment, quality, and quantity of output, one Soviet accountant asks: "Cannot this instrument also be used in our Socialist economy?"[31]

PREPARATION OF GOODS FOR MARKETING

Standardization and Grading

Due to the historical production orientation of the Soviet economy, consumer goods are rigidly standardized. This standardization is coming to

[29] Editorial, "Meet Production Plans for Assortment," *Izvestia*, September 19, 1954; *CDSP*, October 20, 1954, p. 8; and N. Voronov, "The Artist and Everyday Life," *Izvestia*, July 21, 1957; *CDSP*, August 28, 1957, p. 13.

New goods made from artificial fibers, such as stretch socks, stockings, and shirts with wrinkle-proof collars, as well liked and in high demand. However, production enterprises are slow in reorganizing to keep pace with the changing fashions to meet the demands of consumers (Serebrennikov, *op. cit.*, p. 36). The demand for new goods grows rapidly, but the organization of their production on a large scale is slow (Partigul, "Demand and Supply under Socialism," *op. cit.*, p. 14). It is simply easier to meet the gross output plan if no time is lost for reorganization of production of new products.

[30] V. Vokovich, Special Correspondent, "How the White Sandals Fell Out of Step with Fashion," *Izvestia*, February 19, 1964; *CDSP*, March 11, 1964, p. 36.

[31] O. Volkov, Chief of Technical Economic Accounts Bureau of Likhachev Automobile Plant, *Pravda*, August 23, 1964, p. 2; *CDSP*, September 23, 1964, p. 20.

be considered as a shortcoming for trade purposes[32] since the lack of variety impedes the adjustment of goods to individual tastes. To the shortcomings of strict standardization is coupled the failure of grading.[33] According to decrees, Soviet consumer goods should be produced in first grade only. But, as the following example indicates, this is not currently being accomplished. A team of experts was called in by the State Department Store (GUM) in Moscow to check the quality of 1628 alarm clocks, received from a Yerevan Clock Factory. It was found that 1595 clocks, or 96 percent were defective.[34] The existing product-guarantee system does not help the situation either, since the individual enterprises are not responsible for the costs involved in servicing the guaranteed products. Consequently, it is advocated that "the existing guarantee system should be changed: all the expenses connected with correcting production defects should be borne by the plants and factories themselves out of the enterprise fund."[35] The enterprise fund is part of the profit which is left for the enterprise to dispose of as it sees fit, except for minor restrictions.

Packaging

Soviet consumer goods packaging is mainly protective in its nature and its shortage has always been chronic.[36] Therefore, each plant makes its own boxes and packages.[37] Soviet writers, however, have come to recognize the value of prepackaged goods in increasing labor productivity, saving the buyers considerable time, and assuring the customers true weight,[38] as well as providing the customers greater satisfaction since they have shown a preference for prepackaged items.[39]

An attempt has recently been made to solve the packaging problem in Moscow by centralizing packaging production.[40] Nevertheless, packaging remains a problem.[41]

[32] Zhukov, op. cit., p. 3.

[33] A. Bagdasanyan, "Faceless Merchandise," Izvestia, November 30, 1957; CDSP, January 8, 1958, p. 28; F. Feoktistov and B. Glushkov, "Follow a Proven Course," Izvestia, April 18, 1959; CDSP, January 8, 1959, p. 28; editorial, "Produce Attractive, High-Grade Goods," Pravda, September 5, 1954; CDSP, October 20, 1954, p. 8; and editorial, "Raise Trade Standards, Improve Service to Consumer," Izvestia, July 12, 1958; CDSP, August 20, 1958, p. 23.

[34] Serebrennikov, op. cit., p. 36.

[35] Pravda's collective correspondent editors of Ekonomicheskaya Gazeta, "Let the Enterprise Answer for the Assortment and Quality of Products," Pravda, May 16, 1964; CDSP, June 10, 1964.

[36] N. Koshelev and K. Lyasko, Special Correspondents, "Millions on the Barrelhead," Izvestia, July 17, 1962; CDSP, August 15, 1962, p. 28.

[37] V. Kurasov, "Without a Fulcrum," Izvestia, January 14, 1964; CDSP, February 5, 1964, p. 30.

[38] Maslov, op. cit., p. 41.

[39] Maslov, op. cit., pp. 41, 42.

[40] Kurasov, op. cit., p. 30.

[41] Ibid., p. 31.

HANDLING OF MERCHANDISE

Storage

In 1930 the wholesaling system and intermediate warehousing were suspended in Soviet Russia.[42] But when the distribution system from producer to retailer failed, wholesaling and intermediate warehousing were reinstated into the distribution system. Although reintroduced, intermediate warehousing was neglected, however, and storage space did not increase in proportion to the increasing volume of trade. Thus, while commodity stocks between 1940 and 1959 increased 6.7 times, the storage facilities increased only 67 percent. Consequently, the tendency for consumer goods to concentrate at the retail level is continuing: 56 percent in 1941 and 75 percent in 1959.[43]

Carried by the inertia of the former shortage of goods, certain Soviet finance and trade officials still consider that the more goods there are in the retail network, the better.[44] It is nevertheless being realized by others that this diffusion of goods among a vast number of retail outlets limits the possibilities for maneuvering the commodity stocks and prevents the wholesaling system from carrying out its main function of rationally distributing the goods throughout the different parts of the country, thereby providing a proper assortment to each member of the retail system.[45] The growing Soviet awareness of the importance of storage becomes even more meaningful when we consider that the USSR, which is larger than the United States in terms of population and territorial space, has substantially less wholesale space. In 1961 the USSR had 25 million square feet of wholesale space[46] as compared to the 1370 million square feet, 448 million cubic feet, 132 million bushels, and 405 million gallons of storage space available in 1954 for U.S. wholesaling.[47]

FINANCING

To facilitate the movement of some slowly selling goods, installment credit was introduced in 1958 on an experimental basis[48] and in 1959 on

---

[42] Leonard E. Hubbard, *Soviet Trade and Distribution* (London: Macmillan and Co., Ltd., 1938), p. 41.

[43] Lifits, *op. cit.*, p. 35.

[44] Denisov, *op. cit.*, p. 32.

[45] Lifits, *op. cit.*, p. 35; and Denisov, *op. cit.*, p. 32.

[46] S. Partigul, "Statistical Study of Population Demand," *Vestnik Statistiki*, November 6, 1961; *P of E*, December 1961, pp. 33-36.

[47] Paul D. Converse, Harvey W. Huegy, and Robert V. Mitchell, *Elements of Marketing* (6th ed.; Englewood Cliffs, N.J.: Prentice-Hall, Inc., 1958), p. 194.

[48] Marshall I. Goldman, "Marketing—A Lesson for Marx," *Harvard Business Review*, Vol. 38, January-February 1960, p. 85.

a permanent basis.[49] It was met with enthusiasm both by consumers and trade personnel, and it *did* start moving expensive items of good quality, which hitherto could not be sold.[50] The usefulness of consumer credit is recognized and credit sales are spreading at a rapid pace. Thus, in 1961 credit sales constituted slightly more than one percent of total Soviet retail sales[51] and in 1962, 4.9 percent of the Russian Republic sales.[52]

RISK AND INCENTIVE

Since Soviet enterprises are state owned, business and economic risks in the USSR are assumed primarily by the Socialist society as a whole[53] and do not weigh as heavily on the individual enterprises as is the case in a Capitalist society. Yet, even in such a system, managers have to be motivated to achieve. For a long period of time the emphasis had been on social and moral forms of incentive. However, they did not work well, and in 1961 Nikita Khrushchev censured this form of incentive:

> . . . neglect for the material requirements of the working people and the concentration of emphasis on . . . social and moral forms of incentive and reward has retarded development of production and rising of the living standards of the working people.[54]

In 1962 the widely publicized proposal by Professor Liberman to make profit the main index of success appeared in *Pravda*.[55] He urged that free pricing and profitability do the job of creating interest in higher plan assignments, improved operations, and better assortment of improved quality goods.[56] This proposal was greeted enthusiastically[57] for it was foreseen that "then not only the central planning agencies but the enterprise itself, its collective, will have an interest to an even greater degree in the daily progress. . . ."[58] Even Khrushchev agreed that "with-

---

[49] *Ibid.;* and Golden, *op. cit.,* p. 362.

[50] P. Borisov, "Installments? Yes, Installments," *Izvestia,* May 30, 1959; *CDSP,* July 1, 1959, p. 22.

[51] Golden, *op. cit.,* p. 362.

[52] D. Korolev, Russian Republic First Deputy Minister of Trade, "Do Not Distress the Customer, Make Him Happy," *Pravda,* November 18, 1962; *CDSP,* December 12, 1962, p. 24.

[53] Boris Brutzkus, *Economic Planning in Soviet Russia* (London: George Routledge and Sons, Ltd., 1935), p. 11; and Miroshnichenko, *op. cit.,* p. 20.

[54] *Kommunist,* No. 1, 1961. Reference to Khrushchev's statement as quoted by Erro, *op. cit.,* p. 327.

[55] Y. Liberman, "The Plan, Profits, and Bonuses," *Pravda,* September 9, 1962; *CDSP,* October 10, 1962, p. 13; and I. Malyshev, "Planning Is an Important Link in Socialist Management," *Pravda,* February 7, 1963; *CDSP,* March 6, 1963, p. 19.

[56] Liberman, *op. cit.,* p. 13.

[57] O. Antanov, "For All and for Oneself," *Izvestia,* November 22, 1961; *CDSP,* December 20, 1961, pp. 19, 20; and V. S. Nemchikov, "Plan Assignment and Material Incentive," *Pravda,* September 21, 1962; *CDSP,* October 17, 1962, pp. 3-5.

[58] Malyshev, *op. cit.,* p. 20.

out calculating profit it is impossible to determine the level at which the enterprise is functioning and what contribution it is making to the total fund."[59]

Although central guidance of enterprises through administrative controls was formerly considered to be an essential part of the Soviet Socialist society and there were many objections against the use of profit as an indicator of performance, this does not seem to be the case any more.[60] One article even bluntly states that ". . . it is time to realize that guidance of the enterprises through administrative interference in all details is a most ineffective method, one that cannot yield good results."[61] Conversely, profit is seen as the ". . . index capable of eliminating the contradiction between the interests of society and those of the plant's collective, of saving the enterprise from petty and unnecessary tutelage and of placing technology under the control of economics."[62]

Thus, despite the change in political leadership, the proposal for using profit as the main indicator of enterprise performance and giving the enterprise more autonomy not only has many supporters but is gaining momentum.[63] That the new leadership intends to carry the experiment further was amply shown by the December 26, 1964, announcement to be discussed later.

When Communists of high rank advance profit as the main measure of economic success and the main regulator of economic activity in lieu of planning, this indeed is something new, for it seems to constitute an admission that self-interest is the most important driving force in economic accomplishment. Such an admission on the part of the Communists may be the beginning of a deviation straight into the camp of capitalism, although they insist that this is not the case.

The Soviet writers very insistently, although not necessarily convincingly, emphasize that there is an infinite difference between profit in the Soviet Union and the free enterprise system. Liberman points out that in the Soviet Union profit cannot be converted into private capital and thus

[59] As quoted by I. Birman and B. Belkin in "Prices and Profits," *Izvestia*, November 29, 1962; *CDSP*, December 26, 1962, p. 31.

[60] L. Leontyev, Corresponding Member of the USSR Academy of Sciences, "The Plan and Economic Methods of Guidance," *Pravda*, September 7, 1964, p. 2; *CDSP*, September 23, 1964, p. 22.

[61] V. Belkin and I Birman, Candidates of Economics, "The Independence of the Enterprise and Economic Stimuli," *Izvestia*, December 4, 1964, p. 5; *CDSP*, January 6, 1965, p. 14.

[62] G. Kulagin, General Director of Leningrad Machine Tool Association, "Operational Autonomy of an Enterprise," *Pravda*, September 15, 1964, p. 2; *CDSP*, October 7, 1964, p. 37.

[63] V. Trapeznikov, Academician, "For Flexible Economic Management of Enterprises," *Pravda*, August 17, 1964, pp. 3, 4; *CDSP*, September 9, 1964, p. 13; V. Shkatov, Assistant Head of a Sub-department of the USSR State Committee's Bureau of Prices, "What Is Useful to the Country Is Advantageous to Everyone," *Pravda*, September 1, 1964, p. 2; *CDSP*, September 23, 1964, p. 21; Volkov, *op. cit.*, p. 20; and Liberman, Professor at Kharkov University, "Once More on the Plan, Profits and Bonuses," *Pravda*, September 20, 1964, p. 3; *CDSP*, October 14, 1964, p. 21.

cannot be used for private enrichment.[64] He says that to the Soviets ". . . material incentives signify, along with moral elevation of people of labor, an improvement in their living conditions in accordance with each person's labor contribution to social production."[65] And in general "the proposals for making wider use of profits are aimed not at weakening but on the contrary at strengthening the principle of state-planned management of the economy. . . ."[66] Yet, it seems to be contradictory that the proposed autonomy of enterprises will result in a more effective control of the economy by the state. And, again, one can question if self-interest of a Soviet citizen in the improvement of his economic well-being through increased profit is in reality so different from the situation under free enterprise.

DISPERSION OF GOODS

Advertising

Until recently, due to the extreme shortage of goods, there has been no need for the Soviets to use advertising as an important marketing tool. Simple window displays, if any, were considered sufficient for informing the public of product availability. Advertising was certainly not used for preselling.

Now that some effort has to be expended in selling to the more affluent consumers, more attention is placed not only on window displays[67] but also on billboards, posters,[68] neon strips, newspaper ads, radio, television, and advertising films.[69]

Although Soviet advertising is still primarily of the institutional type, it is dawning on the Soviets that the existing advertising is no longer sufficient for familiarizing consumers with new products or for preselling purposes.[70] The general scarcity of advertising is expressed in a complaint by two Soviet citizens that "miles go by, not an ad strikes the eye."[71]

With the increasing state of well-being the Soviet citizens are eager to spend their money. Public opinion is consequently clamoring for more and better advertising: for advertising that is "bright, memorable, easily

[64] *Ibid.*

[65] Liberman, "Mr. Lackenbach as Tourist, Correspondent and Economist," *Ekonomicheskaya Gazeta,* May 30, 1964, p. 13; *CDSP,* June 24, 1964, p. 9.

[66] *Ibid.*

[67] Y. Staroselsky and L. Tsitsina, "Advertising Is an ART, Too," *Sovetskaya Kultura,* October 7, 1958; *CDSP,* December 10, 1958, p. 9.

[68] *Ibid.*

[69] Elizabeth Swayne, "Soviet Advertising: Communism Imitates Capitalism to Survive," *The Role of Advertising,* ed. C. H. Sandage and V. Fryburger (Homewood, Illinois: Richard D. Irwin, Inc., 1960), pp. 93-97.

[70] Yevgeny Kriger, "Do We Need Advertising?" *Izvestia,* April 25, 1964; *CDSP,* May 1964, p. 25.

[71] Staroselsky and Tsitsina, *op. cit.,* p. 9.

grasped, varied and attractive."[72] And even the prominent Soviet economist V. S. Serebriakov, argues that more specific advertising simplifies
marketing. He points out that "the more the buyer becomes accustomed
to definite trademark of a good, the simpler is the distribution operation."[73] Although the point is nothing new to us, it certainly constitutes
a change of attitude in the Soviet Union.

The realization that advertising can be an effective tool in distribution has resulted in the setting up of advertising agencies. Trade publications discuss advertising and provide practical suggestions for its use.[74]
Even competitive advertising has already made its appearance.[75] Doubt-
less the Soviets are in the process of following capitalism down the road of
advertising.

Product Differentiation and Branding

Soviet advertising may become more feasible and effective since the Soviets are discovering that the complete absence of, or slackness in, product
branding enables some factories to turn out products of poor design and
quality without ever being discovered.[76] This has lately been creating
substantial problems in trade channels. The merchandise of poor quality
and the faulty merchandise can no longer be sold (in contrast to the days
of extreme shortage), neither can they be returned to the manufacturer
since he is very frequently unknown. These goods are consequently piling
up at the retail level and must be sold at a huge loss to the state.[77] Product branding, which was formerly condemned as a Capitalist tool in creating monopolies, is now looked upon as a solution to this problem.

Product differentiation and branding is being advocated not only for
product source identification and for quality control but also for enhanc-
ing the effectiveness of selling through market segmentation,[78] a technique long used by the profit-minded Capitalist merchants who were
always quite willing to respond to customer desires.

Pricing

As in any centrally controlled economy, price is one of the most important means of controlling the Soviet economy. Historically, pricing in
Soviet Russia has always been a matter of politics and was treated as such.

[72] *Ibid.*
[73] V. S. Serebriakov, *Oragizatisiia i Tekhnika Sovetskoi Torgovli* (Moscow: Gostor-
gizdat, 1956), p. 76.
[74] Staroselsky and Tsitsina, *op. cit.,* p. 9.
[75] Goldman, *op. cit.,* p. 94.
[76] Feoktistov and Glushkov, *op. cit.,* p. 26; and Serebrennikov, *op. cit.,* p. 36.
[77] Bagdasanyan, *op. cit.,* p. 28.
[78] Partigul, "Demand and Supply under Socialism," *op. cit.,* p. 14.

Although the 1957 reforms did reduce the pricing centralization, even presently a great portion of wholesale and retail pricemaking and price changing remains in the hands of the USSR Council of Ministers.[79]

The centrally set prices often prove unsatisfactory at the individual transaction level, for they act as mediators neither between producers and sellers nor between supply and demand. But such a role for prices has recently been proposed. For example, "a plant puts out new, high-quality products that are in great demand—high prices would be set for them,"[80] thus providing an incentive to the producers for producing new and better products. Under this suggestion, price would become a means not only for recouping the initial investment, but also for making a larger profit. Even a stronger suggestion for freer pricing is one stating that "for all goods not in mass production, prices could be set by the enterprises themselves under conditions of strict adherence to an approved method for calculating such prices."[81]

With the stronger advocacy of profit as the main index of enterprise performance, it is not surprising that a more flexible pricing system is considered as a corollary.[82] It is interesting to note that prices for unique products even now are negotiated with the consumer. However, it is being advocated that "this system should be extended (also) to serially and mass produced items."[83] To some extent this has already been done: the directors of Bolshevichka and Mayak firms, described in the following pages, have been granted the right to establish retail prices.[84]

Because of the central position of price in the economic system this attitude toward freer pricing seems to be an especially significant step in the Soviet transition from the strict control by the state into the direction of free economic activity by the individual economic enterprises.

Selling

Personal salesmanship in the Soviet Union is still of a very poor quality and very opportunistic in its nature: salespeople are concerned only with fulfilling their quota rather than with pleasing the consumer.[85] The attitude of the salespeople, however, is presently under criticism, which was

[79] M. F. Solodnikov, "Costs of Production in Local Industry and Problems of Pricing." *Vestnik Leningradskogo Universiteta, Seria Ekonomiki, Filosofii i Pravda,* Issue 3, No. 17, 1959; *P of E,* April 1960, p. 22.

[80] *Pravda's* collective correspondent editors, *op. cit.,* p. 11.

[81] V. Nemchinov, Academician, "Socialist Economic Management and Production Planning," *Kommunist,* No. 5, March 1964; *CDSP,* May 27, 1964, p. 5.

[82] Trapenznikov, *op. cit.,* p. 14.

[83] Volkov, *op. cit.,* p. 20.

[84] Veselovsky, *op. cit.,* p. 7.

[85] B. Vetluzhanin, "About Little Things," *Sovetskaya Belorussia,* September 26, 1957; *CDSP,* December 18, 1957, p. 29; A. Ryutchi, "I Walk Through the Town," *Sovetskaya Russia,* April 7, 1960; *CDSP,* May 4, 1960, p. 26; Zhukov, *op. cit.,* p. 10; and Maslov, *op. cit.,* p. 40.

not the case somewhat earlier. Thus G. Sakhnovsky, the Ukraine Republic Minister of Trade, points out that "in conditions of sufficiency, selling
fabrics, clothing, and shoes is a far from simple matter. In addition to
professional skills, the salesman must have good taste and an ability to
advise the customer and to help him select the most suitable thing."[86]
The beginnings of consumer-oriented service is reflected in the recently
introduced, but not yet prevalent, progressive selling methods, such as
self-service and selling without salesclerks,[87] as well as providing faster
service to the customers instead of the previously used "three-line" arrangement: "To stand in one line for inspecting the products and inquir-
ing as to their price, to stand in a second line to pay for the desired products, and to stand in a third line for picking up the products."[88]

CONCLUSION

The failure of the Soviet planned economy to adjust to changes which
occurred in the consumption sphere and the success of some modifications
lately introduced lead to an increasing number of suggestions for even
more drastic changes in Soviet distribution. Thus, Comrade Dymshits,
Chairman of the USSR Council of the National Economy said, ". . . if
the output of low-quality goods is to be halted, it is necessary to create
an economic system in which the enterprises have a direct interest in
good-quality output and the trade organizations can exert stronger influence on industry."[89] Furthermore, said Khrushchev, ". . . a system should
be introduced under which factories and firms are directly answerable
to the consumer for the quality of their output, so that the enterprise or
firm works not for the store but through the store for the consumer."[90]
Others rather bluntly propose that the time has come to change the Soviet
distribution from the planned-allocation procedure to the free buying
and selling of goods.[91]

The above is not merely an exercise in theorizing—this is indicated
by the fact that the USSR Council of National Economy recently adopted
a decision to organize (as an experiment) in a new way the planning and
marketing of two clothing production associations, the Bolshevik in Moscow and the Beacon in Gorky. Under the new method the production

[86] Sakhnovsky, op. cit., p. 28.

[87] A. Dementyev, "Some Questions of Trade Service for the Public," Voprosy
Ekonomiki, No. 8, August 1959; CDSP, October 14, 1959, pp. 13-15.

[88] Marshall I. Goldman, "Retailing in the Soviet Union," Journal of Marketing,
April 1960, pp. 13, 14.

[89] Report: "Excellent Goods for Soviet Consumers!" Ekonomicheskaya Gazeta, No.
27, July 6, 1964; CDSP, July 24, 1964, p .5.

[90] Pravda's collective correspondent editors, op. cit., p. 11.

[91] Denisov, op. cit., p. 32; and M. L. Zak, "Role of Supply and Demand in the
Soviet Economy," Vestnik Moskovskogo Universiteta, Seria Economika, Filosofia, No. 1,
1961; P of E, September 1961, p. 27.

plans were not to be established from above, but by the associations themselves on the basis of orders they accept and contracts they conclude with stores. The associations' directors were to negotiate with trade enterprise officials on the quality, styles, models, colors, and delivery schedules for clothing items and bear full responsibility for their sale. They were also to make their own independent decisions as to the source of raw and other materials and the wage fund—with extensive powers for giving bonuses to the workers. The retail prices were to be set by the officials of the associations using the existing official price lists but with the cost of improved finishing and other additional operations taken into account. Finally, the basic indicators for evaluating the associations' operations were to be the volume of output sold on the basis of accepted orders and fulfillment of the profit plan.[92]

The experiment started July 1, 1964.[93] The changeover by the enterprises was accomplished with remarkable enthusiasm. For example, when the Bolshevichka Production Association learned of its new status, it immediately expanded its marketing and designing departments, visited the best showrooms in the country and selected the best styles for their products, and improved the quality of its inexpensive suits. The two associations also raised prices slightly to compensate for the increased expense of producing better quality suits. The demand for their products exceeded expectations.[94]

Now the two associations are famous, for their products (suits, raincoats, and dresses) are no longer gathering dust in the stores.[95] After a four months' operation the results were found to be so outstanding that late in 1964 the Collegium of the USSR Council of National Economy approved measures aimed at shifting a number of light industry enterprises to work according to direct contracts with trade organizations and stores.[96] It was proposed "that 31 percent of the enterprises in the garment industry, 17 percent of the textile enterprises, 33 percent of the shoe factories and 10 percent of the leather plants in Moscow, Leningrad, Gorky and certain other cities be shifted to the new system."[97]

It is worthwhile to note that at the beginning of 1965 in the Lvov Economic Council the experiment was not only to have been started in consumer production enterprises but also in the industrial production enterprises. In the latter ones the Economic Council was to set only the

[92] K. Michurin, "Production, Trade, and Demand," *Pravda,* May 17, 1964; *CDSP,* June 10, 1964, p. 13.

[93] "Experiment under Examination," *Izvestia,* October 21, 1964; p. 1; *CDSP,* January 20, 1965, p. 25.

[94] Kuznetsova, *op. cit.,* p. 12.

[95] Veselovsky, *op. cit.,* p. 7.

[96] "Experiment under Examination," *op. cit.,* p. 6.

[97] "Direct Ties," *Ekonomicheskaya Gazeta,* October 28, 1964, p. 4; *CDSP,* November 11, 1964, p. 9.

output volume and assortment, everything else was left to be worked out by individual enterprises.[98]

In summarizing, it may be said that, as yet, the manner of all six marketing functions in Soviet Russia is greatly inferior qualitatively and quantitatively to performance in the United States. In the performance of the various functions, there seems to be a disproportion between the input and the results obtained. This may be attributed not only to the nature of the system, which is ideologically adverse to marketing, but also to the lack of a proper proportion among the various economic activities.

The evidence, presented on USSR marketing, seems to confirm the hypothesis that, as society becomes more economically advanced and complex, all marketing functions become more important and their performance increases qualitatively and quantitatively. At the beginning of the Soviet period, a great majority of the Russian people was engaged in agriculture and generally tended to be self-sufficient. For many years there was also a continuous lack of consumer goods. It was therefore possible for the Soviets to simplify their marketing system and organize it on the distribution-from-the-top basis. But with the advance of industrialization and specialization, the Soviet people are becoming less self-sufficient and more dependent on their marketing system to supply their needs. An increasing volume of variety of goods is entering the Soviet marketing system and the distribution-from-the-top is becoming less and less effective. It is therefore not surprising that the Soviet attempts to improve their marketing system have been particularly visible in the last six to eight years—the period when consumer goods became more plentiful. The improvements came about through the introduction of self-service, consumer credit, and more (and increasingly more aggressive) advertising. The increased quantity and improved quality of the performance of marketing functions have somewhat improved the Soviet marketing system and brought it closer to that of the United States, if not in theory, at least in practice.

The space in Soviet literature devoted to the discussion of marketing problems is increasing at an accelerating rate and is a sign of the field's growing importance. If the growing favor shown in this literature (1) for product differentiation and branding, (2) for substitution of free choice instead of allocation of goods among enterprises by decree, (3) for providing incentive to individual enterprises by making profit the basic measure of economic success and letting the enterprises keep a good portion they make, and (4) for continuing towards freer pricing, we may well expect that by 1980 the Soviet Union will have, instead of full communism, a marketing system even less distinguishable than now from those existing in the Capitalist countries.

    [98] V. Vukovich, Special Correspondent, "Experiment Is in Its Starting Phase," *Izvestia,* December 26, 1964, p. 3; *CDSP,* January 20, 1965, p. 25.

49.

MARKETING AND ADVERTISING IN YUGOSLAVIA*

Mihoril Skobe

I WELCOME the opportunity to speak to this distinguished audience about marketing and marketing communications in Yugoslavia.

Let me start by telling you of an incident that happened last year in Zagreb, my home town. We were honored by a visit from an executive of one of the largest American agencies, who expressed his surprise at the existence of an advertising business, with agencies and marketing services. The first thing he wanted to know was how, in the self-management system and social ownership of the means of production, there is an interest in marketing.

The answer goes 15 years back. After a certain period of state management in Yugoslavia, it was decided by the National Assembly, in 1950, that our economic and social system should be developed on the basis of self-government, decentralization and gradual abandoning of state monopoly in the economic, cultural, social, political and other areas of life. The result is a system of management of factories by workers' councils and of self-governing local communities. A further result is the transfer of responsibility for planning to the enterprises, a new method of remuneration and the creation of a free market which proved to be a significant factor influencing the economic life of the country. This shift did not mean a change in the principle which governed the ownership of property. The ownership remains the same—public—but management of the enterprises became the responsibility of the people who worked in the enterprises.

Under the self-management system, enterprises no longer receive production plans or any other direct orders or instructions from higher authorities, but instead, decide on the quantity, variety, and quality of goods to be produced. They now decide independently on price policy, distribution of income, determination of personal earnings and regulation of labor relations in their own enterprises. The financial result of these enterprises is thus determined by their own efforts—and their financial rewards are determined not only on the produced value of goods, but on their sales as well. The result is a broader variety and better quality of

* Mihoril Skobe, "Marketing and Advertising in Yugoslavia," *Marketing and Economic Development,* 1965 Proceedings of the American Marketing Association, pp. 96-101. Reprinted by permission.

goods because the working collectives are vitally interested in producing goods demanded by the market.

Now that I have answered—I hope—the question of how, in the self-management system and social ownership of the means of production, there is an interest in marketing, I can get down to the more specific aspects of my subject. Rather than become involved in theory, I will speak about development and actual practice, based on my own experience and observations.

THE NATURE OF THE MARKET

As you probably know, Yugoslavia consists of six republics, has five nationalities, and a population of over 19 million. There are three related but different languages, writte in two different scripts, Cyrilic and Latin. There are three major religions: Roman Catholic, Orthodox and Moslem, and several national minorities. Besides all these variations there are essential differences in economic, cultural and other standards. There are quite developed areas which are approaching the level of Western Europe, but there are also backward underdeveloped areas.

Yugoslavia came out of the Second World War as a destroyed and devastated country. Material war damages have been estimated at more than 9 billion dollars. Industry, mining, and transport were either damaged or destroyed. About two million buildings and houses were demolished or rendered unliveable. At that time almost 80% of Yugoslav people were peasants, and national income was only about 180 dollars per capita.

Since 1947, when the period of reconstruction was completed and the level of the prewar industrial production achieved, the economic, social and educational development has been rather dynamic. Once predominantly agricultural, Yugoslavia became a semi-developed industrial country, in which today industry accounts for more than 50% of the national income. This is the contrast to the 1939 figure of 9%. The industrial production in 1964 was seven times higher than before the war, and the national income increased almost four times.

The Increase in Consumer Goods and Marketing Communications

Immediately after the Second World War there was no room for marketing. Gradually, as production of consumer goods increased and consumer preferences started to have some meaning, marketing started to grow in importance.

Ozeha, the agency I have been connected with, was established in 1945. Ozeha is short for *Oglasni Zavod Hrvatske,* meaning: Institute for Advertising of Croatia. At that time the agency was small and government-operated, with limited scope of activity. Today Ozeha is the largest agency in Yugoslavia and offers assistance in all phases of marketing from research, packaging, labels, and store displays on to newspaper, magazine, radio and television advertising. Our headquarters are in Zagreb, and we have offices in the chief cities of all six Yugoslavian republics.

The agency is departmentalized along such lines as: account executive, creative, media, market research and accounting. Our creative work we buy from free lance people who have contract arrangements with the agency. Some years ago they were members of the regular staff, but they seem to be happier under the present arrangement, and so is the agency.

Among services we perform, which are foreign to some agencies in other countries, are those involving the preparation of catalogues, fair exhibits, movie slides, neon signs and plans for interior store display. The main source of income is the 15% media commission. There are additional fees for research, testing and other collateral activities. We work closely with the marketing staff of our clients in preparing the basic marketing blueprint, but some of the elements of the marketing mix are the client's responsibility, although the agency is expected to have its own proposals. This is the case for merchandising, pricing, branding, channels of distribution and personal selling.

Companies which do not use agencies maintain their own advertising departments that sometimes run to 30 people. In such cases the advertising function varies from company to company, and only rarely does the chief of the company concern himself with it directly, although he usually takes an intense interest in the final plans. More commonly, advertising comes under the wings of the chief marketing executive, who in our country is called commercial director. Sometimes the head of the information service is responsible for the advertising department.

What Kind of Products Are Advertised in the Country?

One big publisher reported that in his newspapers, weeklies and monthly magazines, the volume of advertising, according to the product groups could be classified this way:

- Electrical appliances
- Detergents and cosmetics
- Classified advertising
- Books
- Food products
- Ready-made suits, dresses and textiles
- Shoes, tires and other products

Advertising Campaigns

I can cite some successful campaigns which benefited consumers, advertisers and society as a whole.

1. A couple of years ago it was the custom in the city and in the country to prepare soup at home. That meant lots of time, work and expense. Today, in the towns, almost everywhere canned soups are commonplace dishes and nobody bothers to prepare them at home.
2. Some successful campaigns succeeded in increasing the sale of books by 100 per cent and reducing prices by twenty per cent.
3. Here is an example from the industrial field. The wooden packing case was the predominant method for shipping goods, both within the country and abroad. This was obviously a very expensive way to do things, but nobody was willing to switch to paperboard packing because people distrusted the protective powers of paper and cardboard. But the campaign which promoted the use of the comparatively new packing material was so effective that it did not take long for orders to exceed production capacity.
4. In the international field, the success was for the promotion of tourism. Yugoslavia has many beautiful resorts and other attractions but the country was really *terra incognita* for foreign tourists. Publicity and promotion get a good share of the credit for increasing our foreign tourist traffic from six hundred thousand in 1958 to two million and three hundred thousand last year.

Advertising Media

Newspapers, radio and television are the leading media. Coverage of national and local daily and weekly newspapers is relatively good. Predominantly advertising space is used by manufacturers but in some papers, classified advertising accounts for one third of total lineage.

The number of radio subscribers increased twofold between 1958 and 1963, and the number of TV subscribers grew even faster. In three years from 1960-1963, TV subscribers increased seven times. This is the reason that television could very soon be the leading medium. The most used form for commercials is the one minute spot announcement.

It is of some interest to mention that advertising is not the most important source of revenue for radio and television stations and newspaper publishers. Owners of radio and TV sets have to subscribe to the program and pay about one dollar a month for television and 40¢ for radio.

Subscription, advertising and other sources cover expenses for operating television or radio stations. This is the reason why advertisers do not have influence on programs, and there are no commercials interrupting programs. To reach large audiences, commercials are aired between natural breaks in the program.

Other media used by advertisers are: business publications, outdoor advertising, direct mail, transit advertising, movie screen ads and fairs and exhibits. Among these secondary media, fairs and exhibits are very developed in Yugoslavia. There are 17 fairs in the country, most of them specialized for certain groups of products. One of the largest and well known internationally is the International Zagreb Fair, which last year attracted more than 5000 foreign and 1200 domestic exhibitors and one million seven hundred thousand visitors.

Fairs are an important factor in international and domestic trade. There, actual products are available for inspection and demonstration. The fairs also provide a meeting place for buyer and seller and offer possibility of comparing competitive products—in the same place.

Other Institutions Serving Marketing

The Marketing Research Institute supplies economic organizations with services such as: Marketing research of consumer goods including sales possibilities for new products; analyzing the consumption and competitiveness of various products; research of consumption trends and forecasting of consumption; testing the consumers' image of various products and producers; testing of advertising methods and results; prepares and negotiate marketing research in foreign countries for the domestic client and does marketing research for foreign clients in Yugoslavia. There are some other research organizations such as: *Foreign Trade Research Institute* and *Market Research Bureaus.*

Agency for Publicity Abroad has the main task to promote our exports through International Fairs and Exhibits and publicity. The agency is partly subsidized by the government. This agency organizes publicity for products which are on exhibit; publishes the monthly paper "Yugoslavia Export," and yearly publications "Foreign Trade Almanac," "Directory of Export-Import Enterprises," etc.

Institute for Quality Research gives brands tested in their laboratories special citations for high and permanent quality.

The Yugoslav Oscar for Packing. To promote better packaging and better design, every year there is an organized contest by the Center for advancement of trade and packaging. There are several prizes for best designs.

Advertising Association is an organization of marketing and advertising practitioners and educators. The task of the Association is to improve practice in the whole Advertising industry and to initiate specialized courses at schools and universities.

The industrial design centre is one of the youngest institutions which cooperates with industrial firms in creating designs for new products and in improving the old ones.

CONCLUSION

Last month Yugoslavia introduced wide reform in the economic system. The basic aims of the reform are:

—Further stabilization of the economy;
—Further strengthening of workers' self-management of enterprises and widening of its material base, as well as the strengthening of the independence of enterprises;
—Lessening of state role and intervention in economic life and giving more freedom to the influence and free play of economic forces;
—The wider inclusion of Yugoslavia's economy into the international division of labor and world market, and more direct competition of foreign goods on the domestic market in order to bring more effective and rational production within the country.

It is expected that the reform will bring more responsibility and greater importance to marketing institutions in the country—and at the same time provide an opportunity to show that marketing can contribute toward a higher standard of living in the whole society.

50.

RETAILING IN POLAND: A FIRST-HAND REPORT*

J. Hart Walters, Jr.

RETAILING in prewar Poland was once characterized as having been "particularly underdeveloped (and) primitive with respect to its technical facilities, organizational forms, and method of operation."[1]

The retail structure consisted of numerous, small-scale, highly specialized establishments. During the interwar years Polish retailing became fragmented into yet smaller establishments, so that by 1938 fully 70% of retail outlets were not classed as "permanent localized establishments," that is, shops.[2] This same 70% of establishments accounted for less than 25% of the nation's total retail sales volume.[3]

The picture has changed sharply since the end of World War II. "Socialist ownership" in the form of State and cooperative trading enterprises has replaced private enterprise, which has virtually ceased to exist as a significant force in the retailing of consumer goods. The socialized sector, moreover, has stressed development of a network of shop-type retail outlets including, especially in recent years, such "modern" forms of retailing as self-service.

Demise of the Private Sector

The shift from predominantly private to overwhelming socialized retailing was rapid. In 1946, almost 90% of retail establishments were owned privately.[4] By 1949, about 60% of retail sales volume was conducted by outlets in the socialized sector, which then controlled but 40% of Polish retail establishments.[5] The private sector's role continued to decline; by 1960, it controlled about 12% of the nation's retail establish-

* J. Hart Walters, Jr., "Retailing in Poland: A First-Hand Report," *Journal of Marketing*, Vol. 28, No. 2 (April, 1964), a publication of the American Marketing Association, pp. 16-21. Reprinted by permission.

[1] A. Hodoly and W. Jastrzebowski, *Handel Wiejski w Polsce Międzywojennej* [Rural Trade in Interwar Poland] (Warsaw: PWG, 1957), p. 3.

[2] Mały Rocznik Statystyczny: 1938 [Statistical Annual: 1938] (Warsaw: GUS, 1938), p. 93.

[3] Same reference as footnote 2.

[4] *Rocznik Statystyczny: 1947* (Warsaw: GUS, 1947), p. 84.

[5] *Rocznik Statystyczny:1950* (Warsaw: GUS, 1950), p. 69.

ments with less than 3% of total national retail sales volume.[6] Table 1 gives further information.

The virtual demise of private retailing can be attributed in part to both the closing and nationalizing of existing enterprises. But the major methods of "socializing" retail trade were: (1) developing of a new network of State stores in cities and towns; (2) expanding on the nucleus of cooperative societies, especially in the countryside; and (3) discouraging private trade by heavy taxes and rigorous licensing procedures.

TABLE 1—STRUCTURE OF RETAIL SALES IN POLAND, 1948-60,
BY OWNERSHIP FORM OF ESTABLISHMENT[a]
(Millions of złotys, current prices)

| | | Socialized Sector | | | | |
| | | | | Cooperatives | | |
Year	Total Poland[b]	Total	State stores	Rural	Other	Private Sector
1948	32,400[c]	13,000[c]	1,700[c]	11,300[c]		19,400
1949	38,900[d]	23,340	8,403	14,397		15,560[d]
1950	49,757	40,857	13,262	11,624	15,971	8,900
1951	57,308	51,858	20,340	13,590	17,928	5,450
1952	65,866	60,766	24,902	16,450	19,414	5,100
1953	97,323	93,523	39,118	25,694	28,711	3,800
1954	108,341	104,441	45,048	29,740	29,653	3,900
1955	116,181	112,681	50,454	32,238	29,989	3,500
1956	133,914	130,814	62,867	37,683	30,264	3,100
1957	168,715	160,715	77,981	44,639	38,095	8,000
1958	183,756	176,056	84,267	49,269	42,520	7,700
1959	204,307	197,107	95,438	54,202	47,467	7,200
1960	211,527	205,877	99,699	56,859	48,965	5,650

[a] Sources: *Rocznik Statystyczny: 1961* (Warsaw: GUS, 1961), pp. 252-253; *1960*, p. 272.
[b] Excludes for the years 1950-60 sales of consumption articles not classified as retail trade.
[c] Estimated and computed.
[d] Total Poland and private sector estimated. See M. Napieralski, "Rozwój sieci handlu detalicznego w Polsce,"*Handel Wewnętrzny,* Vol. 3 (1961), p. 72

In marked contrast with private retailing, the socialized sector has stressed the development of *shops*—selling points in fixed, indoor locations. This emphasis reflected Poland's rapid postwar urbanization, in which metropolitan population doubled while the rural population declined. The quick growth of the urban population provided a substantial new market for expanding city retailing facilities of the shop type. The position of the private sector was weak because of its traditional

6 M. Napieralski, "Rozwój sieci handlu detalicznego w Polsce," [Development of the Retail Trade Network in Poland], *Handel Wewnętrzny*, Vol. 7, No. 4 (1961), p. 72.

concentration in petty, nonshop operation. Moreover, the politics of the socialist environment made it impossible for private traders to amass the capital necessary for larger-scale retailing.

STRUCTURE AND ORGANIZATION

Socialized retailing in Poland is not conducted by a single, monolithic, highly centralized organization, but by a rather complex, well-differentiated structure of retail enterprises under several control centers. These may be divided broadly into (1) cooperative and (2) State enterprises.

The Cooperatives

Continuing a development that had achieved some importance during the prewar period, the present regime has stimulated the growth of cooperatives as a major part of the socialized sector. Unlike the State stores, cooperatives pay taxes, but have greater independence in the disposition of operating profits. Cooperatives engaged in retailing can be classified along three main lines.

   A. *Rural Cooperatives.* The rural cooperatives have a virtual monopoly of socialized retailing in the countryside. The basic unit is the local cooperative society at the *gmina* (commune) or *gromada* (township) levels. The local societies are membership organizations, and are affiliated through *powiat* (county) and/or *województwo* (state) federations to the central organization of farm cooperatives (*CRS—"Samopomoc Chłopska"* —Peasants Self-help).

   Besides operating retail stores and wholesaling facilities, the rural co-ops are engaged in farm supply, as well as playing a major role in collecting farm products for sale to State and cooperative processing factories and to other State and cooperative purchasing agencies. Since *CRS* and its affiliates operate some wholesale houses, the retail units are in part supplied as integrated organizations, although they also draw on State wholesaling enterprises, State and cooperative factories, and directly from local farm sources. *CRS* affiliates account for over 27% of Poland's retail trade in consumer goods.[7]

   B. *Urban Consumers' Cooperatives.* The urban consumers' cooperatives, frequently organized under sponsorship of municipal government bodies, operate retail "chains," primarily food stores in the towns and cities. They are affiliated to a national organization (*ZSS*—Union of Consumer's Cooperatives). The larger societies operate some wholesaling facilities, but the supply sources for the retail units are more typically State wholesaling enterprises and cooperative or State producing enterprises.

---

[7] *Rocznik Statystyczny: 1961* (Warsaw: GUS, 1961), pp. 252-253.

C. Other Cooperatives. Production and processors' co-ops, such as dairy producers' cooperatives, operate retail outlets in the cities and towns. In some cases local producers' or processors' cooperatives of a given commodity group are affiliated with a regional or national organization. A substantial proportion of Polish handicraft products is distributed through this type of outlet.

State Stores

In addition to the cooperatives, there are the State stores, which conduct slightly less than half of Poland's total retail trade. They can be classified into two major categories.

A. Manufacturers' Retail Outlets. Various State-owned manufacturing enterprises operate retail outlets, primarily in the cities. For the most part the offerings of such outlets are confined to products of a single factory or group of factories under one enterprise. They are highly specialized by commodity line. The manufacturer's branch store is not necessarily the sole retail outlet of a factory, which also may deliver output to other retail enterprises (both State and cooperative) and to wholesaling enterprises.

B. State Retail Trading Enterprises. Except for a few centrally-controlled organizations, most enterprises of this category are under direct control of the "trade division" of the "Peoples Council" *(Rada Narodowa)* of the political subdivision (usually *województwo*). These are enterprises set up for the specific purpose of conducting retail trade as their main business.

They are organized along lines of commodity specialization within the given geographical unit of control. State retail trading enterprises under this type of regional control account for almost one-third of Poland's retail trade in consumers goods, and include over 500 different enterprises operating about 22,500 shops and over 6,500 small-retail selling points.[8]

Local Control of State Stores. Local or regional control, rather than central control, over the State retail trading enterprises is most aptly shown by the example that the grocery stores of a given locality are controlled by the trade division of the local Peoples Council *along with other retail enterprises handling different commodities.*

Such a food store enterprise has *no organic, line relationship* with other food store enterprises in neighboring localities. Poland has no direct counterpart of the *A & P* or *Safeway* chains in the all-important food field.

---

[8] *Wyniki Ekonomiczne Przedsiębiorstw Państwowych* (Operating Results of State Enterprises), Vols. 1/7 (Warsaw: Instytut Handlu Wewnętrznego, 1961), pp. 2–249.

This local control of State retail enterprises seemingly flouts the commonly accepted rationale of vertical integration, in that the division along political lines tends to restrict the scale of operation achievable by a given firm. While the State retail trading enterprises in some cases operate wholesaling facilities, State wholesaling *enterprises* under direct *central* control are a major supply source.

This form of retail organization apparently is necessitated by and logically consistent with the character of decentralized economic planning in Poland. National plans for consumption and the corresponding plans for retail trade volume are broken down regionally and incorporated into the regional economic plan.

In effect, the *województwo* plans how the total consumption available to it shall be broken down into, say, food and shoes, rather than the central authority planning precisely how much out of national food and shoe consumption shall be allocated to different regions. Since the retail enterprises are the eventual instruments of plan-execution, their organization along regional lines is not inconsistent with this pattern of planning.

The placing of State retail trading enterprises under regional control does not appear to have resulted in over-large entities that are too unwieldy for an economical scale of operation. This problem is largely avoided by the simple expedient of dividing, for example, the retail grocery trade in a large city into several distinct enterprises. In the smaller towns the scale of operation (as indicated by average sales per establishment) is usually of a considerably lesser order than in larger population centers.

There is no apparent relationship between sales size and either gross margin or net profits of enterprises within any given branch of retailing.[9] Probably the rather narrow range of margins and profits among enterprises is a consequence of the rigid, fixed prices set by the central authorities.

ASSORTMENT AND CONVENIENCE

Except where otherwise noted, the following discussion is drawn from observation over an 11-month period in 1961-62, mostly in the city of Warsaw.

Assortment

More similar to European than to American patterns, Polish retail stores are highly specialized in their consumer goods assortments. Assortments tend to be manufactured-ordered rather than along lines of consumption

[9] Same reference as footnote 8.

characteristics. As a result, the Polish consumer typically needs to visit several retail outlets to fulfill daily, normal needs.

The latter phenomenon differs little from that existing in much of Western Europe, but for some puzzling inconsistencies among assortments offered by different shops of the same retail branch. For example, general grocery store "A" might stock item "X," a common enough article of every-day shopping. General grocery store "B," several city blocks away and presumably serving a different clientele, might very well not carry the item in question. Unless by chance the consumer has information about the precise location of item "X," he might have to undergo a considerable "searching" effort, even though the article is in ample supply to the extent that store "A" is overstocked.

The same thing is often even more true for goods not in the normal course of daily shopping. The store in which the customer expects to find, say, a certain appliance may be out of stock; but he has no way of knowing that another store might have the item, or that a new shipment has arrived elsewhere. Advertising by individual units of a "chain" is virtually unknown.

Sensitivity to Consumers

These examples suggest that *de jure* managerial autonomy in making such decisions as assortment-choice has not yet been accompanied by sufficient *de facto* sensitivity to consumer preferences and habits.

In all fairness, the manager's ability to exercise choice is often limited by "spottiness" in availability of supplies. At the same time some degree of insensitivity to consumer needs seems to be involved, even though greater decentralization and more managerial autonomy might presumably mean a greater, rather than lesser responsiveness to customer preferences.

Polish economists have suggested two basic categories of cause for this apparent lack of sensitivity to the consumer's need for more adequate services to accompany goods that the economy can actually make available.

Controlled Prices. The first explanation links the traditional "buyers' market-sellers' market" analysis to socialist institutions of controlled, rigid prices.

In a capitalist, market economy, it is reasoned, a pressure of demand on goods that are in short supply at current prices would stimulate price increases and the restoration of equilibrium or liquidation of the "sellers' market." But under contemporary socialist conditions in Poland, prices are fixed and rigid and, therefore, do not automatically rise under pressure of the "sellers' market" that is said to prevail. Since prices cannot be increased, the seller can easily afford to be indifferent about providing services—the resulting phenomenon is termed "minimization of services" *(minimalizacja świadczeń)*.[10]

Conflicts in Incentives. Another factor tending to generate "minimization of services" is some conflict in the enterprise's incentives to maximize profits, share profits among its employees, and to incur the expenses necessary to improve services.

The drive to maximize profits is reflected in the enterprise's attempt to keep costs low. Since the State retail firm is effectively limited in manipulating prices in either direction, its low, largely fixed margins preclude the incurring of expenses that would be designed to increase sales at existing prices and margins, even though it is to the firm's benefit to sell more than its "norm" or goal.

The overall situation of short or "spotty" supplies inhibits managerial attempts to stimulate demand through any form of nonprice competition. The same situation of short supply, along with the high degree of assortment-specialization on which retail organization is based tends to limit assortment-variation as a "competitive" tactic. "Socialist competition" still exists largely on the theoretical level, and not in practice.

Methods of wage and salary payments also tend to restrict improvements in service. The wages fund available to an enterprise is related basically to sales volume rather than to the number of employees.[11] There can thus be considerable pressure from an enterprise's labor force to limit the number of employees, a dearth of which can critically affect the speed with which people move through retail establishments, especially clerk-service stores.

Although compensation formulas provide incentives linked to sales volume (workers receive more if the shop's "norm" is exceeded), the ambitious and lazy worker in the same job classification share equally in the added proceeds. This gives little *personal* incentive for the individual clerk, except of course to receive promotion to a higher position in the job classification scheme.

Improvements

Along with other branches of the economy, retail trade suffers from the general shortage of skilled and trained labor in Poland. However, labor shortages have induced a rapid growth in self-service retailing. In the period 1958-60, the numbers of self-service retail establishments grew

[10] W. Jastrzebowski, "Rynek nabywcy " (The Buyer's Market), *Handel Wewnętrzny*, No. 6 (1959), pp. 3-4 (of reprint).

[11] M. Górny, *Ekonomika Handlu* (The Economics of Trade), Part 4 (Warsaw: PWG, 1960), pp. 23-25.

from 235 to about 10,000.[12] The number of retail trade employees per head of general population also increased somewhat.[13] At the same time the number of persons of population per retail establishment declined, so that fewer people had to "move" through each establishment.[14]

The improvements cited here were partly offset by the fact that per capita retail sales increased enough so that on a hypothetical average trip to an average store a Polish consumer in 1960 would be buying about one-third more goods than 10 years previously.[15]

The Queue Problem and Service

Queues, a normal part of the daily experience of Polish consumers, have been the subject of much misconception in the Western press. Queues form for goods that are in short supply, or for items that are infrequently available, such as fresh oranges and bananas during the winter months.

But their almost universal existence is not always linked directly with shortages of *goods,* because queues are in evidence for goods with an adequate supply. Other explanations must be sought for situations in which supply is adequate for the demand at prevailing prices.

In such situations queues reflect a disequilibrium in the demand for and supply of *marketing services.* Given the present organization and level of efficiency of Polish retailing, there simply are not enough shops and retail clerks for the volume of goods and the numbers of people that pass through retail establishments.

Although the average Polish retail establishment and sales clerk serve more people than do their Western counterparts, it can be argued that on the basis of sales volume there are sufficient facilities for the population. Why, then, queues?

In the first place, while the total square footage used by retail establishments may be adequate, this footage is broken up into physically-small shop units. These are not conducive to the fast movement of large numbers of people during the "rush hours" in which urban shopping, in particular is concentrated. With a substantial proportion of wives and mothers employed, shopping is highly concentrated in the late afternoon and early evening hours. Such a time-space configuration should require large stores on the American pattern, rather than the more typically European picture of small shops.

Second, the vast majority of Polish consumers shop on foot or use public transportation. For the most part their homes (especially urban

12 Napieralski, same reference as footnote 6, at p. 74.
13 Same reference as footnote 7, at pp. 13 and 266.
14 Same reference as footnote 7, at pp. 13 and 258.
15 Calculated from material cited in footnote 7, at pp. 13, 252-253, 266.

apartments) have little storage space. Refrigeration is not yet prevalent.

Transactions, especially for food, are small and numerous, so that the equivalent of an American one-stop supermarket "shopping basket" would require two to three trips for the Polish consumer; and except for the very few supermarkets in operation, visits to several different stores would be necessitated. Polish consumers favor food that can be bought "fresh" and used the same day.

As a result, Polish retailing is characterized by a high amount of traffic and a large number of transactions in relation to sales volume. With a comparatively smaller sales force and with fewer shops per person than is the case in most of the West, it is impossible for Polish retailing to offer the convenience of quick service.

This will continue to be the case unless there are marked changes in the physical size of retail units, the numbers of retail units and employees, and the shopping patterns of Polish consumers.

TABLE 2—ADJUSTED GROSS MARGIN OF POLISH
RETAIL TRADE, 1948-61[a] (Per cent of retail sales,
including restaurant sales)

Year	Unad-justed Margin	Adjustments for Purchasing, Assortment, Tax[b]			Adjusted Margin
1948	17.0				
1949	16.3				
1950	14.7				
1951	11.0				
1952	10.6				
1953	8.8				
1954	9.0				
1955	8.9	0.5			9.4
1956	7.7	0.5			8.2
1957	7.4	0.5			7.9
1958	9.8	0.5			10.3
1959	10.0	0.5	0.7	1.7	12.9
1960	11.4	0.6	0.7	1.7	14.4
1961	11.4	0.6	0.7	1.8	14.5

[a]Sources: (For margins) Z. Krasiński, "Marża handlowa," *Handel Wewnętrzny,* Vol. VII, No. 1 (1961), p. 22; *Wyniki Ekonomiczne Przedsiębiorstw Państwowych,* Vol. 1/7, pp. 352-359, and Vol. 1/11, pp. 344-351 (Warsaw: Instytut Handlu Wewnętrznego, 1961 and 1962).

[b]The adjustments include purchasing activities of wholesalers and retailers, a reweighting of Polish assortments to correspond more closely with American assortments, and an estimate for incidence of the turnover, or excise tax. An appendix showing the method of adjustment and appropriate calculations is available from the author.

MARGINS AND PRODUCTIVITY

By American standards, retail gross margins in Poland are low. Adjusted for compatibility with American data, they average about 14.5% on sales.[16]

However, the trend in recent years has been upward, reflecting higher prices for some commodities after 1958, a greater proportion of sales of higher priced nonfood items, and some increases in both costs and profits of retail enterprises.

It is difficult to evaluate Polish data on retail productivity alongside of material from other countries because of a dearth of comparable data, and the problem of a really valid *złoty*-dollar exchange rate. As indicated in Table 3, however, the trend in retail sales per employee is strongly upward, due to greater sales volume, price increases in some lines, and growth of self-service retailing.

TABLE 3—SALES PER EMPLOYEE IN RETAIL TRADE IN
POLAND, SOCIALIZED SECTOR, 1955–60[a]
(Thousands of złotys)

Year	Sales per Employee
1955	556
1956	634
1957	774
1958	749
1959	808
1960	800

[a]Source: Calculated from following issues of *Rocznik Statystyczny:* 1961, pp. 252, 266; 1960, p. 285; 1959, p. 249; 1958, p. 281; 1957, p. 228. Figures are in current prices.

In contrast with labor productivity, the trend of inventory turnover has been unfavorable. From a rate of 7.8 in 1956, the average number of stock turns per year had declined to 6.6 in 1960.[17] In part, the decline reflects a shift in consumer purchasing toward more nonfood items, with their characteristically slower rates of turnover.

16 See Table 2 for derivation of Polish margins; also H. Barger, *Distribution's Place in the American Economy Since 1869* (Princeton: Princeton University Press, 1955); J. B. Jefferys, *The Distribution of Consumer Goods* (Cambridge: The University Press, 1950); M. Rives, *Traité d'Economie Commerciale*, Vol. 3 (Paris; 1958).

17 *Rocznik Statystyczny: 1957* (Warsaw: GUS, 1957), p. 223; and *1961*, p. 256.

Because of the short time periods for which productivity data are available, trends are difficult to assess. The 6-year trend in sales per employee has been favorable; but plans to accelerate the increase in the labor force in marketing, if realized, could stabilize or even reverse this trend. The continued rapid expansion of self-service stores, including supermarkets, may help to maintain the favorable trend and at the same time improve the service and convenience offered the consumer.

In all likelihood the rate of stock turnover will continue to decline, along with increases in the proportion of nonfood sales. This trend can be reversed or arrested only by basic changes in methods of handling inventory, or else by increases in the scale of operation, or both.

If recent trends are indicative, distribution costs and margins in Poland can be expected to increase further. However, some of the elements of increasing cost that have characterized marketing in developed, private-enterprise economics are largely absent or negligible. These include the cost of land as expressed in ground rent, as well as cost that can be attributed primarily to competitive institutions and practices.

The Polish distribution system does not involve competitive advertising, sales promotion, and personal selling—all significant marketing cost elements in advanced private-enterprise economies. Also Poland's *production* costs are relatively high. This means that even if marketing costs were to remain constant, they would increase as a *percentage* of sales as production costs dropped, presuming the drop to be reflected in retail prices.

CONCLUSIONS

While the total number of retail outlets is not as numerous as in prewar Poland, the numbers of permanent, localized retail establishments have increased considerably under the postwar regime.

The evolution toward a network of modern shops, including self-service, is largely a consequence of the nation's rapid postwar economic development. One of the factors has been the growth of a large, new class of urban consumers.

The socialized sector has almost totally replaced private retail trade in consumer goods; but marketing organization is relatively decentralized along regional and commodity lines. However, organizational decentralization is not fully accompanied by operational autonomy in some important categories of decision-making. With its purchase prices and margins defined centrally, the Polish retail enterprise is effectively prohibited from setting its own resale prices. Shortages and the very method of retail organization along strongly-defined commodity lines give the store manager little scope for varying assortment, unlike his Western counterpart who may "scramble" merchandise at will.

Services and convenience have improved substantially, especially since 1956; but they cannot be compared favorably with those in the West. But distributive margins and costs are lower than those in Western private-enterprise economies.

Recent trends indicate that Polish marketing margins are increasing, while productivity is remaining stable. Should this trend continue, Poland will have exhibited a pattern not dissimilar to that of private-enterprise economics that have left the "production era" and entered the "marketing epoch."